TO SEE GREAT WONDERS

TO SEE GREAT WONDERS

A HISTORY OF XAVIER UNIVERSITY
1831–2006

Roger A. Fortin

Scranton: University of Scranton Press

(c) 2006 University of Scranton Press

All rights reserved.

Library of Congress Cataloging-in-Publication Data

(Has been applied for but is not available at time of publication.)

Distribution:

The University of Scranton Press
Chicago Distribution Center
11030 S. Langley
Chicago, IL 60628

PRINTED IN THE UNITED STATES OF AMERICA

DEDICATION

To Xavier members of the Society of Jesus, past and present, for their many contributions in the life of the university, and particularly to Francis (Frank) C.
Brennan, S.J., Xavier's Academic Vice President from 1974 to 1982,
for his enlightenment, inspiration, and friendship.

TABLE OF CONTENTS

FOREWORD

Initially articulating his vision during a speech at the University of Santa Clara in October 2000, Jesuit Superior General Peter-Hans Kolvenbach continues to argue persuasively for a radical new way of evaluating the effectiveness of Jesuit colleges and universities. How are Jesuit schools to be graded? Not by the size of their endowments or by the publications of their faculty; not by their graduation rates or the academic quality of their incoming classes; and not by their position in *U.S. News and World Report* rankings, their alumni giving rates, their reputation amongst other college administrators, or by any of the other usual metrics we customarily use to slice and dice colleges and their quality. Instead, Father Kolvenbach argues that the true measure of a Jesuit university ought to be who its alumni become. Not so much the livelihoods they earn, but rather the lives that they create—and even more so, the ways in which they positively interact with the lives of others.

This way of gauging the success of the Jesuit educational enterprise would have made immediate sense to St. Ignatius Loyola, the founder of the Jesuits. Ignatius created what has become the tradition of Jesuit higher education by fusing the educational forms of the classical world with the emerging educational needs of the Renaissance, thereby grounding men destined for active lives in the civic marketplace with the wisdom of the ancient world. In this way, Ignatius believed, his schools would shape men of virtue and learning who would bring to contemporary problems habits of mind and heart honed over centuries, and these virtuous citizens would in turn shape virtuous societies, ready for—or, at least, open to—the loving influence of the Gospel.

The tradition begun by Ignatius of Loyola is alive and well at innumerable worldwide institutions of learning that bear the broad stamp of Jesuit education. It is especially alive and well in the United States, among the 28 member institutions of the Association of Jesuit Colleges and Universities—including Xavier University. The vision that unites these schools is far more important than any accidents of time, place, or history that divide them. Common to all of them is an important cluster of deep and distinctive convictions: that God may be found in all things; that human beings are called for the more and the greater; that the requirements of justice and the demands of the Gospel always go hand in hand; and that men and women only realize their true identities when they sacrifice themselves in service to their neighbor, especially their neighbor in need. The Jesuit colleges and universities in the United States are united by one more thing. Since the mid-1970s, all of them have been engaged in a process of renewing their distinctive Jesuit identities and, as a result, sharpening their abilities to fulfill in our modern context, the high hopes that motivated Ignatius when he founded his original schools.

Dr. Roger Fortin's delightful history of Xavier University is a case study of the foundation, growth, and current flowering of one of these American Jesuit schools. Its history makes the point that each and every one of the Jesuit schools, at least in the United States, has resulted from a lengthy sort of dialogue, one that has gone on between the broad tradition of Jesuit education and the particular and specific needs and opportunities of the communities in which these schools have grown up. Their histories become windows through which we can observe this interplay, and much else besides—the histories of cities and communities, of dioceses and archdioceses, and ultimately, of the Catholic community in the United States itself.

On the eve of its 175th anniversary, Xavier University has much to celebrate and much to look forward to. The same can be said for her Jesuit sister schools in the United States. Together, these colleges and universities constitute a distinct and important voice in American higher education and a lively and crucial apostolate for the Catholic Church in the United States.

Michael J. Graham, S.J.

President, Xavier University

ACKNOWLEDGEMENTS

As Xavier University celebrates the 175th anniversary of its founding as a Catholic and Jesuit institution, its future is promising. Under the leadership of Michael J. Graham, S.J., who assumed the presidency on January 1, 2001, the university is positioned to continue to grow in academic stature. There have been pivotal moments in Xavier's history and this is potentially one of them. The university is entering a new epoch, a novel and distinctive phase in its history. It is undertaking a major transformation in the way it conducts teaching and learning, in the way it relates to its external communities, and in the way members of the university community relate with one another. While carving out new and fresh directions, the institution is rekindling its rich Catholic, Jesuit tradition. Consistent with its mission, it is seeing "great wonders," making it possible for students to seek meaningful and fulfilling achievements in their lives.

By engaging in original archival research, as well as consulting major secondary works, I have attempted to provide a portrait of the major activities, trends, and developments in the life of Xavier University since its beginning in 1831. This study could not have been completed without the able assistance of scores of individuals and offices at the university. I must express a special gratitude to Michael J. Graham of the Society of Jesus and President of Xavier University who, from the start, proved most encouraging and supportive. Moreover, my administrative colleagues at the university provided considerable information and support for this study. In particular, I am grateful to my former and new administrative assistants, Mary Walroth and Claudia Fladung respectively, for their patience and skillful assistance. My gratitude also extends to the staff at the Midwest Jesuit Archives in St. Louis, Missouri, and at the Xavier University Library, especially Timothy J. McCabe, who helped guide me in the selection of illustrations. In addition, special thanks to Gregory Rust, Xavier Director for Photography, Tom Eiser, Xavier Associate Althletic Director for Media Relations, and Katherine St. Denny, University Director for Creative Services, for their professional assistance. I am also thankful to my three students—David Endres, Laura Hoag, and Danielle Langfield—or their careful examination of the university's students' newspapers, and to the alumni, like Joseph Bunker, class of 1956, and John Kelly, class of 1960, for providing helpful information.

Significantly, I am very indebted to my faculty colleagues Dr. Ernest L. Fontana, professor of English, and J. Leo Klein, S.J., professor of Theology and vice president for mission and ministry, for their reading and careful analysis of the entire manuscript and for their invaluable suggestions. I am also grateful to Dr. Charles J. Cusick and Dr. David C. Flaspohler, professors emeriti and former deans at the university, for reading portions of the manuscript and responding with helpful critical comments. Special thanks to Michael J. Conaton and Gerald J. DeBrunner, Xavier University trustees, for meeting with me and providing insights on more recent events at the university. Lastly, and most importantly, I am very thankful to my wife Janet for her love and for her ongoing support of this study.

Roger Fortin
Academic Vice President and Provost
February 1, 2006

Introduction

Xavier University has a story to tell, and when President Graham asked me to write a history of our institution, I shared his enthusiasm about telling that story. This saga chronicles how Xavier achieved its distinguished and distinct place within the gallery of American colleges and universities, beginning with its inauspicious founding 175 years ago.

Xavier's story, like that of other institutions of higher learning, is one—especially during the past century—of constant change and adaptation. In every period of its history, the university has been influenced by the growth, flux, and ferment in society. Xavier's expansion from a small downtown college numbering fewer than 200 students in 1831 to an urban university with a current enrollment of over 6600 involved more than geographical expansion, physical growth, and academic development. Recounted here are Xavier's adventures, its ups and downs, its struggles, trials, challenges, and accomplishments, all as part of two simultaneous and complimentary story lines: Xavier's considerable achievement in higher education and the successful establishment of its Catholic and Jesuit identity and reputation.

This story will also take into account Xavier's unique combination of institutional prerogatives, such as its tradition, geographical setting, students, faculty perspectives, sources of financial support, and the leadership of its presidents and trustees. Throughout its 175 years Xavier has encountered new constituencies, engaged in new tasks, and stretched its resources to support new ventures, all the while affirming and sustaining its Catholic and Jesuit heritage. (1)

While working on this project, I was reminded that the historian generally finds it more difficult to measure the intellectual, moral, and spiritual development of an educational community than assess its material growth. Institutional histories, including this one, pay more attention to administrative decisions, buildings and budgets, planning groups, and other general activities largely because more information about these topics and events is available. Consequently this history provides an incomplete representation of the university as a community of scholars and learners. It does not do full justice to the teaching excellence, scholarship, and service of scores of dedicated faculty members in the university's various disciplines.

Like Xavier, most of the colleges and universities founded in the United States before the twentieth century had a strongly religious character. Most of these institutions, which were usually Protestant Christian, have no significant religious identity today. Among the most well-known are Harvard, Yale, Princeton, Chicago, Stanford, and Duke. In the wake of the Civil War, the leading individuals in these institutions subscribed to the idea of creating a national, nonsectarian Protestant public culture. As the institutions became more secular, religious sentiment became identified more with public service, religious beliefs became more the object of scientific study, and many of the institutions abandoned any legal relationship to the founding denominations. In contrast, Xavier University, like many other Catholic and Jesuit colleges and universities, is characterized by its growth as a multi-purpose institution that continued to add functions and responsibilities without disregarding older commitments to its Catholic and Jesuit identity. (2)

Throughout its history, Xavier University also assumed a strategic place in greater Cincinnati. It became a model of service to the diverse economic and social interests of the community. One of the most formidable challenges faced by Xavier, like other Jesuit colleges and universities, was adapting its European Jesuit educational heritage to an American milieu. Maintaining a balance between those two dynamics was and continues to be a central theme of the Xavier saga, and this history will tell how, while it remained committed to its religious and educational tradition, the university always proved flexible enough to provide the education essential to the needs and dreams of its students and necessary to meeting the skills expectations of their potential future employers. In the process it always attracted students from less privileged socioeconomic backgrounds.

Twelve moments proved pivotal in the history of the university. The first came in 1840 when, upon the invitation of Bishop John Baptist Purcell of Cincinnati, the Society of Jesus assumed control of the diocesan college, called the Athenaeum, and renamed it St. Xavier College. The second came in 1850 when the Jesuits, in the face of financial difficulties, considered abandoning the college and decided instead to close the boarding school and conduct a day college only. A third significant moment occurred in December 1888 when two dozen alumni formed the Alumni Association, which became (and continues to be) an enduring source of support and strength to the college.

A major turn of events took place in 1911 when Jesuit officials bought 26.7 acres of property in Avondale, on the eastern edge of Cincinnati, to move the college from its downtown location to a new suburban campus. In the 1920s six Tudor buildings in Gothic style were erected, and in 1930, St. Xavier College became Xavier University. The new campus and name change significantly altered the image of the institution. The fifth pivotal moment occurred when the university, in the wake of the Great Depression and World War II, saw its enrollment increase substantially with the return of the war veterans, established a graduate school, and began expanding its facilities.

The sixth moment was when university officials, in the midst of surging enrollments, affirmed the institution's long-established Jesuit commitment to its classical course of studies by establishing in 1948 the honors bachelor of arts program, Xavier's first honors program. The seventh telling moment witnessed, from the mid-1950s to the early 1970s, the modernization and unprecedented expansion of the university. Under the guidance of President Paul L. O'Connor, S.J., the university saw a huge increase in enrollments, especially at the graduate level, a corresponding increase in the number of lay faculty, growth and diversification of academic programs, and the erection of eight new buildings on campus.

From 1969 to 1972, three significant changes comprise the eighth special moment in Xavier's history. During that period the university became fully coeducational, the Board of Trustees elected six laymen to the board, and also launched the first capital campaign in the history of the institution. The ninth pivotal moment was when the university in the late 1970s and early 1980s acquired properties on Ledgewood and Herald Avenues, on the eastern side of campus, and purchased Edgecliff College, formerly Our Lady of Cincinnati, from the Sisters of Mercy. While the new properties opened up opportunities for future expansion, the acquisition of Edgecliff College enabled the university to broaden and enrich its course of studies.

In 1979, six years after the university dropped intercollegiate football, Xavier successfully invigorated its athletic program by making a pledge to build a competitive Division I men's basketball program, as well as to comply fully with federal guidelines for women's athletics under Title IX. This tenth pivotal moment increased the quality of Xavier athletics and enhanced the national visibility of the university. The eleventh key moment consisted of the university's decision in the late 1980s to help sustain and nurture Xavier's Jesuit identity by initiating and fostering greater collaboration among Jesuits and lay people, and the subsequent decision by the board of trustees in 1990 to establish a permanent Jesuit Identity Committee to maintain and promote the Jesuit character of the university.

Under the leadership of President James E. Hoff, S.J., the university in the 1990s raised its "sights and expectations," and experienced not only significant renovation, physical growth, and the most successful comprehensive financial campaign in its history, but also a dramatic, unprecedented change in its self-esteem and stature. Building upon Hoff's foundation and inspirational legacy, in 2001 the trustees and President Graham helped launch what promised to be an academic renaissance, potentially the thirteenth pivotal moment in Xavier's history.

As the university celebrates its 175th anniversary, it proudly acknowledges its tradition. It is clear about its identity, its past, and its future goals. In its own special way each generation of faculty, students, administrators, alumni, trustees, and friends has sought to retrieve and reinvigorate the sacred values of the university's Catholic, Jesuit tradition and bring them to bear on the challenges and demands of their times. In the nineteenth and early twentieth centuries Xavier cared about its local reputation. Throughout much of the twentieth century its administration carefully formed, sustained, and enhanced Xavier's regional and national reputation. In more recent years, Xavier programs have attracted even greater public attention because of various marketing and promotional strategies that have become a permanent part of the university's governance.

The commitment and dedication of its people have been and continue to be the strength of Xavier University, providing examples for future emulation. The attachment of the faithful alumni to their alma mater has been exemplary. My hope is that in some small way this book will provide enjoyment and a better understanding of Xavier's history, as well as help each generation deal with future challenges, strengthen affiliations, and affirm the university's distinctive qualities as a Catholic and Jesuit institution.

PART I

The Formative Years of St. Xavier College, 1831–1910

Introduction

In 1831, ten years after the founding of the Catholic Diocese of Cincinnati, Bishop Edward Dominic Fenwick established the Athenaeum, a diocesan boarding and day college dedicated to the study of religion and the liberal arts. As the first Catholic institution of higher learning in the Northwest Territory, the Athenaeum, located on Sycamore Street in Cincinnati, sought to educate laymen and serve as a nursery for vocations to the priesthood. Faced with the increased pastoral demands of his growing diocese, Bishop John Baptist Purcell, who had succeeded Fenwick in 1833, could no longer spare the priests needed to teach at the Athenaeum. So he offered the school to the Society of Jesus. Though there were some reservations and concerns about the acquisition, especially among Jesuits in the Kentucky mission, in the fall of 1840, three hundred years after the founding of the Society of Jesus, it took charge of the school and renamed it St. Xavier College. John Anthony Elet was appointed Xavier's first Jesuit president.

In the first half of the nineteenth century American colleges were mostly small, parochial, and inherently religious in outlook. Religion, especially evangelical Protestantism and, to a lesser extent, Catholicism, substantially influenced the small colleges that dominated American higher education prior to the Civil War. Twenty-nine American colleges were established in the 1840s, 84 in the 1850s, and 92 in the 1860s. Most of these institutions were closely tied to the local culture and responsive to the economic ambitions of citizens and students. St. Xavier's enrollment consisted of both Catholic and non-Catholic students and reflected Cincinnati's ethnic diversity, especially the English, German, and Irish communities. While affirming its Catholic identity and commitment to the traditional Jesuit curriculum, the college not only placed a strong emphasis on the classical course of study but also offered a commercial, mercantile course in the evening. Barely tolerated at most Jesuit schools in the nineteenth century because it was seen as a threat to the classics, St. Xavier introduced a commercial course as a response to American urban culture. (1)

The large number of new colleges founded in post-Civil War America reflected Americans' faith in the future of their country. Sixty-one colleges were founded in the 1870s, 69 in the 1880s, and 51 in the 1890s. The denominational college was still the characteristic institution of higher education, but the trend was diminishing. According to the U.S. Bureau of Education, in 1890 there were 415 colleges and universities with a total enrollment of 44,414 students. Among those institutions, 99 lacked formal church ties, 74 were associated with some form of Methodism, and 51 were Catholic colleges. Among the 35 colleges in Ohio, St. Xavier College had the twelfth largest enrollment. The total enrollment at St. Xavier, which had a combined high school and college program—based upon the European model—was 419, consisting of 348 pre-college pupils and 71 college students. (2)

Catholics and Protestants in nineteenth century America founded colleges for a similar purpose: to provide education rooted in religious faith. As more and more Roman Catholics emigrated to the United States from Europe, establishing specifically Catholic colleges that became an integral part of their contribution to building the new American society. Before 1850 these schools were founded to provide a Catholic liberal education and especially to prepare students for the seminary. After 1850 the emphasis shifted to educating a learned laity, providing an education appropriate for the Catholic community. From 1850 to 1890 an average of 33 Catholic colleges were opened each decade. Seventy percent of these schools eventually closed. Between 1890 and 1910 the newly-opened Catholic colleges closed at the unprecedented rate of 85 percent. (3)

Among the more than 500 American colleges that had been established by 1860, less than 250 were functioning. Because of declining enrollment at St. Xavier College and consequent financial difficulties in the late 1840s and 1850s, the Jesuits also considered closing the college and abandoning their parish in Cincinnati. In 1854 St. Xavier officials decided to close the boarding school only. As a consequence, the college became exclusively a commuter college serving Greater Cincinnati students. (4)

In the aftermath of the Civil War, St. Xavier entered a more promising period academically. In addition to seeing its enrollment jump from 190 in 1865 to 451 in 1900, it witnessed the erection of three new buildings on Sycamore Street: the Hill Building (1868), Moeller Building (1885), and Memorial Hall (1891). As in the majority of American colleges in the second half of the nineteenth century, St. Xavier faculty supplemented and enriched the college's extracurricular programs. In addition to joining the debating and literary societies, students could also participate in dramatic presentations, written competitions, and choir. In 1887 St. Xavier officials began sponsoring a series of evening lectures that were open to the public as well as to the academic community. A few years later the college formed the Athletic Association, which helped promote outdoor interschool athletic games.

During the last quarter of the nineteenth century there was also considerable growth in research, graduate study, and new academic disciplines in American higher education. The Morrill Land Grant Act of 1862, which had granted federal land to the states for agricultural and mechanical schools, helped stimulate higher education's growth in a technological direction. Some colleges expanded the scope of offerings while others entered entirely new markets, such as the education of teachers. Professionalizing the faculty began earlier and proceeded more rapidly at the universities than in the liberal arts colleges, such as St. Xavier. In addition to the spread of scientific research, many faculty members in academia reduced their involvement with religion, while others adopted a service-to-the-community role or valued research and the advancement of knowledge as ends in themselves. Schools of business, journalism, engineering, architecture, pharmacology, dentistry, agriculture, education, psychology, and sociology, among others, took their place alongside law and medicine. Except for the business courses taught in the evening and the introduction of a modest offering of graduate courses in English and philosophy in the 1890s, St. Xavier College was not yet ready to include other professional courses or programs in its curriculum. (5)

By 1900 many new developments and features had been introduced in American higher education. Combined high school and college programs, the predominant model throughout much of the nineteenth century, succumbed to the pressures of a more standardized American system. St. Xavier College separated its two programs and divided its college classes into freshman, sophomore, junior, and senior years, rather than the traditional divisions of poetry, rhetoric, and philosophy. That change, along with the modification in 1886 of the college's daily class schedule to accommodate Cincinnati's suburban growth, the publication the following year of St. Xavier's first collegiate paper, and the establishment of the Athletic Association were signposts of the college's gradual Americanization. However, St. Xavier did not follow the trend in higher education to move from the traditional classical curriculum to the elective system, made popular by Charles Eliot, president of Harvard University. From the time of the Jesuit takeover of the diocesan college in 1840 through the turn of the century, St. Xavier College remained true to its Jesuit classical curriculum.

Another significant development in the life of the college and in the perpetuation of its Catholic and Jesuit traditions was the establishment of the Alumni Association in 1888. Committed "to make the college prosper," the association members played a pivotal role during the 1890 Golden Jubilee—the fiftieth anniversary of the Jesuits coming to Cincinnati—in planning for the expansion of the college. In 1906, to better serve the growing number of people leaving the central city and moving to the hilltop suburbs, the college established a branch school in Walnut Hills, east of downtown Cincinnati. St. Xavier officials, faculty, alumni, and friends also began exploring the possibility of a new and permanent location in the suburbs. (6)

— 1 —

FOUNDING OF A COLLEGE

I n the mid-1820s there was considerable religious growth in the Catholic diocese of Cincinnati, founded in 1821 with the American-born Edward Dominic Fenwick, a Dominican, as its first bishop or ordinary. At the time, in addition to the state of Ohio, parts of Michigan and the Northwest Territory, now Wisconsin, were placed temporarily in the jurisdiction of the diocese. On Easter Sunday in Cincinnati in 1822 there were fewer than a dozen Communions in the St. Peter in Chains Cathedral, located near the center of the city on Sycamore Street between Sixth and Seventh Streets. Four years later there were at least three hundred on the same feast. As the cathedral became too small to accommodate the growing Catholic population, the cathedral congregation supported the idea of building a new cathedral. The diocese purchased a lot adjacent to St. Peter's for the sum of $1,200. The lot was to accommodate both the cathedral and a future seminary. (1)

Upon completion of the new cathedral in 1826, the original frame church and Cincinnati's first Catholic church built on Vine and Liberty Streets was moved to the rear of it and was converted into a temporary seminary. The seminarians as well as priests were to live there. But the building of the new cathedral had exhausted the bishop's funds and Fenwick was unable to sustain a seminary. This was a temporary setback. Before the end of the decade, however, the diocese would have its theological seminary. (2)

As Fenwick expanded missionary work in the diocese, he was in dire need of more priests. One of the major drawbacks of the early American church was the scarcity of priests. The few clergy he did get from Europe did not meet the needs of the diocese. In the early 1820s Fenwick appealed to Father Stephen T. Badin, a contact in Europe, to invite Jesuits and Benedictines in England to come to Cincinnati.

Fenwick was particularly anxious to obtain both German- and English-speaking missionaries to attend to the growing German and Irish immigrant communities. Badin, who thought the Jesuits were the most supportive of foreign missions, appealed to them to establish a foundation in the Diocese of Cincinnati. They declined, informing him that they could not at the time spare any missionaries for Fenwick's diocese. Badin received a similar response from the Benedictine order. (3)

Not long after the dedication of the new cathedral in 1826, the diocese proceeded to build a seminary, parochial schools, a college, and a newspaper, institutions essential to enhancing the Catholic faith in the diocese. The bishop made plans for a diocesan seminary-college to train his own priests-to-be, believing that a college and seminary were essential for the welfare of religion in his diocese. "Without a seminary," Fenwick wrote, "I see only distress for the future. I am, therefore, fully determined to direct all my efforts to this object." He thought it was "of the greatest necessity." The total number of clergy under his charge being eleven in 1829, he thought he needed more personnel. Though he could continue to obtain priests from Europe from time to time, he knew they would "always be too few in number," he wrote, "to answer the needs of the diocese." Moreover, he wanted priests who were sensitive to American culture. "If I have a seminary," he added, "I shall be able to form a native clergy brought up according to the habits of the country, accustomed to the rough roads, [and] acquainted with the language." (4)

On May 11, 1829, Fenwick opened a theological seminary, dedicated to St. Francis Xavier, in the old wooden frame church in the rear of the cathedral. The seminary began with ten seminarians: four in theology and six in the preparatory class. Fenwick appointed the Dominican Stephen H. Montgomery first rector of the seminary. He enlisted the best faculty possible. Keeping a watchful eye on the seminary, the Cincinnati ordinary hoped to "secure" within a short time "seven or eight seminarians" to teach first "the rudiments of Latin to a few children; . . . but I tremble when I consider the expense." Because he had insufficient funds "for the construction of the building . . . [and] to furnish board and lodging to the seminarians and perhaps most of the children," he thought that would "probably put obstacles in the way of building the college." (5)

After his trip to the first provincial council of Catholic prelates in Baltimore in 1829, Fenwick turned his attention to establishing a college, staffed preferably by Dominicans. Donations from European Catholics made it possible. Fenwick was hopeful, writing to the Association of the Propagation of the Faith, a lay organization in Lyons, France that sought to raise and distribute funds to aid missionaries in foreign countries, that he would "be able to convert the seminary into a college and in this manner obtain means to better our condition and set up other establishments, useful or necessary. I shall thus exert some influence in the instruction and education of the youth of this state, a thing that would . . . [be] to the advantage of religion." (6)

While some Protestants expressed concern over Catholic growth in the region, in the spring of 1830 plans for the building of a new college and seminary in the diocese were well under way. By this time the number of seminarians had increased to thirteen. The old frame church, which housed the bishop's residence and the seminary-college, could not adequately serve their purpose any longer. A new and larger building was necessary. Funds obtained from European Catholics enabled Fenwick to buy a lot measuring 100 by 195 feet, north of the cathedral. Despite the expense, he intended to build a college for laymen and a seminary on it. "I will do all I can to build there," he wrote to a friend. Fenwick retained the services of Alphaeus White, a convert and one of Cincinnati's early renowned architects, to build the new college on Sycamore Street, parallel to the cathedral, some fifteen or twenty yards north of it. Fenwick envisioned the seminarians teaching in the lower classes of the college. On May 14, 1830, the cornerstone of the new college, named the Athenaeum, was laid and dedicated by Father James Ignatius Mullon. Born in Ireland in 1793, he came to the United States as a child. He later became a school teacher in Maryland, and eventually was ordained a priest. Almost a year after the dedication, Bishop Fenwick's cousin, Benedict Joseph Fenwick of Boston, Massachusetts, congratulated the Cincinnati bishop on "the starting of [his] college . . . [that] must be of incalculable benefit for firmly planting our Holy Faith in the valley of the Mississippi." The Athenaeum was one of fifty colleges established in the 1830s. Unlike most of them, which were located in or near small towns, the diocesan college was situated in a city. (7)

Opening of the Athenaeum

On October 17, 1831, two and a half years after the establishment of the seminary, the Athenaeum, at a cost of about $11,500, was opened. St. Francis Xavier, the great Jesuit apostle of the Indies, was named patron and protector of the Athenaeum. Only more money and missionaries were needed, Frederic Rese, Fenwick's vicar general noted, "to see again the glorious days of St. Francis Xavier in Ohio and Michigan." Even though Bishop Fenwick's health and strength were failing, he felt "obliged," he wrote, to perform the duty of the presidency himself. A year earlier the old frame church had been razed and the new bishop's house and the seminary were completed. The college, which was the first and only Catholic college in the Northwest Territory, was built parallel to the cathedral and joined to the seminary and the bishop's residence. Fenwick now had a college and seminary in operation, both under the direction of diocesan priests. Upon the completion of the Athenaeum, the seminarians were transferred there. (8)

The new college building, 125 feet long and 50 feet wide, topped with a gilded cross, was two and a half stories high. It consisted of classrooms, a study hall, library, students' chapel, rooms for the faculty, and an attic that served as residence for the seminarians. This initial building housed everything associated with the college. "The College," wrote the Jesuit James Oliver Van de Velde, visiting Cincinnati on his way to St. Louis, "is a building somewhat similar to the Church, but of modern style. It has, like the Church, a small . . . steeple, which looks very pretty. The Bishop's house, which is rather small, joins the two other buildings. The whole, taken together, presents an imposing sight. The college is ample enough to receive a large number of students. The rooms are large, but the dormitory, though spacious, does not admit enough fresh air. The boys will suffer from this cause in the summer." A missionary from Vienna described the building as "beautifully well-proportioned, large and substantial," and envisioned the college becoming "a permanent and incalculably great benefit to this country bereft of Catholic educational and scholarly institutions." Later the diocese erected a building between the cathedral and college that accommodated both the seminary and episcopal residence. (9)

The diocesan college, at times called the "Literary Institute," began its institutional life at a time when the country was consistently expanding westward, and Cincinnati was enjoying the benefits of this expansion. Internal improvements facilitated the city's economic development and growing population. In addition to the Ohio River, two roads from the east gave immigrants access to Ohio. In the 1820s the National Road crossed through Ohio. Paddlewheel steamers plied the Ohio River and expanded river traffic. In the 1830s the Miami-Maumee Canal and the Ohio Canal were built, connecting Cincinnati with the eastern part of the state on Lake Erie. The Little Miami Railroad, chartered in 1836, ran from Cincinnati to Springfield, Ohio, where it connected with another line that extended to Lake Erie. This gave Cincinnati access to the Great Lakes. (10)

Fenwick intended the Athenaeum to serve as a day and boarding school for Catholic boys who sought higher education as well as a nursery for vocations to the priesthood. Over the door of the building was the Latin inscription "Athenaeum Religioni et Artibus Sacrum," which meant "The Athenaeum, dedicated to religion and liberal arts." Frederic Rese was the vice president of the college and dealt with admissions and day-to-day operations. Tuition, which included board, washing, and mending, was $150 per year. The Athenaeum provided a six-year course of studies, as there was then no formal division between high school and college training. The curriculum included mathematics, geography, history, rhetoric, moral, natural and experimental philosophy, chemistry, the Greek and Latin authors, as well as the English, Latin, Greek, French, Spanish, Italian, and German languages. The latter two courses each cost $25 extra. The absence of religion courses in the curriculum helped reassure some non-Catholic parents that their sons could receive a college education without being subjected to "conversion-to-Catholicism" tactics. "Like every similar institution, which much depend, for success, on the patronage of the Public," the school's prospectus read, the Athenaeum would "make every exertion to merit the patronage of a liberal and enlightened Public." A contemporary author also noted that "a sufficient number of teachers . . . attend[ed] closely to all the pupils, both during their hours of study and recreation. This feature, in which most of our prominent seminaries are defective, gave the school a reputation which induced a number of Protestants to prefer it to any of our other schools for the education of their sons." (11)

From the beginning, a large proportion of the students who attended the Athenaeum were non-Catholic. Few of the 60 students enrolled in 1831–1832 were Catholic. "Full of respect for the religious feelings, and religious freedom of others," the prospectus read, "never in our own establishment, shall we manifest a spirit of sectarian proselytism." On the other hand, Catholic parents were assured of a Catholic atmosphere and religious influence in the school as the faculty members were mostly priests and seminarians and there was a students' chapel in the college. Initially all the members of the faculty were to come from the diocese. Though he wanted a native clergy, Fenwick realized that it would be difficult to staff the college with only diocesan clergy. (12)

On October 22, 1831, five days after the opening of the Athenaeum, the Cincinnati ordinary founded the *Catholic Telegraph*, the diocesan newspaper, with Father James Mullon, rector of the seminary, as editor. The newspaper was born on the same site as the Athenaeum, the location of the present St. Francis Xavier Church. The *Catholic Telegraph* was the second Catholic paper in the country, the first west of the Alleghenies. Two months later the Cincinnati bishop wrote to a friend in London that his "flourishing" diocese now contained "twenty-four priests, missionaries, twenty-two churches, and several more congregations without churches, whereas fourteen years ago there was not a church." Moreover, the diocese now had a seminary, college, and a weekly paper. (13)

Fenwick directed the college for about half a year. His ecclesiastical duties, however, required him to frequently travel throughout the diocese. So because of his long absences from the see city, on April 21, 1832, Fenwick appointed James Mullon the first president of the Athenaeum. Mullon's tenure was short, lasting less than two years. (14)

About a month before Fenwick died of cholera in September 1832, the Cincinnati ordinary had tried to secure the appointment of a coadjutor for his diocese. Impressed by the Jesuits he had met, which included his cousin Enoch Fenwick at Georgetown College in Maryland, Bishop Fenwick had requested that Rome appoint the Jesuit Peter Kenny, official visitor and overall superior of the Jesuits of Maryland, his coadjutor bishop. However, John Roothaan, who three years earlier had been elected the Jesuit superior general, often called father general, and had authority over the worldwide Society of Jesus, opposed Kenny's appointment on the grounds of age and infirmity. The officials of the Sacred Congregation of the Propagation of the Faith in Rome, which had been put in charge of the direction of the Catholic Church in the United States, shared these reservations. There was also a concern that the Dominicans, who made up the majority of the clergy in Ohio, would not welcome a Jesuit as their bishop. (15)

Bishop John Baptist Purcell and the Athenaeum

When the Irish-born John Baptist Purcell was installed as Bishop of Cincinnati on November 14, 1833, he inherited a diocese that under Edward Fenwick's leadership had organized mission activities and established those institutions essential to a new see. Almost four months before Purcell took over, James Mullon had written a letter to him expressing concern over the future of the college. "When you accept, which I humbly beg you will," he wrote, "notify me, that I may make the necessary arrangements for continuing the college, which never could be reopened with respect, with the present members. Its prospects are fair and even flattering; but Rt. Rev. Sir, I entreat you, for its support to use your efforts to send some four or five efficient and exemplary young men to assist us in the duties of it—the present with the exception of *three* are anything but what you would expect to see in Seminarians." (16)

Shortly before leaving Emmitsburg, Maryland, where he had served as president of Mount St. Mary's College, Purcell noted that it would "be among the greatest pleasures and holiest occupations of my present station to exert renewed energies that the students frequenting the [secular] College of Cincinnati," which had been established in 1819, be surpassed by the students at the Athenaeum "in talents, in love of science, morality, and virtue." About two months after Purcell's arrival, Mullon left for New Orleans. Purcell assumed Mullon's classes in theology and philosophy during his absence. (17)

When classes at the Athenaeum began in August 1834, Purcell, a diocesan priest and former seminary president and professor, assumed direction of the college as president. "He will not hold the office, as sinecure," the *Catholic Telegraph* wrote. Purcell made arrangements "to spend a considerable portion of every day among the students," lecturing occasionally on theology to the seminarians. If at any time his bishop's duties required "his temporary absence from the school," a diocesan priest was authorized to "serve in his place." (18)

When Purcell became bishop, Cincinnati's population was still predominantly non-Catholic. The growth of the local Catholic Church, largely because of increasing immigration and missionary work, generated uneasiness among some Protestants. What in particular had helped intensify the spirit of anti-Catholicism in Cincinnati was the fact that in the fall of 1830 there were more Protestant pupils than Catholic at St. Peter's Catholic School on Sycamore Street. The Sisters of Charity, who operated St. Peter's, were the first community of women religious native to the United States. They had come from Emmitsburg in 1829 to establish a foundation in Cincinnati. As Catholics took pride in the increasing number of conversions in the diocese, Protestant ministers had legitimate concerns about Catholics possibly influencing and even converting some of their children. In the summer of 1831 the *Christian Journal*, a local anti-Catholic newspaper, warned Cincinnati residents against the "increase of Papists in the United States." It urged Protestants not to place their children in Catholic schools, fearing that the West was fast becoming the pope's domain, and it would soon be all under his control. Bishop Purcell knew that Protestantism was the dominant force in the community, as was true of the whole country. (19)

Organized anti-Catholicism was a major force in the 1830s. The significant increase in the Catholic population, churches, and schools doubtlessly reawakened fear and intolerance among some non-Catholics. As Protestant books and weekly newspapers played on Protestant fears, they invoked images of a Church that was largely a traditional, hierarchical, undemocratic institution that took orders from a foreign power, namely the pope. They viewed the Catholic religion as being irredeemably foreign and intrinsically opposed to the democratic principles of American civilization. A work that received much publicity in the Midwest was Lyman Beecher's *Plea for the West* (1835). Beecher, who had left Boston in 1832 to take over the presidency of Lane Theological Seminary in Cincinnati, argued that part of his ministry was to fight the pope in the Midwest. (20)

Concerned over the increasing wave of anti-Catholicism and the "bigoted and misguided zealots" in the community, Purcell exclaimed that Beecher "is persecuting us fiercely, here. I seriously believe the hour of persecution," he wrote to Bishop Joseph Rosati of St. Louis, "is not far distant." Though anti-Catholicism in the Ohio Valley never reached the intensity that it did in the East, Catholics nevertheless felt the effects of anti-Catholic prejudice. There was "no country, claiming to be free, in which there is more underhand persecution than in America," the *Catholic Telegraph* editorialized, "nor is there a city in proportion to its population, where more instances can be produced of this vulgar bigotry, than in our fair town of Cincinnati." Partly in response to nativism and to the needs of immigrant life, Catholics became increasingly defensive. (21)

Within a few months in his presidency of the college it became obvious that while attending to diocesan matters, and more particularly to Athenaeum issues, Purcell was overextended. "He is overpowered by being obliged to attend all sorts of offices and functions, which would keep several men very busy," wrote Stephen Badin, who had come to Cincinnati to give the bishop a hand. "He must perform all the duties of a Professor of Divinity in the Seminary and of humanities in the College. . . . He must trouble himself with a variety of temporal affairs and domestic economy and government, besides the discipline of the College and Seminary." By the mid-1830s it became clear that Purcell should be relieved of his administrative duties at the college. (22)

In September 1835, Stephen H. Montgomery, a Dominican who had joined Fenwick as a missionary in Ohio in 1819, was named president of the Athenaeum. During Montgomery's presidency, the college encountered difficulties. While visiting Cincinnati in 1836 Badin observed that the Athenaeum was "without rule" and also without a "ruler," as Montgomery was on a trip to New York at the time. When Purcell returned from the meeting of the Third Provincial Council of Baltimore in the summer of 1837, he dismissed Montgomery from his duties as president of the Athenaeum. Edward Purcell, the bishop's brother, who would soon be raised to the priesthood, became the principal of the day school and Father Josue M. Young, the prefect of studies. Largely due to the 1837 financial panic in the country, the Athenaeum was reduced from a boarding school to a day school during the years 1837, 1838, and 1839. (23)

With the growth of Catholicity in Ohio, Bishop Purcell needed more clergy. Even though by 1838 he had seen the number of priests in the diocese of Cincinnati increase from fourteen to thirty, there was still a dire need for clergy. The Cincinnati ordinary, like other bishops in the Midwest, made repeated petitions to Church leaders in Rome for European priests. Purcell was very much concerned with the ability of the diocese to establish parishes and build churches rapidly enough and supply them with clergy to meet the needs of the fast-growing ranks of the Catholic population and to address anti-Catholic sentiments. He believed he could establish twenty new parishes if he had the priests. Because the Cincinnati church was in need of more priests to carry out its ministry, including the staffing of the college, Purcell decided to offer the Athenaeum to the Society of Jesus. (24)

Jesuits were no strangers to the Midwest. The society's missionary efforts in the area had begun as early as 1763, almost two hundred years after the Jesuits' 1566 arrival in Florida. In the spring of 1823 Bishop Fenwick, after hearing that some Jesuits were going to St. Louis College, which had been established as St. Louis Academy in 1818, had sent a letter to his Jesuit cousin at Georgetown College, "I wish I could hear of some of them coming into my diocese," he wrote, "where nearly as much can be done." During the next 15 years Cincinnati became a convenient place for Jesuits to stop on their way to parishes and Indian missions in St. Louis. In 1825 Stephen Badin made an appeal to the English Jesuits to open a house in the Diocese of Cincinnati. "I should be happy," Nicholas Sewall, the English provincial wrote, "if I could find any zealous missionaries for Dr. Fenwick's diocese; but at present we are so distressed for want of men, that it is impossible." (25)

Coincidentally, three days before the Athenaeum opened on October 17, 1831, the Jesuit James Oliver Van de Velde visited Cincinnati on his way traveling from Georgetown to join the faculty of St. Louis College. In 1828 St. Louis College had been placed under the direction of the Society of Jesus. Four years later it became a university. Though Van de Velde and his two Jesuit companions spent but a day in Cincinnati they did meet with Fenwick. The bishop had gone to their hotel and invited them to his residence for dinner. After dinner they visited the cathedral and the Athenaeum. Fenwick hoped to appoint Van de Velde president of the Athenaeum and petitioned the Jesuit provincial of Maryland to that effect. However, his services were seen as more urgently needed in St. Louis. (26)

Though Van de Velde, of Flemish origin, was impressed with the growth of Catholicism in the region, he had some reservations about some of the city's inhabitants. He noted that before leaving Cincinnati one of the Jesuits had "lost his Italian boots. It is probable that they were stolen from him," he wrote, "for they say that there are many thieves in Cincinnati, and especially in the [Cincinnati] hotel in which we lodged." He had previously lost his cane and one of his companions his reading glasses. (27)

The Jesuits Arrive

In need of more priests, religious, and money for his diocese, Purcell in 1838 went to Europe seeking assistance. "My chief object in going [to Europe]," Purcell wrote to Archbishop Samuel Eccleston of Baltimore, "is to obtain a colony of Jesuits for a college" as well as obtain women religious and monetary support. His predecessor, Bishop Fenwick, had hoped to start a college staffed by Dominicans. Now, the diocese turned to the Jesuits. Purcell sailed from New York on June 16, arriving at Liverpool on July 7th. Seven months later, in February 1839, his journey took him to Rome, where he had a special audience with Pope Gregory XVI. The Cincinnati ordinary also had a profitable visit with John Roothaan, the father general of the Society of Jesus. In his meeting, Purcell, who had long had a high opinion of the order, extended an invitation to the Jesuits to take over Cincinnati's diocesan college. As the bishop wrestled with the problem of getting qualified priests and laymen on his college staff, he came to believe that the progress and stability of the Athenaeum would be better provided for by entrusting it to the care of the religious order. Moreover, the college was tying up scarce manpower, which he needed elsewhere. Purcell was ready to close the struggling school if the Jesuits did not take charge. After the national financial panic in 1833 the student enrollment at the Athenaeum had begun to decline. In addition to closing the boarding school for three years in the late 1830s, the college temporarily suspended classes at the end of the 1838–1839 year. In his meeting with Purcell, the Jesuit general promised that the next house established by the order in America would be in the Diocese of Cincinnati. (28)

On December 26, 1839, Roothaan wrote to Peter J. Verhaegen, the Jesuit superior of the Missouri mission in St. Louis, informing him that Purcell had petitioned the society to take over the Athenaeum. In 1823 the Society of Jesus had established the Missouri mission west of the Mississippi. Coinciding with Purcell's petition, the bishop of Detroit, Frederic Rese, formerly of Cincinnati, had made a similar request for his college. "What does your Reverence think?" Roothaan asked. "[W]hich of the two colleges do you prefer? The harvest is great." Two and a half months later, Verhaegen responded. "I realize that our Society will do much good in Cincinnati college [sic] as also in the college begun by Bishop Rese in Detroit; but your Paternity knows," he wrote, "that we cannot provide both colleges with professors. If your Paternity were to send four competent men, we could add to them four younger men and some coadjutor-brothers. This number would suffice for the two colleges together, at least for a beginning. And if both colleges cannot be accepted by the Society, acceptance should be made of one of the two." (29)

In mid-May 1840, Roothaan informed Verhaegen, who was now a vice provincial—as two months earlier the Missouri mission had become a vice province—that as to "the colleges of Cincinnati and Detroit, I hope to be able to send this year not indeed as many trained men as your Reverence desires, but at any rate . . . two or three." The vice provincial or provincial superior had authority over a specific geographical and administrative unit called a "vice province" or "province." Roothaan recommended that the Jesuits take charge of the Athenaeum and thus relieve the diocesan clergy of the responsibility of operating the college. "Cincinnati holds out some promise, not so Detroit," he wrote. "Cincinnati is consequently to be preferred." (30)

Verhaegen, less than enthusiastic, wrote to Purcell on August 10, 1840, informing him of Roothaan's decision and inquiring about the arrangement and conditions at Cincinnati. Before he could accept the bishop's offer "I deem it necessary," he wrote, "that I should be thoroughly acquainted with your views on the subject before I take any step. If, therefore, nothing has occurred to change your mind in relation to this important affair, please inform me of it, and during the ensuing vacation one of our . . . [Jesuits] will pay you a visit and learn from you in person everything we ought to know in regard to the affair in question." (31)

Purcell replied within a week. "I lose no time in telling you of the joy" your letter "has afforded me," he wrote. "There is no mistake *about* or *within* the matter—Ohio with a population of 160 or 170,000 souls and Cincinnati with 45,000, double what it had ten years ago, are worthy of an University conducted by the Society of Jesus, which I have ever reverenced and loved with devotedness and sincerity. I need not tell you of the place which this state occupies in the map of the United States and its immense resources of every description. It could furnish," he argued, "*three hundred pupils* and still find a plenty to spare for Kentucky, if wanted, and for Missouri, if it did not laugh at the idea of wanting buckeye patronage, when its numerous youth are not capable of being accommodated at home." (32)

The Cincinnati ordinary then responded more directly to Verhaegen's inquiry. "I propose then," he wrote, ". . . *to give you up forever*, on condition that they should *ever* be held sacred for church and school, the College, Seminary and Church, with the real estate on which these buildings, which I now occupy, are located—that you may have there a college and a parish church to be served by your Society in perpetuity." He further pointed out that the college was "in good repair, at present, having been newly shingled." Having just imported from France a new cabinet of natural philosophy for two thousand dollars, he was turning that over to the Jesuits as well. He also informed Verhaegen that the diocese would "employ . . . as Teachers of the College" twelve seminarians if that would be of interest to the Jesuit order. He assured him that the "school would be well patronized here after the first clamor of the heretics would be put back—down their own throats. . . . [Y]ou would meet . . . again and again . . . with the most cordial cooperation. I desire only the glory of God by the right education of youth, the confusion of heresy and the conversion of heretics and sinners." (33)

Demonstrating his strong interest in securing Jesuit presence in his diocese, he offered Verhaegen alternatives to the college site in downtown Cincinnati. "In addition to, or instead of the foregoing, just as you please, I would give you 500 acres of land in Brown County, forty miles from Cincinnati. . . . I should think," he added, "a college in the country indispensable—or instead of this in Brown County, you can have sixteen hundred acres or 2000, as you prefer, in Gallia County, 12 miles from the Ohio river. . . . All I would ask is the support of five or six seminarians annually, or in equivalent. But of this, no more now." (34)

Among some Jesuits, however, there were misgivings about taking over the Athenaeum. "I do not see," Van de Velde wrote to Roothaan on August 22, "how the college is to be begun. Certainly no one can be sent from St. Louis University. All who might be suited are quite necessary here. . . . So, unless [Jesuits come] from other sources, it would be a risky thing to begin the college of Cincinnati. It is better that the thing be not done at all than that it be done badly and turn out badly." There was much concern among the members of the society in St. Louis over the shortage of Jesuits in the face of increasing demand for their services. "Every now and then," John Anthony Elet, president of St. Louis University, wrote to Roothaan three days later, "there is talk of opening a new college in Cincinnati. They also speak of starting a residence in New Orleans. In both places a most extensive field lies open with promise of the most abundant fruit. But the workers are wanting and will continue to be wanting unless serious thought be given to a Seminary for Ours completely separated from the college of St. Louis." (35)

Within a few days of Purcell's letter to him, Verhaegen brought the bishop's offer to the attention of his consultors in the vice province. On August 31, 1840, they unanimously agreed to take over the Athenaeum and to keep the college in the city, following the counsel of their founder, St. Ignatius, to place colleges in the cities. The Jesuits' takeover of a diocesan college was the third in thirty-five years since the Society of Jesus had first assumed control of Georgetown College in 1805 and then St. Louis College twenty-three years later. The consultors differed only on the question whether control of the Athenaeum should be assumed at once or be postponed to a later date. Verhaegen recommended taking over the institution without delay, even though only a single Jesuit could be spared for the fall session. Elet and Van de Velde, on the other hand, argued that the opening of classes be delayed a year so as to afford time for the Jesuits to communicate with the father general. They hoped to obtain through his intervention some

Jesuits from other provinces, either to staff the Athenaeum or to replace those professors who would be transferred from St. Louis to Cincinnati. Verhaegen's view prevailed. They decided to take over the Athenaeum during the 1840–1841 year. Elet, who had been President of St. Louis University from 1836 to 1840, was appointed president of the new college. On September 1, 1840, Verhaegen, accompanied by Elet, left St. Louis for Cincinnati to meet with Purcell, who had earlier invited him to visit the city and to make plans to take over the college. (36)

Upon their arrival in Cincinnati they met with Purcell at his house where he served them, the bishop later wrote, "red & white wine." After Mass on September 6, the bishop announced to the cathedral congregation the transfer of the Athenaeum to the Jesuits. The Jesuits changed the name of the Athenaeum to St. Xavier College in honor of St. Francis Xavier under whose patronage Bishop Fenwick had originally placed the Athenaeum. Verhaegen then preached to the assembled congregation. News of the transfer spread quickly. From "this time on, we trust in God," the *Catholic Telegraph* editorialized six days later, "the Athenaeum will be worthy of its motto: 'Sacred to religion and to arts.' The building is being fitted up, extensive improvements are going on in it and around it, and as soon as they are completed the school will commence on a scale not hitherto reached by the institution." The warranty deed of the transfer of the college property did not take place until six months later on March 31, 1841. At that time the Diocese of Cincinnati conveyed for one dollar the Sycamore Street property "to have and to hold to the said Elet, Verhaegen and Van de Velde, the survivors forever—in trust to set apart a portion for a church or a chapel for the permanent accommodation" of the Society of Jesus in Cincinnati. (37)

The diocesan paper praised the Jesuit takeover of the college. "No one," the *Catholic Telegraph* further noted, ". . . ever regreted [sic] that their sons were educated under their direction, for the society is justly celebrated for success in developing the minds of youth, in leading them to the acquisition of every branch of knowledge, and sending forth men into the world, who have been enriched with the purest lessons of morality and fitted for the highest circles of society." The transfer of the college to the Jesuits "thrilled through the heart of many a parent, for this auspicious event had been long fervently prayed for and most anxiously expected." Purcell, who became the first person in charge of the St. Xavier College Board of Trustees, was hopeful that by November 1 classes would "be reorganized in the most efficient manner" and that 25 to 30 boarders would be accommodated. (38)

Rivalry caused some Jesuits to disapprove of the acquisition of the Athenaeum. Members of the French province's mission in Kentucky were about to open a school in Louisville and were surprised that the Flemish St. Louis Jesuits would be taking over the college. William Stack Murphy, Jesuit superior of the mission in Kentucky, expressed concern to his provincial in Paris and to Roothaan. "[W]e fear," he wrote, "it may hurt Louisville much. . . . [W]ithout our being given the least intimation of it, we learn from the papers that our Fathers of Missouri have just accepted in Cincinnati, the bishop's college. . . . This college is going to open November 1 next. Cincinnati being only twelve hours from Louisville, a trip one can make at any moment thanks to 300 steamboats, would our two establishments perhaps be to[o] close together?" For some time the French Jesuits had expressed interest to expand northwards from their Kentucky mission. The presence of the Flemish Jesuits in Cincinnati naturally blocked this plan. It had been the wish of some French Jesuits that the eastern states would be administered by the American Jesuits, the western by the Flemish fathers, and the central portion of the country by the French. Now the French Jesuits' plan had suffered a setback. (39)

While some Jesuits did not think that Cincinnati was "suited for a boarding school," a Jesuit from St. Mary's College in Kentucky impressed upon the Jesuit superior general that "a great field [was] open to their zeal in Cincinnati, the 'Queen City.'" With a population of 60,000 souls, he pointed out that the city was "steadily increasing" and that Ohio, "the *chef-d'oeuvre* [masterpiece] of American colonization, without slaves and without assassins," contained within its limits "the elite of the German and Irish immigrants." (40)

On September 24, shortly after returning to St. Louis, Verhaegen informed Roothaan that all arrangements regarding the college had been made. Six days later, the first contingent of Jesuits, consisting of Peter Gleizal, a priest, and the Jesuit scholastic John Baptist Duerinck, and Brothers Sebastian Schlienger and John Dugan, left St. Louis to begin work at the college. A Jesuit scholastic was a seminarian studying to become a priest. On October 18 Elet, accompanied by the scholastic Maurice Van den Eycken and Brother Peter de Meyer arrived. The Jesuit priest Aloysius Pin came a little later. These eight Jesuits constituted the college's Jesuit community during its first year.

In keeping with Purcell's offer, Verhaegen expected some of the seminarians in the diocese to assist the Jesuits in teaching as long as would be necessary. (41)

In mid-October 1840, Purcell, pleased with the arrival of the Jesuits, wrote to Bishop John Hughes of New York that the "bigots have not so far shewn [sic] many of their teeth, but I presume they are on an edge." As early as 1834, six years before the Society of Jesus took control of the Athenaeum, the *Catholic Telegraph* had printed an article praising and defending the Jesuits. "The Society of Jesus, (we are far from intending to disparage the other religious orders, which have also, their good *quantum* of merits) the most learned and religious body of men the world ever saw," it wrote, "has been and is yet equally misrepresented by Protestants and Infidels, who betraying a want of confidence in their own tenets and principles, and sensible of the great learning and controversial powers of that body exert themselves to destroy by calumny and persecution, those whom they cannot approach with argument." (42)

The Jesuit seed had been planted in Cincinnati. The ministry of the members of the Society of Jesus would help fulfill the order's aspirations of attending to the intellectual, moral, and spiritual needs of students in the college, as well as to the spiritual and temporal needs of parishioners and residents in the community.

JESUITS TAKE CHARGE, 1840–1865

W hen the Jesuits opened St. Xavier College in the fall of 1840, Bishop John Purcell expressed great faith in the development of the "Queen City of the West," which he described as "a calm, beautiful City, having great facilities of access and as thriving as any other in the Republic." In his correspondence with the father general of the Society of Jesus and with the provincial of the Missouri vice province, he elaborated at length on the growth of Cincinnati and the Midwest. Since the acquisition of the Louisiana Territory by the United States in 1803, the country had been consistently expanding westward. In 1845 John O'Sullivan, writing in the *New York Morning News*, coined the phrase "manifest destiny," suggesting that the country was destined to expand "from sea to sea." That year the United States annexed Texas. The following year the country waged war with Mexico. The tremendous movement of people westward helped make the river metropolis one of the fastest-growing urban centers in the country. In 1846 the Catholic population in Cincinnati was twenty-five thousand, approximately one-third of the city's total population. "Our city," Bishop Purcell wrote, "is increasing rapidly. I suppose 2000 houses in progress of building. Mechanics all employed—Journeyman, carpenters, masons, plasterers—from $1.50 to 1.75 per diem." The city's growing population and rapid economic development stimulated social and cultural growth. (1)

No longer a frontier settlement, the burgeoning city had become an important western river community. Steamboats on the Ohio River and the opening of canals had provided the foundation upon which Cincinnati grew. Heavily industrialized by mid-century, Cincinnati was a place where banking services, hog slaughtering and packing, and furniture manufacturing, clothing, and iron- and metalworking industries prevailed. By the 1850s it was the third largest manufacturing center and the sixth largest city in the United States. (2)

From the mid-1830s to the end of the Civil War in 1865, new immigrants, principally from Germany and Ireland, would significantly change the population of Cincinnati. In the first half of the nineteenth century, Cincinnati's population nearly doubled every ten years. The Catholic Church in Cincinnati steadily was becoming a church of immigrants, and because of the needs of immigrant life, local Catholicism increasingly developed religious and ethnic solidarity and institutional separatism. St. Xavier College, largely staffed by immigrant faculty and administration, attended to the intellectual and spiritual needs of the sons of mostly first generation immigrants. (3)

Beginning of St. Xavier College

As the first Jesuit president of St. Xavier College, John A. Elet also served as the rector or the local superior of the Jesuit religious house or community. Born in St. Amand, in what is now Belgium, on February 19, 1802, he completed his studies at the College of Mechlin in Belgium. He was one of nine young Flemish, who at the invitation of the Jesuit Charles Nerinckx, an influential missionary from Kentucky, left their native land and volunteered as missionaries in 1821 in spreading Catholicism in the United States. He entered the Society of Jesus that year. He was still a novice in the Jesuit novitiate at White Marsh, Maryland, when Bishop William Dubourg of New Orleans went to Georgetown College to secure Jesuits for the northern part of his diocese that extended all the way to Missouri. In response to his invitation, seven novices, all Belgians, and two priests set out for the West in the spring of 1823 and founded at Florissant, Missouri, the Missouri mission of the Society of Jesus. That year he was subsequently ordained and began working as a missionary among the Indians. When Elet came to Cincinnati to take charge of St. Xavier College in 1840 he had had four years of administrative experience as president of St. Louis University to guide him in establishing the college on a more solid basis. He referred to his new college as the "child of my predilection." In addition to helping establish it on a firm foundation, his pastoral sense would also have a significant influence on the spirit of the college. (4)

St. Xavier's first prospectus, approved by the provincial of the Missouri province and the father general of the Society of Jesus in Rome and sent by John Elet from St. Louis, appeared in the *Catholic Telegraph* on September 26, 1840. The provincial and the superior general were key figures in the governance of the Jesuit colleges. For the naming of the Jesuit president and other major officials, initiating or modifying academic programs, changing admission requirements, building and constructing programs, among others, the provincial had to apply to the superior general for permission. The prospectus sent to the diocesan newspaper announced that St. Xavier College, scheduled to open as a boarding and day school on the first Monday in November 1840, was under the direction of the Society of Jesus and the patronage of Bishop Purcell. During the months of September and October, before school opened, with the help of carpenters, bricklayers, and painters, the Jesuits overhauled the Athenaeum building. They refurnished the classrooms and dormitory rooms for the students and equipped the kitchen with a new stove. To generate much-needed revenue, they sold the three old stoves at an auction. (5)

Founded on the principles developed by St. Ignatius of Loyola, a Basque nobleman and former soldier of fortune, who founded the Society of Jesus in 1540, St. Xavier College echoed the belief of its founder. When Ignatius left soldiering for a life of penance, prayer, and the service of God and his fellow men, he found his lack of academic education a handicap in fulfilling his aspiration. In his thirties he pursued academic studies and at the age of forty-three he earned the degree of master of arts at the University of Paris. There he joined his friend and later fellow Jesuit, Francis Xavier, who had also acquired the master of arts degree. When Pope Paul III approved the Society of Jesus, Ignatius became the first superior general. Manifesting their convictions, he and his fellow members emphasized the importance of learning by establishing houses of study for the society's younger members. In 1549 the members committed themselves to the education of other youths as well. In Part IV of his *Constitutions of the Society of Jesus* Ignatius clearly underscored the importance of education. (6)

The *Ratio Studiorum* became the Jesuits' "Plan of Studies," the basis for Jesuit education. Published by the Society of Jesus in 1599, the *Ratio* was based on the University of Paris model that Ignatius of Loyola so admired. It stressed humanities, philosophy, and theology. By the end of the sixteenth century the Society of Jesus had established the first educational system in the world: that is, an organization of schools that remained in close contact with one another, reviewing, sharing, and evaluating educational experiences with one another. The institutions were highly flexible and adapted themselves to circumstances of times, places, and persons through constantly shared reports and evaluations. Throughout the seventeenth century the Jesuit schools easily adapted the *Ratio* to whatever culture in which they found themselves. To be true to the tradition of Jesuit education, Jesuit institutions provided an education to help prepare men to live in their culture critically, intelligently, and spiritually. The Jesuits attended to their mission for almost 200 years until the society was suppressed by papal order in 1773. Until that time, it guided a network of 845 educational institutions worldwide. (7)

During the nineteenth century, Jesuits in America continually adopted the main points of the *Ratio Studiorum* and modeled their curriculum after the six- or seven-year programs in a number of European universities. The first three years in the program were called first, second, and third humanities, and the last three were poetry, rhetoric, and philosophy. Colleges in Europe and in the United States provided a comprehensive education that included primary, secondary, and college instruction. Eventually, in the twentieth century, the first three years of humanities in America would become the equivalent of a high school curriculum. In the nineteenth century, however, the integrated six-year program was considered a "college" program of Jesuit education. The general age for admission to St. Xavier College was from eight to sixteen years old. So more than half of the students enrolled at the college were actually at a pre-college level.

The renovated school opened as a Jesuit institution on November 3, 1840. It had eight Jesuits and five assistant tutors. In keeping with its Catholic and Jesuit heritage, St. Xavier College symbolized revealed religion and the humanist tradition. It subscribed to the belief that God gave each person a task in life—a career, a vocation, a challenge, a mission, and a belief that God wanted each individual to make a contribution to society, to make the world a better place, and to be a man for others. The *Ratio* supplied the college's central paradigm. The traditional offerings of Latin, Greek, philosophy, ethics, history, chemistry, and natural science, among other disciplines, contained the heart of Jesuit education. The course of studies, which constituted a demanding program, had a four-year curriculum that included three years of Latin and Greek and two years of rhetoric and mathematics. Natural philosophy (chemistry and physics) was offered in the third year, while logic, metaphysics, ethics, and moral philosophy were offered in the fourth. Interspersed were a variety of classes in history, ethics, logic, and religion. In addition, the college offered Spanish and German language courses without any additional charge. Students in each year's class studied the entire curriculum together. The teachers often called upon them to recite their lessons in the classroom, as oral recitation was a preferred pedagogical device. (8)

Throughout the nineteenth century the college curriculum placed a strong emphasis on the humanities, the arts, and the sciences. Typically, private religious colleges in the 1800s had a classical curriculum. The Yale Report of 1828, published in the prestigious *American Journal of Science and Arts*, proved helpful to denominational colleges. A well-reasoned defense of traditional classical education, the Yale Report quickly became the most widely-read and influential pronouncement on education at the time. It was an excellent assertion of the humanist tradition. It helped justify a curriculum that offered courses in science, fine arts, the humanities, and social studies. America's well-established colleges placed a strong emphasis on classical languages, rhetoric, mathematics, logic, and moral philosophy. Classical studies were justified for the knowledge they provided and for the mental discipline and cultural refinement for later life. They also retained their practical purpose to help prepare students for the professions of law, medicine, and ministry. St. Xavier officials insisted that students in the classical program study not only the achievements of ancient Greece and Rome, but also the skills of language, rhetoric, and critical thinking. Emphasizing the importance of both knowledge and virtue, the program aimed to educate students intellectually, artistically, and morally, while preparing them for lives of service. The faculty believed that the right kind of education could improve character. In many ways, the college would serve society through the dedicated lives of its graduates. (9)

In an attempt to attract more day students, in December 1840 the college established a mercantile department in order to provide students a business education. The mercantile course of studies was partly in response to the desire of working class parents that education be more practical. At the same time that there was considerable appreciation for the prestige of a classical education, some expressed a desire for more practical and accessible non-classical courses as well. "At the solicitation of many parents and citizens," Elet advertised in the January 9, 1841, issue of the *Catholic Telegraph*, "St. Xavier College has agreed to enlarge the Day School attached to the institution. By this arrangement the College will afford to the youth of the city an excellent opportunity for acquiring a business education. . . . The plan of instruction is organized on an extensive scale and well calculated to prove useful to Public. The institution begins to flourish, and bids fair to be numbered [before] long among the best Literary Establishments of the West." (10)

As a multipurpose college, which was a variant of the classical college, St. Xavier sought to educate a learned laity as well as a learned ministry. The classical course of studies, which constituted the core of the college, began to be surrounded by non-degree commercial subjects in evening classes. There was a growing belief in America that college should also be a place for non-degree students. The mercantile course of studies included classes in the English and French languages, writing, geography, history, arithmetic, and bookkeeping. These offerings gradually became more apparent across America. Under much public pressure, Ohio University in Athens, Ohio, moved away from the traditional course of study and emphasized more practical and useful courses for contemporary life. Fifteen years before the Jesuits took over the Athenaeum, Miami University in Oxford, Ohio, substituted applied mathematics and political economy for ancient subjects. The transition from a frontier to a market-driven society in antebellum America was especially rapid in Ohio, where there was considerable canal building and railroad construction. In 1860 the state had the third largest population in the country. (11)

In its first year, the college, serving both as a day and a boarding school, had 76 students, 50 of whom were boarders. Among the enrolled students, 29 were registered in the classical course and 47 in the mercantile. Records show that the first student to be registered was thirteen-year-old Joseph Musick of Florissant, Missouri, on October 14, 1840. He stayed at the college for two years, but as the notes in the college register indicate, he was shot accidentally in St. Louis during the summer of 1842. A year later he recovered and returned to St. Xavier, where he graduated in 1845. The college's first catalogue, then called *Calendar of St. Xavier College*, declared that the "religion professed by the Teachers and by the majority of the Pupils" was that of the Roman Catholic Church, "yet Students of all denominations are admitted." William Mitchell Neubold from Summerville, Tennessee, was the first Protestant to register at St. Xavier. (12)

The early college catalogues specified that certain kinds of clothing were essential. Each boarder was expected to have "at least two suits of clothes for each season (summer and winter) to be worn on public occasions," along with eight shirts, eight pairs of socks, six napkins, six towels, four pairs of shoes or boots, a black fur hat, a cap, a cloak or overcoat for winter, a knife, fork, spoon, tumbler, combs, and brushes. Students were prohibited to have money in their own custody. With regard to pocket money, college officials insisted that no student be allowed more than twenty-five cents a week and that the money be deposited with the designated agent either in Cincinnati or New Orleans, Louisiana. Parents who lived at a distance were requested to appoint an agent in Cincinnati and New Orleans, who helped interpret the college's mission and oversaw the payment of all student expenses. The agent in New Orleans acted as regular agent of the college for the southern states of Louisiana, Tennessee, Mississippi, Alabama, and for Mexico and Cuba. College authorities also warned that all letters written to the students, to President Elet, or to the agents "must be directed free of postage, or they shall be liable to remain at the post office." Moreover, all letters sent or received by students, unless to or from their parents, were "subject to the inspection of the President." (13)

The Jesuit officials at Xavier, seeking from the outset to recruit out-of-area students, especially from the South, emphasized the educational benefits of both Cincinnati and the College. Cincinnati was "peculiarly advantageous to the mental improvement and bodily comfort of the Student," they wrote, "affording him the opportunity of attending many interesting lectures on the Arts and Sciences . . . in this city." Moreover, it gave him "the advantages derivable from regular and well supplied markets, and enables him, in case of sickness, to obtain the best medical attendance." (14)

By the mid-1840s school authorities tightened supervision over day students and a pattern of campus life began to emerge. In order to make certain that they were "at all times . . . under the supervision of a responsible and trustworthy person, none will, in [the] future, be admitted as day scholars, unless they live with their parents or some near relatives, and if orphans, with their guardians." The college provided a rationale for these rules. "The culture of the heart and mind of youth," the college catalogue stipulated, "constitutes the end of this institution, and this important object can only be attained by establishing order and [a] systematic course of procedure. . . . These rules are not imposed with the design of subjecting the students to a heavy and a toilsome yoke, but of promoting their advancement in virtue." Authorities insisted that "the discipline is firm but paternal," which they interpreted to mean "affectionate and conciliatory." (15)

The first celebration at St. Xavier College took place on December 3, 1840, the feast day of St. Francis Xavier. The faculty and Catholic students attended Mass in the college chapel. Immediately after the Mass they assembled in the study hall where William X. Guilmartin, a student, delivered an address. On February 22nd students and faculty celebrated George Washington's birthday and Guilmartin delivered a eulogy on the "Father of his Country." Every year throughout much of the nineteenth century there was some form of oratory as a tribute to the first president of the United States. The college also integrated the traditional holidays of Christmas and Independence Day into the campus life. (16)

During its initial academic year, the college introduced its first extracurricular program. On January 19, 1841, some upperclass students formed a debating society. Two students, John Goodin and George Guilford, met with President Elet "for the purpose of soliciting his cooperation" in forming a club. Elet agreed immediately. A few days later the students held a meeting in a classroom and drafted a letter to officials at St. Louis University, requesting information on their debating society. At the same meeting they named the debating group the Philopedian Society (from the Greek: "Those Devoted to Education") and elected William Guilmartin president. The society held its first official meeting on February 24th. From that point on the students met regularly to improve their public speaking by means of discussions and debates. The college provided them with a library and a room in the Athenaeum building. The members dealt with such contemporary topics as the impact of immigrants from Germany and Ireland on America, the rise of American nativism, the moral responsibilities of elected representatives, and the abolition of slavery.

Ohio was a free state, and the residents of Cincinnati were much aware of the practice of slavery that existed in neighboring Covington, Kentucky, just across the Ohio River. During the Mexican War, 1846–1848, the members of the society also faced squarely the political issue of the day and debated whether or not the war was just. A debate, which at times commanded more interest than in the knowledge that it imparted, implied a winner or a loser, and there was "an element of rivalry or sport" in the exercises. In the judgment of one scholar on American higher education, the debating society was the "first effective agency of intellect to make itself felt in the American college." First appearing at Yale in 1753, virtually every college in the first half of the nineteenth century had a debating club, with a name that could be traced to Greece. (17)

A sign of a promising educational relationship of St. Xavier College with the community was the cooperation between the Philopedian Society and the local Woodward Library Society in Cincinnati. In February 1844 the Philopedians invited members of the Woodward Society to attend the celebration of the birthday of George Washington at the college. The following month St. Xavier debaters attended an exhibition at the Woodward Society. The speeches delivered by members of the Philopedian Society were at times quite elaborate. An address on "The Influence of the Church on Society," delivered on February 22, 1847, at the Washington Birthday celebration was published in three consecutive issues of the *Catholic Telegraph*. Forensic displays and oratorical contests were often seen as good practice for teaching, law, and the ministry. (18)

A month after the formation of the Philopedian Society, the *Catholic Telegraph* on February 27, 1841 announced another important beginning at St. Xavier College. "At the request of some young gentlemen, who are desirous of learning the German language, and who have expressed their wish to attend at night, after hours of business," the diocesan paper wrote, "a German Class and also a Bookkeeping Class, will be opened at St. Xavier College on the 1st of March next, and will be taught every evening toward candlelight." Partly in an attempt to attract local students, the college offered evening classes in bookkeeping and German literature for those who worked during the day. Seeking to supplement the traditional humanities education with a business program, it started an evening school in order "to afford both to the students and to persons engaged during the day in mercantile pursuits an opportunity for frequenting these classes." Though mainly an urban day school, St. Xavier College had a number of part-time students. By offering its first night courses, the college—through its evening school—began a tradition of providing an important service to the community of serving the unique needs and schedules of professionals or aspiring professionals in greater Cincinnati. From the beginning the commercial studies were kept separate from the classical course of studies. Students who completed the mercantile course received certificates of qualification and earned one academic credit. (19)

Although St. Xavier was off to a good beginning, there were financial concerns. From the start, the college faced a financial challenge, trying to balance operating expenses with revenues from tuition charges. In its first year the college had a financial deficit of $310. Nevertheless, Peter Verhaegen, Jesuit superior of the Missouri mission, was hopeful. "The beginnings would be a little difficult," he wrote, "but we should soon have a goodly number of subjects." (20)

At the end of the college's first year, Bishop Purcell was optimistic of its future. In June 1841, shortly after receiving papal approval of the transfer of the Athenaeum to the Jesuits, Bishop Purcell thanked John Roothaan, father general of the Society of Jesus, for taking over the college. "[I]t is an occasion of joy shared with me not only by all the faithful of this city, but also by not a few non-Catholics," he wrote, "who realize that the sceptre of education of school-going youth can nowhere be entrusted to or held by more skillful hands, the experience of three centuries to witness." The Cincinnati ordinary was hopeful that in mathematics and physics, as in the other sciences, St. Xavier College would "not only equal but even surpass . . . the [f]lourishing colleges conducted under the auspices of heretics." Anti-Catholic sentiments in the city concerned Purcell deeply. In early September he again wrote to Roothaan, hoping that he would not be "unmindful of our needs, for the enemies of the Holy Name of Jesus Christ are making every effort to endow schools and colleges in which *per fas et nefas* [justly or unjustly] to bring the Catholic cause to ruin. But with God, the most Blessed Mary and the dear Society straining every effort in opposition, nothing whatever will they be able to effect." (21)

College Activities and Organizations

On March 5, 1842, the Ohio legislature passed an act incorporating St. Xavier College. Private colleges that were founded by a religious group appointed a number of trustees from within or outside the denomination and applied to the state for a charter to do business. Such charters were readily granted. That year 185 students attended the college. Authorizing the trustees of St. Xavier College to confer "such Honors and Degrees as are usually conferred by Colleges and Universities," the initial charter was good for thirty years, after which time it would have to be renewed. Since the Jesuits' takeover of the college, there had been six members on the Board of Trustees, consisting of a president, vice president, secretary, treasurer, and two other members. As trustees they were "held individually liable for all debts" of the college. Bishop Purcell was *ex officio* president of the board, while Elet, the rector or president of the college, was *ex officio* vice president. (22)

In early May the members appointed a committee to draft a constitution and by-laws to govern the board's proceedings. Though Purcell was absent from the city and Elet chaired the first meeting, there is no evidence that the bishop ever attended a board meeting during his tenure. The bishop's authority over the affairs of the college was minimal, almost non-existent. Later that month the trustees approved the documents. Beginning that year, the annual meeting, held in the college library, took place on the second Thursday of July. "Secrecy may be enjoined on the Board for a short period of time," one of the by-laws read, "whenever the majority deem it necessary or expedient." By 1844, when enrollment was 260, which was an increase of 38 students over the previous year, and consisted of 93 boarders and 167 day students, there were seven members on the board. A year later enrollment reached its highest level at 291. (23)

As the Board of Trustees oversaw the general direction of the college, the administration focused on day-to-day activities. The matriculation fee for St. Xavier College boarders and half-boarders, those who had breakfast and dined at the school, was ten dollars; for day or commuting students, five dollars. Resident students paid $130 per year for tuition, room, and board with an additional $15 for washing and mending, $5 for stationery, and $5 for physician's fees. At the time, the rate for resident students, contrary to today's standards, did not include bedding, towels, napkins, knives, forks, and spoons. For those students who spent their summer vacation of a month and a half at the college, they paid an additional charge of $20 for board and lodging. Half-boarders paid $100 per year. Thinking that the college was located in a flourishing Midwestern river community and was easily accessible from all parts of the country, Jesuit authorities hoped to attract boarders. Day students enrolled in the classical course of studies paid $40 per year for tuition, while students in the mercantile program paid an annual tuition of $24. The college charged additional fees for science laboratory breakage and for extra courses in vocal and instrumental music, dancing, and drawing. Tuition continued at these prices until 1863, when inflation and the depreciating value of money during the Civil War required an increase. (24)

Once a month, resident students were permitted to visit their parents, guardians, or relatives "residing in the city or its vicinity." College officials prohibited any other absence during the course of the academic year "except in cases of necessity." At the end of each quarter the college sent bulletins to the parents or guardians "to inform them of the conduct, health and proficiency of their sons or wards." In many ways St. Xavier College served as a substitute guardian to the young undergraduates, who, in their parents' judgment, were in need of some parental guidance. Students were expected to conform to an exacting list of regulations. Officials would notify parents of excessive absences, which could lead to dismissal. In order that the students would at all times be under the supervision of a responsible and trustworthy person, the college announced in 1844 that no day students in the future would be admitted unless they lived "with their parents or some near relatives, and if orphans, with their guardians." (25)

Beginning in 1842 the college enforced a daily schedule, which if judged by the standards of today's college students might be considered difficult and rigorous. Resident students normally rose at 5 a.m. At 5:30 they went to prayers and attended Mass, followed by an hour of study. In most Catholic institutions in antebellum America, morning prayers and Sunday Mass attendance were mandatory for resident students. Commuting students at St. Xavier College were required, as far as practicable, to attend the morning study session. Breakfast followed, and then there was a half-hour recreation period. Classes began with English at 8, followed by Latin and then Greek. At 11:30 there were a variety of available courses, such as writing, bookkeeping, history, and geography. The junior students attended history, mythology, and geography classes while the seniors studied chemistry and physics. After the mid-day meal at 12:15 there was an hour of recreation. Then came a study period that was followed by a period during which the students attended a class in French, German, or metaphysics and then a class in mathematics. At 4:30 there was another half-hour period of recreation, followed by a two and one quarter hour study period. The school day ended at 7:15, usually with a moral lecture. Dinner was served at 7:30. The day culminated in prayers at 8:30, followed by "lights out." There were no classes on Sundays nor on the mid-week holiday on Thursdays. Saturday was a school day, a practice that would continue into the twentieth century. In its first catalogue the college announced that it would make certain that students were "punctual in attending School." The academic year usually began on the first Monday in September and almost always ended during the first week in July. The year ended with public examinations in all classes, followed by a rigorous commencement week program. (26)

All classes were taught in the Athenaeum, a two-story brick building with a basement and attic, which fronted Sycamore Street and ran back parallel to St. Peter in Chains Cathedral about two-thirds the length of it, leaving space for a yard in the rear. The cathedral stretched from Sycamore Street back to an alley, a half block. Between these two buildings was the bishop's residence in the center. Shortly after Purcell transferred the college and seminary buildings to the Jesuits in 1840, he embarked on the ambitious project of building a new and more imposing cathedral at a new site on Eighth and Plum Streets. Upon completion of the new cathedral five years later, the old cathedral with a tall spire surmounted by a cross was turned over to the Jesuits who, with members of the old parish, then formed St. Francis Xavier Church and parish. By the 1850s the front part of the Athenaeum had private rooms and offices and the rear was divided into halls for class purposes. A stairway and a wide corridor to the yard and St. Xavier Church separated the Jesuit residence portion from the halls. "But a religious community of between 30 and 40," a scholastic recorded in his diary in 1865, "needed a different arrangement." In the rear, except the study hall on the first floor, which also served for an assembly hall for private exhibitions, the Jesuit community occupied half of the hall space next to the church for refectory, library, and recreation room, leaving a large classroom in the basement and a chapel on the second floor, looking on the yard, for the students. Three classics classes were held in the front part beside the faculty offices on the first floor or in the basement. (27)

St. Xavier College's first commencement exercises were on Thursday, July 29, 1841. It began at 8:00 a.m. and continued until early evening. The program listed eighteen events and activities, the briefest of which might have been about ten minutes. It was the custom then for college students to display some of the knowledge they had learned during the preceding term and deliver public addresses. Senior orations were the culmination of these exercises. The initial program had two presentations in French, two in Latin, one in Greek and in German respectively, a eulogy on George Washington, a debate on the influence of the theater in England, musical selections, and the distribution of academic awards. The following year the commencement lasted two days. There were presentations in English, French, German, Latin, and Greek, debates in both English and French, and musical selections.

In addition to an address in German on the love of one's country and a French ode on Truth, there was an ode to George Washington given in Latin. The college conferred the master's degree on William Guilmartin, the first graduate of St. Xavier College. The degree of master of arts was given to a student who, after having completed his collegiate course, had devoted at least two years to some literary pursuit. (28)

In the summer of 1843 there was a three-day commencement, again with the appropriate music, debates, dramatic readings, and addresses in various languages. There was a debate on capital punishment, followed by a "Comic French Polylogue," an English speech on Ireland, and a German discourse on poetry. Musical interludes separated the presentations. Exercises on the following day began with a debate on the "Relative Advantages of Monarchy and Republicanism," which was followed by a discourse on the French language and a metaphysical dialogue. On the third day there was a debate on the "Comparative Merits of Greece and Rome." The 1843 commencement ended with the conferring of St. Xavier College's first baccalaureate degrees to students at the end of their classical course of studies. The first students to receive the degree of bachelor of arts at the college were John Goodin and Timothy O'Connor, natives of Cincinnati. By 1849 students who "eminently excelled" in their studies graduated *cum distinctione* [with distinction]. Those whose studies were not "so distinguished" graduated *sine distinctione* [without distinction]. (29)

The early administration set the tone not only for academics but for student life as well. What was traditional in all Jesuit colleges was the establishment of the students' Sodality of the Blessed Virgin, later called the Sodality of the Immaculate Conception, which was the first non-academic student organization at St. Xavier, having received its charter from Rome on December 8, 1840. The purpose of the sodality was to foster devotion to the Mother of God. It offered a program of regular devotion. In response to a request from the Xavier sodality, the queen of France arranged for the donation of a painting of the Assumption of the Virgin Mary from King Louis Philippe's private gallery to the college. The painting arrived in Cincinnati in March 1847 and was installed in the sodalists' chapel. In gratitude for this splendid gift the sodalists in early May received Communion from President Elet and prayed for the welfare of their royal benefactors. (30)

In addition to the students' Sodality of the Blessed Virgin and the establishment of the Philopedian Society, Jesuit officials—in response to the students during the 1841–1842 academic year—formed the

Philhermenian Society or Junior Literary Society for the younger students, enabling them "to speak with ease and fluency." When the Philopedian and the Philhermenian Societies petitioned the board of trustees in 1842 "to legalize their existence as connected with the literary department" of the college, the board referred the matter to the faculty who subsequently approved it. In addition, the college established in 1842 the Euterpean Society, offering students with musical talents an opportunity "to add solemnity" to the celebration of various festivals, and to offer to qualified students the advantages of performing in a regular college band. This group provided the music for the extended two- and three-day commencement programs at the college. Eight years later the band performed the "St. Xavier Quick Step," composed by H. Bollman, professor of music and director of the band, at an honors convocation. In 1847 the college formed the Himiroletic Society to help its student members improve in the speaking of French. In addition to these offerings, the college also introduced, at additional cost to the students, optional classes in music, drawing, dancing, and fencing. (31)

During its first year 1840–1841 the college had "a large library," a contemporary wrote, "containing four or five thousand volumes," predominantly in classical studies and philosophy and mainly for the use of the faculty. Two years later there were six thousand volumes. In 1848 college officials established a students' library. Most American colleges at mid-century had few volumes in the library, some but a few hundred books. Only eight institutions had over ten thousand volumes. Reflecting continuing growth and development, in 1865 the St. Xavier library had ten thousand texts. These works were either purchased with college funds or obtained by private donation. The college, for about sixty years, charged a modest fee to students for use of the library. Moreover, during this period the college had a museum with an extensive collection of specimens of botany, conchology, and mineralogy, as well as chemical and philosophical instruments. (32)

From the beginning, lay faculty assisted the Jesuit priests, brothers, and scholastic seminarians in the classrooms. In the second year two laymen, both former students of Xavier, William Guilmartin, professor of rhetoric and English literature, and John Bernhard Stallo, professor of German language and literature, joined the six priests as faculty members. Stallo would eventually become one of the most distinguished members of the faculty. A native of Oldenberg, Germany, he arrived in Cincinnati in 1839 at the age of sixteen. In 1840 he published an elementary textbook for teaching German. In addition to being a faculty member, he was in charge of the Music Society at the College. At the 1844 commencement the college conferred the Master of Arts degree on Stallo. This upset Bishop Purcell since Stallo had previously accused the ordinary in the press of having misappropriated funds sent from Europe for German parishes to bankroll the building of his new cathedral. Upon graduation Stallo took a teaching position as professor of physics, chemistry, and mathematics at St. John's College, now Fordham University, in New York. He was twenty-five. Four years later his book on *General Principles of the Philosophy of Nature* was published in Boston. This strongly Hegelian book introduced Hegel to the New England intellectual Ralph Waldo Emerson. In the summer of 1848, Stallo returned to Cincinnati and became a lawyer. When Purcell in the fall brought suit in a civil court to recover church property claimed by the pastor of Holy Trinity Church on West Fifth Street in Cincinnati, Stallo was counsel for the defendant. In 1852 he was appointed judge of the Common Pleas Court. Continuing his work in philosophy and science he became a prominent figure in a group called the Ohio Hegelians. In 1881 he completed his most important work, *The Concepts and Theories of Modern Physics*. Four years later President Grover Cleveland appointed him U.S. Ambassador to Italy. (33)

Purcell Mansion

By 1843 the boarding students made use of a villa house, called the Purcell Mansion, located on Ingleside Avenue in Walnut Hills in Cincinnati, about two and a half miles east of the college, for their regular recreation time on Thursdays. Originally acquired by Bishop Edward Fenwick in 1832 as a possible site for his seminary, Purcell sold it to the Jesuits in 1845 for $9,000. The property consisted of a large house with some farm outbuildings on a rolling and tree-filled site of seven-and-a-quarter acres overlooking the Ohio River. On one of Cincinnati's most elevated heights, it provided a panoramic view of the surrounding countryside. The grounds at the Purcell Mansion were laid out and divided into garden, vineyard, pasture, grove, and ample play area for the exercise and amusement of the students. The Jesuits first used it as a farm and holiday villa until the summer of 1847, when the building was remodeled for a boarding school. During the presidency of John E. Blox, of Flemish origin, who succeeded Elet in August 1847, it became the home of the preparatory department of the college, separating the younger boys, eight to thirteen years of age, from the older ones. College officials were hopeful about the prospects of the preparatory department in Walnut Hills. (34)

On July 20, 1847, Elet, St. Xavier College's first rector, had announced to the board of trustees his intention to resign the presidency of the college, and that Blox, who had been on the faculty as chaplain since 1846, should succeed him. The board accepted his resignation. In the nineteenth century there was no presidential search committee. The selection of St. Xavier College's second Jesuit president, however, was anything but simple. On August 4th, following a meeting held in St. Louis, Blox was named president of St. Xavier College. But on the following day, James Oliver Van de Velde, the provincial, rescinded the appointment. He assigned the Jesuit John Druyts to the post. Purcell, displeased with the removal of Blox from Cincinnati, protested on his behalf. Two weeks later, on August 19, Van de Velde renamed Blox president of St. Xavier College. Blox, a Belgian, became the second Jesuit president. Though a member of the Maryland province of the Society of Jesus, he had served as the first Jesuit pastor of St. Xavier Church in 1845. Elet held office until his departure in early August to represent the vice province of Missouri in a meeting of procurators at Rome. While in Rome he was appointed religious superior for the Jesuits of the Midwest, serving in that capacity until his death in 1851. (35)

The Purcell Mansion students "under the age of thirteen years," the 1846–1847 college catalogue pointed out, "are kept entirely separate from those who are more advanced in life, the former live in the country, the latter in the city." That separation, deemed advisable by college officials, had been impossible on Sycamore Street because of the cramped quarters. Some thought that separating the younger boys from the older ones would facilitate greater discipline among the younger boarders. At this period the institution enjoyed unexampled prosperity, and the number of pupils was greater than at any previous time. "There is probably no College in the United States, which has advanced so rapidly in public favor, with all classes, as St. Xavier," the *Catholic Telegraph* noted in 1848. " . . . No men could be more attached to their pupils, or more devoted to their improvement, than the Jesuit Fathers, and parents have learned how to appreciate their merit." Another observer pointed out that the college provided "not only a good but liberal education, fitting" the young men "for practical and useful life [and] giving them high intellectual culture, with a well improved moral sense free from sectarian bigotry." (36)

By transferring the rhetoric and grammar classes to the countryside, "removed from the noise and distraction of the city," college officials argued that the youth would not only enjoy "the country life, [but] acquire a fondness for industry and perseverance, which may render them one day, honorable, useful, and influential members of society." The annual room and board fee was $130. Students who spent their vacation at the mansion paid an additional fee of $20. By the fall of 1847, two Jesuit faculty members and two Jesuit seminarians attended to 25 students at the mansion. Herman Aelen, S.J., was president for the first session in 1847–1848 and George A. Carrell, S.J., former president of St. Louis University and pastor of St. Xavier Church, in 1848–1849. Partly because of the transfer of the preparatory department to Walnut Hills, enrollment at the college in 1847–1848 increased to 330. (37)

The college maintained the preparatory department for only two years, returning it to the city in the summer of 1849. It is conceivable that the combined effect of the annual cholera outbreaks, which developed into major epidemics in the Midwest, and the prohibitive distance to the main campus contributed to the closing of the department in Walnut Hills. In the 1849–1850 academic year student enrollment in the college declined to 242 students, 108 boarders and 138 day students. This was a decrease of 17 students from the year before. The Jesuits retained the grounds and buildings in Walnut Hills until 1873, continuing to use it as a vacation site for the boarding students on the regular Thursday holidays and as a villa for outings and excursions. "Our recreations were always cheerful and pleasant," a scholastic wrote. It was customary for students to walk to the Purcell Mansion when it was "not too warm, otherwise" they would go by a horse-drawn "omnibus." college officials assured the parents that their sons were "attended by several prefects, whose presence is a security against every species of disorder." Julius D. Johnston, a Jesuit seminarian and prefect of studies at the college in 1850, recorded in his diary observations of the autumn scenery at the Purcell Mansion. "Took notice of the great beauty of the woods and their various colored hues," he wrote. " . . . What a subject of poetry! What thoughts! What feelings! What a union of Beautiful and the Sublime. Beauty in the gorgeous dies that cover the trees, sublimity in the deep suggestions of the Future and the Infinite." (38)

The year that the preparatory department closed, a cholera epidemic raged through the Midwest. It had a devastating effect on Cincinnati, where over 4,600 people out of a total population of 116,000 fell ill.

In a nine-day period in June, 398 of 506 burials in the city were Asiatic cholera victims. On June 27, St. Xavier College students, under the leadership of Cheri Nouges, a student from New Orleans, gathered together and placed themselves under the special protection of the Blessed Virgin Mary. All the students but one agreed to the following resolution: "Holy Mary, ever Virgin Mother of God, . . . in consideration of the danger to which we are exposed during the prevalence of the dreadful sickness with which it has pleased Almighty God to afflict the earth, having the fullest confidence in thy power and willingness to protect us, . . . do solemnly vow and promise to Almighty God, and to thee, that if thou shalt so exert thy power in our behalf that none of us may fall a victim to the cholera at this season." They resolved that they would have two gold crowns placed on the chapel statues of the Blessed Virgin and the Infant Jesus, whom she carried in her arms, if the students were not harmed by the plague. The college year ended quickly and "the greater part" of the commencement exercises and the conferring of degrees were postponed "till the opening of the next session" in the fall. According to one account, a Xavier student fell victim to cholera during his journey home and was buried along the banks of the Mississippi. He was the only student cholera fatality and Xavier legend has it that he was the only student who had not agreed to the resolution to the Blessed Virgin. (39)

The cholera epidemics also claimed the lives of Jesuits. In 1849 Angelus Masselle, pastor of St. Xavier Church and a native of Belgium, was the first Jesuit to succumb to the disease. He had filled various posts in the college, including minister and professor of physics, mathematics, and rhetoric. As chaplain to the city hospital, he was exposed to the contagious disease and died at the age of thirty-eight. The following summer Christopher Genelli, an Austrian, died within two days of his arrival at Xavier. In 1851 the Jesuit seminarian Julius Johnston died. He had been a teacher of rhetoric and belles lettres at the college, as well as secretary of the board of trustees. A Virginian, he had been reared in the Protestant religion. He became a lawyer, married, and had two daughters. After the death of his wife he entered the Society of Jesus in 1846. His stay at St. Xavier was brief. (40)

Ethnicity and Enrollment

St. Xavier's ethnic composition during the 1840s and 1850s reflected the growing ethnic diversity of the region's population. The city's rich ethnic profile was reflected in the names of the 185 students enrolled for the school year of 1841–1842. Among the students were a Reinlein, Rieckelmann, and Stuntebeck together with a Gilligan, Murphy, and O'Connor. That year slightly over 50 percent of the student body was of English, Scottish, or Welsh descent, while Irish-Americans accounted for approximately 21 percent. German-Americans were the next largest group with about 9 percent, and those of French ancestry numbered nearly as much. The student body was distinctly Anglo-American. Twenty years later, students of English and Scottish parentage had declined to less than 20 percent of the enrollment. From the 1830s to the 1860s, thousands of German Catholic immigrants made their way to the "German Triangle," extending from Milwaukee to St. Louis to Cincinnati. By 1847, Cincinnati, which then had more German-speaking Catholics than any other diocese in the country, already had six German parishes. Moreover, the potato failure and famine in Purcell's native land of Ireland (1845–1847) brought waves of Irish English-speaking immigrants to American shores, particularly to Cincinnati, where St. Xavier Church largely attended to Irish and English-speaking Catholics. Well into the second half of the nineteenth century, among the immigrants, the Irish and German Catholics had the most visible impact on the local church and on St. Xavier College. After the Irish and German immigration had coalesced, it resulted in a dramatic increase in German and Irish students, and by 1861 one in four students was an Irish-American and nearly half, 46 percent, were of German parentage. Among the 132 students that year, 113 were from Cincinnati and 14 from Covington and Newport, Kentucky. (41)

In the 1840s the majority of the boarders at the college came from the Southern states and a few from Mexico and Cuba. Louisiana students, some of whom were French-speaking Creoles, were the fastest-growing group during the decade, and by 1850 they accounted for 46 percent of the boarding students. Enrollment reached a high point in 1847—330 students, with 112 boarders and 218 commuters. Forty-four students, nearly 40 percent of the 112 boarders, were from Louisiana. St. Xavier College had grown from less than 100 students in 1840 to over 300 in seven years. Within two years, however, enrollment dropped by nearly 100 to 242, including the loss of 80 day students. Of those students enrolled in 1847, 54 percent of the boarders and only 36 percent of the day students attended St. Xavier the following year. (42)

For the next three years, boarder enrollment remained relatively constant as the declining number of students from the South was partly offset by new enrollees from New York, Michigan, Pennsylvania, and Mexico. The birthplaces of the St. Xavier resident students listed in the 1850 census included ten states and four foreign countries: Mexico, Ireland, England, and Germany. Six in ten still came from the South and 10 percent were foreign born. The students ranged in age from eight to twenty-four, averaging just over fifteen years of age. At the time, the general age for admission was from eight to sixteen years. In 1851 the age for admission increased to ten years. The popularity of the other Jesuit colleges and the opening of St. Joseph's College in Bardstown, Kentucky by the Jesuits in 1848 may have contributed to the declining and shifting enrollment. (43)

The first catalogues of St. Xavier College reveal that in the 1840s French and English were spoken "indiscriminately during the hours of recreation." However, with the exception of the Latin, French, Spanish, and German classes, and in the philosophy course where Latin was spoken, English was the ordinary language of communication in all the classes. The prefect of studies' diary for October 15, 1850, points out that the rector "directed something to be done to restrain the Creoles from speaking French and appointed [a Jesuit] . . . to establish some rule for it." More liberty in that regard appeared to have been allowed the students in the first years of the college. Perhaps as an effort at greater cultural assimilation in response to the rise of nativism, locally and nationally, English became the ordinary language of communication during recreation. (44)

At mid-century the Jesuits at the college also enriched diversity in the city. They were natives of Belgium, Austria, Ireland, Germany, and Cuba. The Cincinnati Jesuits mirrored the ethnic diversity of the Jesuits in the Missouri vice province, whose territorial boundaries stretched from Ohio to the Rocky Mountains and from the Canadian border to the Mexican border. In 1846, the 154 Jesuits in the vice province represented eight countries of origin. Forty-five members were from Ireland. The Belgians, who dominated the provincial leadership until 1870, accounted for forty-two members, including the largest number of priests. In addition, sixteen Jesuits were from Holland, sixteen from the United States, thirteen from Germany, eleven from Italy, nine from France, and two from Spain. All told, there were 137 Europeans and 16 Americans. (45)

Jesuit superiors advised their members to be sensitive to ethnic differences. They urged them not to speak about politics or become embroiled in ethnic issues. In order for the members of the Jesuit community to be more effective in the classroom and church pulpit, an effort was made for them to master the English language. Similarly, Bishop Purcell urged the non-native priests in his diocese to master English in order to extend "their usefulness to American Catholics and Protestants." In one instance, a Jesuit who chose the Bible for his model to acquire a good English style, one day in class sought to quiet a student who was speaking out of order by instructing him to "come and stand in the midst thereof." The class laughed out loud. He did not realize that "the Biblical style was not in fashion." (46)

As in the Athenaeum in the 1830s, a large percentage of resident students at St. Xavier College were non-Catholic. Though the day students appeared to have been largely, and in some years entirely Catholic, in April 1844 Elet estimated the proportion of non-Catholic boarders at one-half. "If we admitted only Catholic boarders," he said, "religious instruction and exercises of piety would suffer less embarrassment." Consistent with their ministry, there was satisfaction in the way of conversions. "The Protestant children," he said, "cannot resist the influence of good example and during the last thirteen months eleven of them have been converted." (47)

In the early years of the 1850s the college saw a continuing and greater decline in enrollment for both day students and boarders, dropping from 242 in 1849 to 170 in 1852. What might also have contributed to a decline in the number of boarders, in addition to the possible popularity of other Jesuit colleges, was the social instability that prevailed in Cincinnati. This period saw bitter disputes and rioting between ethnic groups, immigrants, and the native-born. These tensions culminated in the rioting that occurred in December 1853 and January 1854 in response to the visit of Archbishop Gaetano Bedini, the pope's nuncio, or ambassador, to the Imperial Court of Brazil. Sent by the pope to visit the United States, he was "to observe the state of religion . . . , the conduct of the clergy and the abuses that have crept in," among other things. On his tour he was subjected to several anti-Catholic demonstrations. On December 23rd, while in Cincinnati, he visited St. Xavier College. After celebrating Mass in the college chapel, he met with the students in the study hall. Later he dined with the Jesuit community. Two days later on Christmas Day, Bedini preached in St. Peter in Chains Cathedral. That evening a riot broke out. A person was killed, 15 were wounded, including a policeman, and 65 were arrested. (48)

Throughout the 1840s and 1850s, Catholics in Cincinnati, and Jesuits in particular, had to contend with anti-Catholic sentiments. In the fall of

1843, John Quincy Adams, former United States president, visited Cincinnati for the cornerstone dedication ceremonies of the Astronomical Observatory in one of the hilltop neighborhoods east of the city overlooking the Ohio River. On Thursday, November 9, there was a gigantic parade, and since Thursday was a regular weekday holiday at St. Xavier, it is more than likely that students from the college marched in the parade. Adams delivered the main address and helped lay the cornerstone.

On that day members of the Philopedian Society declared Adams an honorary member of their society and invited him to visit the college and meet with them. There is no evidence that he came. More than likely he did not, because of what happened the following day, Friday, November 10. That morning Adams addressed a crowd of more than three thousand people in the Wesley Methodist Episcopal Chapel on the north side of Fifth Street between Sycamore and Broadway. He spoke for almost two hours on the history of astronomy. Before he concluded his talk, the former president lamented the persecution of Galileo at the hands of the Inquisition. He claimed that Ignatius of Loyola, founder of the Society of Jesus, under the influence of "religious fanaticism" had invented the Inquisition. Calling the Jesuit order "an engine of despotic power," Adams concluded that, unlike Galileo, Newton was fortunate to have lived in a country with "no college of Cardinals to cast him into prison." The diocesan newspaper, the *Catholic Telegraph*, denounced Adams's remarks, pointing out that the Inquisition was established three hundred years prior to Ignatius's birth. The paper called his remarks a "sad commentary on the astounding ignorance which prevails among Protestants." (49)

One of the earliest political and social issues that Catholics faced in Cincinnati in pre-Civil War America was nativism. The increased Catholic immigration in the 1840s and 1850s that swelled the Catholic population to record numbers stimulated anti-Catholic sentiments. Fearing a papist takeover, some Protestants and the Cincinnati press harangued against Catholics for their alleged "undemocratic" practices. In 1846 the *American Protestant*, a No-Popery newspaper, was started in Cincinnati. A year later an article on "Popery in the United States" in the *Christian Observer* pointed out that in the Diocese of Cincinnati there were the seminary of St. Francis Xavier, St. Xavier College, three convents, four female seminaries, and approximately ten charitable institutions with a combined population of approximately 10,000 pupils. "A great proportion of the teachers in these institutions are Jesuits," it wrote, "the bitterest foes of civil and religious liberty who breathe the air of heaven." It further argued that the Jesuit "leader in the Western States is the President of St. Xavier's College in Cincinnati." (50)

Some of the anti-Catholic sentiments in the archdiocese spilled over into education and politics. In 1853 the Ohio legislature debated a school bill that, if passed, would have required all school-age children to attend the public schools for a minimum of three months of the year. The Ohio bill was defeated and subsequently dropped. During this same period Ohio Catholics petitioned the legislature for a share of the school fund. Purcell, who had three years earlier been appointed archbishop of Cincinnati, mounted a campaign against mandatory attendance of public schools and published a forceful pastoral letter concerning the April 1853 elections and the issue of public funds for Catholic schools. The local elections centered on the propriety of state funding and developed into a significant confrontation between immigrants and "native Americans." Protestant and secular papers responded sharply and angrily to Purcell's pastoral. The 1853 election marked the first time that an election hinged on the issue of religion.

Both Catholics and Protestants claimed victory in the elections, and for about two years there were renewed charges that Purcell had interfered in local politics. During this period there were a few outbreaks against the Catholic churches in the archdiocese. Occasionally stones were thrown at the cathedral. In 1854 a mob hurled a cobblestone at the St. Xavier College president's window facing Sycamore Street. Notwithstanding the furor of anti-Catholicism in Cincinnati at the time, the college retained the support of a number of Protestant parents who enrolled their sons at St. Xavier. (51)

As the heated election took its toll on the archbishop and Cincinnati Catholics, the Jesuits were under suspicion as well. An article on "Vulgar Ideas of the Jesuits," published in the September 23, 1854 issue of the *Catholic Telegraph*, reflects some of the sentiments of the time. "We have been studying anti-Catholic 'public opinion' for some time, and with extraordinary diligence, in order to discover" the prevalent view "of the character of the Jesuit," the editor wrote. "We have read," he continued,

> many newspapers which otherwise we would never have read, and listened with interest to many remarks which, in other circumstances, would have provoked our laughter. We present the fruit of these labors to our readers today.
>
> In the first place, it would seem that the Jesuits are a *secret* society. This absurdity is paraded in a hundred country papers, and repeated in a thousand conversations. . . .

In the next place, the Jesuits are a society comprising laymen, as well as priests. The laymen are not those harmless innocents known to us as 'lay-brothers,' but men of the world—merchants, lawyers, tailors, shoemakers, etc.,—married men. Only the other day a Catholic merchant of this city was told by an 'intelligent' fellow-merchant that he was a Jesuit! Nay, even women are members of this terrible Order: Irish and German servant-girls . . . are thought to be members of the secret body, and privy to its cunning councils. And yet the society is secret!

Furthermore, the Jesuits know everything that is going on. They pry into the secret conversations of their enemies; they have the census of all the men, women, and children in the country; and each Jesuit knows all their names by heart—their education, family prospects, the amount of their liabilities, the worth of their estates.

In accordance with this extraordinary knowledge, they possess a super-human sagacity and self possession. They never act without design. If they look pleasant in a railroad car, it is but a trap to inveigle into the meshes of the Romish net the elderly lady to whom they resign a comfortable seat. All that is done among Catholics is first planned by them. Whatever business a Catholic engages in, he engages in it at their bidding. A grocery keeper cannot sell a pound of tea, except it promote their interest, and is done under their direction.

By the middle of the decade the anti-Catholic demonstrations in Cincinnati had subsided and Archbishop Purcell was pleased to write to an episcopal colleague that "[a]ll is quiet now." (52)

The Jesuits, the Seminary, and the Community

After the Jesuits acquired the college in 1840 and the bishop transferred it and the original seminary building to them, Purcell moved the seminary to St. Martin's in Brown County, about forty miles east of Cincinnati, in order to make room for the Jesuits at the college. He initially preferred the rural location for the seminary, thinking that the pastoral setting would be healthier for the seminarians. Two years later Purcell persuaded the Congregation of the Missions, more popularly known as Vincentians or as Lazarists, to operate the seminary. From 1842 to 1845 the Vincentians discharged all the duties of the seminary. Because of the distance from the city and the difficulties of slow travel, some thought Brown County was an undesirable location for a seminary. The bishop and the Vincentians, moreover, did not always agree on the operation of the seminary. As a consequence, in summer 1845 Purcell brought the seminarians back to Cincinnati. He housed them temporarily in the scholasticate attached to St. Xavier College. The seminarians stayed with the Jesuits for about two years. In compliance with Bishop Purcell's initial offer to the Jesuit provincial in 1840, between 1843 and 1845 four or five seminarians, under the direction of a Jesuit, taught some of the classes at the college. In August 1845 Purcell requested that Leonard Nota, S.J., a St. Xavier professor of mental and moral philosophy, be named superior of the seminary. James Oliver Van de Velde, Superior of the Vice Province of Missouri, argued that such appointment would first have to be approved by the father general. However, he agreed that Nota should teach theology to the seminarians and in general direct them in their studies. Two months later Purcell again requested that Nota be named superior. Van de Velde and his advisers first demurred, but finally, in March 1846, complied with the bishop's request. Nota remained superior until 1848. (53)

The living quarters at the scholasticate on Sycamore Street must have been crowded. It accommodated the Jesuit faculty, seminarians, and the boarding students, which numbered 92 in 1845–1846 and 101 in 1846–1847 respectively. In the summer of 1847 Purcell converted the top floor of his residence at Eighth and Plum Streets, adjoining the new cathedral, into a dormitory and study hall for the seminarians. They remained there for four years, studying philosophy and theology under the supervision of the Jesuits. Before long, the bishop challenged local Catholics to build a new seminary, subsequently erected in 1851 on top of Price Hill on the west side of Cincinnati. Its name was changed from St. Francis Xavier to Mount St. Mary's of the West Seminary. (54)

When Purcell in 1840 had proposed to transfer the college and to make a donation of the land and buildings to the Society of Jesus, he thought he was not going "beyond the bounds of moderation" to ask that the Jesuits feed and clothe the seminarians who would teach about three hours every day in the college. But after the provincial informed him that it could not be done "and that the Society had never accepted the gift with a perpetual burden," Purcell then turned over the property to the Jesuits outright without any burden on the order. "In return for this good faith of mine," Purcell later wrote, "I certainly ask for nothing except that God be honored through our Lord Jesus Christ to the great gain of souls and particularly those of boys." Thus, when a claim was later made that the college was under obligation to board a certain number of seminarians gratis, Elet wrote to Purcell in 1847 that no conditions had been imposed upon the order by its acquisition of the college and church. Nevertheless, "it has been complied with from the second year and more so at present than ever," he wrote. In addition to free tuition and board for three resident students and free tuition for six day students, amounting to $584, the seminarians were admitted at the "low terms [of] . . . $80 for a whole year's board [and] $20 for light, fuel, room, washing, [and] mending." Thus, he argued, "your Lordship must be convinced that we do contribute our mite towards the support of your diocese." (55)

As part of their ministry, Jesuits also assisted the Diocese of Cincinnati in attending to the Catholics at the city hospital and in doing parish work. While devoting themselves to the spiritual growth of the parish they established various sodalities and societies. In 1846, six years after the Jesuits' arrival, the *Catholic Telegraph* wrote that it "is extremely gratifying to witness the great increase of piety in that quarter of the city where the church of St. Francis Xavier is situated. Two years ago there was only a small chapel in that part of town, and now the spacious accommodations of the Church of the Jesuit Fathers are scarce sufficient for the numerous congregation that attends it." That year the Jesuit administration lengthened St. Xavier Church forty feet to accommodate the needs of the growing population. "The rapid increase of this congregation," the diocesan paper further noted, "is a subject of frequent remark" by Catholics, and the ". . . instruction given at this church on Sundays . . . attracts a great many Protestants, who listen with marked attention to the familiar . . . exposition of the Catholic faith and morals [that] is usually delivered by the President of the [College]." (56)

Writing to John Druyts, president of St. Louis University in 1847, George Carrell, pastor of the St. Xavier parish, pointed out that if "you stand in need of exercise, you can petition to be one of the pastors of St. Xavier's, Cincinnati, at the end of your presidential career. You will not have reason to complain of a sedentary life. There is no end to our parish—it embraces the length and breadth and depth and height of the city." Moreover, he pointed out that few have "seen poorer or more wretched abodes—poverty and intemperance prevail here to a frightful extent." (57)

Purcell, in need of clergy, also asked the Jesuits to assist or take charge in other parishes in the diocese. In the period 1841 to 1851, Jesuits served St. James Church in White Oak, and St. Mary's and Corpus Christi churches in Covington and Newport, Kentucky, respectively.

Newport and Covington at the time were part of the Diocese of Cincinnati. In 1847 Jesuits were assigned to the two Catholic parishes in Chillicothe, Ohio, and to St. Mary's parish school in the Over-the-Rhine district on the eastern side of Cincinnati. Joseph Patschowski, S.J., oversaw the Sodality of the Blessed Virgin, which was an outward expression of religious piety, organized a choir that soon became one of the best trained choirs in Cincinnati, and served as pastor of Corpus Christi Church in Cincinnati. St. Xavier clergy also performed parochial duties as late as 1869 in Immaculate Conception parish in Newport, Kentucky. In addition to doing parish work, the Cincinnati Jesuits served as retreat masters and chaplains. (58)

A leading figure in the parish missions in the Diocese of Cincinnati was the Jesuit and Austrian-born Francis Xavier Weninger, who arrived in the see city in 1848, joined the St. Xavier faculty as a professor of scripture and Hebrew in 1849, and began preaching in local German parishes in his spare time. Generally he delivered two types of sermons, one directed to all members of the parish, and the other to separate groups of married men, married women, single women, and single men. Weninger's first mission in the diocese took place at St. John the Baptist Church on Green Street in Cincinnati between Christmas Day 1848 and New Years Day 1849. In time the Jesuit, who preached in French as well as in German, also wrote his own doctrinal and devotional literature. Weninger, who helped raise "considerable" funds to help finance the college, continued his successful parish missions throughout the Midwest. (59)

In the spring of 1849 Weninger invited the Brothers of the Society of Mary, an order founded in 1817 at Bordeaux, France, to come to Cincinnati and operate a school for boys in his parish. The Society of Mary accepted the invitation and sent Father Leo Meyer and Brother Charles Schultz to the diocese. When they reached Cincinnati in the summer, during the cholera epidemic, Purcell asked Meyer to temporarily assist Father Henry Juncker in Dayton. On September 1, 1850, Meyer and three Brothers of the Society of Mary opened St. Mary's School, a boarding school for Catholic boys. In 1857 the school became known as St. Mary's College, which later became the University of Dayton. Like St. Xavier College, the second college in the Diocese of Cincinnati opened as a day and boarding school. (60)

In the mid-1850s the Jesuits began making plans to replace their little wooden St. Xavier church on Sycamore Street in Cincinnati. Even though a few years earlier Purcell had bought the Methodist Episcopal

Church on Sycamore Street to take care of the overflow at St. Xavier, the congregation needed a larger church. In February 1860 the work of dismantling and demolishing St. Xavier Church, section by section, began. During the demolition one of the walls fell, crushing thirteen laborers. All thirteen men were members of the parish. News of the tragedy spread through the city and a crowd of approximately ten thousand, who in part blamed St. Xavier College officials for the catastrophe, gathered on the scene. City officials took the situation promptly in hand. The local police surrounded the college, preventing any forced entry. During the next several weeks various Catholic congregations and relief committees throughout the city took up a collection for the relief of the families. A few weeks later demolition work continued. On January 20, 1861, the new St. Xavier Church was dedicated. (61)

Notwithstanding the varied Jesuit contributions in the Diocese of Cincinnati, by the mid-1840s there was some friction between Bishop Purcell, who was ex officio president of the Board of Trustees, and the society. At the same time that Purcell appreciated and often praised the work of the religious orders in his diocese, having been personally involved in bringing some of them to the diocese, he was concerned over any diminution of episcopal authority. His concern was typical of a diocesan clergyman's reaction to the separate orders. A letter written by President Elet to Purcell in 1845 suggests that there was tension between the Jesuits and Purcell and that the bishop appeared indifferent or cool toward the society. No specific reason was given. Grateful that the bishop had given the Jesuits use of the Purcell Mansion for vacation, it was done "on the condition," Elet wrote, "of working in it for the good of your flock from morning early until late at night; and I ask confidently did we not comply with it? We thank y[ou]r Lordship for having opened a field to us, and we ask but one more favour, to be permitted to work with it in peace. I am grieved beyond expression at the unfortunate change that has taken place in y[ou]r Lordship's mind with regard to us. . . . God is my witness," he concluded, "that during the 5 years that I have spent in your diocese, I have studied to please y[ou]r Lordship, not *from political views*, but from a thorough devotedness to y[ou]r Person and a desire of promoting the M[ajor] D[ei] G[loria]." (62)

Despite some early disagreements between the Jesuits and the bishop, Purcell often praised the Jesuits for their work. Writing to Archbishop Samuel Eccleston of Baltimore in December 1845, Purcell noted that the Jesuits "are, individually, most exemplary & edifying priests. . . ." But, he added, "it is their too great zeal . . . for their society that is at fault." Over time relations between the bishop and the society steadily improved. Apparently the estrangement in the mid-1840s was short-lived. Writing to the father general in Rome in February 1847, Elet commented that "Purcell shows himself every day more and more benevolent in our regard. I wonder why after his splendid gift to us of this college and the church annexed to it he has not been enrolled among [our] prominent benefactors by a diploma of affiliation." It also appears that Elet brought the matter up to John Roothaan, Jesuit superior general, in his visit to Rome in 1847. A document signed by Roothaan on March 16, 1848, not only acknowledged Purcell as the founder of St. Xavier College, but indicated that he was entitled to the Masses and other spiritual suffrages guaranteed by the Jesuit Constitutions to distinguished bene-factors of the society. "By this document," Van de Velde, the Missouri vice provincial, wrote to Purcell, "your [Lordship] becomes a partici-pant in all the prayers, good works and merits of all the members of our Society—*in perpetuum*, during life and after death." (63)

Dedicated to the education of their children, Cincinnati's immigrant Catholic families and Bishop Purcell joined efforts to build parochial elementary schools throughout the diocese. Jesuits at the college assisted the diocese in this effort. By the late 1840s, 80 percent of the parishes had Catholic schools, largely operated by women religious orders. In July 1847, St. Xavier College officials purchased a lot sixty by one hundred feet on the west side of Sycamore Street, north of Seventh Street, at a cost of a hundred dollars a foot to promote "the establishment of a Free School in the eastern part of the city for the education of the Catholic youth." By the end of the month parishioners met in the college hall and pledged $600 towards the purchase of the school lot and organized themselves into the Catholic Free School Society. Blox, president of the college, was elected president and John Duerinck, S.J., treasurer. The parish succeeded in raising money for the new school. A building was started and finished in time for occupancy at the beginning of the next school year. On May 29, 1848, St. Xavier parish opened the tuition-free elementary school with the Jesuit Angelus Masselle, professor of mathematics and physics, as its first director. It had an enrollment of about 100 students. The parochial school enjoyed a steady growth due partly to the increase of Irish immigrants. (64)

During the summer of 1848 the Maryland province recalled Blox. During his brief tenure in office, lasting a little over a year, the college had opened a short-lived preparatory school in Walnut Hills and

St. Xavier parish had established two free schools for boys and girls. The Jesuits appointed John DeBlieck, another native of Belgium, their third president of St. Xavier College on February 17, 1849, the day after his twenty-eighth birthday. Though DeBlieck was in the second year of his theological studies at St. Louis University, the Maryland provincial decided to promote the scholastic to the priesthood with the idea of appointing him president of the college. Elet, now religious superior of the Jesuits in the Midwest, wrote to Bishop Purcell, who had a high opinion of Blox, that DeBlieck was "vastly superior to Father Blox as a scholar and as a manager." DeBlieck served as president from 1848 to 1851. (65)

During his presidency DeBlieck taught philosophy to the scholastics. He acquired the reputation of being an astute and independent thinker, which sometimes caused him problems with the officials of the vice province. In the spring of 1851 Elet discussed with his consultors probable action to be taken against DeBlieck because of complaints that in his lectures to the scholastics he subscribed to unpopular neo-scholastic philosophical opinions, not authorized by the father general of the society. Elet admonished him to espouse more conventional philosophical opinions. Overall, his position was never so extreme as to jeopardize his professorial status. He continued to teach philosophy at St. Xavier and, in later years, in other Jesuit colleges. His correspondence in the late 1850s with Orestes A. Brownson, a talented and famed lay scholar from Boston and a convert to Catholicism, testifies to DeBlieck's neo-scholastic disposition. They both agreed that due to lack of free and independent thinking, no true philosophy was being taught in American colleges and universities. (66)

In June 1851, George Carrell, a native Philadelphian who became a Jesuit in 1835, succeeded DeBlieck as president of the college. He was the first American-born Jesuit to hold that position. Carrell was no stranger to Cincinnati. He served as pastor of St. Xavier Church in 1847 and as principal of the preparatory school at the Purcell Mansion for a year. Early in his presidency, the college erected the Carrell building on Sycamore Street, at right angles to the Athenaeum building. It housed a chemistry laboratory in the basement, a museum and physics cabinet on the first floor, grammar classes for the commercial course on the second, and the preparatory department on the third floor. Notwithstanding this latest addition, St. Xavier College was about to experience, as one observer later noted, its "darkest hour." (67)

The Closing of the Boarding School

Ten years after the Jesuits assumed control of the Athenaeum, the financial condition of St. Xavier College was precarious. The constantly decreasing number of boarders was a major problem. When William Stack Murphy, S.J., the Missouri vice provincial, visited the college in 1852 for a personal assessment, he found the situation "far from promising. The faculty, its younger members especially," he wrote to John Roothaan, the father general, "were discouraged. . . . The day college and the boarding school are going down right before one's eyes. This institution has never been flourishing in the true sense of the word. During its first years it enjoyed a factitious prosperity produced by means that were artificial, and, so to speak, blustering. This could not last. To begin with, a boarding school is entirely out of place there," he continued; "the premises anything but suitable, sombre-looking dormitories under the roof, poorly lighted and sunken class-rooms. Our poor scholastics find themselves imprisoned as it were with some sixty pupils." Moreover, Murphy was concerned about President Carrell's capacity for leadership. "He is not of that class of people who . . . know[s] how to put a good face on bad fortune," he wrote. ". . . He has more or less a resigned air and makes no effort to fortify and encourage his community. For the rest he is exact, regular, restrained, well-thought of by everybody, paternal towards those under him, but full of firmness." Less than a year later Carrell resigned as president to become the first bishop of the Diocese of Covington in Kentucky. It is alleged that he had long been unhappy as a Jesuit, not able to adjust well to the large ethnic membership in the order in the Missouri province. Isidore Boudreaux from Louisiana and the first student of St. Louis University to become a Jesuit succeeded him as president of St. Xavier College in December 1853. (68)

That winter Murphy and the province consultors explored two options regarding the future status of the college: they could close the boarding school and conduct a day school only, or abandon the college and St. Xavier Church altogether and leave the city. In Murphy's judgment it was hard to justify the assignment of fourteen teachers to teach Xavier's 124 students. Before the Civil War most American colleges were small, and those with St. Xavier's enrollment size typically had as few as four or five instructors.

St. Xavier classrooms were generally small, situated almost underground and poorly lighted. Like most classrooms in American colleges

in the antebellum period, they were bare and unadorned, poorly ventilated during the warmer months, and ill-heated in winter. Revenue
from the small enrollment was inadequate to maintain the buildings
and to operate the college. Relatively short stays by the students and
the inability of some of them to pay full tuition exacerbated revenue
uncertainty problems. The idea of closing a college like St. Xavier was
not unusual. Eighty-one percent of colleges in the United States closed
before the Civil War. (69)

Later that winter Joseph Keller, S.J., the prefect of studies at
St. Xavier College, wrote a detailed letter to the father general urging
him to close the entire institution. Such a move, he thought, would
relieve the strain on the Jesuit personnel in the vice province and would
make it easier for the Society of Jesus to staff the schools in St. Louis
and Bardstown, Kentucky. Keller thought closing St. Xavier would
also make it possible for several Jesuit faculty members at the college
to pursue their studies in divinity. "I reproach no one, I blame no one,"
he wrote, "for it is evident that practically all are working to their full
capacity. But I regret keenly that things in our vice province have come
to such a pass that the name Jesuit in this part of the country has
become little more than a name. Certainly the situation should be otherwise and could be if our men were not tied down by so many occupations." (70)

In January 1854 Jesuit officials at the college and in the Missouri vice
province, after consulting with Purcell, decided to close the boarding
school and admit only day students. "We have dissolved the boarding-
school here," wrote Peter DeSmet, the highly respected Jesuit missionary and treasurer of the Missouri vice province on July 25, 1854, "in
order to spare men and money." Until then, the majority of the students
had mostly been boarders. The resident students were encouraged to
continue their education at the Jesuit boarding schools in St. Louis or
Bardstown. However, unlike conditions at St. Xavier, the color line was
strictly drawn at the two schools. "Cincinnati," Murphy wrote to the
father general, "being in a State where slavery does not exist and where
the blacks are better received, a number of Louisianians sent thither their
children of mixed blood. Bardstown and St. Louis could not receive
them without offense. Moreover, all the white pupils would leave at
once." Though the Ohio legislature in 1842 had incorporated St. Xavier
College as "an institution for the education of white youth in the various branches of useful knowledge," college officials knowingly admitted
students of "mixed blood."

On September 9, 1854, the *Catholic Telegraph* announced that St. Xavier College had opened five days earlier "FOR DAY SCHOLARS ONLY." That was "the beginning of a new era, or rather it was equivalent to beginning anew," reported *Woodstock Letters*, a recorder of events connected with the Jesuit colleges and missions in the United States. (71)

Despite closing the boarding school, the college continued to have financial problems. Day student enrollment was a problem for much of the decade. During the 1854–1855 and 1855–1856 academic years, with a faculty of nine Jesuits, there were 109 and 135 students enrolled respectively. Low enrollment and a fluctuating student population affected the size of the operating budget and made it difficult for the rector and the treasurer to run the school efficiently. There continued to be much concern over the status of St. Xavier College. Annual budgets at the college before the Civil War, when Jesuits did most of the teaching and administrative work, were around $20,000. Bank failures and uncertain economic times in Cincinnati also adversely affected St. Xavier's enrollment and finances. (72)

In March 1855, Murphy, as vice provincial, argued that "St. Xavier's being the sick child required immediate attention." Some Jesuits, especially those stationed outside of Cincinnati, continued to have doubts about the viability of the college. They urged that the day school also should be suspended. They recommended that the Jesuit faculty be sent to other colleges or work in parishes. Consequently, there was growing concern among the Jesuits in Cincinnati about their possible withdrawal from the city. However, Peter DeSmet, as treasurer of the vice province, continually opposed the abandonment of St. Xavier College and Church. "The financial state of the college gives us a great deal of concern," he wrote to the father general in January 1855. At the time the debt was $25,068, which had been largely incurred to renovate the church, to buy two pieces of property for the possible addition to the College, and to purchase a villa. According to DeSmet the money had been raised chiefly "from petty depositors or creditors, most of them workmen who can come any day to call for their deposits." He was concerned that should "any rumors of a disquieting nature be started against us, say, of an attack on the college by . . . anti-Catholic[s] or something similar, a great many of these petty creditors would come and call for their deposits and the Procurator would find himself unable to meet the calls." He argued that the college's real estate would be sufficient to cover the debt in full. Thus, he recommended taking a loan on the real estate and for the college to place itself "under shelter of one or two good Catholic creditors." (73)

Significantly, DeSmet further argued "that the Society does an immense amount of good in this great town," emphasizing the important religious work of St. Francis Xavier Church and its accomplishments. "It would be a veritable calamity, to my mind," he asserted, "were we to abandon this place which our Fathers have bedewed with their sweat for many years and with good results." Writing a few months later to John Duerinck, S.J., former St. Xavier faculty member and now at St. Mary's Potawatomi mission in Kansas, he argued that "[m]uch good is done in Cincinnati and the day college promises very fair." (74)

On September 8, 1856, Boudreaux resigned to become master of novices in the region, a position he would hold for the next twenty-five years. The Board of Trustees appointed Maurice Oakley (an English translation of his Flemish name, Van den Eycken) the sixth Jesuit president of St. Xavier College. He had come to America from Belgium with a party of five young men in 1834. Former rector of St. Charles College at Grand Coteau, Louisiana, in the mid-1840s, he was known for his artistic temperament and tastes, and he was a skillful mathematician. Oakley aimed to build Xavier on a firmer foundation. However, that would not happen. (75)

Serving but a few months in his new post and reflecting the thoughts of his predecessor, Oakley became pessimistic about the future of the college. In the fall and winter months of 1856 he "appeared," a colleague observed, "somewhat in the blues with regard to the situation of St. Xavier College." But the college "will and must flourish," DeSmet wrote to Oakley in January 1857, "and must and shall continue in spite of the petty little obstacles and prejudices raised by prejudiced minds to hinder its progress." Though the college had but 90 students in June 1858, DeSmet, who continually championed the cause of the struggling college, remained optimistic.

At the time, Ohio had 22 colleges with an average enrollment of 85 students. St. Xavier had 130 students in the fall of 1858. DeSmet pointed out to Jesuit officials in Rome that Oakley "allows himself to be too easily discouraged and sometimes manifests a desire that this house be given up. This would be a great misfortune for the city and a very sad occurrence for the Society." What also had to help the case for keeping the college open was the fact that almost one third of the seminarians in the vice province had been educated at St. Xavier. (76)

In the fall of 1860, Felix Sopranis, a Jesuit official visitor from Rome touring the United States, paid a visit to the college. At the time enrollment was 133. His favorable evaluation of the situation proved decisive for Jesuit officials. A review of the previous July commencement in the diocesan newspaper might have contributed to his positive assessment. "The debate on the respective merits of Ancient and Modern Civilization, written by the students . . . , was characterized by solid, manly Christian thought, and by a finished rhetorical delivery," the *Catholic Telegraph* observed. After commenting on various performances it concluded that St. Xavier "bids fair to be one of the most successful educational institutions in the West." After careful examination of the college, Sopranis, like the provincial, praised the academic work being accomplished and recommended keeping the institution open. Jesuit officials in Rome concurred. (77)

Before the end of the decade, the faculty at the college had solidified course offerings. During the late 1840s and 1850s there had been growing concern over the classical course of studies. Some individuals charged that courses were not taught in the proper sequence, high grades were given for mediocre work, "[a]cademic honors were being bestowed on the unworthy," and that the program was "in disarray." Beginning in 1859 students in the final three years of their six-year classical course of studies continued their work in poetry, rhetoric, and philosophy. Students in poetry focused on composition and more advanced work in Latin and Greek prose and poetry, and rhetoric students concentrated on classical orations. Third-year students took their philosophy courses in Latin and also enrolled in "Natural Philosophy," which at St. Xavier consisted of chemistry and physics. Moreover, the former mercantile course became known as the commercial course with the classes designated as first rhetoric, second rhetoric, first grammar, and second grammar. As interest in business education grew in the 1850s, there were individuals who questioned the value of studying the classics. "It will take time to convince the youth of America," a Jesuit argued in 1860, "that the study of the ancient language is of any use to them; we shall never be able to get along without teaching a special course for such as are preparing for business." (78)

As St. Xavier College struggled to stay open in the 1850s, the Archdiocese of Cincinnati had three short-lived efforts in higher education. In 1855 it opened St. Peter's College in Chillicothe, Ohio, which lasted only one year. The following year Mount St. Mary's of the West

Seminary in Price Hill began accepting regular non-seminarian college students into its baccalaureate program. The college component of the seminary closed in 1862. In 1859 Purcell started the Catholic Institute of Cincinnati, a polytechnical school with liberal arts and commercial goals that lasted but six years. Cities in Ohio and throughout the Midwest during the antebellum decades tended to be graveyards for colleges. Cincinnati College, chartered in 1819, had operated intermittently. When a fire destroyed the college building in 1845 and a new building was erected, the trustees suspended its academic department and provided a series of lectures and a form of adult education. The Protestant University of the United States in Cincinnati, chartered in 1845, never opened. The Farmers' College, founded outside Cincinnati in 1852 to provide a practical collegiate education for business and farming, faced continual financial problems and lasted less than forty-years. (79)

St. Xavier College and the Civil War

When the Civil War broke out in April 1861, total enrollment at St. Xavier College was 133 students in the six-year classical program and the four-year commercial course. Jesuits assigned to the college worked in the classroom, the pulpit, and in the parish. At the time there were eleven priests, eleven brothers, and three seminarians. There were four lay faculty members who conducted classes in drawing, architecture, and music. Because of the early wartime conditions, college officials ended the school year a month earlier in June 1861. (80)

A month later the religious superior of the Midwestern Jesuits appointed John Schultz the tenth president of the college. Schultz, the seventh Jesuit president of St. Xavier, succeeded Oakley as rector on July 16 and was named ex officio vice president of the board. A native of Alsace-Lorraine, Schultz had come to the United States to work with the Native Americans. Within a few years he was put in charge of the Potawatomi mission in Kansas. Pleased to learn of his appointment to St. Xavier he wrote to a fellow Jesuit. "Very seldom has it befallen any of Ours who has spent ten years among the rude, uncivilized Indians," he said, "to be called thence suddenly and set over a college in a very populous city. But how precious a thing is the virtue of obedience, I realized on this occasion." (81)

The vice province of Missouri included territory claimed by both the Union and the Confederacy in the Civil War. So William Murphy, the Jesuit religious superior, instructed the Jesuit faculty under his jurisdiction not to show partiality to either side. "Granting that every citizen is free to adopt the view entertained by the State in which he resides and to which he belongs for the time being," Murphy wrote, "it follows that so far as Missouri and Kentucky are concerned, the sovereignty of the General Government exists—and consequently residents of these two States are bound to consider it as the only lawful Government. According to the same doctrine, Ours residing in Free States are obliged to recognize its authority." Accordingly, Cincinnati Jesuits complied with the laws of Ohio and remained consistently loyal to the nation. (82)

Since most St. Xavier students were too young for active service, President Abraham Lincoln's call in 1861 for volunteers had little impact on the 133-member student body. However, the few older tudents who were eligible to serve in their local home guard unit caused some difficulties in maintaining regular classroom activities. (83)

Despite reductions during the first two years of the war, Xavier's enrollment in 1863 was 153. Like its counterparts in Ohio, St. Xavier College maintained generally the same pace and curriculum of the antebellum years. Catholic students attended Mass at 8:00 a.m., followed by classes until noon. After a two-hour break for lunch, classes resumed at 2:00, lasting until 4:45 p.m. They continued to attend the 2:30 p.m. devotions on Sunday and Holy days of obligation. They were also expected to make their annual retreat. (84)

When Confederate troops captured Lexington, Kentucky in early September 1862, Ohio Governor David Tod requested federal troops and issued a call for volunteers. Approximately 30,000 troops from the South were reported marching toward Cincinnati. On September 2nd the governor issued a proclamation to Cincinnati. "Our southern border," he wrote, "is threatened with invasion. I have, therefore, to recommend that all loyal men of your counties at once form themselves into military companies and regiments. . . . The soil of Ohio must not be marched over by the enemies of our glorious government." The response in Cincinnati and neighboring communities was immediate. It is probable that accommodations were made at the college enabling St. Xavier students to comply with the governor's request, because only 90 students attended classes during the emergency. In addition, some of the non-Jesuit faculty members were absent, and French, German, and writing classes were canceled. Later that day General Lewis Wallace in the Northern army proclaimed Martial Law in Cincinnati, Covington, and Newport. The general's proclamation included the order that all schools be closed.

Within a week, however, as Confederate troops retreated south, communities and schools in Cincinnati and northern Kentucky returned to normal. A good example of the return to normalcy is the St. Xavier College prefect of studies's diary entry about three weeks later. He wrote not of another threatened attack, but of the football game to be played by the students on their Thursday holiday. (85)

Notwithstanding Congress's passage of the Enrollment Act of March 3, 1863, known as the "military draft law," the 1863–1864 school year began on a note of optimism. There were 156 students for a faculty of twelve Jesuits and five lay people. Tuition was increased from $40.00 to $60.00 per year for the first time since 1840. High prices on certain items and the depreciated value of money during the war necessitated the increase. By the end of the fall semester, however, the draft law, which imposed quotas on the states, presented a problem to the college. The Enrollment Act included all born in the country, naturalized citizens, and those awaiting naturalization proceedings. Protestant ministers, rabbis, Catholic priests, and religious were not exempt. In addition to several St. Xavier College students being conscripted, in January 1864 three Jesuit priests and two scholastic seminarians were listed for the draft. One of the seminarians did not pass the physical examination. The college could not afford to lose faculty members in the middle of the school year. Moreover, the parish needed their pastoral services. During the Civil War the federal government allowed draftees to pay a $300 conscription exemption fee. The college did not have the $1,200 needed to obtain exemption for the Jesuits, so parishioners raised the money. (86)

During the Civil War, Jesuits of St. Xavier Parish cared for the sick and wounded veterans in hospitals, while others conducted chaplain duties in the jails and prisons. Like the many women religious orders who generously volunteered their services during the war by becoming more identified with their commitment to Christian living and humane concerns, the Jesuits helped enhance a more positive view of Catholicism. On campus, members of the Philopedian Society debated such topics as whether or not secession by the eleven Southern states from the Union was justified, or whether African Americans should be admitted as citizens, or the white soldiers of the Civil War were superior to the black soldiers. In the March 1865 convocation of the Philopedian Society, "Patriotism," "Heroes," and "Worth Dying For" were the titles of some of the Latin and English presentations. These reflected the political climate prevalent in the North. (87)

In 1865, after enduring a decade of fiscal problems and near collapse in the 1850s, and weathering the stress of the Civil War, St. Xavier College was more sure of itself and more confident of its future. That year the student body numbered 190, the largest enrollment since the closing of the boarding school. The classical course of studies had five classrooms, the commercial three, and the preparatory one. As the country sought to reunite its people, St. Xavier College sought to build more firmly upon its Catholic and Jesuit foundation. (88)

A MORE SECURE
ST. XAVIER COLLEGE,
1865–1911

On December 3, 1865, Walter Hill, S.J., a forty-five-year-old native of Kentucky, became the eighth Jesuit president of St. Xavier College. At the time there were fifteen Jesuit faculty, three lay professors, and 262 students, the biggest enrollment in seventeen years. Students in the four-year commercial course attended classes in the newer Carrell Building on Sycamore Street. Those enrolled in the six-year combination high school and college classical course of studies met in the older two-story Athenaeum, which stood parallel to St. Xavier Church on Sycamore Street. In the aftermath of the Civil War, St. Xavier College entered an academically very promising era. Moreover, it began to make its mark in the community where Xavier alumni could be found in various professions, in the business sector, and in the ranks of the clergy. (1)

By this time the college had a pressing need for more adequate living quarters for the Jesuit faculty and additional classrooms for students. Once considered "a marvel of architectural beauty," Jesuit authorities saw the Athenaeum building as "but a relic of the past." James J. O'Meara, a twenty-year-old Jesuit scholastic from Missouri who had just arrived at the college in 1865, described the classroom situation in the Athenaeum. The basement accommodated classrooms for chemistry, drawing, and music. In the "long dark hall," he wrote, "imagine 50 boys sitting along three sides of the classroom, before old style desks or rather a continuous desk down the length of the hall, with a long continuous bench without rest for the back." The teacher's desk stood beside the door. The first floor of the Athenaeum contained living rooms for pastors and faculty. Toward the rear was a spacious study hall that served also as a classroom and as a hall for the annual commencement exercises. On the second floor were living rooms for the faculty on both sides of the corridor, the library, and the students' chapel. Above the second floor was a spacious attic. In 1863, responding to the need for improved facilities, and seeking a site for possible construction of a new building, the college paid $18,500 for property at the southwest corner of Seventh and Sycamore Streets. During the next four years it also acquired the adjoining lots, increasing the property to two hundred feet square, north of the church. (2)

Early in 1867, Hill, who, according to a contemporary "had a sagacious eye for improvements," provided a realistic assessment of St. Xavier College and of its needs. "Our college," he wrote to the father general, "has never been very successful; our buildings, class-rooms and yard are very poor, the house standing just in the northern shadow of the church, rendering gas-light necessary in the rooms for most of the day." The debt of the college was about $40,000, while its possessions were valued at $80,000 to $100,000. "Our Fathers who have lived in this house," he continued, "have long seen that no extensive good can be done here unless we provide a more spacious and commodious building." He proposed to erect a new building on property farthest from the church and remove the Carrell Building, using the site as part of yard or court. He "[c]onfidently believe[d]" the college could "borrow most of [the] money from people [in Cincinnati] interest free." On his last visit to the college the provincial had recommended to St. Xavier officials that they "endeavor to provide a building that would be more extensive and more inviting to the people than the present rude one." (3)

The college, which had a record enrollment of 337 students, then began raising funds for a new faculty residence and classroom building, and solicited contributions to fund professorships and "annual prizes for excellence in the ancient and modern languages, and in the sciences." In the first year there were several donors, including "one zealous clergyman," St. Xavier officials noted, who subscribed ten thousand dollars; another cleric who gave one thousand dollars; and a Catholic layman who donated an additional one thousand. These gifts were combined with a few smaller amounts from other clergymen. (4)

Four months later on Sunday, May 12, the administration laid the cornerstone for the new building. "An immense crowd," the *Catholic Telegraph* wrote, "assembled in the streets, and in all the houses from which a sight of the spot was to be had." The procession, led by the scholastics John Moynihan and James O'Meara, was composed of church dignitaries and various sodalities and associations connected with St. Xavier Church: the Young Men's Sodality, the Sodality of the Holy Family, the Orphan Society, about three hundred students from the college, and 436 boys and girls confirmed earlier that day by Archbishop John Purcell, "all with banners and flags, and headed by a band of musicians." After blessing the cornerstone, Purcell congratulated the college on progressing from the stage of a "one-horse institution." Some of the scholastics "felt that as a slur," O'Meara wrote in his diary, "but the antecedents explained it, as well as the hard times of the Civil War." For the college officials it remained to be seen "whether, in the completion of the undertaking, the founding of Professorships, . . . there are persons who will emulate the generous founders of numerous non-catholic institutions. It is to be hoped that the work may be speedily finished and thus an Institution be here permanently established, in which will be taught the branches of higher education." (5)

On June 25, 1868, the college dedicated the new massive four-story building, extending back about 120 feet from the road on Seventh Street, with heavy and intricately carved oak doors and moldings and an ornate stone porch facing Sycamore Street. Built at a cost of $150,000 the faculty building became known as the Hill building. It "looked like a palace compared to the old Athenaeum, which was still in use for class-rooms," O'Meara wrote. "It was heated by steam; and every room was supplied with marble wash-basin with hot & cold water; and the toilet was inside on every floor." Beforehand, the privy was outside across the yard. The Hill building symbolized enormous confidence in the future of St. Xavier College. With its construction, enrollment increased from 263 in 1865 to 358 students by 1868. (6)

About the time of the dedication of the new building, a Jesuit, assisted by some students, renovated the Athenaeum's attic and provided an entertainment and lecture hall as well as a meeting room for the Philopedian Society and other student functions. Another Jesuit faculty member recalled the day when "some mischevious [sic] boys, while exploring the recess between the Philopedian Hall and the roof, broke through the ceiling and rained down a shower of plaster on the heads of members of a literary society that was then in session." (7)

On May 7, 1869, less than a year after the dedication of the Hill Building, the General Assembly of the State of Ohio issued a perpetual charter to St. Xavier College, with all the rights of a college, replacing the original thirty-year charter issued in 1842. Thirteen days later the

Board of Trustees met to reorganize itself under the proposed new document. At the meeting the members suggested repealing that part of the constitution that made the archbishop of Cincinnati ex officio president of the board. The new charter called for seven members on the board. The only qualifications required for the office of trustee were residence in Hamilton County, where the college was located, membership in the Society of Jesus, and United States citizenship. Also, the trustees were "liable individually for the debts of their college . . . in excess of the value of its property."

By May 31, at a special meeting of the Board of Trustees, the members unanimously accepted the provisions of the act passed by the Ohio legislature. This led to the formation on September 2, 1869, of the first all-Jesuit as well as in-house Board of Trustees, with Walter Hill, president of the college, as president of the board. The Jesuit religious community and the Jesuit institution were one and the same entity. The president served as head of the college and rector of the Jesuit community. As rector-president he acted as one. Usually four Jesuits were appointed as house consultors to assist him in his deliberations on various courses of action, such as the management of the property. These same consultors, the president, and two additional Jesuits formed the Board of Trustees. Two of the trustees served as treasurer and secretary respectively. Management of the institution meant Jesuit control in deciding academic, religious, and financial practices and policy. A Jesuit institution was legally incorporated and the members of the Society of Jesus formed the corporation as trustees and officers. This remained the policy for a century. Whenever a trustee was appointed elsewhere and left the city he resigned from the board. (8)

The year after St. Xavier College acquired its new charter, the Municipal University Act passed by the Ohio legislature established the University of Cincinnati, which united the old Cincinnati College, the Cincinnati Astronomical Society, organized in 1842, and McMicken University, established in 1859 by a generous gift from Charles McMicken, a local merchant. In 1871, the Fathers of Holy Cross from Notre Dame, Indiana opened St. Joseph College on West Eighth Street in Cincinnati. St. Xavier's total enrollment declined from 358 students in 1868 to 317 students in 1871 at the time of St. Joseph College's opening. St. Joseph College continued until 1920, at which time the religious order closed the college due to mounting financial liability. (9)

The first significant action of the St. Xavier Board of Trustees under the new charter was "selling the Purcell Mansion" in order to raise additional revenue and offset the declining enrollment. Initially the members agreed to sell the property at the price of $75,000. The following February, however, they decided unanimously to subdivide the Purcell Mansion property, "offering it for sale at public auction." They thought they could get "10 to 15 thousand dollars more . . . by subdividing the property [than] . . . could be realized . . . from its sale as a whole." A novena was made to St. Joseph for a quick sale. At the auction, held two months later, the house and ground were sold by lots and "they went flying," the trustees' minutes read, "realizing $89,229.03." The college ended the school year financially solvent, largely because of the sale of the mansion. But in the fall of 1873, student enrollment declined further, falling to 284. It was the first time since 1867 that it was less than 300. Both the city and college were affected by the country's economic depression. (10)

In preparation for the nation's centennial in 1876, St. Xavier College introduced military drill among the students in the fall of 1875 and secured the services of a regular drill sergeant. The administration organized the St. Xavier Cadets, complete with uniforms, to contribute "to the physical training of the students [and] to add solemnity" to the celebrations. Regular army officers from Newport, Kentucky, conducted drill exercises twice a week. This program lasted until the end of the centennial celebration in 1877. About a decade later the college consultors discussed the formation of a military company at St. Xavier but decided against it. (11)

During the centennial, the Philopedian Society, which continued to foster literature and eloquence, met once a week to practice debating and from time to time to entertain the public by reciting poetry and prose selections in English and in German. The college held its June 1876 commencement at the Pike's Opera House, which opened in 1859 and served as the home of the Cincinnati Symphony Orchestra, in downtown Cincinnati. Red, white, and blue printed programs commemorated the ceremony. In an effort to establish closer relations with Cincinnati's academic community, Rudolph Meyer, S.J., vice president and prefect of studies, also invited the superintendent of public schools and other local dignitaries to an honors convocation presented by the college students. Two students presented their Latin essays on "Cincinnati, the Queen of the West." (12)

The Philopedian Society's public programs continued for several decades. Shortly following the U.S. naval victory at Manila Bay on May 21, 1898, during the Spanish-American War, the society presented a special program and later debated whether the United States should retain permanent possession of the Philippine Islands in the Pacific. At times it overspent its budget and relied on the college to cover the additional costs. Two years earlier, the consultors of the Jesuit community had agreed to cover the additional expenses for the performance of *Henry IV*, but informed the Philopedian Society that if it were to claim "the honor and credit of similar performances, it should . . . assume the expenses." (13)

Enrollment grew, and in January 1884 the Board of Trustees began planning for additional classroom space to supplement the Hill building. Despite the continuing decline in enrollment in the 1870s, from 272 in 1874 to 224 in 1879, the tide turned in the 1880s. By the middle of the decade the number of students had increased to 293. On February 19, 1884, Samuel Hannaford, a local architect, agreed to prepare "all necessary drawings, specifications and details required to construct" an addition to the Hill Building. A year later in March the consultors approved the plans and accepted bids for the work to be done on the new structure, which would later become known as the Moeller Building. The Carrell Building, between the Hill and the Athenaeum buildings, was razed in the summer of 1885. The new building was joined to the Hill building in the front and consisted of classrooms, a study hall, and an exhibition hall with a stage for dramatic presentations. The Athenaeum, Hill Building, and the Moeller Building constituted the campus. (14)

Curricular Changes

Walter Hill served as St. Xavier's president for almost four years. In mid-September 1869 he announced "that duties required his presence elsewhere" and therefore offered his resignation, which the board accepted. As head of the college he had provided considerable leadership. The library increased its holdings to more than 14,000 volumes, which was an increase of 17 percent in two years, while the museum increased its conchological, geological, and mineralogical specimens. Hill moved on to St. Louis University where he taught philosophy for the next thirteen years. Author of two textbooks, *Elements of Philosophy* (1874) and *Ethics* (1879), Hill was an excellent philosopher. He was the first St. Xavier president to produce any noteworthy literature. (15)

The trustees then elected Thomas O'Neil, a native of County Tipperary, Ireland, and former president of St. Louis University during the Civil War, Xavier's ninth Jesuit president. During his two-year term, 1869–1871, St. Xavier revamped and strengthened its course of studies. Instead of the traditional six-year classical program, officials lenghened the course of instruction leading to the degree of Bachelor of Arts to seven years. The classical course of studies, which reflected the educational system of the *Ratio Studiorum*, continued "to impart a thorough knowledge of the English, Greek, and Latin languages, of mental and moral philosophy, of pure and mixed mathematics, and of physical sciences." For the first time the academic and the collegiate departments were clearly separated and identified as such in the college catalogue. The first, second, and third academic years corresponded to high school; and philosophy, rhetoric, poetry, and humanities corresponded respectively to the senior, junior, sophomore, and freshman classes of college. In the judgment of one contemporary St. Xavier faculty member, the curricular change constituted "a wise move for the prestige of the college." In addition to having a structured seven-year classical program, the texts for the courses in the various branches were also specified by title and name of author. Because of the demand of the curriculum, college officials urged parents "to insist on their sons studying at home for two or three hours every evening." (16)

The college classes were held on the first two floors in the Hill Building. Poetry and humanities courses were on the first floor in inside parlors. Though the parlors contained two windows and were larger than the adjacent private rooms, they seemed "small," a scholastic wrote, "for a class of 30 boys." The philosophy and rhetoric classes were on the second floor, where the students sat in rows of double desks. Significantly, in the fall of 1869 a change took place inside the classrooms. The college installed stoves to provide more heat in the winter. (17)

For almost three decades from the time of the Jesuit takeover of the Athenaeum in 1840, the scholastic year usually began on the first Monday of September and ended in early to mid-July, mostly at the beginning of July. Beginning in 1868, however, it ended at the end of June. Moreover, it was the custom in the post-Civil War period for the college to cancel classes on special occasions. In September 1871 it granted a half-day holiday in honor of Ulysses Grant, president of the United States, who visited Cincinnati. In October a full holiday was granted in order that the students might attend the dedication of the Tyler Davidson Fountain, then located on Fifth Street between Walnut and Vine Streets in Cincinnati. (18)

In late November 1870 an event occurred that briefly upset the daily schedule. It was after 4 p.m., and classes had been dismissed. A man ran down the corridor calling for the treasurer, Michael Lawlor, S.J. He came out and walked "up and down the corridor with the crazed man," a scholastic observer wrote, "[and] tried to reason with him and get him out" of the building. But the man demanded chalices and treasures that he thought were hidden in the building. "That moment," the eyewitness wrote, "out sprang the Rector [President O'Neil] and pounced on the man halfway up, catching him by the arms. But though pinned, the mad man drew knives from under his sleeve slashing our brave Rector on both arms. . . . Presently two Brothers ran up to the rescue and they dragged him down head foremost. Hearing the scuffle . . . boys came out of the classroom and they helped to carry the man like a corpse out on the porch." Firemen, stationed across the street, brought a wagon and took the man to jail. At the subsequent trial the man was declared insane. O'Neil, "the hero of the debacle," the scholastic wrote, suffered "deep cuts on his arms." (19)

It was also customary for the Jesuit faculty members, who participated in monthly meetings to discuss academic matters, to teach all the branches of their respective classes. "[G]ood order," a teacher wrote, "depended on one man, who had the chance to observe the characters of his pupils." From the time of the arrival of the Society of Jesus in Cincinnati, Jesuits dominated the faculty at St. Xavier College. The number of Jesuits working in the school fluctuated with enrollment. By 1878 there were 12 priests, 9 scholastics, and 11 lay brothers. Growing enrollment, however, necessitated the hiring of lay instructors. Two of them had charge of the music department, and two others conducted classes in architecture and mechanical drawing. In August 1882 the college engaged a teacher for a grammar class at $50 per month and a bookkeeping and penmanship teacher at one dollar per hour. The following year it hired two commercial teachers, "five hours per day—at the salary of $60 per month." Until the 1890s the number of lay faculty never exceeded five in any one year. As St. Xavier offered more professional courses, a few more lay people joined the faculty. In the mid-1890s salaries of lay faculty members varied from $45 to $69 per month. (20)

Every month there were convocations, dramatic presentations, and written competitions in every branch, which enabled the faculty members to see the progress of each student and of the whole class. Academic grades were still sent to the parents each month and awards were given for academic proficiency. During the presidency of Leopold Bushart, who succeeded O'Neil in the summer of 1871, the new president offered a special award of a gold fountain pen in the spring and summer and a pair of ice skates in the winter for the highest class average. A native of Belgium, Bushart (formerly spelled Buysschaert) served as president for three years. In the post-Civil War period, more and more American colleges introduced prizes as a way to stimulate interest in academic studies. At Williams College in Massachusetts, an alumnus awarded a prize to the student who won the most prizes. Through the end of the nineteenth century St. Xavier College officials at times exempted all students who had maintained "honors" work for the year from the annual examination. (21)

Over a fourteen-year period from 1874 to 1887, St. Xavier College had six different presidents, two of whom were not new to the office. When Bushart was appointed president of St. Louis University in 1874, Edward A. Higgins succeeded him as St. Xavier's eleventh Jesuit president and served until 1879, Born in 1839 at Carlow County, Ireland, he came to America ten years later and was ordained in 1869. Higgins was familiar with Cincinnati, having taught there a few years earlier. On January 1, 1879, Higgins was named provincial of the Missouri province and Thomas O'Neil was appointed to an interim term as president of the college. O'Neil's previous experience as president meant that he could make an easy transition to this interim position. Seven months later he tendered his resignation to the board and Rudolph J. Meyer, a native of St. Louis, was elected a member of the board of trustees and appointed president. (22)

Fifty-two-year-old John J. Coghlan, a native of Ireland, succeeded Meyer on July 31, 1881. Having been a parish missionary, he appeared at first to be more conversant with pastoral than with college work. Nevertheless, he was well prepared both to deal with Xavier's 262 students and faculty and to help develop St. Xavier Church and parish. During his three-year presidency he did much to help raise the academic standards and to develop scholarship among the students through an awards system.

In the summer of 1884 the provincial called Coghlan to St. Louis, and Henry Moeller, a native of Covington, Kentucky, was chosen president A member of the class of 1866, Moeller became the first alumnus president of the college. A year and a half later, Edward Higgins returned for a second term as president, succeeding Moeller who, on Christmas 1885, became president of St. Louis University. (23)

On recreation days in the post-Civil War years, some of the Jesuits walked over the hills to Eden Park in Mt. Adams or to Walnut Hills through the fields or by Mt. Auburn Avenue to the Vine Street hills.

In the spring of 1870 the college purchased for $18,000 a forty-three-and-a-half acre farm in Campbell County, Kentucky, approximately six miles from downtown Cincinnati and four miles upstream just beyond Newport. The trustees hoped that the newly-acquired "country place . . . might serve as a Villa, where the professors could spend their vacation." On high land overlooking the Ohio River and opposite the mouth of the Little Miami River, the property had an eleven-room house and a stable. Called St. Thomas Villa, it provided facilities for vacation time and for the regular Thursday holidays during the school year. To facilitate transportation, college officials provided a buggy, a spring wagon, and a horse affectionately named "Bob." During summer vacations, some of the scholastic seminarians and Jesuit priests and brothers visited the farm. At times they "walked there," O'Meara recorded in his diary. "Altogether it was a very enjoyable place for the summer vacations," he wrote, "and often we spent our Thursdays there." At times they made the trip in a rowboat, rigged with sails and christened the "Maris Stella." School authorities sold the property in 1886 for $10,000. (24)

While expanding academic and social activities at the college, officials always remained focused on the classical course of studies. Committed to its Jesuit tradition, the college published fifty additional pages of curriculum in its 1876–1877 catalogue and eighteen additional pages the following year. In response to a request made by the Ohio College Association, a society of Ohio college professors founded in 1867 and whose membership favored a classical course of studies and required an academic program of four years in Latin and Greek, President Edward Higgins agreed to share the principles of the Jesuit plan of studies. The association gathered its members every winter vacation to have them share their experiences in the classroom. At the December 1877 annual meeting in Cincinnati, Jesuit faculty members gave talks on "The Jesuit System of Teaching the Classics" and "The Importance of a Knowledge of Philology to the Teacher of Classics." Under the guidance of George Hoeffer, S.J., prefect of studies in the 1880s, the college raised the classical course of studies "to its founding standard," O'Meara noted in his diary. In the summer of 1886 the Jesuit consultors petitioned the provincial that "a uniform course of studies be followed in every college of the province." The following year, all midwestern Jesuit colleges adopted St. Xavier College's curriculum. A St. Xavier alumnus later recalled in *The Reveries of an Alumnus* some fond memories of his classical studies at his alma mater. He wrote:

> How well I remember the old college days
> The studies and tasks; the professors; and all
> The hardships of Latin; the Greek's puzzling maze
> Those memories now I can fondly recall. (25)

In 1881 when the college celebrated the fiftieth anniversary of its founding, two contemporary Cincinnati historians wrote that "'Old St. Xavier' is a name that is today in many mouths, and that awakens pleasant recollections in many hearts. It has educated hundreds in the city which it adorns. Its graduates are to be found in honored places on the bench and at the bar. The medical profession," they continued, "counts many of them among its members, some well known to fame and others fast rising into prominence. To ministers of the religion it professes it has given birth by scores. But we can give no more practical illustration of its work as an educational institute than by presenting its course of studies." (26)

In the fall of 1886, because of Cincinnati's suburban growth, changes were made in the daily class schedule. Until then college doors had opened at 7 a.m. with daily Mass for Catholic students at 8. Classes were from 8:30 to 4, with an hour-and-a-half lunch break for any student who chose to walk home on the uneven brick sidewalks bordering the bumpy cobblestone streets. There were classes Monday through Saturday, and Thursday remained the regular weekly holiday. "Owing to the extension of the city into the suburbs," the St. Xavier catalogue reported, "the double session has become an inconvenience to the majority of the students who come from a distance, and a hindrance to the proper preparation of class work at home." The college set up a new daily schedule. Study halls now opened at 8:00 a.m., Mass for the Catholic students was at 8:30, followed by classes until 2:30 p.m. Only a half hour was allowed for lunch.

Students now could get home earlier in the afternoon. However, since the midday meal was the main meal of the day for many families, a large number of parents insisted—some even sent physicians' notes to support their position—that their sons be dismissed early to go home for lunch. The resulting class disruption created confusion and disorder. So in the fall of 1903, college officials introduced another slight change in the daily schedule of activities. They ended the morning session at 11:45 a.m and classes resumed an hour later. (27)

In 1887 the college expanded both its academic program and community outreach by sponsoring a series of evening lectures by its faculty in the new College Hall in the Moeller building. The lectures, given on Wednesdays of January and February and intended to be "chiefly for the old students of the college and for those who are interested in the Catholic treatment of important questions in history and philosophy," provided an important service to the community. The subjects generally included philosophical and historical criticism, as well as literature and ethics. In the first year the series consisted of six lectures, of which two were delivered by President Higgins. The program paralleled the post-Civil War Chautauqua religious lecture series in New York, which had become popular throughout the United States. The most popular lecture, "The True Philosophy of the Land Question," presented by Higgins, a man known for his reserve and who usually kept his emotions to himself, consisted of an exposition and refutation of the theories of the economist land reformer Henry George in *Progress and Poverty*. Higgins's talk, first given in the College Hall, was later repeated at a theatre in the city. His lecture was so popular that not only was it favorably reviewed in the newspapers, but it was also printed in pamphlet form and sold for the benefit of Cincinnati's poor. Rabbi Isaac Wise of Cincinnati noted in the *Israelite* that Higgins's pamphlet contained "much that is worth reading. True, it is tinged with Christian doctrines and the views natural to a priest of the Roman Catholic Church, but the philosophy is sound, and a perusal of the brochure will furnish many an argument to refute the socialistic theories which are just now epidemic." (28)

In April of the same year, students at the college wrote and produced the first St. Xavier College newspaper, *The Collegian*. They intended it to be a monthly publication edited by the poetry class. "Published under the auspices and with the full approval and encouragement of one of the oldest and best institutions of learning in the land," the editors of the new publication wrote, "*The Collegian* goes forth animated with the confidence which the character of its venerable patron cannot fail to inspire." The columns were open to any St. Xavier student, as well as "to students of any institution," the newspaper wrote, "who may not be of our religious creed." One of the purposes of *The Collegian* was "to let the public know just what lessons in the matter of morality young men are taught within St. Xavier's hallowed walls. By a good education," the editors continued, "is meant religious and mental training so blended together that they become inseparable." They expected a wide circulation because "Old St. Xavier has multitudes of friends." (29)

The five issues of *The Collegian* provided an interesting contemporary view of academic life at St. Xavier. The first publication provided an extensive sketch of the college, while its editorial reflected the enthusiasm and optimism of the students. The essays, historical sketches, fiction, and poetry reflected the literary flavor of the day, while the "Notes and Comments" section was filled with reports about the students' extracurricular activities of football, baseball, and handball, as well as the accounts of the various student societies. The newspaper ceased publication in the fall of 1887. Five issues had appeared and then, without notice, the paper ceased publication. Though the students in 1894 petitioned St. Xavier officials for a "college journal," there would not be another student publication until about twenty years later. (30)

The college's academic growth and standards were sometimes reflected in the graduation exercises. On June 27, 1887, school authorities held its forty-fifth annual commencement at Pike's Opera House. In the rich commencement tradition of the college, the graduates conducted the literary part of the program. "The subject which they selected," the *Catholic Telegraph* reported, "was whether the poets or philosophers of pagan and Christian times gave the better idea of a future state of rewards and punishments, . . . illustrating with vivid pictures and apt quotations from the choicest literary men of all times," such as Plato, Socrates, and Virgil. In the editor's judgment, the St. Xavier graduates "showed that their college course had stored their minds with a great amount of erudition and scholarly attainments." (31)

Except for some courses in business, mostly in the evening, there was generally no provision at the college for professional or graduate instruction. For a brief moment in the 1880s, St. Xavier's commercial course set up a hypothetical business community, including a bank, post office, railroad office, and insurance company. Students were supplied with "a Cash Capital of College Currency and a stock of Merchandise" and engaged themselves in business. In 1894 the college offered some extension courses, and, two years later, initiated a post-graduate course of study in philosophy and literature. The latter, which could be completed in three years, enabled St. Xavier's "own graduates to continue their philosophical and literary studies." Because of more pressing needs of academic departments and the limited resources at the disposal of the faculty, at the turn of the century the college discontinued the graduate courses. Like many American colleges, St. Xavier, at the time, was too small to offer much breadth in curriculum. (32)

Among the 35 colleges in Ohio in 1890, St. Xavier College ranked twelfth in enrollment. The great majority of colleges in the state as well as in the country were small. The average collegiate enrollment in Ohio was 105, compared to a national average of 106. The largest college in the state was Oberlin, with a co-ed enrollment of 609. At the time, the University of Cincinnati and Ohio State University in Columbus had 120 and 221 co-ed students respectively, while St. Xavier College, with an overall student population of 419 men in its combined high school and college program, had 71 college students. Collegiate enrollments in Ohio rose from 3,681 in 1890 to 5,807 in 1900. However, 73 percent of the additional students could be accounted for in three institutions, Ohio State, Cincinnati, and Western Reserve in Cleveland. St. Xavier's total combined enrollment increased slightly from 419 to 425. The following year, in 1901, the school reached record enrollment of 458. (33)

At the turn of the century St. Xavier's collegiate enrollment, like that in other Jesuit colleges and universities of the Missouri province, represented approximately one-fourth to one-third of the total enrollment in the school. Below are enrollment figures at these institutions in 1903. The first column displays the total enrollment in the combined seven-year plus programs, and the second column presents the number of students enrolled in the college or university sections of those programs:

St. Ignatius College, Chicago	535	121
St. Xavier College	400	108
St. Louis University	371	85
St. Mary's College, St. Mary's, Kansas	274	70
Creighton University, Omaha, Nebraska	273	83
Marquette College, Milwaukee	258	93
Detroit College, Detroit	201	80 (34)

Xavier's administration was experiencing increased pressure to abandon the European model and adopt the American system that separated high school and college programs. In 1910, Jesuit Superior General Francis Xavier Wernz approved a plan by which St. Xavier divided its college classes into freshman, sophomore, junior, and senior year, rather than humanities, poetry, rhetoric, and philosophy classes. Notwithstanding the fact that some province and college consultors were "decidedly adverse" to the idea, the change mandated "promoting the best boys of the 4th" class in the high school "into a newly-organized Freshman class." Though influenced by the standardized organization of American higher education, St. Xavier and other Jesuit colleges did not adapt their curriculum to the American norms. (35)

In the gradual transformation of American higher education after the Civil War there was a conflict between tradition and modernity, between religious and secular forces, and between localism and nationalism. In a period of organizational expansion and diminishing sectarianism, most of the colleges were denominationally based and locally focused. A movement for greater technological and scientific education, which had begun before the Civil War, helped produce new and more popular colleges. The Morrill Federal Land Grant Act of 1862, in an effort to provide agricultural education, made it possible for state governments to develop the land-grant colleges, institutions with a popular and practical orientation. In addition, the American state university, which began in the South, was in the post-Civil War period mainly prevalent in the Midwest and West. Land-grant and other state colleges were to small-town America what municipal colleges and universities were to the cities. (36)

In the process, there developed a controversy between the classicists, who would accommodate some new academic subjects, and others who seemed, at times, to only want to endorse practical or technical education. In October 1899 President Charles William Eliot, the first president of Harvard University to earn a national reputation, had written an article in the *Atlantic Monthly* that challenged the classical curriculum and proposed the adoption of an elective system in higher education. He challenged traditional administrators and faculty committed to the idea of a fixed, uniform classical curriculum required of everyone. He recommended that students have more freedom to select from among different classes and utilitarian courses of study. In the process he attacked the Jesuit curriculum. He argued that only direct revelation from on high could justify a uniform or required curriculum.

The renowned Harvard historian, Samuel Eliot Morison, wrote about half a century later that "[i]t is a hard saying, but Mr. Eliot, more than any other man, is responsible for the greatest educational crime of the century against American youth—depriving him of his classical heritage." Led by Eliot, an increasing number of nonsectarian colleges and universities introduced a vast array of utilitarian courses of study by the end of the century and substituted a broad elective course of studies for the traditional classical programs. St. Xavier College, however, while offering a few commercial courses in the evening, was resolute in its commitment to its classical course of studies. Holding tightly to the *Ratio Studiorum,* St. Xavier remained committed to the systematic study of Latin and Greek, ancient history, literature, metaphysics, philology, and rhetoric, among others. (37)

Community Outreach

About two decades after the demolition of the old St. Xavier Church in 1860, the congregation experienced a tragedy. On Good Friday morning, April 7, 1882, a fire destroyed the interior of St. Xavier Church and steeple. William Henry Elder, then Cincinnati's coadjutor bishop, wrote about the church's "blackened walls and charred timbers." He noted that the crowds of English-speaking Catholics, who "every Good Friday had made a pilgrimage to kiss the big crucifix," now gazed

> on ruins, bewailing, crying—not figuratively, but literally. The big wooden cross, 16 feet long, from the top of the steeple, falling and lying on the sidewalk, [was] muddy with the water of the engines. Spontaneously some good soul knelt and kissed the broken cross lying on the pavement. Others followed and almost all day they were kneeling on the curbstone, a dozen at a time, to kiss that cross; emblem of the ruin of their Church, and of the love of their Saviour.

During the fire the Athenaeum building "was often in danger from the flying embers," a Jesuit faculty wrote. "So, the furniture was hastily carried into the yard." All told, only the four walls, foundation, and the tower of the church, "with its outside damaged by the heat and water and its inside lining corroded by the flames," remained. The total loss amounted to about $200,000. Under the leadership of the Jesuits and Charles Driscoll, who would serve as pastor for over thirty-five years, immediate steps were taken to rebuild the church. Contributions came in generously. Within two weeks they raised over $40,000. By March 1883, less than a year after the fire, the Jesuits reopened the church for service. The formal dedication took place on Ascension Thursday, May 3. (38)

As part of their religious ministry, the Jesuits of St. Xavier Parish, which then extended from the Ohio River north into the country beyond Avondale, expanded their community outreach. They devoted themselves to the spiritual growth of the parish and the students of the college. In addition to the daily Mass requirements for the Catholic students, in the late 1880s the Jesuits instructed their students in the faith and provided frequent devotional and retreat opportunities. Even those enrolled in the commercial program were subject to catechetical instruction. The largest society at the school during this period was the Acolythical Society, dedicated to assisting the Jesuits at Mass, especially on Sundays and feast days. In 1887, its members numbered 38 and it claimed to be the "best-drilled altar boys' society in the city." (39)

The Jesuits were especially concerned over the welfare of the newly-emancipated African Americans. On May 10, 1866, St. Xavier Church bought property on Longworth Street between Race and Elm Streets in the west end of Cincinnati. Under the leadership of Francis Xavier Weninger, the Jesuits helped organize St. Ann's Colored Church and School, the first parish founded in the archdiocese to meet the needs of African Americans. At the time there were fewer than 6,000 blacks in Cincinnati, and only a few of them were Catholic. In 1868 Weninger founded the St. Peter Claver Society, named after the Jesuit who, in the early 1600s, converted and cared for the pastoral needs of thousands of slaves in Colombia. Members of the Claver Society, a predominantly white group made up of German Americans, provided assistance and helped spread the gospel to African Americans. Moreover, that same year a primary school under the supervision of the Sisters of Notre Dame de Namur was opened for black students. (40)

In January 1873 the St. Xavier board of trustees discussed an offer made by the United States Express Company on Longworth Street to buy St. Ann Church for "300 dollars cash per front foot." St. Xavier's treasurer, Michael Lawlor, S.J., argued that "the effort to establish a separate colored church . . . had been a failure, and now when an opportunity so favorable presented itself of getting rid of what he would mention to call 'an Elephant,' common sense dictated that they should avail themselves of it." Driscoll opposed the sale. Arguing that St. Ann "had not proved a failure," he pointed out that there "had been over 100 converts made in that church, and he thought the pastor should be questioned on the work really done in the church, which should not be taken on vague rumor." But President Leopold Bushart and other members of the board each asserted "that the attempt was a failure." Though the trustees authorized Bushart "to sign all necessary papers for the transfer of the property," the sale was never consummated. Twelve years later the Missouri provincial inquired "whether it would be advisable to cease to do the pastoral work at the Negro church." In response to his inquiry, the Jesuits at the college argued that "as long as there was to be a negro congregation and church within the limits of our parish, it should remain under our control." In 1908 diocesan priests took over the apostolate to Cincinnati's black Catholic community. (41)

In addition to the parish duties of celebrating Mass and visiting the sick, the Jesuit pastoral staff also oversaw the activities of more than 1,000 pupils in the parish elementary school, established residences for working boys and girls, conducted sodalities for married men, married women, single men, single women, and for the younger children of the parish, and served as chaplains for the hospitals and city jail. At times, as in 1873 at the urging of St. Xavier President Bushart, students at the college gave public dramatic exhibitions in Mozart Hall on Fourth Street, the net proceeds of which were given to the Little Sisters of the Poor, who had arrived from France five years earlier and attended to the poor in the southwestern end of the city. (42)

Diocesan Bank Collapse

In 1878, St. Xavier College officials had to deal with a financial scandal unprecedented in the history of the Archdiocese of Cincinnati, when a devastating financial failure struck the informal private banking operation of Fr. Edward Purcell, Archbishop Purcell's brother. For approximately forty years the archbishop had delegated to his brother total responsibility for diocesan financial matters. Fr. Purcell had been accepting deposits for safekeeping from Catholics in the archdiocese and from other Ohio residents. As confidence in the local banks was shaky and news spread of Edward Purcell's banking business, more and more people found comfort in placing their savings in the hands of the archbishop and his brother. Over a forty-year period, perhaps as much as twenty-five million dollars were deposited in the bishop's bank. (43)

Since the national panic of 1873, a series of financial crises had occurred in Cincinnati. By 1878 a number of small banks were forced to close their doors, causing panic and a run on Purcell's bank. To make matters worse, the city's leading bankers no longer accepted

Purcell's notes. The archbishop's brother had used personal notes from individuals to whom he had loaned money as collateral to secure loans from banks to help meet demands from his depositors. Although by November Edward Purcell had paid out over $100,000, he could not meet all the requests from the depositors. (44)

On December 18, 1878, some archdiocesan clergy met at St. Xavier College to draw up crisis management plans to help the archbishop. They formed a committee, consisting of William J. Halley, pastor of the cathedral and chancellor of the archdiocese, John Albrinck, pastor of Holy Trinity Church, Ubald Webersinke, provincial of the Franciscans, and Edward Higgins, president of St. Xavier college, to meet with the archbishop. They met with Purcell at the college. As a way of restoring public confidence, the committee urged the archbishop to make a public statement "to the effect that he holds himself . . . responsible for all financial claims against his brother." They also proposed that he provide "as security for such claims and liabilities, . . . all the assets, of whatever kind or value, that belong to him, as well as all the properties" that belonged to the diocese. If there appeared "an excess of liabilities over the assets," the four clergymen pledged themselves "to cooperate cordially with the Most Reverend Archbishop in providing means to meet all the demands, and pay off all debts." Later they realized that in their resolve to pay the entire debt they had, as Albrinck put it, "undertaken a fool's task." Moreover, their recommendation to pledge the local church's property as security for the liabilities of the bank failure would later be discounted by the court. The following month Higgins, now religious superior for the Jesuits of the Midwest, presented Purcell with a $1,000 bond to help support the diocese in its financial crisis. (45)

By spring 1879 auditors estimated the loss from the diocesan bank failure to be over three-and-a-half million dollars. The depositors filed a suit against the diocese, arguing that all property held in Purcell's name as archbishop should be auctioned to pay the creditors. By early 1881 every church in the archdiocese had been assessed by Archbishop William Elder, Purcell's successor, to meet the expense of the pending diocesan lawsuit. Assessment on the Jesuits' three churches was $125 for St. Francis Xavier, $12.50 for St. Thomas Church on Sycamore Street, and $10 for St. Ann. Considering "the state of the public mind," which was understandably upset over the financial scandal, the St. Xavier board of trustees decided not to take up a collection in the three churches, but "to pay the amounts privately and by three separate drafts." (46)

The celebrated Mannix V. Purcell trial, known as the "Church Case," since the archdiocese was the defendant, began on April 4, 1882, and ended about nine weeks later on June 24. The judges then deliberated on the matter for almost a year and a half, rendering their decision in December 1883. The court decided in favor of the archdiocese of Cincinnati, declaring that the local church was not liable for the bank's debt. It concluded that Archbishop Purcell had held various churches' "properties . . . in trust for charitable and pious uses." Though head of the local church, the court decided that Purcell was the trustee and not the actual owner of the properties and therefore could not sell what he did not own. On January 14, 1889, the Jesuit community donated $25 to the creditors' fund, which had been established to provide some assistance to the creditors. (47)

Extracurricular Activities

Increased extracurricular offerings, including debates, theatrical programs, oratorical competitions, and honors convocations four times a year became regular features of the campus calendar. In fall 1865 the administration established the Student Library Association. Three years later students organized the German Literary Society, better known as the German Academy. Its mostly German-American members met weekly for the purpose "of acquiring ease and fluency" in the use of the German language, by means of debates, essays, and oratorical compositions. When in March 1878 Archbishop Purcell and the papal envoy to Canada visited the college, students not only gave speeches in English, Latin, and French, but also in German. In the late 1880s the German Academy, which later became known as the Heidelberg Club, had twenty-four members. (48)

By the mid-1880s the college expanded students' musical and literary opportunities. In the spring of 1884 it formed a choir to enable students to improve themselves in vocal music and to perform publicly at "Religious and Literary Festivals." The following June the choir performed at the commencement ceremonies. One of the major contributors to the music program was musician Otto Juettner, an 1885 graduate. On Sunday, September 20, 1885, students organized the Xavier Lyceum, a literary society. The previous spring the students had presented a literary and musical program. "[W]ith the power of knowledge" and the "quickness of wit," one of the members wrote, the Lyceum aimed "to rout in intellectual warfare" those who would attempt to attack the

"Holy Catholic Church." The newly-formed society used the College Hall for literary performances. When in February 1891 the Philopedian Society celebrated its fiftieth year of existence, the active members and alumni commemorated the event by a social union and a literary entertainment. The Lyceum remained active until about the mid-1890s. (49)

During this period the college sought to prevent the young men from intermingling with the young ladies in dramatic and musical performances. In the late 1880s and early 1890s the administration prohibited members of the Young Ladies' Sodality in the Diocese of Cincinnati from participating in the school's Christmas play. "[It] did not seem proper," the house minutes read, " to [the Jesuits] for ladies to appear on our stage." In 1906 Archbishop Henry Moeller, who had been ordained archbishop of Cincinnati four years earlier and was an alumnus of the college from the class of 1869, informed his alma mater that Rome condemned "all dancing" and that he personally advocated "elimination of female voices from the choir." (50)

Through the 1890s and into the new century, St. Xavier College continued to sponsor oratory and elocution contests and classical and contemporary dramatic presentations. In addition, students participated in the Intercollegiate Latin and English Essay Contests between the Jesuit schools of the Midwest. In each of the contests it was customary for the seven schools collectively to submit over 150 papers. Occasionally a St. Xavier student captured the gold medal award and first place in the competitions. A good performance also could lead to a school holiday. (51)

In the post-Civil War period, as American colleges and universities began to realize the importance of intercollegiate relations, it was impossible for them to ignore the growing national popularity of intercollegiate football. The Princeton-Rutgers game of 1869 is considered the first intercollegiate football game in America. Since the early 1860s, Xavier students had been "fond of playing football" on school grounds, but it wasn't until 1900 that organized intercollegiate football debuted at the college. Two years earlier the school catalogue had listed for the first time the St. Xavier Athletic Association, whose purpose "was to encourage and promote outdoor interschool athletic games." Only those students who achieved "a requisite standard of proficiency in their studies" were allowed to participate in football and baseball. In the fall of 1901 the St. Xavier College football team went undefeated and won the Interscholastic Football League championship. The *Cincinnati Enquirer* awarded it the championship banner. The students celebrated by participating in a rally at the school. Other schools in the league—Woodward, Walnut Hills, Franklin, Hughes, and Technical—which were exclusively secondary schools, protested the fact that St. Xavier players were college-age students. As a consequence the league was disbanded and the following year St. Xavier had to add new teams to its football schedule. (52)

Alumni Association and Golden Jubilee

Through the years, suggestions had been made to unite the St. Xavier College alumni. Commencements had provided occasions for alumni reunions. In 1872 the first complete list of St. Xavier graduates appeared in the school catalogue. That initial list reveals that medicine, law, business, and ministry—both Jesuit and diocesan—were the major professions of the alumni. In the July-August 1887 issue of *The Collegian* the editors called for the formation of an alumni association. On December 12, 1888, in response to an invitation from Henry Schapman, St. Xavier's seventeenth Jesuit president, twenty-four alumni met in the College Hall.

The college consultors had announced at their August 28, 1887, meeting that Schapman was the "newly appointed Rector of St. Xavier College and Church." On October 6 Schapman, a native of Holland, former pastor of a parish in Kansas, and vice president of St. Louis University, formally succeeded Edward Higgins, who had been named president of St. Ignatius College in Chicago. In response to Schapman's encouragement and pledge of support, those present at the December 1888 meeting in the College Hall, founded the Alumni Association and elected Francis H. Cloud, a member of the class of 1863, its first president. (53)

During the next four months the members held several meetings, selected additional officers, drew up a constitution and by-laws, and made preparations for the first alumni banquet, which was held on May 1, 1889 at the college. The evening ceremony was an overwhelming success. A local newspaper observed that the College Hall "was handsomely decorated" with potted palms on the stage, "and from the horseshoe dining tables hundreds of spring blossoms gave forth their fragrance." Moreover, "[t]he hall was filled with music, light and banners," it continued, "and cheers for 'old St. Xavier' fluttered the banners frequently during the night. . . . It was the first annual dinner of the alumni of St. Xavier and the Alma Mater was wined, cheered and serenaded until her old head must have ached." Alumni and faculty members gave talks on St. Xavier's past, present, and the future. The main speaker, Cardinal James Gibbons of Baltimore, reminded the alumni that he had been a student at St. Xavier in 1855 and that "the memories of those pleasant days would never be effaced." Though the editors of *The Collegian* two years earlier had described the discontinuation of the boarding school in 1854 as the "beginning [of] a new era" and perhaps the college's "darkest hour," they were optimistic about St. Xavier's future. "[W]ith renewed energy," they argued, "the Fathers labored on to make the College prosper in its new sphere." (54)

In the spring of 1890, the alumni, working with St. Xavier College officials, faculty, students, and parents planned for the celebration of the fiftieth anniversary of the Jesuits in Cincinnati. It is interesting to contrast this celebration with the scarce attention that had been given nine years earlier to the fiftieth anniversary of the 1831 founding of the Athenaeum. By 1890 the St. Xavier College administration and the Alumni Association had elevated the college's Jesuit origin and identity to primary position in its institutional memory. "[U]nder Jesuit control," *Woodstock Letters* noted, St. Xavier "always maintained a reputation for scholarship and piety." (55)

Over a fifty-year period the college had conferred 235 bachelor of arts and 90 master of arts degrees. This was an average of four to five baccalaureate graduates and one to two master of arts graduates per year. Since the graduate totals were so low, the Alumni Association, in order to increase membership, did allow non-graduates of the college whose education had been interrupted by the Mexican War, the Civil War, or financial hardship, to join.

The trustees thought that the college should celebrate its Golden Jubilee "with great solemnity at the close of the scholastic term." They selected commencement week as the most appropriate time for the commemorative events. The provincial authorized the school to close for one week and conduct a series of programs from June 16 to June 22. Beginning with an alumni Mass at St. Xavier Church, celebrated by Archbishop William Elder of Cincinnati and the bishops of Wheeling, West Virginia, and Covington, Kentucky, the festivities included musical recitals, speeches, a banquet attended by about 150 alumni and guests at a local hotel, commencement exercises, and a parish anniversary Mass. According to a local newspaper, the Mass for the Alumni Association "was one of the most impressive in the history of the city. Admission was by card only." The commencement took place at the Grand Opera House on Vine Street in Cincinnati on Wednesday evening, June 18. In attendance were civic and religious leaders, including Governor James E. Campbell of Ohio. The week of jubilation ended with solemn pontifical vespers on Sunday evening, June 22, celebrated by Archbishop Elder. (56)

In the winter of 1889 the Jesuit consultors and the provincial of the Missouri province had opposed "putting up more buildings" at the college. St. Xavier authorities nevertheless persisted in their request to replace the Athenaeum building with a new classroom building as part of the Golden Jubilee. The following spring, upon receiving approval from the provincial, college officials hired an architect and began inspecting and discussing sketches for a new building to be called Memorial Hall. President Schapman appealed to the alumni and the newly established Alumni Association in St. Xavier's fund-raising drive. During the Golden Jubilee year, a friend of the college offered to donate $10,000 for a new building if the alumni would do the same. The Alumni Association responded enthusiastically to the challenge. In 1890, *Woodstock Letters* announced that St. Xavier College "is putting up the last wing of the college, which will complete the magnificent plans begun by Fr. Hill" about twenty-five years earlier. In the fall of 1891 the college dedicated Memorial Hall. During the excavation for the construction of Memorial Hall, the Athenaeum, the original college building that had been used for sixty years, was demolished. (57)

The new five-story classroom building connected to the Moeller building and extended as far as St. Xavier Church. It contained classrooms, scientific laboratories, a gymnasium, a chapel, and a large exhibition hall. It was the center piece of the college. At the dedication, the alumni held a reception for over 200 guests in the library, adjoining Memorial Hall. The Cincinnati Orchestra furnished the music. During the ceremony members of the Jesuit community showed visitors the nearly completed chapel, whose interior soared three stories to a Romanesque ceiling and a skylight. (58)

On December 29, 1891, Archbishop Elder dedicated the new chapel. That day Memorial Hall, later called Alumni Hall because of the $4,000 donation from the former students of the college, was formally opened to the public with an alumni presentation of scenes from six plays of Shakespeare. Moreover, St. Xavier College spent $400 in fitting up a gymnasium in the hall and engaged a regular athletic instructor to work with the 145 college-level students in gymnastic exercises. "Those of Ours who believe that we should not neglect the physical culture of our pupils, while training their minds and hearts," *Woodstock Letters* wrote in 1892, "will be deeply interested in the result of the experiment." Students were especially pleased with the well-equipped new gymnasium on the premises. What "the Students' Library does for your intellectual faculties the Gym does for your bodies," a student publication wrote, and that the college intended "all her sons to go out into the world thoroughly sound in mind and body. If you want to be an athlete, what you need most is the gym." Seven years later the college engaged a trainer for the gymnasium. (59)

Two-and-a-half weeks after the dedication of the chapel, the provincial, John P. Freiden, paid his annual visit to the college. While visiting the new classroom building and meeting with the students, he pointed out that electric or gas light "should be put into the class-rooms and study-halls, sufficient to enable the students to read without straining their eyes." By 1906 the college placed "electric lights in all the class-rooms" as well as "disinfectants in boys' closets." (60)

From its founding, the Alumni Association took an interest in the intellectual life of the campus. Working closely with college officials, it sponsored social and cultural events to reflect the main purpose of a St. Xavier education. Henry Schapman, who had been instrumental in the formation of the Alumni Association, was appointed president of the University of Detroit in 1893. His successor at St. Xavier, Alexander J. Burrowes, S.J., proved to be an equally strong supporter of the Alumni Association. Burrowes inspired confidence and had a keen sense of humor. He initiated an evening lecture series and invited alumni to speak. Regular participation by Burrowes, faculty members, and alumni helped make the series popular for years.

"'Old St. Xavier's,' as this college is familiarly and affectionately called," *Woodstock Letters* reported in 1896, "has reason to be proud of her alumni, because of the active interest which they ever display in enhancing her record before the public. . . . [E]vidence is afforded by their frequent participation in literary exercises planned under her inspiration and direction." In the winter of that year, the association sponsored ten public lectures, eight presented by alumni of the college. Most of the subjects, sometimes presented with illustrated slides, reflected each alumnus's profession or business. The topics ranged from "Odd Points of Law" by Denis F. Cash, class of 1887, and "Early English State Trials" by Edward P. Moulinier, class of 1887, to "Modern Medicine" by John E. Greiwe, M.D., class of 1886, and "Principles of Socialism" by President Burrowes. In 1903 the Alumni Association inaugurated an annual spring dinner series. (61)

On November 10, 1896, (the same year that Burrowes put in a telephone, thinking it was "advisable to give it a trial,") the college started an evening graduate program. About fifty graduate students enrolled for the weekly classes, which were limited to philosophy and literature. The principal professor was John Poland, S.J., lecturer on ethics and literature. Since 1842 St. Xavier had been conferring the master's degree on those students who successfully studied philosophy for an additional year. In June 1897 seven graduate students received the degree that was presented by their graduate professor, Michael J. O'Connor, S.J., who was also the newly appointed president of the college. The following fall the school enrolled 60 students in the graduate program. The college discontinued the program in 1902 in order to better meet the needs of other academic departments. Four years later officials reopened it with 45 students. (62)

That same year, St. Xavier officials established a scholarship fund, which was the beginning of the institution's endowment. At the time, 171 American colleges reported no endowments. This number included public and Catholic colleges and most of the small colleges in the South. Patrick Poland, the owner of a local wholesale grocery business, died and left his fortune to his sons, John A. and William F. Poland of the Society of Jesus. The estate valued at $60,000 "assure[s] us," Michael O'Connor wrote to the provincial, "of a yearly income of . . . $2,700, the greater part of which, comes to us from the rental" of a store on Third Street in Cincinnati. (63)

O'Connor, who would be president for four years, established the scholarship endowment fund in order for "the four College Classes of St. Xavier College, [and] the Philosophy Class [to] . . . be declared free *for all time to come*." It is significant to note that the purpose of O'Connor's plan, entitled "Scheme for the Endowing of the Class of Philosophy," was "to make philosophy free to [the] pupils without pecuniary loss to the College. . . . A free Philosophy," he wrote, "would probably hold over for graduation many who would otherwise go to the Seminary, after Rhetoric. Perhaps the chief recommendation of this scheme is that without pecuniary loss we would keep boys longer under our influence; this alone would seem to approve this thematical panacea; if it be true that our *only reason* for teaching is the influence we can exert on our pupils." (64)

But O'Connor's goal was never realized. Beginning with the first session of the 1897–1898 academic year, only $1200 was set aside annually from the income of the fund to help pay tuition fees. The college added the remainder of the income to the principal of the fund, "until such time as the increased capital make it possible for us to take further steps looking to the full endowment of the college course." By 1918, when the principal had grown from $60,000 to about $300,000, the William F. Poland Scholarship Fund was in place, largely made possible by William's patrimony. In the beginning the scholarships were granted to seniors only, but later juniors were included. But the U.S. economic depression of the 1930s greatly diminished the principal. (64)

Expansion to the Suburbs

By the turn of the century, more and more people left the older parts of the city and moved to hilltop neighborhoods and suburbs. Such technological improvements as the horse-drawn omnibus, electric streetcar, incline, and automobile helped facilitate the movement away from the city. In the face of commercial expansion and aging housing, like other middle-class Cincinnatians, Catholics who could afford to move to the suburbs did and the Catholic Church followed them. St. Xavier College authorities considered moving out of the city as well.

The downtown College, surrounded by office buildings, was restricted in its development. The noise of the factories, the congestion, the dirt, and the smoke made it desirable to move to a more spacious and healthier location. From the time of the Civil War through the end of the nineteenth century St. Xavier College enrollment, on the average, was about 300. Part of the reason for the small enrollment might "be attributed to the position as well as location of the College" downtown, the editors of *The Collegian* wrote in 1887. "The building had grown old and dilapidated—quite behind the time, in fact—so that even under the most favorable circumstances it was inadequate." When the new St. Xavier Church in 1883 was built close beside it, "one-half" of the school "was left in almost Egyptian darkness. It was no unusual occurrence to carry on school by lamplight, even in the middle of the day." If the weather happened to be rainy, a person indoors in the inner city could scarcely read with ease at midday. Moreover, a great deal of damage was "done by smoke and soot to the valuable works of the College Library, as also to the many paintings and other works of art which adorn the corridors and halls," *The Collegian* added. ". . . To make matters worse, the portion of the city in which the College is situated, is becoming deluged with factories, the smoke of which, when the wind blows strong, can almost be carved with a knife." In addition to being a "smoky" city," a scholastic wrote, from Sycamore Street "up towards the hill [the city] was lined with slaughter houses which gave [Cincinnati] the nickname of Porcopolis; as a drove of pigs passing up from the levee up front of the College was not an unusual sight." (65)

In the summer of 1904, William Poland, one of the consultors of the Jesuit community, wrote to Joseph Grimmelsman, the Missouri provincial, that he had personally visited "the hills on the side streets between the Reading Road and the bluffs . . . and from there to Eden Park," east of the city, for the possible establishment of a branch school. "There is little ground left unoccupied," he continued. "All things considered it would take a long process to come to a decision on the placing of a school somewhere on the hill. It would take longer to find the suitable spot which could be gotten possession of. The case is so distant and intangible and so full of complications, that on consultation with my mother it was decided to drop this future possibility." But the matter was not dropped. (66)

The following spring the consultors discussed "the matter of a branch school" in Walnut Hills. They were convinced, however, that the provincial "would insist on a *church* and *branch college.*" They decided to present the matter to Archbishop Henry Moeller. Later that day President Albert J. Dierckes, a native of Ludlow, Kentucky, who had succeeded Michael O'Connor as president of St. Xavier College in February 1901, visited the archbishop and requested permission to establish a school in Walnut Hills. Though predisposed to favor the establishment of a "branch college," the archbishop, reflecting the concern of the diocesan clergy over boundary limits, did not support the idea of the Jesuits "having a church on the Hill tops." The archdiocesan consultors, however, favored neither. They did "not see any need of more colleges in town" and advised "against the move." Authorized by the archbishop, Francis Dutton, the chancellor of the archdiocese, informed Dierckes that in the judgment of archdiocesan officials a new college "is scarcely necessary." Notwithstanding the initial refusal of the archbishop and his consultors, the idea of expanding the school to the suburbs remained a vital topic among Jesuit officials at the college. (67)

Church boundary disputes and parish raiding in the late nineteenth and early twentieth centuries in the Archdiocese of Cincinnati had intensified tensions between the archbishop and the clergy priests who were members of religious orders. During this period Archbishops William Elder and then Henry Moeller revamped the organizational structure of the archdiocese and fostered more centralized control over church affairs. At the turn of the century, the Jesuits had two parishes in Cincinnati, St. Francis Xavier on Sycamore Street and St. Ann in the west end. St. Xavier was the largest parish and one of the most prosperous in the archdiocese, whereas St. Ann, the black parish, was among the poorest. As more and more people who lived within the boundaries of St. Xavier Parish gradually took up residence in the suburbs, the prestige of the church attracted transient worshippers. The diocesan clergy complained to the archbishop that Jesuits at the St. Xavier Church stole marriages, funerals, and parishioners from them. Though the Jesuits may not have actively solicited Catholics from other parishes, they did not turn them away when they sought membership on their own. (68)

Almost a year after President Dierckes had visited Moeller, the archbishop in February 1906, "of his own accord," inquired whether the Jesuits wished "a branch college still." However, he did not approve the establishment of a church, either parochial or collegiate, and ruled "out Evanston and Norwood," east of Cincinnati, as possible sites for their branch college. In early March the St. Xavier consultors met and declared that the "main difficulty is the question of a church." While expressing various opinions, they came to no conclusion as they had to wait to hear from the father general in Rome as to the necessity of having a church with the college. In the meantime, Dierckes, accompanied by John Poland, met with the archbishop and informed him that "the reason for delay in answering his proposition was the necessity of hearing from higher superiors." Moeller again insisted that Norwood and Evanston were "forbidden ground" and that "a college only [was] to be considered." In mid-March the college officials informed the provincial accordingly. A month and a half later the chancellor, on behalf of the archdiocesan consultors and the archbishop, informed Dierckes, to his surprise, that St. Xavier was "at liberty to erect a Branch College anywhere in the suburbs, provided that you do not take boys till after their First Communion, and that the . . . [private chapel] in the buildings be not used save by the inmates, and on days of study, by the students." Dierckes and fellow Jesuits were prepared to move accordingly. (69)

In late May the father general approved St. Xavier College's request to "buy" the proposed site, with an old-style mansion on it, at the intersection of Gilbert and Lincoln Avenues in Walnut Hills, east of Cincinnati, for a branch preparatory school. At a special evening meeting of the consultors of the Jesuit community on July 11, they saw a good opportunity for securing the house and land for less than $35,000, and unanimously agreed to take "advantage of the opening." About six weeks later, on August 24, the Board of Trustees met in President Dierckes's office and authorized him to purchase the property at a cost of $31,600. The house contained seventeen rooms, of which two were large enough to serve as classrooms with little alteration. On October 1, 1906, the college opened two classes with sixteen students in the mansion on the property. By the end of the year there were thirty students. In the second year there were seventy-six. Tuition was $80, rather than the $60 charged at the college downtown. William A. Mitchell, S.J., who had just arrived from St. Louis, became prefect of studies. Taught by two scholastics, the classes provided the first and second year high school students a preparatory training equivalent to the eighth grade of grammar school. (70)

Enthusiastic over the recent acquisition, some Jesuit officials thought that St. Xavier College had also "secured a most desirable site for a future College in Cincinnati." All the car lines on the "hill-tops" met at Gilbert and McMillan Avenues, only a few minutes walk from the new school. They thought there was "every prospect of more than doubling the good which is being done there by placing an additional college on the 'distinctively residence part of the city.'" In early January 1907, Dierckes and the consultors considered a possible "addition to the 'Branch College,'" sometimes called St. Xavier on the Hill. They all urged "action as soon as possible." Two weeks later they called the prefect of studies in to explain a rough sketch of the proposed addition to the school. (71)

During the spring and summer months, St. Xavier College officials consulted with the provincial, retained an architect, and drew up plans for a permanent addition. In November the provincial inquired whether the lot on which "the Walnut Hills Branch High School" stood would "be sufficiently large to build all that we need, in case we located there permanently," and was there any possibility of securing the adjoining house and lot. Though the consultors thought the lot would answer their needs, they were convinced they "would be slightly cramped with regard to the *campus*." Notwithstanding that, they urged that the property "be clinched as soon as possible." Lastly, the consultors argued that "the erection of new buildings would cost more than the acquisition of the adjoining property." Though the father general eventually gave permission for St. Xavier to buy the property, the administration never reached an agreement with the seller. (72)

On March 3, 1908, Joseph Grimmelsman, the forty-five-year-old native of Cincinnati, former president of St. Louis University, and Missouri provincial, became the twenty-first Jesuit president of St. Xavier College. Sixteen days later he was formally elected president of the board. By the fall and winter of 1908 he and other college officials became more convinced that the Walnut Hills property, even with the adjoining property and lot, was too small for the college. They proposed securing a larger plot of land. (73)

In the meantime, Archbishop Moeller was willing to consider the relocation of the college on the condition that a more effective priest be put in charge of St. Ann Parish. Though the archbishop found the current Jesuit pastor to be a "very good man," he was, in his judgment, "old and not able to do the work that is required to make the colored folks do their duty." Moeller further pointed out that "[e]ven if you keep the parish of St. Xavier, you will have only two, while the Franciscans have five."

Rudolph Meyer, the provincial and former president of St. Xavier College, informed Moeller that the terms were acceptable and that he had a priest that understood "the negro character" of St. Ann. "But I do sincerely hope that, even if we have no charge of the colored people," he continued, "you will see your way to letting us have a new college and parish in a suitable locality. . . . [I]f your Grace and the clergy of Cincinnati expect us to educate the youth of the city properly and save them from the contaminating influence of secular institutions, you must allow us to use the means necessary for the purpose. Now, as you are aware, the locality of St. Xavier's is no longer suitable for a college, and it will be less suitable still as the city develops."

He further argued that "in the past some of your excellent clergy, so many of whom are former students of St. Xavier's, have been enabled to follow the call to the ecclesiastical state. It is our hope that by offering similar conditions in the future, many more may be enabled to do so." Meyer concluded by pointing out that for financial reasons the college should not "abandon" St. Xavier Church "until . . . the new parish church and the new college have been established on a firm basis." The latter would not in the beginning "add much to our income," he wrote, "but [would] add very much to our outlay." (74)

In spring 1909, Grimmelsman, a tall and inspiring figure, wrote to the provincial regarding a possible new location in the suburbs for the college in place of the Gilbert Avenue property. "There seem to be only two possible openings and meagre ones at that. I went out towards

Rose Hill beyond Avondale but will have to go again to examine this section more carefully. Then there is possibly another place between St. Francis de Sales Church and Hyde Park. We are having so much rain that it is hard to get a good afternoon. Going to any of these places means an afternoon." The direction of the city's growth continued to point to the suburbs. Attempting to adjust to the changing environment, Meyer had declared several times that the school should either acquire more property at the Gilbert Avenue branch or purchase more property in another area. As the provincial and college officials leaned toward the acquisition of new property for a relocation of the school, they helped set the stage for a new era at St. Xavier College. (75)

PART II

"A New Life for Old St. Xavier": A University is Born 1911–1945

Introduction

Between 1910 and 1945 American higher education experienced unprecedented change as scores of students enrolled in postsecondary education. Not all institutions, however, benefited by the increase in enrollment. On the eve of World War II fifteen percent of the institutions with 150 or fewer students in 1900 had become junior colleges, and an additional forty percent had either closed their doors or merged with other institutions. While a number of small colleges survived, some, like St. Xavier College, grew to small- or mid-size universities and occupied a meaningful place on the American higher education scene. (1)

For its future growth and development, St. Xavier College had to leave its downtown location and move to the suburbs. With the purchase of the Avondale Athletic Club, east of downtown Cincinnati, in 1911, school officials, faculty, and alumni began drafting a new vision for the College. Four years later the College launched a fund-raising campaign, its first major public appeal to the people of Cincinnati for financial support, to give "old St. Xavier. . . a new life." Following the move to Avondale in 1919 the College erected six buildings in ten years – Alumni Science Hall, Hinkle Hall, Elet Hall, Schmidt Library Building, Schmidt Fieldhouse, and Albers Biology Building. In particular, both Elet and Albers made important statements about the future of the College. They were markers pointing to a new St. Xavier. Upon completion of Elet Hall in 1924 St. Xavier College became a residential community once more and aspired to become a regional college. In 1929, when Albers Hall was completed, the faculty energized its science curriculum and developed a pre-medical course of study that would become an acclaimed academic program.

By this time St. Xavier College had established a School of Commerce and Finance, a summer school for women religious, a coeducational College of Law in the evening, and had been accredited by the North Central Association in 1925. In 1930, in recognition of its already proud tradition and with optimistic and hopeful anticipation of continued future success, the college changed its name to Xavier University. Indeed, Xavier had much to be proud about when it celebrated the centenary of its founding in 1931. It had assumed a significantly new identity. St. Xavier of old had become a multi-school university of the modern American type. (2)

In the first half of the twentieth century, extracurricular activities on American campuses, including Xavier's, also changed dramatically. By the time of World War I athletics, social clubs, campus newspapers, theater groups, and student magazines had become even more prominent in American colleges and universities. They were seen as contributing to make students "well-rounded," forming character, and encouraging socialization. Before the end of World War I in 1918 St. Xavier College had established a permanent students' newspaper, a literary magazine, and a new dramatic society. It had also adopted the schedule of American high schools and colleges, making Saturday, instead of Thursday, the regular weekday holiday. By going residential and enrolling additional students in the 1920s the College fostered new dramatic, musical, and vocal performances and new religious observances and activities. Like their counterparts on many college campuses the students attended the junior prom and began electing beauty queens. As the institution became more competitive in the major sports of football, baseball, and basketball, it adopted the nickname Musketeers and the "one for all and all for one" motto. As student governments during the first quarter of the twentieth century had become widespread on American college campuses, St. Xavier students by 1923 had formed a student council. By the 1930s Xavier University students also promoted Catholic doctrine and social action in their opposition to communism and "materialistic education." In 1935 the University established the Reserve Officers Training Corps, which became mandatory for all new undergraduate students. (3)

During the economic depression of the 1930s the financing of American colleges and universities suffered. Xavier University, like most of its counterparts, underwent some retrenchment. In addition to introducing cuts in salaries, it reduced the number of lay faculty members and administrative personnel. In 1934, the same year that the University lost its accreditation for one year because of athletic irregularities, it closed the College of Law. Though enrollment increased during the latter part of the decade, throughout the depression years the University contended with operating deficits. By 1943 the University faced a more serious challenge. Because of a significant decrease in student enrollment during World War II the University had to secure a contract with the federal government or consider closing its doors. That year a contingent of United States Army Air Corps cadets joined the fewer than 100 students on campus. The University weathered its financial woes and, upon a successful end to the War in 1945, began planning for a brighter future.

— 4 —

A NEW CAMPUS, 1911–1931

I t had become apparent in the last quarter of the nineteenth century that the future growth and development of St. Xavier College required the acquisition of additional property, which was not possible in its downtown setting. Though the need for expansion was partly realized with the purchase of property for the branch school on Gilbert and Lincoln Avenues in Walnut Hills in 1906, St. Xavier officials acknowledged that the newly-acquired property was inadequate for any extensive expansion of the college. On March 2, 1911, Rudolph Meyer, the Missouri provincial, wrote to President Joseph Grimmelsman regarding the possibility of acquiring additional property or possibly a new site and moving the college to the hillside. Though Archbishop Henry Moeller of Cincinnati, after several months in opposition to the idea, now approved the move and the establishment of a new parish, he did so, however, "with the understanding that later on the present St. Xavier [Church] would have to be given up." His consultors opposed giving the Jesuits a second parish. But "later on," Meyer noted, "is a very elastic term. It may mean *very late*— perhaps never. [The archbishop] cannot and, I think, will not ask us to give up St. Xavier's until we have built up a new parish; and, by that time, no secular priest will be found willing or capable of taking care of the present St. Xavier parish district." (1)

In light of Moeller's concession and the potential for the college, Meyer urged Grimmelsman to act quickly. "[W]e can and must hold the Archbishop to his promise and concession. It will play an important part in the question you will have to solve concerning the 'Academy on the Hills.'. . . I am afraid, unless we bestir ourselves," he wrote, "we may lose our only chance of development on prudent lines.

Hence my anxiety in the matter. It is difficult nowadays to get a foothold or to expand in any diocese, where and as we would like . . . Please discuss *your situation"* with your consultors. In mid-March St. Xavier consultors met and renewed their discussion on the future of the college. During the course of four months they pondered what to do with the branch school in Walnut Hills. Should the site be retained and improved or should a better site be secured for "the collegians of St. Xavier" and a new parish established? (2)

In early July 1911, as Jesuit officials discussed the future of the college, the provincial re-assigned Xavier President Joseph Grimmelsman to Milwaukee to serve as president of Marquette University, and on July 5th Francis Heiermann, S.J. succeeded him as president of St. Xavier. Distinguished as a scholar in the field of classical languages, this president of St. Xavier College emigrated from Germany in his youth, joined the Society of Jesus, and eventually became president of St. John's College in Toledo, Ohio. Six days after his appointment as president of St. Xavier, college officials agreed to make "an effort to secure the Avondale [Athletic] Club," which had been dissolved in 1903, "as the site of a future location in preference" to the one in Walnut Hills. Formed in 1897, the Avondale Athletic Club had been during its short existence one of the city's most exclusive organizations. The club room and banquet halls in the red brick, three-story Georgian style house, centrally located in the park district at Dana Avenue and Winding Way in Avondale, had made it a popular social center, the scene of many festive gatherings. Its football and baseball teams had been the champions of the area. The club's spacious and attractive grounds were situated on either side of Northside Avenue, later named Victory Parkway, between Winding Way and Dana and Herald Avenues. The first part of the tract of land consisted "of a brow of hills with a deep valley," Heiermann wrote to Meyer, "which contains, [in the western section], a fine baseball field in good condition. The other section [to the east], separated by a proposed boulevard, is on high ground. The site is such that, being far away from existing churches, later on the erection of a parish would not be excluded, but we thought best, for the present not to mention this at all." The western section contained the clubhouse, "a solid building, . . . which with small expenses," the president added, "could be fitted up to answer all the needs of the academy for some few years." The Avondale Athletic Club was a five-minute walk from the Reading Road trolley car and about seven minutes from the Norwood streetcar, both affording easy transportation to the city.

Heiermann further noted that the property was also enhanced by the fine residences in the area. At the time Avondale was seen as the center of the expanding city and its suburbs. (3)

The Jesuit consultors thought the site was "admirably suited to [their] purposes" and sought "to learn the names of the owners" and the asking price. This information "had to be secured in a cautious way," Heiermann wrote to Meyer, "as the proprietors might easily object to the purchase on the part of St. Xavier's." By the third week of July they learned that the asking prices were $50,000 for the western section of the Eugenia H. Bragg estate on which the building stood, $12,000 for the lot and house that adjoined the estate, and approximately $30,000 for the eastern section. The Board of Trustees, hoping to get a loan of $100,000 to meet all emergencies, authorized Heiermann to enter into negotiations for the purchase of the Avondale Athletic Club. It did so with the understanding that the property should not be acquired at the expense of St. Xavier Church. The provincial had earlier suggested that in order to obtain a new parish on the hills it might be advisable to consider a future transfer of St. Xavier parish to the archbishop, "trusting that when the time came" the college "would not be called upon to fulfill the agreement." The consultors were, as one of them wrote, "unalterably opposed to any arrangement that would look to such a step." They had no intention "of giving up St. Xavier Church," which had "an assessed valuation of four hundred and seventy five thousand dollars." (4)

At the time the college had no debts and had to its credit $20,000 in securities. Heiermann was hopeful that the property on Gilbert and Lincoln Avenues could be sold at a price around $35,000. He then asked the provincial's permission to take up a loan of $100,000 and to sell the Walnut Hills property, arguing that the indebtedness of the college after the sale of the property would be about $65,000, the interest of which would be covered by the annual revenue. The anticipated annual surplus of revenues over expenses in 1911 was between $4,000 and $5,000. Though there was talk in Cincinnati that the city might demand the Avondale Club property for a park, Jesuit officials had been assured "on good grounds" that that would not be the case. A definite decision was expected by August 1. "Formal negotiations cannot be opened by our real estate man before that date," Heiermann explained, "but he is willing to get an option in *his own* name as soon as possible. Delay should be avoided." In the meantime the president consulted with a number of intimate friends and advisers to the college and all favored the Avondale Club property. (5)

At the same time that Heiermann requested the provincial's permission to purchase the Avondale Athletic Club, some of his consultors also wrote to him agreeing with their president that the "Branch College" situated on Gilbert Avenue was not the ideal site either for a college or for a prospective parish. "[T]here is no room for extension," a consultor wrote. They all favored the purchase of the Avondale property. "It is far enough away from any parish," another wrote, "to encourage the hope, should the mind of Ecclesiastical Superiors change in our favor, of some day getting *another* parish—without, of course, giving up St. Xavier's. . . . It is the most desirable site left. Some steps must be taken soon to provide for the future. This is our best chance. I might say our only chance—as another site farther away—that has been mentioned—is not to be considered in comparison." A third consultant argued that the large piece of property "seems to be most desirable to . . . allow us to begin to show signs of life." A fourth Jesuit, Francis J. Finn, who favored "removal of the collegiate department from the factory district," thoroughly agreed with those assessments. To him the change was "inevitable." (6)

In late July, Meyer and his province consultors agreed with the views of those of the Jesuit House at the college. At a dinner on July 31, the feast day of St. Ignatius of Loyola, Archbishop Moeller approved the purchase. Heiermann then drafted a letter to the father general, requesting permission to purchase the Avondale property. On September 11 Heiermann received a cablegram from Rome, approving the acquisition. (7)

A week later the St. Xavier Board of Trustees secured a mortgage from Cincinnati's Western and Southern Life Insurance Company in the amount of $70,000 at 5½ percent interest, payable in ten years. Heiermann then entered into a contract with Eugenia Bragg, the proprietor, for the purchase of the Avondale Athletic Club property. The next day, on September 19, 1911, the college purchased the 26.747 acres of the Avondale property for $85,000.

It was a giant step forward for the college. Archbishop Moeller congratulated Heiermann and the Society of Jesus and felt "deeply grateful" that the college had "secured the beautiful and suitable site in Avondale, in order to extend the sphere of its educational activity. . . . We fondly cherish the hope that, ere long, the site will be adorned not only by a large and flourishing college, but also graced by a Catholic University, forming the keystone in the system of Catholic education in the Archdiocese." (8)

One of the clauses that the Bragg estate insisted on in the sale of the Avondale property was that a double boulevard would be dedicated to the city in order to accommodate the newly developed automobile. St. Xavier College officials soon learned to their satisfaction that the board of park commissioners was willing to run one of the boulevards on the edge of the property instead of through it, thus saving the property from being divided into three sections. Consistent with the purchase agreement, college authorities donated the property for the boulevards through their newly-acquired grounds, with the understanding that St. Xavier would not be responsible for paving and upkeep of them. (9)

Though the primary intention of the purchase was to provide for the future expansion of the college, students at the Walnut Hills branch school, which accommodated both high school and preparatory classes, were the first students on the new campus. College officials remodeled the clubhouse as a high school and continued it as the Avondale Academy under the direction of George McGovern, S.J., who had previously conducted the school in Walnut Hills. Renamed Xavier Hall, Archbishop Moeller dedicated and blessed the renovated clubhouse building on December 28, 1911. The college divided the ballroom into several classrooms, converted part of the banquet hall into a chapel, and kept the bowling alleys intact. At the noon recess, school officials provided a warm meal in the cafeteria, described as a "cozy luncheon room." In addition to Xavier Hall, the new property also included five tennis courts, a swimming pool, and a large athletic field suitable for football and baseball. On Friday, January 5, 1912, classes began for the 87 enrolled students. (10)

The Alumni Association and St. Xavier's Diamond Jubilee

Renewed with enthusiasm over the purchase of the Avondale Athletic Club, the Alumni Association took a hand in launching the college with a new vision and a new destiny. President Francis Heiermann, "a man of spare build" who had, a contemporary observed, "great energy," used part of that energy to challenge the Alumni Association through the influence of their moderator, William J. Harrington, S.J., to improve the Avondale property. With the aid of the alumni, "especially in keeping [the college's] needs before the Catholics," the president established a fund for new construction. Prominent in the alumni movement was Walter Seton Schmidt of the class of 1905, who became one of the outstanding benefactors of the institution and a foremost alumni leader. A man of diverse talents, he was a quarterback on the early St. Xavier football teams, played the violin well enough to be a member of a symphony orchestra, and became a leading local real estate professional. (11)

At the twenty-fifth anniversary of the Alumni Association on January 5, 1913, the members "thronged" the Jubilee Mass in the morning and the reception in the evening. Following the Mass, Harrington summoned the guests to Memorial Hall by ringing the handbell that had been used in earlier days to call the students to their classes. During the ceremony they recalled how the association was founded "for the fostering of college spirit among the alumni, the cementing of friendships formed in college days and assisting of the college in its work."

Ten days later more than 100 alumni attended the jubilee banquet held at the Business Men's Club in downtown Cincinnati. Francis Cloud, first president of the Alumni Association, spoke on the "Role of the Alumni." As the St. Xavier graduates looked forward to what lay ahead for the new Avondale campus, an officer of the association expressed these sentiments: "Would it be too much to hope that in the not too distant future some Alumnus, wandering back from the East or West, to take part in a celebration something akin to this one, might take his stand upon one of the nearby hills and gaze with brightening eye and throbbing heart upon the different lecture halls and colleges that dot the spacious acres of St. Xavier University?" On their way home following the banquet, four alumni "discussed the debt which St. Xavier men owed to their Alma Mater, and decided that it was time to show their gratitude by actions instead of mere words." During the next few weeks they helped form a group of twenty-six alumni, with William C. Wolking as chairman, to help make plans with college officials for the transfer of St. Xavier to Avondale. (12)

The Jesuits had been particularly anxious to move the college to the suburb. During his December 1913 visit, former president of the college, Alexander Burrowes, who was now religious superior of the midwestern Jesuits, urged St. Xavier officials to move at the earliest possible time. In the spring, the consultors met and began developing "a long plan . . . to move the College to Avondale . . . [and] to think seriously of the location of buildings." The following May, Burrowes visited the Avondale site to help select the location for the new buildings. Realizing that Walter Schmidt was eager "to have something definite to tell the alumni as an incentive to stir up" a fund-raising drive, the consultors informed him that "whatever money the alumni would turn in would go to the erection of buildings at Avondale." That same year the Alumni Association directed Otto Juettner to compose a college song in honor of the alma mater. He wrote "Xavier For Aye," and presented it at an alumni celebration on George Washington's birthday in 1915. (13)

Since 1915 marked the seventy-fifth anniversary of the Jesuits accepting control of the Athenaeum, the Alumni Association and the college decided to commemorate the occasion with a fund-raising campaign. Though St. Xavier officials had previously raised funds for specific projects, this was the college's first major public appeal to the people of Cincinnati for financial support. The goal of the campaign was $75,000, $15,000 of which was raised at the committee's first meeting in January 1915. The target date for the completion of the campaign, announced in the *Diamond Jubilee Bulletin*, was the feast day of St. Francis Xavier, December 3, 1916.

The architectural firm of Joseph G. Steinkamp and Brother drew up plans for the new buildings on the campus. The first set of plans for the east side of the campus between Northside and Herald Avenues called for a faculty building, student dormitory, and classroom building; for the west side between Northside and Dana and Winding Way the plans included the former clubhouse, a gymnasium and outdoor swimming pool, tennis courts, basketball courts, handball courts, football and baseball fields, and an oval running track. "Old St. Xavier, your Alma Mater, now in her Diamond Jubilee year," Heiermann wrote, "is entering upon an era of much-needed expansion." (14)

From late summer 1915 through the spring of 1916, the Diamond Jubilee Committee met regularly. Through its *Diamond Jubilee Bulletin*, sent mainly to the alumni, it invited the St. Xavier graduates and friends of the college "to present a substantial testimonial of their loyalty to their Alma Mater on the occasion of her Diamond Jubilee. This testimonial," the committee wrote, ". . . would be used towards cancelling the debt, or for erecting new buildings in Avondale, or for the founding of scholarships." While every donor could specify a donation for any one of the three purposes, or for any other particular need "towards the great cause of Catholic higher education," Heiermann announced "that all the funds so far deposited or to be deposited, without specification, shall be used for the erection of the new College Building in Avondale." The initial estimate for the building was $200,000. Officials planned to use half of the building for classrooms, study hall, and science lecture and laboratory rooms. The other half would serve as a faculty building, which the college planned to convert into classrooms whenever a separate faculty building could be erected. (15)

At the time, St. Xavier's mortgage debt was $97,000, largely incurred by the purchase and improvement of the Avondale Athletic Club. It was not possible for the college to accumulate any funds from its day-to-day operation, as it had hoped it could have done, to help pay the debt, as the expenses were about equal to the income. "This is due partly to the low tuition fee exacted," the committee wrote, "but chiefly to the fact that every year from *fifty to one hundred* deserving young men are educated by the Jesuit Fathers of St. Xavier College FREE OF ALL CHARGE." Because in its finances, St. Xavier Church was "entirely distinct" from the college, tuition fees provided the main income of the college. "If it were not for the fact that the teachers . . ., as members of a religious order, serve without salaries," they wrote, "it would be impossible to maintain the college financially." Officials still hoped, however, to reduce the mortgage debt by the sale of the Gilbert Avenue property. Though two years earlier in 1914 the consultors of the Jesuit community had decided that "the old building" on Gilbert Avenue "was not worth repairing and should be torn down," over several years parts of the property were sold, with the last parcel disposed in 1923. (16)

The *Diamond Jubilee Bulletin* concluded on an enthusiastic note. "Nothing in years has so stirred the enthusiasm of St. Xavier men as the purchase by the College of the former Avondale Athletic Club property," it wrote. "'A new life for old St. Xavier,'" it continued,

> is the first thought of every alumnus. The site on which rises a greater St. Xavier is a fine tract of twenty-six acres. . . . The ground itself is ideally suited to college purposes. On the east and west are high level plateaus, between which extends a broad valley—one of nature's beauty spots. The athletic fields are in the base of the valley, . . . a campus perfect. The steep hills, covered with virgin growth, rise on each side of the athletic fields, forming a natural amphitheater. . . . The new St. Xavier will thus rise in a wild and picturesque spot, surrounded by parkways, yet in a location which was chosen first because it was the very center of Cincinnati and its suburbs. For the future, what may we not hope? Medical and scientific buildings, an arts department, a library— massive piles rising on the eastern eminence—these are prospects

which the years shall realize. Dangers indeed must be braved in a launching of new departments. But the time is ripe; the support of St. Xavier's loyal sons and the guidance of her able rector, who already has done so much, spells sure success. May that not be a distant day, when we behold old St. Xavier a university in very truth. (17)

St. Xavier's Diamond Jubilee became a resounding vote of confidence in the future of the college.

Curricular and Extracurricular Developments, 1911–1920

A major step toward achieving university status occurred on October 9, 1911, during President Francis Heiermann's first year, with the opening of the St. Xavier evening school, sometimes referred to in the college catalogue as the Department, School, or College of Commerce, Accounts, and Finance. Classes were held five nights a week from 7:30 p.m. to 9:30 p.m. Although business courses had been taught in the evening since 1841, and the day college had long had a commercial department, neither of these programs led to a bachelor's degree. Except for some courses in business, there was generally no provision for professional or graduate instruction, with the exception of some brief moments in the 1890s when St. Xavier College offered some extension lectures and a few graduate courses. In the latter part of the nineteenth through the first quarter of the twentieth centuries, following the founding of the first collegiate school of business at the University of Pennsylvania in 1881, there was a rapid rise of business education and an incorporation of white-collar professional programs in the structure of American higher education. St. Xavier College was no exception. (18)

Since the founding of the college, the central piece in St. Xavier's curriculum was its classical course of studies. Influenced somewhat by the curriculum in the School of Commerce and Finance at St. Louis University, the St. Xavier School of Commerce, Accounts, and Finance made it possible for young men, "irrespective of their religious adherence, who have brains, energy, and the ambition to succeed in business, and who realize that thorough preparation is essential to success," to complete a full college program by taking evening classes and be awarded the degree of bachelor of commercial science. About 100 students were enrolled in the new program. The first graduation class, consisting of 12 students, was in 1914. Alumni and local businessmen played an important role in the development of the School of Commerce, Accounts, and Finance. Only three Jesuits, namely Aloysius McCormick, professor of ethics and political economy, John Morrissey, professor of economic resources, and Francis Heiermann, professor of classical languages and president, served on the faculty. Alumni and laymen from the Cincinnati business community taught the rest of the courses in accounting, sales, business management, investments, bookkeeping, and commercial German or Spanish. The lay faculty in the business program constituted about one-third of the college staff. In the fall of 1914 St. Xavier College, under the direction of a local newspaperman, introduced a new School of Journalism and Advertising. As in the School of Commerce, Accounts, and Finance, classes were held in the evening. The new degree program offered a bachelor of commercial science in journalism. In 1915 the two programs had a combined enrollment of 209 students. Four years later, however, probably because of declining and low enrollment, the college discontinued the School of Journalism and Advertising. (19)

In December 1915, during the First World War, the School of Commerce began publishing *The Xaverian News*, a fortnightly newspaper of student activities. As the newspaper voice of the students on campus, it intended to knit student activities in the day college and in the evening division. Published by a board of student editors under the supervision of a faculty moderator, *The Xaverian News* changed its name to *Xaverian News* in the fall of 1919. It became a weekly newspaper in 1925–1926. With the exception of the first years of the newspaper, in which it was published under the auspices of the evening division, the editors and writers of the student newspaper typically represented the interests of the day school. (20)

By 1918 the evening programs in commerce and finance and in sociology were incorporated in the Department of Liberal Arts, which "added . . . immeasurably," college officials noted, "to the reputation and general standard, as well as to the influence of the college in this vicinity." While the academic discipline of accounting became a special feature, ethics and political economy formed the groundwork for the study of business, and the course on commercial law broadened the outlook and "offered a safeguard in business pursuits." The enhanced reputation of the college and its growing student body emboldened some students to refer to St. Xavier College as the "Harvard of the West." (21)

In the fall of 1919, St. Xavier College further enhanced its academic image by opening a coeducational College of Law in the evening division. It began at the request of alumni and prominent members in Greater Cincinnati who thought it would serve a need in the community. As early as the summer of 1912, the college consultors had discussed generally the possibility of starting a law school. Two years later a local attorney visited President Heiermann and informed him of the alleged low academic standing of the Young Men's Christian Association (YMCA) Law School in downtown Cincinnati. That information, and the fact that many Catholics were attending the law school, indicated it might be an opportune time for the college to open a law school. During the next four years, college officials consulted several local lawyers and alumni, and though there were concerns expressed over the inadequacy of the library and the lack of professors and finances, they all favored it. (22)

By early 1919 the new president of St. Xavier College, James McCabe, S.J., and a contingency of alumni headed by Walter Schmidt, strongly recommended to the Board of Trustees the establishment of a night law school. A native of Ireland and a former student at St. Xavier in 1878–1879, McCabe succeeded Heiermann in January 1917, becoming the college's twenty-third Jesuit president. He was formerly president of St. Mary's College in Kansas and Marquette University. McCabe wrote to the provincial that because the YMCA Law School had a very low standing and in general had "a pretty dark cloud over them, [t]he present time is deemed favorable for competing with them." Though a number of the consultors thought that "St. X has no money to try a L[aw] S[chool]," he continued, "Walter [Schmidt] . . . maintains that there is absolutely no risk in this undertaking—that on the contrary, besides prestige, it will be sure to bring in money. He told me that if there were a deficit, he would himself make up that deficit, but he felt certain that the school would pay. . . ." The board subsequently approved the establishment of the law school. (23)

Since the members of the Jesuit faculty were not qualified to teach the necessary courses, it was up to the alumni and members of the Cincinnati Bar Association to make up the faculty. Edward P. Moulinier, an alumnus, became the first dean of the law school, as well as the first lay dean in the history of the college. Classes were held from 6 p.m. to 8 p.m., Monday through Friday, during the school year. During the day, students were often seen attending sessions of the courts of Hamilton County, the Municipal Court, and the Federal

Court. In addition to joining the Schools of Commerce and Sociology in the evening division and adding a professional presence to the college, the law school also enhanced the professionalism of women in the community. A fall 1922 article in the *Xaverian News* boasted the accomplishment of a woman student whose score on the Ohio bar exam was third highest among the 376 test takers. (24)

Notwithstanding the addition of professional programs in the evening division, St. Xavier College remained true to its Jesuit educational tradition in the liberal arts. Professional and occupational aprograms curricula grew alongside St. Xavier's liberal arts curriculum. As a Jesuit Catholic institution, the college insisted on the cultivation of Christian virtues. Thorough instruction in the principles of religion formed an essential part of the curriculum and activities in the day college. Though students of any denomination were admitted, all were required to show a respectful demeanor during the ordinary exercise of public prayer. The college required Catholic students to attend the classes in Christian doctrine, to be present at Mass on class days and at other chapel exercises whenever held during the week, to make an annual retreat, and to approach the sacraments at least once a month. The Sodality of the Immaculate Conception, organized in 1841, continued to draw large numbers of students to its meetings and devotional activities. Among its principal activities were the distribution of Catholic literature, collection of donations for the missions, and performance of charitable works in the community. Overall, in its moral training the college aimed at building the conscience of its students for the right fulfillment "of their civil, social and religious duties." On occasions, civic activities and events were interspersed among academic events. (25)

Committed to the Jesuit curriculum, college officials maintained that the institution "had grown strong in the conviction that the classics or classical studies are—even in the twentieth century—the best means of developing the student's mind." The course of studies consisted of a four-year program of English composition and literature, Latin and Greek with the reading of the authors, algebra, geometry, history, sciences, civics, elocution, and physical culture. Each year's subjects were so "correlated and connected," they wrote, "as both to expand and draw together the various branches, thus securing in each year a well-balanced development of mind." Convinced that attaining a degree of Bachelor of Arts "is the best preparation for the professions and the higher business pursuits," they discouraged students "to attempt professional courses before acquiring that culture and mind-training" made possible in the arts and sciences. "No greater benefit can be conferred on a young man now-a-days," Heiermann wrote to the parents in 1913, "than a full college education rounded out by a course in philosophy and crowned by the degree of Bachelor of Arts." (26)

Like their predecessors, the college administration and faculty still expected the students to perform three hours of homework each day during the school week. "All the work prescribed," the 1916 booklet on *Regulations and Practical Suggestions for the Students of St. Xavier* read, "must be ready in the morning before class commences. Attention in class and application to the proper amount of homework must of necessity bring results and engender in the student a real interest in studies." Students whose academic average in each of the principal branches was less than 67 were not allowed to advance to a higher grade, and students who failed in one of the principal branches were warned and would not be promoted until they completed a satisfactory examination. (27)

To help foster greater appreciation of the humanities, the college introduced two new student activities. In March 1912 it founded *The Xavier Athenaeum*, a quarterly literary magazine. "We are pleased that you have resolved to call the new college magazine, the *St. Xavier Athenaeum*," Archbishop Moeller wrote to Heiermann, "as thus will be perpetuated the name of the old Athenaeum." The faculty and college officials hoped to stimulate literary effort among the students. St. Xavier honor students, who participated in the intercollegiate English essay competition among Jesuit schools in the Midwest, formed the staff. During the 1912–1913 academic year, the college also started a new dramatic society, the Buskin Club. Its first production, presented in Memorial Hall, was *A Person of Distinction*, a dramatization of Molière's *Le Bourgeois Gentilhomme*. (28)

Since 1814, American Jesuits had followed the European model for the scheduling of classes in the curriculum, providing a midweek holiday after three days of classes. In mid-May 1917, St. Xavier College authorities took a vote regarding the change of recreation day from Thursday to Saturday. Adopting the schedule of American high schools and colleges, they made Saturday the regular weekday holiday. President James McCabe referred the matter to the provincial who subsequently gave permission. Beginning in the fall, Thursday became a regular class day. (29)

Because of the coal shortage during the First World War, U.S. government regulations had required that St. Xavier College, like many other colleges and universities, close from January 15 to January 22, 1917. Students used the time to prepare for the midyear examinations. For similar reasons, the school also closed on January 29 and February 6. In late spring, after the United States entered the war, St. Xavier College started military training, which took place after school hours. Almost all the students took part. *The Xaverian News* published letters from alumni in training camps and on the battlefield. (30)

In addition to its established course of studies, college authorities continued their support of intercollegiate sports. In 1911, St. Xavier participated in two intercollegiate sports, football and baseball. That year, 35 of the 46 day students tried out for the football team. The St. Xavier College Athletic Association, led by five alumni, printed a souvenir season program for the football games. Because faculty in American colleges at the turn of the century generally withdrew from the growing complexity and management of football, the alumni associations seized the opportunity. They achieved domination of college athletics and became involved in the recruiting, coaching, feeding, and care of the athletes. In the fall of 1911, St. Xavier played against five college teams, including St. Mary's Institute (University of Dayton). Not having any football facilities on campus, the team often trained on the banks of the Little Miami River. As the college's football program grew in popularity and talent, in 1917 the team went undefeated. Alumni interest in the program grew accordingly. In many American colleges, including St. Xavier, football became the sport that inspired the most enthusiasm among graduates and friends. (31)

Despite not having a home floor for basketball games or practice, the college's Athletic Association decided to field a basketball team during the 1914–1915 academic year. This was about two decades after James A. Naismith started the new sport in Springfield, Massachusetts, in 1891. The school's gym was too small, so the team used the gym floors of nearby St. Francis de Sales and St. Aloysius parishes for practices. Upon President Heiermann's request, the majority of the consultors agreed "to permit night games of basketball." The 1915–1916 season ended with a 6 and 4 record, and the team celebrated its season with a banquet at a local hotel. For two years during World War I, Xavier did not field a basketball team. (32)

Largely because of the rising wartime costs, college officials, who had discussed several times between 1912 and 1914 the possibility of increasing tuition, in 1917 raised tuition to $80 per year. Tuition had remained at $60 annually for over half a century since 1863. The low tuition and an increasing number of endowed scholarships, mainly through the Poland Family Fund, made it possible for a large number of qualified students, especially juniors and seniors with at least a "C" average, to acquire a free college education. For a time, college officials hoped the Poland fund would be sufficient to endow the two highest classes or grade levels of students. Estimating the maximum number of students for both classes to be about thirty-five, at $60 each— before the tuition increase—officials had hoped the fund would generate $2,100 in revenue. That goal never materialized. The treasurer of the Missouri province convinced his authorities that the revenue from the endowment account was too small and that "the uncertainty of it," he said, "makes it clear to me that we must allow the fund to increase to a considerable amount, much greater than it is now." Though it never achieved its primary intent, in the succeeding decades the Poland endowment account would continue to help fund scholarships. (33)

On October 1, 1918, during the last year of World War I, the college inaugurated the Xavier unit of the Student Army Training Corps (SATC), established two months earlier by the Congress of the United States to prepare students for possible military service. Run as a full-time army training facility, St. Xavier housed the 232 young men, largely from Ohio and Kentucky, at the seven-story Fenwick Club in downtown Cincinnati. College officials modified the curriculum to meet the needs of the future army officers. The teaching faculty consisted of eleven Jesuits and twelve lay faculty members, including a woman who taught part-time in the evening. Four officers formed the army staff. Virtually every day the young men marched to and from classes. Army drilling and forced marches took place in the fields of Deer Park, northeast of Cincinnati, and along the cobblestones of Reading Road in the city. At the end of the fall semester in 1918, shortly after the war ended in November, the college disbanded the St. Xavier unit of SATC. (34)

During the war eleven Jesuits and two alumni diocesan priests served as military chaplains. According to available records, eleven Xavier alumni were killed. George W. Budde of the class of 1916 has been traditionally regarded as the last person to die in action. While out on a mission he was hit by enemy machine-gun fire and died on the morning of Armistice Day, November 11, 1918. (35)

The Move to Avondale

During the Diamond Jubilee fund drive in 1915, St. Xavier College authorities had considered several plans for the new campus and concluded that one "new building at Avondale [was] possible as soon as $75,000 is collected." By mid-November the alumni had subscribed $61,944, of which $49,373 was already in hand. During the next three years the Alumni Jubilee Committee met regularly with members of the St. Xavier administration and continued to raise funds, collecting an additional $50,000. (36)

In January 1919, President James McCabe emphasized the importance of beginning construction in Avondale. "It is maintained," he wrote to the provincial, "that we will never get going without starting (which seems reasonable enough), and that the plant down here has fallen into a dry rot. . . . St. X certainly does not cut much of a figure here in Cincinnati at the present day. It is maintained, too," he continued, "that we can not hope for much of a College here without getting new blood from outside. Our own H[igh] S[chool] does not furnish enough of material for a good college. We have seen, in the S.A.T.C., that if we had a chance to take boys from out of town we could get plenty of them. The plan therefore includes the gradual development of the dormitory system." Echoing the sentiments of most of his Jesuit colleagues, including the provincial's, McCabe argued strongly for St. Xavier College to become a residential college once more. He further insisted that the college students "must be separated" from the high school students. McCabe was convinced that by separating them, enrollment in the college "would increase." The college students did not like to be associated with the younger students "or to be taken as one of that class," he wrote. In addition, some Jesuits feared that harm could be done to the younger boys by continuing contact with the older ones. (37)

Proposed construction at St. Xavier College was consistent with the emerging trend in society. In the aftermath of World War I and throughout the 1920s, a building boom dominated the landscape of American higher education, both private and public. Depending most on their alumni for financial support through fundraising efforts, a number of colleges and universities erected new buildings. Laypeople and alumni, especially through their respective alumni groups, took pride in their institutions. Officials at St. Xavier knew that the college also had loyal alumni and warm friends. Walter Schmidt, who McCabe thought had "as wise a head on his shoulders as any man in Cincinnati," had convinced him and other members of the board of trustees that the college could "put up enough of a building to get a start," that "[g]etting a start is essential for the life and development of St. X," and that when "the people see that we are doing something, they are apt to come and help. They will do nothing as long as they see we do nothing." For his part, McCabe was convinced "that unless we do something . . . , St. Xavier's is doomed. Its reputation now is that of a H[igh] S[chool]. The people of Cincinnati see mostly H[igh] S[chool] boys attend here, and that is our rating in the public mind." What he proposed "is only the rational and legitimate development of St. Xavier," he said. "It is not only the 'esse' [to be] but the 'bene esse' [to be well] that is necessary: for if we can not have the latter, we will not long have the former." (38)

What helped hasten the decision to begin construction in Avondale was the donation in the spring of 1919 of $100,000 by Mrs. Frederick W. (Mary) Hinkle to the building fund. This was the first six-figure gift in the history of the institution. The students also contributed $1,300 to the fund. The board subsequently approved the plans for an administration building and a science hall on the east side of the campus. Work on the science building began on June 24, 1919. Construction of the administration building began two weeks later on July 7. (39)

At the end of August, Jesuits at the high school covered the St. Xavier College sign above the school's front door on Seventh and Sycamore Streets with the name of St. Xavier High School. For the 1919–1920 school year St. Xavier College officially moved to the Avondale campus and used the former clubhouse building for classes until the new buildings were completed. Moreover, in that first year the college did not separate entirely from its historic downtown roots, as all the science classes were still held on Seventh and Sycamore Streets. Both the students and the faculty temporarily commuted back and forth to classes at the two sites. (40)

In the summer of 1920 there was a rush to complete both buildings under construction on the new campus in time for September classes. The college borrowed $80,000 at 6½ percent interest, payable in ten years, in order to complete the two buildings. Two months later it carried an additional loan to grade "the new buildings" at an estimated cost of $10,000. At the downtown location, college officials renovated new classrooms for the evening School of Law and the Schools of Commerce and Sociology as well as for some daytime high school activities. Classes for these schools, as well as extension courses, continued to be held downtown. In early fall the college also explored a possible merger or affiliation with the Queen City College of Pharmacy in Cincinnati, whose officials expressed interest in the new science building. Though the previous year St. Xavier trustees had established a night law school and had space on the new campus for additional expansion, they voted against "buying the Pharmacy College, or affiliating with the Pharmacy or hiring out scientific rooms to the Pharmacy College." (41)

The first building completed at the Avondale site was Alumni Science Hall. Completed in 1920, it housed the departments of biology, chemistry, and physics with accompanying classrooms and laboratories. As a memorial of the Diamond Jubilee, alumni gave the major portion of the $150,000 necessary to erect the Tudor-Gothic building. On September 14 the 103 students in the college took classes in Alumni Hall. The former clubhouse of the Avondale Athletic Club provided additional classrooms, a cafeteria, a temporary library, and recreational space. In November, St. Xavier officials brought the administration building, Hinkle Hall, at a cost of $240,000, to completion. The three-story Tudor-Gothic structure, whose towers resembled those of the thirteenth-century Francis Xavier family castle in Navarre, Spain, had forty-one rooms for the Jesuit faculty, a chapel, a recreation room, a library, and offices. There were also parlors in which to entertain visitors. In the afternoon of November 14, at the blessing of the new St. Xavier College buildings, Archbishop Henry Moeller gave the main address from the landing of the grand staircase leading to Hinkle Hall. To the invited guests, which included Mary Hinkle and members of the Diamond Jubilee Committee, he expressed his earnest desire to help the Jesuits in the development of St. Xavier College into a well-equipped institution and of his plan to establish at the college a normal school for the training of parochial school teachers. After the blessings the college opened the buildings to the public for a tour. Ten days later, the college's Jesuit faculty took their last evening meal together at Seventh and Sycamore Streets and headed for their new home in Avondale. Their first meal on the new campus was on Thursday, November 25— Thanksgiving Day. A year later the college installed a marble altar in the Jesuit community chapel on the first floor of Hinkle Hall. (42)

During its first year in Avondale, college officials outlined a plan for a "Greater Xavier" and envisioned as many as ten buildings, in addition to the three already standing, being erected on the property.

Planning to put academic buildings on the east side of campus and athletic facilities on the west, they hoped to construct a new library, chapel, gymnasium, biology laboratory, classroom building, administration building, and four dormitory units at $150,000 each. All buildings were to be in the Tudor-Gothic style. At the end of its first academic year on the new campus, St. Xavier was reported to be the largest Catholic college in Ohio. Its enrollment included 80 students in the College of Law, 395 in the evening School of Commerce and Sociology, 111 students pursuing the liberal arts degree in Avondale, and 175 students, mainly women religious, pursuing studies on a part-time basis. Part-time and evening students outnumbered the full-time day students by more than five to one. (43)

In the fall of 1922, on October 22nd, the college dedicated the $40,000 football stadium, known as Corcoran Field, in honor of John and E. B. Corcoran, generous local contributors to the stadium fund. The grandstands on the west side of the field had been erected a year earlier. In addition to the stadium, Corcoran Field had facilities for baseball, tennis, track, and calisthenics. To accommodate the growing popularity of organized sports, especially football, many colleges and universities built facilities. Athletic departments now had their own budgets, and a number of institutions in the 1920s erected massive stadiums, a decade in which stadium or fieldhouse building reached its apex. Sporting events, which helped fill the pages of the newspapers, also helped connect the alumni to the institution, sustaining their loyalty and their donations. Football generated among the alumni unprecedented emotional and financial investments. The St. Xavier College football team, which had been accepted as a member of the Ohio Athletic Conference in November 1920, was coached by Joseph (Joe) A. Meyer, known to most of his friends as "The Chief." In addition to football, he also coached baseball and basketball from 1920 to 1937. (44)

Shortly before the college embarked on its second phase of construction in Avondale, on April 1, 1923, Hubert F. Brockman, who had received his early education at St. Philomena School on East Third Street in Cincinnati and later entered St. Xavier High School and then St. Xavier College, where he graduated in 1896, became president of the college. As head of St. Xavier High School he was somewhat surprised that he was put in charge of his college alma mater. "When I found out you were to take my place downtown," he wrote to Herbert

C. Noonan, S.J., at St. Ignatius College in Chicago, "I was somewhat amazed," because of Noonan's previous college administrative experience, "to realize that it is not the opposite way, namely, that you should succeed Father McCabe and I remain here." He was installed as president of the college at dinner on Easter Sunday. The following evening the Alumni Diamond Jubilee Committee sponsored an informal reception and dinner for McCabe. At the gathering the guests subscribed $70,000 toward the building of a dormitory. (45)

In the fall the newly-installed president, who was destined to have a significant impact on the college, officially announced the drive for funds for a new residence hall in order to attract out-of-town students. The new campus solved the problem of congestion, which had physically handicapped the college in its two buildings downtown. The Avondale site afforded adequate facilities for the expansion of the college, which it was prepared to do in order to help meet some of the growing educational demands. College officials, consistent with the increasing practices of American colleges and universities since the Civil War, thought that a curriculum, a library, a faculty, and students were not enough to make a college. Having a residential student community became a high priority. Though two years earlier some people in the school and the Jesuit community had questioned the need for an on-campus residence, the editor of the *Xaverian News* answered the criticism by citing the need for the college to serve as a model educational institution not only for the city of Cincinnati but the entire region of the "middle south." In November, with the provincial's support, President Brockman submitted a formal application to the father general for the building of a dormitory. Upon his approval, construction began in December. (46)

The Alumni Association, which figured prominently in the campaign, formed the Dormitory Fund Committee, with Harry J. Gilligan of the class of 1912 serving as chairman. "The need of funds," Brockman wrote to the college community, "to take care of the normal expansion of the college and its work is most urgent—to say nothing of the splendid opportunities for good which lie immediately before us." In need of additional operating funds that year, the college increased tuition for the second time since the Civil War, raising it from $80 to $125. The treasurer made clear that the college's revenue had not been "covering expenses by some thousands of dollars." Since the Civil War most small colleges, including St. Xavier, had overspent virtually every year and had to deal with deficits. The new and substantial facilities on campus seemed to justify the 25 percent increase in tuition. (47)

Early in 1924 the college distributed a pamphlet on "The 'Why' of a Dormitory" to the alumni and friends of the college. "Experience has shown," it read, "that it is impossible to have a Catholic college large in numbers, if it depends solely for its students on the city in which it is located. . . . It must have a large radius." For seventy years St. Xavier had drawn students exclusively from Cincinnati and the neighboring Kentucky cities. "As a result," it continued, "St. Xavier has always been small and in consequence the influence of the Jesuit educators for good has been sadly circumscribed." Many young men living in Ohio, Kentucky, Indiana, West Virginia, and Tennessee had sought admission at the college, but had "been refused," it further noted, "because there was no way for caring for them. Thus the dearth of Catholic college graduates in this part of the Middle West has been almost appalling." The pamphlet also pointed out that the proposed dormitory would "offer the necessary facilities for doubling the number of Catholic college graduates and double the efficiency of the teaching staff. The need for representative Catholic laymen is the crying want of the day. . . ." There were eagerly optimistic plans to complete the building before the beginning of classes in the fall. (48)

Construction of the residence hall continued through much of 1924. The college used the excavated earth for the dormitory to rebuild the automobile drive that circled the rear of the clubhouse. With the September 1924 opening of Elet Hall, named after St. Xavier College's first president, John A. Elet, the college once again became a boarding institution. Because of the new dormitory, enrollment in the fall of 1924 was 249, an increase of 65 students. The alumni handed over the residence hall, built at a cost of $175,000, free of debt, challenging the college to furnish it at a cost of approximately $8,000. Like Alumni Science and Hinkle buildings, Elet Hall was of the Tudor-Gothic type of architecture. It had a temporary chapel, pending the erection of a college chapel, separate from the Jesuit community's chapel in Hinkle Hall on the campus. Lounging rooms, parlors, and recreation facilities also afforded ample space for indoor recreation. The rear of the dormitory was a few yards away from the spacious Corcoran Field. The Recreation Hall-Library, the former clubhouse, also adjoined the new residence building. (49)

The formal opening of Elet Hall took place on October 4th. The ceremonies started at 1:30 p.m. when a procession of clergy and alumni left the Recreation Hall-Library building and winded its way over to the new building, where the blessing took place. "With its beautiful

Tudor-Gothic exterior and modern homelike apartments," *Woodstock Letters* recorded, "Elet Hall, . . . that crowns the hill overlooking the campus, fills a long-felt want at St. Xavier. Ample room is afforded 100 student guests, with accommodations for recreation, study and social activities and a temporary chapel where daily Mass, a long-forgotten privilege, has been resumed. The interior represents the latest development in the line of hotel construction and tasty decoration. Heat is supplied by a battery of oil-burning boilers with automatic control, while hot water for toilet purposes is furnished from a recently improved gas heater." (50)

The opening of Elet ushered in a new era for the college. In addition to helping to increase enrollment, it helped expand the number of student organizations and athletic programs. The first residents came from various parts of Ohio, Kentucky, Indiana, and Illinois. They were impressed by the new facility and quality of life on campus. One student commented in the newspaper that "few hotels can boast better accommodations" and that the meals served in the cafeteria were excellent. "Instead of the 'take it or leave it' meals at other boarding schools," he wrote, "one finds a large assortment of attractive calorie producers arrayed before him." Whether it was the amenities of the new residence hall or the college's growing academic reputation, by 1927 Elet Hall was filled to capacity. (51)

After only five years on the Avondale campus, St. Xavier College's physical plant, now consisting of four buildings, had changed dramatically and had more of a college appearance. Alumni Science Hall contained classrooms and had thoroughly-equipped laboratories for the three sciences. It also housed the editorial room of *Xaverian News* and the office of the Dean of the College of Liberal Arts. Hinkle Hall, the faculty building and administration hall, had in 1924 over forty Jesuit living quarters, a dining hall, a chapel, recreation rooms, the office of the president, and a large roof garden. The combined Recreation Hall-Library in the former Avondale Athletic Club contained the student dining room, the student library, and the dressing rooms for athletic teams, in addition to a two-alley bowling course. Corcoran Field embraced the football stadium, the tennis courts, the baseball field, and running track. The stadium with concrete stands seated 5,000 people, while wooden stands on the field accommodated an additional 5,000. In 1926, St. Xavier College held its first commencement outdoors on Corcoran Field. (52)

During the next few years college officials and alumni planned for a more expansive campus. Though they considered the possibility of making the northwest corner of the property on Marion Avenue and Winding Way available for a new St. Xavier High School, they chose to focus instead on the needs of the college. Brockman hoped to make St. Xavier College "the foremost Catholic College. . . . I am doing all I can to get real service out of our marvellous body of alumni," he wrote in 1924. "I am working day and night to enlist them one by one into a service such as W[alter] S[schmidt] . . . and others are rendering." Brockman made this his primary focus. Notwithstanding his "serene chapel countenance," a Jesuit colleague observed, he was a man full of "energy. He seemed never to have a lazy bone." (53)

In early 1924 Brockman encouraged alumni to join him in planning for new construction. While on a trip to London in the spring, Walter Schmidt wrote to Brockman that he and a companion "have gotten many ideas on building in the course of our trip, and I think can be of considerable help in the matter of the chapel, library, etc." Earlier that year Schmidt had turned over a 20-year life endowment policy for $40,000 to the college while pledging to keep up the annual payments of $1,750. While Schmidt was in Europe, Brockman wrote to father general, pointing out that the St. Xavier College alumnus and a companion would be in Rome in early March and asked that they be treated very well. Brockman hoped that the Jesuits' House would give them a "cordial reception . . . and encourage them in the splendid work they are doing for S[t.]X[avier]C[ollege]." Schmidt's "heart," he wrote, "is in SXC." Upon his return to Cincinnati in mid-May he, some alumni, and Brockman engaged in more serious discussions. Six months later the board agreed to build a new library and sought father general's approval, which he granted on the condition that "no debt is incurred." (54)

In late fall a group of alumni and civic leaders, headed by Schmidt, established the Xavier Foundation, a committee of alumni and friends of the college, numbering about forty, who were united for the purpose of gathering funds for the building program. Among the new buildings planned were the library, chapel, and gymnasium. The nucleus of this committee was derived from the old Diamond Jubilee Committee that had functioned for a similar purpose during the previous decade. The goal of the Xavier Foundation, which held regular monthly meetings at the college, was to raise one million dollars. This was not a public drive or campaign, but a system of private solicitation of funds. During the fall months it raised, in addition to pledges, an average of $12,000 each month. By this means the college gathered over $200,000 in 1925 alone, which helped meet some of the needs of the growing college. (55)

The college broke ground for a new library in March 1925. To help raise funds for the new facility, St. Xavier authorities sponsored various events, such as the presentation of W. S. Gilbert's *The Mikado* at the Emery Auditorium on Walnut Street in downtown Cincinnati. Actual construction of the library building began in the spring and was completed at a cost of $175,000 in time for the fall term in 1926. Situated between Hinkle Hall and the Alumni Science Hall on the east side of Victory Boulevard, the new library contained a large main reading room, 40 by 80 feet, stack rooms to accommodate 150,000 volumes with room for expansion, and a fine arts room and a reference room for philosophy, history, and sociology. At the time the college owned slightly more than 50,000 volumes. The new library building also had a chapel and some classrooms. The college dedicated the Tudor-Gothic building in May 1926, and three years later named it the Walter Seton Schmidt Library Building in honor of the alumnus who had been the principal benefactor for the project. (56)

In the summer of 1925, in the midst of all the construction activity, college authorities reinforced their Jesuit connection by establishing a seminary in Milford, Ohio, on 100 acres of land about fifteen miles from the Avondale campus. In August, twenty-seven seminarians arrived to continue their studies at the Milford division, which was a part of the College of Liberal Arts. The first seminarians took courses in classics, sciences, history, English, and pedagogy. (57)

That same summer the college remodeled the Recreation Hall-Library at a cost of $50,000 and renamed it Union House. It would later become more popularly known as the Red Building. After renovating the basement and removing the bowling alleys, the Union House now contained quarters, including showers, for 100 athletes. The first floor had a small library that was also used as an assembly room. The second floor contained a large new dining hall. The students used the rooms on the top floor for billiards and other indoor recreations. Offering both commuter and resident students the opportunity to engage in common activities, the student union became the site of student meetings, dances, and performances. The Union House also had offices for the *Xaverian News*, recently moved from the Alumni

Science Building, and the *Musketeer*, the college yearbook, established in 1924. (58)

Later that year the college acquired approximately seven acres of "property lying north of Hinkle Hall," between Victory Parkway and Woodburn Avenue, part of which later became Ledgewood Avenue. Also included in the purchase was the acquisition of 750 feet on Herald Avenue, opposite Hinkle Hall, on which the college had signed a lease about four years earlier. "This should give us," Brockman noted, "plenty of building space for our needs for the next twenty-five years." While providing for future expansion to the north, it also excluded "undesirable neighbors." In the fall of 1922 the board of trustees had considered the property on Herald Avenue "a menace to the privacy for the residen[ts] of Hinkle Hall." The Jesuits had hoped to secure control of the property. Brockman reminded the trustees in 1925 of the college's lack of funds and that for several years it had suffered "an appreciable deficit." He was concerned over the amount of extra indebtedness that the college would have to carry. In March the board opted to borrow $350,000 in order to refund existing indebtedness of the college and to provide additional funds for new construction. A few months later the trustees decided to lease the newly-acquired property north of Hinkle Hall. (59)

As the college campus continued to grow and alumni support became more critical, early in 1926 a group of St. Xavier College women graduates met with President Hubert Brockman and proposed the establishment of the Alumnae Association, comparable to the Alumni Association established in 1888. Since 1914 women had been attending the college in the evenings, weekends, and summers. Under the leadership of Catherine Carter—a graduate of the School of Law—these women drafted the Alumnae Association constitution and elected officers. Carter became its first president. Luella Sauer, a charter member of the Alumnae Association, soon helped establish an annual scholarship to be awarded in the name of the association. Along with the Xavier Foundation and the Alumni Association, women graduates helped raise funds to meet the needs of the college. (60)

That same year Walter Schmidt, in honor of his parents, donated $250,000 for the construction of a gymnasium fieldhouse. Providing a security note, he agreed to pay about $10,000 a year interest and to provide in his will the capital portion of his gift. "In consideration of St. Xavier College proceeding with the construction of a gymnasium fieldhouse building upon the security of [my] note," Schmidt wrote,

"I hereby agree, on or before January 1, 1960, to pay to St. Xavier College the sum of $250,000 . . . with interest thereon at the rate of (5%) five percent per annum . . . to commence from the date of completion of the building." The only condition imposed by the provincial for the construction of the new facility was that "private individual showers" be installed instead of "open showers." Construction of the fieldhouse began in the spring of 1927. (61)

St. Xavier College dedicated the Schmidt Memorial Fieldhouse, built at a cost of $325,000, on March 7, 1928. It had a total seating capacity of 12,500. Five thousand of the seats were permanent and 7,500 were movable. The ceremony took place on the evening of the first basketball game against the University of Cincinnati, the first athletic contest between the two schools since a football game a decade earlier. Walter Schmidt and Herman Schneider, acting president of the University of Cincinnati, were Brockman's special guests. At 7 p.m., following the ceremony, the doors of the fieldhouse were opened. By 8:15 there was not even standing room to be found. St. Xavier College faculty, alumni, students, other Ohio colleges' and universities' faculties, administrators, and athletic directors, as well as many representatives of Jesuit institutions were among the attendees. Bands and cheerleaders of both schools entertained the crowd. "Fine spirit was shown at the game," it was noted, "and it may mark the beginning of permanent athletic relations." The packed crowd in the fieldhouse witnessed St. Xavier's victory over its rival by a score of 29–25. Prior to construction of the campus fieldhouse, the basketball team had played its home games in a local gym. Four years earlier the 1923–1924 basketball team had played the first extended schedule with a 12–4 season. (62)

At the time of its completion, the fieldhouse was the largest basketball facility and sports arena in the state, as well as the largest assembly building in Cincinnati. It had facilities for most indoor sports and special provisions for winter practices of outdoor athletic activities. In addition to being the home of the basketball team, the new fieldhouse provided facilities for physical education and intramural athletics. It marked an important step in the development of the student health program at the college. In June 1929 the college held its commencement in the fieldhouse. (63)

In the mid-1920s college officials resumed discussion about the building of a church and parish in Avondale. In January 1927 Archbishop John T. McNicholas of Cincinnati, who had succeeded

Henry Moeller in 1925, approved the request. For over two decades archdiocesan officials had denied the Jesuits' proposal for another parish. Shortly after learning of McNicholas's approval, former President James McCabe, who was at Creighton University in Omaha, Nebraska, advised Brockman to negotiate the parish limits "through the Archbishop quietly but firmly, and that you be as suave and as non-committal in your dealings with the enraged pastors as you know how. . . . Don't make too much of the anger or enmity of the pastors. Most of them carry that under their vests anyway. The Jesuit is 'tolerated,' not liked by the clergy, and usually because he can do things that they can not do." (64)

Construction of Saint Robert Bellarmine Church on the first floor of the Schmidt Library Building began in April. Named after Robert Bellarmine, the seventeenth-century Jesuit saint and scholar, it would serve as the church until a separate building could be constructed. Many of the interior furnishings were donated and erected in memory of deceased Jesuit priests and scholastics who had once labored in the college or had been pastors at St. Xavier Church. James O'Neill, S.J., served as pastor. The first Mass and first baptism for the new parish were held on Sunday, April 24. The first marriage took place two weeks later. (65)

In the fall of 1927 St. Xavier College conducted a $300,000 fund-raising campaign to complete construction of the east stands in the football stadium at Corcoran Field. It justified the addition in terms of the intrinsic value of sports on a college campus and the growing alumni and public support for football. The new construction increased capacity to 15,000. Myers Y. Cooper, a Cincinnati realtor and busi-nessman, served as the executive chairman of the drive. On October 2nd the legendary Notre Dame football coach, Knute Rockne, deliv-ered the main address at a successful benefit dinner at the Sinton Hotel in downtown Cincinnati. At the dinner Cooper helped raise $20,000 in twenty minutes. "To raise over $300,000 by popular subscription for a Catholic athletic project is absolutely unbelievable to men who know the difficulties confronted in such an undertaking," an alumnus and auditor of the fund drive said. At the December meeting of the Xavier Foundation, which at the time consisted of fifty Cincinnatians, Brockman presented Cooper with a gold watch. "In one of the largest single enterprises attempted in our history," Brockman said, "he brought magnificently to our cause a practical and effective business talent. . . . Your name is written in the long history of St. Xavier College amongst those who gave their best to sustain and enlarge its labors for the good of Cincinnati and our beloved country." (66)

The college completed the stadium addition in November 1929 and dedicated it on November 23, the day of the homecoming game against Denison University. Mayor Murray Seasongood of Cincinnati spoke. Visiting engineers called the renovated and expanded stadium "an architectural gem." Regarded by some as one of the finest stadiums in the nation, it was constructed entirely of concrete, and its seats made of California redwood. One of the highlights of the football season was Xavier's annual game for the Governor's Cup with the University of Dayton. "It is a game in which Cincinnatians, and most particularly Xaverians take great pride," a trustee wrote. "Not only because we can extend a welcome to Ohio's foremost citizen, but because the possession of his trophy is at stake." (67)

In 1928 Myers Cooper, who had led the successful fund-raising drive for the football stadium, was the Republican party candidate for governor of Ohio. His opponent's political campaign exploited Cooper's association with St. Xavier College and its Catholic identity. In the 1920s the Ku Klux Klan organized hate campaigns against African Americans, Catholics, and Jews, and burned crosses in front of Ohio churches and on the front lawns of some Catholics' homes. When Alfred E. Smith, a Catholic from New York, sought the presidency of the United States in 1928, that also generated widespread anti-Catholic sentiment.

Although Cooper was not a St. Xavier alumnus, he had been unanimously voted an honorary member of the Xavier Foundation because of his leadership in the fund drive. A tribute to him had also appeared on the front page of the *Xaverian News* on January 4, 1928. During the political campaign some political opponents had the front page of the *Xaverian News* reprinted. To make sure that the readers would understand the source of the reprint, they inserted the word "Catholic" in the masthead to read: "Published weekly by the students of St. Xavier CATHOLIC College." They sent reprints of the article to the predominantly rural and Protestant sections of the state.

In response to Cooper's candidacy for governor, Brockman pointed out on the eve of the election that it had "been the policy of the College . . . to stay out of politics. . . . However, Mr. Myers Y. Cooper, whose admirable personality has captivated all our groups because of his personal contact with us, has drawn practically all the St. Xavier group to his side. His leadership of our Stadium Campaign is an additional reason for a very high devotion to him on the part of all who feel that he has all the qualities for a worthy and capable Governor of our . . . state." Notwithstanding the bigotry, Cooper was elected governor. (68)

In February 1928, college officials had begun making plans for a new biology building. Ten years earlier, before construction began at the Avondale campus, the college consultants had concluded that in order to enhance the reputation of St. Xavier College "certain expenses were necessary to enlarge and equip the science department." In the spring of 1928, William H. Albers, who requested anonymity at the time, pledged a gift of $150,000 to the college for a biology building, which would later be named after him. In the fall the consultors received the father general's approval for construction of the new structure. (69)

The Biology Building, located north of Hinkle Hall, was completed on July 1, 1929, at a cost of $250,000. Dedicated on November 10, it was St. Xavier's seventh building in the Tudor-Gothic style. The general building contractors and furnishers, who were alumni, erected the building practically for the cost value of materials and labor. This was their unadvertised gift to the college. The new facility spurred an increased interest in scientific research and the education of students for careers in medicine and dentistry. That same year the faculty and administration inaugurated a three-year premedical program. In 1930 Professors Alphonse Land and Martin Phee, S.J., began research to isolate the "cancer germ," a project that they hoped would prove beneficial to medical research as well as bring fame to the college. (70)

When the facility first opened, the biology and physics departments shared the building. Two biology laboratories completely equipped for 100 students, technicians' rooms, a culture room, and an office for the department head occupied the third floor. The physics department with its laboratories was on the second floor. A large lecture hall with more than 150 seats and some smaller lecture rooms occupied most of the first floor, while the remaining space consisted of a suite of three rooms for the president's office, and a lobby and museum for mounted specimens. On September 23, the college consultors, who convened once a month, met for the first time in the president's new office. Cincinnati's State Senator Robert J. O'Brien, a close personal friend of President Brockman, had paid for the furnishings in the new office. At about the same time the college converted the former president's office in Hinkle Hall into a chapel with three altars. The chemistry department became the sole occupant of the space it had formerly shared with the department of biology in Alumni Science Hall. (71)

In order to secure a proper entrance to the new building, the college authorized a fill of fourteen feet in front of the building and the widening and extension of the private roadway down past it. In addition, the administration in the summer of 1929 made improvements by introducing other changes in the front of Hinkle Hall. They removed the concrete stairs formerly approaching it and built a rustic wall six feet high extending along the whole width of Hinkle Hall. In place of the former staircase they erected two shorter staircases in the same rustic pattern at the opposite ends of Hinkle Hall that led up from the road to the terrace in front of the building. The following year the college landscaped the lawn sloping from Hinkle Hall to Victory Parkway. The "jovial Irishman" Robert J. O'Brien spent about $30,000 "on landscaping a part of our College grounds last fall," Brockman wrote in February 1930. "He built beautiful wide staircases on the grounds and ornamented them with . . . planted shrubbery and tall juniper trees." In his honor, that area of campus became known as the O'Brien Terrace. (72)

The new landscaping and the completion of the Biology Building, including the new and more spacious president's office, helped generate renewed optimism in the future of the college. "I had to put up with a few quips and thrusts because, being a poor lowly Jesuit, I was established in such palatial quarters," Brockman wrote to O'Brien on the day following his first consultors' meeting in his new office. "Oh boy! They had fun with me. But I could afford to keep my chin in the air. Who couldn't? Every one of them is looking for the job of Rector. We are going to have more candidates for President of St. Xavier College than this institution ever had in the hundred years of its existence. . . . I immediately said that if I leave here, everything goes with me. Under such a possibility, they were all ready to resign as candidates for President." On a more serious note he emphasized the college's growing reputation. "Between you and me and the lamppost," he continued, "let me add that never before was this group [of consultors] so ready to consider the development of the College on big expansive lines. I am convinced that the psychology of having a rich and beautiful office brought about this state of mind in them. . . . It is my ambition to make this Catholic College an outstanding one in the city and state. I have no doubt either that it is on the way to being known throughout the country. Already the Associated Press carries many items about the College throughout the country. They are beginning to want news about St. Xavier." (73)

Brockman's vision of a more expansive St. Xavier College remained strong throughout his presidency. While he was particularly proud of the institution's accomplishments in a relatively short period of time, he thought more could be done. Because of the "overflow of out-of-town boys," he and his consultors thought a wing should be added to Elet Hall. By the end of the decade the resident students represented twelve states, and St. Xavier authorities opened a new residence facility, Finn Lodge, on the Herald Avenue side of campus east of Victory Parkway. At the time approximately one in six St. Xavier College students was a campus resident, the greatest number coming from high schools in Cleveland and Chicago. (74)

Brockman was also pleased with the prudent and cautious investments made by the college. "We have built up a very beautiful college in Avondale," he wrote to Bernard Henry Kroger, founder of the Kroger grocery store chain, in 1930. "It is built economically and efficiently without the loss of an inch of space in any of the buildings, and at a cost that is ridiculously low. No college in the country," he insisted, "has succeeded in doing what we have done with the same amount of money." In an attempt to enhance further St. Xavier's educational mission, Brockman asked Kroger for his assistance. "What we need immediately is an expanded program in our Business Administration courses," he wrote. "We have fine teachers and trainers in commercial and industrial courses. The students are ambitious and determined. You can see it in their eyes. My heart sinks when I realize that owing to the lack of equipment, I cannot provide bigger and better training. We need more room for Business courses." What he hoped for was a business administration building. "You can't get the effects which we are able to produce," he concluded, "without a special building." (75)

Additional construction, however, was not forthcoming. Not withstanding St. Xavier's accomplishments and Brockman's optimism regarding the future growth of the college, because of the Great Depression and World War II there would be no further construction on campus until almost two decades later.

St. Xavier College Comes of Age

As the St. Xavier campus expanded in the 1920s, so did the college's extracurricular and athletic activities. Proud of the college's accomplishments and its Jesuit identity, *Xaverian News* in December 1920 published a poem emphasizing both the correct pronunciation of the name "Xavier" and the school's commitment to "good behavior." It wrote:

> A word beginning with an 'X'
> Must never sound to rhyme with necks.
> No, no, this X pronounced should be
> Exactly like the letter 'Z'
> And that's why our dear name St. Xavier
> Must always rhyme with good behavior.
> In all the seasons, in all weather.
> The two are always found together. (76)

Once the college had established roots in Avondale, it instituted over half a dozen new student organizations and activities. In 1921, on the six hundredth anniversary of the death of Italian poet Dante Alighieri, the college established a new student organization, the Dante Club, whose purpose was to spread the knowledge and appreciation of the Catholic classic, *The Divine Comedy*, and to promote interest in other classic literary works through public lectures on campus. In addition, the college established the "X" Club, composed of young men who earned their athletic monogram. It was initiated to encourage a close bond of friendship between the lettermen. That same year the administration established the Catholic Students' Mission Crusade (CSMC) unit of the College of Arts and Sciences. CSMC, a national grassroots lay ministry with its national headquarters in Cincinnati, helped generate thousands of vocations to the priesthood, the religious life, and service to the Church. The students held weekly meetings and took up weekly collections for the benefit of the missions. By the mid-1920s, 93 students in the College of Liberal Arts, over half of its enrollment, were members. (77)

During the years between 1850 and 1930 school officials assumed that the vast majority of St. Xavier students would be active participants in the Roman Catholic faith. Catholic students in the day college were required to attend the annual three-day retreat, as well as certain weekly chapel assemblies and Masses. The retreat in the 1920s consisted of various spiritual exercises, including Mass, benediction of the Blessed Sacrament, the Way of the Cross, and talks on spiritual matters by the Jesuits conducting the retreat. In 1924 the college established the Knights of Columbus club for the purpose of fostering the spirit of that national Catholic fraternal organization on campus. Among the student organizations the sodality was the largest. It helped organize impressive displays of public piety, such as the 1925 Sodality Convocation at Corcoran Field attended by over 10,000 people. St. Xavier students were also active participants not only in the Catholic Students' Mission Crusade but also in the annual parade of the Holy Name Society, whose object was to discourage profanity, indecency, and vulgarity in speech. (78)

Another activity established during the college's second year in Avondale was a radio club. By way of a newly-licensed St. Xavier College wireless station, the voice of the college could be heard in the Midwest and sometimes as far away as Massachusetts. The wireless also made it possible for the students to receive messages and news from stations on the East Coast. That enabled the students to report the news almost as soon as the events occurred. Two years later, college officials also organized the Xavier Masque Society, whose purpose was to foster dramatic, literary, and musical interests. Each year the society produced a classical play. In 1925 the Book Lovers organization, composed of friends of the college, was founded to improve the reading and research facilities of the library through the purchase of books. (79)

In the fall of 1926, John King Mussio, class of 1924, and a teacher at the college who later became a diocesan priest and bishop of Steubenville, helped organize the Clef Club, whose members practiced an average of two hours a week and received instruction in musical theory and correct interpretation. Each year the club performed one or more numbers for public entertainment. That fall, Frank Dowd, a student, organized the band. It marched for the first time at a football game the following year. By the end of the decade, the college also had an orchestra which provided opportunities for student ensemble playing. Ten years after the move to Avondale, the Masque Society, orchestra, band, and Clef Club sponsored dramatic, musical, and vocal performances on campus. Doubtlessly, St. Xavier's new residential community had helped expand the range of social life and development on campus. (80)

During the 1920s dances became the most popular form of social entertainment for St. Xavier students. Student organizations at both the day school and evening college sponsored their own dances. The junior prom, however, was the major student event sanctioned by the college. Although forbidden by the provincial about a decade earlier, once it was inaugurated by the class of 1921 the prom became the social highlight of the year, attracting as many as 600 couples. The prom was held in various downtown hotels until 1931, when the administration transferred the event to the Lodge Reading Room in Schmidt Library.

It had come to the attention of the administration that some students were drinking at the dances. In 1931, Prohibition under the Volstead Act was the law of the land. The change in venues allowed more supervision of the students. Despite the disapproval of some of the students, the editor of the *Xaverian News* wrote that the administration had good reason to move the prom to campus, as students in the past had made "monkeys out of themselves . . . [with] the aid of many bottles of gin." The administration hoped that the prom would help "develop" the young men's "social side." Other annual dances held on campus included the freshman-sophomore hop and the senior ball. The evening school also sponsored dances that were well-attended. (81)

In the nineteenth century, students had a limited voice in extracurricular matters. Throughout the 1920s students in American colleges, including St. Xavier, took measures to increase their role in decision- and policy-making. As social and cultural activities at the college grew in the 1920s, so did the students' voice on aspects of student life on campus. Beginning the first year on the new campus, St. Xavier students held biweekly general assemblies to allow the students to voice their opinions to school officials. In 1921, Xavier officials denied a student request to establish a student council, stating that "the conditions at the present time do not warrant such a body." Two years later, however, the administration changed its mind. It discontinued the student assembly and approved the establishment of a twelve-member student council and its involvement in extracurricular activities. At first a large number of students expressed their displeasure in the decision, arguing that the student council alone was not conducive to the participation of the majority of the student body. Over time, however, students more readily accepted the role of the student council on campus. By 1925 student governments had become widespread in American colleges and universities. (82)

During the decade, St. Xavier officials continued to enforce a number of student regulations. The college forbade gambling and chewing tobacco under penalty of dismissal. Student smoking was allowed only in the basement of Alumni Science Hall. A controversy developed concerning whether freshmen should be subjected to a set of "freshman rules" as a means of introducing them to college life. Throughout the decade, most editorials in the *Xaverian News* disapproved of the proposed rules, arguing that they would undermine school unity and harmony. Nevertheless, in 1930 the student council adopted the freshman rules, requiring the first-year students to wear caps at all times, sing the school song on command, and stay seated in the chapel until all upper-classmen had left. An upperclassmen "vigilance committee," known as the Kangaroo Court, was responsible for punishing freshmen offenders, often through paddling. (83)

St. Xavier College conducted classes both on the Avondale campus and in downtown Cincinnati. The College of Liberal Arts, located in Avondale, offered four-year courses that led to degrees of bachelor of arts, bachelor of science, and bachelor of philosophy. In addition, premedical students took sufficient work in two years to educate and equip themselves properly for medical school. The college also offered a two-year pre-legal course. Without attempting to supplant the evening School of Commerce downtown, in the late 1920s the College of Liberal Arts also offered day business courses in Avondale. Six years later it initiated a bachelor of science in commerce degree in accounting. Classes were offered on Saturdays. At the time there was talk about the possibility of permanently establishing a school of business administration with day degree courses. (84)

Notwithstanding the introduction of some professional courses in the day curriculum, President Brockman made clear in the college publications that the "Jesuit faculty of St. Xavier follows the *Ratio Studiorum*, famous educational rule of the black-robed sons of Loyola." The college tried to balance the traditional classical curriculum with some new so-called practical courses. Brockman further pointed out that in "the age of unrest and radical 'isms' St. Xavier stands firmly for the great truths underlying our present order. Its graduates are not parlor Bolshevists or embryo Socialists or slinking Pacifists, but go forth with a high respect for authority and for the rights of property—imbued with the ambitions of usefulness, contentment, and service. Right thinking men, regardless of creed, appreciate the saneness of its philosophic teachings." In compliance with the expressed wish of Archbishop McNicholas, by the late 1920s the college offered a weekly course on apologetics to educate laymen for the public defense of Catholic principles. (85)

St. Xavier also offered evening classes in the College of Law and the Schools of Commerce and Sociology at a St. Xavier High School building downtown on Sycamore Street. In addition to courses in commerce and finance, lectures were given in literature and philosophy. Though in the College of Law those individuals who wanted to follow the profession in Ohio were required to complete two years of college work, the course leading to the degree of bachelor of laws required two additional years of study. Degrees of bachelor of commerce and of master of commerce were awarded in the School of Commerce. The former degree was given at the end of four years' work. Diplomas in the School of Sociology were awarded upon successful completion of a two-year course. (86)

In March 1925 the North Central Association of Colleges and Secondary Schools (NCA), the midwestern educational accrediting organization, admitted St. Xavier College. For about a decade the provincial had urged Jesuit colleges of the Missouri province to adapt their educational standards to American higher education norms and to "seek admission." Acting as quasi-governmental entities, accrediting and professional associations examined and influenced academic standards, faculty-student ratio, laboratory and library size, and staff qualifications. To comply with NCA requirements, the college discontinued admitting freshmen into its College of Law. In addition, the on-going construction of a new library that year was an important and timely addition for the NCA review. (87)

In the fall of 1925, shortly after a meeting of the Jesuit Seismological Association, whose members operated Jesuit seismograph stations, James Macelwane, S.J, a seismologist at St. Louis University, wrote to Brockman about the possibility of establishing a station on the St. Xavier campus. Less than two years later the college established a station, which was set up in a vault in the basement of the new Schmidt Library Building. Several long and short period seismographs recorded every tremor of the earth's surface. St. Xavier's station was the only one between Washington, D.C., and St. Louis. It provided daily reports to the United States government, the daily press, national services, and scientific agencies. In 1928 Joseph Wilczewski, S.J., became director and served in that capacity for about three years until he was transferred to Marquette University in August 1931. The station remained shut down until the arrival in February 1932 of a new director, Victor Stechschulte, S.J., who had received his doctorate in seismology at the University of California. (88)

During its first decade on the Avondale campus, St. Xavier College, like many other colleges and universities, pursued greater visibility in society not only in intellectual and social areas but in intercollegiate athletics. Football was the most popular intercollegiate sport at the college, drawing a large number of fans to its games and serving as an important source of tradition and pride for the school. The tradition of homecoming began on November 25, 1922, when St. Xavier played

Otterbein College before a crowd of 4,000 at Corcoran Stadium. Over time, homecoming included a student dance and a pep rally or bonfire the evening before the game. Students held some of the pep rallies on Fountain Square in downtown Cincinnati. Another important athletic event was the annual Thanksgiving Day game against the Haskell Institute of Kansas held each year from 1919 to 1935. (89)

In the 1920s more and more students supported intercollegiate and intramural sports activities. It was during that decade that students in the stands at the stadium sang the chorus of their new football song:

> March on, march on, old Xavier;
> Thy Royal Sons and true
> We rally round, thy praise to sound,
> To pledge our hearts anew,
> Give a cheer, a rah, rah, rah;
> Give another and a tiger, ah:
> For the noble White and Blue
> In proud acclaim, shout, shout her name,
> Old Xavier: Hurrah!

Intramural sports competition also began on campus in 1923 when basketball and bowling leagues were introduced. St. Xavier officials believed that physical activity was a benefit to student morale. By 1930 two-thirds of the students in the day school had signed up to participate in either baseball, basketball, handball, horseshoes, tennis, or track. (90)

In addition to increasing student interest in intercollegiate and intramural sports, athletics got a boost from its supporters. In the summer of 1923 the Athletic Council increased its membership "in order to obtain a more widespread interest in athletics at the College." The council, a self-elective body of men, mostly alumni, directed the athletic activities of the school. They subsequently prepared a constitution and "asked a certain number . . . interested in the College to become members of the Athletic Association." The object of the association, the constitution read, "shall be to control and govern athletics at Saint Xavier College; to cooperate with the Student Body in handling all athletic activities; to suggest to the Faculty ways and means of improving the physical condition of the students." Membership was limited to thirty, consisting of faculty, alumni, students, and other friends of the college. The majority of the officers were members of the faculty. (91)

In the spring of 1925, *Xaverian News* sponsored a contest to find an appropriate nickname for the athletic teams. On October 7 the paper announced the name Musketeers as the winner. Francis J. Finn, S.J., a faculty member and trustee, submitted the nickname Musketeers because he thought the "one for all and all for one" motto that was attached to the legendary characters of France ought to reflect the spirit of the athletic teams. Beginning with the academic year of 1925–1926 the spirit of D'Artagnan, the seventeenth-century Musketeer and heroic member of the king's guard who had died in battle in 1673 would be emulated by Xavier's athletic teams.

The widely-known author of twenty-one books for boys—which were translated into dozens of languages—Finn was also a lecturer in literature and poetry, an assistant pastor of St. Xavier Church, active in sodality work, director of the St. Xavier parochial school, the first free endowed parochial school in the country, and a founding member of the Community Chest. In such books as *Percy Wynn*, *Tom Playfair*, and *Claude Lightfoot*, he made the American Catholic boy a reality. Finn died in 1928, and even in death he manifested his vow of poverty, for he was buried in his old and worn cassock. One cold day he had allegedly asked a teacher to be sure to let him know if any child needed shoes or clothing. The teacher, glancing at the priest's shoes, saw that they were so badly worn that Finn's toes almost protruded. (92)

Finding an appropriate nickname for St. Xavier's athletic teams was one challenge; finding competition for them was another. "The great difficulty about arranging a schedule is the necessity of going down on our knees and asking College teams to play us," President Brockman observed in 1925. St. Xavier's athletic director had experienced considerable difficulty the previous year in scheduling five football games in the Ohio Conference. When he had scheduled two games and "complained of the apathy of the other Colleges," a delegate from Western Reserve University in Cleveland argued that the football conference "ought to disclose its mind openly in reference to its attitude towards St. Xavier and say whether it was on account of religious feeling or whether they were afraid of the athletic ability of St. Xavier College that they refused to play St. Xavier." In 1925 the college succeeded in getting only one conference game. That meant it had to schedule non-conference teams who were "either entirely too heavy for us or very much our inferiors," the St. Xavier president noted. (93)

In 1926 Brockman initiated an effort to establish a Midwest Jesuit athletic conference. Though this idea had been proposed before,

St. Xavier's proposal was the most comprehensive and ambitious to date. There were seven Jesuit colleges and universities in the midwestern region: Detroit, St. Louis, Marquette, Loyola, Creighton, John Carroll, and St. Xavier. He hoped that at least four of them would be willing to start a conference. Having "given a great deal of thought and attention to the matter of athletics in our Catholic Universities," he wrote to John P. McNichols, S.J., president of the University of Detroit in January 1926, he argued that the Jesuit "institutions are not desired as members of the different Conferences in their territories. Even if admission to such Conferences was practical yet when our institutions join them religious feeling or some other cause disposes the other Institutions to slight our own." As a consequence, the Jesuit colleges or universities were more or less independents and had to take games where they could get them. "It is my best judgment," he continued, "that this forces an 'inferiority complex' even on our own institutions and the boys in them. . . . To remedy this situation," he contended, "I offer the suggestion that the Jesuit Universities of the Middle West form a conference, using themselves as a nucleus and if possible joining to themselves sufficient other representative non-Catholic Institutions to form a group of ten or twelve." That action, he thought, would not only assure maintenance of high scholastic and athletic ideals, but also make it possible for the Jesuit institutions to "no longer have to beg for games." He recommended insuring four football games in conference and eight in basketball. "I might point out," he concluded, "that the different Institutions mentioned are each in a big city, and practically cover all the big cities of the Middle West, which is an additional reason why the Conference mentioned would come to have real prestige." Brockman also sent a copy of his letter to the other Jesuit presidents, inviting their thoughts on the matter. (94)

During the next two weeks the presidents of St. Louis, Creighton, and Loyola expressed interest in establishing a conference. Though Jeremias O'Callaghan, the provincial, gave his full "support" to the idea, he thought that some "of our Colleges will hold back." McNichols of Detroit not only had reservations about a conference, but resented the provincial's interference. "I am surprised that the Provincial should proceed to any measure which would coerce colleges into the league which you propose," he wrote to Brockman. Opposed to the idea, McNichols argued that playing Jesuit schools would not draw a crowd large enough to pay "the guarantee. . . . You can talk all you want about building up public opinion," he wrote, "but when the building up of that public opinion means a deficit running into thousands of dollars each year, over a period of years, I think it is asking too much." In his judgment, non-Jesuit competitive teams generally drew larger crowds. If "Detroit has to pay its own bills, it must get into a league which will bring crowds to the game. Possibly you consider my position selfish, and it is. When there is question of coin of the realm, each one of us has to look out for himself." (95)

Notwithstanding Brockman's efforts, the proposed Jesuit athletic conference never materialized, largely due to lukewarm support or outright opposition from some of the presidents and resistance from the athletic directors at the larger schools, namely Marquette, Detroit, and Creighton. It became clear, as one Jesuit colleague from Loyola University in New Orleans observed, that "because of the conservative attitude of some of your Universities in the Missouri Province, each one is trying to get recognition from the big non-Catholic schools and seems afraid that by too friendly associations with their sister Jesuit Colleges they may be ignored by the Big Ten. It is our unfortunate condition to always suffer from this inferiority complex."

Though a few presidents met twice in Chicago in August 1926 to try to keep the concept of a conference alive, the meetings were in vain. When four years later there was interest on the part of some schools, including St. Xavier College, to form a basketball conference with the Jesuit and Catholic schools, Brockman was not hopeful, as there did not appear to be any interest among athletic directors. "It all seems," Brockman wrote, "an ineffective procedure." As he suspected, the proposed basketball conference also did not happen. (96)

During the next few years there was continued concern by the administration and alumni of St. Xavier College over the growth and level of athletic competition and its relationship to the reputation of the college. "Athletics at your college are at a critical stage," the president of the St. Xavier College Alumni Association wrote to the members in 1927, "where we must take our place with nationally known teams or go back among and be identified with the little 'jerk-water' colleges. Practically squeezed out of the Ohio Conference . . . ," he continued, "there are but two ways left—advance above [such] conferences, or sink beneath them. As an alumnus you want to see your college grow. The best way to grow is through athletics, which are not self supporting." He urged the alumni to continue to support athletics and their alma mater. (97)

Teachers' College

In February 1914 the Ohio legislature enacted the Morris Educational Bill, approving the issuance of state teaching certificates without examination to individuals who had completed high school and an approved college program. In order for the Catholic elementary schools to obtain state recognition, their teachers had to be certified. Most of the teachers at the 110 parochial schools in the Archdiocese of Cincinnati, serving approximately 30,000 pupils, were religious sisters who sought certification. At the request of Mary Florence, mother superior of the Sisters of Charity in Cincinnati, in June 1914 St. Xavier College conducted its first summer school for nuns. Two years earlier Marquette had become the first Jesuit university to be granted permission by Jesuit officials to admit "ladies and even nuns" to its summer courses. The St. Xavier classes, under the auspices of the college and mostly taught by its faculty, were held at the sisters' Cedar Grove Academy in Price Hill on the west side of the city in the evening, on Saturday morning, and in the summer. Sixty-four women religious enrolled in the six-week program. For the first time in its history the college was coeducational. Though St. Xavier College officials considered requiring a full year's enrollment in the college for the sisters, it never happened. A letter written by a Brown County Ursuline sister in the spring of 1915 echoed the sentiments of the women religious communities that St. Xavier College would be "too strict in requiring a year's residence in the college," especially when a year's residence was not required in some other places and that the work could "be done in summer sessions entirely." (98)

For the next two summers the courses were held at St. Xavier College on Sycamore Street. While more and more American colleges created education as an advanced field of study, the Archdiocese of Cincinnati and St. Xavier College were among the first in the country to attempt to establish a normal school for teaching women religious. A number of professional groups, economists, librarians, educators, and psychologists, among others, insisted that before entering practice people gain appropriate scholarly knowledge and become certified. Like a number of academic institutions, St. Xavier College seized on the opportunity and began educating the professional educators for certification. The faculty designed course offerings to provide credit toward college entrance requirements or toward a degree, as well as to meet the requirements for state teaching certification. "I need not assure you," a mother superior wrote to President Francis Heiermann, "that every Sister in the School is most thankful to you and the good Fathers for the sacrifices they so generously made in our behalf." Nevertheless, in the summer of 1917 classes were back at the Cedar Grove Academy for the convenience of the members of the Sisters of Charity and other women religious communities. (99)

Because of the increased demands of state regulations on teachers, St. Xavier College officials explored new possibilities for expansion of its academic programs. In addition to summer classes and courses on Saturday mornings from 9 to 12, offered over thirty weeks, the college added afternoon classes. In the fall of 1917, ninety-three sisters from nine different religious communities enrolled in the college. A year later, three Sisters of Charity were the first women graduates of St. Xavier College. They had matriculated in the summer and extension course program and each received the bachelor of arts degree. (100)

In September 1918, St. Xavier's School of Commerce evening division also opened its doors to women students. During the First World War, 1914–1918, a growing number of women in the Greater Cincinati community replaced men in the work force, which had a positive influence on the scope of business education at St. Xavier. The college provided other women, in addition to the nuns in greater Cincinnati, with more practical and specialized education because of the increasing demand in the business community for professional women. To meet the need for trained social workers, the School of Sociology provided theoretical and practical training in social service. Furthermore, for the first time, part-time women faculty members taught courses in the evenings, summers, and Saturdays at the college. Admission of women to the education and business programs of the college was a giant step. Doubtlessly, discussions over the proposed Nineteenth Amendment to the U.S. Constitution, which ultimately would give women the right to vote, helped enhance the beginning of a movement for fuller educational equality. Though Jesuits' attitudes regarding the presence of women in college activities and programs had changed since the nineteenth century, there would continue to be no coeducational classes in the day school, which was the Jesuits' primary educational focus. (101)

In the summer of 1919, when 175 students—all but eight of them women religious—were enrolled in the college's teacher training program, President James McCabe and Francis Finn, S.J., renewed conversations with Archbishop Henry Moeller regarding the program. They proposed creating a full-fledged teachers' college for the sisters at the new Avondale campus. Given the large number of religious

congregations teaching in the metropolitan area, they thought enrollment would not be a problem. In June 1920, McCabe submitted a formal proposal to Moeller for his consideration.

The college hoped to erect a building or two on the Avondale campus, north of Alumni Science Building and Hinkle Hall, which were
under construction. Officials planned to have the science faculty and
facilities at the service of the women religious for half of the school day
and available for the traditional day students the other half day. "This
is considered to be a very great economic advantage for the Sisters'
School," McCabe wrote to the archbishop, "since the erection of a
separate scientific plant and securing fit Professors would evidently
entail great extra expense and difficulty." He made clear that the college contemplated the undertaking of the project "on condition that the
Sisters' College and Normal School be located on the St. Xavier
College grounds at Avondale," be owned by the college, and "be an
integral part of the St. Xavier College plant." The president further
proposed "that the funds necessary for the construction and equipment" of the teachers' college, which was estimated at $500,000, "be
collected by the Alumnae of the various Sisterhoods." Convinced that
the archdiocese would be "the chief beneficiary" in the result of this
arrangement, "since the parochial schools and Academies are to reap
direct benefit from it, we do not think," he concluded, "we are asking
too much from you when we ask you to approve and further this good
work." (102)

In September, Moeller responded by submitting a plan of his own.
While acknowledging that the educational policy should be in the
hands of St. Xavier College, he argued the buildings should not be
located on the college campus and that "the ownership and control be
vested in the archbishop of Cincinnati." While submitting "a plan of
bilateral control," Moeller further insisted that the archdiocese had the
right "to supplant the Jesuit Fathers by other teachers" if it should
become "advisable." (103)

Austin G. Schmidt, S.J., Dean of the Graduate School at Loyola
University in Chicago and a former professor of education at St.
Xavier College, responded critically to the archbishop's plan, arguing
that "dual control might invalidate the issuance of credits and degrees"
and might prove unacceptable to the North Central Association.
Jesuits "have learned by experience," Schmidt wrote, "that the ownership of a school and the control of its educational policies can not be
separated." He insisted that "[w]hoever owns the school, controls the

money; whoever controls the money, can cause the school to be taken off the North Central's accredited list; whoever does that, does serious injury to us in Cincinnati and elsewhere. Nor is money the only thing. We could lose our standing, for example, if the curriculum were tampered with; if degrees were given under lax standards; if professors of a certain type were employed." Regarded as one of the most learned American Jesuits of his time, especially in the field of pedagogy, Schmidt further contended that the primary purpose of the teachers' college was to meet legislative requirements, and that St. Xavier College "must serve the interests of Catholicity here by creating a school whose credits and degrees are recognized everywhere." (104)

In late October 1920, Moeller sent a tentative agreement to McCabe, contending that as the archbishop he would "have the right to demand that the curriculum of studies" in the proposed teachers' college "be entirely in conformity with the requirements of the Church and State for teachers in the schools, . . . that all members of the faculty shall be sound in doctrine [and] good morals and . . . the judgment as to these qualities to rest with" him. Under his agreement the college would also have to insure "that all books, texts etc., to be used in the college" met his approval. While now conceding that the property could be owned by, and located at, St. Xavier College, Moeller's proposal further stipulated that if the Society of Jesus were to violate any of the stipulations in the agreement, it would turn over to the archdiocese "all the money, real estate or other goods of this institution or college acquired from donations, contributions or alms" for the project. (105)

Though Schmidt found the archbishop's "conditions . . . irritating," he nevertheless thought they would not cause the college "any trouble." While acknowledging that "the obligation of restoring the money is a thing that will probably scare the Provincial and General, to all intents and purposes," he wrote to McCabe, "the archbishop has surrendered. The building can be on our ground, and we own it. He doesn't have his dean there to pester us. He can't fire us at will, but only for three specific causes (faulty curriculum, refusal to use approved texts, and an immoral faculty) which we can easily avoid. His control is nugatory. He keeps just enough to save his face, and that really is what he probably was aiming to do." (106)

Notwithstanding Schmidt's favorable review of the archbishop's proposal, in early November McCabe and the St. Xavier Board of Trustees protested against dual management. "If acceptance of dual management is a necessary condition of your Grace's permission and approval of the project and the plans by which the project was to be realized," McCabe wrote to Moeller, "then St. Xavier College must respectfully step aside. . . . I find it impossible to understand why the proposed arrangements concerning the Sisters' Normal School are so unacceptable, when a parallel arrangement has been in operation here at St. Xavier Church since the time the Jesuits first took charge." He pointed out that St. Xavier Church, though owned and operated by the Board of Trustees of St. Xavier College, was "as real a unit of the archdiocese as any other church in the archdiocese, and has an unbroken record of loyalty to the archbishop and devotion to the work for which he stands." He contended that if St. Xavier Church could carry on so successfully, it seemed to him "strange" that the proposed teachers' college, organized under similar conditions, "should prove an element of disturbance, or engender a fear of dissatisfaction or inefficiency at some future time." (107)

The administrative and financial differences between St. Xavier College and the Archdiocese of Cincinnati over the proposed teachers' college were never resolved. Although Archbishop Moeller encouraged the Jesuits to raise the funds and construct the building for the proposed college, he wanted to retain some degree of control over the buildings, faculty, and curriculum. Jesuit authorities balked at the idea. The restrictions upon the college's freedom of operation were in the trustees' opinion too great. When Moeller's proposal was sent to the father general in Rome in 1921 for his consideration, he rejected it. Thus, the college abandoned the idea, at least temporarily, and the summer and Saturday classes for women religious continued as before. (108)

Though the archbishop never approved the Jesuits' proposal for a teachers' college, it did not stop St. Xavier College officials and the Alumni Association from praising him at an alumni banquet in Februay 1924. His support for the eventual removal of St. Xavier College from Sycamore Street to Avondale was very much appreciated. Moreover, they acknowledged his overall accomplishments and for being "the most distinguished son of our common Alma Mater." The Alumni Association then added that for "four score years and more . . . our Alma Mater . . . has instructed our youth in wisdom and truth and the grace of God. She has ever held high the torch of Catholic piety, morality, and culture. She has ever cooperated with the efforts of your Grace and your Grace's illustrious predecessors to spread the light of faith." Moeller responded that he was "pleased with the attitude of sympathy and cooperation which the Jesuits of Cincinnati are showing towards him." Writing to Jesuit officials in Rome later that month, Hubert Brockman, who had succeeded McCabe as president of the college in 1923, pointed out that the archbishop "has not always done what I thought he ought to do and has even taken what might be termed an opposite attitude; but I have been patient with a far eye to ultimate results." (109)

Shortly after John McNicholas's installation as archbishop of Cincinnati in August 1925, President Brockman revived discussion about a possible teachers' college. In late fall he had, in his judgment, "a very profitable conversation" with the archbishop, who appeared receptive to the possibility of erecting a separate building on the Avondale campus for "teacher training." Brockman, who thought the teachers' college "is today . . . more imperative than ever," hoped to elevate the teacher training school, which was largely being conducted in the summer, "from a second class to a first class and on an equal level with the Liberal Arts College." The faculty and administration prepared a curriculum of studies and a schedule of classes for six days of the week, including a day for practice teaching in the parochial schools under the supervision of the superintendent of Catholic schools. "I have from the beginning," Brockman wrote, "spoken only of the necessity of having a first class school both to the archbishop and to the professors. If we are not to have a first class school the Jesuits will not undertake it." (110)

The Ohio Department of Education in Columbus, Ohio endorsed St. Xavier College's proposal. Based on his experience as former president of the college, James McCabe, who was then at Creighton University, interpreted the Ohio department's support as "a good thing." In his judgment "Columbus can hold the whip over reluctant and incompetent churchmen. The schools will be the better for it," he wrote to Brockman in January 1927. While believing that the teachers' college should belong to St. Xavier "and run as an integral part of the institution," he feared, though, that the women religious orders would "establish convents for their sister students out around" the college. He cautioned Brockman to restrict them "to those parts from which the good sisters can't look into our house." In addition to a teachers' college, McCabe thought a graduate school was "absolutely essential." A teachers' college and graduate program, "when fully established and running," he argued, "w[ould] give S[t.]X[avier]C[ollege] an incomparable prestige," and would be, "to my mind, the real FOUNDING of S[t.]X[avier]C[ollege]." (111)

On the last day of March, Brockman, archdiocesan officials, and members of the various women teaching orders met. Though he suspected that the archdiocesan officials were not disposed to turn over any more of the control of the recommended teachers' college than was necessary, Brockman, like his predecessor James McCabe, nevertheless proposed that the college should have control of the finances, since it was "to be responsible for the standards." He recommended "that the school be conducted for a year by way of experiment." Following the meeting, Brockman received letters of support for his proposal from mother superiors in the community.

Two weeks later the state's supervisor of teacher training also endorsed St. Xavier's proposal and urged McNicholas to reorganize the programs for training teachers as conducted by the various women religious orders in his diocese. "It has occurred to me," he wrote to the archbishop, "that a good substantial program of training can be provided through affiliation with St. Xavier College. This institution already is in good standing with various standardizing agencies, . . . and affiliation of training with such a reputable institution would make possible permanence and growth, in which you are doubtless vitally concerned." For a "Sisters' College" to be "successful" and to "get state recognition," McCabe observed, "St. Xavier seems the only hope." The college was already attending to the academic needs of a number of women religious. Among the 134 graduates in 1927, 80 were women and most were nuns. (112)

In early summer, McNicholas approved, "by way of experiment," St. Xavier College's request to open a "Normal School" for the training of women religious. Brockman wasted no time. Three days later he informed the mother superiors that St. Xavier College would be conducting a full-time teachers' college for the preparation of diocesan teachers for elementary grades in compliance with the new state requirements. On September 20 the college opened the school in Avondale, beginning with freshmen and sophomore classes. Tuition was $100 a year. (113)

However, the teachers' college conducted classes for only one year. In the spring of 1928 McNicholas established a teacher training school, called the Athenaeum of Ohio, to educate the members of the teaching communities of sisters, lay teachers, priests, and seminarians, as well as to prepare organists and music teachers in the archdiocese. "[T]he work was so peculiarly a diocesan affair in its purpose," McNicholas wrote to Brockman, "that he thought it could best be done under strictly diocesan auspices." The Diocese of Covington also opened a teacher training school for its religious communities. The teachers in the two dioceses were required to attend their own respective schools. Consequently, sisters' enrollment in St. Xavier's education courses decreased and the college's teacher training program suffered a major setback. (114)

In the fall the college expanded its graduate program by offering, "for the present," Brockman wrote, "only a Master's degree. We anticipate that Education, English and possibly Chemistry will be the Major subjects" in demand. Anticipating a program for the training of principals, assistant principals, and English and science teachers, St. Xavier College now awarded the master of science degree in addition to the master of arts, bachelor of arts, of science, of philosophy, of commerce, and of literature degrees. By the end of the decade the evening school and graduate program had over 350 students with 21 faculty members. The Jesuits almost exclusively taught in the day college, while most of the laymen taught in the College of Law and Schools of Commerce and Sociology. In the first twenty years on the Avondale campus, less than 25 laymen taught in the College of Liberal Arts. (115)

University Status

When Jesuit officials contemplated moving St. Xavier College to the Avondale campus in 1919, they gave some thought to the idea that the college be named a university. But Francis X. McMenamy, S.J., the Midwest Jesuit superior, urged caution. "I should prefer 'Xavier College' or 'Avondale College' to Xavier University until the institution takes on the dimension of a University," he wrote to President James McCabe. "There is a strong feeling against calling a college a university. St. Xavier's is making a fine start towards a university, but I feel we should not burden it with too big a name." (116)

In early January 1922, about fourteen months after the completion of Hinkle Hall, the Alumni Association adopted a resolution in support of a name change. "Be it resolved by the St. Xavier Alumni Association," the resolution read, ". . . that the matter of a change of name of St. Xavier be suggested to the College authorities for consideration and action at some appropriate future time, and that a copy of this resolution be transmitted to the Reverend Rector of the College." About three weeks later *Xaverian News* reported inconclusive results of interviews that the staff had conducted with students, alumni, and faculty about a possible name change for the college. There was evidence that at times Cincinnati residents and visitors to the city confused St. Xavier College with St. Xavier Church, St. Xavier High School, and St. Xavier Parochial School. In February an alumnus recommended to the newly-installed president, Hubert Brockman, that the Jesuits change the name of the school. "Very likely," Brockman replied, "Xavier University will be the ultimate choice. I believe however at the present time that the change should come at the time we are ready to raise the status of the college to a university. I hope the day of this consummation is not far distant." (117)

Sporadically during the next two years the Board of Trustees discussed various possible name choices. Students, faculty, and alumni made several suggestions, ranging from "Dixie University" and "Bellarmine University" to "Sheridan University" and "Fenwick University." Writing in confidence in 1926 to President John P. McNichols at the University of Detroit, Brockman pointed out that St. Xavier "is planning to take the name University with a suitable prefix." However, there was some "reluctance to change" and no consensus could be reached by the trustees. As the college continued to grow physically and in academic stature, eight members of the St. Xavier Foundation in December 1927 reaffirmed the Alumni Association's resolution of 1922. Although they did not recommend a definite name for the university, they suggested that the name St. Xavier College could "be retained for the Classical School." To many alumni, the college designation implied smallness, sectarianism, and perhaps insignificance. Moreover, midwestern Jesuit schools in St. Louis, Milwaukee, Detroit, and Cleveland were universities. (118)

In early 1930, Brockman, on behalf of the Board of Trustees, requested permission from the father general in Rome to change the name of St. Xavier College to Xavier University. He sent a detailed five-page letter, along with newspaper clippings and supporting letters and documents from the Ohio Department of Education, Xavier Foundation, Alumni Association, and Athletic Association. The main argument for the name change was educational. St. Xavier was becoming a multi-school university of the modern American type. The various academic programs in the separate divisions of the school, consisting of the Arts and Sciences in Avondale; Law School, School of Commerce and Finance, and afternoon, evening, and Saturday classes at the downtown campus; and the Jesuit seminary department at Milford, provided a convincing argument in favor of the university designation. Furthermore, the state and regional accrediting associations had been consulted, and all agreed that if the school chose to be called a university the name would be approved. As early as January 1927, the head of the Department of Education in Columbus had complimented President Brockman on the "notable achievement in the steps which you have taken toward the organization of what is virtually a Catholic University of Cincinnati." Moreover, editorials in the local newspapers and many friends of St. Xavier College, including Governor Myers Cooper of Ohio and the former mayor of Cincinnati, Murray Seasongood, supported the name change. According to Brockman and fellow administrators, the change in name would also add prestige to the approaching centenary anniversary of the school in 1931. (119)

On June 4, 1930, St. Xavier College officials received Rome's permission to change the name of the college to Xavier University on the condition that the archbishop of Cincinnati also approved "the change in writing." About six weeks later McNicholas agreed to the name change. On July 31 the Board of Trustees unanimously resolved that the name of St. Xavier College be changed to "XAVIER UNIVERSITY." Four days later, on August 4, by an act of the Ohio Department of Education, St. Xavier College became Xavier University. The following year the trustees changed the wording of the official seal from "Collegium" to "Universitas." Xavier's new status affirmed the meaning of the new school seal that the Board of Trustees had approved two years earlier. Its motto, "Vidit mirabilia magna," "He has seen great wonders," was, in Brockman's judgment, "a good motto for our students, seeking, as it were, great achievements in their lives for the glory of the Faith." (120)

About to celebrate the centennial of its founding, Xavier had much about which to be proud. After a decade of phenomenal growth, physically and academically, the university seemed positioned to reach a higher level of distinction. Indeed, the move from Sycamore Street in downtown Cincinnati to Avondale had given "new life for old St. Xavier." During the next fifteen years, however, the challenges presented by the Great Depression and World War II would greatly test the university.

— 5 —

DEPRESSION AND WAR, 1931–1945

Xavier President Hubert Brockman died from pneumonia on February 12, 1931. President for almost eight years, Brockman had made an indelible mark on the history of the university. The bricks and mortar phase of his presidency produced the greatest physical plant expansion in Xavier's first 100 years. When he took office in 1923 there were three buildings on the Avondale campus. Completion of Elet Hall in 1924 was one of the first achievements during his term. Although the plans and preliminary work for this building had begun before he took office, he helped accelerate the construction process. The Schmidt Library building was next and became an important link in the east campus chain. Schmidt was also home to the seismograph station and Bellarmine Chapel. The $300,000 campaign for a new stadium and the construction of a new fieldhouse at the college were projects to which Brockman gave unstinted service and counsel. Brockman also oversaw the remodeling of the Union House, which was the center for student recreation and dining halls. The Albers Biology Building on the east campus was the last building erected in the 1920s. Under Brockman's leadership, St. Xavier College developed its facilities as well as its academic reputation. Appropriately, the college became a university during his tenure. (1)

On the day of Brockman's death, the university trustees appointed George R. Kister, S.J. acting president. He had been director of Xavier's summer program and former president of Marquette University. On April 23rd, Hugo F. Sloctemyer, S.J., was named president and installed during private ceremonies in Hinkle Hall. A month later he was elected president of the board of trustees.

Sloctemyer at the Helm

Born in 1884, Hugo Sloctemyer, like Brockman, was a native of Cincinnati. He was an alumnus of Xavier where he majored in physics and mathematics. In 1902 he had entered the Jesuit novitiate at Florissant, Missouri. Having a strong interest in geology, he spent several summers in the mountains of the United States and Canada as a member of geological expeditions. He taught physics and mathematics at the University of Detroit School of Engineering and served as dean of men and vice regent of the School of Philosophy at St. Louis University for ten years before being appointed president of St. Ignatius High School in Chicago, a position he held until the Xavier appointment.(2)

"There have been so many vast improvements since my own college days at Xavier," he said at his installation, "that this growth is one of the remarkable features of the institution. It shall be my policy to continue the policies and programs that have made Xavier University a growing institution. . . . There will be no 'sweeping changes' of any kind in the immediate future and it shall be my policy to maintain a program that is for the best interests of Catholic education, for the welfare of our city and for the needs of our growing student enrollment." In his initial address to the students he expressed his deep gratitude to the university. "Permit me to say at the outset," he said, "that I am very happy to be with you. To be detailed to a term of service to my Alma Mater is always a satisfaction to one who has been schooled in the ideals of Xavier." (3)

At the graduation exercises on June 11, 1931, Sloctemeyer delivered a President's Report, the first such report recorded in the annals of the university. In that report the new president renewed the institution's commitment to its Catholic and Jesuit heritage. Emphasizing the 1931 centenary, he said the university offered "herself at the beginning of her second century to the city of Cincinnati and to the surrounding territory as a producer of Christian ideals in youth. . . . She begins the second century with a stout and brave heart, full of confidence in the genuineness of her mission, impelled with the spirit of her founder, my own predecessors in the chair of her Presidents, and the long list of hardworking and self-sacrificing members of her faculty, who have brought the torch of Catholic education, flaming and beautiful, down to the present day as a guarantee of the steadfastness of her purpose and the continued realization of her hopes." (4)

Sloctemyer made special note that after 100 years those specific things that defined and expressed Xavier's Catholic identity continued to be an integral part of campus life. He described how frequent celebration of the Mass for resident and non-resident students, and devotional exercises such as benediction of the Blessed Sacrament and sodality meetings, "enhance the spiritual life of the students." The student's "zeal for the faith and its spread find activation in Mission Club work, in the activities of the Dante Club, the Eucharistic League, the Catholic Students' Mission Crusade, and in other works of a religious nature." (5)

The university's commitment to its Catholic identity and tradition did, however, pose a challenge at times. In the fall of 1931 one person requested that Xavier stop selling meat sandwiches at the Friday night football games. At the time the Catholic Church forbade Catholics to eat meat on Fridays. In that person's judgment, the practice of serving meat on Fridays was "disedifying and scandalous, smacking of compromise and indifferentism." The Athletic Council took up the issue. The "consensus of opinion," a member of the council wrote, "was that we should not attempt to regulate the morals of our patrons. . . . It is true that the affairs are held on the grounds of a Catholic institution but it must also be remembered that only one of our six local opponents [is a] Catholic college," and the other five opponents had "followers who not only are privileged to eat what they please, but who also would probably ridicule us if we tried to prevent the sale of such things as 'hot dogs,' etc." He viewed it as a minor matter. "I would hesitate being a party to any action," he wrote to President Sloctemyer, "that would attempt to regulate this matter as it smacks too much of Methodism and the policies of the Anti-saloon League." Agreeing with the Athletic Council's interpretation of the situation, Sloctemyer did not intervene. (6)

By the time of its centenary, Xavier's enrollment had grown and its academic reputation was strong. In the fall of 1930 and 1931, enrollment in the day school was 470 and 469 students respectively, a marked increase from 1929. Total university enrollment in the centennial year was 1,339. In addition to the 469 in the College of Liberal Arts, there were 493 in Education, 332 in the Schools of Commerce and Finance, and 45 in Law. For the fourth straight year the university had been singularly favored in having won most-outstanding ranking in the combined Latin and English contests held among Jesuit colleges and universities in the Midwest, in which several thousand students participated.

This was an enviable record, and as Xavier continued to excel in these competitions it demonstrated the high standing of academic work in the classics and English. Throughout much of the decade the university also had orientation lectures each Tuesday for freshmen. The academic dean gave the September lectures on aspects of college life. The other lectures dealt with various professional careers. The administration and faculty were hopeful that these lectures would assist the students in planning their careers. (7)

The university also continued to offer evening courses in the downtown School of Commerce and Finance on Sycamore Street. Business and cultural courses were offered at convenient hours for approximately 400 men and women. It provided technical training in such business courses as accounting, economics, commercial law, advertising, business English, and salesmanship. Moreover, since 1927 the university had offered business courses for day students on the Avondale campus. The faculty and administration thought prospective students in the college "who contemplate a business career, or . . . wish . . . to acquaint themselves with the intricacies of modern business methods" would find the courses beneficial. In 1931 the university conferred its first degrees of bachelor of science in commerce. (8)

The summer sessions and the late afternoon and Saturday classes at the university continued to show a steady growth in enrollment and in course offerings. This extended program met a much-needed demand and afforded an opportunity for teachers in area elementary and secondary schools and academies to pursue their academic and professional training and to earn college degrees. Whereas Xavier faculty and area professionals taught the classes on Saturdays and late afternoons, during the summers the administration also hired a few faculty members from other Jesuit colleges and universities to teach some of the courses. (9)

During the academic year 1930–1931, the Crosley Radio Corporation, based in Cincinnati, hosted a series of ten- to fifteen-minute lectures over station WLW in commemoration of the university's one hundredth birthday. The centennial celebration had begun with the graduation exercises the previous June. Over fifteen speakers participated in the radio broadcasts. President Brockman introduced the series, followed by nine academic addresses, among which were such topics as "An Unpublished Hawthorne Diary," "Church and Evolution," and "Going to the Theater." During the winter months of the same year the Alumni Association sponsored a course of scholarly lectures in the Mary Lodge Reading Room of the Walter Seton Schmidt Library. (10)

The university during its centenary year witnessed growth in its academic programs and continued to sponsor various social and cultural activities and events. The band continued to perform, mainly during the football season, and the Clef Club did artistic work throughout the year. In the climax to the successful 1931 season, the club appeared in a concert with the Mount Saint Joseph's College for Women at a hotel in downtown Cincinnati. The Musketeer Orchestra, the newest of Xavier's musical organizations, entertained at many university functions. The X-Club, working with the student council, helped elevate student perceptions and attitudes about "the honor there is in wearing the University's initial letter." In 1931 the Xavier Masque Society produced eleven plays. The Dante Club made presentations at 40 different venues in Ohio, Kentucky, and Indiana, focusing on the lives of heroes and heroines in the Catholic Church. In February of that year, the university established the Mermaid Tavern, a literary society. Limited initially to thirteen students of high scholastic rating and literary ability, the members of the society discussed English literary masterpieces at their meetings. (11)

At the dawn of its second century the university's needs were "many and various," Sloctemyer wrote. "The most pressing of them," he thought, was "the establishment of an endowment fund, which will make more secure and stable the physical and scholastic progress of the university." Though the economic depression dampened his and the university's enthusiasm, "Xavier is more than willing," he said, "to await the coming of better opportunities to accept the philanthropies of her many friends and well-wishers." (12)

Teacher Training, 1931–1934

In 1931 the university's teacher training program had a small enrollment. The diocesan college, the Athenaeum of Ohio, had taken its toll on the university's program. However, that fall there appeared to be some sign of hope. The Ohio Department of Education again encouraged both the Archdiocese of Cincinnati and Xavier Univeristy to join forces. In November the associate supervisor of teacher training in Ohio wrote to Father Francis J. Bredestege, the archdiocesan superintendent of schools, and hoped that within a year there would be a "single Catholic teacher training agency . . . in the Cincinnati area." He urged officials at the Athenaeum and Xavier to "cooperate" in this effort. (13)

On the evening of December 10, Sloctemyer and Archbishop John McNicholas of Cincinnati met. "I found his Grace," Sloctemyer wrote, "very willing to discuss the matter." Though McNicholas continued to think that teacher training should be essentially diocesan in nature and should be handled by the authorities of the diocese, he saw "great difficulty in their handling it" and saw it as a "great financial burden" to the archdiocese. On the other hand, the Cincinnati ordinary also argued "that the establishment of a teacher training department on the Xavier campus would also be frought with difficulty." Convinced that the diocesan teacher training program was "not a success" and was "noted for its disorganization and general inefficiency," Sloctemyer was hopeful that the work could "be done [at Xavier] efficiently under a system of joint control." The president's optimism, however, was unfounded. The archbishop remained committed to the Athenaeum and its teacher training program. (14)

Notwithstanding McNicholas's decision, Sloctemyer and the archbishop maintained cordial relations. Sloctemyer regarded the local prelate as a "great friend." Writing to Paul L. Blakely, S.J., editor of *America* magazine in 1932, he pointed out that "[w]e get along famously and I have made every effort to cooperate with him in everything. . . . He and I have much to do with each other and seem to get along well together." Earlier that year at a dinner McNicholas had acknowledged publicly that the Jesuits "had done marvellous work" in Cincinnati "in building up a strong Catholic body." In particular, he recognized "the immense debt the diocese owed to the Society of Jesus by educating so very many of its Priests" and that Xavier University "had saved the diocese hundreds of thousands of dollars in bearing the expense of higher education for a century." (15)

At the beginning of the fall semester in 1934 there were only three students enrolled in the university's teacher training school downtown. The dioceses in northern Kentucky and in Cincinnati continued to mandate that women religious orders send sisters to their own respective diocesan training colleges. "This is particularly distressing for, if left to their own choice," Sloctemyer wrote to a colleague at John Carroll University in Cleveland, "they would flock to Xavier. They are, however, not left free and so the difficulty remains both for them and for us." By the end of September, Xavier officials decided to discontinue the teacher training program, and the three remaining students were sent to the Athenaeum. Though Sloctemyer thought the decision was a "logical one," the university continued to offer "liberal arts courses among which," he wrote, "we shall include our usual number of educational courses." (16)

As the university continued to provide a few graduate English and education courses to teachers in the community, women religious in northern Kentucky requested a more extensive graduate program. In early May 1934, sisters at the St. Anne Convent in Melbourne, Kentucky, and the local superior at the provincial house in Covington, wrote to Sloctemyer, requesting that Xavier sponsor summer graduate courses. The new Kentucky School Code required teachers to have a master's degree in order to obtain a certificate to teach in the elementary grades. "You are aware, no doubt," Mother M. Lucy, superior at the St. Anne Convent wrote to Sloctemyer, "that the latest rulings . . . demand . . . an M.A. degree for teachers in the Grades." (17)

Xavier faculty and administration, however, could not oblige under such short notice. "I referred the matter of starting a graduate school to a committee about a month ago," Sloctemyer wrote a few days later to the superiors of the three women religious orders in northern Kentucky, "and they returned the verdict that the time was entirely too short to successfully plan and prepare for a work of such importance. The provisions for a permanent graduate school personnel and policy, the securing of adequate library facilities and the gathering of a capable faculty," he argued, "are quite out of the question for the coming summer." He further pointed out that if a graduate school "is to be begun it must be begun on such a high scale of scholarship as to command the respect of the educational world. To begin a weak school would be of no consequence neither to the students nor to our own institution." University officials decided to consider inaugurating a graduate school at a later date and, if they were to do so, to start it "on a solid basis." In the meantime, they continued to offer a few graduate courses in English, education, and chemistry. (18)

The Athletic Issue and North Central Association

The growth in the 1920s of intercollegiate athletics, and football in particular, generally increased public interest in American colleges and universities. Football games inspired considerable enthusiasm from potential donors, increased public support and visibility, and kept many alumni in touch with their respective institutions. All too often it

appeared, as one historian noted, that "the basis of that sense of kin-
ship and allegiance had less and less to do with academics, and more to
do with an institution's ability to field a winning team." (19)

Xavier's 1931 athletic teams continued to be competitive in the
major sports of football, basketball, and baseball. Starting with the
1930–1931 basketball season, the success of the Musketeers, behind
the coaching of Joe Meyer and then Clem Crowe, helped elevate the
profile of basketball at the university. The attendance at games "was a
hundred percent greater," Sloctemyer wrote, than the previous year. In
football Xavier gained momentary national recognition in the fall of
1933 when it played Indiana University, the first appearance of a Big
Ten football team in Cincinnati, and won 6–0. Though outweighed
twenty pounds to a man, the excited homecoming crowd witnessed the
Xavier team outgain its opponent 150 to 105 yards rushing and 103 to
64 yards passing. Earlier that year the Xavier University stadium had
been fitted with lights to permit the playing of football at night.
"Prominent lighting engineers have observed," Sloctemyer noted
proudly, "that the Xavier Stadium is better lighted for such playing
than perhaps any other stadium in the country." The university was
also becoming more competitive in track, tennis, and golf. Xavier's
intramural sports program also became more complete, organizing
leagues that were properly supervised in various team sports as well as
conducting tournaments in such individual sports as handball, tennis,
dart, and golf. "Practically every student enrolled in the University," it
was noted, "competed in some sport during the year, may[be] in two or
three." (20)

Indeed, athletics figured prominently in the Jesuits' general education of students. For close to "a century," Sloctemyer said in 1931,
reflecting on what he thought were the sentiments of past Jesuit administrations, Xavier officials "have felt that sports are the expression of
one of the most refreshing and humanizing of human interests. Athletic
competition tends . . . to raise the standards of intellectual life at the
University [and] . . . to increase the high mission of the University." In
addition to developing muscles, cultivating good team spirit, and incul-
cating sportsmanship, "[s]ports here," Sloctemyer argued, "are truly a
part of an educational career. . . . Play, relaxation, spontaneity, and the
mental nourishment of games round out the life of the Xavier collegian." Insisting that intercollegiate and intramural sports at the
university should not be "susceptible to commercialism," he further
argued that they "are so worked out as not to be corrupted." (21)

However, early in 1933 Sloctemyer questioned the practices of the Athletic Council, more particularly its granting of what he called "athletic scholarships." The council sponsored a grant-in-aid program for athletes and took care of the recruiting, scheduling of games, and maintenance of the athletic stadium. Having complete charge of the finances of the athletic department, which included setting the price of admission and handling the gate receipts, it bought the uniforms and paid the coaches' salaries, all at virtually no cost to the university. In mid-February Walter Schmidt, who chaired the Athletic Council, responded to Sloctemyer's inquiry and insisted that no "scholarships were given to athletes." Rather, payment was made "to a number of men for work done." In his judgment it was a "serious injustice to discriminate against a student merely because he is an athlete and that is the policy towards which you are tending." He further argued that in terms of tuition it "seems distinctly unfair," the former St. Xavier College quarterback wrote, "to rule out a better class of men from receiving help because they are red-blooded enough to wish to enter into athletic competition." (22)

In the summer Sloctemyer inquired further into the council's practices. More specifically, he expressed concern over Xavier's methods regarding the preseason try-out period for football athletes and the distribution of money to them. He wanted to ascertain that the university complied with the rules of the North Central Association (NCA), which required that football candidates be admitted first as students in the institution before any try-out. Xavier had been a member of the accrediting organization for eight years. "I fear," Sloctemyer wrote to Henry Bunker, a member of the Athletic Council, the "consequent action of the North Central Association, if they find out that these try-out periods were held. I believe that the [Athletic] Council should assure itself that this system will not endanger the position of the school with the Association." While urging that candidates be instructed to send their credits to the university registrar for approval before being told definitely to come for the try-out, he also insisted that the try-out period be limited to ten days. "In case of difficulty with the North Central," he wrote, "we can say that the fitness of the boy as a student was determined before his qualifications as a player. It is good practice independently of the North Central. The boy comes here as a student first." (23)

Sloctemyer's concern over the profile of the student athlete was a high priority for him. He strove "for a well-balanced athletic program," he wrote in a report to the university community, "which will assist studies and not retard them." His concern was not his alone. Four years earlier Daniel M. O'Connell, S.J., dean of the College of Liberal Arts, had written a letter to President Hubert Brockman regarding the football team. In addition to being critical of the long evening practices of the football squad on the field that interfered, in his judgment, with their studies, he expressed concern over their academic status. "Unless we are going to have a further distinction between athletes and other students, something must be done," he wrote. "As it is, we distinguish between them on eligibility. We demand 32 hours a year and 32 points ("C") from the other students and only 24 hours (without points) from the athletes. In fact, some athletes have not the last qualification." (24)

Sloctemyer also thought there were "serious difficulties" regarding the method of distributing the money to the athletes and the payment to the university. It appeared that members of the coaching staff had made some of the boys, especially those who received financial assistance, work harder on the field. "Remarks were made with very bad effect both upon those who were being assisted and those who were not," he wrote. He also contended that the system had kindled "the spirit of commercialism . . . and the [p]ossibility of dishonesty in the use of money given to players for expenses." Furthermore, he was concerned over the council's tardiness in attending to the students' bills. He emphasized that the university could "not board and lodge these boys for the greater part of the year without being recompensed fairly promptly." The Athletic Council had worked out a tuition and room and board discount for student athletes. The athletes' bills were sent regularly to Walter Schmidt who then paid them with the proceeds of the athletic department. If the amount were not sufficient, the university bore the "temporary expense." Though Sloctemyer understood that the Athletic Council during the economic depression was hard pressed for funds, the university's "finances are in a more desperate condition now than ever," he argued, "and I fear a total collapse of the athletic activities if we can not get ourselves out of this hole." (25)

Moreover, the president issued an additional requirement. He stipulated that "[n]o Non-Catholics are to be invited to attend" the preseason try-out. "Catholic boys," he argued, "are in many ways preferable to Non-Catholics. The reasons are evident. We fear the possible results of a few 'bad eggs' in the dormitory. It takes too long to learn them. In the meantime much harm may be done." In the absence of Walter Schmidt, Henry Bunker turned over Sloctemyer's letter to Art Leibold, vice chairman of the Athletic Council. "We feel certain," Leibold wrote to Sloctemyer four days later, "that your wishes in this matter will be faithfully carried out by those in charge." (26)

In February 1934, almost a year after Sloctemyer's initial inquiry into the practices of the Athletic Council, the North Central Association informed him that an official visit by them would be necessary if Xavier University wished to remain on the list of accredited schools. NCA officials had decided to visit private institutions that experienced budget constraints and had a small endowment. In addition to Xavier, among the Jesuit schools to be visited were Loyola in Chicago, John Carroll, and the University of Detroit. Xavier University then operated at an annual deficit of $30,000 and its endowment was less than $300,000. The two examiners visited the campus in early March. (27)

Though generally complimentary of the educational programs, they pointed out that a "careful examination" of academic grades showed "a markedly skewed distribution towards A and B in a majority of the courses." They recommended that "this condition should receive the careful attention of the administration." The evaluators' concern was consistent with the Jesuit provincial's request, a few years earlier, not "to give grades above eighty-five percent to . . . more than one-third of the students in each of their classes." In light of the NCA recommendation, the faculty discussed the matter at great length at the fall general faculty meeting. Nevertheless, the grade inflation issue persisted. Five years later John J. Benson, S.J., dean of the College of Liberal Arts, still insisted "that the grades in general were too high." In his judgment, compared to American public and private institutions "Xavier was on a higher level according to its grade distribution." He urged each faculty member "to make a self-examination in the matter of grading." (28)

But the more critical point of the North Central Association examiners' twenty-two page report, five pages of which dealt with athletics, criticized the administration of athletic activities. In particular, they expressed concern over the university's policy regarding the admission of student athletes. However, notwithstanding their concern they recommended to the NCA Board of Review that Xavier "remain on the accredited list." Less than a month later, on April 17, upon the request of the members of the Board of Review, Sloctemyer appeared at their spring meeting in Chicago. The board focused exclusively on Xavier's athletic program. Concerned over the potential gravity of the student athlete issue, they informed Sloctemyer that they would send a consultant by train to Cincinnati that evening for a second and more focused examination. Following his one-day visit on campus, the consultant concluded "that athletes are being favored financially at Xavier University and that the athletic eligibility standards as announced in the bulletin of the University are not being enforced." Three days later the Board of Review recommended dropping Xavier University from the list of accredited institutions because of the "athletic situation." The next day the NCA Executive Committee officially removed Xavier from its accreditation list, arguing that the school and faculty "did not exercise sufficient control and direction of . . . athletic activities." While both Loyola and John Carroll weathered the site visits successfully, Xavier and the University of Detroit, which was on the verge of bankruptcy, did not. (29)

Losing accreditation, which had been Sloctemyer's fear for over a year, was a serious matter. Shocked by the news, the faculty and administration expressed specific concern over the future status of graduates applying to medical school and graduate programs. A distinct advantage of membership in the North Central Association was the fact that academic credits earned were mutually recognized without examination by member colleges. Concerned over the university's public relations and future enrollment, Sloctemyer immediately tried to soften the news of Xavier's expulsion from the NCA. "[A]s far as entering or graduating students are concerned," he said in the *Catholic Telegraph* on May 1, "there will be no effect whatever. As you know, this institution has been given first-class rating scholastically and it is to be hoped that whatever difficulties are thought to exist in the conduct of athletics will be cleared within a short time. . . . Xavier's whole record," he argued, "is of such outstanding merit that it is not conceivable that any school would underrate us for whatever is conceived as out of order in our athletic situation." (30)

About three weeks after the NCA decision, Raymond Walters, president of the University of Cincinnati, confirmed Sloctemyer's suspicion. He assured him that the NCA ruling would have no bearing on the admission of Xavier students to post-baccalaureate programs. "Graduates and students of the College of Liberal Arts of Xavier University," he wrote, "will be considered for admission to the graduate, professional, and other colleges and schools of the University of Cincinnati on the same basis as in past years." Shortly thereafter Xavier officials issued a press release. "We understand that the credits of the graduating class of this year will be recognized," the release read, "and the University should have no difficulty, if it so desires, in obtaining readmission before the end of the ensuing scholastic year, so that none of the students need be concerned. However, a stigma has been placed upon the good name of Xavier which it is our intention to see removed." (31)

Though encouraged to protest and appeal the Board of Review's action, President Sloctemyer was convinced that the NCA "will not change its decision. . . . It becomes," he noted, "a matter of moral certainty for them and a denial of the same for us." Nevertheless, the university drafted a lengthy protest and, as Sloctemyer had predicted, it had "no effect upon them." About the same time, the president, writing to a colleague in late May, noted that the "excitement about our North Central difficulty has considerably subsided. We are laughing about it now since there does not seem to be any particular disadvantages for us in not being of their number. We are sure of having our better students accepted, without examination, into any schools to which they may care to go." (32)

At first Sloctemyer and a number of Jesuit colleagues at the university were reluctant to implement the changes necessary for Xavier's readmission to the North Central Association. The changes, as required by NCA, meant the abolition of the Athletic Council and dismissal of the members who had devoted so much of their time, effort, and finances, not only for the athletic program but for many other university programs. The Athletic Council's chair, Walter Schmidt, was the principal benefactor for both the library building and the fieldhouse. By mid-December the university consultors unanimously recommended postponing Xavier's "application for readmission for one year." Four days later, however, Charles Cloud, S.J., Chicago provincial, urged the university "to make an attempt to apply *this year* for readmission." In early January the Xavier administration complied with Cloud's wishes and sought readmission. (33)

In late February, upon receipt of the university's readmission application, the North Central Association sent another two-person team of examiners to the campus. Prior to their arrival, Sloctemyer had met with the faculty and outlined the steps the university had taken toward "gaining readmission." Thinking that the Athletic Council had "directed its own interests entirely" far too long, he established a five-member Board of Athletic Control, consisting of four Jesuit faculty members and one layman from the Department of Economics. The president authorized the new board to determine the athletic policies of the university and to execute them through working committees under the direction of its chairman, Terence Kane, S.J. "THE DELIBERA-TIONS OF THIS BOARD," he emphasized in capital letters, "SHOULD BE KEPT ENTIRELY CONFIDENTIAL BY EACH MEMBER. THIS IS A NECESSITY." Sloctemyer also added, without the power to vote, two lay consultors to the board. They were Walter Schmidt, chair of the old Athletic Council, "as one who is intimately connected with the athletic history of the University," he wrote, and Coach Joe Meyer, because of his familiarity with the university's athletic relations. Moreover, Sloctemyer, with the approval of the board of trustees, initiated a change in the role of the Athletic Advisory Council, formerly the Athletic Council, and in the selection of its members. To show confidence in the members of the former Athletic Council, as well as to lessen criticism of his new directive, Sloctemyer appointed all of them to another year of service on the newly-established Advisory Council. The faculty, who had complained about the previous athletic practices, were pleased with the new regulations. (34)

In early March, the NCA team, upon review of the new athletic administrative structure, finances, faculty, instruction, student services, physical plant, and athletic program recommended that Xavier be accredited. Shortly after the second NCA team had completed its visit, Xavier University received a new president. Sloctemyer, who had been in ill health for some time, had completed the normal three-year term for Jesuit rectors in the spring of 1934, but continued to serve until the appointment on March 10, 1935, of Dennis F. Burns as the university's twenty-sixth Jesuit president. Burns arrived on a Sunday morning and the announcement of his appointment by the father general, Wlodomirus Ledochowski, S.J., was made at a private ceremony in the Jesuits' dining room preceding the evening meal. Two weeks later he was elected president of the Board of Trustees. Educated at St. Ignatius College in Chicago, Burns received his B.A. and M.A. degrees from St. Louis University, entered the Jesuit order in 1908, and was ordained to the priesthood in 1922. (35)

In early April, Xavier's newly-installed president attended the spring meeting of the North Central Association Board of Review. The NCA directives were clear. Burns faced the situation coolly. All athletic finances were to be integrated in the university's budget and all athletic receipts, expenditures, and accounts were to be handled by the treasurer. In this manner, the faculty and administration of the university would exercise greater control of athletics. Upon satisfactory review of the university's new regulations, which were consistent with the NCA directives, the North Central Association readmitted Xavier. In mid-April, Henry Bunker, a member of the former Athletic Council, congratulated Burns "on the successful termination of the North Central matter. We are all most happy." That spring the University of Detroit also regained its accreditation. (36)

Shortly after the university received the official word from the North Central Association, Burns called a meeting of the Athletic Advisory Council. Ten members attended, including Walter Schmidt. He informed them of the NCA directives and the university's new regulations. The first comment by a council member at the meeting questioned "the right of the North Central" to impose such regulations. Interpreting it as "an asinine remark," Burns pointed out that university officials "were not sitting in judgment on the North Central, that we have to remain in that association, and that we mean to live up to the regulations." Though some of the members concurred with the NCA ruling, most of them were unhappy with the new regulations. Throughout the meeting, Walter Schmidt "appeared 'flabbergasted,'" Burns later wrote to the provincial, "but gave no indication of hostility." (37)

Twelve days after his meeting with the Athletic Advisory Council, Burns learned from Schmidt himself "that he had assembled the [former] Athletic Council" without any of the Jesuits present. Burns disapproved of Schmidt's action. The former chair of the Athletic Council explained to Burns that "the impression the Athletic [Advisory] Council got from [the] first meeting was that they were being put out, that it was 'another ecclesiastical move,'" and that though Burns was "nice and gentlemanly," they were convinced that he was sent to the university "to do away with football altogether" and that he was appointed president because he "was at Loyola when football was dropped there!" When Burns explained that there was no foundation to these allegations, Schmidt "again seemed quite satisfied," Burns wrote to the provincial. His read of Schmidt's reaction, however, would soon be proven wrong. (38)

The following evening three other Athletic Advisory Council members called on Burns, and they, too, apparently left satisfied. "Candidly," he wrote to the provincial on May 14, "I believe a few ringleaders among them are trying to bluff us out of the stand we have taken, hoping they will be able to continue with the old policy of the past. . . . I intend to leave nothing undone to keep the goodwill of all our alumni and friends, but not at the sacrifice of our new policy." In subsequent meetings, Burns, who regarded the athletic situation as his "biggest problem," his "bête noire," made it clear that the Board of Control would directly handle all athletic matters and that the Athletic Advisory Council was not to proceed as it had in the past. (39)

In the summer, the controversy over the administration of athletics at the university escalated. Walter Schmidt criticized more strongly and openly the new arrangement. "It looks to me," he wrote to Burns, "as though this whole situation is headed for a nasty mess, which will have serious repercussions on not only the Athletic activity, but upon the Institution and the Jesuits." Though he acknowledged that it was "the perfect right of the college to operate its Athletic affairs as it sees fit," he argued that unless the council was "fired with enthusiasm and the feeling that it has some place in the picture, possesses your confidence and some measure of authority in its work, . . . I fear that trouble is in store for Xavier and for your administration." More specifically, he feared that "the whole Athletic program will collapse and the work of a great many years go for naught, either because the Institution will be forced to discontinue Athletics entirely, or go so far downward . . . that they would have better been entirely discontinued." In response, Burns reiterated the obvious, namely that the faculty and administration were required to "direct and control" athletics. (40)

On August 20, Burns wrote to all the former members of the Athletic Advisory Council who had served as chairmen of various committees of the council and thanked them for their many contributions. He then invited each one to continue his activities under the supervision of a newly-appointed faculty moderator. That same day the *Cincinnati Times-Star* reported an "Athletic Shake-up at Xavier," editorializing that the suspension of Xavier by the North Central Association "was a lot of poppycock." It argued that the university had not "indulged in over-emphasis" in athletics any more than "the majority of its slightly-too-sanctimonious brethren. . . . A few months ago, the North Central Association . . . restored Xavier to good standing. Everybody congratulated everybody else, but behind it all," it continued, "was the impression of the faculty, men more interested in creating good citizens than in creating good halfbacks, that, after all, athletics, particularly football, might be deflated somewhat. From now on, the dope has it, Xavier's athletics will be directly under the faculty, with little, if any, interference brooked from the old grads. A new Athletic Council may be appointed, but if so, it will be purely ornamental." (41)

The following day, Burns, who was supported fully by the faculty, sent a letter to the alumni, encouraging them to support the football activities of their alma mater. He saw "no reason why an alumni body as numerous as that of Xavier cannot make sure that the spirited representatives of their school this fall will not play to empty or half-empty stands." Notwithstanding Burns's public statements in support of the athletic program, some alumni assumed incorrectly that the proposed changes in its management would mean a downgrading of athletics at the university. The situation was exacerbated by the resignation in October 1935, in the middle of the football season, of Joe Meyer, football coach and athletic director. He thought the university's new athletic policy would weaken the football program. In an effort to generate letters of protest to the faculty, football supporters had sent letters to alumni groups and to the Cincinnati newspapers, expressing dissatisfaction with the changes in Xavier's athletic program. Burns became known as the football "hatchet man," since it was alleged that he had been president of Loyola University in Chicago when it eliminated football. However, Xavier's Alumni Association soon learned that this allegation was false. In fact, Burns had actually been teaching at St. Louis University. Through all this, Burns became more convinced that "the real trouble-makers in this whole business" were the members of the former Athletic Council "who still resent our taking over control, especially of the athletic finances." (42)

In mid-October, Burns wrote a letter to the provincial, describing Coach Meyer's incident and the alumni letters to the newspapers. Waiting until "the smoke of 'battle' cleared," he wrote, "I really believe we are on the right road to setting our house entirely in order. . . . You will be glad to hear that the [reactions] have been most favorable to Xavier. In fact outside of a mere handful of disgruntled alumni . . . everyone is very outspoken in telling us that it is the best thing that ever happened at Xavier." Burns also had a bit of good luck—the football team went 6 and 3 for the 1935 season, and 5 and 5 the following year. That seemed to silence some of the critics that the new changes in the athletic program would spell the end of football at the university. During the next five years, however, financing of the athletic program and the status of athletics both continued to decline. Since the fracas over the NCA directives and new university regulations, there were fewer alumni supporting athletics. (43)

Notwithstanding negative comments on the university's focus regarding athletics, more particularly football, in December 1937 a committee of Cincinnati citizens requested that the University of Cincinnati enter into athletic relationships with Xavier University. Since 1927 the two schools had scarcely competed in sports. For example, after the initial basketball game between Xavier and Cincinnati in 1928, they had not played each other again. In late fall the council of the city of Cincinnati had passed a resolution requesting that "athletic relations in the way of competition in football, basketball, golf and baseball should be resumed and entered into at as early a date as possible between Xavier University and the University of Cincinnati, all in the interest of co-operation and for the good of both educational institutions and for the benefit of the citizens and taxpayers of this city." The Xavier Board of Trustees declined the request, arguing that "in view of the reorganization of the Athletic Department of the University and the appointment of a new football coach, it does not seem advisable to enter upon such relationship at this time." (44)

The following year, when athletics lost $18,000, President Burns and the university consultors considered dropping intercollegiate football. However, that "would probably mean closing Elet Hall," the consultors' minutes read. They thought "it would be extremely difficult, if not impossible, to induce enough out-of-town students to come here" and reside on campus if there were no football. Two years later athletics were "[f]inancially worse off . . . than [in 1938]," consultors noted, and they hoped to find a "possible way of winning back friends lost five years ago." They voted to continue football, "but at no greater expense." (45)

In January 1940, the city extended another offer to Xavier University to play the University of Cincinnati in sports. This time Xavier officials responded positively. The improvement in relations between Xavier and its two neighboring universities helped change the trustees' opinion. In 1939, Burns had given an address at a faculty and student convocation at Miami University in Oxford, Ohio, and had presented the invocation at the June commencement at the University of Cincinnati. Times had changed. Two decades earlier Archbishop Moeller had discouraged Catholic leaders from attending events at the University of Cincinnati, fearing that would "compromise" their position.

Shortly after the city's appeal to President Burns, two businessmen and friends of Xavier University approached him about the possibility of arranging a football game with the University of Cincinnati in the fall. They recommended that "part of the proceeds" be used to help "liquidate the debt . . . on the [football] stadium." Then they pointed out that aside "from any direct profit we might make from the game by taking a percentage of the gate, it would be to the advantage of the school to form athletic relations with U.C." The Xavier consultors agreed on the condition that the "school derive some direct profit to help pay the expense of the team, about $5,000." Gradually, in the 1940s, Xavier University and the University of Cincinnati resumed their rivalry and these games became, as the *Cincinnati Enquirer* later noted, "city 'classics.'" (46)

In the early 1940s, the Xavier University administration and faculty remained committed to intercollegiate and intramural sports. They were acutely aware that these programs added a valuable dimension to a Jesuit education and helped enhance the image of the school in the community. "[A]thletics does advertise a school and creates interest in the school," a Jesuit faculty member observed in 1941. "The growing publicity and increased interest in this year's basketball team is a good example." He was also pleased that the basketball program was finally "paying for itself . . . he first time I witnessed that." The team's 1940–1941 record was 13–9, compared to 6–17 the previous year and the football program also realized "a net profit . . . of over 7,000 dollars." (47)

By early 1943 Xavier's policy regarding athletics at the university was made abundantly clear. The athletic program was "for the whole student and the whole student-body," the policy read, which meant "that the program of intercollegiate athletics must not be developed to the exclusion of a representative intra-mural program." University officials then charged the athletics department with the development of a physical program for the entire student body. (48)

The Great Depression and the University

During the Great Depression of the 1930s the financial condition of American colleges and universities suffered. Capital spending disappeared almost entirely. From 1931 to 1933 faculty salaries declined by around 15 percent and across-the-board institutional cuts were prevalent. Alumni giving also declined. However, higher education overall suffered less during the depression than did many other social institutions. Few institutions closed. Between 1934 and 1936, among the 1,700 colleges and universities 31 closed and 22 merged. Nevertheless, within most institutions of higher learning, including Xavier, there were continuing fears of impending financial disaster. (49)

Xavier University consultors and trustees had numerous meetings dealing "with economies and retrenchment." At the time of Sloctemyer's appointment in 1931, Chicago provincial Charles Cloud, S.J., urged him to "look into the financial situation . . . as soon as possible. It must not be that another deficit should be incurred since the debt has already become large. You must find ways and means of curtailing the expenses to such a point," he said, "that the income will more than care for them." That year Xavier had an operating deficit in excess of $20,000. Cloud feared that the financial problems of the various universities and colleges in the province would increase as the Depression continued. "You must make it plain to all those who are in charge of the administration at Xavier," he said, "that expenses must cut down below the revenue if disaster is to be averted." (50)

In the fall of 1931 the administration reduced faculty and administrators' salaries by 10 percent and reduced the number of lay professors in Avondale from 17 to 9. The university discharged the director of intramural athletics and instructed Coach Joe Meyer to "take full charge" of the program. At the time "[a]ll students" were expected "to participate in some form of intramural athletic activities." The university saved money by holding the annual junior prom in the reading room of the library, rather than at a downtown hotel, and reduced expenses by discontinuing the baseball team. It raised money by renting the fieldhouse to organizations for events, including a dog show on one occasion. By 1938, the university, whose tuition was already the lowest among American Jesuit colleges and universities, had to reduce its student activity fees as well. The reduced annual fees were $6 for university athletics, $5 for intramural, $2.50 for library, $1.50 for the school's newspaper, $1 for the Debating Society, and $.50 for the Masque Society. There were also lower food prices in the cafeteria. For thirty cents students could buy a lunch that included a choice of meat, two vegetables, bread and butter, and a choice of beverage. (51)

During President Hugo Sloctemyer's first year in office, Cincinnati's archbishop urged his pastors to recommend Xavier and other Catholic institutions of higher learning in the archdiocese to Catholic high school students. Although Xavier's enrollment was fairly stable in the early years of the Depression, the administration expressed concern over enrollment in the subsequent years. In the fall of 1932 total enrollment decreased by 124 students and university officials discussed the possibility of "admitting coeds" at the undergraduate level. They decided not to pursue the matter, however, because of their concern that increased competition for female admissions might negatively effect the financial welfare of the existing Catholic colleges for women. As an enrollment strategy the newly-installed president, knowing that the institution needed "students badly," suggested an "Inspection Day" when prospective freshmen could visit University facilities. The administration chose a Sunday afternoon at the end of May as "a suitable time" for the classrooms, laboratories, fieldhouse, and dormitory to be opened to give the "young men a chance to see what Xavier can offer." In his 1932 Presidential Report Sloctemyer noted that the University, "with its customary resourcefulness of spirit and energy. . . , goes forward with the hope that the dawn of a new day is not far distant and that with the coming dawn will arise new opportunities for service to the youth of this community and surrounding territory." (52)

Despite their concern over low enrollment, Xavier officials maintained the University's policy against admitting blacks. Throughout the 1920s and into the 1930s most Catholic colleges and secondary schools in the country were racially segregated. When in the fall of 1928 two "colored gentlemen" applied to take classes in the School of Commerce they were denied admission. In the fall of 1931 Father Leo Walsh, pastor of Holy Trinity Chuch – a parish newly dedicated to work among black people in the lower west end of Cincinnati –, submitted the applications of "two high type colored students," according to the consultors' minutes, but the University denied them admission. They noted that the University's charter, issued before the abolition of slavery in 1865, "specifies 'white.'" Though some Jesuit universities like Detroit and John Carroll admitted black students, Xavier consultors voted down a proposal "that colored boys be admitted at Xavier as a 'policy' not to exceed 10%." The consultors, aware that the University had resident students from Kentucky and the South, argued that "Xavier at this crucial time," cannot risk losing, say, 50 students." (53)

University officials continued to explore ways to reduce operational expenses. During the 1932-1933 academic year the consultors also discussed plans for refinancing the University's debt and asked the provincial's permission "to float one large loan to wipe out present floating indebtedness." That year Sloctemyer established for the first time in the University's history an advisory finance board of five laymen. "I must again insist with you," the provincial wrote, "that you must be absolutely relentless . . . in cutting down every expense until you are sure that you are able to meet all your obligations." Because the University had again experienced a deficit, Cloud warned that "[a]t that rate complete ruin and closing of Xavier faces you." He urged Sloctemyer to "be absolute in the elimination of every deficit. . . . So please use all your authority to bring things into proper shape." At some point, he thought, the university may have to consider "bankruptcy." A few days later Sloctemyer and his consultors declared the university's "financial situation [as] desperate." Not only was "[m]aterial expansion . . . quite impossible under the present circumstances," the president wrote, but "serious limitations" were placed upon budgets, ranging from curtailing activities in various departments to not sending "any Christmas cards." (54)

Throughout the Depression, the university had an annual operating deficit ranging from $20,000 to $40,000, which meant that certain budget restrictions were required. For example, the university was unable to provide sufficient "offices for the professors." While the university's total enrollment in the fall of 1932 had decreased by 124 students, full-time enrollment in the College of Liberal Arts had remained steady at 466. A year later enrollment increased by about 10 percent to 514: 422 students at Avondale and 92 at Milford. That was the largest enrollment ever in the day school. That same year there were 828 evening students. The university's total enrollment had increased by 137 students over the previous year. The related increase in tuition revenue helped temper the deficit crisis. Xavier's increase in full-time enrollment was in contrast to the 8 percent decline in enrollment nationally from 1932 to 1934, but in keeping with the overall increase in attendance at Catholic colleges. Hoping to sustain and increase Xavier's enrollment, some of the Jesuits patronized activities and canvassed students at some of the Catholic high schools. (55)

In light of Xavier's annual operating budget deficit, the provincial's strong warning, and economic uncertainties posed by the Depression, the university reviewed professional programs in the evening division. Even though in 1933 Sloctemyer took pride in the fact that the College of Law was "making a substantial contribution to the legal life of the city," a year later he and the trustees terminated the program for academic and financial reasons. Neither the American Bar Association nor the Association of American Law Schools would grant recognition to any school that offered law classes only in the evening. Faced with uncertain financial conditions and the administration's unwillingness to invest additional resources in the professional program, the trustees decided not to open a day division of the Law School. In addition, university officials discontinued the School of Sociology.

The university limited its evening course offerings to liberal arts, commerce, and finance. For students in the commerce course of studies, the faculty and administration started a cooperative program, in which a twelve-week period of employment followed a twelve-week classroom period. To assist students enrolled in the School of Commerce and Finance evening classes, in 1934, the university appointed Florence C. Albers dean of women. Albers, who had earned her bachelor's and master's degrees at Xavier, was the first woman admistrator in the history of the university. She served as dean for sixteen years. In the summer of 1935, school authorities moved the evening division from Seventh and Sycamore Streets to the St. Xavier Commercial School building south on Sycamore Street, between Fifth and Sixth Streets. By 1935, Xavier's academic organization consisted of the College of Liberal Arts, the School of Commerce and Finance, day and evening divisions, the Milford Novitiate for the training of Jesuit scholastics, and the downtown division of the College of Liberal Arts that conducted Saturday morning classes and a summer session. Through these units, the university granted the following degrees: bachelor of arts, of literature, of philosophy, of science, of commercial science, and master of arts and sciences. (56)

In an effort to address the annual operating budget deficit, the university introduced new fiscal strategies. In 1936, when interest rates were lower, with the help of its advisory finance board, the university refinanced its $280,000 loan, negotiating a rate reduction from 5 percent to 4 percent. Shortly thereafter it initiated the Dads Club, Xavier's first annual fund-raising program. To "foster relationships which may be helpful," President Dennis Burns wrote, and "to better the financial condition of the university," at the end of the decade the trustees appointed an "Advisory Board of Prominent Laymen" to advise the university on "business matters." University consultants took comfort in the knowledge that the alumni were "making an impression in the community. . . . Many 'bigmen' in the city," the consultants' minutes read, "are X.U. grads." (57)

The increase in overall enrollment, from 1,163 students in 1936 to 1,409 in 1938, was not enough to eliminate the annual operating deficit. The university was unable to hire all the additional lay faculty members it needed, especially for business courses in the School of Commerce. On the main campus there were 27 Jesuits and 11 lay faculty members, hired mainly to teach mathematics, modern languages, and the sciences, while downtown there were 7 Jesuits and 24 part-time lay faculty.

In January 1939 the faculty and administration again expressed the need for "more teachers, 2 in accounting and 2 in economics." About one-third of the students were enrolled in these courses. Though authorized initially to recruit two faculty members in economics, Burns "invited" the School of Commerce "to pass on the hiring of . . . new teachers for economics." However, the consultors reallocated $5,600 they had saved by not renewing the contracts of two non-business faculty and hired two lay faculty members in business, stressing the need "of good men in the C[ommerce] & F[inance] course, which has now the largest enrollment." (58)

Campus Life in the '30s

At the beginning of the decade the university required all resident students to attend daily Mass. Though it was not compulsory for commuter students, each Catholic student was expected to attend Mass in his home parish. Traditionally the university canceled the first class on the first Friday of each month to allow all students to attend Mass as a group. By 1934 each grade level had an appointed day in which its members attended one of the three daily Masses in the Elet Hall chapel. The administration monitored attendance of resident students at daily Mass until 1940. At that time faculty supervision ended and approximately one-third of the student body attended daily Mass voluntarily. (59)

The 1930s were characterized by worldwide activist movements. Xavier students began to perceive themselves and the university as a microcosm of that larger reality. As their perceptions shifted, students became more involved in the political and ethical issues of the day. A good example of that was the politicization of *Xaverian News*, the student newspaper. In 1936, Xavier students founded the Jesuit College Newspaper Association as a means of promoting Catholic doctrine and social action in their opposition to communism, neo-paganism, and "materialistic education." Xavier became the headquarters for the twelve-member association, and *Xaverian News* was a leader in the transformation of school newspapers into a "more elaborate medium for Catholic action."

Inspired by Pius XI's 1929 encyclical *Mens Nostra,* a large number of Catholics in the 1930s became identified with the Catholic Action movements. Catholic Action members committed themselves to more fervent religious practice, a study of Catholic doctrine and social principles, and community engagement. In 1937 the editor of the student newspaper, now called *Xavier University News*, stated that the paper's mission was "to urge a campaign for Catholic social action on the campus, and to reflect an atmosphere positively and unmistakably representative of a Catholic college." To many Xavier students, the university's Catholic and Jesuit identity was of extreme importance. (60)

Other student organizations became attentive to social action and sought to counter the threats of the modern world with an authentically Catholic perspective. The sodality, which had been apolitical throughout its history, argued for the rights of African Americans, supported the Catholic Worker Movement, opposed atheism and communism, and engaged in a study of America's "unethical monetary system and its administration." Even the Dante Club and Masque Society became more closely associated with the propagation of Catholicism. The former now identified itself as an "influentially Catholic group with a distinctively Catholic ideal" while the Masque Society took pride in the performance of *Father Malachy's Miracle*, considered "the best in Catholic drama." In 1936 another student group was formed to attend to political and religious realities of the period. The Marian Brigade, a national crusade of prayer among Catholic students against the growing menace of communism, sought to combat it through prayer to the Blessed Virgin Mary and helped prepare students to engage in street preaching. (61)

With an eye to increasing enrollment, the board of trustees approved President Burns's recommendation that the university apply to the U.S. Army to establish a Reserve Officers Training Corps (ROTC) program for the young men on campus. On December 27, 1935, the War Department approved the application, and in the fall of 1936 a contingent of Battery B, 19th Field Artillery from Fort Benjamin Harrison in Indiana arrived on campus to inaugurate the ROTC program. It consisted of Major A. M. Harper, commanding officer, two other officers, and eight non-commissioned personnel. For three years the university even provided rent-free lodging to the commanding officer, until the house was needed for teachers' use in 1939. (62)

The ROTC program became mandatory for all new undergraduate day students. Although upperclassmen enrollment was voluntary, a poll indicated that 78 percent of the student body planned to enlist in ROTC. The program consisted of five hours of class and drill work per week for all physically fit freshmen and sophomores. Successful completion of the advanced course of the program qualified the candidate for a second lieutenant's commission in the Officers' Reserve Corps.

In addition to their academic and military duties, the cadets performed other functions. In January 1937, when the Ohio River flooded, some cadets assisted at relief centers throughout the city, while others supported the Red Cross and National Guard relief work. Two years later the university, under a contract with the Civil Aeronautics Authority, established a new student pilot training program at the Cincinnati airport. In two years' time, 108 students had graduated from the program. (63)

Looking ahead to the 1940 centennial anniversary of the Jesuits' arrival in Cincinnati and seeking ways to celebrate its Jesuit identity, the university in April 1939 established a local chapter of Alpha Sigma Nu, the national honor fraternity for students of Jesuit colleges and universities. The following spring, Cincinnati Jesuits began celebrating their local centennial, as well as the quadricentennial anniversary of the 1540 founding of the Society of Jesus. In April they presented a pageant of that 400-year history at the Taft Auditorium on Fifth and Sycamore Streets. At the alumni Mass on September 22, Monsignor Fulton J. Sheen of New York gave the sermon, which was broadcast over two local radio stations. A week later the university celebrated both anniversaries with a Mass in the Schmidt Memorial Fieldhouse. Archbishop John McNicholas of Cincinnati delivered the sermon. In late November, university officials closed the Centennial Jubilee with a dinner at the Netherland Plaza Hotel in Cincinnati. Over 1,400 guests attended at $1.50 each. Among the special guests who gave talks were James A. Farley, former U.S. postmaster general, Governor John Bricker of Ohio, and Mayor James Garfield of Cincinnati.These funds helped reduce the budget deficit and capital debt. The university raised approximately $60,000 during the centennial year. (64)

In the midst of the celebration on August 26, 1940, Burns tendered his resignation as president of Xavier University. That day Celestin J. Steiner, former vice president at the university succeeded him. During Burns's five-year term, the university accomplished much. In addition to being reinstated in the North Central Association and investing control of athletics with the faculty and administration, the university established the Dads Club, installed an Army ROTC unit and a Civil Aeronautics Authority pilot training program, and saw its overall enrollment increase by about 25 percent, from 1,241 to 1,577 students. (65)

Born in Detroit, on February 7, 1898, Steiner attended the University of Detroit and entered the Society of Jesus in 1918. He studied in the United States, as well as in England, Belgium, France, and

Holland, where he was ordained to the priesthood. He returned to the United States in 1933 and was assigned to Xavier University. He served variously as freshman counselor, general director of student activities, and later vice president. In 1937 the provincial appointed him president of St. Xavier High School. Three years later the forty-two-year-old Steiner returned to Xavier University as its twenty-seventh Jesuit president. A year into his presidency he suggested "that this might well be made a 'test year' regarding the possibilities of increased enrollment and of academic expansion." He hoped to make Xavier a more renowned "liberal arts" institution with a quality faculty and bigger enrollment. However, Dean Benson of the College of Liberal Arts soon informed him that the entrance requirements were "lower for Xavier than any other [Jesuit] college in the Chicago [and] Missouri Provinces." (66)

The idea of establishing a full-fledged graduate school at Xavier had been discussed for over a decade, and an ad hoc Jesuit committee had already done some preliminary investigation into the matter. Steiner, however, considered undergraduate academics the chief university priority and thought the launching of a graduate school posed several problems. In addition to the problem of admitting women in graduate studies on campus, it "would involve [financial] increments," Steiner said, "in a . . . number of academic departments, . . . in the (first-class) faculty, [and] . . . in the library." He doubted that the university, which then had a $20,000 deficit, could find the funds to finance the additional expenditures. The new president advised that a clear definition of the university's position "is needed, since we cannot continue as we are, losing every year." Concurring with Steiner, a trustee suggested that the university should "[g]o slowly" on this matter. In the meantime, the university consultants, echoing Steiner's sentiments, proposed making "Xavier a first-class liberal arts college."

At the time there were 37 faculty on the main campus, with Benson as dean, and 19 in the downtown division, with John C. Mallow, S.J., as dean. There were faculty members in Evanston who also taught in the downtown school. At the Milford division, where students pursued advanced courses in Latin, Greek, English, modern languages, history, and also courses in Hebrew, philosophy, pedagogics, and public speaking, there were 10 faculty members, with Allan P. Farrell, S.J., as dean. (67)

Early in his presidency Steiner made clear that in order for Xavier to become a first-class liberal arts institution, teaching and scholarship mattered the most. While not opposed to faculty members taking "an active part in civic life," they were expected to be "scholarly professors, . . . experts in the classroom in imparting information and inspiring our boys." In an address to the faculty, Steiner employed unmistakable terms, saying that the university's "first duty is clearly to our class-room," giving "our boys our best in and out of the classroom." Being judged "first and foremost by students and alumni, . . . [w]e must make that our masterpiece." Once that first duty was met, "we place our-selves, our time and talents . . . where there is [the] greatest need always in the interests of Xavier." (68)

The University and World War II

On Sunday December 7, 1941, Japan attacked Pearl Harbor. That event not only changed the course of history for the nation, but also the focus and direction of Xavier University. Like most other colleges and universities, Xavier began adapting its educational programs to the national war effort. In early January, President Steiner attended a con-ference of representatives from the army and navy, the Selective Service Board, the National Resources Planning Board, and the U.S. Office of Education. After retuning to campus, he held a general faculty meeting to discuss plans for an accelerated program that would make it possi-ble for students to graduate before they reached the draft age of twenty years. Before the end of the month, the university offered additional courses as well as Saturday classes for seniors and juniors, and made plans for an extended summer school program. Through the evening division it also offered an accelerated program in mathematics, modern languages, and economics for students interested in government serv-ice. Though a poll conducted in 1939 by *America* magazine had indi-cated that 97 percent of Xavier students opposed the United States entering the war in Europe and that 78 percent would not volunteer to serve if the country went to war, Japan's attack on Pearl Harbor instantly changed students' attitudes. (69)

By March 1942 approximately 150 former students and alumni were serving in the war. In addition to the regular academic and ROTC classes, that spring the university had a Civilian Defense program. Xavier students and volunteers from the Hamilton County Defense Corps used university facilities to prepare for their participation in the war effort. On May 29, Xavier officials sponsored a ceremony at the football stadium for the more than 6,000 graduating members of the corps. (70)

Despite the war, in the fall of 1942 the university experienced a record enrollment on the Evanston campus. Among Xavier's 592 day students, 129 were resident students. About two years later some of them lived in a new university residence, acquired in the fall of 1943, on Marion Avenue, across Victory Parkway on the west side of campus. Three hundred forty-five of the day students joined the Enlisted Reserve Corps. Among them were 135 freshmen, 69 sophomores, 74 juniors, and 67 seniors. Only three seniors and five juniors were not members of the corps. In January, at the end of the fall semester, students enrolled in the corps were called to active duty. (71)

That same month, the consultors, at their regular Friday meeting, discussed "the future of the University in consequence of events owing to the war." The departure of students for active military service had its effect on enrollment. Only about 300 students were registered for the second semester, which was a decline of over 250 students from the fall semester. The university suffered the effects of the war. The new draft law, which now affected eighteen-year-olds, would take most of the returning students. Increasingly concerned about the welfare of the institution, Steiner and his consultors became convinced that the university would have to get a contract with the federal government or close its doors before the end of the academic year. Government officials had already proposed possible contracts to schools and universities for the use of their facilities in training young recruits for the army and navy before being shipped overseas. Steiner strongly recommended that the university get started by securing lodging "so as to be ready when the government asked our aid and offered a contract." (72)

By the middle of the month, Steiner officially offered the university as a site for a government training program. "It appeared," Steiner informed the university community, "that it was either getting a government contract or closing" the school. On January 30, 52 seniors graduated in the school's 103rd commencement, the first mid-year graduation in the history of the institution. Four days later the United States Army Air Corps selected Xavier to train cadets. On the first day of March, 260 cadets of the 30th College Training Detachment (CTD) aircrew from Maxwell Field, Alabama arrived. Xavier was among the first 281 colleges approved by the armed forces for cadet instruction.

A contemporary later recalled that the aircrewmen "debarked from the shuttle buses cold, tired, hungry and uneasy in a strange new surrounding. It was late afternoon and they assembled outside the college dining room in the snow and slush, waiting for orders to file in for their first meal at Xavier. No situation was better calculated to make friends for Xavier," he continued. "They were marched, single file, into the warm, cheery dining room, where they had a choice of wonderful food, served on china, and they sat down to tables covered with tablecloths." That year the university also offered the Army Specialized Training Program (ASTP). (73)

To accommodate the influx of cadets, the Jesuit priests, brothers, and scholastics vacated Hinkle Hall. Some moved to the Marion Avenue residence, now called Marion Hall, some went downtown to St. Xavier High School, and a few rented nearby homes. The second contingent of 250 aviation students arrived on April 1 and began classes four days later. All told, the detachment numbered about 500 trainees. Half of them lived in Hinkle Hall and half in Elet Hall. Cadets remained four to five months on campus. The university operated the cafeteria in the Union House as an army mess hall. The cadets and the few civilian students danced to the music of the jukebox and enjoyed the bowling and other recreational facilities in Union House. (74)

Shortly before the arrival of the second unit of cadets, the university had found other facilities for the civilian students housed in Elet. It obtained quarters at the Fenwick Club, a Catholic men's residence downtown. There the Xavier students, with two Jesuit priests in charge, had a section of the building to themselves. They had at their disposal a chapel, a large social hall, reading room, swimming pool, gymnasium, and other athletic facilities. Breakfast and the evening meal were taken at the Fenwick and lunch was served on campus. For the convenience of the students, the university—at its own expense—arranged for transportation to school in the morning. A special bus waited at their door to take them directly to the campus. "The only real inconvenience," Steiner wrote to the parents in March 1943, "[was] the distance from the Campus," which was about a fifteen-minute ride from the city. He further assured them that "[n]o matter how long the war lasts, Xavier will always provide a Jesuit home for its out-of-town students." (75)

Xavier provided the aircrewmen, who wanted to be pilots, navigators, or bombardiers, courses in physics, mathematics, history, geography, and English. Victor Stechschulte, S.J., who taught physics, oversaw the academic program. In addition to the cadet accommodations on the Xavier campus, courses in navigation, meteorology, civil air regulation, and dual flight instruction were taught at the Cincinnati airport in Sharonville, north of the city, and at Lunken Field, east of the university. "We were in class constantly," Marty Goldfarb, a 20-year-old air corps cadet later said. "The Jesuits taught us all they could. They were very good to all of us. . . . We had physical training two hours every day. Father Raymond Mooney, a tough but very gentle man, used to run us through our paces. By the time we left Xavier, we were in great shape, which was necessary for combat."

The army divided the trainees into groups of one hundred, so that when a group finished and left, another one hundred arrived. In addition to supervising physical training, Mooney, as auxiliary chaplain, also coordinated religious services for the Catholic, Protestant, and Jewish cadets. A faculty member later recalled: "We were quite busy under a rigorous program directed by Fr. Stechschulte. . . . [O]ne of the big thrills that I shall never forget," he said, "was to see in early morning, from the second-story window of Albers Hall that overlooks the Hinkle Hall terrace, the fine young cadet unit marching in cadence from Elet Hall on its way to classrooms in Albers, and bursting into 'Xavier for Aye' as it approached Hinkle Hall." The CTD, known for its precision marching, was in constant demand for public demonstrations. Concerned that the marching cadets might cause traffic problems in neighboring Avondale and Evanston, Cincinnati's city manager convinced Steiner that at night the cadets should carry a number of lanterns as a precautionary measure. The predominate number of aircrewmen utilized almost all of Xavier's facilities. (76)

On July 11, 1943, four months after the arrival of the first contingent of aircrewmen, the university dedicated the Shrine of Our Lady, Queen of Victory and Peace to the Xavier men serving their nation. Located in front of Alumni Science Hall, it became a favorite campus spot for Sunday afternoon snapshots. Everyday at noon during the month of October, the student body, including cadets, gathered at the shrine for the recitation of the Rosary. The special intention was to maintain "a union of prayer with X-men in the service throughout the world." (77)

In the fall the university enrolled 94 civilian students in the day college: 4 seniors, 7 juniors, 21 sophomores, 59 freshmen, and 3 unclassified. This was a decline of 47 students, or 33 percent, from the previous semester. The war, as predicted, had taken its toll. The evening division remained on the regular semester plan, but the College of Liberal Arts in the day division adopted the trimester plan, with sessions beginning in July, November, and March. During the next years only a few student organizations continued to accommodate the smaller student population. The Student Council, Philosophy Club, Biology Club, and Mermaid

Tavern were reorganized and continued in operation. Though the administration discontinued the *Xavier University News* and *Musketeer Yearbook*, it initiated a mimeographed newsletter entitled *Xavier News: A Student Publication*, first issued on September 19. For eighteen months, the newsletter, published close to two dozen times, went out to the men overseas in the military camps, as well as to some other members of the Xavier family. All told, its distribution included approximately one thousand men in the service, the civilian student body, the air corps trainees, the alumni, alumnae, and some friends of the university. Moreover, members of the Mermaid Tavern sent *Tavernews* regularly to the graduate and undergraduate members of the student organization in the military. The Xavier Choral Group, war-time successor to the Clef Glee Club, made its first public appearance in the fall of 1944. (78)

In accordance with the university daily order and rules, during the war years students rose at 7:30 a.m., had breakfast at 7:50, lunch at 12:50 p.m., dinner at 6, studied from 7:30 to 9:00, recessed 9 to 9:30, and got ready for bed by 10:45. All students attended Mass on Sundays and Holy Days. Daily Mass and frequent Communion were "strongly recommended." The first Friday of each month was monthly Communion day for all. On regular study nights no student could leave the premises after 7:30 p.m. Before attending academy meetings, glee club practices, or other activities, each student had to check his name, cite reason, and record the time of return in the office of the prefect. On Friday, Saturday, and holiday evenings that were not followed by a class day, students could stay out until midnight. On Sunday and on holidays followed by a class day a student had to be in by 8:00 p.m. unless he received the rarely rewarded prefect's permission to remain out until 10:30. Students were forbidden to have any "OBJECTIONABLE pictures" on the walls. Obscene pictures or books, drunkenness or the possession of intoxicating liquor, and gambling were causes for dismissal. (79)

During the course of the war the university sponsored special events to support Americans in battle, as well as for peace in the future. Students curtailed several campus social events as they focused on the war effort. They sponsored a "Red, White, and Blue Dance" to collect defense stamps and took part in a scrap drive competition with the University of Cincinnati. As a consequence, the Xavier football practice field soon became covered with golf clubs, refrigerators, safes, tires, stoves, furnaces, and automobile parts. Xavier collected 70 tons of scraps, 6 tons more than its counterpart, and used the $1,792 in proceeds to purchase war bonds. On a Sunday afternoon in early October 1943, more than 7,000 persons gathered in the Xavier fieldhouse, which had been converted into a cathedral for the St. Francis Peace Day observance. Archbishop John McNicholas of Cincinnati delivered an address on "America's Peace Aims." Alumni Homecoming, the Booklovers Library benefit party, and the Dads Day event, which in previous years were scheduled as separate fall functions, combined to sponsor a card party and dance at a local hotel in downtown Cincinnati in November. A radio broadcast, which originated at the hotel, transmitted a salute from the assembled guests to Xavier men in the service in Europe and in the southwest Pacific. By beaming the salute all around the world, Xavier officials identified the broadcast as the university's "first Universal Xavier Day." (80)

The war also took its toll on Xavier athletics. Military regulations prohibited CTD and ASTP cadet participation in intercollegiate sports. In the summer of 1943 the football coach, Clem F. Crowe, had to recruit his 28 players from approximately 80 civilian students, most of whom were sixteen or seventeen years old and under 200 pounds. With the exception of a few sophomores who were trying their hand at playing college football for the first time, all were fresh out of high school. Not a single member was from the 1942 team, and only 13 had previous experience. Notwithstanding the limitations, Xavier's decision to continue with an intercollegiate sports program met with excellent public response. The *Cincinnati Post* sports editor in his August 24 column pointed out that the university was "doing something very noble indeed. The men in charge at Xavier didn't have to put themselves to all this trouble. They could have taken the easy way out like a lot of other colleges did by simply announcing: 'We quit football.'" The university appeared to be fulfilling a promise made about nine months earlier by Steiner when he informed the guests at a football banquet "that so long as 11 students remained at Xavier there would be a football team." That fall the football team scored only one victory in its seven-game schedule. (81)

Upon the recommendation of the Xavier faculty board of athletic control, the end of the 1943 football season also marked the end of all intercollegiate athletics at the university until after the war. Though Steiner had pledged that the university would continue intercollegiate athletics as long as there were enough students interested in joining the teams, the impact of the draft made it highly improbable that the civilian student body would be sufficiently large during the coming fall and winter semesters to provide teams in either football or basketball. The few civilian students were not capable of supporting a full and competitive athletic program. Shortly after the football season ended, the university granted Clem Crowe, athletic director and head coach of both football and basketball, a leave of absence to join the coaching staff at the University of Notre Dame for the duration of the war. (82)

In late March 1944, the army announced that it would withdraw all air corps men from Xavier by June 30. "What do we do now?" Steiner asked his consultors. "Shall we wait for, hope for an armed service program, and meanwhile plan nothing else?" The Jesuits agreed not to "move back into Hinkle Hall until [they] were absolutely sure that [they] would not get an armed service program." The enrollment problem remained acute. During the 1943–1944 academic year the university, with a faculty of 28 Jesuits and 21 laymen, most of whom taught part-time, awarded only thirteen degrees from all its divisions. "It is with regret," Steiner said, "that Xavier views the closing of the Army Air Forces Base." If unable to secure another armed service program, a majority of the trustees thought they should take seniors from St. Xavier High School. (83)

Following the exodus of the air corps unit from Elet Hall, 14 day students moved into the first floor. When classes began in the fall, there were approximately 75 students in the day school and around 800 part-time students downtown. Only two laymen, Richard Garascia in chemistry and William Marcaccio in physics, taught in the day division. To compensate for the departure of the cadets, as well as to make use of the facilities on campus, the entire senior class of 148 students of St. Xavier High School moved to the Evanston campus. Though the transfer of the senior class helped relieve crowded conditions at the high school, Jesuit authorities at St. Xavier High School, the provincial wrote, "helped the university." While the students remained under the care of the high school officials, the university provided the teaching. The two schools adopted the same arrangement the following year. (84)

The air corps men remained on campus sixteen months until June 30, 1944. Upon termination of the CTD program in late September, the Jesuits returned to Hinkle Hall. In all, the university educated and helped train 1,808 military personnel before they moved on to active duty in western Europe, North Africa, the Pacific Rim, or southeast Asia. "We feel confident," Steiner said in his farewell address to the remaining air corps men, "that we have given them something of the

Xavier spirit and that we have adequately provided for them an important phase in their training.'" In the process the university had grossed approximately $150,000 each five-month period, which helped sustain the institution, as Steiner and the trustees had hoped, during the war years. (85)

In the summer and early fall of 1944, Xavier officials began preparing for the postwar period. In June an academic committee, which had deliberated throughout the month of May, submitted to President Steiner recommendations that anticipated the needs of high school graduates, discharged service men, and adults who wished to further their education. In addition to providing a curriculum reflective of its Jesuit tradition, it proposed a two-year course in industrial chemistry that would prepare analysts for industrial plants, factories, and hospitals; special courses in physics including electricity, radio, and meteorology; courses in business correspondence and report writing, advertising, salesmanship, journalism, accounting, economics, typing and shorthand; and pre-college courses for veterans of adult age who wished to complete high school work and qualify for college entrance. (86)

That same summer, Xavier authorities, confident in the university's future, built new entrance gateposts that flanked University Drive at the Dana Avenue entrance. The fieldstone and the design harmonized with the stone construction of the O'Brien Terrace and the Memorial Shrine. Large bronze lamps surmounted the gateposts, and bronze tablets on the sides identified the buildings on the east campus. In the fall the university opened the Labor School, under the directorship of Richard T. Deters, S.J., minister of the Jesuit community, as part of the Institute of Social Order for the study of labor-management problems. "The purpose of the Labor School," Deters wrote, "is to train honest, upright, forceful, and truly progressive labor leaders, men who know their rights and duties and who are prepared to face their problems with understanding and a sense of justice." It offered courses in a variety of subjects ranging from labor ethics and labor legislation to the history of organized labor and principles of economics. There was no tuition charge and the teaching staff worked without salary. The faculty, consisting of four Jesuits, a Dominican, and four laymen, taught the courses two evenings a week. (87)

In January 1945 the U. S. Maritime Commission named one of the new victory ships in honor of Xavier University. It was one of several vessels named after colleges and universities that went into service during the year. The Alumni Association donated a plaque and an aerial photograph of the university to be displayed on the new cargo ship, named *S.S. Xavier Victory*. Before its launching at Richmond, California on the evening of March 7, 1945, Dan H. Heeking, an alumnus and naval lieutenant stationed at Berkeley, California made a presentation. "May the *S.S. Xavier Victory*," he said, "sail safely and triumphantly as a unit of the greatest fleet in the world and may the men of her crew know the same spirit which inspires the men of Xavier whose motto is 'All for One and One for All.'" (88)

After surviving the Depression years and with the end of the war imminent, Xavier University cautiously began planning for a brighter future. Under the leadership of Presidents Sloctemyer, Burns, and Steiner, the university had successfully cleared academic, athletic, and financial hurdles, and now it anticipated a more promising era.

PART III

A MODERN UNIVERSITY 1945–1990

Introduction

At the end of World War II the United States was one of the most powerful nations on earth. Released from the grip of the Depression, the country's population and economy continued to expand. During the four decades after World War II Americans witnessed the beginning and end of the Cold War, the demise of the Soviet Union, an aging population, increased participation in education at all levels, more women in the work force and higher education, and more children being reared in single-parent homes. It was also a period of mass higher education, as enrollments, finances, and institutions expanded. Indeed, changes in American higher education in post-World War II America need to be considered in the context of the massive readjustment in society. (1)

In the 1960s and 1970s social and political tumult raged across America and confrontation and interchange between differing ideas and values dominated our culture. Women's rights, concern for the environment, racial justice, and a desire for peace became part of American mainstream consciousness. When Pope John XXIII convened the Second Vatican Council in Rome in 1962 no one could foresee its impact on the Catholic Church and its influence on society. In particular, Vatican II helped reinvigorate the role of the laity in the church as well as in American Catholic higher education. As a new ecclesiology replaced the authoritarian and clerical concept that had traditionally prevailed in American dioceses, a new model of authority, which included greater participation of lay people, also emerged in most Catholic colleges and universities, including Xavier.

In the wake of World War II federal legislation exerted considerable influence on higher education. One of the most influential was the Servicemen's Readjustment Act of 1944, more popularly called the GI Bill, provided educational benefits to veterans of the armed forces. In 1950 the Housing Act provided loans to construct college residence halls. The 1958 National Defense Education Act authorized loans and fellowships for college students and funds to support foreign language study. The Higher Education Facilities Act of 1965 provided grants for several types of college services, including libraries and undergraduate programs, and construction of facilities. (2)

Stimulated by the new federal legislation and the population increase of the postwar baby boom, American colleges and universities experienced an expansive cycle of enrollment and physical growth throughout the 1950s and 1960s. Higher education became available to more and more students. Before World War II access to American higher education had been more a privilege than a right. That changed after the war. In 1960 about 40 percent of all high school seniors were being accepted into college. By 1970 it was 52 percent and by 1990 it reached approximately 61 percent. This was quite a contrast from the early 1900s when only about 2 percent of young people between the ages of eighteen and twenty-four went to college. (3)

A consequence of this growth was the creation of the multiversity, a larger and more complex university enrolling 25,000 or more students. These unprecedented enrollment levels contrasted sharply with the college population before World War I, when only a handful of colleges enrolled as many as two thousand students. In the wake of World War II there was a faster pace of growth among public institutions. Student collegiate registrations increased from 2,000,000 in 1946 to 8,500,000 in 1970, 2.1 million of which were in private schools and 6.4 million in public institutions. Enrollment in Catholic colleges and universities jumped from 450,000 in 1970 to 609,000 in 1980. Xavier University's growth was equally significant. Its total enrollment increased from 1,625 in 1945 to 4,115 in 1960 and 6,680 in 1990. (4)

From the end of World War II to 1990 the trend toward secularization in higher education was evident. More than 600 public institutions were opened. 500 of them were two-year colleges. 650 private institutions were started, but half as many closed, for a net gain of 325. The percentage of public institutions increased from 35 to 44 percent of the total number of colleges and universities, while enrollment in public institutions went from 49 to 79 percent of the total student population in American higher education. The greatest competition for students was within the private sector. In order for many private colleges to survive or fare better, many of them began offering graduate or professional programs. To accommodate the increasing enrollment in the graduate professional programs in education and business administration, Xavier University established a Graduate School in 1956 and a College of Business Administration in 1961. By 1968 the University enrolled more graduate students than undergraduates. At that time Xavier's graduate program was the fourth largest in Ohio and third among the 28 Jesuit colleges and universities. Some institutions, in the process of emphasizing professional programs, diluted their traditional undergraduate core of study. Xavier, however, revitalized its traditional Jesuit undergraduate curriculum and established the Honors Bachelor of Arts program, with intensified courses in Latin, Greek, and philosophy, in 1948, and the University Scholars program, a more general honors course of study, in 1975. (5)

During this period Xavier, like most American colleges and universities, experienced unprecedented new facility construction. The ROTC Armory, completed in 1949, was the first new building on campus since the erection of the Albers Biology Building twenty years earlier. The Thomas J. Logan Chemistry Building and Hubert J. Brockman Residence Hall were built in 1954. Eight new buildings were constructed during the presidency of Paul L. O'Connor. S.J., (1955-1972). These additions—Karl J. Alter Classroom Building (1960), St. Robert Bellarmine Chapel (1962), University Center (1965), Harry J. and Edna D. Husman Residence Hall (1965), Walter A. and George McDonald Memorial Library (1967), George H. and Rose Kuhlman Residence Hall (1967), George J. Joseph Building (1968), and Walter E. Schott Memorial Building (1970) – constituted the biggest building phase in the history of the University. During the tenure of President Robert W. Mulligan, S.J., (1972-1982) the University erected the Paul L. O'Connor Sports Center in 1976 and the College of Business Administration Building in 1981 and also acquired two acres of property, between Ledgewood Avenue and Victory Parkway, in 1979, and 19.8 acres in Norwood, a community east of the campus. The new acquisitions, along with the 1980 acquisition of Edgecliff College, formerly Our Lady of Cincinnati College, provided new educational opportunities for the University.

Another startling change in Catholic higher education in the 1960s was the rise of the laity within the ranks of faculty, administrators, and trustees. Previously, religious communities and bishops had directed Catholic higher education seeking little or no consultation with laypersons. In 1960 members of founding religious communities were predominant at their respective institutions. Thirty years later they constituted a minority among faculty and administrators. This shift had a dramatic impact on religious identity at many Catholic colleges. The predominance of lay men and women in Catholic colleges by 1990 meant that the relationship of the institutions to the Church no longer had the clear canonical character that prevailed under the care and governance of religious communities. Post-Vatican II Catholic colleges and universities more often articulated the character of their institutions in terms of ecumenism and collegiality rather than with such phrases as "education for service to family and church" or "formation in Christian values." (6)

Boards of trustees, comprised of an increasing number of lay men and women, assumed greater control of Catholic institutions. In 1972, Xavier University ended its 130-year-old tradition of strictly Jesuit governance by electing six laymen to the board of trustees. By 1990 the Chicago province of the Society of Jesus and the University trustees, a majority of whom were lay persons, approved a sustaining agreement, by which the University became separately incorporated. The board of trustees, which had legal control of the properties and policies of the University, accepted the responsibility of sustaining the Catholic and Jesuit character of the institution.

In the 1960s the mission statements of Catholic colleges and universities were almost interchangeable, emphasizing a commitment to liberal arts, character formation, and a campus community rooted in the Catholic faith. As the institutions sought to improve their status in the academic world, there was an increasing attempt to professionalize the faculties. More and more Catholic universities, including Xavier, gradually embraced secular academic standards and distinguished themselves in American higher education circles by caring about the level of advanced degrees and scholarly publications of the faculty. Xavier also established new vice presidencies that significantly changed its administrative organization. (7)

As Xavier experienced significant growth between 1945 and 1990 it also increased its tuition. From 1946 through the 1970s, tuition increases in American colleges and universities averaged slightly more than the rate of inflation. By the 1980s the situation changed. Tuition increased nationally much more rapidly than either inflation or family income. In the 1980s the median family income increased by 50 percent whereas tuition in public and private institutions rose by almost 90 percent. At Xavier tuition jumped from $150 per year in 1945 to $2,990 in 1980 and $9,000 in 1990. (8)

During this period the University witnessed other significant changes. It discontinued compulsory participation in the Reserve Officers Training Corps Program in 1969; terminated intercollegiate football four years later; introduced coeducation at the undergraduate level in 1969 and faculty development initiatives in the 1970s, and hired an increasing number of women and minority faculty members. In each generation, scores of students addressed social justice issues and participated in community service. The University conducted three capital campaigns that increased its endowment from $350,000 in 1945 to $21,000,000 in 1990. The dramatic changes in American society, the Catholic Church, and higher education helped contribute to Xavier's overall growth and expansion.

— 6 —

THE UNIVERSITY'S POSTWAR CHALLENGES, 1945–1955

S hortly after the war with Germany in Europe ended in May 1945, the Xavier administration and faculty began planning for the university's postwar future. President Celestin Steiner, with support from a group of greater Cincinnati businessmen, announced a local fund-raising campaign with an ultimate goal of one million dollars. Steiner hoped that 40 percent of the goal would be secured before the end of the year "so that Xavier might be ready" for the return of war veterans. "Xavier stands today as yesterday and always," the university declared in its appeal to the local community, "a bulwark against communism, nazism, socialism, and every 'ism' that strikes at the heart of our American way of life. This community and the nation have the absolute assurance that no un-American philosophy will ever be tolerated at Xavier." (1)

A few months earlier Steiner and Jesuit colleagues had discussed their role in the greater Cincinnati community. "Before we make any plans about the buildings we need," Steiner said, "we ought to know what we Jesuits can do here in Cincinnati. This antecedent knowledge is necessary in order that we may see what the buildings themselves are meant to do." He thought that during the next twenty-five years the Jesuits at the university would be well-advised to shy away from vocational programs and professional fields like engineering, and focus instead on continuing "our regular college courses, [e]xpand . . . the select liberal arts school, [and] . . . [e]nter into a large scale, far-sighted social program." Steiner insisted that those activities the Jesuits "could probably do best, since our training best prepares us for that." But where should the new buildings be erected? That, in Steiner's judgment, constituted a "fundamental problem. Our maintenance and operation is [sic] rendered extremely difficult here," he said, "because the buildings are so far apart, and separated by a deep valley. Should we dispose of Elet Hall and the Union House, and concentrate our entire plant, excepting the field house, on [the eastern] side of the boulevard?" The trustees favored the new construction on the eastern side of Victory Parkway. (2)

The purpose of the fund drive was two-fold: to take care of the operating deficit and to provide funds for additional buildings. Like many other American universities, Xavier ran a deficit largely because of the war years' depletion of the student body. In 1944–1945 the operating deficit was approximately $70,000, which was larger than the annual operating deficits throughout the Depression years. Steiner planned to use 15 percent of the amount raised in the fund drive to cover operating deficits, 55 percent for urgently needed postwar construction, such as a science building, auditorium, and dormitory wing, and 30 percent for faculty research, scholarships, and reserve. (3)

In addition to the endorsement of the university's fund appeal by the local newspapers, Archbishop John McNicholas of Cincinnati urged his pastors to assist Xavier University in two ways. "First, all in this community who are interested in a solid Christian education in which moral values are given their proper place," he wrote, "are asked to enable Xavier to have an enrollment in postwar days of 1,000 students." Furthermore, "all who can should help the University to build up a reserve fund," he continued. "It is incredible that in more than 100 years generous benefactors have not been found who would insure Xavier University of a worthy endowment fund." To show his support he personally sent $1,000 in the name of the priests of the archdiocese. (4)

At the time, the university's assets, exclusive of grounds and buildings and equipment, amounted to approximately $315,000. While the endowment provided some income through interest, it was offset by the fact that the university had to pay interest on a debt of about $575,000. "Our chief endowment," Steiner wrote, "has been, and is, what we call the *Living Endowment of Men*." He was thankful for the contributed services of the Jesuit faculty and administration. Not unlike religious in other Catholic institutions, the Jesuit community used only those funds that were necessary for maintenance of the priests and returned the rest to the university at the end of each fiscal year. He pointed out that while a lay faculty member on the average was paid an annual salary of

$4,000 the actual cost of a Jesuit to the university was between $1,000 and nothing. The saving was therefore between three and four thousand dollars. By multiplying that amount by the number of Jesuits engaged in teaching and administrative work, he estimated a saving between $75,000 and $100,000 per year, "or the equivalent," he wrote, "of approximately two million dollars in endowment." Moreover, the concept of the religious as a "living endowment" had been used as needed by accrediting agencies when they required evidence of a level of endowment. (5)

In the aftermath of the surrender of Japan that ended World War II in August 1945, Xavier University began planning for its postwar future with renewed vigor. Steiner outlined the university's educational goals in a small pamphlet entitled *Xavier Must Be Ready When They Come Back*, which was sent to all alumni and friends of the university. "Xavier faces the great task of being in readiness for the returning servicemen who will be eager to continue interrupted educations," he wrote. "Knowing her responsibility in the postwar world, Xavier University is now making plans—plans that are equal to the challenge." (6)

In the fall Steiner hoped "to revivify the drive" that was lagging because of the sudden ending of the war and its temporary adverse effect on the economy. He hoped to find a donor that would help build a convocation center for the production of dramas, lectures, concerts, and other forms of entertainment that would house an auditorium with a capacity of 1,000 to 1,500, a basement lounge room and snack bar that would serve as a student union building, and offices for administration. Though there was also a need for a science building, he thought that would come from the Logan fund. Thomas J. Logan, former Cincinnati clothing manufacturer, had bequeathed $335,000 to Xavier for a science building at his death in 1930. Economic difficulties in the 1930s and low enrollment during World War II, however, precluded the erection of a new building. In early spring 1946 the board of trustees, though supportive of Steiner's proposed auditorium building, thought that "the first of the building program be a science building." Limited success in fund-raising delayed construction of the new building for another six years. (7)

In April, William H. Albers, chair of the Individual Special Gifts in Xavier's campaign, extended an invitation to several individuals to attend a luncheon at the Queen City Club, a businessmen's club in downtown Cincinnati. He hoped to help insure Xavier's position as a strong cultural influence and a valuable business asset in the community. In addition to Mayor James G. Steward of Cincinnati, Raymond Walters, president of the University of Cincinnati, also attended the luncheon to help support Xavier's campaign. That same month the City of Cincinnati Council passed a resolution endorsing Xavier's fund drive. The university, which had to revise its fund-raising goal because of postwar economic considerations, now hoped to raise $400,000. (8)

That spring Steiner emphasized the need to reinvigorate alumni financial support. Due to the economic depression, the feud over control of athletics, and World War II, alumni support had declined. He was convinced that "[a]lumni work is the most neglected and perhaps the most promising of the fields in which we can carry on our work." At the time the university had an alumni office, established in the early 1930s, staffed by a part-time secretary who managed the business of the office, maintained records, sent mail, kept a year-round social program for the alumni, and edited alumni publications. Steiner saw the need to appoint an alumni director who, he thought, should "be closely tied in with the university administration," especially the director of public relations. He argued that the university "can't get sustained financial support from [the alumni] without a well-thought-out program that is *built up and calculated.*" To help generate additional alumni financial support, in the summer of 1946 the university established a "loyalty fund" to replace the system of alumni annual dues, "so that those who have greater means will have a suggestion and a stimulus each year to make a sustaining contribution to the school. We have learned," Steiner wrote, "that the Alumni can give more than we ever dreamed of, and yet are potentially capable of much greater than we have achieved." The fund drive, completed in 1946, raised about $500,000. (9)

Through the remainder of the decade, the Alumni Association continued to support the university in a variety of ways. In the fall of 1948 it sponsored a drive for the installation of a set of electric carillonic chimes, at a cost of about $4,000, on campus. The following year the alumni added the names of the 75 Xavier students and 65 members of the 30th College Training Detachment who were killed in action during World War II to the Shrine of Our Lady of Victory and Peace on the terrace fronting Alumni Science Hall. Visits to campus often included the shrine. Homecoming, often called H-Day, sometimes included a post-football game visit to the shrine. (10)

Enrollment Growth

Immediately after World War II, Xavier's enrollment increased substantially as a result of the Servicemen's Readjustment Act of 1944, more popularly known as the GI Bill of Rights, which helped usher in the era of mass higher education. It provided several benefits to war veterans who attended school, including a year of unemployment insurance, medical care, counseling services, and tuition, books, and living expenses. Each serviceman was entitled to one year of schooling plus an additional month for each month served in the armed forces. Thus, a veteran with two years of active duty could complete a four-year college program at governmental expense. Irvin F. Beumer, a 1941 alumnus who served as Xavier's director of veterans' education, certified qualified veterans for admission consideration at the university. (11)

In September 1945, Xavier had 525 full-time male students on campus, 75 percent of whom were returned veterans, and had a resident population of 150 out-of-town students, 115 more than the previous January. The enrollment of 525 was 67 students shy of the 1942 record enrollment of 592. Eleven hundred men and women, 25 percent of whom were veterans, were enrolled in the downtown evening division. The average veteran was twenty-three years of age and had more than three years of military service. (12)

That fall, Steiner, with the assistance of Victor B. Nieporte, S.J., class of 1931 and dean of the College of Liberal Arts, initiated a study estimating the revenue from 500 full-time students and the amount of salaries and wages that the university would have to pay to the faculty and staff. Though the president "wanted all to receive a just compensation, [he] believed that there were inequalities when some of the laboring help," he argued, "received much more than teaching or clerical help. . . . We may not always be able to do," Steiner said, "all the good we see can be done and that we would like to do." The following year Steiner thought it was "imperative" that the university's Committee on Rank and Tenure, established in the fall of 1945, "immediately become active" concerning salary and professional matters.

The committee consisted of Vice President Frederick N. Miller, S.J., and five faculty members, three laymen and two Jesuits, all appointed by the president. Steiner thought it was important to draw up some sort of salary scale as soon as possible, for he was concerned over "the raiding by wealthier schools of college and university" personnel. He argued, however, that it was "even more important that we study our statutes on Rank and Tenure and relate these provisions to our present faculty." Steiner also issued instructions to academic departments to hire full-time male Ph.D.s whenever possible. At the time, the university had a policy that would continue into the 1950s of not hiring women teachers in the undergraduate day school. "[W]e have never had a [full-time] woman on our faculty," Steiner wrote to a female applicant, "since Xavier is not a coeducational institution." In some cases, however, it employed women part-time in the evening division. In the fall of 1947 the board of trustees authorized that the academic help be paid "approximately the same wages as those in other schools." Noting that maintenance help was paid union wages, or slightly higher, and that clerical salaries were high, the trustees argued "it is up to the individual in charge of offices to see that the help are kept busy." (13)

In response to growing enrollment and increasing demand for a full-fledged graduate program, especially by local women religious, in the spring of 1946 university officials established a coeducational graduate division for the offering of master's degrees in the arts and sciences. Earlier that year the Cincinnati archbishop had encouraged Xavier to introduce graduate work in order to meet the demand for Catholic postgraduate education. Though the administration suspected that there would necessarily be a few women graduate students making up academic credits at the undergraduate level on the main campus, the board of trustees nevertheless approved the new division. Reiterating the sentiments of President Hugo Sloctemyer twelve years earlier, the university seemed poised to inaugurate a graduate program "on a solid basis." William P. "Bud" Hetherington, Jesuit professor of classical languages, was the first director. Raymond McCoy from the Department of Education succeeded him the following year. He oversaw graduate programs, which offered courses in the late afternoons during the week and on Saturdays for thirty years. "At first, almost all our students were members of religious orders," McCoy said. "Out of those first 135 students, 122 were nuns and 5 were priests. We had very few laymen and no laywomen [on the faculty]." In the beginning, the graduate division had five departments: chemistry, classical languages, education, English, and mathematics. (14)

In the fall of 1946 there were 1,486 undergraduate students, including 900 freshmen in the day school, the largest first-year class in Xavier's history. The unprecedented size of the first-year class, representing twenty-four states and four foreign countries, posed a challenge to the faculty. "Due to the tremendous student load placed by present registration on the three history instructors—900 freshmen, plus about 100 upper classmen," minutes of the Department of History read, "it was recognized that ordinary tests and quizzes could not be used in customary frequency." Over 77 percent of the total student body, 1,150 students, were veterans. The university's total enrollment of 2,771 included 1,120 part-time students in the downtown Evening College, formerly the evening division, 40 graduate students, and 125 students in the Milford Seminary division. About 90 percent of the students were Catholic. These numbers far exceeded any previous enrollment levels. That year veterans' enrollments grew nationally to 1,080,396, 51.9 percent of the total college population. A year later the figure reached a peak of 1,122,738, constituting 48 percent of the population. Faculty generally found the veterans to be more mature, more serious, more highly motivated, and more career-oriented. Indeed, the GI Bill had a highly significant impact on American higher education and more particularly on Xavier University. From 1946 to 1950, higher education enrollment was double its prewar level. Over two million veterans attended college in the six years following the war. At the same time, colleges and universities became more inclusive, enrolling more persons from racial, ethnic, gender, and socioeconomic groups that previously had been neglected or underrepresented. This new impetus helped develop the belief that everyone with proper qualifications could go to college. (15)

Anticipating enrollment increases, Xavier University officials in 1946 contracted with the federal government for the construction of "temporary housing" on campus for both single and married students. Federal authorities had promised housing for the veteran students. There were to be fourteen apartments for the married students and ten buildings for the single students. However, the barracks, as the temporary housing units came to be known, were not finished in time for the beginning of classes in September. School officials arranged temporary housing in the fieldhouse for the single students scheduled to live in the barracks and put J. Peter Buschmann, S.J., in charge. They set up 194 army cots in 12 rows with a chair alongside each bed and placed lockers and study tables at strategic points for the students' use. Generally at the end of each school day the students were in the fieldhouse by 7:30 p.m., unless they were in the library, Union House, or at a meeting. They were expected to be "quiet . . . in order to give all an opportunity to study. . . . Never was a study hall like this," Buschmann later wrote, "with men sprawled on beds or sitting where they could with book in hand and others in small groups talking together in subdued voice, with the comparative quiet occasionally broken by the sharp click of a typewriter perched on a trunk." At 10:30 p.m. Buschmann turned out the floor lights. Eight-and-a-half hours later at 7 a.m., students awakened to the sound of a whistle. "In a trying situation like that," Buschmann wrote, "one could expect pandemonium, chaos, and rebellion. But the opposite was true. . . . Only once or twice did some of them display a short-lived impatience. A spirit of true camaraderie prevailed." (16)

Students stayed in the fieldhouse for five to six weeks. In October the ten housing units that accommodated 250 students were completed and the students moved in. The residential barracks were located at Ledgewood Drive and Herald Avenue. For the next seven years the units were filled to capacity—twenty-four students to a building, housed three to a room. Because of the temporary nature of the structures, maintenance and heating were not economical nor very efficient. Four oil-burning stoves in each unit provided the only heat that was quickly dissipated through the thin roof and siding. The students found it difficult to read or study in the rooms because the thin walls permitted sound to travel from room to room. These temporary buildings together with the fourteen family units, Elet Hall, and Marian residence made it possible for the university to offer housing facilities on campus to approximately 450 persons. The university also put up two other barracks. South Hall, located left of the University Drive entrance, provided students with a snack bar and campus theater. North Hall, on left just beyond Albers Hall, also on University Drive, had classrooms and science laboratories. (17)

The veterans, who outnumbered the traditional undergraduate day students, felt very much a part of the institution. "When I returned to Xavier after the war," a veteran later recalled, "I remember the campus being overloaded with people who, like myself, were returning from the war. There was a great camaraderie among the veterans on campus, not only because we shared classes after the war, but because we were all a part of the same experience." The administration, faculty, and staff had much to do with that. Steiner was personally convinced that the university should "make every effort to provide educational facilities for veterans and non-veterans whose *right* to education is a matter of supreme concern to the present and future of our country and the world. In these days when charges are being made and substantiated that forces destructive of our American way of life are finding their way into churches, schools, colleges, etc., it gives us consolation to know that few, if any, young men or young women have ever left Xavier Communists, Nazis, Fascists, or socialists." If there were any, he thought, "it was *in spite of*, and not because of Xavier education." (18)

In October 1946 the administration placed the younger students in Elet Hall under the supervision of a Jesuit prefect. Earlier in the spring, the Board of Trustees had initiated a student proctor system in the residence hall. This was consistent with the 1943 memorial from the provincial recommending that a minimum of Jesuits "be required to prefect dormitories." He urged presidents of boarding colleges to devise a system where Jesuit prefects would not be required to wait up all hours of the night for the return of the boarders after dances and night permissions. In the place of the usual second and third floor prefects, reliable students now performed certain duties such as the maintenance of order during study periods, checking attendance at certain functions, and assisting the Jesuit prefect. The university assigned three Jesuits to reside in Elet, noting that it could not assign that many to future residence halls. (19)

Indeed, in the aftermath of the Second World War, Xavier University had to cope with the burden of a rapidly-expanding student body. Only two years in Xavier's history saw more than 500 students in the day division. The university now had to turn away hundreds of students who applied for admission. More than 400 students were from out of town and lived on the campus. A faculty member observed that "though Xavier needed more than a century to acquire five hundred students, she had grown in four days from five hundred to fifteen hundred." Classes ran from 8:30 a.m. to 8:00 p.m. Tuition, which was almost the lowest in Ohio, also increased. It rose from $75 per semester to $8.50 per credit hour, an increase from $75 to $127.50 for the average fifteen-hour load each semester. The influx of veterans and the tuition and fees that they brought with them helped pull Xavier out of its financial doldrums. (20)

New Programs and Construction

During the postwar period the maintenance and preservation of the university's identity as a Jesuit and Catholic institution was an important issue to the students. The religious aspect of a Xavier education differentiated it from other schools, and many students valued this difference. In a 1946 article in *Xavier University News*, which had resumed publication on March 1, the editor commented that it was necessary for man to learn religion in order to have a full education. Many Xavier undergraduates thought that their education was superior to most secular institutions because the university, they believed, educated the whole person and nurtured him morally. One student in 1954 commented that Xavier graduates stood out among the rest because of their high moral principles and ability to integrate knowledge provided by their background in philosophy and theology. This moral formation was a crucial element in the students' decisions to attend Xavier. When graduates were asked in the mid-1950s why they chose the university, the school's Catholic tradition was one of the top responses. In a survey sent out to the class of 1959 two years after their graduation, 52 percent wrote on the survey that "moral and religious guidance" were a major asset of the university. None of the survey questions had mentioned the religious aspects of the school, yet these former students thought it was important enough to refer to it in their responses. (21)

Xavier's Catholic identity was evident in many ways. The school's newspaper constantly urged the students to act in accordance with Catholic norms and doctrine. Each academic year began with the Mass of the Holy Spirit, attended by all the students. The university required students to attend Mass once during the week and the prefect of discipline enforced the rule. Absentees were warned, and if they continued to be absent were subject to suspension from school. There was also an active Angelus group, which commemorated the mystery of the Incarnation and urged students to pause as the bells rang out at noon and to say their prayers to Mary. In addition, there was a movement to carry out Mary's Fatima plan, which included praying for Russia's conversion from communism. In February 1948, several Xavier students arranged to have the Rosary constantly recited each day by having students sign up for a fifteen-minute time slot. (22)

The young men were also expected to act in accordance with Catholic morals in all their actions, whether directly related to life on campus or not. Swearing was seen as a vulgar, adolescent behavior in which Xavier men should not engage, because it reflected poorly on them and on the university. Editorials in the school's newspaper regularly reminded the students to act with Catholic morals, manners, and virtues in all their activities. In response to a contemporary national survey that stated that "the younger generation of today has no moral standards," *Xavier University News* challenged the students to prove this statement wrong and to be active in their faith. (23)

In addition to being concerned over proper behavior, students at times protested against certain campus practices. During the 1948–1949 academic year two freshmen, representing nearly 300 dissenting fellow classmates, presented a petition before the student council, objecting to the extension of the time period that freshmen were required to wear their "beanie" caps. This event was the first-known instance of a group of students rebelling against action taken by the student council since its formation twenty-five years earlier. The practice of wearing the caps, however, continued into the 1950s. (24)

Another important aspect of campus life was community service. As a Jesuit institution, university officials instructed students on the importance of helping others and promoting social justice. In a March 1946 issue of *Xavier University News,* the editorial remarked that "[t]oo often we merely attend classes, never realizing that a complete and separate community is in full swing all around us. We want every member of the student body to become a citizen of that community." There were numerous appeals in the postwar period to donate money to help rebuild Europe and to help the poor. During the Korean War in the early 1950s, students donated 134 pints of blood in a blood drive for the armed forces. (25)

In post-World War II America, Xavier's Catholic identity also touched the lay faculty. Like many Catholic colleges in the country, the university issued contracts prohibiting faculty from teaching anything contrary to the tenets of the Roman Catholic Church. For well over a century, American Catholics, including those in the Archdiocese of Cincinnati, had been taught to avoid contact with non-Catholics and their institutions. In the mid-1950s, Xavier faculty members and administrators concurred that academic freedom at the university "operates within the context of American patriotism, Catholic belief, and the educational philosophy of the *Ratio Studiorum.*" As more authoritarian and clerical control prevailed in Catholic colleges and universities, including Xavier, academic issues were usually handled behind closed doors. Through the decade, Xavier's president, like his counterparts in other Catholic colleges and universities, could unilaterally remove a troublesome faculty member. These decisions were informal and secret, and there is no official documentation of the university's dealing with critical or nonconforming faculty members. (26)

In the immediate aftermath of World War II, the faculty, especially lay members, gradually grew in influence and authority in academic affairs. At the November 1946 general faculty meeting, attended by

19 Jesuits, including President Steiner, and 21 full-time lay faculty members, Steiner asserted "that it is of vital importance that Xavier has laymen." Acknowledging the importance of each lay faculty member in fulfilling the mission of the university, he further declared that "[i]f a layman should prove himself superior to a Jesuit faculty member, the layman will receive the position in question." At the time a number of departments were headed by laymen. He and some of his Jesuit counterparts came to terms with the fact that lay faculty members were an important part of the Jesuit operation. While assuring his lay faculty colleagues fair and professional treatment in terms of salary, rank, and tenure, Steiner expected of them "complete loyalty, initiative, industry, assumption of responsibility, scholarship and outstanding teaching." (27)

In his talk the president also encouraged the chairs of the various academic departments to produce plans "to strenghen their departments." He promised additional equipment and financial assistance in order "to bring these plans to fruition. There is no reason . . . why each department should not become as strong as the best in the country." Steiner also encouraged the faculty to become active members in national and state associations. He had set an example earlier in the spring by accepting Ohio Governor Frank Lausche's invitation to serve as a member of a higher education committee in the state. (28)

Following his opening remarks at the general faculty meeting, Steiner turned over the meeting to the chair, Dean Nieporte, S.J. After briefly stating the new policy of rotating the chairmanship of the faculty meetings among the members of the lay faculty Nieporte then introduced Raymond McCoy from the Department of Education. "[M]y chairmanship is easy," McCoy said. "I am to present to you the attitude and plans of the Academic Council on a matter which it considers the most significant task which we, as a faculty, face this year—the re-examination and strengthening of the undergraduate academic program." The Academic Council, which had been established in the fall of 1945 and dealt with general academic matters, had argued that a review of the academic program did not pose a threat to the university's Jesuit and Catholic tradition. "[T]his year, when we have 900 freshmen," McCoy said in 1946, echoing the sentiments of the council, "is the time for the faculty of the institution to take stock of the situation, re-examine the whole academic program, see to it that requirements are in line with our purposes, and generally strengthen our program so that these freshmen shall be offered a unified program the features of which represent a logical and orderly extension of our purposes as a Catholic University." He did not think it meant "starting anew or casting out the old." Since the university between 1941 and 1946 had seen its enrollment "change from 400 to 600 to 1000 air force men to about 35 civilians and then suddenly up to 600 and 1500 in one year," it had to make "basic decisions here or there because of necessities," he said, that contributed to "some inconsistencies, inadequacies, or anachronisms in its academic program." (29)

Earlier in the semester a few departments had recommended substituting a comprehensive examination for the thesis requirement in the students' senior year while many faculty members debated the significance of a core of general studies. Though there were faculty members in the business administration course of studies who wondered if the students in the program should start with economics and accounting in their freshman year and take these subjects each year in order to become better prepared professionally, the majority of the faculty at the general faculty meeting preferred to help the students become "generally competent individuals who . . . developed some specialty in economics and bookkeeping principally in their last two years." They argued that the educational curriculum "must flow logically from the basic purposes of Xavier as a university." (30)

After the meeting the university formed an Institutional Purposes Committee "to review, accept, modify, or expand" academic programs and submit their recommendations to the Academic Council. Chairs of the various academic departments, after consulting with their respective faculty members, then met and recommended what they thought would constitute the best set of curricular requirements for academic majors and minors. The following fall, university officials introduced the major and minor system. Students had to have a major, a minor in a subject approved by the chairman of the student's major department, and a second minor that generally was philosophy. The major meant a minimum of eighteen hours of upper division work after completion of a minimum of six hours of lower division work. A minor supposed at least twelve hours of upper division work after completion of at least six hours of lower division courses. Philosophy was an automatic minor since all graduates needed eighteen hours of philosophy. A student had to have a "C" average in his lower and upper division courses for a major and minor. In the business administration program all freshmen had to major in either economics or accounting and minor in the other. (31)

In addition to introducing new academic features, the university expanded its outreach into the community. In the spring of 1947 it established an "Institute on Family Life," hoping to help "preserve the home and family life of our people, Catholic and non-Catholic." There was concern that, due to the increasing divorce rate and its effect on home life, the American family was in jeopardy. The university held its first Family Life Conference in the summer. At the sixth conference in 1953 more than 1,000 persons attended. (32)

The following fall Xavier also began the Great Books of Discussion Series, under the direction of Harold C. Gardiner, S.J., literary editor of *America* magazine. Made popular by the University of Chicago, the university intended the series to be a service to the greater Cincinnati community. The series lasted but a couple of years. In February 1948 the Xavier Masque Society and the International Relations Club staged a dramatization about the United Nations. With 5,000 spectators in the fieldhouse, the program was, in Steiner's opinion, "good advertising, the best kind of publicity" for the university. In 1949 Xavier established the annual Operation Youth, a one-week citizenship training program for high school junior and senior students, held at the beginning of each summer. John A. Moser, class of 1933, was its first director. By 1955 Operation Youth had won three times the Freedoms Foundation National Award for its "outstanding" contribution to the better understanding of the American way of life. (33)

Like many universities and colleges in post-World War II America, Xavier University was in urgent need of additional facilities. That was the principal reason for the fund drive in the mid-1940s. By 1946, when undergraduate day enrollment had leaped to 1,486 students, every room that could be used for instruction was pressed into service. Steiner expressed the need both to remodel the university fieldhouse in order to handle the enlarged physical education program and for the construction of an armory because of the significant increase in the student population and to relieve the crowded condition in the fieldhouse. Moreover, Xavier's unit of the Reserve Officers Training Corps (ROTC) field artillery had grown. Though ROTC officials in 1945 had expressed concern over the fact that the university had fewer than the minimum of 100 students, two years later the corps had more than doubled in size. The rooms and storage space previously used in the Xavier fieldhouse were no longer adequate. "It seems most certain," Steiner wrote, "that the good of the colleges in the future will be tied up with some army training program." In the fall of 1946 the university began exploring the possibility of building an armory "that would house all the military facilities." (34)

To assist the university in its building program, which included the proposed armory, Steiner helped professionalize business practices on campus and secured outside professional advice. In the fall of 1946 the president established a central purchasing office to oversee parts of the budget. The following January, Steiner, following President Hugo Sloctemyer's precedent of having an advisory board of laymen, also formed a board of lay advisers composed of nine business and professional leaders from the greater Cincinnati area. Acknowledging the importance of lay participation in the direction of the university, Steiner reported at a general faculty meeting that the "advice and counsel of this . . . group [should prove] . . . invaluable, because the University is on the eve of the greatest era of service to the community and to the nation." When he sought the lay board's advice on the building of an armory at a time when construction costs were high, the members pointed out that "there would be no advantage in waiting, for wages and materials would not come down within the next few years." (35)

At the end of July, Steiner, who thought the university would need city space for the construction of an armory, wrote a letter to the mayor of Cincinnati, Carl W. Rich, pointing out that Xavier had "every reason to believe the large student enrollment, particularly of returned veterans, will continue for the next four or five years." He argued that it was "urgently necessary that we build an armory." The U.S. Office of Education and the Federal Works Agency had provided a sum of approximately $45,000 to assist Xavier if there were a building completed by February 1, 1948. In order to take advantage of the grant, university authorities needed to proceed immediately. Fortuitously, an opportunity presented itself to the university to obtain material that had been fabricated for a navy building at Camp Perry, Virginia, during the war. The Federal Works Agency, as a part of the veterans' educational facilities training program, made the material available to Xavier. A university planning group designated a plot of ground immediately adjacent to the fieldhouse on Winding Way as the ideal future location for the armory. (36)

To help secure the location, the university purchased the residence at the northeast corner of Marion Avenue and Winding Way, named St. Barbara Hall, for use by the military department. The entire property was to the northeast of a short dead-end spur of Marion Avenue that separated that tract from the newly-acquired property. Since the university would own both sides of the street and it ran dead-end to a bluff overlooking the baseball playing field, Xavier petitioned the Cincinnati City Council to abandon the street and thus permit the university to extend the armory building 150 feet from the fieldhouse over to St. Barbara Hall. On November 19, the city council issued an ordinance vacating Marion Avenue east of Winding Way, and turned it over to Xavier University. Seven years later the university acquired the deed for Sycamore House, formerly called Elet Hall Annex, between Elet Hall and the fieldhouse. Xavier now owned and used all six buildings on the west end of campus from the Red Building, formerly the Avondale Athletic Club on Dana Avenue, to St. Barbara Hall. (37)

Because of unavoidable delays in the construction of the armory, the university received an extension from the government until July 1948. Seven months later, in February 1949, the armory was finished, built at a cost of $150,000, which was more than twice the original estimated amount. Completed in time for second semester classes, the new facility, located between the fieldhouse and St. Barbara Hall, provided additional space for the military department and more classrooms for the academic departments. It became the first permanent building erected on campus since the Albers Biology Building in 1930. Earlier in the academic year the university had approved membership in the National Society of Pershing Rifles, whose purpose was to develop, to the highest degree possible, outstanding traits of leadership, military science, military bearing, and discipline within the framework of a military-oriented, honorary fraternity. Within five years Xavier's rifle drills squad won two first prizes in the competition with ROTC units of nine other midwestern universities. Though the building was primarily for ROTC purposes, all rooms were made available for general university use. In addition to accommodating a rifle range for the university's rifle team, it became the regular scene of student dances and official convocations and receptions. During the 1949 commencement the university also turned it into a dining room when it served breakfast to 255 graduates and their families. (38)

In the immediate postwar years, enrollment continued to climb. In the fall of 1947 President Steiner, Paul L. O'Connor, S.J., dean of the Evening College, and the mayor of Cincinnati welcomed the largest class in the history of the school. The university registered over 1,650 students in the day school, 1,100 in the evening, 180 at Milford Seminary, and 75 in the graduate division, for a total of 3,190 students.

A year later its enrollment increased to 3,501: 1,884 in the College of Liberal Arts, 1,286 in the evening, and 130 at Milford. The graduate division, just three years old, had 301 students. There was an increasing number of students from out-of-state and from foreign countries. In the fall of 1949 the university greeted 400 freshmen and 1,300 returning upperclassmen. Only 400 of them were veterans. From 1947 to 1951, Xavier enrolled an average of 500 out-of-town students representing 28 states. The "street car" university label no longer applied to Xavier. (39)

As undergraduate enrollment grew significantly in the postwar years, Steiner and his Jesuit colleagues sought to build upon Xavier's rich Jesuit tradition and, in the process, raise the bar of academic excellence. In the fall of 1948 William Hetherington, S.J., associate professor of classical languages, established the Honors Bachelor of Arts program for students of exceptional academic ability. With Steiner's backing, Hetherington recruited 22 high school graduates with four years of Latin and promised them "an ideal liberal education." In addition to offering intensified courses in Latin, Greek, and philosophy, which included four years of Latin and two years of Greek, the classical honors program required twelve hours of mathematics, ten hours of chemistry, and eight hours of physics. The student's average class load was twenty hours per semester. In its second year, the honors course of studies scored one of its first measurable accomplishments when Xavier took top honors among the eight Jesuit colleges and universities at the Intercollegiate Latin Contest. In its first six years HAB students won first place five times in the contest. (40)

The faculty designed the honors AB course of studies not only to help improve the quality of education for the students in the program, but also to respond to the challenges of the age. "We live in startling and troubled times, amid great scientific advances and dreadful international crises," Hetherington wrote in a booklet describing the program. "We have reason to fear for the very existence of our civilization and way of life. We feel that we may in very truth be standing on the brink of an abyss. Yet in the midst of times like these we at Xavier have seen fit to institute a starry-eyed, idealistic course of studies for youths who are to face the unknown world of tomorrow." Then Hetherington raised a question that he proceeded to answer himself. "Why have we embarked on such a venture? We have done so," he wrote, "not only because of our abiding faith in such a course of studies; not only because such a curriculum has been traditional for centuries in Jesuit universities wherever and whenever students could be found; [and] not only because of the need of modern men for Christian humanism. . . . We do so," he continued, reflecting the sentiments of many Catholic educators concerned over the cultural crisis of the age, "because we know from history that in so doing we are fighting the never-ending fight of man against barbarism and the forces of dissolution." To help underwrite scholarships for students in the Honors AB program, Hetherington came up with the Mardi Gras dance, an annual fund-raising activity held shortly before Lent. (41)

In the late 1940s the university also enhanced its mission by addressing additional student needs. During the 1949–1950 academic year Xavier began providing counseling and placement services to students on a full-time basis. Through the counseling service students received guidance in choosing courses of study, plans of action, and careers suited to their particular aptitudes and personality traits. Through the placement service the university assisted current and former students by bringing their capabilities to the attention of prospective employers. That same year Xavier established the Chaswil Foundation Student Loan Fund, a gift of Charles F. Williams, member of the university's board of lay advisors. Through the Chaswil Fund, undergraduate students could borrow interest-free money for their education and delay repayment for five years. As a revolving fund it was designed to be perpetually available to benefit students with financial need. The following year approximately 40 students availed themselves of the opportunity. Through the 1950s the fund continued to provide interest-free loans to Xavier undergraduates. (42)

In the fall of 1952 the university initiated the master of business administration (MBA) program. Seeing the need for providing the same kind of graduate education for "executives in service" that was available for "teachers in service," the new program made it relatively easy for an employed person to study for his master's degree by scheduling courses in the late afternoon, evening, and on Saturday morning. Among the more than 250 students enrolled at Xavier that year for graduate studies, 89 enrolled in the MBA program. The following year it began offering graduate courses in business administration in the summer sessions. (43)

In the fall of 1954 the university scored an historical first in Cincinnati when it offered through the Evening College the first college course for credit on television over the city's educational television station, WCET. James V. McCummiskey, S.J., professor of philosophy,

Xavier

Photo Album

1831-2006

Edward Dominic Fenwick, O.P., 1768-1832, first Bishop of Cincinnati and founder of the Athenaeum, the precursor of St. Xavier College

John A. Elet, S.J., first Jesuit President, 1840-1847

The Athenaeum, 1831

St. Xavier Church and College, circa 1919

Jesuit faculty, circa 1880

President's office downtown Cincinnati

Francis H. Cloud, 1863 graduate and the first President of the St. Xavier Alumni Association (1880-90)

Philopedian Society, a student debate club, circa 1900

St. Xavier Alumni Association, 1904

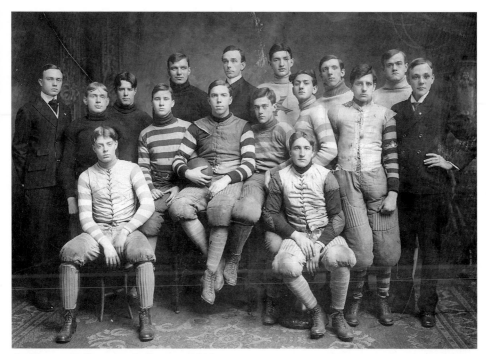

St. Xavier College football team, 1903

Xavier Avondale campus, circa 1911 – panoramic view from the site of the proposed
College buildings

Hinkle Administration Hall (left)
and Alumni Science Building
(right), circa 1920

Evening Division, Xavier University, 1930's

Preparing for a festive dinner, Union
Building cafeteria

South Hall dining facility

Crossing to Elet Hall, 1924

Commencement procession, 1936

Library, downtown Cincinnati

Night School pre-prom party, January 1937

Academic scene, 1938-1939 academic year

Aerial view of campus, 1940's

Reserve Officers Training Corps (ROTC) Review, 1940

Crowd cheering at a Xavier football game, October 1948

Salad Bowl football champions, 1950

Logan Chemistry building opened in 1953

Mary Lodge Reading Room, Schmidt Library

Fr. Raymond Allen, S.J., teaches mathematics class

Xavier Musketeers – National Invitation Tournament champions, 1958

Fr. Paul L. O'Connor, S.J., third from left, tours with group on campus, circa 1964

First coeds in Xavier's undergraduate day division

Student registration, circa 1970

Graduation: Anticipating the future

Women's basketball has been played
at Xavier since the early 1970's

Xavier's Academic Mall, remodeled in 1996

Multifunctional Cintas Center opened in 2000

Michael Graham, S.J., Xavier's 34th Jesuit President (2001 -)

Electronic classrooms facilitate learning

taught a course on ethics entitled "Why Be Moral." The following spring the college also sponsored a course on consumer economics. (44)

Concurrent with the post-World War II growth of academics at Xavier were developments in athletics. Students participated in a variety of intramural sports, which included bowling, football, baseball, basketball, tennis, and boxing. After a lapse of two years during the war, in the fall of 1945 the university reinstated basketball. First coached by Ed Burns in 1945–1946 and then Lew Hirt for the next five years, the Musketeers went through a couple of lean years. During the 1945–1946 and 1946–1947 seasons the team earned 11 victories and suffered 33 losses. In Hirt's second campaign, however, the Musketeers reached national prominence when they compiled a 24-8 winning season and took fourth place in the National Association of Intercollegiate Athletics (NAIA) tournament in Kansas City, Missouri. That tournament, which included a field of 32 teams, marked the first postseason participation by the Musketeers, and also the first time a Xavier basketball team traveled to a game by air. (45)

By the fall of 1946 the university reinstated other intercollegiate sports and the Xavier band. However, the football team's first season was deplorable. It had a record of 3-7, losing 70-0 to the University of Kentucky. According to newspaper sports writers, Xavier officials had to decide whether they wanted to continue to try and compete with larger schools or "drop several rungs down the collegiate football ladder and tackle the smaller fry." The following summer Steiner momentarily considered dropping the sport. He argued "if the revenue from the rental of the field, the fieldhouse, and other sources did not cover [its] expenses, it was [his] opinion . . . that [the university] should drop it." Within three years, however, the program reached its highest peak. In 1949 the football team defeated the University of Louisville and the University of Cincinnati en route to a 10-1 season and its only bowl game, a 33-12 win over Arizona State in the Salad Bowl on January 2, 1950. From 1949 to 1951, the football team won 27 games, lost 2, and tied 1. (46)

In the immediate postwar years, first-year students could not be members of the varsity teams of the major sports of football, basketball, and baseball. Veterans, however, were an exception. Of freshman standing or not, they could be members of the varsity teams. Any student whose scholastic standing was below a quality point ratio of 1.5 on a 4.0 scale for each session of the first year, and below 1.75 for each session of succeeding years, was automatically placed on academic probation, which excluded the student from participation in any form of extracurricular activity. (47)

In January 1948, President Steiner was surprised to learn that the basketball team played two games during the week of examinations. "It is simply unjust to expect students to do justice to their examinations under such circumstances," he wrote. "I suppose the only role I can play is the pitiful role of Pilate washing my hands of the whole matter, even while I realize that an injustice is being done." He then notified the business manager of athletics that "from February 1st, 1948 on . . . [t]here are to be no athletic contests during time of examinations or retreat. No matter who has signed agreements to the same, I shall use my authority to cancel what has been agreed upon." (48)

Three years after World War II, the university's enrollment, academics, and athletics had grown significantly. Encouraged by this growth, university officials contemplated further expansion. On the eve of the construction of the armory, Steiner outlined the university's vision in a document entitled *Xavier Steps Into the Future*, printed in the spring of 1948. "We believe that we have a bigger job to do than at any time in the past," he wrote. "To that end, we have prepared this visualization of Xavier—an expression in brick and mortar of a great tradition, a great present and a greater future." The university called for a $4,300,000 plant expansion according to a ten-step plan. Steiner's priority list included additional dormitories, a new classroom building, science building, student union, swimming pool, student health center, and student chapel. Some of his administrative colleagues, however, had reservations. They regarded the list as too ambitious. Paul O'Connor, S.J., newly-appointed dean of the College of Liberal Arts, questioned "whether it was good to ask for so many things when the one great need of a new classroom building is so evident." Though Steiner left Xavier in 1949 to become president of the university of Detroit, significant parts of his vision document set the tone for much of Xavier's growth during the next decade. On September 6 the university hosted a farewell reception for Steiner at the armory building. City officials attended. (49)

The Steiner years, 1940 to 1949—the longest term of office up to that time for any Xavier president—were noteworthy. He had worked hard and conscientiously, proved to be a resolute leader, and guided Xavier through the economic depression years. Although the number of civilian students dropped to less than 100 during the war years, he brought in the air force's 30th College Training Detachment and provided a program under which more than 1,800 cadets were educated and trained. The veteran surge after World War II brought the university its greatest enrollment growth to date. The enrollment in 1948–1949 totalled 3,500 students, with 1,890 in the day division, significantly higher than the enrollment of 1,572 with 502 in the day division when he took over in 1940. (50)

Two academic milestones were accomplished during Steiner's administration. The first was the opening of the graduate division in 1946. In three years' time it grew to an enrollment of more than 300 students. The second was the establishment of the undergraduate honors bachelor of arts program. In addition to these accomplishments, the university purchased a residence at Dakota and Marion Avenues and established Marion Hall for dormitory use, and purchased property at Marion Avenue and Winding Way for use by the military department. In addition, Steiner established the Xavier Board of Lay Advisors and oversaw a number of campus improvements, the largest of which were the new ROTC Armory Building and the remodeling of the university's fieldhouse. Temporary barracks were also erected to handle the postwar veteran enrollment. (51)

Another important characteristic of Steiner's administration was the university's greater involvement in the Cincinnati community. He encouraged the establishment of the Xavier Forum that each year brought to the city speakers of national repute on topics of public interest. Other notable projects included the formation of the Institute of Social Order for the study of labor-management problems, the Family Life Conference, and the Great Books Lecture Series. Regarded as a "friendly" community leader and one of Cincinnati's best-known citizens, Steiner was a member of the boards of directors of several civic organizations. He also served as president of the Ohio College Association and on various committees of the Association of American Colleges. He was a consultant to the executive board of the National Catholic Educational Association. Steiner was also widely-known for his spiritual work in the community. He gave scores of retreats, conferences, and days of recollection in the high schools, colleges, and convents in the Midwest. (52)

On August 21, 1949, two-and-a-half weeks before Steiner's farewell reception, James F. Maguire, S.J., became Xavier's twenty-eighth Jesuit president. Born on March 8, 1904 in Chicago, Maguire completed his early education there, graduating from St. Ignatius High School. After two years of study at the University of Detroit he entered the Society of Jesus in 1918 and was ordained to the priest-hood in 1935 at St. Mary's in Kansas. Maguire came to Cincinnati from West Baden College at West Baden Springs, Indiana, where he had served for six years as rector of that Jesuit seminary. His simple installation ceremony took place in the early evening in the Jesuit community dining room at the university. The "event was an instance of history repeating itself," the *Cincinnati Enquirer* noted. Nine years earlier, almost to the day on August 26, 1940, Maguire had succeeded Steiner as president of St. Xavier High School while Steiner, who had been dean of men at Xavier in the mid-1930s and president of St. Xavier High School from 1937 to 1940, simultaneously took over the presidency of Xavier University. While assuming the presidency at Xavier University, Maguire also became pastor of Bellarmine Chapel. (53)

The Maguire Years, 1949–1955

At the half-way mark of the twentieth century, four months after Maguire assumed the Xavier presidency, the university had much to celebrate. Since the turn of the century its growth, like that of many American colleges and universities, had been phenomenal. In 1900 only 238,210 students were attending colleges and universities in the United States. In 1950, the total was 2,439,910. In 1900, twenty students graduated from St. Xavier College. In 1950, 245 students graduated from the university's College of Liberal Arts, 25 from the downtown and Milford College divisions, and 22 were awarded master's degrees from the graduate division.

Three months after his installation, Maguire, like his predecessor, affirmed his commitment to liberal education. In an address to the faculty in December 1949 he reminded them of the university's "sacred trust . . . to endow our students [not] merely with the treasures of a Liberal Education," but with "Christian education" as well. Critical of the elective system and the mass production and educational assembly lines in higher education, he emphasized the importance of the Jesuit core of studies and the cultivation of "intellectual excellence [and] . . . Ignatian spirituality" in educating leaders. "As faculty members," he said, "your contribution to this supreme function of Xavier University is as essential as it is vital." Encouraged by the newly-established honors AB program, he pointed out that "few faculties are in a more favored position than [the faculty at] Xavier . . . , with its relatively small student body, to realize to the full the magnificent potentialities of a truly Christian, Liberal Education." (54)

Early in Maguire's presidency the administration also made plans to launch a new fund drive to help fulfill the university's mission. In 1951 the university began the $1,000,000 three-year Fund and Good Will Campaign. Rallying the support of Cincinnati leaders, the university's financial goal was more than twice that of the 1945 Xavier drive, but considerably less ambitious than the ten-step plan laid out by his predecessor three years earlier. Influenced by President Steiner's preliminary study of campus needs, the objectives of the new campaign included the erection of a chemistry building and replacement of the temporary barracks with permanent campus housing. (55)

The postwar increase in enrollment meant that the university needed more classroom space and dormitory facilities on campus. The use of army barracks provided only a temporary answer to the need for student housing. The $1,000,000 campaign, with the alumni quota set at $200,000, progressed well. In the first year the alumni donated $121,775.20. In the spring of 1947, Xavier had formed an Alumni Board of Governors, consisting of fifteen members, who guided the activities of the Alumni Association. To lay a more secure foundation for the association, as well as to generate greater interest among alumni, Xavier formed chapters where geographic concentrations of alumni warranted them. By the spring of 1953 the university had six alumni chapters in Ohio and one chapter in Indiana. On March 10, leaders of these regional chapters met on campus for the first Alumni Chapter Conference. (56)

The 1951 fund-raising campaign, which was the principal campus project during Maguire's presidency, provided construction funds for the Logan Chemistry Building and a new residence hall. It was admiration for Xavier alumni that in large part had prompted Thomas Logan to make his gift twenty-one years earlier to the university. Campaign funds were added to his original bequest of $335,000 to insure completion of the $750,000 Logan Building. There were signs in 1951 that the slight decline in undergraduate enrollment following the postwar surge had halted. Almost 320 freshmen were beanie-capped in the first week of school, an increase of approximately 50 students from the previous year. "[W]e can again look to growth in our undergraduate totals," Maguire declared in 1953. In the fall of that year the Logan Chemistry Building opened for classes. The university dedicated it on May 22, 1954, and the president of the United States, Dwight D. Eisenhower, sent a letter of congratulations to honor the occasion. At the dedication, university officials placed a century depository of materials of scientific interest in front of the building. The university set an atomic clock, scheduled to open the depository on May 22, 2053. *The Xavier Newsletter* sent to alumni proudly reported that the new Tudor-Gothic building added "impressiveness to the line of university structures on the brow of the hill to the east of Victory Parkway." Upon its completion a large shuffling of space took place in other buildings on campus and North Hall on University Drive became the maintenance department headquarters. (57)

The residence hall problem was also a long-standing one. In the immediate postwar period Elet Hall, Marion Hall, and the temporary barracks provided housing for resident students on campus. In February 1952 the Board of Trustees approved the planning of a new residence hall on Ledgewood Avenue, where three barracks had stood since 1947. A year later the university secured a $600,000 loan from the United States Housing and Home Finance Agency, and broke ground for Brockman Hall, named after Hubert F. Brockman, S.J., Xavier's former president. On May 21, 1955, as part of the annual Xavier Family Day, Archbishop Karl J. Alter of Cincinnati, who had succeeded McNicholas five years earlier, dedicated the new hall. Built at a cost of $900,000, Brockman Hall, a residence for 300 students, opened in the fall. Campaign funds supplemented the government loan. (58)

In the early 1950s, President Maguire and Xavier administrators worked with the Alumni Board of Governors and alumni chapters to help invigorate relations between the alumni and their alma mater. On December 3, 1952, the 400th anniversary of St. Francis Xavier's death, the university established Universal Communion Sunday, as an annual event, to be held on the Sunday nearest the December 3 feast day. Sponsored by the Alumni Association, Xavier graduates everywhere were invited to participate. Eighteen alumni groups attended Mass and Communion as a body on Sunday, December 7. In Cincinnati approximately 700 alumni participated in a Mass at the fieldhouse. All told, more than 1,300 alumni participated in the observance. At the third Universal Communion Sunday, Xavier introduced the St. Francis Xavier Medal awarded to persons who exhibited in their lives exemplary qualities that distinguished the patron of the university. (59)

In his efforts to build stronger support for the university, Maguire, consulting with the Alumni Association, helped set up a plan of annual giving whereby business and industry, the alumni, parents, and other members of the university community helped support Xavier. In the first Blue and White Derby annual fund campaign in 1953, alumni gave $15,000, which enabled the university to equip the graduate research laboratory in the newly-built Logan Chemistry Building. The Dads United for Xavier Club, formerly the Dads Club, through its appeal, also equipped a laboratory. In 1953 the university started the Living Endowment Fund (LEF). In its first year there were 830 donors. The class gifts of 1951, 1952, and 1953 made possible the erection in 1953 of the statue of St. Francis Xavier on the O'Brien Terrace, facing Victory Parkway. That same year, friends of the late Albert D. Cash, alumnus, former mayor of Cincinnati, past-president of the Alumni Association, and former director of the Dads Club, provided a memorial conference room in Logan Hall in his name. In 1954 the university inaugurated the Businessmen Mobilized for Xavier (BMX), also an annual fund-raising appeal. The administration divided the funds derived from the several fund-raising appeals amongst capital improvements, faculty salaries, and student services. (60)

In January 1954, Maguire and Fred C. Lamping, class of 1926 and president of the Xavier Alumni Association, announced jointly the formation of an Alumni Fund Council. With a maximum membership of twenty-five graduates, its purpose was "to encourage the alumni and others to make gifts of all types to the University" as part of an annual alumni fund drive. Favoring this new approach, in August of that year the Alumni Association discontinued collection of annual dues. The net effect was one appeal made annually to alumni for support of the university. There was ample made precedence in the history of other universities for the change. The university saw the number of alumni participating in the alumni fund appeals increase from 835 in 1953 to more than 1,300 in 1955, and contributed amounts from $24,124.28 to more than $40,000. In 1955 the percentage of alumni participation in the fund was over 33 percent, placing Xavier in the top echelon in alumni giving among Catholic men's colleges. At the time there were approximately 3,300 alumni, located in forty states and eleven foreign countries. During the 1954–1955 academic year the university raised $294,379.07 in gifts and bequests from the Businessmen Mobilized for Xavier, the Alumni Living Endowment Fund, and the Dads United for Xavier. (61)

While alumni membership and contributions grew during Maguire's first five years as president, the value of the university plant also increased by nearly $2,000,000 through the improvement of buildings, the erection of the Thomas J. Logan Chemistry Building and the Hubert J. Brockman Residence Hall, and the acquisition of additional property adjacent to the campus. Maguire helped establish a chapel in Elet Hall and a lounge in the Union Building for the primary use of resident students. In addition, in 1950 the university equipped Albers Hall for music performances and lectures. Two years later he dedicated the Fine Arts Room on the first floor in Albers Hall to the memory of Dorothy Albers, a benefactor to the university. (62)

In addition to brick and mortar projects and work with the alumni, Maguire helped lay the foundation for faculty governance in the life of the university. He supported the effort by the faculty to establish a Faculty Committee. On March 9, 1952, lay faculty members met in the Fine Arts Room "for the purpose of determining the feasibility and practicality of establishing a faculty organization." Dr. Charles F. Wheeler, professor of English, chaired the exploratory meeting aimed "at discovering the 'why and wherefore'" of a faculty group. At the time there were about 88 full-time faculty members, approximately 67 of whom were lay. Not knowing what would be the full scope of the charge of the faculty group, there was some discussion of the faculty "banning together to buy staple items collectively." Throughout the spring and next academic year, a committee of seven faculty members studied "the advantages and disadvantages" of establishing a faculty organization and drafted a Faculty Committee Constitution. (63)

In early fall 1953 the faculty approved the committee's work. The purpose of the Faculty Committee, as set forth in the constitution, was "to promote the good of the University in all matters which pertain directly to the faculty, especially in such areas as scholarship and research among the members of the faculty, promotion of excellence in teaching, orientation of new faculty members, conditions of service which affect the faculty as a whole, and liaison between the faculty and the administration." Dean Paul O'Connor pointed out to Maguire in late September that such a committee would make the faculty members "feel they belong, . . . [would] do much toward advancing the interests of the faculty and the University, . . . and have some faint voice in determining policy." Maguire recommended that seven faculty members, including three Jesuits, serve on the committee. "To get [it] on the right foot," he wrote, "I suggest that the first members of the Committee be appointed by the President, and after that vacancies be filled by election." On the last day of September, Maguire appointed the faculty to the committee, which he viewed as "the official advisory board of the dean of the College of Liberal Arts," then regarded as the chief academic officer, and as "the official representative body of the faculty when called upon for advice in matters of policy by administrative officials or committees." At the first meeting the seven faculty members elected the chair of the committee. (64)

The Faculty Committee met ten times in its first year. Two days before each meeting, the committee members posted the agenda on the faculty bulletin boards. The notice also included an invitation to the faculty to attend the meetings. Within seven months of the Faculty Committee's birth, however, O'Connor, who placed "great importance on its work," noted in a meeting with the members that "liaison between the faculty and the Faculty Committee had not been as effective as he had hoped for." He also thought that the committee's "communications with officials of the University . . . had not functioned at a high level of efficiency." Notwithstanding the dean's initial concerns, during its first year the Faculty Committee began working on a faculty handbook and dealt with the question whether academic classes should begin at 8 or at 8:30 a.m. The faculty voted to keep it at 8:30. (65)

After a six-year term in Cincinnati, in the summer of 1955 James Maguire became president of Loyola University in Chicago. Under his leadership Xavier had experienced remarkable growth and development. He came on the scene in 1949 when enrollment had reached its peak because of the large number of veterans seeking education. Thereafter he had to cope with uncertain annual revenues caused by fluctuating enrollment. His careful administration kept Xavier's budget in the black every year but one. He crusaded vigorously for the cause of private education and was particularly supportive of religious education at the university. With his support, the faculty in the Department of Religious Education changed the department's name to Theology, reorganized the major, and offered more upper-level courses. In 1954 Maguire set up an academic committee of department heads and senior faculty members to develop a blueprint for the university's development in the next decade. Like his predecessor Maguire also set the example for university administrators and faculty by constant participation in civic affairs. (66)

It was also during Maguire's tenure that the university's membership in the Chicago province underwent a change. In 1954 the Jesuit father general in Rome authorized a reorganization of the Chicago and Detroit provinces. While Loyola University and Xavier were housed in the Chicago province, the University of Detroit and John Carroll University became part of the Detroit province. The growth of these schools had been most pronounced since World War II. Xavier, in particular, rose from a pre-war enrollment of approximately 1,200 to approximately 3,000 full- and part-time students in 1955. (67)

XAVIER UNIVERSITY TRANSFORMED: THE PRESIDENCY OF PAUL L. O'CONNOR, S.J., 1955–1972

O n the evening of July 31, 1955, in the refectory of Hinkle Hall, with the reading of a message from John Baptist Janssens, the Jesuit father general, Paul Lynch O'Connor became Xavier University's thirty-second president and the twenty-ninth Jesuit president. Born August 10, 1909 in Joliet, Illinois, O'Connor attended Loyola Academy and then Loyola University in Chicago for two years. In 1929 he entered the Society of Jesus at the Novitiate of the Sacred Heart in Milford, Ohio, to begin his training as a Jesuit. In 1932 he earned the bachelor's degree in literature from Xavier. Six years later he received the master of arts degree in English from Loyola University. In 1941 he completed his studies for the priesthood at West Baden College in Indiana. From 1942 to 1944 he served as dean of freshmen at the University of Detroit. Before joining the Xavier University staff in 1946, O'Connor served two years as a navy chaplain. His tour of duty took him to the shores of Japan. He was chaplain aboard the *U.S.S. Missouri* when the Japanese representatives in Tokyo Bay signed the peace treaty that ended the war in September 1945. Upon release from military service he joined the university. (1)

At the beginning of the fall term in 1955, the forty-six-year-old O'Connor, who had a fine sense of humor, Irish wit, and a great capacity for work, delivered his first message as president. Reflecting the university's rich Jesuit tradition, he emphasized the importance of educating students intellectually, morally, and spiritually. "In the Providence of God," he said, "you are in a university that will prepare you, if you cooperate, not only for the economic and social challenges but also for the more important problems of your inner life." Three months later he argued that "all true education . . . implies the evolving and unfolding of a young mind into mental and moral maturity." For that to happen, however, a quality faculty was essential. "I am absolutely convinced," O'Connor said, "that the heart of all education lies in the teacher in the classroom." A teacher himself, he would stop to chat with students, at times about his favorite Jesuit poet, Gerard Manley Hopkins. (2)

In O'Connor's judgment the greatest challenge that he faced as head of the university was "meeting the tidal wave of enrollment ahead." Xavier's total enrollment of approximately 3,400 students in the fall of 1955 surpassed even the height of the post-World War II veteran enrollment period of 1948–1949, when there were approximately 3,300 students. Though there were slightly fewer full-time students, the big difference was in the graduate division where there were over 670 students, compared to 125 in the fall of 1948. The university's facilities were being pushed to the extreme. Notwithstanding the erection of the new Brockman Hall, the residence facilities on campus were completely filled. It even had been necessary to authorize off-campus residence for some upperclassmen. In addition to the need for more residential facilities "[w]e need a great deal of classroom space," O'Connor said. "While we do not intend to start costly professional schools like medicine and dentistry, engineering and law, in competition with already established schools in the vicinity, we do intend to increase, in quantity and quality, what we already have." (3)

During O'Connor's first year as president, the university celebrated the 125th anniversary of its founding. In April, O'Connor delivered an address entitled "125 Years of an Unchanging Vision." That same month the *Xavier University News* published a special anniversary edition and the Department of Philosophy hosted the national convention of the American Catholic Philosophical Association. In the fall, special events marked the anniversary. On October 17, the actual date of the founding of the Athenaeum in 1831, administrators, faculty, students, and friends of the university gathered in the fieldhouse for an anniversary convocation. Among the speakers were Bishop Clarence Issenmann of the Archdiocese of Cincinnati and Mayor Charles P. Taft of Cincinnati. In the evening Archbishop Karl Alter celebrated a High Mass in St. Francis Xavier Church. In November, shortly before Thanksgiving, the Cincinnati Symphony Orchestra presented a "Birthday Party" concert in the fieldhouse. Peter Paul Loyanich, alumnus, and John Reinke, S.J., of the psychology department, presented piano solos. A specially-commissioned musical fantasy titled "Xaveriana," based on Xavier songs and written for two pianos and orchestra, was also part of the program. (4)

Three years later in December 1959, O'Connor proudly described the university seal and the rationale behind Jesuit education. Suggesting a multitude of themes, "[i]t has," he said, "the name of the University—'Universitas Xaveriana'; our city—'Cincinnatensis'; and the date of our founding—'1831'." On the upper right was the black-robed right arm holding the cross of Christianity, "suggesting," he wrote, "the Jesuit Order which has operated Xavier University since 1840." On the lower right were three pink shells suggesting the spectacular missionary journeys that St. Francis Xavier, the patron of the university, made to India and the Far East in the mid-sixteenth century. Above the shield was a compressed circle with the letters IHS for the name of Jesus. Below it were the letters AMDG that stood for the Jesuit motto—Ad Majorem Dei Gloriam—For the Greater Glory of God. In O'Connor's judgment the "educational philosophy of the men who founded Xavier University and of those who have carried it down to this very moment can be distilled into one great idea—the great idea of the Christian Revelation—the awesome fact that man has a supernatural destiny." This educational philosophy carried the conviction that students had to "be educated to live not only in time but in eternity. They must be educated both for life and for an after-life. . . . The *Ratio Studiorum*," he continued, "is simply the rationale of the educational program that we think is distinctive of Jesuit education." Reflecting later on the distinctive letter "X," he pointed out that it stood "for Xavier, a name of fame. . . . 'X' men," he argued, echoing the sentiments of his Jesuit colleagues, ought to "display the highest qualities of intellect and character." Throughout his tenure O'Connor insisted that a "Jesuit education is not satisfied with a merely learned man. It proposes to train a man in virtue and character. . . . [It] takes into account not only man's complete growth and the totality of his relations, but also and essentially his elevation to a supernatural destiny." (5)

A More Modern Campus in the Making

During the 1956–1957 academic year, the graduate division, which had soared to an enrollment of 923 in just ten years of operation, was given the status of graduate school. At the same time, the University changed the designation of the College of Liberal Arts to the College of Arts and Sciences. To reflect the growing size and complexity of the business administration offerings, Xavier officials also established a new division of business administration with Thomas J. Hailstones, associate professor of business administration and economics, as director. For the first time in its history, the university created an executive vice presidency and appointed Victor Nieporte, S.J., to the position. Its purpose was to facilitate more efficient handling of administrative tasks connected with the president's office. The following year the school's enrollment reached a record high of 4,058 students, which was over two hundred more than were registered the previous fall, also a record semester. These increases taxed all classroom facilities. A significant factor for the increase in enrollment was the success of the master of business administration (MBA) program. Since its establishment four years earlier there were 688 students enrolled in the MBA program, giving Xavier the largest such program in the area and also the largest among Catholic universities in the United States. (6)

To accommodate this growth, O'Connor, who had a vision of expanding the campus, thought the university needed additional facilities. In the first decade after World War II the ROTC Armory, Logan Chemistry Building, and Brockman Hall had represented a new phase of construction. Early in O'Connor's presidency the university began planning for a new and more ambitious campus building program. In June 1957, before any plan was laid out, the university appropriately conferred the honorary doctor of laws degree to Walter S. Schmidt, one of the university's most generous benefactors. "Our proudest boast on this memorable occasion," O'Connor said, "is that you are a son of Xavier." The degree, conferred in the Schmidt Fieldhouse, which had been erected almost three decades earlier as a memorial to his parents, paid tribute to what Schmidt had done for his "Alma Mater as advisor, benefactor, and leader," O'Connor said. ". . . Our modern campus," which Schmidt had helped secure "in concept and largely in realization, bears witness to your capacity for bold planning and fearless execution." (7)

The January 1958 meeting of the presidents of the 28 Jesuit colleges and universities, held at Georgetown University, also helped plant the seed for the new crop of construction at Xavier. The presidents adopted a statement on "The Current Role of Jesuit Education." Though concerned over the Cold War, and especially the production of ballistic missiles, they argued that "the basic response of education to today's pressures lies not in a program of better ballistics (despite its importance) but in one that produces better men." Convinced that the Jesuit institutions in the 1960s would expand their physical plant "to accommodate their proper share of the large college population expected," they envisioned a collective ambitious construction program of over $100 million that would provide more than 90 new buildings on Jesuit campuses. Wanting to be "significant players" in modern higher education, the Jesuit presidents were confident they could realize their goal because of the loyal support of some 600,000 alumni, generous benefactors, industry, and philanthropic foundations. The Board of Governors of the Jesuit Educational Association, which was founded in 1934 and provided the administrative oversight of American Jesuit colleges and universities, hoped to build "autonomous expanding" institutions. (8)

Two months after the presidents' conference, O'Connor appealed to the university's alumni and friends for support, pointing out that Xavier's greatest immediate needs were "the maintaining of improved faculty salaries, the balancing of the current operations budget, and the building of a classroom building." From the time he became president O'Connor thought that Xavier's annual solicitation would provide the necessary funds. Though in the 1950s the usual procedure of private schools when faced with a need for expansion was to mount a capital gifts campaign, O'Connor had well-placed confidence in the three chief supporting bodies of the university: Alumni Association, Dads Club, and local business and industry. The university had come to rely on the proceeds from these annual drives to fund special projects. "We will continue this annual solicitation," he had written in his first year as president, "and we feel sure that as we make known our increased needs, . . . industry in this area, our alumni, and our friends will see that we are given the tools to do this most important work." (9)

In the spring of 1958 the university introduced a new feature in its efforts to stimulate alumni giving. Through a telephone hookup in twelve cities east of the Mississippi River it conducted its first alumni meeting by telephone, called "Operation Partyline," which originated in the old Red Building on Dana Avenue. "So once again," O'Connor informed the alumni, "you are out in front. . . . As I visualize these telephone lines radiating in all directions out from the campus, I feel suddenly that Xavier's campus has exploded into a great circle a thousand miles across." (10)

That same year a faculty committee appointed by O'Connor developed a campus construction plan calling for a classroom building, multipurpose student center, Jesuit faculty residence, and a chapel. Executive Vice President Nieporte coordinated the campus building program. A year earlier, anticipating a substantial increase in enrollment during the coming decade, the university's academic departments in separate meetings had underscored the need for additional classrooms. The administration began raising money from business and industry in the community, alumni, parents, and other friends of the university. There was considerable discussion about the new building's location, since that would likely affect future plans for the campus. The university administration and faculty chose a site on the east side of Herald Avenue, behind Albers and Logan Halls. They also proposed that a student center, Jesuit faculty residence, and chapel be erected in that general area. To address safety issues for students and faculty as well as to reduce the traffic noise, university officials petitioned the Planning Committee of the Cincinnati City Council to close Herald Avenue between Dana and Ledgewood Avenues. On July 2, 1958, the City Council enacted the ordinance to vacate a portion of Herald, thus opening up the land to the east for maximum development. (11)

In the fall of 1958, the Board of Trustees approved plans for the construction of the new classroom building. "[T]his is the foundation stone of a whole new campus development," O'Connor wrote. "For the first time in these forty years on this campus we will have sufficient classroom space at our disposal," he said. The new classroom building was dictated in part by the growing popularity of summer school. In the summer of 1959, when construction began, there were well over 1,200 students who attended the two summer terms. (12)

University authorities considered several names for the new classroom building, including Founders Hall, Xavier Hall, and Loyola Hall. In September 1960 they decided to name it after Karl Alter, archbishop of Cincinnati. Three months later, with the archbishop presiding, the university dedicated the new classroom building, in time for the start of the second semester. It was the first air-conditioned building on campus. Constructed at a cost of $1,175,000, Alter Hall contained a 300-seat lecture hall, eventually named Kelly Auditorium, underwritten by a Detroit supporter of the university, and thirty-three classrooms, which doubled classroom space on the campus. Other features included a central records office, offices for the academic deans and their staffs, a student lounge, and a communication arts laboratory. The proceeds over a four-year period from the Businessmen Mobilized for Xavier, Living Endowment Fund, and Dads United for Xavier paid for the new classroom building. With the addition of Alter Hall, the library in Schmidt Hall retrieved approximately 60 percent of the space that it had "devoted to other uses." (13)

In anticipation of the new classroom building, in the fall of 1960 university officials transferred the Evening College, which had been located in downtown Cincinnati on Sycamore Street since 1911, to the main campus. The new location provided more classrooms and more parking facilities for the evening students. Being on the main campus also afforded them a wider course selection and access to the main library and scientific laboratories. The evening students secured Xavier ID cards that enabled them to attend sporting events, plays, and various campus activities at a discount. The 1961 summer school enrollment of 1,631 students set a new record for summer enrollment and was more than a 20 percent increase over the previous year. The addition of evening courses to the summer curriculum contributed to this increase. (14)

That same year, St. Xavier High School at Seventh and Sycamore Streets moved to a new location on North Bend Road, northwest of downtown Cincinnati. That move ended 120 years of uninterrupted Jesuit educational activity in the downtown area. Though the building, for many years the site of both St. Xavier College and High School, was razed, St. Francis Xavier Church and the rectory remained at the original Sycamore Street location. In 1961 Milford College, where the Jesuit seminarians studied, was the only college of the university not located on the main campus. "We have found this consolidation of day and evening colleges on one campus to be most advantageous," O'Connor said. ". . . [M]aking maximum use of one's facilities is a cogent argument with me against a split campus." Eleven years later the university changed the name of the Evening College to the College of Continuing Education. The initial title had been developed when the Evening College conducted only evening classes. By the early 1970s there were late afternoon classes, a full schedule of Saturday classes, and special seminars and programs that were conducted totally in the day. (15)

In anticipation of the future expansion of university facilities, Xavier officials acquired additional property. In the fall of 1961 they secured a ten-acre plot of land from the Toms River Chemical Corporation. The new tract to the north of Herald Avenue at Tibbles Street was located relatively close to the two most recently-erected campus buildings, Brockman Hall and the Karl J. Alter classroom building, and the Herald Avenue playing field used by Xavier students. The new addition of land brought the total campus area to 65 acres. University authorities hoped to erect a new chapel and student activities center on the newly-acquired property. (16)

In June 1960 the children of Elizabeth R. and Charles F. Williams gave the university $200,000 for the construction of a new chapel in honor of their parents. Dedicated on December 16, 1962, the new chapel replaced the one which had graced the first floor of the Schmidt Building for thirty-four years. The new chapel was a departure from the traditional style of church architecture. Flashed with aluminum, the saddle (hyperbolic paraboloid) roof, the first of its kind on a church in the greater Cincinnati area, featured a unique support system and seemed to soar into the air. Serving both the Xavier student body and nearby St. Robert Bellarmine Parish, the new chapel, adjacent to and north of Alter Hall, became a focal point of the expanding campus. (17)

The next phase of the campus development plan, proposed by the faculty in 1958, included the erection of a multi-purpose student center on the large area north of the chapel, a classroom building, and a Jesuit faculty residence. In early 1963 O'Connor announced that "as its next steps" the university would also renovate or expand the library. Later in the year the university considered erecting a new residence hall. Success in annual fund appeals had made it possible for the university to build the classroom building without a capital gifts campaign. O'Connor hoped that the proposed new buildings would be partially financed in the same way. (18)

In 1963 Congress passed the Higher Education Facilities Act (HEFA) in order to help expand college facilities. The university applied for and received a $1,250,000 loan to supplement the $1,000,000 raised from donors to help build the student center. Over a five-year period Catholic colleges received over $125,000,000 from HEFA grants for facilities. The university broke ground for the new center in December. Less than two years later, on October 31, 1965, with Archbishop Alter presiding, university officials dedicated the new facility. The University Center provided a dining room and Musketeer Grill, a theater, meeting rooms, a bookstore, activities offices, recreation areas, and administrative offices. A top floor meeting room, appropriately called the Board Room, served as the regular meeting room for the Board of Trustees sessions. It was the "costliest building in the history of this institution," O'Connor said, "and also one of the most needed. . . ." Upon its completion O'Connor noted that the university had "achieved a major break-through in terms of our physical plant. Finally, after 40 years of developing the present campus," he said, "we have a complete facility, ready in all its essential parts to serve our education program." (19)

During the construction of the University Center, Xavier began building a new residence hall. In the spring of 1963 the University received a gift of $350,000 from Harry J. Husman, a Cincinnati businessman and alumnus, which enabled University authorities to consider construction of another facility. Xavier had needed a new residence hall for several years, since only 525 of its nearly 800 out-of-town students could be accommodated in campus housing facilities. Lack of funds had delayed construction. A growing number of applications from students living outside greater Cincinnati had also underscored the need for an additional residence hall.

In order to temporarily address the shortage in student housing, two student organizations in the late 1950s had each successfully leased a house and operated it under the supervision of a faculty member. In 1958 the students' Knights of Columbus Council opened a residence facility on Reading Road, less than a mile from campus. The following year the second off-campus residence facility opened on North Crescent Road, about four blocks from the university. Residents of the two houses pitched in to clean and maintain the premises. For the first time in over a century, in the fall of 1963 out-of-town undergraduates outnumbered local students. The following summer the university received an anonymous donation of $250,000. With these funds plus the Husman gift in place, the trustees authorized the university to begin negotiations to construct the Husman residence hall. (20)

The following January the university negotiated another government loan of $500,000 to cover the required interim financing during the construction. A year later the trustees secured a twenty-year mortgage for the same amount at 5 percent interest from the Federal Housing Administration (FHA). Xavier officials dedicated the new Harry J. and Edna D. Husman Hall, with room for 292 students and built at an approximate cost of $1,300,000, on November 28, 1965. That fall the school had a record enrollment of 5,194, with 2,223 undergraduate students, 2,072 graduate students, and 899 students in the Evening College. That was an increase of 531 students over the previous year. The undergraduate day division experienced a 15.5 percent increase, which included a record freshman class of 782 students, nearly 100 greater than in 1964. "There is an explanation to this undergraduate growth," O'Connor said. "In recent years we have had to turn away hundreds of out-of-town students because of the lack of housing on the campus." (21)

When applying for the government loan in late 1965, FHA authorities had discovered a discriminatory provision in the original 1840 Articles of Incorporation that limited the mission of the university to the "education of white youth." The university administration and trustees in the 1960s were unaware of the clause. Government officials pointed out that the articles had to be changed before the loan could be authorized. Although the university, upon the strong recommendation of Archbishop John McNicholas of Cincinnati, had been admitting a small number of African American students since the 1940s, it had done so in violation of its own Articles of Incorporation. As a consequence, on February 3 the trustees made the necessary change. Two days later the university filed a Certificate of Amendment to its articles, indicating that the corporation existed for the purpose "for the education of youth in the various branches of useful knowledge and an understanding of the liberal arts." (22)

As the University Center and Husman Hall were being built, the faculty and administration discussed whether South Hall, the former barracks and student center at the entrance of University Drive, should be demolished. There was, trustees argued, "much to be said for tearing down South Hall." A poll of the faculty, however, recommended that new faculty offices be installed in the former barracks. At the time a number of faculty shared offices. In the spring of 1965 the board agreed to erect new faculty offices in South Hall. At the same meeting the trustees also voted to expand the biology department to the second floor of Albers Hall and move the physics department, which had been occupying that floor, to Alumni Hall. (23)

In early November, John D. Malone, S.J., associate dean of the College of Arts and Sciences, reflecting the sentiment of some of his administrative colleagues, sent a letter to President O'Connor "strenuously" opposing "providing equipment for just *some* faculty members in South Hall," the ones moving into the newly-erected offices. The question of furniture and supplies for the faculty had come up before, but it had always been postponed pending their potential move to more suitable quarters in Hinkle Hall upon the possible erection of a new Jesuit residence. "However," Malone wrote, "recent mutterings that have come to my attention cause me to question the wisdom of any further delay in providing better equipment for the faculty." A "way to dispel" their concerns, he argued, "would be for a formal assurance from the President that . . . the faculty . . . are indeed vitally important, and so considered by the administration, [and] . . . to provide them *now* with . . . new desks and chairs." Three days later Jeremiah O'Callaghan, S.J., dean of the College of Arts and Sciences, and who had also become dean of faculties in 1961, supported Malone's request. He had been appointed dean of faculties largely because the faculty, O'Callaghan later observed, "began to expect more attention to their needs and were becoming suspicious that other areas of the University were getting undue attention, influence, and power." Not knowing precisely why the request for furniture "came at this time," O'Callaghan wrote to O'Connor, "I conjecture, with reason, that it resulted from observation of many physical improvements" on campus. Moreover, the desks and chairs "presently in use," he argued, "[are] strictly second class." A week later the trustees unanimously approved the purchase of new chairs and desks for all faculty members in South Hall. (24)

In the spring of 1966, a few months after the dedications of the University Center and Husman Hall, the university hosted the formal opening of the Fine Arts Gallery, located in the Carriage House of Marion Hall. A two-story structure at the back of the Marion property, the Carriage House could be reached by a winding drive that passed under the porte cochere of the main house. Of prime interest in the new gallery was the value and size of the fine arts collection, which Hubert Brockman had begun to acquire for the Avondale campus. His successor Hugo Sloctemyer continued the effort and placed particular emphasis on Cincinnati artists. The result was a collection of canvasses by a number of famous local artists such as Frank Duvenek and Edward Potthast. At the opening of the Fine Arts Gallery, the university exhibited works by Cincinnati artists, over 75 paintings from the Renaissance, the seventeenth-century Dutch and Flemish schools, the English portraiture school, the Barbizon school, the French Impressionists, and works by nineteenth-century Americans. The gallery also displayed antique and modern porcelains, bronzes, and other works of art. (25)

While construction of the new student center and residence hall were underway, the trustees in the fall of 1964 had also approved the building of a new library at a cost of approximately $1,800,000. The Walter A. and George McDonald Foundation, interested in making a significant contribution to higher education in Cincinnati, had given $1,000,000 to the university. The Schmidt Library, which had been conceived in the mid-1920s as adequate for a student body of 700 was no longer sufficient. In 1964 there were more than 4,600 students. Having "made phenomenal strides on both the undergraduate and graduate levels in recent years," O'Connor said, he thought Xavier could "double that number in another decade." The university chose a site on the newly-developed Xavier University Mall, which extended from Herald Avenue, for the building of the three-story library. That same fall the university received $572,608 from the Ohio Board of Regents, which distributed federal funds to Ohio colleges and universities under provisions of the federal Higher Education Facilities Act of 1963, to help improve its library facilities. (26)

On May 7, 1967, the university dedicated the McDonald Memorial Library, and Archbishop Alter blessed the building. Built for approximately 400,000 volumes, which was five times the book capacity of the library in the Schmidt Building, it had a seating capacity of slightly over 700 people. A garden in the rear provided an area for relaxed study and thought. The Schmidt Building library had served the university community for 40 years. The vacated space was used for classrooms, the bursar's office, a computer center, and temporary faculty offices. (27)

In November 1965, as the university celebrated the dedication of Husman Hall, the trustees considered the feasibility of constructing another residence hall. Based on the fact that both the University Center and Alter Hall could accommodate more students, they authorized O'Connor to proceed with the planning of a new facility. Projections of continued increases in undergraduate enrollment compelled the trustees to approve the new project. There was a "critical need," they thought, to build the new residence hall "as soon as possible." Temporarily easing university housing practices, the dean of students, Patrick H. Ratterman, S.J., in response to the shortage of residential space on campus, had been permitting many more students to live in apartments off campus. On December 10, 1967, the university blessed and dedicated the new residence hall on Herald Avenue. Named Kuhlman Hall in honor of George H. and Rose Kuhlman, parents of Leo G. Kuhlman of the class of 1911 and Lawrence B. Kuhlman of the class of 1914, it was connected to Husman Hall by a breezeway. A seven-story building, the university's first high-rise, Kuhlman Hall had room for 432 students. The infirmary rooms of the McGrath Health Center, on the first floor of the new building, provided health services for the members of the university community. Upon completion of Kuhlman, the residence facilities on campus provided room for over a thousand students. (28)

In the spring and summer of 1966 the University Mall, on which five of the newest university buildings faced, underwent landscaping. By the fall, school officials closed and decided to tear down the sixty-eight-year-old Red Building on Dana Avenue. As the original building on the campus, the Georgian-style structure with the gleaming white cupola resting atop three stories of red brick had served as the club-house for the Avondale Athletic Club; as Xavier Academy (1912–19); and as a college classroom building (1919–20) until Alumni and Hinkle halls were completed in the fall of 1920. It then later served as the university cafeteria and activities center. Indeed, different generations of Xavier students knew it respectively as the academy, Union Building, chapel, cafeteria, library, recreation center, bowling alley, and a little theater. (29)

Originally the university had planned to remodel the Red Building into a demonstation Montessori school for preschool-age children and install counselling rooms, classrooms, and audio-visual facilities. Beginning in June 1961 the Graduate School offered the nation's first university-level graduate school training program in Montessori educa-tion. However, to refurbish the building for the education of small chil-dren and to be in compliance with the strict building code of the City Building Commission was not economically feasible. Sentiment grew to build a new structure. By the spring of 1967 the Board of Trustees opted for a new three-story building for Montessori education at an estimated cost of $475,000. "There is a lot of tradition connected with the old building," O'Connor said. "Because of this and the beauty of the structure itself, we would, of course, prefer to keep it standing. However," he continued, "our land is at a premium now due to our rapid campus expansion. We have no choice but to remove the build-ing and make new use of the site." On December 1, 1968 the university dedicated the new George J. Joseph Building, home to the Center for

Human Development. Used by educators in preschool development, the center also helped prepare counselors, psychologists, and reading specialists. (30)

The final piece of the campus development plan proposed in 1958 was the Jesuit faculty residence. For several years university officials explored the possibility of building a new home for the Jesuits on campus. In 1966 it became an objective of the Living Endowment Fund (LEF) campaign. In a series of talks to the alumni in the fall, O'Connor referred to the Jesuits' inadequate living conditions on campus and hoped to ease overcrowding by building a new planned residence. Pointing out that he had "no intention of downgrading Hinkle Hall," for it had been for over 45 years "a dignified and impressive campus symbol . . . and a good home for the Jesuits, today," he argued, "Hinkle hall is crowded. In fact it is overflowing." In addition to Hinkle, five neighborhood residences on Dana and Ledgewood Avenues housed members of the Society of Jesus. Community dining and recreation for all the Jesuits were no longer possible because Hinkle Hall could only accommodate 35 residents. (31)

When Jesuit visitors visited the university it was difficult to find appropriate accommodations on campus. "As the pressures for space have been mounting," O'Connor said, "one of our community wags recently suggested that we remove Isaac Jogues and Ignatius of Loyola from the niches on the front of the building to make way for two living Jesuits." Moreover, Hinkle's location "at the crossroads of this busy campus is much too public to be ideal as a Jesuit home," he explained. There were many instances when students and faculty used the Hinkle Hall corridor on their way to classes in Albers or Alumni Hall on a rainy day. Though he sympathized with them, "I also know," he said, "the awkwardness of having your chapel and dining room open onto a thoroughfare that resembles Broadway at Times Square." As he argued for a new Jesuit residence next to the library that was under construction, O'Connor was confident that he could find a new and highly important function for Hinkle Hall. He proposed, as he had promised the faculty, using it to provide offices for its lay members. At the time they were sharing facilities in South Hall, whose "density of occupancy," he said, "is just about intolerable." (32)

For thirteen months, March 1966 to April 1967, the Chicago provincial and Xavier's Jesuit community exchanged opinions on the cost and the nature and scope of the proposed building. Though at first the provincial had reservations about each Jesuit having his own private bath and facilities he agreed in mid-March 1966 that "as far as he was concerned there was no certain objection to having toilets and showers in the rooms." The plans, however, had to go to Rome for father general's judgment, which, in the provincial's opinion, was "not predictable." Xavier's Jesuits' Planning Committee oversaw the plans for construction and was hopeful to see the building begun toward the end of the year. In September, however, the provincial recommended a reduction of "the size of the private rooms." Disappointed by his suggestion the local planning committee subsequently met and voted to hold firm to the size of the rooms. That same month the Walter E. Schott Family Foundation, a Cincinnati foundation, gave Xavier a gift of stock and cash in the amount of $750,000 to be used toward the construction. These funds, along with those contributed by alumni through the LEF drive, made it possible to build the new Jesuit residence hall as soon as plans were finalized. (33)

In October the North Aurora scholastics in Aurora, Illinois, criticized Xavier's construction plans, referring to "unnecessary and luxurious furnishings." In light of the newly-erected Bellarmine Chapel on campus they considered the proposed chapel in the new building unnecessary. Moreover, there were Jesuits in the Chicago province who were concerned about the size of the rooms, the resultant cost, and the height of the building, estimated to be ten stories high. As a consequence, the Xavier Board of Trustees decided to delay final action until all issues were addressed and to wait for the provincial's decision. (34)

In late December 1966, O'Connor learned that the father general also had reservations about the private baths, the community chapel, and the height of the building. Members of the local Jesuit community again met and discussed their predicament. Although some thought that they should not eliminate the individual baths, the majority of them agreed to do so in order to secure general approval of the plans, which included the community chapel and the high-rise. "[C]ontrary to the belief of some," a few Jesuits argued, "people . . . would be surprised if we did not have [a chapel]." When the trustees met in January and the following spring, however, notwithstanding the one concession by the Jesuit community, they found the overall recommendations of the building committee, including the high-rise, individual rooms equipped with private baths, and the community chapel to be sound and "fundamentally favorable." (35)

O'Connor then informed the provincial of the trustees' deliberations and how the university planned to finance the building. In addition to the Schott Foundation gift of $750,000, the university had raised $969,000 and had surplus funds of $428,000 for a total of $2,147,000. The following month the provincial approved the plan, including the private baths, with a strong recommendation that the chapel wing, which extended out beyond the rest of the building, be incorporated into the rest of the building. "If your reason for building a high-rise was to save space," he argued, "it seems to me that you have defeated your purpose in extending the chapel. . . . If you are going to use up all this space, it would be more advisable to extend your whole building. This would eliminate the need for such a high building." Five days later O'Connor telephoned him, pointing out that incorporating the chapel would "require scrapping the present plans and starting over again. To attempt simply an adaptation would result in a hodge-podge. This effort would, of course, be very expensive and would take a long time." The provincial gave permission to proceed with the building as planned. Later that day the trustees unanimously approved the construction of the Walter E. Schott Memorial Building. About three years later, on February 22, 1970, the Jesuits moved from Hinkle Hall into their new ten-story residence that could accommodate 68 Jesuits. The new Jesuit residence was the eighth major structure erected on the Xavier campus since 1960. (36)

In the spring the Board of Trustees, through the university's attorney, assigned the Schott Jesuit Residence, commonly called Schott Hall, to the Jesuit community of Xavier University for their sole use for as long as the Chicago province assigned a "reasonable number of Jesuits" to teach, administer, or counsel at the university. The reason for the arrangement was the provincial's worry "about the future," O'Connor wrote, "when possibly some lay Board of Trustees would want to get rid of the Jesuits." At the time there was discussion over the possible addition of laymen to the board. In return for the Schott building, the Jesuit community, which bore all costs for the maintenance of the building, agreed to return to the university a percentage of their university salaries. O'Connor was pleased with the agreement. It insured "that the University," he wrote, "would receive some kind of monetary return from it and therefore be able to justify in our own consciences the turning over the building to the Jesuits." (37)

As the university proceeded with the construction of the last building in the university's campus development plan, Xavier authorities approved additional renovation of the University Mall. In the fall of 1968, members of the class of 1962, 1964, and 1968 respectively contributed to the building of the Musketeer Plaza, directly across from the entrance to Alter Hall in the Mall. Since 1951 each senior class had collected a sum of money from its members as a farewell gift designated for a specific project and presented to the university on commencement day. Even though Xavier's Musketeer tradition was thirty-seven years old, it was the class of 1962 that asked itself whether Xavier had given appropriate visibility to the Musketeer, the symbol of its athletic team, and made a class gift toward that purpose. The university committee charged with carrying out the terms of the gift set out to get a meaningful statue. Then an article appeared in the *New York Times* pointing out that the town Auch, in the province of Gascony in southern France, was the birthplace of the most famous of all Musketeers— Charles de Batz-Castelmore, the Musketeer D'Artagnan of seventeenth century France. The younger son of a royal family, D'Artagnan had contributed many soldiers to the French army. The piece further pointed out that millions of people had become acquainted with him through reading Alexandre Dumas's novel, *The Three Musketeers*, published in 1844. But not until the mid-1960s was it discovered that D'Artagnan had really existed. It was also learned that in 1933 the town had honored the soldier by erecting a bronze statue of him. (38)

Xavier officials pursued the possibility of the university obtaining a reproduction of the Musketeer D'Artagnan. In the summer of 1964, Joseph Bourgeois, chair of the Department of Modern Languages, and his wife, Jeanne, visited France and the town of Auch. The visit resulted in photographs of the statue and contact with the mayor of the town. Shortly after their return to Cincinnati, Jeanne Bourgeois received a letter from the mayor, pointing out that the town officials had decided to offer to Xavier University a copy, reduced in size, of the statue. It arrived in the spring of 1965. Made of terra cotta, with a bronze finish, it stood about one-third life-size. The university placed it in a special niche in one of the main rooms of the new University Center. In the fall of 1966 the Xavier community received the history of D'Artagnan in artistic form through a huge mural affixed to the walls of the Musketeer Grill in the University Center. (39)

In addition to the miniature statue and mural in the University Center, the members of the class of 1962 decided to erect a large and more visible symbol of the Musketeer on campus. Following lengthy negotiations between the mayor of Auch and the celebrated French sculptor Andre Tauziede, the university signed a contract for sculpting a life-sized reproduction statue of D'Artagnan. While the negotiations progressed, members of the class of 1964 also decided that a suitable location should be selected for the American flag on campus. On November 2, 1968 members of the class of that year also made it possible at the Musketeer Plaza dedication to mark a spot on campus with the letter 'X,' symbolizing both the university's patron, St. Francis Xavier, and Christ. The statue of D'Artagnan stood on the Musketeer Plaza flanked by two symbols of its past—one was the tile entrance inscription from the lobby of old St. Xavier College at Seventh and Sycamore and the other was the terrazzo floor insignia that recalled the Red Building's original use as the Avondale Athletic Club. "This is a great moment in the history of Xavier University," O'Connor said at the dedication. ". . . Tradition is the golden thread that binds a community like Xavier into a unity spanning the years." (40)

The University's New Profile

With new facilities being built in the 1960s and an increasing number of students enrolling in the university, the Xavier administration also underwent a significant change. In early spring 1966, O'Connor proposed a new administrative organization to the trustees. The president had nine people reporting directly to him. "This appears," O'Connor said to the board, "to be clearly too many. . . . It now seems to be time to rethink and tighten up [the] chain of command." Moreover, he hoped the new administrative structure would also help "decentralize authority and responsibility." After some discussion the trustees created four new university vice presidencies. Two of the vice presidents were laymen, the first non-clerics to hold such high posts in the history of the school. Irvin beumer, Xavier's first lay business manager, became vice president for business and finance; Jeremiah J. O'Callaghan, S.J., academic vice president; Patrick H. Ratterman, S.J., vice president for student affairs; and Edward P. VonderHaar, vice president for public relations and development. Nieporte continued as executive vice president. "I am especially pleased to be able to appoint the lay vice presidents," O'Connor said. In light of the changes in the Catholic Church brought about by the Second Vatican Council, which had convened in Rome in 1962, he argued that the appointment of lay administrators was "in keeping with the new emphasis on the importance of the laity in the Church and in the works of the Society [of Jesus]." (41)

The new administrative organization dramatically changed the operations of the university. Over the years the structure of the university had become more and more complicated with day and evening divisions, graduates and undergraduates, colleges of arts and sciences and business administration, and extension courses. In addition to the increased complexities of Xavier's academic organization, there was also growth in student services, complicated by the impetus given these services with the opening of the University Center. All the responsibilities had rested on the dean of faculties, who was also responsible for the academic leadership of the entire university.

Like most colleges and universities, the university divided its administrative structure into four general functions: academic affairs, student affairs, public relations and development, and business affairs. The academic vice president, formerly called the dean of faculties, devoted himself entirely to strengthening academics in the university. Academic Vice President O'Callaghan's direct reports were the academic deans, librarian, registrar, and director of admissions. The student affairs office supervised housing and food services, counseling, placement, student organizations, student health, and athletics. The director of public relations, the moderator of the alumni, and the director of development, who previously all reported directly to the president, now reported to the vice president for public relations and development. This arrangement promised to provide greater efficiency and bring a more orderly chain of command to the entire division. Similarly, the business manager and the treasurer, who previously reported directly to the president, now reported to the vice president for business and finance, who also administered the buildings and grounds, security, purchasing, and mail divisions. (42)

The physical expansion and renovation of the campus in the 1960s were done partly in anticipation of increasing enrollment at the graduate level. By 1968, Xavier University enrolled more graduate students than undergraduates. Under the leadership of Dean Raymond McCoy, the Graduate School grew from 135 students in the summer of 1946 to 2,643 in the fall of 1968. Its growth was due in part to the philosophy and long tradition of the university to make it most convenient for the part-time student to attend classes. While 86 percent of the total enrollment pursued master's degree studies on a part-time basis, the overall graduate population nevertheless represented 28 states. By the end of the decade, Xavier's Graduate School was the third largest among the Jesuit schools. Only St. Louis University and Loyola University of Chicago graduate schools were larger. In Ohio it was the fourth largest. In the summer of 1969 the university topped all Jesuit colleges and universities in summer school graduate enrollment, totalling 2,748. The following year on June 3, 1970, Xavier's 132nd annual commencement ceremonies, conducted for the first time as a two-part production, afternoon and evening in the university fieldhouse, had a record graduating class of 1,605. Graduate enrollment of 3,147 in the spring semester of 1970 was the largest ever. Undergraduate enrollment, on the other hand, fluctuated from 1,781 in 1964 and 2,223 in 1965 to 2,022 in 1970. Indeed, "[t]o a newcomer to the campus, or, more accurately, to one who has returned after a long absence," *Xavier Alumnus* magazine observed, "today's university is an exciting place." Xavier "is certainly not the same school or the same campus that existed . . . five years ago or fifty years ago." (43)

A short article entitled "An Outsider Looks Inside Xavier" in the October 1969 issue of *Xavier Alumnus* pointed out that more "important to most alumni than the physical characteristics of the campus" and all the other changes were "traditions." Many thought "that these should remain completely unchanged," especially the "authoritarian nature of the university." Liking the idea that the "ultimate power of decision still resides with the president of the university," they nevertheless noted that the student and faculty voices were "more discernible." The magazine further observed that there was among the faculty "an obvious ferment of thought, . . . a continuing conversation . . . among the holders of differing points of view. All of this is, no doubt, good for the university. . . . Amid all change and prospect of change," it concluded, "it is sometimes difficult for the returnee to recognize the campus he left some years ago." (44)

Indeed, by the mid-1960s the faculty voice had become more evident. In the judgment of President O'Connor, upon completion of the university's first faculty handbook in 1956, the faculty had "developed the spirit of an elite corps, courteous, generous, effective, [and] representative." As the university experienced significant enrollment and facility growth in the 1960s, faculty members—who were at the heart of the academic enterprise and had participated in the development of a campus building master plan in the late 1950s—sought even "greater participation" in the affairs of the university. During the 1965–1966 academic year the Faculty Committee, formed a dozen years earlier, submitted "A Plan for Enlarging the Role of the Lay Faculty in the Administration of Xavier university." For two years Faculty Committee members in their informal meetings with the president had discussed "possible broader Faculty involvement in University affairs and policy." In the process they sought "to know more precisely the role of the Faculty Committee in advancing this objective." While the December 1965 faculty strike at St. John's University in New York highlighted many faculty grievances in American colleges and universities, which included inadequate faculty salaries and benefits and overall dissatisfaction with university administrations, it focused principally on the faculty's lack of participation in decision making. At Xavier, St. John's strike reflected the absence of structures by which lay faculty could participate more fully in the governance of the university. At a time when Jesuits at Xavier, like their counterparts in other Jesuit colleges and universities, were firmly in control of the administration of the school, many of them feared that laymen might disregard or break with the goals and spirit of the Society of Jesus. (45)

Like many of their colleagues in other colleges and universities, by the spring of 1966 Xavier faculty members sought to enlarge their role in the life of the university. Encouraged and influenced by two lay administrators, Raymond McCoy in the Graduate School and Thomas Hailstones in business administration, they pressed for more control over faculty hiring and tenure. When the American Association for University Professors censured St. John's in the summer of 1966, it sent a message to all institutions of higher learning of the need for faculty handbooks, committees on promotion and tenure, and faculty senates with recognized authority over curriculum.

That same summer President O'Connor and the Board of Trustees granted the faculty's request for the Faculty Committee to appoint "instructional faculty members" to the Academic Council, Admissions Committee, Graduate Council, and Rank and Tenure Committee, but denied the request to appoint Jesuit faculty to the Board of Trustees. Financial crises in American colleges and universities provided another reason for faculty to become engaged in the governance of the institution. That summer the president approved the committee's recommendation that the university form a Budgetary Review Committee with faculty members appointed to it. In the fall there was greater integration of faculty and administration on committees as the faculty began electing colleagues annually to various university committees. At the time there were about 250 full- and part-time faculty members attending to approximately 5,700 students, which was an increase of 50 full- and part-time faculty in four years to teach the additional 1,664 students. (46)

In the summer of 1970, President O'Connor sent to the trustees a copy of Dean McCoy's Report of the Committee to Study a University Senate, recommending the establishment of a Senate in order to enlarge university governance. In August the trustees approved the report's recommendation. The University Senate, which was advisory to the president, consisted of 41 administrators, faculty, students, and staff. There were 14 members of the faculty (all but two elected), 9 students (all but two elected), 10 members of the administration (*ex officio* members), 4 alumni, 2 representatives of the Jesuit community, and 2 elected to represent the staff. The president presided over all sessions. "[I]t gives all sectors of the University," a university administrator said, "an opportunity to speak out on important issues." The University Senate addressed a variety of issues, ranging from the university's fund-raising efforts, campus life, and athletic programs to academic life, recruitment objectives, and budgetary matters. While strongly endorsing what it called a "tripartite senate" the Faculty Committee nevertheless continued to insist "that a purely *faculty* voice should be maintained and that the Faculty Committee should continue to function." (47)

Curricular Developments

During the late 1950s undergraduate student groups and organizations remained active. In the spring of 1957 the 117-year-old Poland Philopedian Debating Society hosted the highly-regarded Robert S. Marx National Invitational Debate Tournament. During the 1958–1959 academic year the Masque Society's offerings of two plays by Molière and Shakespeare, an original musical, three one-act plays, and a week-long presentation of *Treasure Island* for the Cincinnati Children's Theatre set a new level of accomplishment for the organization. That same year two Xavier University students, majors in physics and mathematics respectively, followed Russian satellite accomplishments with interest. As satellite observers they formed a moonwatching team on campus. (48)

Under the leadership of the faculty and administration there were several academic innovations and programs during O'Connor's presidency. In June 1957 the Institute of Hispanic Studies completed its first year of operation with a special six-week language program in the summer for a large contingent of Latin American students from the Caribbean area. During the following academic year the university introduced the tutorial system in the sophomore and junior years of the honors bachelor of arts program. Instead of meeting for class three times a week, each sophomore or junior—either singly or with a fellow student—met the professor once a week. That year the administration also designated the two-story property, known as Marion Hall, as the principal residence hall for the students enrolled in the honors course. In the same year the university, under the leadership of Raymond Allen, S.J., chair of the mathematics department, also introduced a cooperative program in mathematics with area high schools desiring to accelerate the progress of their academically talented students. Moreover, school officials established a hospital administration program that embraced graduate and undergraduate degree work and summer workshops. Within five years, 70 full-time students were enrolled in the graduate hospital business administration program, one of only fifteen institutions of higher learning in the country that offered such a program. During the 1959–1960 academic year the campus radio station broadcasted on 600 KC within the confines of the campus, employing the electrical current as its carrier. In addition to airing music and news, the station, with its studio in Albers Hall, carried play-by-play accounts of the freshman football games played in the Xavier stadium. In 1964 it moved into new studios in the basement of Alter Hall. This move also enabled the faculty to strengthen the communication arts curriculum. Six years later Xavier's new educational FM radio station, WVXU-FM, under the leadership of Lawrence J. Flynn, S.J., went on the air. (49)

In the fall of 1961 the university, under the leadership of Professor Vytautas Bieliauskas, chair of the Department of Psychology, initiated a master's degree program in psychology. In addition, the division of business administration, established five years earlier, became a separate college with Thomas Hailstones as dean. The mercantile department, which was started with the arrival of the Jesuits in the fall of 1840, had grown into a college. The university now had five major divisions: College of Arts and Sciences, College of Business Administration, Evening College, Graduate School, and the Milford division. With 136 credit hours required of each business student in the undergraduate four-year program, 60 credit hours were in business subjects. He could concentrate or major in accounting, economics, finance, marketing, management, or industrial relations, disciplines that formerly belonged in the College of Arts and Sciences. The concentrations consisted of 24 credit hours of study, leaving 36 hours for other required business courses. Among the colleges and universities in the country, Xavier had one of the highest ratios of non-business subjects to business subjects for business administration students. In addition, business students were required to take the core subjects of English, philosophy, theology, history, mathematics, science, psychology, and military science. Five years later the College of Business Administration established the Institute for Business and Community Service to provide programs and services to professionals in the metropolitan area. (50)

For one week in October 1962, six of the most distinguished physicists in the world participated in Xavier's Conference on the Foundation of Quantum Mechanics. Participants included Nobel Prize winner Paul A. M. Dirac of Cambridge University, Boris Podolsky of the Xavier faculty, and faculty members from Princeton University, Harvard University, Yeshiva University, and the Israel Institute of Technology. (51)

Two years later Aline Fredin, in honor of her parents, made a gift of nearly $200,000 to the university for Xavier students to pursue studies in France. Born in Cincinnati of French parents, Aline Fredin studied piano at the Cincinnati College of Music and then spent a number of years in Europe studying music. The Fredin bequest made it possible for the university to endow the gift and award scholarships to students. At first Xavier students attended the University of Lyon in east-central France for an entire academic year. Later the administration changed it to the Xavier Fredin Summer Program in France, which provided scholarships for study during the summer months, and then expanded it so that the scholarship recipients could spend not only the summer but their complete junior academic year at the University of Paris (Sorbonne). (52)

In the fall of 1964 a university committee headed by William J. Larkin III, associate professor and chair of the Department of Mathematics, submitted a proposal to Dean O'Callaghan for the establishment of a computer center, subsequently approved by the Board of Trustees. Room 10 on the first floor of the Schmidt Building had a new look. The room, which over the years had been the site of numerous public lectures, was converted into the computer center. Under Larkin's directorship, the center assisted all kinds of programs and activities— academic research, personnel, payroll, development records, alumni list, and the grading of examinations. A number of graduate and undergraduate students served as operator-programmers. (53)

In January 1970 Xavier University was thrust into the national spotlight when it added a $750,000 General Electric 430 time-sharing computer, making Xavier a pioneer in the field of academic time-sharing computation. The university and Applied Computer Time Share, Inc. entered into a cooperative effort, serving as a source of time-sharing for educational institutions in greater Cincinnati. Campus terminals that could use the time-sharing computer were located in Alumni Hall, in the Graduate School office in Alter Hall and in Logan, Elet, and Albers halls. The Department of Marketing pioneered the classroom application of the time-sharing computer. (54)

In 1966 the College of Business established the Center for Management and Professional Development as an extension of its professional offerings to the regional business community. It began offering a selection of publicly advertised programs each semester to corporate, government, and nonprofit institutions that needed to provide their supervisory and management staffs additional skill and professional development.

A significant accomplishment during O'Connor's presidency was a revision of the university core of studies. During the 1966–1967 academic year the university established nine faculty core curriculum study committees. Students, administrators, and alumni joined the faculty as "resource persons." The committees, whose collective charge was to revise the core curriculum, met almost weekly. "What combination of disciplines," they asked, "produces the best citizen, the best scholar, the person most likely to make an important contribution to society, the person most likely to live an intellectually rewarding life, the person most prepared to fulfill the purpose of his existence?" In his presidential address at the June commencement in 1967, O'Connor was hopeful that the committees' work would "influence the direction of this University for all time to come." At the time students were required to take eight credit hours in Christian culture, twelve in English and literature, six in history, six in mathematics, six to twelve in modern languages, eighteen in philosophy, eight in science, two in speech, and eight (four for non-Catholics) in theology. (55)

At a two-day administrative workshop in the fall, the participants reviewed and discussed reports of the core curriculum study committees. Some faculty and administrators were hopeful a proposal would come out of the working session that would possibly lead to a modification of the philosophy and theology requirements. "The ideal core," some thought, "[would] be one that permits a student to prepare liberally as well as professionally." In the spring of 1968 the trustees approved the recommendation of the Academic Council, consisting of administrators and faculty who dealt with undergraduate matters. The new core now required students to take twelve credit hours in philosophy, twelve (six for non-Catholics) in theology, twelve each in the humanities, mathematics and science, and social science, nine to ten in foreign languages, and three in English composition. Though three years later the Academic Council recommended reducing the number of philosophy and theology hours to nine hours each, with a three-hours swing between them, the requirements remained at fifteen and twelve respectively. Counter to the movement in American higher education toward fewer curricular requirements, Xavier still retained a demanding required curriculum. (56)

On many Catholic campuses in the 1960s faculty members studied and debated the nature and significance of their respective institution's core requirements and Catholic identity. In particular, they focused on the role of religion courses. By the late sixties the Society of Catholic College Teachers of Sacred Doctrine, founded in 1954, evolved into the College Theology Society. At Xavier, like on many campuses, the religion program since 1950 was called theology; on some campuses, "religious studies." Until the 1960s the task of college teachers of religion or theology was assumed to be one of instruction in Catholic faith and practice. The spirit of ecumenism, which especially grew out of Vatican II, gradually influenced and modified course offerings. During the decade many Catholic institutions, including Xavier, introduced a broader selection of courses, including studies of religions and theologies other than Roman Catholic. While some Catholic faculty continued to offer neo-scholasticism as a unifying agent for contemporary culture and religious faith, the university offered a curriculum that dealt with myriad aspects of human life. (57)

At a meeting at Land O'Lakes in Wisconsin in 1967, convened by President Theodore Hesburgh of the University of Notre Dame, the participants produced a document entitled "The Nature of the Contemporary Catholic University." Acclaimed by some as a statement of independence from the Church by Catholic colleges and universities in the United States, it argued that for a Catholic institution of higher learning to perform its teaching and research functions effectively it "must have a true autonomy and academic freedom in the face of authority of whatever kind, lay or clerical, external to the academic community itself." It further stipulated that "the Catholic university of the future will be a true modern university but specifically Catholic in profound and creative ways for the service of society and the people of God." (58)

As Xavier's academic programs and physical plant expanded in the 1960s, university trustees and administrators considered the possibility of once again sponsoring a college of law. In early January 1966 the dean of the Salmon P. Chase College of Law had met with President O'Connor to inform him that the school's Board of Trustees was considering offering the law school to Xavier University. Having to move out of its quarters at the YMCA in downtown Cincinnati, Chase officials were anxious to get some university affiliation. The University of Cincinnati had previously turned down their offer and negotiations with Miami University in Oxford, Ohio appeared doubtful. Though in 1968 the Xavier Board of Trustees declined the offer for the Chase College of Law to become affiliated with the university, during the next three years Xavier administrators and faculty continued to explore the possibility. In December 1970 the university trustees decided that they would consider affiliation on the condition that the law school "provide [money] to Xavier University . . . for the erection of facilities on [the Xavier] . . . campus . . . or for endowment." No agreement was ever reached and discussions eventually stopped. (59)

As the faculty was at the heart of the institution and largely determined its academic health, the university during O'Connor's presidency gradually increased faculty salaries. Over a two-year period in the mid-1950s, the university on the average increased salaries by $1,000, moving from $4,900 to $5,900. At the time the minimum salary for an assistant professor was $5,500 to a maximum of $6,500; for an associate, $6,500 to $8,000; and for a professor, $7,000 to $8,000. In the summer of 1956 the Ford Foundation awarded Xavier a grant of $390,000 for the purpose of improving lay faculty salaries. Xavier was one of twenty-three Catholic colleges and universities that received funds from the foundation. The grant helped provide an increase of 15 percent to the salary base. During the next fifteen years average salary increases ranged from 5 to 8 percent per year. By 1963 the average lay faculty salary had more than doubled since World War II. Significantly, too, in the spring of 1962 the university, in addition to continuing to grant full tuition remission for courses taken by its employees, had changed its policy of 50 percent tuition remission for dependent children of faculty and staff to 100 percent. To recognize outstanding achievement in teaching, which was the primary responsibility of every faculty member, two years later the Xavier chapter of Alpha Sigma Nu, Jesuit honor society, inaugurated a Teacher of the Year award. Presentation of the first award was made in May at the 25th annual dinner of the chapter to Edward B. Brueggeman, S.J., who had joined the Department of Theology two years earlier. (60)

Prior to the summer of 1966, faculty contracts were for twelve months, and faculty teaching loads were fifteen hours per semester. In the spring of 1965 a survey had been sent to the 110 full-time faculty, 82 lay and 28 Jesuit, regarding desirability of ten-month contracts. Among the 68 respondents, 59 favored it, 4 were opposed, and 5 were indifferent. Some faculty members thought the proposal did not affect them personally, while a few others, "in considering the common good," did not know whether the ten- or twelve-month contract would be better. Upon the recommendation of the Faculty Committee, Academic Council, and Committee on Rank and Tenure, consisting of administration and faculty who made recommendations on salary increases to the president, the following January the trustees, notwithstanding the dean of faculties' "misgivings," approved both the issuance of ten-month contracts with no lowering of salaries and the reduction of teaching loads to twelve hours per semester. For summer teaching, which was no longer part of the annual contract, instructors now received $900 per course, assistant professors $1,100, associate professors $1,300, and professors $1,500. Three years later salaries for full-time faculty in the summer school were paid for each course on a basis of 1/8 of their current salaries. (61)

Beginning in 1966 the university published the faculty salary scale in the American Association for University Professors bulletin. By 1970 the average salary range for the faculty was $14,750 to 15,984 for professors, $12,769 to 13,888 for associates, $10,916 to $11,879 for assistants, and $8,722 to $9,603 for instructors. At the time there were 27 professors, 35 associate professors, 46 assistant professors, and 18 instructors, for a total of 126 tenured or tenure track faculty members, which was an increase of 16 full-time faculty in two years. Part-time faculty rate for two 3-hour courses was $500; after 3 years, $520; and after 6 years, $550. (62)

Mounting university costs in the 1960s required the university to increase its tuition. "It is a fact of life," O'Connor wrote in 1963, "that Xavier operates in the same economic framework as other American educational institutions. Operating costs of these educational institutions have risen sharply in the last two decades." The addition of salaried lay teachers, retention of staff members against inducements of other educational institutions as well as business and industry, expansion of student services, such as placement and advising of students, plant expansion and resultant increase in maintenance costs, and the need to operate in a competitive economy were reasons for the steady increase. At the time the university charged $25.00 a credit hour in the undergraduate college and $26.00 a credit hour in the Graduate School. In the mid-1960s Xavier's overall undergraduate tuition was $969 per year, an increase of $819 since the end of World War II. (63)

Throughout O'Connor's presidency there was no established deadline for student applications. The university accepted applications from out-of-town students until the residence facilities were full. The instructional facilities were ample, especially with the completion of Alter Hall. For the fall 1961 class, Xavier applicants hailed from 46 states and 18 foreign countries. A deposit of $25.00 accompanied the application, and for a student requiring housing, the university charged an additional $25.00 room deposit. In addition to having a transcript of his high school academic record sent to the director of admissions, the applicant had to take the College Entrance Examination Board Scholastic Aptitude Test and have the scores sent to Xavier. In the spring of 1962 the Xavier University trustees, who regularly met in the fine arts room on the first floor in Albers Hall, approved the centralization of financial aid in one office, thus making it possible for the university to better allocate its scholarship aid based on need. (64)

Campus Activities and Issues

During the 1950s and 1960s Xavier University students compiled an impressive academic record. Graduating seniors averaged nearly one fellowship to graduate school for every three graduates of the undergraduate day division. Scores of Xavier graduates went on to medical, dental, or law school. In 1961 twelve Xavier students had straight "A" averages during the first semester to head the dean's list of honor students. One hundred and eighty-nine students qualified to be on the list by achieving averages of 3.25 or better, representing approximately 11 percent of the student body. Among the colleges and universities in Ohio and Michigan, Xavier ranked fifth in the production of Woodrow Wilson scholars, sponsored by the Woodrow Wilson Foundation, during the years 1945 to 1963. In 1963 alone twelve fellowships were won in nationwide competition—seven Woodrow Wilsons, three National Science Foundations, one Danforth Foundation, and one Fulbright Foundation. From the late 1940s through the 1950s Xavier placed first in the Intercollegiate Latin Contest among Jesuit schools nine out of twelve times. Xavier students had participated in this competition for more than half a century. "[E]xcellence in the classical languages," O'Connor said, "is the hallmark of a Jesuit university and superiority in competition with other Jesuit universities is a real joy to a Jesuit president." In 1969 the university won the Jesuits' Intercollegiate Essay Contest, which began in 1888, by placing its three entrants in the top five. (65)

In the immediate postwar era through the 1950s, Xavier students' single largest political concern was communism. Many issues of *Xavier University News* contained articles expressing concern over the teachings of Karl Marx and the spread of communism. In 1952 one of the student authors maintained that "freedom—academic or otherwise—does not include and cannot survive freedom to conspire to overthrow our government." Ironically, two years earlier Harry Gold, a Xavier alumnus of the class of 1940, had been arrested for distributing atomic bomb secrets to the communist leardership in Russia and pleaded guilty to the charge of espionage. Though at the time the school's newspaper carried little national news, students supported the efforts of Senator Joseph McCarthy of Wisconsin to combat communism. The period from 1945 to 1955 proved to be one of the most intense periods of anti-communist investigations and activities in the history of the United States. Sodality and other student groups in the university often sponsored drives for collections of anti-communist books and magazines to be sent to countries subjected to communism. Several students also expressed concern over the atomic bomb and the need for the United States to pursue a more aggressive foreign policy, especially in relationship to the Soviet Union and China. In response to campus awareness of these issues, the students in 1956 formed a Contemporary Affairs Club. (66)

During the social and cultural upheavals of the 1960s, American campuses, in contrast to the 1950s, did not experience a quiet time. Many Xavier students, like their counterparts in American colleges and universities, reached out beyond issues on campus. Student protests targeted many issues including the war in Vietnam, race, poverty, and the environment. *Xavier University News* often supported the "Young

America for Freedom" programs, maintaining that "there should be a prominent place on the college campus for organizations devoted to political discussion." In the early 1960s the students replaced the Contemporary Affairs Club with the Political Forum. In the fall of 1966 students aired national and international issues in the weekly discussion meetings known as Faculty and Students Talk (FAST), held in the Musketeer Grill in the University Center, and Faculty and Dorm Students in Conference (FADSIC), held in residence halls. (67)

A racial incident occurred that affected the basketball program and, more generally, the university. The success of the basketball program in the post-World War II period had earned it an invitation to the Sugar Bowl Holiday Tournament in New Orleans in 1962. First invited to the National Invitational Tournament (NIT) in 1956, by March 1958 the team, coached by Jim McCafferty, won the NIT by defeating in overtime the University of Dayton in the championship game, which was the first national championship ever won by an Ohio college. The next day approximately 10,000 people greeted the basketball team at the greater Cincinnati airport as they returned from their victory. Because of the success of the team, the following year the majority of the home basketgall games were played at the Cincinnati Gardens, a larger arena about five miles northeast of the university. Xavier continued its winning ways, appearing in the National Collegiate Athletic Association Mid-East regionals for the first time in 1960–1961. The invitation to the Sugar Bowl Holiday Tournament, however, posed a challenge to the university. Early in 1962 it had signed a contract for the basketball team to participate in the tournament. In accordance with Louisiana state law the seating in the basketball arena separated whites and non-whites. Furthermore, Mississippi State, one of the teams in the tournament, was forbidden by the Mississippi legislature to play against a team that had non-whites on the squad. (68)

Xavier University officials, faculty members, the Athletic Board, and the Student Council met separately to discuss the team's participation in the Sugar Bowl Holiday Tournament. Some students thought that going to the tournament would go against the school motto, arguing that Xavier would not be "all for one and one for all" if its African American basketball players were discriminated against. There were others who thought that the university was compelled to compete, regardless of race issues, because the school had signed a contract and that breaking it would tarnish the university's integrity. In early October the Student Council passed three resolutions protesting the university's participation in the tournament on the grounds that it fostered segregation practices. Student leaders urged the university not to participate in the tournament and "to make a public statement declaring its positive position on integration." Various organizations, such as the Cincinnati AFL-CIO Labor Council, the Cincinnati branch of the National Association for the Advancement of the Colored People, the National Catholic Conference for Interracial Justice, the Cincinnati Congress of Racial Equality, and the Student Nonviolent Coordinating Committee, concurred with the students' resolutions. (69)

Ten days later O'Connor issued a statement explaining the university's decision to participate in the tournament. "We believe . . . that it is better that those of us who condemn racial segregation," he argued, "visit the South than not. As one newspaperman pointed out, with our contact go our ideas. It is a matter of judgment which method will succeed better in breaking down racial prejudice." O'Connor further explained that the main reasons for participation in the tournament were to enhance the athletic reputation of the school by playing in a nationally-recognized tournament and to provide a homecoming for friends and former associates of Coach Jim McCafferty, who had spent fifteen years coaching in New Orleans. In McCafferty's 1962–1963 final season at the helm of the Musketeers Xavier won the National Catholic College Championship when it defeated Creighton and St. Bonaventure at Freedom Hall in Louisville, Kentucky. McCafferty then turned over the coaching reins to assistant Don Ruberg in order to devote full time to his duties as athletic director. Eight years later, in the spring of 1970, the university celebrated fifty years of basketball on the Avondale and Evanston campus at its final home game of the season. It honored 54 former players at halftime by inducting them into the Xavier University basketball hall of fame. (70)

In addition to the race issue, students addressed other social causes. In the summer of 1963 thirteen Xavier students and a Jesuit priest, Charles E. Ronan, spent two months in Mexico to help construct, without pay, a children's hospital and a nurses' home in San Cristobal, Chiapas, the southernmost state of Mexico and about 150 miles from the Guatemala border. To help finance the trip the Xavier student council gave $500 toward the cost of $2,500, and the remainder came from mission collections at the university and in Cincinnati churches. The following summer five students spent two months in Mexico building a trade school in the tiny Indian village of Huistan, also in the state of Chiapas. When the Ohio River flooded in the spring of 1964, over

100 Xavier students worked as volunteers to the Red Cross. As part of the federal government's War on Poverty program in the mid-1960s, Xavier students in 1965 acted out the university's mission by sponsoring trips to Appalachia. (71)

As another way to affirm its Catholic and Jesuit identity and acknowledge social action, the university continued to bestow the St. Francis Xavier Medal each year to a recipient for distinguished service, especially in Catholic education and thought. Recipients of the medal in the late 1950s included Auxiliary Bishop Fulton Sheen of New York and Carlos Romulo, ambassador from the Philippines. In October 1959 Xavier awarded the medal to Dr. Thomas A. Dooley, the so-called "Jungle Physician" of Laos. The late President John F. Kennedy, who was assassinated on November 22, 1963, became the first person ever to receive the St. Francis Xavier Medal posthumously when O'Connor conferred it on him the following month on Universal Communion Sunday. (72)

In the fall of 1963 the university established the Xavier Forum Lecture Series, formerly the Alumni Lecture Series, and adopted as its theme that year "Social Conscience of the Sixties." The series included such topics as Russia, religion, race, justice, and Vietnam. When in January the university refused to allow Mississippi Governor Ross Barnett to speak on campus because of his segregationist views, many students criticized the administration's decision. Concerned over academic freedom, they questioned if university officials were any better than the Southern governors if they used their power to keep "undesirables" from having their voice heard. The students further argued that the governor had committed no crime except having a different opinion than the Xavier administration. Later that month, after having met with members of the Student Council, the Faculty Committee recommended to President O'Connor that a committee be set up "to examine and make recommendations on a statement with respect to speakers on campus." (73)

Two weeks later O'Connor responded by pointing out that he had "enough confidence in the good sense and judgment" of the faculty not to change what he considered "to be a wise and sensible policy." Since the late 1940s the university policy and practice had been to put "the authority and responsibility of approving speakers in the hands of the Faculty," especially those who were moderators of organizations. All student organizations on campus had faculty moderators. Arguing that it was "practically impossible to draw up regulations which would cover every situation," O'Connor further insisted that he would "rather leave . . . [it] up to the good sense and taste of the members of the Faculty rather than bind them with minute regulations." The policy, which encouraged "discussion on all sides of a controversial issue which is current and intellectual," provided for the right of appeal to the dean of faculties and ultimately to the president and the Board of Trustees. Over a fifteen-year period the faculty moderators had approved speakers who, they thought, contributed "to the educational betterment of the student and the community," O'Connor observed, but "have refused to approve speakers whose views are immoral, subversive or educationally barren." In sponsoring a speaker on the campus "the University does not state," he concluded, "that it agrees with every statement made by the speaker. Much less does it expect that every faculty member will agree with every statement. I think this is generally recognized." In 1966 the university, on the recommendation of the Student Council and faculty, established a University Speakers Committee, composed of faculty and students, to invite "controversial speakers to campus." (74)

As Xavier students protested against a number of campus and social issues, like most students on American college campuses, they engaged in a variety of pranks. A noteworthy one for Xavier occurred in January 1957. Shortly after final exams, unknown students came up with the idea of putting the Jesuit residence up for sale. They placed the following classified ad in the *Wall Street Journal*: "APARTMENT BUILDING FOR SALE: Must be disposed of rapidly. The Hinkle Building, three-story stone structure containing 53 furnished units. Elevator and intercommunication system, adequate parking facilities. Suburban atmosphere with direct community to downtown Cincinnati. Write, wire or call Paul L. O'Connor, Hinkle Building, Victory Parkway, Cincinnati 7, Ohio. Redwood 1-2341." The students billed the ad to Xavier. O'Connor received about fifteen inquiries. His search for the culprits was unsuccessful. As part of a memory exchange at reunion weekend in June 1998, Tim Wooner, class of 1958, confessed. He and his associates presented the university with a check for $25 to cover the cost of collect calls from prospective buyers. (75)

Moreover, students also rebelled against the university's dress code. In the fall of 1959 the university had initiated a new student dress code, requiring students to wear jackets and neckties to classes, convocations, and in the dining halls. By the early 1960s an increasing number of students did not conform with the code. In March 1964 the chair of the Faculty Committee alerted the dean of men, Patrick Ratterman, S.J., to the seriousness of the matter. "Last week I had occasion to go to one of the classrooms in the Alter Building. I could not but notice," he wrote, "that far less than half of the students in the classroom were dressed in conformity with the Code of Dress." After checking other classrooms along the third floor corridor he observed that "fewer than fifty percent of the students in any room were dressed according to the Code." Having been approved by a large majority of the faculty just five years earlier, he argued that faculty cooperation in enforcing the code, which had "started out quite good," he noted, "has obviously dwindled, extremely spotty at best." In his judgment the situation had become acutely embarrassing for the last year or two "when the first warm days come. . . . Out come students in sport shirts and shorts simply flouting the rule." Not wanting "to antagonize members of the faculty," he concluded, he hoped to meet with Ratterman to prevent seeing "something about which everybody was so enthusiastic just five years back go down the drain." Two days later the dean of men met with the Faculty Committee to discuss enforcement of the policy. But abandonment of the code seemed almost inevitable. After circulating a questionnaire to the faculty, which showed that less than half of the faculty favoved it, in January 1966 the university—to the students' satisfaction—officially discontinued the dress code.(76)

In the spring of 1967 Xavier students also generated a lot of interest through their newly-established Experimental Academic Community. They offered a variety of noncredit courses aimed at personalizing their education. In one of the few experimental education credit programs, approximately 60 students enrolled in the university's first integrated nine-hour cross-disciplinary approach to learning in history, philosophy, and science. Three faculty members taught the course entitled "Revolt Against Formalism." The following year the course, under a different title, aired on a local television station. (77)

Students' interests, rights, and freedoms became more prominent and reached a high point in the late 1960s. At the September 1967 administrative workshop, participants discussed religious issues on campus and student rights. The "old ways of doing things just can't work now," a commentator said. "Student attitudes toward Catholicism and the Church are more questioning. The students want reasons and question authority." Xavier administrators, like their counterparts in most Catholic colleges, concluded that they could no longer govern students "in loco parentis." However, when in the fall of

1968 a large number of Catholic students did not attend the compulsory November 12 Memorial Mass in the university fieldhouse for deceased alumni, faculty, and students, the university imposed fines on the students. (78)

Acting on the recommendation of the Xavier Student Council and the Religious Development Committee, headed by Thomas G. Savage, S.J., chair of the Department of English, a month later university officials changed the university policy regarding compulsory attendance for Catholic students at special Masses during the school year. Faculty and administrators on Catholic campuses in the 1960s, reflecting the Second Vatican Council's strong emphasis on individual freedom, had been questioning if the students had enough freedom. Wanting students to have the right motive for attending Mass, the Jesuit father general in Rome had wondered as early as 1962 if a college should use disciplinary sanctions in connection with compulsory Mass attendance. The Xavier Mass of the Holy Spirit, which regularly celebrated the opening of each new scholastic year, and the Memorial Mass were now scheduled for student participation on a voluntary basis. Though the Student Council proposed the remission of fines incurred by those students who had not attended the November 12 Memorial Mass, O'Connor decided, after consulting with administrators and students, that the fines would be assessed for unexcused nonattendance at the Mass inasmuch that it was the rule of the university when the boycott action was taken. (79)

The following February, the trustees, upon the recommendation of the Religious Development Committee, announced that religious retreats were also now voluntary for seniors and juniors, but remained compulsory for sophomores and freshmen. A year later, and again upon the recommendation of the committee, they declared all retreats "non-obligatory for a period of two years." In addition to retreats, the university began sponsoring "other creative programs of spiritual development." (80)

As the university community debated students' rights in the late-1960s, the question of student activism became a central issue on campus. By this time *Xavier News* regularly published articles that advocated change and reform in society and equated student activism with being a responsible member of society. In 1968 the university gave preliminary approval for students to form a chapter of the most well-known student activist group in the country, the Students for a Democratic Society (SDS). The chapter generally advocated students' rights, civil rights, and ending the U.S. involvement in the Vietnam War. After just six months, however, the students broke their affiliation with the national organization because of SDS demonstrations and violence. Xavier students renamed the former SDS chapter Students for a Progressive University. (81)

Just as anti-communism was the dominant student issue on campus in the 1950s, the conflict in Vietnam was the main issue in the mid- to late 1960s. While some students traveled to other university campuses and to New York City to participate in protest demonstrations against the war, there were others who thought that anti-Vietnam demonstrations were anti-American and traitorous. Moreover, while a number of students thought that demonstrations for or against the war were acceptable if they were nonviolent, some were completely apathetic. By the late sixties the Vietnam War polarized the campus. Faculty members as well as students were divided on the issue. As part of a national movement, 14 Xavier faculty signed a petition to Lyndon Johnson, president of the United States, calling for a cease-fire and negotiations. About the same time the Student Council joined 99 other schools in signing a letter to President Johnson objecting to various aspects of the war. In keeping with the Catholic tradition, some students also questioned whether or not the war was just. (82)

When in the spring of 1968 Xavier students marched on campus in support of the Vietnam War, they were met by a group of anti-war protesters. According to the *Xavier News*, whose editorial board opposed the war, the counter-demonstrators were concerned that "a unilateral demonstration would be giving the city a one-sided view of Xavier thinking on the war." A year later, the university, upon students' request, cancelled classes and sponsored the Xavier Day of Community Awareness on Vietnam. A complete 24-hour educational program began with a vigil service at midnight, followed by a series of lectures, seminars, panel discussions, liturgy, and a closing debate between 'pro' and 'con' speakers regarding U.S. involvement in Vietnam. Though some members of the greater Cincinnati community criticized Xavier's administration for caving in to students' demands, President O'Connor rejected the complaints and encouraged the open and free dialogue. The program was a success. "The Xavier Students' Day Awareness, a product of their own initiative and concern," the editorial in the *Cincinnati Enquirer* wrote, "underscored in good fashion the students' assessment of contemporary scholasticism that the pursuit of knowledge and the ability to evaluate cultural and political environments are the immediate responsibilities of every member of an academic community." During the 1968–1969 academic year Xavier officials established a Student Rights and Responsibilities Committee, consisting of administrators, faculty, and students, to help give students more voice in the university. Like their student counterparts in other American colleges and universities who had gained a greater voice in academic management, Xavier students gained seats on a number of university committees. (83)

Early in February 1969 the Academic Council, consisting of four administrators and seven faculty members and chaired by the academic vice president, met and unanimously recommended, after surveying the faculty, students, and administrators, that Xavier's Reserve Officers Training Corps Program (ROTC) be made voluntary. Their view was consistent with a national trend away from compulsory ROTC. The growing unpopularity of the war in Vietnam, coupled with the widespread movement on college campuses for fewer administrative restrictions and regulations, contributed to the trend. A year earlier the Student Council had voted to make the program voluntary. Whereas in the mid-1950s all the students surveyed had stated that ROTC was beneficial because of its instillation of discipline and preparation for war, Xavier students in the late-1960s, like most of their counterparts across the country, thought differently. Slightly over 70 percent of the students polled preferred a voluntary ROTC program. "The faculty," the Academic Council informed the Board of Trustees, "are heavily in favor of voluntary ROTC." Since its establishment on campus in 1936, two years of study in the basic course had been mandatory for all students. The advanced program for juniors and seniors always had been on a voluntary basis. Though four years earlier the trustees had approved unanimously the dean of faculties's recommendation to keep the ROTC program intact, on February 25, 1969 the trustees unanimously voted to make the ROTC program voluntary. When consulted, Xavier's Department of Military Science thought "the University [could] support a voluntary program." (84)

In the late 1960s the university continued to address race issues. In the fall of 1967 the students held an integration forum to discuss race relations in the city. Later that fall the *Xavier News* published a special issue on "The Inter-Racial Community" that stressed the need for mutual respect and cooperation. In one faculty member's opinion "the image of Xavier in the negro community was non-existent." He regarded that "state of affairs . . . deplorable since we have the space and talent available for a highly successful liaison between the University and the negro community immediately surrounding us." Moreover, with O'Connor's approval, the faculty and students formed a Committee on Racial Justice and Charity, whose purpose was to focus on better race relations on campus and in the surrounding areas, as well as attracting more African American students. In 1969 the university established a Center for University and Urban Affairs and named John L. Henderson, former assistant dean of men and the first African American administrator at the university, coordinator of university and urban affairs. At the request of Xavier's Afro-American Student Association (AASA) the university also added $20,000 to the scholarship fund for minority and disadvantaged students. (85)

From the mid- to late-1960s there had been a growing interest among young African Americans in their history and culture. This interest, sparked to a large extent by the urban and racial unrest in society, in turn generated greater interest in political and social issues. In addition to establishing a program to extend services to the neighboring black community, Xavier's African American students, echoing the sentiments of many of their counterparts in other colleges and universities, recommended the establishment of black studies courses, hiring of more African American faculty and administrators, and the recruitment and retention of more African American students. In 1969 the university had 184 black students enrolled in its graduate programs and 30 in its undergraduate day division, along with 55 in the Evening College for a total of 269 in a student body numbering approximately 6,000. At the time there were two full-time tenure track African American faculty members on campus. In February 1970 Xavier's AASA, with Kenneth Blackwell as president, inaugurated its program, "Black Awareness Week," to run concurrently with National Black History Week. Members of the association thought "that it was both necessary and timely for Xavier to educate itself and the surrounding communities on the culture, history and present attitudes of black people." About two years later the university formed an Affirmative Action Committee to address race issues on campus. (86)

Alumni and Development Growth

Xavier's increasing student body in the 1960s presented a new challenge to the university. The Alter classroom building and the University Center were major structures toward which the Alumni

Living Endowment Fund (LEF) had made a significant contribution. At the time that these buildings went up in the 1960s, prominent benefactors also came forward to support other projects. As a result the university erected the Williams Memorial St. Robert Bellarmine Chapel, the Husman Residence Hall, and the McDonald Memorial Library. Moreover, because of successful annual appeals the university added 19 acres to the campus mostly in the area it called the North Campus, east of Ledgewood Avenue and north of Herald Avenue. There the university developed the major parking area for the campus and some recreation fields for the resident students. Since the beginning of the decade the university had been acquiring houses as they became available on Ledgewood, Dana, and Herald Avenues. (87)

By the mid-1960s the university had come to rely on four sources of income. The first was the students' tuition and fees, which represented less than 50 percent of the total income. The second source of income was the small endowment of approximately $1,000,000 that yielded about $50,000 a year. The third source was the endowment of contributed services provided by the 45 Jesuits who were administrators and teachers at Xavier. At the time about 30 percent of the faculty were Jesuits. They served the university without any pay except for their minimum requirements of lodging, food, clothing, and incidentals, such as transportation. The value of their contributed services annually was over $300,000. "It would take more than $6,000,000 in invested capital," O'Connor said in 1964, "to provide this amount." When asked five years later what the Jesuit salaries and the contributed services that were returned to Xavier meant to the university, O'Connor replied: "Merely a matter of life or death." In a note to the Jesuit community that year the president further elaborated on its significance. "To give you some idea of just what this Endowment of the Jesuit Order means," he wrote, "is that it is carried on our books as an Endowment for Unrestricted Income of about $10 million. I would say that if this income did not come from the Community each year, our accreditation by the North Central Association would be in jeopardy." The fourth and final source of income consisted of gifts, such as provided by Businessmen Mobilized for Xavier (BMX). "I can tell you quite frankly," O'Connor said, "that Xavier could not operate in the black, that it would be out of business in a few short years if it were not for gifts. But I am proud to say that the institution was actually founded on the premise that gifts would always be forthcoming. All of our buildings have been built through gifts—from groups or individuals."

He further pointed out that it had long been "the spirit of the Jesuit Order that so far as possible the education offered to the students [would] be free." However, that "was the idea 400 years ago. In today's world," he said, "when modern educational practice requires ideal environment—heated, lighted, ventilated buildings, entirely free higher education is beyond the ability of the Jesuit Fathers to provide. But we go as far as we can by giving our own services and relying on the gifts of generous people." (88)

In particular, alumni financial support had grown considerably over the years. The percent of alumni making gifts to the university ranged from 24.2 in 1953 to 62.2 in 1962, with a high of 66 percent in 1959. The number of donors grew from 830 in 1953 to a high of 4,546 in 1962, while gifts ranged from $30,890 to $158,159 respectively. By its sixth year in 1958 the Alumni Annual Fund developed into one of the leading college appeals in percentage of participation. Alumni giving reached and maintained a percentage of participation above 60 percent—to place among the nation's alumni leaders. It was first among Catholic men's colleges and rated among the top 5 percent of funds among all American colleges and universities. According to the American Alumni Council, Xavier University's 66 percent alumni participation was the highest among all the private men's colleges who reported in the 1959–1960 survey. The alumni fund, regarded as the "bell cow" of the university's annual support program, together with the parents' program and the appeal to local business and industry, furnished by 1961 over $400,000 annually to Xavier. That year the administration established a Committee for Estate Planning to help meet long-term needs of the university. (89)

By 1964 Xavier had four major annual appeals—the Alumni Living Endowment Fund, the Dads United for Xavier, Businessmen Mobilized for Xavier, and the Musketeer Annual Athletic Appeal, formed in the mid-1950s. "Our four campaigns . . . have now been providing a grand total of $450,000," O'Connor said in 1964, "which would require invested capital of $9,000,000." That year Xavier officials established the Alumnae Living Endowment Fund as a new pattern of annual support for the university. For more than four decades the Alumnae Association had financed its projects through membership dues and fund-raising social activities. (90)

In the summer of 1967 Xavier added $1,000,000 it received from the estate of Thomas J. Walsh, former Cincinnati railroad executive, to the endowment. Within two years the endowment was valued at approximately $2,750,000. Despite the growth in principal, however, the relative effectiveness of endowment income, which was used primarily for scholarships, had diminished because enrollment had grown to more than 6,000. The Jesuit-contributed services endowment had remained fairly constant since no additional Jesuit manpower from the province was assigned to the university. (91)

The Alumni Living Endowment Fund by 1971 had raised $2,688,250. Founded eighteen years earlier, "I think you know," O'Connor wrote to the alumni, "that Xavier is one of the few institutions that has steadfastly endeavored to avoid capital campaigns for building purposes and has relied upon these annual efforts to achieve its building goals." Notwithstanding the early success of the fund, the percentage of participation in LEF declined steadily from 1966 on, from 59 percent in 1966 to 31.7 percent in 1971, raising $162,691 that year—less than $200,000 for the first time in five years. Roughly during the same period, however, the BMX annual drive grew steadily. In 1958 it averaged $100,000 annually. Ten years later it surpassed $200,000 for the first time in its fourteen-year history. In no uncertain terms "[t]hese men and women constitute our endowment," O'Connor said, "a living, ever renewing endowment." By the fall of 1969 no longer did the majority of Xavier's alumni reside in the Cincinnati area. For the first time over 50 percent were outside the metropolitan area. (92)

Consistently throughout this period O'Connor relied on annual funds to finance new construction. In 1967, however, the university sent out a questionnaire to twelve schools inquiring about capital gifts campaigns. At Xavier's fall administrative workshop, participants discussed the potential merits of a capital gifts campaign. Some argued that such an approach, in contrast to the annual giving campaign, would ordinarily net more, but the amount of planning was considerable. There was also a fear that a hard-hitting capital campaign could undermine Xavier's successful annual fund appeals. Nevertheless, there was general support for a capital campaign. Moreover, the participants at the workshop agreed that a long-range plan regarding future strategies had to be developed as soon as possible. (93)

A year later the university set up a Planning and Development Committee to begin work on a five-year plan that would help drive the university's campaign. To help lay the foundation for the campaign O'Connor hired the professional consultant services of the George A. Brakeley Company to conduct a feasibility study. In the meantime the Planning and Development Committee formed 35 committees made up of faculty, administrators, and students, to examine every basic assumption on which the university was founded, on which it operated, and from which the university would project its future. From the separate reports the members of the Xavier administration, Board of Trustees, and the faculty developed a five-year action program. By February 1969 the program's major goals were coeducation in the undergraduate colleges, a modified Board of Trustees to provide for lay participation, greatly improved athletic facilities for intramural programs, a college of business administration building, doctorate programs in some departments, endowed chairs for distinguished visiting professors, and endowed scholarships to counterbalance the rising tuition charges. In April the trustees reviewed the proposed five-year plan for the university and the consultants' feasibility study. About a year later the academic departments reviewed the plan and submitted their recommendations to the administration. In mid-June 1972 the trustees launched the university's first capital gifts campaign, the Advancement Fund Campaign, at the Queen City Club. Based on the Brakeley Report they hoped to raise $30,000,000 over a period of ten years, half of it in five. (94)

During O'Connor's presidency the university relied heavily on gift income not only to help finance the construction projects but to help balance the budget. Operational costs had steadily mounted in the 1960s. In 1964 the total budget for the year was $3,697,228. Four years later it was $6,879,000 and the faculty salaries amounted to $1,994,000, or approximately 28.9 percent of the budget. From 1960 to 1972, with the exception of the 1964–1965 academic year when the university had a surplus of $40,772, the university had annual operating deficits ranging from $42,000 to $457,734. In 1968–1969 and 1969–1970 Xavier operated with a financial deficit of over $400,000 each year, except for 1968–1969 it balanced the budget by transferring gift money to it. When that year's financial report revealed a net operating deficit of $457,734, largely due to a decrease in undergraduate enrollment by 150 students, O'Connor transferred all the development funds of $373,264.43 to reduce the deficit to $84,470.45. Only through gifts, O'Connor thought, would the university be able to meet its obligations. He feared the rising costs for salaries, supplies, and services. Unless some new steps were taken, university officials projected that the deficit for the 1970–1971 fiscal year could reach $1,000,000. "A privately operated institution," O'Connor said in 1970, "whose only ordinary sources of income are tuitions, income from endowment which at

Xavier is mainly the contributed services of the Jesuit Community, and gifts from individuals and foundations, cannot long endure on such a deficit economy. So, Xavier University, concerned with maintaining its scholastic excellence, its many out-of-classroom services to its students, and its vitality for development and growth, . . . must continue to be circumspect about the expenditure of its resources. It must regularly review all of its sources of income and strive with all its might for improvement." In the absence of a significant endowment, that fiscal mindset would for the foreseeable future be a continuing imperative in the life of the university. (95)

The University Becomes Fully Coeducational

The idea of transforming Xavier University into a coeducational undergraduate day institution developed in the 1960s. Though there had been sporadic discussions of it earlier, the idea crystallized in the latter part of the decade. In the mid-1950s several students in the school's newspaper had recommended that Xavier become coeducational. A few years earlier three Jesuit universities—Creighton, St. Louis, and Gonzaga in Spokane, Washington—had obtained formal permission from the Jesuit superior general to admit women students in their colleges of arts and sciences. One Xavier student argued that having female students in the undergraduate day programs would make the boys "dress nicer," act "more civil," and study harder so that they would not be outsmarted by girls. Early in his presidency Paul O'Connor maintained that there was no need for Xavier to be completely coeducational because there were already fine Catholic colleges for women in Cincinnati. He did concede, however, that having young women present on campus would doubtless bring out the best in the young men and possibly decrease interfaith marriages. (96)

In the fall of 1961 the trustees began considering whether the undergraduate day division should be coeducational. At the time there were women students registered in the Evening College, summer sessions, and Graduate School. Two years later they petitioned the Jesuit provincial, who at the time disapproved of coeducation, that women be admitted to the College of Business, emphasizing that "there are no suitable Catholic facilities for business education on the college level available to girls in the city of Cincinnati." Notwithstanding the provincial's earlier assurance to President O'Connor that under such conditions "Roman permission for coeducation is readily given," he denied Xavier's request. Despite the disappointment over the provincial's decision, in 1967 O'Connor pointed out in a talk in Indianapolis that Xavier would "continue to strive for excellence" in its undergraduate programs, as well as "search for new programs that will add to our educational service to individuals. This may include," he said, modifying his position of a decade earlier, "women in the near future." At their spring board meeting that year the trustees again discussed whether they "should come to a definite policy favoring coeducation." No action was taken. (97)

While the Xavier trustees and administration entertained the question of coeducation, President O'Connor in 1967 granted permission to several students from Our Lady of Cincinnati College (OLC), a women's college on Victory Parkway about four miles south from the Xavier campus, to take day classes. The Sisters of Mercy had opened the college, which overlooked the Ohio River, in 1935. O'Connor referred to the OLC students as "special exceptions." The following year the administrations of Xavier University and Our Lady of Cincinnati College agreed on a cooperative experimental program whereby students from both colleges could elect to attend certain day classes on either campus. In announcing the plan, which was subject to renewal each year, Paul O'Connor and Sister Mary Honora Kroger, OLC president, pointed out that it was "not to be construed or viewed as preliminary to a merger. The identity, autonomy, and independence of each institution are in no way impaired by this agreement." They hoped ultimately that a consortium embracing all area institutions of higher learning would be achieved. (98)

As the two institutions engaged in the cooperative venture the university's Student Council in the fall of 1968 conducted a survey of the undergraduate student body concerning the possibility of coeducation at the university. Among the 943 respondents, 22 percent were freshmen, 28 percent sophomores, 28 percent juniors, and 22 percent seniors. There was a uniform and affirmative trend in the answers among commuters, resident students, and students throughout the four classes. Among the respondents, about three-quarters of whom had attended all-male high schools, 64 percent of them wanted Xavier "to extend coeducation to the undergraduate day division," while 19 percent did not and 17 percent were indifferent. (99)

Three months later a university-wide committee, chaired by Dean Thomas Hailstones of the College of Business, submitted a preliminary report on coeducation to the Board of Trustees. The majority of the trustees thought that by going coeducational the university could both increase the quality of the students and help its financial position. At the time the university faced a $600,000 deficit. They advised O'Connor to confer with Archbishop Karl Alter of Cincinnati and the presidents of the two Catholic women's colleges, Our Lady of Cincinnati College, which was scheduled to change its name to Edgecliff College on February 3, 1969, and the College of Mount St. Joseph, before they made a proposal to the provincial. (100)

During the holiday season O'Connor met with all three individuals. "Sister [Mary] Honora at Edgecliff [College]," O'Connor informed the board, "thought that this move of ours would hurt them during the first and possibly during the second year. But she thought in the long run it would not make too much difference." He then added in parentheses that he did "not know how many of her faculty would agree with her." Honora and the Sisters of Mercy had expected Xavier to make "this move long before this time," he explained, "and that they had been preparing for it." Moreover, he continued, "Sister Adele [Clifford] at Mt. St. Joseph also did not think it would make much difference one way or the other." Though the archbishop at first seemed worried about the effect it might have on the women's colleges in the city, he was satisfied with the discussions O'Connor had had with the two presidents. He did think, however, that if the Jesuits were going to put up women's residences, they "were letting [themselves] in for a lot of trouble." O'Connor informed the archbishop that it was not in the university's immediate plans. (101)

At the January 1969 meeting of the Board of Trustees, O'Connor cited reasons why he thought "it would be advantageous" for Xavier to go coed. Arguing that the number one reason for Xavier to admit women at the undergraduate day level was to provide "a more normal and natural environment for learning and living," he contended that it would also give Xavier "access to a number of excellent students heretofore denied to us." While not thinking women were "naturally more intelligent than men," he insisted that "experience has shown that . . . colleges who have gone coeducational find their women students in general ranking higher than the men." The presence of bright women students in a class, he further argued, might "spur on the male students to better accomplishment." (102)

While maintaining that there were valid academic reasons for the university to become fully coeducational, he also underscored the potential financial benefit. O'Connor argued that for Xavier to become financially solvent it needed "more day undergraduate students," as young men were not attending in sufficient numbers. Not unlike many other Catholic colleges and universities in the late sixties Xavier's financial picture was bleak. The unprecedented growth in the college-going population in the early part of the decade led the university, like many other institutions, to enlarge faculties and make extensive additions to facilities on the campus. As a consequence, expenses soared, loans were secured, and significant deficits were incurred. Moreover, the unexpected declining enrollment in the latter part of the decade had also contributed to the deficits. (103)

According to O'Connor's best estimate, the university could function most efficiently with about 2,500 day undergraduate students. He was hopeful that going coed would help achieve that goal. In addition, he pointed out that the archdiocesan school office worried about a number of their Catholic women graduates attending the coeducational secular universities. "[A] goodly number of these graduates stated quite flatly," the president said, "that they wanted a coeducational school and were tired of 'all girls' schools taught by Nuns." Lastly, there was "also the fact," he declared, "that the presence of women on the campus seems to have a civilizing influence on the men students, but I would not press this point too far." (104)

Shortly after O'Connor's presentation the trustees unanimously voted to admit women students to the undergraduate day division, thus discontinuing the 138-year-old single sex undergraduate admission policy. "It was to be clearly understood," they noted, "that it is the mind of the Trustees that the University remain a Jesuit university, not less than at present, and it does not mean that we expand simply for the reason of having greater numbers." Like O'Connor they hoped to secure and maintain an undergraduate enrollment of approximately 2,500 students. About three weeks later Father General Pedro Arrupe wrote to the Chicago provincial, Robert F. Harvanek, approving Xavier's request to admit women students. "Let us pray that the admission of women," he wrote, "will relieve the financial embarrassment of Xavier and elevate academic standards as well." (105)

In the fall of 1969 the undergraduate day college of the university became coeducational. Xavier was among the last of the 28 Jesuit colleges and universities to become totally coeducational. That fall 52 women, including 23 first-year students and 29 transfer students, signed up for day classes. Two months earlier, on July 1, Mary Louise Faeth had been named the university's first dean of women in the undergraduate day school. Since the end of the nineteenth century coeducation had helped to save many small denominational men's colleges whose existences were severely threatened by competition from state institutions in the Midwest and West. In the 1970s almost all of the remaining Catholic men's colleges and some women's colleges went coed. (106)

Though a 1968 campus survey had indicated that about two-thirds of the undergraduate student body preferred coeducation, some students opposed the change. "If we have equal numbers of girls and fellows, hardcore intellectual thinking will be lost," a male junior student said in 1969 in an interview by the *Xavier News*. When the administration planned to open the fifth and half of the sixth floors of Kuhlman Hall to women in 1970, there was an avalanche of outrage in the student newspaper. "Our university has condescended to allow women to enroll in day and night classes," a male student said. "But to allow them in our dorms! Never!" (107)

Notwithstanding some male opposition and reservations, women students immediately became engaged in curricular and cocurricular activities. They were active in campus organizations including Student Council, the weekly *Xavier News*, the drama group, volunteer work, and liturgical activities. In the fall of 1969 Kathy Keating won two Ohio women's swimming championships, 50-yard and 100-yard breaststroke titles, at a meet held at Denison University. While the women's rifle team zeroed in on practice targets, other women students helped organize a marching drilling team. (108)

As the university went coed, it had to change the way it did business. Father Albert B. Bischoff, a member of Xavier's campus ministry staff in 1969, noted "that the cafeteria service had a habit of cooking for men. It was all starches and heavy stuff, lots of greasy meat, no salads. The women's dietary needs were overlooked." At times when he accompanied the women to the cafeteria he observed that the young men were less likely to whistle or make catcalls in his presence. "I was like their guardian angel. They were noble, courageous souls." In 1970 only two women taught full-time on the faculty. The university had hired its first temporary woman faculty member in the undergraduate day division in the Department of Biology in 1960. The cultural and social events on campus also had to be reconfigured in the early 1970s. In the spring of 1972 an Ad Hoc Committee on Women's Concerns, in conjunction with the English and education departments and with assistance from the Cincinnati chapter of the National Organization for Women, sponsored a three-day campus seminar featuring a series of lectures and panel presentations, designed to sensitize the Xavier community to the need for an increased awareness of the roles of women in society and, more particularly, on campus. As the institution in the 1970s became more fully coeducational, the few women faculty members, full-time and adjunct, sometimes joined by women support and administrative staffs and students, explored a variety of topics relevant to alternative lifestyles for women as they sought to realize their maximum potential as human beings. (109)

Board of Trustees

From 1865 through the first half of the twentieth century, church influence within many private institutions had declined, especially in colleges that had converted themselves into universities. The modern era at these schools saw the presidency and the ranks of the faculty, once dominated by clergymen, routinely filled by laymen. In the process, these faculties acquired more authority in terms of hiring, curriculum, and degree requirements. Moreover, in many institutions the trustees had become corporate directors for institutional maintenance and the administrators more like business managers. (110)

As the 28 Jesuit colleges and universities entered the 1960s, their presidents remained firm in their opposition to laicization of the boards of trustees. "As administrators of Jesuit colleges and Jesuit universities," they recorded in the Proceedings of the Conference of Jesuit Presidents on January 10–11, 1960, "we readily recognize our responsibility to clearly establish and to spell out in our structural organization the lines of Jesuit leadership and control, particularly in each key spot. We recognize that legal authority must be clearly and exclusively invested in Jesuit hands." Within a few years that attitude changed radically. (111)

The move toward greater inclusion of lay men and women on the boards of the Catholic institutions began around 1964. According to the Charles Ford and Edward Roy study in *The Renewal of Catholic Higher Education*, published in 1966, the "number two problem" after finances cited by the presidents of the colleges and universities surveyed in the mid-1960s was "the ambiguous role of the religious community." There were times when religious community and university leaders did not agree, and when that happened religious community opinions took precedent over the university. Prior to this time a Jesuit college or university was identified with the religious congregation, namely the

Society of Jesus. A Jesuit institution of higher learning meant one corporate body and the Society of Jesus owned and operated the entire establishment. Moreover, the United States provincials, acting as the Board of Governors of the Jesuit Educational Association (JEA), were the key individuals in the governance of Jesuit colleges and universities. They had to apply to the father general in Rome for a variety of permissions. (112)

At the March 1966 meeting of the Xavier University Board of Trustees, President O'Connor urged his Jesuit colleagues to consider adding lay people to the board. At the time a number of Jesuit colleges and universities explored the possibility of reorganizing their boards. Some Xavier trustees, however, were "wary of any move which would take the authority of the University out of Jesuit hands." Three months later O'Connor attended the two-day Jesuit presidents' meeting at Gonzaga University in Spokane, Washington, where the participants discussed the make-up of their boards of trustees and considered whether a board of control should be made up of principally nonmembers of the institution. The North Central Association had recently expressed concern over the exclusive religious composition of the boards of Catholic institutions, arguing that strictly Jesuit control "denies a perspective which could be gained by having outside people on the Board" as well as escape the criticism of being dominated by religious. In their judgment, if personnel decisions were made by religious superiors rather than by rank and tenure committees, how could an institution defend itself in courtrooms and foundation boardrooms where there was concern over sectarianism? At the time St. Louis University, under the leadership of President Paul Reinert, S.J., explored setting up a combined board of trustees that would include Jesuits, some from within and some from without the university, and laymen. The president, however, would continue to be a Jesuit. (113)

By the spring of 1967, O'Connor began publicly discussing the possible laicization of the university's Board of Trustees. The "question of lay trustees," he noted, "has been uppermost in many minds." He pointed out to the Indianapolis chapter of the Alumni Association that "Xavier has never been afraid of lay participation. Through almost our entire history we have had lay teachers. In later times we have had lay deans, lay administrators, and lay advisors." At the time Xavier had three lay deans and two lay vice presidents. "I am not averse to having laymen on the Board of Trustees and I certainly shall give it full consideration," O'Connor said. "I believe the lay voice is being heard and listened to at Xavier and I really don't think there is a feeling of either side to rush into any reorganization that would materially change the university's governing structure." (114)

By the fall of 1968 Xavier trustees began addressing more seriously the whole governance issue. A year earlier Rome had given permission to St. Louis University to set up a Board of Trustees of both laymen and Jesuits who would hold legal title to the university. They were also given permission to incorporate separately the Jesuit community. St. Louis University and the University of Notre Dame were the first Catholic universities in the United States to initiate a fundamental shift in governance. This was the beginning of the process of giving boards of trustees of Catholic colleges and universities full authority, drawing up new by-laws for university governance, and separating corporations. Though there was a fear that the shift would be interpreted as moving toward secularization, in the judgment of those who favored the change "laicization" was a matter of "declericalization" and not "secularization." (115)

Conversion in governance at the board level usually followed a few steps. First, the institution added laypersons to the existing board. Then it enlarged the board's agenda. Finally, it adopted a new structure of power and established separate corporations for the college and the religious community. As a champion for the laicization of the board of trustees and for separation of the college and the Jesuit community, the Jesuit Paul Reinert and many of his colleagues adopted the explanation provided by Father John McGrath, a canon lawyer at the Catholic University of America, regarding the nature of the "public trust." In his book *Catholic Institutions: Canonical and Civil Law Status*, published in 1968, McGrath argued that the properties and other assets of the college were held "in trust" by the board of trustees and that donations and grants were given to the college and not to the religious community. As a group, American bishops did not object to McGrath's explanation. (116)

When several other Jesuit colleges followed St. Louis University's lead and applied for a like permission, the father general sent a letter to JEA containing a number of questions that he wanted answered before he would grant further permissions. "As I see it for Xavier University," O'Connor wrote to the trustees on the eve of their October 4 meeting in 1968, "we have three possibilities for the composition of the Board of Trustees." He suggested that the trustees could replace some members of the board with Jesuits from outside the university, replace some or all of the local Jesuits with laymen, or replace some with Jesuits from outside the university. "A definitely distinct, though very closely inter-related question," he further thought, "is whether or not we should incorporate the Jesuit Community at Xavier University as a separate corporation from the University." (117)

The next day the Xavier trustees devoted their meeting almost exclusively to a discussion of the governance of Jesuit institutions in preparation for the joint meeting with the province consultors scheduled two weeks later. First, they discussed advantages of having all Jesuits on the Xavier board. It would "assure Jesuit control . . . [and] safeguard the intent of the University," some argued. Others suggested that they could have two Jesuits from outside the university as a first experience. While strongly disclaiming any intent of approaching "the aims and procedures of a secular university," they further thought that they could introduce some laymen in a gradual manner. They denied as the principal reason for a change in the composition of the board the fact that the lay members would be a source of obtaining money. Though that "would be a reason," they insisted, it would "not necessarily be a principal reason." Not believing that adding lay people was "inevitable, . . . [t]he question remains," they said, "whether it is advisable." (118)

At the same meeting the trustees also discussed the possibility of establishing a separate corporation for the Jesuit community. While some members feared it "could minimize the Jesuit influence in the University," there were others who thought "it could make clear the Jesuit equity in the University community." Some trustees expressed concern that separate incorporation could also result in the Jesuits "having less of a feeling of involvement in the University. At present," the board minutes read, "the Jesuits do feel, in some degree, that they are members of a society which owns and operates the University." Moreover, some Jesuits expressed concern over the possible decline or diminution of Jesuit identity on campus and were reluctant to transfer authority over the legal and fiscal affairs of the university to an independent Board of Trustees. The following winter a fellow trustee suggested to O'Connor that in the future the university "draw up a document which stated our Jesuit purposes, which every applicant for a faculty position could read, and then sign before we hired him or her. A catalog statement is not enough," he wrote. ". . . Until we take care of this faculty problem we can have Jesuits on the Board of Trustees, as deans, and as faculty members, and yet gradually see our institutions become non-Jesuit. . . . Because we have been remiss in this in the past our institutions have tended to become less and less Jesuit." (119)

In the summer of 1969 the Board of Trustees voted to add Jesuits from outside the university to the board in the near future. In the fall it also agreed to eventually add lay associates to the board. "Clearly," the minutes read, "the [lay] board members . . . should bring an added objective view. . . . Their presence . . . would interest them in fund raising, and, of course, their knowledge would be helpful in general." The motion passed with one abstention. This decision was in keeping with Vatican II and with the 31st General Congregation of the Jesuits held in 1965–1966, which recommended "close collaboration" with lay people. The following year a survey of Jesuit college and university governing structures revealed that among the 28 institutions, 13 did not have lay associates on their boards. John Carroll had as many as 21 among 28 trustees and St. Louis 21 among 32. According to a study conducted that year, the 66 Catholic institutions who were members of the Middle States Association of North Central had governing boards that included both religious and lay members. (120)

At the fall 1969 meeting the trustees also decided to relieve President O'Connor, who was ill, of some of his duties, thinking that he needed "assistance, . . . especially during the [anticipated] fund campaign." On February 2, 1970, by order of the provincial, Richard Deters, S.J., became the first independent rector of the university's Jesuit community. Since 1840 Xavier's president had also served as rector. That latest change also helped lighten O'Connor's duties. In the fall O'Connor formed a committee, chaired by Dr. Harvey A. Dubé, professor of chemistry, to conduct a search for a provost. The trustees intended the provost, who would assist O'Connor in carrying out some of his administrative duties, to succeed him to the presidency in a year or two. Earlier the president had informed the trustees "that the most important duty and obligation of a member of the Board of Trustees is to select a new president since so much of the future of the University depends upon this selection." The following January the trustees unanimously chose Robert William Mulligan, S.J., as the university's first provost. He was no stranger to the Jesuit community and to some members of the academic community. Eight years earlier Mulligan, then academic vice president at Loyola University in Chicago, had been the guest speaker at Xavier's annual President's Faculty Dinner. (121)

The first phase of the board's reorganization was effected on January 10, 1971, when for the first time in the history of the university, Jesuit members from outside the Xavier Jesuit community became trustees. Since 1840 the governance of St. Xavier College and later Xavier University had rested in the hands of the representatives of the local Jesuit community. Three seats had become vacant because of the transfer or retirement of some local Jesuits on the board. Using its self-perpetuating power, the board extended invitations to three out-of-town Jesuits. The next day, the trustees again discussed adding laymen to the board. But as they planned to recruit influential laymen for an anticipated fund-raising campaign, they deferred their selection to a later time. Though the Board of Trustees was bound legally to meet at least once a year, ordinarily the nine-member board had met once a month. Beginning that January the trustees began meeting four times a year. (122)

At the April 1971 meeting of the Board of Trustees, the members discussed whether they should have one or two boards. Having two boards would have meant the establishment of a Jesuit corporation board with vested rights to university trusteeship and a second board that would be responsible for controlling the operation and management of the university property and operations. This was another effort by some trustees to give more secure control to the Jesuits. Convinced that two boards would not attract the most qualified lay people, the trustees decided to stay with one board. They did, however, expand the board. The trustees amended the university charter so that there would be not fewer than fifteen and no more than twenty-five members on the board, a majority of whom had to be members of the Society of Jesus. On July 18, 1972 the Board of Trustees appointed six laymen to the board. They were Michael J. Conaton, Harry J. Gilligan, John T. Murphy, Fletcher E. Nyce, William S. Rowe, and William J. Williams. By this time most American colleges and universities had a significant number, often a majority, of lay trustees. By the end of the decade 77 percent of the Catholic institutions had adopted the new format. (123)

During their deliberations in the spring and summer of 1972 the trustees also drew up and approved a Certificate of Amendment to the university's Articles of Incorporation. According to the new document the president of the university was ex officio a voting member of the Board of Trustees. In addition, the board members had general responsibility for the administration of the university, including the power and authority to adopt a constitution or statutes for the university and to elect a president, who had to be a Jesuit, and such officers of the university as the trustees deemed necessary or advisable. The officers of the Board of Trustees consisted of the chairman, vice chairman, and secretary of the corporation. In accordance with the university statutes the trustees appointed an Executive Committee, presided over by the chairman of the board. In May the board approved the Certificate of Amendment and filed it with the Ohio secretary of state. (124)

After the addition of outside Jesuits and lay members to the university's Board of Trustees, Xavier's governing body became increasingly more professional in exercising its authority. The board's Executive Committee prepared agendas for the regular quarterly meeting of the Board of Trustees and had the authority to act for the entire board when necessary. It also nominated all committees and new officers. The Academic Affairs Committee met quarterly with the academic vice president and reviewed academic programs and policies as they related to the mission of the university. The Finance and Audit Committee met with the financial vice president, reviewed the annual financial statement, and made general recommendations regarding fiscal policies. The Development and Public Information Committee reviewed the policies and programs of the university related to fund-raising and to publicity. The Nomination Committee recommended nominations of new members to the Board of Trustees as vacancies occurred. The Student Life Committee reviewed extracurricular programs and policies related to student activities, including intercollegiate sports and residence hall regulations. The Plant and Building Committee made general recommendations regarding maintenance, major renovation, and new construction to the Board of Trustees. In keeping with modern university practice the board separated its policy-making function from the internal administration of the university. (125)

The Football Issue

As early as 1961 the Board of Trustees had discussed the status of football and its cost, estimated to be $17,600 a year. That was a lot of money "to pay out," some trustees then argued, "for an activity which contributes not one thing to the academic well-being of our students—the primary end of our university." They thought it better for the university to use the money to meet academic needs, such as starting a Department of Sociology with two full-time faculty members. Moreover, they pointed out that Jesuit schools like Fordham, St. Louis, and Georgetown had not suffered academically because of the loss of football. These trustees, however, were in the minority. The board agreed "to push ticket sales to make up for any deficit accruing from the . . . program." (126)

Nine years later, at the December 1970 board meeting, the all-Jesuit membership again considered the football issue. Based on an Athletic Board commitment to increase revenue, effect greater efficiency in the internal operation of the football program, and operate with a balanced budget, the trustees unanimously decided to keep football. However, notwithstanding the board's favorable decision to retain the sport, a special task force of administrators, faculty, and students continued to review the program. After a loss of $419,013 during the 1970–1971 fiscal year there was considerable discussion on campus about its possible discontinuation. (127)

Concerned over the university's financial woes and declining faculty morale, Mulligan, the newly-appointed provost, proposed reexamination of the football program. An anticipated 1971 university operating deficit of over $500,000, which was close to the financial losses from football that year, prompted talk on campus of a possible freeze on salaries for the next academic year. Declining enrollment and the nearly 100 empty beds in the residence halls had contributed to the deficit. In February, Mulligan wrote a confidential letter to O'Connor. Though the trustees, in view of the depressed state of the national economy, had decided not to increase tuition because they thought "it would be risky," he nevertheless recommended that the Rank and Tenure Committee's proposal for a 5 percent salary increase be approved. "General experience seems to indicate that when faculty are given no salary increases their morale suffers badly," he wrote, "and this at times is communicated to students. The failure to give any salary increases," he added, "might [also] suggest to some that Xavier is in desperate financial straits . . . [and] would harm, rather than help, a campaign for funds." Although his knowledge of Xavier's financial history was limited, it was his impression that the university's financial condition, "while unfavorable, is far from desperate." Mulligan also feared that some competent teachers would leave if there were a salary freeze. As a way to help improve the university's financial condition, Mulligan proposed scaling down the football program. (128)

In October 1971 the task force charged to review the football program indicated to Mulligan that they would in all probability recommend discontinuing the sport. "We are losing our shirt on the sports program and in other areas too," a faculty member on the task force said. "[W]hy should we be penalized for that?" In mid-October a student survey conducted in all four residence halls revealed that from a random sample of 265 students, 23 percent of them wanted to retain football at the current level of competition, 39.5 percent opted to de-emphasize football—which meant competing with colleges of Xavier's size—, 19.1 percent wanted to drop football as an intercollegiate sport, and 2.3 percent had no opinion. In response to the question "Did the fact that Xavier has major college football influence your decision to come to Xavier?" 25.3 percent said "Yes," while 74.7 percent said "No." To the question "Do you attend most of X.U.'s home football games?" 79 percent answered "Yes" and 21 percent "No." When those students who attended most of the games were asked would they "be willing to pay an additional $15 to attend Xavier's home games next year?" 24.9 percent answered "Yes," 75.1 percent "No." A few weeks later, however, the Xavier Alumni Association Board of Governors recommended that the university "maintain its current level of intercollegiate football competition," arguing that "the Xavier concept of education was, and should continue to be, a total approach concept, and that football plays a vital role in such a program." The members also cautioned the trustees "that any reduction in the level of the football program" could impede future alumni financial support. (129)

Notwithstanding the Alumni Association's recommendation, Mulligan informed O'Connor that at the December meeting of the Board of Trustees he would recommend changes in the football program. "As you know," he wrote, "in recent years both our football and . . . basketball programs have involved serious financial losses." He proposed a gradual phasing-out of football scholarships as well as reductions of the football coaching staff and personnel in the athletic director's office. Since football scholarships and contracts were normally granted in mid-December, Mulligan argued that the action had to be made before then. (130)

Despite the adverse impact of football on university finances, not everyone supported the provost's position. In mid-November Ed VonderHaar, vice president for public relations and development, responded to Mulligan's proposal and echoed the sentiments of many alumni. "I need not labor the point that football has been a part of the Xavier University image for the past 50 years. . . . Except for a few years during World War II, the activity has been continuous," he wrote. "There is no question that the . . . fund-raising will diminish to a much smaller figure if we are not to support football. . . . Can we afford to have our public visibility dropped? What do business and community leaders talk about most of the time at the Banker's Club, Luncheon Club, Golf Club, etc.? Sports events? Do we want to be left out of the conversation?" He concluded by pointing out that many "alumni leaders involved in alumni fund-raising are products of our football program." (131)

As expected, in December 1971 the task force recommended to the Board of Trustees that the university decrease its financial commitment to intercollegiate football. The trustees accepted their recommendation and initiated a three-year program to reduce costs. Beginning in the fall of 1972, freshmen became eligible to play on the varsity team. That decision eliminated the need for freshmen squad coaches and the costs involved in freshmen games with other colleges. The board also reduced foolball grants from 73 1/2 to 50 percent over a three-year period, cut budget items by 25 percent over the same period, and eliminated one full-time coaching position. Concerned over faculty morale, the trustees were hopeful that the faculty would accept keeping football as long as there was a significant reduction in expenditures. (132)

On September 8, 1972, the trustees appointed Robert Mulligan Xavier's thirtieth Jesuit president. Three weeks later he was appointed chairman of the Board of Trustees for one year. Paul O'Connor, who had been president for seventeen years, the longest tenure of any Xavier president, became chancellor at the university. The title of chancellor, "as far as I can find out," O'Connor said, "means roughly translated 'otium cum dignitate' ('leisure with dignity')." In his new position he continued to assist the university in public relations and fund-raising. In November O'Connor left for a few weeks vacation in Ireland. (133)

Xavier University underwent a major transformation during Paul O'Connor's presidency. It witnessed the biggest building spurt in the history of the university, erecting eight buildings in ten-and-a-half years. In the process it saw overall enrollment grow from about 3,400 students in 1955 to 5,990 in 1972, with the most significant increase occurring at the graduate level—670 to 3,120 students. Committed to Xavier's Catholic and Jesuit traditions, O'Connor also oversaw the revision of the university's core curriculum, establishment of the College of Business Administration, installation of a new administrative organization with four new vice presidencies, issuance of ten-month faculty contracts and reduction of teaching load to twelve hours per semester, and enlargement of the role of the faculty in the life of the university. While affirming students' rights and freedoms, the university discontinued the student dress code, compulsory ROTC, compulsory Mass attendance and retreats, and authorized the beginning of Black Awareness Week. Moreover, under the president's leadership Xavier University launched its first capital gifts campaign, became fully coeducational in 1969, and laicized the Board of Trustees in 1972. As the university thanked O'Connor for his leadership and steadfast commitment to Jesuit ideals, it made plans for an even brighter future.

ADJUSTMENTS AND CONFLICT: A MATURE UNIVERSITY IN TRANSITION, 1972–1990

I n his inaugural address at his installation on December 3, the
feast of Xavier University's patron, St. Francis Xavier, President
Robert Mulligan renewed the university's commitment to its mission and long-established Catholic and Jesuit tradition. In the spirit of
St. Francis Xavier he insisted that the university "should be a place
where not only should we learn, but a place where we should love, and
a place where we should love to be. So it is in this spirit today," he said,
"that I call upon the friends of Xavier, the staff of Xavier, the students
of Xavier, the faculty of Xavier, to join together to continue the great
traditions of Xavier as a happy place, a place of joy, a place for God's
people."

The mood on campus was very upbeat. The Advancement Fund
Campaign had just started, and the university seemed positioned for
significant changes. From the beginning, Mulligan—who had earned
his doctorate at Louvain in Belgium—stressed the need to develop
stronger academic programs by means of a renewed emphasis on the
humanities and a strengthening of the core curriculum: "Only when we
say that a Xavier graduate is a person who not only thinks well, but
who also reads well, writes well, and is mature in a good sense of the
word, will we really be fulfilling our purpose." He insisted that through
the core curriculum, Jesuit education sought to educate the "whole" person, "instilled with Judeo-Christian ideals." When asked in an interview

if an institution like Xavier could "still be identified as Catholic in orientation and outlook?", the fifty-six-year-old Mulligan responded unequivocally. "To be a Catholic university," he said, reflecting the 1967 Land O'Lakes statement, "an institution must first concentrate on being a good university." (1)

A new aspect of the inaugural ceremony was the investiture of the president's medallion. A symbol of the office and an affirmation of the university's identity, it included the Xavier University seal, which reflects the institution's origin and character. Imprinted on the seal are "Cincinnati," "1831," and the motto "Vidit Mirabilia Magna," which affirms that the individual who has "inquired into righteousness has seen great wonders." The scallop shell setting for the seal is the universal symbol of the pilgrim-traveller and underscores the significance of St. Francis Xavier's travels and his relentless search for truth that led him to his total dedication, to God and his fellow human beings. Lastly, it includes a chain that, with its repetitive elements, connotes the unbroken succession of scholars and saints whose contributions manifest a continuous commitment to educate students intellectually, morally, and spiritually. (2)

The End of Football

During the last years of Paul O'Connor's presidency, the administration and faculty had been concerned about mounting deficits and dipping enrollments in the two undergraduate colleges. The annual operating deficits from the 1968–1969 academic year to 1971–1972 were $84,480, $576,250, $339,275, and $132,900 respectively. Though in 1972–1973 it had just about "broken even," with a surplus of $32,500 after internal transfers of $171,600, President Mulligan pointed out that "[it] would be illusory, however, to think the University has 'turned the corner.'" The university continued to reduce operational expenses by not replacing some of the personnel leaving the university. (3)

A major financial strain on the budget was the declining enrollment of full-time undergraduate students. It had dropped markedly. In the fall of 1967 the College of Arts and Sciences (A&S) had enrolled 1,591 men and the College of Business Administration (CBA) 696, for a total of 2,287 students. Despite the admission of undergraduate women students in 1969, in the fall of 1972 only 1,351 men and women were enrolled in A&S and 590 in CBA for a total of 1,941, in contrast to 2,287 three years earlier. That was a decline of 346 full-time students. (4)

The university reduced the number of full-time faculty and staff and introduced severe budgetary restrictions, such as deferring major maintenance and repairs on campus. It also resorted to short-term borrowing to meet payroll and operating expenses. However, "[i]t has not been necessary to ask anyone who has won tenure at Xavier to resign because of the decreased enrollment and income," Mulligan wrote. "I hope this will never be necessary. At Xavier, as elsewhere, tenure is won only with great difficulty. It is seldom abused. Tenure protects faculty against arbitrary action, and it is but a small privilege to grant to a highly conscientious profession that is badly underpaid. . . ." What also helped prevent the deficit from getting bigger were the contributed services of the Jesuit community that amounted to approximately $300,000 in the early 1970s. (5)

In the midst of these financial challenges, the football program again came under review. Despite officials' efforts in 1971 to scale down the program and to increase ticket sales and booster club donations for the 1971–1972 season, football program losses reached almost $300,000. For the 1972–1973 season it exceeded $250,000, not including the indirect costs related to overhead and stadium maintenance. In addition, the football team had had several continuous losing seasons. To compound the problem further, student sentiments in the *Xavier News* were largely critical of the football program. The editorial staff recommended dropping the athletic program entirely because its "win at all costs" attitude, which—in their judgment—mistakenly placed ambition above both students and academic excellence, ran counter to Jesuit ideals. (6)

Though "the public image of Xavier as a loser on the football field is a concern," Mulligan pointed out to the trustees at the September 1973 board meeting, of greater concern to him and many others in the university was the expense of the program. When he had been asked in an interview early in his presidency about the future status of football, Mulligan had responded instantly and encouragingly. "Football," he said, "is a tremendous asset to any university. A sense of unity arises from athletic programs. . . . Football is . . . a part of college life that cannot be divorced from the educational process." But the continuing precarious state of the budget concerned him greatly. The previous December the academic members of the Budget Review Committee had recommended the discontinuation of football as soon as possible. In June 1973, Roderick Shearer, vice president and dean of student development, had reported that though the University Senate, consisting of faculty, students, administrators, and staff, had decided not to support its ad hoc committee's recommendation to drop football, nevertheless the members were concerned about its cost. Mulligan urged the trustees at their December meeting to evaluate again the "expenses and benefits" of the football program. (7)

On December 19, 1973, the board at its regular meeting revisited the football issue. After citing "the high cost of the program," Mulligan stated his difficulty of "defending [its] financial loss, . . . which was the same amount of money last year," he said, "as that spent on the library." His greatest concern was "the deficit recurring year after year." The president then asked Shearer to present a recently completed report on the football program. Endorsed by the University Senate, the Alumni Board of Governors, and the Athletic Board, the report identified five possible alternatives: maintaining the program at the present level of competition with a possible conference application; maintaining it at the level of the National Collegiate Athletic Association Division III with a possible conference application; maintaining Division III level with a possible conference level with, however, only partial scholarships granted from a much-reduced operational budget; maintaining only a club level football program; and discontinuing intercollegiate football. The three groups could not "in conscience recommend the discontinuation of football," the report said. It recommended reducing "the cost to a minimum," dropping to the Division III level, and maintaining "a program [that] gives Xavier a chance of winning and keeps fan interest." (8)

After Shearer's presentation the trustees discussed the "pros" and "cons" of football at the university. Jeremiah O'Callaghan, S.J., academic vice president and a senior member of the board, stated that he had thought for fifteen years "that the football program should be dropped." He now argued that "the point has been reached at which many people agree with him." He then asked for Mulligan's opinion. Acknowledging that many alumni thought Xavier should keep football, but on a lower level, the president nevertheless was "convinced that reducing it very gradually can never be done." While football provided some benefits to the university community and to the quality of campus life, he argued that "the amount of money spent in relation to 1,900 [undergraduate] students is prohibitive." He thought a budget limit had to be set at once by the trustees in order to bring the football program down to a lower division. During the course of the session, three Jesuits and five of the six lay members on the board spoke in favor of discontinuing the program. The other lay member, Mulligan, and O'Connor favored retaining the program on a smaller scale. By a vote of fifteen in favor and three against, the board voted to discontinue football at the university effective January 1, 1974. Mulligan called the board vote "a difficult decision." In his annual report to the university community he left open a window of possibility for football's comeback. "If some assured means could be found to fund the sport, as by an endowment," he said, "I would support its return, provided that student and community interest, which has waned notably during the last decade, could also be revived." (9)

For the first time since World War II, in the fall of 1974 there was no football at Xavier University. There appeared to be little concern about its absence on the part of the resident students. Most turned their attention to new sports—soccer, women's volleyball, and rugby, among others—and other activities. The intramural programs recorded an all-time high in participation, with women's flag football holding the highest interest. Another encouraging sign was the fact that 850 basketball season tickets were sold by December 1974, more than ever before. By June 1976 the university for the first time in about ten years ended the fiscal year with a modest surplus of $29,619. (10)

Despite the board's decision, interest in resurrecting football continued. Four years to the month after the board's decision to discontinue the program, the trustees approved the Athletic Board's request to conduct a feasibility study with the possibility of introducing the sport at the Division III level, where no scholarships were given. A marketing survey conducted in the winter of 1976–1977 had indicated some interest in football. The interest, however, was insufficient "to justify any steps towards its introduction," Mulligan wrote to the board. During the next few years a group of alumni, trying to bring football back, secured pledges of $107,000, an amount insufficient to sustain any football program. In 1984 the board agreed to table the fund-raising effort until the university was in a position to handle the facilities problem posed by the locker rooms and deteriorating stadium. (11)

With football gone, the university's focus in intercollegiate athletics in the 1970s was on men's Division I basketball. During the decade the basketball team not only lost more often than it won on the court, but each year its budget operated in a deficit. In 1978 the university's overall athletic deficit amounted to approximately $100,000. "A more successful basketball program," Michael Conaton, a trustee, argued at the board meeting, "would reduce this deficit, since basketball is Xavier's only income sport." During the next several months the Athletic

Board, chaired by William Daily, associate professor of education, reviewed Xavier University athletics and developed goals for the basketball program, as well as criteria for a new coach. Mulligan concurred with the board's recommendations that there was need to unify the whole management operation in athletics and to establish the momentum needed to develop more viable athletic programs. In the spring of 1979 the trustees and Mulligan hoped that income from a revitalized men's basketball program could cover costs of all athletic programs and "stop the drain from the general fund." The specific goals were to seek a suitable conference affiliation "as soon as possible," win 75 percent of its games at the Division I level after three years, participate in a postseason tournament at the end of four years and, from that time on, make an "appearance at least once every four years." (12)

As a first step, the university terminated the basketball coach, the athletic director, and the intramural director. Intense screening then took place in the search for a combined coach and athletic director. Two months later at the May meeting of the Board of Trustees, the president announced that with the appointment of Bob Staak, assistant coach at the University of Pennsylvania from 1975 to 1979, as the men's basketball coach and athletic director, the "athletic program has been rejuvenated." The trustees planned to revitalize intercollegiate athletics without jeopardizing its 90 percent or better graduation rate among athletes. Moreover, they invested approximately $300,000 in the men's basketball program, $182,000 of which consisted of an increase in operational expenses, about a 40 percent jump from the year before. In 1980 Xavier officials also took the lead in establishing the Midwestern City Basketball Conference. (13)

In addition to making an attempt to put the men's basketball program on a self-supporting basis, the university allocated more money for women's athletics. There was a need nationwide for a "turnaround" in athletics in compliance with federal guidelines for women's athletics under Title IX. By 1979 women's sports at Xavier included basketball, volleyball, swimming, and tennis. Men's athletics consisted of basketball, baseball, soccer, tennis, and swimming.

Two years later in December 1981, the Board of Trustees received an encouraging progress report on the status of the athletic program. According to the study, school spirit concerning the men's basketball team and other men's and women's varsity sports had improved. There was increasing attendance at the games and season ticket sales for men's basketball were ahead of previous years. Commenting on the report, a trustee pointed out that $25,000 had been spent to recruit four basketball players, which was, in his judgment, "a sign of the times." (14)

Academic Programs

When Jeremiah O'Callaghan, S.J., in the fall of 1973 had asked to be relieved of his administrative responsibilities as academic vice president, President Mulligan considered restructuring the academic affairs area and eliminating the office of the academic vice president. Some administrators, like O'Callaghan, thought the university "could economize substantially" by not filling the position. But if there "is some academic Messiah available," O'Callaghan wrote sarcastically to the chair of the Faculty Committee, "and if the University can afford him, well and good." The Faculty Committee countered with the argument that though the members were "in favor of cutting back administrative positions during a time of faculty cut-backs," they "doubted the wisdom of eliminating a position that is assigned twenty-four specific functions in the *Faculty Handbook.*" After consulting with the deans, department chairs, and the Faculty Committee, Mulligan, perhaps to "maintain morale," decided to retain the academic structure. In December the Faculty Committee thanked Mulligan for retaining the position of "chief administrative officer for academic affairs who stands above the decanal offices and is subordinate to the President." (15)

Nine months later, Francis "Frank" C. Brennan, S.J., dean of the graduate school at St. Louis University, became Xavier University's second academic vice president. A few weeks after his appointment Brennan began making plans to help energize academics at the university. At the September board meeting he informed the trustees that the faculty should consider a new honors program in addition to the honors bachelor of arts (HAB) program, which focused mainly on classical languages and philosophy. In 1975 Xavier established the University Scholars Program. A more general honors program than the HAB, the new program also attracted students of high academic aptitude. During the next decade both programs affirmed the finest of Xavier's education. Over 60 percent of the 263 HAB graduates by 1985 were practicing physicians, lawyers, and university professors. The remaining graduates had taken positions in a variety of business, governmental, and religious professions. Students in the program had a 99 percent graduate school acceptance rate. When in 1985 the HAB program had a total of fifteen students with an average of four first-year students admitted each year, the University Scholars Program had 144 students enrolled. From the time of its establishment it remained basically constant with an enrollment of approximately 50 new students each year. (16)

At the fall board meeting in 1974, Brennan, who discussed the importance of developing new areas of concentration at the under-graduate level, such as nursing and social work, expressed particular interest in developing graduate work in theology. "[T]here is need for us to be in this work," Brennan said, "because we are an institution dedicated to religious values." In 1970 the university had graduated its first majors in theology. In the fall of 1978 the trustees approved the establishment of a master's degree program in theology on "a three year trial." It began the following summer, and theology became a new area of scholarly inquiry within graduate education. That same year the board also approved the establishment of a master of arts in humanities program. (17)

Most significantly, the new academic vice president strongly recom-mended at his first board meeting in September 1974 that the university "devise a program for faculty development so that we could reward [the] faculty members and help us to stimulate them to further academic" growth. Three months later the university created an endowment fund of $50,000 for faculty development, which helped provide some "release time" from teaching to faculty engaged in research. Two years later Xavier initiated a modest faculty development program, awarding a few three-hour load reductions to the faculty. Thinking that the faculty had "begun to lose confidence in themselves and in the value of their contri-bution," Brennan hoped "to lift up [their] spirits, . . . [and] to give them much greater pride in the inestimable value of what they [were] doing." To help promote and coordinate faculty development, in 1977 the university appointed a faculty member as assistant vice president for research and academic planning. (18)

That year the University also began offering two graduate extension business programs, one on the campus of Transylvania University in Lexington, Kentucky, and the other on the campus of Ohio Dominican College in Columbus, Ohio. The College of Business intro-duced in Lexington an executive MBA program. The program ran for a year and a half, offering each course one at a time for six weeks each, one full day per week. Two years later Dean Thomas Hailstones, with the approval of the Graduate Council, moved the successful executive MBA program to Xavier's campus. (19)

In addition to the establishment of the University Scholars Program and development of new academic programs, in December 1975 the trustees concurred with the president and academic vice president that they should consult with the faculty and begin exploring "changes and adjustments in the core curriculum of the undergraduate colleges." However, substantial changes that could conceivably alter the character, traditions, and purposes of Xavier's undergraduate colleges were to be submitted to the Board of Trustees prior to official adoption and implementation. Though the 28 Jesuit colleges and universities had long abandoned the traditional *ratio studiorum*, with its emphasis on classical languages, mathematics, philosophy, and theology, Xavier's revised core curriculum in 1976 retained more features of the traditional program than did most other Jesuit schools. It required students to complete a course in English composition, four courses in philosophy, four in theology, four each in the humanities and social science, two each in mathematics and science, and four in a foreign language. The two-year foreign language requirement, however, was for undergraduates in the College of Arts and Sciences only. (20)

In the spring of 1978 the university's core curriculum and faculty development program received support from an unexpected source. In mid-March a five-member team from the North Central Association of Colleges and Secondary Schools (NCA) visited the campus and conducted its regular ten-year review. The North Central report highlighted as positive features of the university the maintenance of a Catholic and Jesuit philosophy of education, primarily through a strong undergraduate core curriculum, and the institutional loyalty of the faculty. It also noted that the quality and scholarship of the faculty had improved since the last NCA site visits ten and twenty years earlier respectively. In 1978, 64 percent of the full-time faculty held a terminal degree compared to 28.8 percent in 1958. In addition, the number of local and Ohio degrees had also decreased, and many more faculty members were engaged in research and publication. Nevertheless, the school still had an "inbreeding" problem, as approximately 60 percent of the faculty members were alumni. Moreover, in an effort to keep up with the best of American secular higher education, Xavier, like other Jesuit colleges and universities, consciously sought to professionalize the faculty. Without compromising the primary importance of teaching, increasingly the university expected the faculty to engage in publishable scholarly research in order to stay current with, and contribute to, the advancement of knowledge. Overall, the North Central evaluation team "found Xavier to be a well-established institution, one with a remarkably long history of service, enjoying excellent rapport with the city and the area around it." Though in its judgment the university had a record of wise financial operation, small indebtedness, and a future that promised stability, it viewed the small endowment of approximately $6,000,000 as problematic. (21)

Of considerable concern to the NCA team were the heavy teaching loads of faculty members and the apparent "absence of organized institutional long-range planning." For the former they recommended a system of sabbaticals for faculty. "[D]espite modest salary levels and heavy teaching and committee loads," the North Central report read, "morale is excellent." The overwhelming majority of the faculty taught four courses each semester, sometimes involving four preparations, plus one or two additional courses in the summer. Moreover, while engaged in a reasonable amount of scholarly work, each faculty member was required to hold office hours for out-of-class student counseling and academic advising, as well as to participate in a variety of university governance and management activities either within a department or in the university at large. In light of the faculty's heavy teaching load and increasing engagement in research and service, the site team recommended the introduction of a modest sabbatical program, whose aim would be to help reinvigorate members of the faculty. (22)

In early fall Mulligan informed the academic community that it was not "financially feasible for the University to establish a system of faculty sabbaticals across the board." However, he was hopeful that it would be possible to broaden the small program instituted by Brennan two years earlier. In the spring of 1979 the academic vice president, joined by faculty, began exploring the possibility of initiating a formal sabbatical program. The following year the university introduced a seniority sabbatical program, with the three most senior faculty members, in terms of years of service, taking leave in the fall semester, and four the following spring. (23)

In his final report to the Academic Affairs Committee of the Board of Trustees in the spring of 1982, Brennan, who had announced his resignation in order to pursue pastoral work, again underscored the importance of faculty development. "Faculty development and improvement," he said, "should be a continuing priority for the administration and for the Board. The vast majority of Xavier's faculty works hard and successfully. Morale tends to be high, and people generally like what they are doing and the environment in which they are doing it.

This is critical. I think that faculty and staff members will continue to respond positively if they sense a genuine concern for their welfare." Faculty Committee representatives also reported to the Academic Affairs Committee that they were "waiting to see what the direction of the new administration will take in this matter" and pointed out that if it continued "to focus on publication and research, then the University must look very carefully at the current teaching load." By 1985 the university committed approximately $346,000 annually for a variety of faculty development activities including sabbaticals, research leaves, reduced teaching loads for research, and summer research stipends. As expectations for scholarship grew and teaching loads continued to be heavy, the newly-revised faculty development program helped enhance teaching, scholarship, and service as well as play a critical role in faculty retention. (24)

Over the years Xavier faculty as teachers, researchers, and academic advisors had had a strong influence on the life of the university. Among them were Paul Harkins, who taught Greek and Latin in the Department of Classics from 1946 to 1975; Richard J. Garascia, professor of chemistry, who taught full-time at the university for 40 years; Karl P. Wentersdorf, specialist in the field of medieval and Renaissance literature, whose scholarly accomplishments were recognized throughout the Western world, taught from the mid-1950s to the 1980s; Thomas Savage, S.J., who served as chair of the Department of English in the 1960s and 1970s, was an intellectual and spiritual force on campus; and Joseph J. Peters, S.J., professor and chair of the Department of Biology, whose research led to 38 publications over a 20-year period. Wearing a laboratory smock over his Jesuit habit, Peters often visited students in the cafeteria and became known as the "cafeteria celebrity." These five individuals, among others, were trusted guides to faculty and students alike and exemplified the high ideals of Jesuit higher education.

During the Mulligan years, the university also considered other ways of enhancing academic life. In the mid-1970s the academic vice president's office sponsored two-day academic planning conferences, one each year, funded by the Danforth Foundation, at the Jesuit Retreat House in Milford, Ohio. Approximately 50 faculty members, students, and administrators participated in small group discussions on a set of topics that considered Xavier's resources, potential, and mission as the university approached its 150th or sesquicentennial anniversary in 1981. Moreover, they explored ways of introducing new academic programs, structures, and community-oriented activities. In the fall of 1975 the university revised the statutes regarding composition of its Board of Undergraduate Studies. It included the undergraduate deans, the associate deans, seven members of the faculty, and three students. Four years later the university established the Graduate Council, consisting of nine faculty members and three administrators. The purpose of the new council was "to give the faculty," Brennan said, "a greater voice in the policy of the Graduate School regarding quality and purpose of graduate programs." By 1977 both the Office of Admissions and Recruitment and the Office of the Registrar, formerly under the jurisdiction of the vice president for administration, reported to the academic vice president. That same year the university changed its academic calendar, which had been a subject of discussion for some years. First semester classes, which had begun late in September with a Christmas break followed by a brief resumption of classes in January before semester examinations, now began earlier and ended in December. Second semester classes now began the second week in January and ended in early May. Among the 1,082 students who responded to a survey of reactions to the possible calendar change, 886 had expressed a preference for starting earlier. The faculty and administration had voted 120 to 13 for the change, which was implemented in the fall semester of 1978. Partly in response to the NCA team's concern over the lack of "institutional planning" at the university, during that academic year a committee of faculty and administrators further considered questions of long-range academic planning. (25)

In the late 1970s and early 1980s the university also explored the possibility of seeking accreditation by the American Association of Collegiate Business Schools (AACSB) for Xavier's College of Business Administration. As the faculty and programs in the college grew stronger, such as with the establishment in the early 1970s of the college's and university's first endowed chair, made possible by the family of D. J. O'Conor, a Cincinnati industrialist, a number of CBA faculty led by Dean Tom Hailstones and Brennan recommended accreditation. Faculty members, however, were "divided in their opinions of the benefits of [AACSB] accreditation," Mulligan said. "Some feel the additional expense of meeting accreditation requirements would be better spent on faculty salaries." In his final report in 1982 to the board's Academic Affairs Committee, Brennan argued that AACSB accreditation was necessary for the future of the university. Though the project would be costly, estimated at approximately $1,000,000, which included the hiring of more business faculty, he pointed out that the university relied heavily on the College of Business Administration and "may have to face the prospect of this leap forward if the College is to avoid falling behind." Much of the growth of the college had been made possible by the strong and steady leadership of Tom Hailstones who, on January 1, 1983, resigned after serving as dean for over 20 years. Notwithstanding the influence that the College of Business Administration had on the life of the university and in the metropolitan area, during the next several years many faculty members, especially those outside the college, thought the proposed AACSB accreditation would cause financial strain and faculty morale problems. (26)

University officials during Mulligan's presidency were very concerned over declining enrollment numbers. The early 1970s was a low point for enrollment in many men's colleges in the United States, primarily because of the draft and the war in Vietnam. From 1970 to 1974, Xavier experienced a decrease of 415 undergraduate students. In 1974, for the first time since 1946, there were fewer than 400 first-year students enrolled. During the same period, the number of students in residence halls, that had a capacity of 1050, dropped from 804 to 703. Moreover, for the first time since the founding of the Graduate School in 1946, there was in 1973 a decrease in enrollment, though slight, in the master of education program. Mulligan was particularly concerned over the declining undergraduate enrollment. Although fully committed to the graduate programs, he thought Xavier's primary mission as a Jesuit university was to concentrate "more efforts and resources on the development of the full-time undergraduate student body than on that of the part-time graduate student." Mulligan hoped to "increase gradually" the number of full-time undergraduates to 2,200, an increase of approximately 400 students. Though one trustee described Xavier's enrollment picture as "very stormy," another observed that because the drop in enrollments was not unusual "compared to American colleges," he cautioned the university not to "panic." (27)

In the summer and fall of 1976, the Corbett Foundation, a local foundation established in 1958 by J. Ralph and Patricia A. Corbett, helped fund an undergraduate admission and enrollment study. Representatives of a consulting company met with Xavier's recruiting staff, studied their recruitment publications, and sent out a questionnaire to students and other groups to find out what they thought of Xavier. As a result of the study, completed in early 1977, the university introduced a number of changes in its recruitment operation, the most significant of which was the retention of a professional firm to develop new literature for prospective undergraduate students. Xavier's goal was to admit 500 to 600 first-year students each year. Moreover, in the spring the university developed an exit-interview system to assist in analyzing its retention rate, which was lower than the typical rate in other universities. To help recruit and retain minority students, the Corbett Foundation also provided $100,000 for assistance to black students in the form of scholarships and special academic advising. (28)

In seeking more undergraduates, university officials found it necessary to lower academic expectations and admission standards. Entrance scores for the first-year class in 1978 were modest. The average verbal Standardized Achievement Test (SAT) score was 457, mathematics 485, a drop of 8 and 19 points respectively from the previous year. Only 36 percent of the first-year students scored above 500 in verbal and 51 percent above 500 in mathematics. Upon the insistence of the administration and faculty, the university provided more remedial academic services. Nevertheless, during the next several years there was dissatisfaction among some faculty who thought the university was accepting too many borderline and probation students. But the high expectations of some of Xavier's academic programs, however, such as the honors AB, university scholars, and pre-med, insured that any class would include students of very high potential and achievement. (29)

By the fall of 1978 total undergraduate enrollment in the Arts and Sciences and Business Administration colleges was 2,052, the first time in six years that it rose above 2,000. The first-year class totalled 574. More than half of full-time undergraduates in 1978 commuted from greater Cincinnati, leaving about 750 students in residence halls. Overall undergraduate enrollment, including the College for Continuing Education, which had replaced the Evening College in 1972, was 2,823. Graduate enrollment was 3,664, making the Graduate School the largest among the Jesuit universities in the country. The previous year, Dean Ray McCoy, who had shepherded the Graduate School for 30 years and had seen its enrollment grow from about 200 to approximately 3,700, resigned. His overall influence in the life and direction of the university during his tenure was substantial. (30)

A year later, enrollment in the two undergraduate day colleges reached 2,256, the largest combined enrollment since 1968. This figure included 637 new first-year students and 130 transfer students. However, whereas from 1970 to 1980 Xavier's full-time undergraduate enrollment grew by 6.5 percent, and first-year applications increased from 1,163 to approximately 1,400, enrollment in American Catholic colleges and universities increased by 16 percent. By 1980 the mix of undergraduates and graduates on Xavier's campus was reversed. For the first time since 1968 the number of undergraduate students (3,931), full-time and part-time, was greater than the number of graduate students (3,405). This trend would continue into the twenty-first century. From 1972 to 1982, undergraduate full-time and part-time enrollment jumped from 2,870 to 3,985, while the graduate population dropped from 3,120 to 2,965. During the same period Xavier witnessed a major change in the gender composition of its undergraduate student population. The male population decreased from 2,168 to 1,801, while women increased from 702 to 2,184, which constituted 54.8 percent of the undergraduate body. The gender distribution in the residence halls, however, was reversed, whereby approximately 58 percent of the students were men. In 1983 total undergraduate enrollment was 4,125, surpassing 4,000 for the first time in Xavier's history. In six years' time the university's new enrollment strategies, which included a lowering of admission standards, had proven successful. Undergraduate enrollment had increased by 1,302 students. (31)

Construction, Acquisitions, and the Expansion of Campus

During Mulligan's presidency the university engaged in two fund-raising campaigns. The goal of the Advancement Fund Campaign, the drive that began in 1972, was $30,000,000 over a ten-year period. The university hoped to raise $15,000,000 in the first five years. The stated purposes in the initial phase of the campaign were $3,825,000 for endowments for grants-in-aid and for improvement of student life; $3,800,000 for endowments for faculty development and physical improvements of teaching facilities; $875,000 for curriculum and to make wider use of Jesuit scholars; $700,000 for strengthening library collections and educational equipment; and $5,800,000 for a College of Business Administration building and a general administration building. (32)

In the spring of 1973 the University Planning and Development Committee noted that there was also a lack of recreational facilities on campus and recommended to the Board of Trustees that a sports complex, with a pool and shower-locker facilities, be built adjacent to the fieldhouse. During the university's commencement ceremony later that spring, Ralph Corbett, head of the Corbett Foundation, asked O'Connor if the university had a swimming pool. Learning that it did not, he immediately suggested that his "Foundation might consider helping build one," on the condition that construction would start prior to December 31, 1975, at which time the foundation expected to discontinue its activities. Enthused by the offer, the trustees began developing plans for the new facility. (33)

On September 16, 1974, six days after Paul O'Connor's death, Corbett suggested to Mulligan that because the last project O'Connor was involved in was the swimming pool, "it would be highly appropriate" to name the new building after him. "If you agree—then I hope you can activate a strong group of men to raise the funds to match our pledge. It should be done as soon as possible—don't you think? The need for this new facility is great—and Paul's memory should be honored!!" While plans were being developed for a new sports complex, the Corbett Foundation also provided approximately $200,000 to develop the university's performing arts, which, Mulligan thought, would "greatly improve the quality of student life on campus." (34)

At the December 1974 board meeting, the trustees approved the construction of a $2,700,000 sports complex, to be called the Paul L. O'Connor Sports Center. In the process they eliminated the general administration building proposal from the Advancement Campaign list of goals, "feeling," Mulligan said, "that a sports center for our students should have a higher priority." To be built in two phases and designed to be an intramural building for student and community use, the first phase of the O'Connor Sports Center included an olympic-size swimming pool, locker facilities for students, faculty, and staff, four racquetball courts, a weight and exercise room, and an all-purpose room for wrestling and gymnastics. At various times since the spring of 1928, when the student newspaper had carried the headline, "Swimming Pool is What the College Needs Most," the university had contemplated building a swimming pool. Forty-eight years later, on September 29, 1976, the university dedicated the Ralph and Patricia Corbett Physical Education Building of the Paul L. O'Connor Sports Center. In order to build the sports center the university relocated the tennis courts in the area behind Kuhlman Hall. Phase II of the sports center complex, which began in 1976 and was completed a year later, consisted of a large gymnasium, two classrooms, offices, and exercise and trophy rooms. (35)

By 1975 it was clear that the university would not meet the initial Advancement Fund Campaign goal of $15,000,000. That fall the trustees discussed the need for more and continuous cultivation of potential donors. A year later the Development and Public Information

Committee of the Board of Trustees met in Mulligan's office and recommended phasing out the Advancement Fund, which had raised a total of $8,600,000. There were a number of reasons for ending the campaign. The popular Paul O'Connor, who had been filling the role of chancellor since stepping down as president, died in 1974. The trustees also regarded the public announcement of the campaign with less than 30 percent of the total committed to have been a mistake. Moreover, they regarded a ten-year plan as inadvisable, since most of the corporate donors chose to contribute over the extended period. Going back for an additional gift proved very difficult. Lastly, neither of the two largest gifts qualifed as the type of gift that would be needed to reach even the first phase with its $15 million goal. Though halted prematurely, some of the funds raised in the campaign made it possible for Xavier authorities to remodel Hinkle Hall for use by the faculty, many of whom moved over from the old reading room in Schmidt Hall, which had temporarily housed most of the faculty previously located in South Hall at the University Drive entrance. (36)

At the full board meeting in the fall of 1976, the trustees approved a new five-year fund drive, called the Sesquicentennial Fund Campaign, that would run through 1981, the 150th anniversary of the founding of the university. Chaired by J. Gibbs MacVeigh of the class of 1955, the new campaign, with a goal of $6,600,000, earmarked $3,000,000 for a new College of Business Administration building and the rest for endowment for the library, scholarships, faculty development, facilities renovation, and improvement of instructional equipment. With over $3,000,000 in hand in the fall of 1979, the university publicly announced the three-year campaign and changed its monetary goal to $8,375,000. It ended successfully in 1981, having raised $8,389,683. Over a five-year period the two campaigns enabled the university to nearly double the size of its endowment from $3,100,000 in 1974 to $6,180,000 in June 1979. During the same period the value of the physical plant increased from $30,000,000 to $52,000,000. (37)

While the university shepherded the Sesquicentennial Fund Campaign, opportunities arose to help expand the size of the campus. In the spring of 1978 the Board of Trustees approved negotiations for the purchase of property between Ledgewood Avenue and Victory Parkway, owned by Dr. Joseph Link, Jr., alumnus and professor emeritus at Xavier. He and his twin brother had attended the university in the early 1930s. The proposed property consisted of two acres, three apartment buildings, and two homes. "Its future proper development is of considerable importance to the University," Mulligan said. The university already owned a number of houses on the east side of Ledgewood. Purchase of the Link property on the west side provided "considerable added assurance," Mulligan said, "of keeping the neighborhood at a reasonable high level of maintenance and of assuring us room for future expansion." Closing on the Link complex took place in January 1979 and the university acquired ownership of the property over the course of ten years. The out-of-pocket cost to Xavier was $254,000. The rest of the payment over the ten-year period came from the rental of the property, which Xavier put in the hands of a professional manager. "I have turned over the six buildings and two acres of land . . . to Xavier," Link said, "in appreciation for the kind generosity of the Jesuit Fathers for helping the Link twins during the Great Depression." (38)

Less than two months after the university signed the agreement on the Link property, Mulligan and the president of the Board of Directors of the United States Shoe Company jointly announced the U.S. Shoe gift of its 19.8-acre Norwood property to Xavier. Adjoining the campus on Herald Avenue, the property, valued at $6,000,000, included several buildings and parking spaces for more than 800 vehicles. "Xavier has been virtually landlocked," Mulligan said, and the gift "opens up great opportunities." The trustees' Plant and Buildings Committee conducted a study of the potential development of the new acquisition that was handed over to the university in 1980. The A. B. Dolly and Ralph Cohen Foundation, a Cincinnati foundation established in 1956, gave the university a grant of $100,000 to be used to renovate the U.S. Shoe property for educational use. In the spring of 1981 the university tore down South Hall, the frame building that had been more recently used for storage, as additional storage space was made possible by the new acquisition. A year later the trustees decided to tear down all buildings on the U.S. Shoe property except for the newer warehouse building, keeping it for use by the university maintenance department, and develop the rest of the land for recreational purposes. The trustees secured a bond issue of $550,000 to cover the estimated cost. (39)

As Xavier officials proceeded with the acquisition of the Link and U.S. Shoe properties, they made plans to realize a more than forty-year-old dream of erecting a business administration building. Though Mulligan in 1973 had approved a feasibility study, plans for the proposed College of Business Administration (CBA) building were not developed until the fall of 1976 at the start of the Sesquicentennial

Fund Campaign. Three years later the Board of Trustees agreed to go ahead with its construction on Ledgewood Avenue, adjoining Alter Hall. The state of Ohio authorized $5,920,000 in tax-free municipal bonds for the facility. By carefully investing the funds at approximately 12 percent interest until they were needed, a surplus remained for the university after it had completed payments on the building. (40)

On April 30, 1981, the university dedicated the new College of Business Administration building. The three-story structure contained five traditional classrooms, two large amphitheater classrooms, two classroom-laboratories, three seminar-conference rooms, a larger conference room, a computer terminal center, the Center for Management and Professional Development, which had changed its name in 1980 from the Institute for Business and Community Service, administrative offices, and student counseling facilities. The new building also freed space needed by other parts of the university. Three years later, school officials erected an addition to the CBA building, providing 23 faculty offices. (41)

The most controversial expansion during Mulligan's presidency was the acquisition of Edgecliff College in 1980. As early as 1969, when Xavier decided to go fully coed, the trustees of the two schools discussed the university's possible acquisition of Edgecliff. In September of that year a local business leader informed President Paul O'Connor that "the Mercy nuns were thinking that they might have to give up Edgecliff" and he wondered whether Xavier "would like to take it over." Edgecliff had an annual operating deficit and two long-term debts. The acquisition "could have far-reaching effects on our future growth," O'Connor informed the trustees in 1969. Though the Xavier trustees were reluctant "to say no to the offer," they thought "the problems in a take over [were] very serious." Nevertheless, they decided to meet with Edgecliff representatives. Nothing came of the meeting. (42)

About a decade later, talks between Xavier University and Edgecliff College officials resumed. President Mulligan and Sister Margaret Anne Molitor, president of Edgecliff, met several times to discuss ways, as Mulligan put it, "on developing a relationship that would benefit both institutions." The university's motivation for possibly acquiring Edgecliff was to "enhance Xavier's services to the community" by adding the "fine arts, nursing, and social services," academic disciplines then offered by Edgecliff but not available at Xavier, to its curriculum. The board authorized Mulligan to pursue the matter further. Xavier University officials were aware of other Jesuit acquisitions of neighboring colleges. In the mid-1970s, when many small women's colleges had large debts, Boston College had purchased Newton College, and the University of San Francisco, Lone Mountain College. In mid-January 1980, Frank Brennan, Xavier's academic vice president, informed the Faculty Committee of "discussions" with Edgecliff College and pointed out that it would "not be possible to speak concretely about any tentative agreement for some time." (43)

By early spring, however, negotiations between Xavier and Edgecliff developed much more quickly than had been anticipated. "[T]he situation at Edgecliff is deteriorating rapidly," Mulligan reported to the board, "and the acquisition would be a very progressive step." The Sisters of Mercy needed an answer by April 1 in order to allow them time to receive approval from Rome to complete the negotiations. Archbishop Joseph Bernardin of Cincinnati had already given his consent. The trustees agreed to respond as quickly as they could to the Sisters of Mercy's request. (44)

To Xavier officials, there were apparent advantages to the acquisition. The university would acquire not only new academic programs, but a twenty-acre campus with seven buildings. Edgecliff had the seven-story Sullivan Residence Hall for 288 students, Corbett Theater building for speech and theater arts facilities, Grace Hall for physical and consumer sciences and modern languages, Administration Building, Brennan Memorial Library, classrooms and art galleries in Emery Hall, and the music department in Maxwelton, a building across the side street from the Administration Building. Xavier would thus "avoid the need," Mulligan said, "to build any additional facilities during at least the next 25 years, which would be a vast saving." School officials were also hopeful that the university would acquire loyal alumni. (45)

Mulligan and Brennan also emphasized to the board that the purchase of Edgecliff would not be a merger. What they proposed to the trustees was the university "acquiring the assets of Edgecliff," Brennan said, "with a view of continuing it as an educational institution." The proposal, already approved by the Edgecliff College trustees, provided for the outright purchase by Xavier of certain Edgecliff assets, such as buildings, land, equipment, supplies, and records, by July 1, 1980, at a cost of $6,000,000. The university would also take over the mortgage indebtedness of approximately $1,600,000 on the properties. A cash payment of $500,000 was to be paid on October 1, 1980, and the remaining total paid over a period of 20 years at no interest. Moreover, Mulligan and Brennan hoped to administer the Edgecliff campus more efficiently by decreasing the size of the administration and faculty, closing small departments, and centralizing services. Fully "aware of the financial risk," the Xavier board knew that "if the operation is not successful in five years," a trustee said, "the buildings and land could be sold to provide sufficient income to meet Xavier's obligations to the Sisters of Mercy." Convinced that it was "a reasonable risk" the trustees authorized the Executive Committee to issue a contract. In late April, Brennan informed the university community of the board's decision. (46)

Within two weeks, however, at the May 1980 board meeting, the trustees decided to abandon the idea of an immediate purchase of Edgecliff College "and to consider only an option to buy." That action, they thought, further minimized the risk. At this point a trustee granted the university the money to make an option payment of $600,000, with the university holding a three-year option to buy by June 30, 1983. According to the agreement the university would make $340,000 yearly payments over 22 years, with a balloon payment in the final year to cover the remaining balance. The Sisters of Mercy agreed to the plan. The trustees at both institutions kept the option contract confidential. Mulligan informed the board that while faculty members "feel the addition of Edgecliff to the University will be a fine addition to the University, . . . [they] naturally have some apprehension." (47)

On July 1, 1980, Xavier University publicly announced the acquisition of the Edgecliff campus and control of the Edgecliff College assets. Edgecliff College, now known as Edgecliff College of Xavier University, became the fourth undergraduate college of the university, joining the College of Arts and Sciences, College of Business Administration, and the College of Continuing Education. At a joint press conference by Edgecliff and Xavier officials, Brennan pointed out that Edgecliff College would "begin a new existence as a constituent college of Xavier University under an administration appointed by and responsible to Xavier University." Roger A. Fortin, professor of history and Xavier's associate vice president for academic affairs, became dean of the new college. While committed "to effecting the necessary economies and to avoiding inappropriate duplication," Brennan wrote, "Xavier will also make efforts to sustain the Edgecliff traditions and to maintain Edgecliff's identity as a college devoted to the fine arts and to human service programs." In addition to the acquisition of the departments of art, music, theatre arts, nursing, and social work, with the purchase of Edgecliff College came the third wave of women in the life of the university. The first two consisted of part-time women in the evening and graduate programs in the aftermath of World War I and the introduction of coeducation in the undergraduate day colleges in 1969 respectively. (48)

In the fall of 1980, university enrollment, including Edgecliff's, totalled 7,336, an historical high point. Daily shuttle service accommodated students on both campuses. A few dozen Xavier University students took courses, especially in the arts, on the Edgecliff campus, while about 100 Edgecliff students enrolled in classes on the main campus. In the beginning the university kept the 2.8 million dollar budget for Edgecliff separate from the budget on the main campus to provide for better monitoring of the revenues and expenses of the new college. Xavier temporarily retained twenty of Edgecliff's faculty members. Of those, ten were women, including four Sisters of Mercy, three of whom joined the College of Arts and Sciences Departments of Biology, English, and History respectively. In addition, six other Sisters of Mercy remained in various administrative or staff positions. From the start many of the approximately 5,000 alumni of Edgecliff College accepted the change well. Their financial contributions in 1980–1981 matched those of the previous year, indicating that much of their loyalty to the college and its tradition had not been lost. (49)

When Xavier celebrated its 150th anniversary in 1981, the expansion of the campus, with the addition of the Link, U.S. Shoe, and Edgecliff properties, had opened up new educational opportunities. A civic breakfast on January 22, 1981, inaugurated the beginning of a year-long calendar of events celebrating the university's sesquicentennial anniversary, the Jesuit work in the high school, St. Xavier Parish, and Jesuit retreat houses in the Cincinnati area. Throughout the year there were academic convocations, a commemorative concert by the Cincinnati Symphony Orchestra, and a special Mass at St. Xavier Church. To help appreciate some of the university's accomplishments over 150 years, Lee J. Bennish, S.J., associate professor of history and archivist, wrote *Continuity and Change: Xavier University, 1831–1981*, published in 1981. A memorable event during the sesquicentennial year was the election of Phyllis Smale, Xavier's first woman trustee. (50)

During the anniversary year the operating costs of Edgecliff College of Xavier University proved higher than anticipated. Primarily due to a lower enrollment than projected, in its first fiscal year the new college suffered a deficit of $150,000. At the same time the overall university budget showed a surplus of $41,000. For six consecutive years the university had operated in the black, recording its most substantial surplus of $433,000 at the end of the 1979–1980 academic year. What continued to sustain the budget were private gifts and grants. In 1980, annual giving totalled $725,000, which constituted 4.7 percent of the operating budget. Significantly, the administration was optimistic about the university's future. While the acquisition of Edgecliff helped enhance Xavier's curriculum, university officials also made fuller use of the satellite campus by hosting various social and academic events on the campus, especially in the art department's Emery Hall, an historic home that once hosted the nineteenth century English novelist, Charles Dickens. (51)

In the fall of 1981, Faculty Committee representatives, concerned over the recent acquisition of Edgecliff College and the U.S. Shoe property, met with the Academic Affairs Committee of the Board of Trustees and expressed their uneasiness over the university's financial resources. Arguing that the institution was expanding too much and too fast, they pointed out that they had received little information on the acquisitions and had no part in the decisions. They feared that in the future the university's limited resources, rather than being appropriated for more pressing academic needs, would be drained by the purchase of Edgecliff College and the renovation of the U.S. Shoe property. More specifically, they recommended a greater commitment of money to the faculty development program and the addition of remedial courses in mathematics and English and services for students admitted with lower test scores. (52)

By 1982, Edgecliff College had fully adopted Xavier's core curriculum. Edgecliff's former degree programs had been reduced from 22 to 5 and the faculty and staff of the college by about one-third to fifteen. The satellite campus now concentrated exclusively on programs in human services and in the fine arts. The nursing program had received accreditation and work had also begun on the development of a graduate course of study. While approximately 300 students from the main campus now took courses at Edgecliff, about 200 from Edgecliff traveled to the main campus. (53)

Notwithstanding some faculty reservations, the administration of the university was positive about the purchase and confident about the viability of Edgecliff College and the future of its programs. "[I]f Xavier continues to develop the . . . programs," Mulligan said, "Edgecliff College can certainly become self-supporting." Brennan also commented on Edgecliff in his final report at the spring 1982 meeting of the

Academic Affairs Committee of the Board of Trustees. "Solution of the problems raised by the acquisition of Edgecliff and the acceptance of the U.S. Shoe property," he wrote, "will require time and expert professional planning. While candidly acknowledging my own involvement in these enterprises, I would also like to state that I believe we made the right decisions, and I hope excessive caution will not lead to the precipitous repudiation of these developments. They will cause some anxious hours for many, but they will be worth it." The Faculty Committee, however, continued to express "grave concern [over] the current expansion of the University," especially regarding the Edgecliff campus. They argued that the university should unload the satellite campus and take care of the Edgecliff students on the main campus. (54)

Later in the fall the university also explored the unexpected acquisition of additional property. The management of Rainbo Baking Company, located across the street from the U.S. Shoe property on Herald Avenue, proposed a gift of its property to the university. Though appreciative of the gift, in light of recent acquisitions by the university some Xavier trustees urged caution. The board authorized Mulligan to work with its Executive Committee in pursuing the matter. It insisted that no real cost be incurred by the university for at least three years. In December 1985 the Company donated the property to the university. (55)

A New President, Charles L. Currie, S.J.

In the summer of 1978, Mulligan informed the Executive Committee of the Board of Trustees that "looking down the road, I think it might be advisable to establish a timetable when a successor could be named." Having served as president for six years, he suggested that a search could begin as early as November 1978, with a new president taking office in October 1979; or begin a search a year or two later and a successor to take office in October 1980 or 1981 accordingly. He thought the latter might be more appropriate, for it would be his 65th birthday as well as the 150th anniversary of the university. In light of the ongoing Sesquicentennial Fund Campaign, the Executive Committee requested that he stay on as long as possible. Mulligan agreed to do so. At the December 1980 board meeting, the trustees initiated the search for a new president. (56)

The search committee, consisting of members of the administration, faculty, and a student, reduced the original list of seventy Jesuit candidates to thirteen by early spring. Five candidates were invited to campus. By late April 1981 they unanimously recommended Charles L. Currie, S.J., president of Wheeling College in Wheeling, West Virginia. Since Currie, who had been president for nine years, had requested complete confidentiality regarding his candidacy, the search committee had not been able to solicit recommendations from individuals of Wheeling College or in the Wheeling business community. However, two Jesuit trustees had made discrete inquiries on a confidential basis from Jesuit colleagues at the college. In addition, Xavier's vice presidents and deans had interviewed Currie. With all this information, committee members were enthusiastic about their top candidate, and cautioned against delaying making a decision, since at least one other Jesuit college was conducting a presidential search. In May the board appointed Currie. Having informed the trustees that he would not be available until the summer of 1982, Mulligan agreed to continue to serve until Currie's arrival. (57)

In his last report to the Board of Trustees in May 1982, President Mulligan commented on the budget and enrollment. He anticipated future deficits. "[I]t is unavoidable for many reasons," he said. The basketball program had lost over $100,000 in 1982, the Center for Management and Professional Development had also lost approximately $100,000, and the graduate enrollment in education had decreased from 1,800 to 1,200 in the last few years. Though undergraduate enrollment had been increasing steadily since 1978, its "future," Mulligan noted, "is not very bright, due to the decline in 18-year-olds, plus the fear of future [federal] reductions in student loans." On a more positive note, the out-going president hoped for an upturn in revenue, pointing out that Xavier's tuition costs were still very low comparatively, 25th out of the 28 Jesuit colleges. Moreover, he was optimistic that as soon as the economy got stronger there would be an upswing in graduate enrollment. He concluded by advising the board that the "faculty should be spoken to frankly and realistically about the resources of the University, since they expect much more than the University can afford." (58)

Much was accomplished during Mulligan's presidency. Influenced by his academic vice president, Frank Brennan, the university initiated a second honors program as well as a faculty development program, which did much to enhance teaching and scholarship and, in the process, faculty self-esteem. While seeing an increase in total enrollment from 5,990 to 6,950, the university witnessed an ineffective fund-raising campaign only to be succeeded by the more successful Sesquicentennial Capital Campaign. Though Mulligan may be remembered more often for the termination of the football program and, to a lesser extent, for the rejuvenation of the men's basketball team, the acquisition of the Link and U.S. Shoe properties, erection of the O'Connor Sports Center and the College of Business Administration Building, and the integration of the Edgecliff College programs in the life of the university significantly renewed hope in Xavier's future.

In early fall 1982 the new president, Charles Currie, expressed his gratitude and appreciation to his predecessor "for the good condition in which he left the University, one of stability and calm," allowing him lead time for planning. Ironically, throughout most of Currie's administration the university would be anything but stable and calm. Currie, who received his bachelor's and master's degrees in the mid-1950s from Boston College and a doctorate in physical chemistry from the Catholic University of America in 1961, was inaugurated on October 22. (59)

From the very start Currie urged the development of a more up-to-date mission statement and a study of space, facility, and academic needs, which included addressing administrative computerization needs and the possible establishment of a new telephone system. In the fall of 1982 the administration offered telephone etiquette seminars on campus to improve the image of the university and developed a standardized new logo and letterhead for all university stationery and publications. In addition, campus planning consultants visited the campus and, working with the University Space Committee, made a proposal for developing a holistic approach to short- and long-term space projects. A gift of $100,000 covered the consultants' costs. (60)

Early in 1983 the university established the Academic Organization Task Force, whose purpose was to study the university's academic organization and consider the best structure for the most effective operation of the academic affairs division. It met from April through December. At the time the university had five academic units: College of Arts and Sciences, College of Business Administration, College of Continuing Education, Edgecliff College, and Graduate School. The following year the university reorganized itself into three colleges: Arts and Sciences, Business Administration, and Professional Studies. While the departments of art, music, and theatre arts, formerly in Edgecliff College of Xavier University, joined the College of Arts and Sciences, the Department of Education in the College of Arts and Sciences and the disciplines of nursing and social work in Edgecliff

College were placed in the new College of Professional Studies. By discontinuing the Graduate School, graduate programs in the three colleges were administered by each respective dean. The College of Continuing Education became the Division of Continuing Education. (61)

In the mid-1980s Xavier's teaching faculty in the university's three colleges consisted of 201 full-time and 169 part-time members, an increase of about 29 and 69 respectively in eight years. Among the full-time faculty, 34 percent were at the rank of professor, 26 percent associate professors, 30 percent assistant professors, and 9 percent instructors. In addition, 62 percent were tenured. Three were Hispanic (1.4 percent) and five—an increase of four in five years—were African American (2.4 percent), 48 were women (23 percent), which was an increase of 46 women in fifteen years. Though progress had been made since the North Central team had evaluated the faculty seven years earlier, the number and percentage of faculty with "in-town" degrees from either Xavier or the University of Cincinnati was undesirably high. Among the full-time faculty 11 percent had master's degrees from Xavier and 21 percent had master's or doctoral degrees from the University of Cincinnati. (62)

Building upon Currie's initial planning efforts, in the fall of 1984 the university established a University Planning Committee. Co-chaired by Frank Hoenemeyer of the Board of Trustees and Dr. John Minahan, who had been appointed academic vice president in 1982, the committee consisted of administrators, faculty, students, alumni, and friends of the university. Charged to review the strengths, weaknesses, opportunities, and threats (SWOT) of each university department, the Planning Committee completed its analysis in December. The SWOT analysis and newly-developed Identity and Mission Statement became the basis for the formation of 3- to 5-year plans. (63)

At that time the university offered fifty-one undergraduate academic programs leading to bachelor of arts and bachelor of science degrees. The core, which had been modified slightly, consisted of a course in English composition and one in fundamentals of mathematics; four courses in a foreign language in most degree programs; four courses in the humanities; four courses in phiosophy; four courses in theology; two additional courses in mathematics; two courses in science; and two courses in social science. "It is the strength of this core curriculum that characterizes the unique elements of Xavier Jesuit education," the University Planning Committee Report said in 1985. "Xavier's primary purpose," it continued, "is to provide undergraduate students with a liberal education in the arts, sciences and humanities within the context of a specifically Christian and Catholic world view of things. Students are provided the opportunity," the report further stated, "to study specific professional and pre-professional disciplines within this liberal arts context with the expectation that they develop a personal sense of the moral and religious order in which they are to pursue their life goals and careers." Consistent with the university's tradition, it concluded that "[s]tudents and faculty alike are expected to develop both their intellectual powers and moral sensibilities in ways that unify rather than diversify secular and religious thoughts. The pursuit of this unity denotes the unique power of a Jesuit education." (64)

At the graduate level in the fall of 1985, the university offered thirty-three master's degrees through the three colleges with a total enrollment of 2,812, 92 percent of whom were part-time students. Five years earlier the university had 3,498 graduate students. Despite the decline of 686 students, graduate education and the business curricula and programs were very large and healthy given their specific purpose of serving the part-time, older adult who was, or aspired to become, employed in a business or education profession. In fact, Xavier's Department of Education and the College of Business masters' programs were each larger than that at any college or university within a 50-mile radius. (65)

That same fall, 33 percent of the 570 first-year undergraduate students were from the upper half of their high school class. They had a grade point average of 2.76 and combined SAT score of 957. The university's total undergraduate student body consisted of 3,973 students, among whom 3,035, or 76 percent, were from Ohio. Among the other students, 11 percent were from the midwestern states of Kentucky, Indiana, Illinois, and Michigan, while 13 percent came from other sections of the nation, primarily the East. Xavier was still primarily a local institution with growing visibility in the Midwest region and minimal visibility in the eastern states. International students comprised an additional 8 percent of the total undergraduate body. Recruitment efforts in other midwestern and eastern states as well as in the nation at large had yielded minimal results. Among the first-year undergraduate students, 246 were from Cincinnati, a decline of 12 percent over four years. According to a survey conducted by the admission office, the most significant reason for the decline of local students was financial, with Xavier's basic tuition cost being over twice as costly as its major local competitors. Overall, 60 percent of the Xavier student population were commuter students. (66)

During the same period there was a net decrease in total aid funds as a percentage of tuition costs available to students. This was largely due to the fact that federal financial aid sources had been decreasing faster than the university's ability to replace them with private funds. While in 1981–1982 federal aid was 48.53 percent of tuition revenue, three years later it was 42.53 percent. Because Xavier was experiencing difficulty in recruiting local area students, the university steadily increased its institutional grants-in-aid budget. Nevertheless, by 1985 first-year student indebtedness for all student loan categories had increased by over one-third since 1981. The average loan amount rose from $1,569 to $2,450. A goal proposed by the University Planning Committee to help improve Xavier's position in relation to local area competition was to increase need-based financial aid to local area students by significantly increasing the endowment, thus partially offsetting the local area tuition differential. (67)

Based on the recommendations of the University Space Committee, the University Planning Committee in its report also proposed new construction and renovation priorities. Prioritizing the goals at the $25,000,000 and $40,000,000 levels, they recommended construction of a new four-level academic science building west of Logan Hall, near the site of the recently demolished North Hall, the wooden physical plant building, and expansion of the McDonald Library. They also recommended recycling the west row central campus academic buildings, which consisted of Logan, Albers, Hinkle, Schmidt, and Alumni Halls. These buildings required substantial renovations largely due to deferred maintenance, rapidly aging utility systems, and energy conservation opportunities. Committee members also proposed a $7 million convocation center, with a seating capacity of about 7,500, for competitive sports and for special events, meetings, lectures, concerts, and convocations. In addition, the committee recommended renovation of the residence halls. "After twenty years of continuous use" and deferred maintenance, the report read, "the current residence halls are deteriorating." Lastly, the University Planning Committee proposed two endowed chairs, one in business ethics and the other in the humanities. Planning to increase the endowment by $18.7 million to $28 million, university officials hoped to reduce its dependence on student tuition and fees from 72 percent to 65 percent by 1990. Over a three-year period, 1982 to 1985, the endowment had increased by $1.8 million to $9.3 million. (68)

Sale of Edgecliff and Programs

In mid-September 1982 the board appointed a small number of trustees to work with the administration to produce a position paper on Edgecliff College. The board had to decide in the coming year whether or not to exercise the university's three-year option to purchase the campus and its facilities. Currie had already met with the Faculty Committee and gone over the situation in some detail. "It is pretty clear," Currie said, "that if the faculty were to take a vote today, they would say 'No' to Edgecliff College." The programs on the Edgecliff campus had a smaller enroll-ment than what had been projected and the college's deficit in 1981–1982 was $72,000. (69)

However, Currie thought the negative reaction could be turned around if the board and administration made a good case for doing so. He had met with the Sisters of Mercy the day before the Xavier board meeting to inquire if they would object to a public disclosure of the terms of the purchase agreement. They did not object. Because it "is almost universally believed," Currie informed the board, that the finan-cial arrangement regarding Edgecliff "has been finalized and that Xavier has acquired the College," he thought a full disclosure of the information would help clear the air on campus. In his judgment, part of the problem had been that the original acquisition negotiations were of necessity conducted in secret, and that the lack of information about it had contributed to the negative reaction on campus. (70)

During the fall semester the administration conducted a feasibility study of the Edgecliff campus, which projected that as a center for con-tinuing education Edgecliff could be operating within two or three years at a surplus of $230,000. However, that still would not be suffi-cient to meet the $340,000 yearly payments for the purchase of the property. Taking into account the findings of the study, the board's Finance Committee considered the acquisition a good long-term invest-ment, but could not say with any assurance that there would be no adverse budgetary impact on the university in a year or two. Whereas a trustee spoke against divided campuses in general and cited advan-tages in concentrating on one campus, it was the consensus of the Finance Committee that the long-term gains by acquiring a valuable piece of riverfront property would more than compensate for the possible short-term problems. After much discussion, Robert Kluener, chair of the Board of Trustees, argued that the board should no longer delay the decision to exercise the option. He urged his colleagues to consider carefully the reaction of the Cincinnati community were the university to drop its option on Edgecliff, stressing that such adverse reaction might seriously hurt Xavier's next campaign for funds. In Currie's judgment there were "more pluses than minuses, but that he could live with the decision either way." After further discussion the board agreed to "proceed with the purchase of the Edgecliff campus," which was consummated a few weeks later. At the board's Academic Affairs Committee meeting in May 1983, members of the Faculty Committee pointed out that while most faculty members realized the admininistration had to possibly go ahead with the acquisition, they still had some concern about finances. (71)

During the 1983–1984 academic year, university finances worsened, and relations between the faculty and some administrators, especially the president, deteriorated as well. In late January 1984 the chair of the Faculty Committee informed the academic vice president that there was "widespread concern among the Faculty about overspending [by the administration] and a proliferation of new administrative positions," about the deans' inability "to come up with travel money for interviewing prospective new faculty," and about the elimination of approved "new faculty positions." Significantly, faculty members were "all the more concerned," he continued, "about already insufficient funds to meet the University's academic needs." The next day President Currie sent a memo on mid-year budget adjustments to the Finance Committee of the Board of Trustees, the vice presidents, and the Faculty Committee. In it he confirmed faculty concerns, pointing out that there would have to be cuts, "about 2% of our budget," which included not purchasing new "classroom equipment" for the remainder of the academic year. While "honest questions about priorities are always in order, let us avoid simplistic and divisive scapegoating," Currie wrote. This would become Currie's characteristic response to growing concerns over his administration. "I have been more impressed," he wote, "with how our vice presidents" have dealt with "questions and priorities" than he was with the faculty. That irritated a number of faculty members. (72)

Concerned over the Faculty Committee's questioning of his administration, Currie wrote another letter to the committee. "I am sure we can do better in communicating and working positively for the good of the university than is reflected in your . . . minutes," he said. "As I hope you realize, I want to work with you to improve communication, trust and participation in the collaborative effort necessary to make Xavier the best it can be. We have to move beyond the level suggested in your . . . minutes if we are to achieve that best." That same day, a member of the Faculty Committee, reflecting the sentiments of many of her faculty colleagues, responded to Currie's latest letter. "Why is it that every question raised by a faculty member has to be taken as a disloyal act? Can't we be thought of as persons," she wrote, "working for a common goal?" Indicating that there was "a lack of trust," on both sides, she pointed out that "[d]irect communication is always the best basis in our search for excellence. Let's begin anew—together." In the face of growing mutual suspicion, however, that would not happen. (73)

In May 1984 Currie informed the trustees of a potential 1984–1985 deficit of between $750,000 and $1 million figured on a $32 million dollar budget. Errors in the 1983–1984 base budget in the amount of $209,000, discovered by Dr. J. Richard Hirté, newly-appointed vice president for financial administration in 1984, and overexpenditures and "discrepancies in estimating fringe benefits and underestimated tuition remission," which added $436,000 to the "shortfall," made it necessary to use reserve funds in order to balance the 1983–1984 budget. To compound the financial problem, there was a larger-than-expected enrollment decline. There were 103 fewer full-time and 170 part-time students than the previous year. To help reduce the anticipated deficit the university eliminated or left vacant new faculty and staff positions. (74)

The bleak financial situation and faculty concerns about the administration intensified friction on campus. The "new administration has introduced changes and calls for changes that have created an atmosphere of uncertainty and tension," the Faculty Committee wrote. It criticized the administration for not articulating clearly "its goals and expectations in terms of the roles of present and new faculty members, student profile, budgetary processes (especially the means of funding all programs), . . . and use and development of physical plant in the short and long term." Making clear that its concerns about change "should not imply that the faculty is against change," the committee's hope was to define the university's "direction clearly and not to lose the benefits of [its] prior accomplishments." Moreover, committee members criticized "the style of the new administration," which, in their judgment, contributed "to a sense of tension among the faculty. Specifically," they argued, the "reorganization of the President's office has created confusion about roles and responsibilities" and how decisions were made. In particular, the appointment of a former assistant from Wheeling College as his administrative assistant proved problematic. Her administrative style, working relationship with the president, and intrusiveness in all divisions of the university impaired the relationship of his office with the Jesuit and university communities. In addition, the Faculty Committee was concerned over the leadership of the academic vice president. "Although desirous of leading the faculty," the committee wrote, "sometimes he appears to be too aggressive and some members of the faculty become concerned about his ability to fulfill his promises." (75)

During the 1984–1985 academic year Currie and the Board of Trustees attempted to boost morale on campus by linking Xavier's strategic planning with efforts to develop significantly more resources for the university by hopefully launching a new capital campaign. At the time, university assets were valued in excess of $93 million and the physical plant maintained over 50 campus buildings, representing 1.2 million square feet of space and 108 acres of property. According to Robert Kluener, chair of the Board of Trustees, Xavier's sights had to be raised with endowment goals. "[A]n $8.9 million endowment fund," he argued in the fall of 1984, "is absurd." In addition, Kluener hoped the administration would review the budget with the faculty, so that everyone would understand the situation. Notwithstanding efforts to improve the mood on campus, the university's financial situation and the president's style of leadership continued to cripple Currie's presidency. (76)

In the spring of 1985 some board members suggested that Xavier consider alternatives for Edgecliff, including the sale or possible lease of part or all of the property to a developer. Kluener stressed the need for a definite plan to solve a two-fold problem—one being short-term, the other long-term. While viewing the selling of Edgecliff as possibly a short-term solution, he envisioned a fund drive to be a long-term solution. At their May meeting the trustees decided to prepay the mortgage on Edgecliff in anticipation of the future sale of the property. Though the university and the Sisters in 1983 had executed a non-interest bearing loan of $5.4 million secured by an open-end mortgage agreement, the prepayment of the promissory note at a 10.25 percent annual discount factor was estimated at approximately $2,003,000. Currie had met with Sister Mary Virginia Sullivan, the first dean and former president of Our Lady of Cincinnati College, and various Edgecliff alumni leaders to discuss the university's decision. The Edgecliff alumni requested that they receive prior notice before any decision was announced publicly, that a special "farewell" event be held, and that "an Edgecliff Room be established on Xavier's campus." (77)

In December 1985 Xavier officials put the Edgecliff property up for sale. During the next fifteen months they negotiated with several developers. On April 30, 1987, the university sold the property to a developer for a price, including interest, of $6,975,000 over three years. Having no continuing obligations on the property, the university established an equity position in excess of $3 million. In the summer and fall of 1987 the administration moved Edgecliff's academic programs to the main campus. In anticipation of the move, the university had renovated approximately 90,000 square feet of space, including the complete renovation of approximately 60,000 square feet of the A.B. Cohen Center on the former U.S. Shoe property, 22,500 square feet of the Rainbo Building, and part of Elet Hall. While the Department of Social Work relocated to Elet, the Cohen Center became the new home for hospital and health administration, art, and nursing. A house on Dana Avenue and several dedicated spaces in Alter and Logan Halls accommodated the music department. The Cincinnati College of Mortuary Science, which had been renting space on the Edgecliff campus, also temporarily occupied space at Cohen. To facilitate these moves the university transferred the maintenance department to the Rainbo Building and the communication arts department from the basement of Alter Hall to a house on Ledgewood. The university paid the renovation costs of approximately $5.6 million from the proceeds from the sale of Edgecliff and the estimated annual operating savings of $750,000 per year. (78)

The following winter the university, in consultation with Edgecliff alumni, developed a scholarship program to benefit Xavier students related to Edgecliff graduates. Shortly after the acquisition of Edgecliff College in 1980, the governing bodies of both the Xavier and Edgecliff Alumni Associations—desirous of achieving fuller cooperation between the two organizations—had placed two Edgecliff representatives on the Xavier Alumni Board of Governors and established the Edgecliff Alumni Committee that guided the activities of the Edgecliff Alumni Association. The latter had been established in 1937 by Sister Mary Virginia Sullivan and Adele Pohl Corbett of the class of 1936, the first alumni president. (79)

President Currie is Removed

Compounding the university's monetary problem was the continuing unrest on campus over Currie's presidency. Despite the planning and collaboration between areas of the university "there persists," the president had informed the board in the fall of 1984, "a malaise or morale problem for some." It was a question of people "wanting things to get better," he said, "but not to change." In Currie's judgment "he had overestimated the openness to change and the willingness to stretch on the part of the University community and that he was pulling back in appropriate areas." Furthermore, he insisted that the discovery of structural problems with the budget was a significant source of morale problems "and the effort to protect those responsible may have backfired by leading to a lessening of confidence in the new administration." Because of the monetary and morale issues, during the 1984–1985 academic year Currie concentrated more intensely on fund raising to help reduce the deficit, then estimated at $858,000, monitored the strategic planning process, and tried "to make people," he said, "have fun at Xavier!" In an attempt to improve relations, he had formal and informal meetings with faculty and with the Jesuit community to discuss growing concerns over his decision-making and leadership. While continuing to insist that the "budget shortfall [was] . . . the main reason for a campus morale problem" he thought there was "also a need for better communication and greater sensitivity to uneasiness with change." (80)

Notwithstanding Currie's good intentions to address administrative and financial issues and to improve faculty morale on campus, his presidency came under greater criticism. The crisis came to a head following an early spring 1985 *Xavier News* interview with the financial vice president in which a salary freeze for 1985–1986 was reported to the faculty for the first time. In an attempt to explain the university's fiscal problem that led to the freeze and to improve relations with his Jesuit colleagues and the faculty, Currie met with Xavier's Jesuit community, the Executive Committee of the American Association of University Professors (AAUP) chapter, and the Faculty Committee. Both the members of the AAUP chapter and the Faculty Committee expressed a loss of confidence in his leadership. By a vote of 79 to 5, AAUP members expressed their "profound concern over the fiscal crisis of the University" and declared that the "President does not enjoy the confidence and trust of the faculty." Larry Biondi, S.J., a trustee and chair of the Academic Affairs Committee of the Board of Trustees, met with members of the Faculty Committee, and Robert Beckman, S.J., a trustee, met with the Jesuit community. Both groups noted a serious morale problem on campus, expressing not only a loss of confidence in the president's leadership, but also concern over priorities that seemed to be "bankrupting Xavier." What had been to many individuals a fairly stable university had now become unstable and financially at-risk. Some argued that the new administration did not understand Xavier, citing the *Xavier News* article on the salary freeze as the ulti-mate example of administrative insensitivity. (81)

At the board's spring meeting, Currie cited two tactical errors for the widespread discontent on campus. His initial pronouncement as presi-dent that all was well at the university, when in fact significant financial problems existed, was his first mistake. The budget problem became the "basis for fear," he argued, "on [the] part of insecure individuals [and] accusations by those upset with changes." His second mistake, Currie insisted, was complying with his academic vice president's request that he "stay away from the faculty." As a consequence, his "base with the faculty," he said, "was severely limited." While empha-sizing the importance of addressing "*all* significant issues, the financial one," in his judgment, "was paramount." He expressed confidence to the board "that the situation could be turned around by addressing both the financial issue *and* substantive concerns of the faculty," though most of the latter, he insisted, "would disappear" if the deficit were removed. After his presentation to the board, Currie left the room and the trustees discussed at great length the president's predicament on campus. The chair took a secret ballot on whether the board had confidence in his leadership. Eleven voted "yes" and six voted "no." The trustees then agreed that the task was to get on with the business of leading the university. They were interested in helping the president in any way they could. (82)

The next morning, Kluener, Frank Hoenemeyer, chair of the board's Planning Committee, and Currie met with Xavier's vice pres-idents, deans, and the Faculty Committee. "Because there have been some concerns expressed about the leadership of Xavier University which have tended to focus on the University's financial picture," Kluener said, "the Board thought it best to report directly" to you. He reaffirmed the board's confidence in the president and "pledged to help in resolving what it is confident are short-term financial difficul-ties." Significantly, Kluener also emphasized "the continuing need for both strong administrative leadership and effective participation by faculty and other members of the University community in the gover-nance and management of the University, and the need always to look for more effective ways to achieve this goal, in ways appropriate for Xavier." (83)

Expressing regret for the "salary freeze," Hoenemeyer was hopeful that the university's financial dilemma could be straightened out in three years or less. The 1985–1986 budget presented to the board caused concern, "but not panic. . . ," he said. "We . . . will look at anything/everything that can be done, which will not harm Xavier in the long run." President Currie then spoke. "We need to bring to the task the best brainpower, the strongest loyalty to Xavier, the most innovative strategies we can muster collectively and cooperatively," he said. "Throughout this effort we need to maintain open communication and trust and to put aside rumors and mistrust. Only in this way can we continually create the Xavier we all want." (84)

Despite the good faith effort by the trustees to help improve the climate on campus, during the next three months relations between Currie and the academic community continued to deteriorate. Notwithstanding the conversations that Currie had that spring with faculty and members of the Faculty Committee, vice presidents, and deans, faculty unrest did not subside. "My summary evaluation at this point," Currie wrote to the Executive Committee of the board in May 1985, "is that while the most vocal faculty will settle for nothing less than full capitulation by me (and the Board), there are still enough people in the 'wait and see' or supportive category to justify working through the situation." He was hopeful that the planning process was sufficiently in place to begin talking seriously about a capital campaign and that there was a workable model for handling the deficit situation, which had been reduced from $858,000 to $588,000. "I will," Currie wrote to the trustees, "be working over the next six weeks to bring that to 0. Thus, while in no way minimizing the gravity of the situation, I feel the worst is behind us and that with continued support we can get the job done." A few days later the Executive Committee and John Pepper, a trustee who served as the liaison for the board's Academic Affairs Committee, met with the Faculty Committee. "Faculty malaise and dissatisfaction [with President Currie] is still strong," the Academic Affairs Committee then reported to the full board at the May meeting. (85)

Two-and-a-half months later on July 30, 1985, the trustees held a special meeting. To avoid possible speculation on campus as to the purpose of the meeting, they chose to meet at a hotel in downtown Cincinnati. The chair of the Board of Trustees began the meeting by reading a letter that he had prepared on the continuing precarious state of affairs at the university. Currie then submitted a proposal to the board that he hoped would help resolve the lingering problems on campus. He recommended the appointment of a provost, arguing that such an appointment would successfully address the problems on campus. "Because of the present high priority need of the University to develop additional financial resources," Currie said, "the President needs to concentrate more heavily on the external dimension of the University, while delegating operational responsibilities for internal affairs to the academic vice president and provost as the second highest ranking official of the University." Contending that he had the support of the deans, vice presidents, and the chair of the Faculty Committee for the proposed change, he envisioned the provost relieving him from most internal duties and thus not bring him in contact much with the faculty. (86)

Though Currie hoped that the appointment of a provost would secure his presidency, Kluener announced that "another agenda item was to be discussed, whether the Board wanted the president to continue in office." He asked Currie to excuse himself. After a debate among board members about such a procedure, the president reluctantly left the room. Following extensive discussion the board invited Currie back in and a summary of the discussion related to his failed leadership was presented to him for his reaction. The chair then called for a vote of confidence or lack thereof in the president. A secret ballot was taken and the vote, 11 to 8, recorded no confidence in the president. Currie then submitted his resignation. After some discussion, the Executive Committee agreed to work with the president on the transition to his successor. Planning to leave the university in early 1986, Currie promised to "continue to do all in his power to leave Xavier in as good a position as possible for his successor." He wanted to stay on for a semester in order "to tie up any loose ends, clarify any areas of concern and restore things to an even keel." Unhappy with the board's majority vote, a few trustees, who had supported Currie, resigned from the board. (87)

In early August the president requested the resignation of his academic vice president, John Minahan, whom he had considered to have been disloyal to him. Minahan complied with the president's request. After consulting with the Faculty Committee and getting its approval, Currie then established the Interim Executive Academic Committee (IEAC), composed of Charles Cusick, dean of the College of Arts and Sciences, Roger Fortin, associate vice president for academic affairs, and Francis Mastrianna, dean of the College of Business Administration. The triumvirate, or troika, as the IEAC was popularly called, assumed responsibilities assigned to the office of the academic vice president as specified in the new Xavier University Faculty Handbook, adopted in 1980. Each member of the IEAC committee assumed certain specific administrative duties. Having a temporary life of one year, it was understood from the beginning that upon the selection of a new president, the university would form a search committee for an academic vice president. (88)

In December 1985, Currie, who at times was "angry and frustrated," addressed the Board of Trustees for the last time. "Calm has been restored to the campus," he said. Wanting "to be as positive as possible about the University," he added, "I also want to be candid and honest, as a way of being helpful to this Board." Then he proceeded to describe the university he had gotten to know. "I came to Xavier enthusiastic for what it is and can be. At times I have felt there has been almost a conspiracy to dampen that enthusiasm and idealism." Currie, who early in his presidency had referred to Xavier as a "sleeping giant," further argued that the university and many of its supporters had "limited vision." An alumnus "once chided me," he said, "for trying to make Xavier a 'champagne university' when it was happy to be a 'shot and a beer' college. I rejected that viewpoint then and I reject it now. It is a repudiation of the generous efforts and dreams of men and women over a proud . . . history." He then noted that "[m]any years of financial limitations have made Xavier less creative, innovative, and responsive than it might be." He urged the board to take "the necessary steps to develop the resources Xavier needs and by continually calling forth the best from the University community." (89)

In a surprising move he then chastised both some members of the faculty and Board of Trustees. In his judgment Xavier was "only partially a community. . . . The events of the past year indicate that while there are pockets of 'community' among us, there is also serious divisiveness, and a number of people not unwilling to use character assassination, dishonesty and intimidation for whatever motivation. If the events of the past year have served a needed *catharsis* for the University, well and good. But Xavier has a considerable way to go to be the community it professes to be, a community of concern, of rational, honest, civil discourse and collaboration." Lastly, he criticized the trustees for their lack of support for him. "The new president," he said, "will have some of the same and some different hopes and dreams for Xavier. . . . I am concerned that he have the full support of the Board, because he too will have to make some difficult decisions and personnel choices. I have spent the past one-and-a-half years seriously hampered by 'end arounds' to this Board. I submit this has to change. . . . [If] faculty and administration are to come to this Board, or to individual Board members, without the prior knowledge of the President, and in hidden opposition to him, I strongly suspect you will be looking for still another president in not too many years. I hope we all have learned from our mistakes." He urged them to give his "successor the support he will need to do his job well. . . . Quite honestly, I don't think I had that. . . . I honestly feel," he concluded, "that Xavier is better in many ways than I found it, and I know my successor will make it better than I left it—but only if you give him the help and support he needs." (90)

At the same board meeting the trustees, in consultation with Currie, appointed Dean Francis Mastrianna acting president of Xavier University. Kluener had earlier contacted Robert Wild, S.J., Chicago provincial, to determine whether an acting president was required to be a Jesuit. The provincial confirmed that it was not a requirement. Mastrianna became acting president on January 15, 1986 and served in that capacity throughout the spring semester. (91)

During the 1985–1986 academic year the university reduced an anticipated budget deficit of $1.2 million to $258,000. To help stabilize the financial condition, the administration improved budgetary controls, outsourced the bookstore to an outside service, and awarded no salary or wage increases for the year. The wage freeze caused the salaries in the various faculty ranks to drop in comparison to comparable schools. Faculty salary increases between 1981 and 1984 had reflected a concerted effort by the university to bring wages to the 60th percentile according to the American Association of University Professors list of schools in the same national category as Xavier. Because of the freeze, faculty salaries dropped from the 60th percentile in rank II in division IIA schools to approximately the 49th percentile and remained pretty much at that level throughout the remainder of the decade. During the 1985–1986 year the university also increased revenue by realizing a 2 percent increase in the annual giving campaign. In light of a year of turmoil on campus that led to the removal of President Currie, the trustees on the board's Development Committee considered the increase in annual giving a "significant accomplishment." (92)

Faculty response to Currie's removal was generally positive. Overall, financial problems doubtlessly contributed to the malaise of his short administration and to his eventual removal. In addition to budget irregularities and overexpenditures, the drop in total enrollment from

6,950 in 1982, when Currie assumed the presidency, to 6,237 three years later compounded the problem. Most significant, however, were the president's poor personal relations with the faculty, his lack of support from some members of the Jesuit community, and what appeared to be his inabilily to come to grips with his own administrative and leadership limitations. Ironically, however, Currie's great expectations and vision of a more modern and upscale Xavier University would later be realized. (93)

Following an extensive presidential search, which had begun in October 1985, in May 1986 the Board of Trustees unanimously chose Albert J. DiUlio, S.J., associate dean of the College of Business Administration at Marquette University, as the university's new president. After receiving his baccalaureate degree at Marquette in 1965 he joined the Jesuit order and was ordained in 1974. Five years later he received his doctorate in economics and education from Stanford University. Two years after his administrative appointment at Marquette, on October 24, 1986 he was inaugurated as Xavier's thirty-second Jesuit president. By that time the emotional pitch on campus during the Currie malaise had subsided. (94)

DiUlio's Presidency

Shortly before his installation DiUlio expressed concern over enrollment and the quality of the undergraduate student body. In his first semester on campus, the number of first-year students was 577, down from 611 the previous year. Total undergraduate enrollment was 2,403, which was 213 fewer students than in 1983 and close to what it had been ten years earlier. Among the day students, 154 were African American (8 percent of the student body), 38 (2 percent) were Hispanic, and 25 (1 percent) were of other races (19 Asian and 6 American Indian). Total university enrollment in 1986 was 6,265 compared to 7,336 at the time of the university's assimilation of Edgecliff College six years earlier. Concerned over "a serious erosion in the full-time undergraduate student population," a trend that he considered "serious for the welfare of the institution," DiUlio initiated a comprehensive review of the university's admission operation, and in 1987 secured a new dean for Enrollment Services. In addition to targeting a first-year class size of 625 for the fall of 1988, DiUlio sought to increase admission criteria, target quality local students, and focus out-of-town recruiting on the 20 to 25 best feeder states. In order to be more competitive, in 1989 the university changed the formula for financial aid from a fixed amount to a percentage of the tuition. (95)

From 1982 to 1988 the growth in enrollment in Catholic colleges and universities was mainly among part-time students. A study based on the 229 Catholic colleges on the Association of Catholic Colleges and Universities membership list reported a total student enrollment of 609,350 in 1988, of whom about 400,000 were full-time students. At Xavier, however, during the same six-year period there was a decrease of 318 and 332 part-time undergraduate and graduate students respectively, but an increase of 112 full-time undergraduate students. The 2,676 full-time undergraduates in 1988 constituted 273 more students than two years earlier. (96)

In addition to addressing enrollment needs, DiUlio pressed for "a stronger financial base." The continuing budget deficit motivated him to terminate nine unfilled faculty positions and to leave five vacant. After a faculty review of a number of academic programs, the university that year discontinued the theatre arts major. The administration out-sourced food service and decided to pay off some outstanding federal loans in the amount of $2 million. By paying these off at a 29 percent discount rate, the university saved approximately $600,000. To further address financial needs, in the fall semester DiUlio identified two priorities. Realizing that the university was heavily tuition-driven, he recommended a larger, more stable and more select group of full-time day students. Second, he recommended a more substantial endowment. "Xavier must proceed with a capital campaign," he said, "and the endowment must grow in real terms." At the October board meeting the trustees echoed DiUlio's remarks and stressed "the urgent need . . . to add much needed dollars to the University's endowment." In their judgment, Xavier's small endowment of $9,700,000 created a dangerous situation for the future. (97)

A gift from Clara Schawe, a local resident and acquaintance of former President Paul O'Connor, presented "an opportunity," DiUlio observed, "for Xavier to change the use of its endowment from a source of income to real growth." Cincinnati's Fifth Third Bank, the executor for the Schawe estate, inventoried the estate in December 1985 and estimated its value at approximately $5,479,000. These proceeds, invested during the probate period, appreciated to $6,899,000 and were distributed to the university in June 1987. In accordance with an existing trust indenture related to the College of Business Administration Building, the university took $1.8 million from the Schawe proceeds and deposited it into the collateral fund. The university then transferred $4.2 million to the endowment, $600,000 to the unexpended plant funds for reserves and repairs, and the remaining dollars to the current operational fund. (98)

Planning for a capital campaign had halted during Currie's administration. When DiUlio renewed interest in a fund drive, he reviewed all previous planning documents. The university mission statement, the strengths, weaknesses, opportunities and threats (SWOT) document, and the university planning document were all completed in late 1984 through mid-1985, so DiUlio directed that they "be reviewed and revised to reflect 1987 realities and thinking." Moreover, since completion of the documents, the university not only had a new president but had changed academic leadership three times. After the discontinuation of the Interim Executive Academic Committee in the summer of 1986 and the appointment of Dr. Robert Murray, professor of classics, as acting academic vice president for one year, in June 1987 Dr. Joan Connell became Xavier's new academic vice president. She was the first woman vice president at the university. In addition, there were "those members of the university community," a report on capital fundraising at Xavier in 1986 noted, ". . . [who] will not accept anything that was a product of the Fr. Currie/John Minahan era, particularly something conceived during the climax of the strife period." (99)

Steps had been taken during the 1986–1987 academic year to develop a consensus on the university mission statement as well as on key academic documents. By early spring university officials had circulated a revised form of the mission statement to faculty in the various academic departments along with a copy of the respective departments' old SWOT analysis. According to the mission statement, as a Catholic institution in the Jesuit tradition, the university's "essential activity is the interaction of students and faculty in an educational experience characterized by critical thinking and articulate expression with special attention given to ethical issues and values." During the spring term the faculty and librarians endorsed the new mission statement and updated their respective SWOT documents.

Two years earlier, when the faculty had worked on the initial SWOT texts, the university had established a Task Force to study the feasibility of doctoral programs at Xavier. Though the Task Force report issued in 1986 concluded that the Departments of Education and Psychology were official candidates to offer doctoral degrees, only the Department of Psychology that year requested permission to conduct a feasibility study for a doctoral degree program. In November, university officials authorized the department to proceed with the study. (100)

Meanwhile, some trustees expressed concern over Xavier's negative financial image in the local press. An article in a local newspaper had referred to the university as "debt ridden." Having gone through what one trustee called the "stressful period" of Currie's presidency, another emphasized "the need for Xavier to clear up all of its internal issues before starting a campaign. He warned that Xavier cannot afford negative press when it is in a campaign mode." School authorities began adopting a more proactive stance to help establish a more positive image of the university in the local media. (101)

Notwithstanding concerns over the negative press, by the fall of 1987 plans for capital fund-raising were progressing well. The university retained the professional services of a local public relations and advertising firm to assist in the planning of the proposed fund drive. Though a $20–40 million goal in the campaign would not meet all of Xavier's needs, DiUlio thought it "would be a realistic and achievable goal." In October the university held a two-day retreat in Lexington, Kentucky, in preparation for the campaign. Two months later the trustees launched the Cornerstone Campaign. (102)

After an extensive review of Xavier's academic programs and the alignment of disciplines in the university's colleges, in the spring of 1988 the Board of Trustees approved the recommendation to reorganize the division of academic affairs. Four years after the university had reorganized itself into three colleges, namely Arts and Sciences, Business, and Professional Studies, it replaced the latter with the College of Social Sciences. The new college included the Departments of Criminal Justice, Education, Health Services Administration (formerly hospital and health administration), Nursing, Political Science and Sociology, Psychology, and Social work. In addition to the graduate programs in education, health services administration, and psychology, in 1990 the trustees approved the initiation of a master of science in nursing in the College of Social Sciences. (103)

That same spring the university established a committee to study Xavier's core curriculum. When the Core Curriculum Committee, consisting of twelve faculty members and three students began meeting in the summer, a National Endowment for the Humanities survey showed that it was possible to graduate from 78 percent of the nation's colleges and universities without ever taking a course in the history of Western civilization; from 38 percent without taking any course in history at all;

from 45 percent without taking a course in American or English literature; from 77 percent without studying a foreign language; from 41 percent without studying mathematics; and from 33 percent without studying natural or physical sciences. Though the Xavier core had strong requirements, many thought it needed to be updated for the 1990s. A survey of faculty opinions indicated that there should be more integration of courses across the curriculum. (104)

In the fall of 1988 the trustees also approved the president's initiative "to develop a long-range planning process." After consulting with the Faculty Committee, department chairs, deans, and vice presidents, the university established the University Futures Committee. Consisting of faculty and members of the administration, the committee held its first meeting in December to begin drafting a plan for the university's future. That same fall the university completed a study of its academic and administrative space needs. The document, which became a resource to the University Futures Committee, identified science space needs and related costs. A year later the trustees authorized the construction of a new physics building and the remodeling of the Albers and Logan science buildings. The total cost was estimated at $7.5 million. By the end of 1989 the silent phase of the Cornerstone Campaign had received $18.3 million in pledges, an increase of $16.6 million over eighteen months. The following spring the science facilities project began with the leveling of land adjacent to Logan Hall for the physics building. By that time the university Futures Committee had completed the first draft of its Working Vision document, which was discussed broadly across the campus. (105)

While launching the new campaign to meet broad goals, the university, under the leadership of academic vice president Joan Connell, also addressed long overdue faculty salary needs. In light of the fact that in 1989–1990 faculty salaries for professors were at the 48 percentile in rank II in comparable division IIA schools, associate professors at the 48 percentile, and assistant professors at the 51 percentile, well below the Xavier target of 60th percentile at the three ranks—due largely to the salary freeze implemented four years earlier during Currie's presidency—the university adopted a three-year goal to move Xavier salary ranges back to the 60th percentile of IIA schools. Moreover, in an attempt to address the university's heavy teaching load, (the overwhelming majority of faculty members continued to teach four courses or twelve hours each semester), the administration in the fall of 1990 made it possible for new tenure track faculty to teach only three courses each term by giving them the option of either a 9-hour load plus specific research responsibilities or a straight 12-hour teaching load. Most chose to teach three courses plus the research option. By this time, research grants, originally available only to tenured faculty, were available to non-tenured faculty with a minimum of three years of full-time service at Xavier. (106)

Another part of Xavier University's long-range planning was athletics. Since the university's commitment in 1979 to build a national level Division I basketball program, the men's basketball team had become increasingly successful and grown in national recognition. Xavier's appearance in the 1983 NCAA Tournament, its first since 1961, and the growing local and alumni interest in the men's basketball program led the administration to review and consider the program's growth and its potential for future success. That year the university brought in a sports marketing consultant, who recommended the addition of a marketing and promotions position, and the appointment of a separate director of athletics. The team's appearance in the National Invitational Tournament in March 1984, with home victories versus Ohio State and Nebraska, also proved to be a major boost for the program as more alumni and friends of the university exhibited renewed interest in the program.

Though the 1984–1985 men's basketball season did not end with a postseason appearance, the program's growth nevertheless continued. The entire home schedule was played at the Cincinnati Gardens, the WLW radio station broadcasted the games, and marketing and fundraising efforts increased attendance and income levels. In August 1985 Coach Staak accepted the head coaching position at Wake Forest University. The subsequent search resulted in the hiring of Pete Gillen, assistant basketball coach at the University of Notre Dame. The next three seasons produced even more growth and success. The men's basketball team, which had become dominant in the Midwestern City Conference, appeared in three consecutive NCAA Tournaments. The resulting increase in interest in the team produced continued increases in attendance, publicity, and revenue. (107)

During the summer months of 1987 the university commissioned two consultants to work with the athletic department to further assess its strengths and weaknesses. They developed a plan to position Xavier athletics to be even more competitive, to bring equity to various intercollegiate athletic programs, and to better serve student athletes and the entire student body. Reasserting that the first priority for Xavier athletics was the men's basketball program, they hoped it would produce the revenue necessary to increase the funding of other sports. Though women's sports had continued to grow, with some success in volleyball (North Star Conference Champion in 1985), soccer, and tennis, and the men's baseball team had won the Midwestern Collegiate Conference Northern Division championship for two consecutive years in the mid-eighties, the non-revenue sports needed more funding in order to be more consistently competitive. In December 1988 the Board of Trustees approved the department of athletics's five-year plan for additional funding, such as scholarships, for both revenue and non-revenue sports. (108)

Student Activities

Building upon the university's Catholic and Jesuit heritage Xavier students affirmed the institution's as well as their own personal values in a variety of ways. In the early 1970s, over 200 students made three-day retreats. Since retreats were no longer compulsory, university officials were encouraged by that level of participation. In the spring of 1974, Xavier's Alpha Sigma Nu chapter of the Jesuit honor society presented a five-part series on the "Idea of a Jesuit University." The views of faculty, students, and outside guest speakers emphasized involvement in the problems of the world. Though by the mid-1970s community service seemed to have reached a low point with Student Volunteer Services, by the end of the decade once again Xavier students became increasingly engaged in community programs. What helped was the call in 1978 by the 32nd Congregation of the Society of Jesus to the "service of faith and the work of justice." Xavier, like other Jesuit institutions, embraced the call. By 1988 the students newspaper reported that "volunteerism [had] become of central importance at Xavier." (109)

As Xavier students in the early 1980s became increasingly engaged in community and social activities, the student government sought to bridge relations between resident students and commuters and build "a sense of community" on campus. In 1975 it resurrected homecoming despite a lack of a football team and founded Tucker's Tavern in Brockman Hall. These efforts, among others, proved successful. In a straw poll of the student body in 1983 on the university's strong and weak points, every student interviewed named the sense of community as one of Xavier's strongest points. (110)

Two major students' protests and controversies occurred on campus during Mulligan's presidency. In December 1974 students protested over the university Budget Committee's tuition recommendation to the Board of Trustees. In anticipation that the deficit for fiscal 1975–976 would reach $549,000, the committee concluded that additional income had to be generated to offset the deficit. It recommended that the university inaugurate a flat tuition rate in lieu of the semester hour or credit hour rate for full-time undergraduate students taking twelve to eighteen hours. The flat rate was rather common across the country and was used in most tuition listings by colleges and universities. At the mid-December meeting of the Board of Trustees, President Robert Mulligan recommended that a flat rate of $1,960, including fees, per academic year be approved. During the meeting a group of students gathered outside the board room on the top floor of the University Center. Victor B. Nieporte, S.J., a trustee and administrative vice president, left the meeting to talk with the president of the student body, who explained that the students wished to meet with the trustees to discuss their displeasure over the fact that they had not been consulted or involved in the decision regarding the proposed change in tuition. Nieporte then reported his conversation to the trustees. After considerable discussion, the trustees decided to deny the students' request to interrupt a board meeting and, through Frank Brennan, S.J., a trustee and academic vice president, proposed to the student leaders that a committee of board members meet with them in the afternoon after the meeting. The students accepted the proposal and made an orderly departure. Subsequently, the board approved the flat rate. (111)

At the afternoon session the students complained "[we have] not been given the necessary data to make intelligent contributions to this and other policy formations. We feel very uneasy in this helpless condition." In particular, they expressed concern over "an atmosphere, that denies or disregards the intelligence, maturity, and concern of Xavier students." At the March board meeting, Brennan remarked that the student discontent "was not directed so much to a tuition increase as to the manner in which the increase was made and . . . without adequate consultation with the students." That spring Mulligan and Brennan began having monthly luncheon meetings with students. By 1981 there were student representatives on the University Budget Committee. Four years later members of the Board of Trustees had dinner with representatives from the student body, toured the residence halls, and had an open discussion with students. It was a success. Every year since then the trustees have had dinner with students, affording them an opportunity to share their experiences and possible concerns with board members. (112)

The second significant student controversy during Mulligan's presidency took place in the spring of 1980 when he decided to close Breen Lodge, a women's center established in 1970 in a house on Ledgewood Avenue. The center, which had become a popular institution at the university, had sponsored programming on women's issues for a decade. The announcement of its closing resulted in a students' rally to save Breen. The president received over 100 letters and 1,500 signatures in protest to the closing. The situation escalated when Mulligan refused to meet with Breen's residents to discuss the issue. Throughout the semester, students accused the president of arbitrariness and insensitivity toward women's issues. The Romero Center for International Students, also located on Ledgewood, replaced the women's center in Breen Lodge for the 1980–1981 academic year. Mulligan argued that the university could financially support only one of the houses and he opted for the Romero Center. When the director for student development later argued that the protest tactics over Breen had insulted the administrators and only solidified the decision to close the house, his remarks ignited another firestorm of complaints about student treatment by the administration. (113)

Other students' concerns in the 1970s and 1980s revolved around social and national issues, world hunger, foreign policy in Central America, abortion, and apartheid. In the early to mid-1970s many students participated in a boycott against non-United Farm Worker (UFW) lettuce. In February 1973 *Xavier News* called for the Food Service Department on campus to buy only UFW lettuce. Views on the boycott ranged from unified support to indifference, with a few involved students pushing the issue. After the *Roe v. Wade* decision by the U.S. Supreme Court in 1973, which declared abortion constitutional, abortion consistently became a topic in the students newspaper. Moreover, in the late 1970s some students were upset over the continued presence of ROTC at Xavier. The strongest protest occurred in 1979 when, as part of a ROTC recruiting effort, a tank was parked on the academic mall for a day. Its driver made the unfortunate mistake of pointing the tank's gun at Bellarmine Chapel. Some students wrote letters to the students newspaper, arguing that ROTC was incompatible with the goals of a Catholic university. But overall attitudes toward United States foreign policy had changed significantly from the Vietnam War days. When President Jimmy Carter announced the Selective Service registration system in 1980, the *News* canvassed students for their opinions and generally made light of it. (114)

Following the assassination of Archbishop Oscar Romero in El Salvador in 1980, many Xavier students and faculty members signed a petition against sending further aid to the Salvadoran government. In the fall of 1981 an estimated 450 students fasted to raise awareness of world hunger. The following year a small group of students advocated a boycott of homecoming because it was held at a building owned by Nestlé, which was criticized for its marketing of baby formula in the Third World. After the students' sponsorship of a South Africa Week in 1984 to promote awareness of apartheid, it became a consistent topic in the *Xavier News*. By the late 1980s a column in the newspaper, which had changed its name to *Xavier Newswire* in September 1985, reflected the growing sentiment on campus that protests were a reasonable part of engaging in peace and justice work. On March 30, 1990, the university community participated in an academic convocation to honor six Jesuits slain in El Salvador. (115)

From the mid-1970s through the 1980s, African American students addressed campus and societal issues and regularly participated in Black Awareness Week. They called for more black faculty and students as well as an increase in academic counseling. From 1961 to 1980 Xavier had three full-time black faculty members. The failure to recruit "more black faculty" and students "has been," Mulligan said, "an ongoing problem at Xavier." In response to black students' concerns, in 1980 Xavier established a task force in an attempt to increase admission of black students and provide better services for minority students. Underscoring the importance of the issue, Mulligan pointed out to the trustees that the university had an obligation to serve the city of Cincinnati, which was 40 percent black, by providing adequate educational opportunities and services for African American students. Of the approximately 140 black students in Xavier's undergraduate colleges, 41 percent were on academic probation. Because most black students "find Xavier very difficult," Mulligan said, ". . . they need better counseling, better screening for admission, and other support services that may require a budget addition." Continuing Xavier's tradition of community outreach, two years earlier Mulligan had established the university's Community Relations Advisory Council to provide greater support to its surrounding communities of Evanston, Avondale, and North Avondale. (116)

By the late 1980s there were several programs and opportunities on campus to assist black students. Among these were the Black Mentoring Program, the Bridge Program, and the Minority Recruiting Day. Also, there was a Black Alumni group formed and committed to helping African American students at Xavier. Notwithstanding good intentions and efforts to enhance the recruiting and retention of black students, the situation did not improve. The number of African American first-year students in the fall of 1989 dropped from 9.1 percent the previous year to 5.5 percent. Among the 6,477 students enrolled in the university, 504 were African Americans, which was 7.8 percent of the total student population. (117)

In the spring of 1987 the Board of Trustees adopted the Burton Elementary School—College Opportunity Program, designed to provide a "viable avenue" for the approximately 50 members of the 1987–1988 sixth grade class attending Burton Elementary School, which was largely populated by African American students, in Avondale, to attend Xavier University after they graduated from high school. By earmarking $250,000, the university, under the leadership of Kenneth Blackwell, associate vice president of community affairs, and consistent with Xavier's mission and its history of community involvement, developed a funding strategy allowing it to offer "last-dollar gap" tuition assistance to students who qualified academically. Moreover, the program provided academic support activities for the Burton students, including Saturday classes on campus. (118)

As the institution's and students' engagement in social activities continued to expand, by the mid-eighties the residence halls sponsored over 300 separate social, cultural, and educational programs, including an Alcohol Resource Fair. During most of this period the university had three large residence halls—Brockman, Husman, and Kuhlman—and used two converted homes as small residence halls. Until its closing in December 1990, Marion Hall provided housing for approximately 40 male students. While Xavier's Dorothy Day House served as the home for the programs on peace and justice, by the end of the decade about 150 students participated annually in a variety of activities, including soup kitchens, rehabilitation of housing for low income persons, tutoring, and clothing drives. The Office of Minority Affairs offered opportunities for the campus to celebrate its racial, ethnic, and cultural richness. By the end of the decade there had been considerable expansion in student services, as well as significant facility improvements in the residence halls. During the 1989–1990 academic year the university reorganized the health and counseling area to expand counseling services, created the Office of International Student Affairs, and opened the new Xavier Village housing complex. The completion of the Xavier Village at the southeast corner of Dana Avenue and Victory Parkway added a new dimension to the campus and provided students with a welcome alternative to traditional residence housing. A 56-unit apartment student facility, the Village opened in the fall of 1989. The two, three, and four bedroom furnished apartments featured a community laundry area, convenience store, mail room, and community lounge area. Brockman Hall also benefited from a comprehensive renovation that improved the student living spaces both aesthetically and functionally. (119)

Sustaining Agreement

Robert Wild, S.J., Chicago provincial, addressed the Xavier University Board of Trustees at their December 1987 meeting. He focused on two issues. First, he emphasized the importance of the board, as the university's final governing authority, "to continue the Jesuit identity at Xavier and to take more responsibility for promoting that identity. Jesuits," he said, "cannot do it by themselves." Second, he stressed the need for a three-way sustaining agreement between the Chicago province, the university's Board of Trustees, and the Jesuit community. With his full support, the Xavier Jesuit community moved toward separate incorporation and established an Ohio not-for-profit corporation that became legally separate and distinct from the university's educational mission while still cooperating with it. The trustees agreed "to activate" the process and establish a Sustaining Agreement Committee to help maintain the university's Jesuit identity and to identify the role and responsibility of the province, Jesuit community, and the Board of Trustees. (120)

In the spring of 1988 Leo J. Klein, professor of theology and the rector of the Jesuit community, and President Albert DiUlio met regularly with the Jesuits to discuss their role in maintaining Xavier's Jesuit identity. Moreover, over 70 lay faculty and staff participated in an Ignatian and Jesuit identity program. They thought Jesuits needed to speak up more about St. Ignatius of Loyola and his method of life and the spiritual exercises. Two years earlier the Faculty Committee had expressed concern "over the declining number of Jesuits" and thought a better effort should be undertaken "to help [lay] candidates understand the mission of Xavier University." In 1987 the Jesuit community had provided and funded Ignatian programs, under the direction of George Traub, S.J., to its employees. Through a series of on- and off-campus forums for new employees, the programs sought to help define Jesuitness at Xavier, to increase understanding of the manner in which

Ignatian ideals related to the university's Catholic and Jesuit identity, and to raise the visibility and presence of the Jesuit influence in the university community. Participation and discussion contributed to individual insights into how a person's particular position—whether administrator, faculty member, or staff—helped fulfill the university's mission. (121)

In the face of decreasing numbers of Jesuits nationally and the increasing professionalism of the lay faculties, there had emerged a strong interest among Jesuits and lay people to work together to sustain the Jesuit character of their respective institutions. The first national meeting on Jesuit-lay collaboration was held at Creighton University in May 1988. This marked a new era in Jesuit higher education. That year, some schools had as few as three Jesuits on their faculties. At this meeting the message was clear. Steps would have to be taken if the institutions were to retain their distinctive Jesuit identity into the twenty-first century. The following year there was also an important meeting at Georgetown University, where more than 900 Jesuits and lay colleagues gathered. At that meeting came the idea to form a National Seminar on Jesuit Higher Education. Through its *Conversations* magazine, issued twice a year, it provided a national forum for the discussion of key issues of concern among the Jesuit institutions and encouraged local discussion of topics of common interest. Moreover, regular regional and province-wide meetings of educators were established. While *Western Conversations* served members on the west coast, and representatives from the Maryland province institutions attended the semiannual Gatherings of Faculties, *Heartland* made it possible for faculty, staff, and administration from the Jesuit schools in the Midwest to come together.

While exploring ways to enhance Xavier's Jesuit identity on campus, the university, provincial, and Jesuit community in the spring of 1989 continued to lay the groundwork for a sustaining agreement, as well as developed plans to move the Jesuit community to facilities that better fit their needs. At the time there were twenty-three Jesuits at Xavier. Thirteen of them were faculty, five were in administration, two in campus ministry, and three worked in a combination of areas. Fifteen years earlier the university and the Jesuits had signed a document giving the university power to initiate a discussion concerning use of Schott Hall if the number of Jesuits in residence was believed to be insufficient. Under the direction of the provincial, the Xavier university Jesuit community became two separate and independent communities. The university renovated the Linkshire apartment building on Victory Parkway on campus to house the Xavier University Jesuit community and transferred the property to it. In addition, the university provided approximately $200,000 for renovating what became known as the Faber Jesuit Community, a building about a mile from the university campus. This new community provided housing for the Cincinnati Jesuits who were not assigned to one of the four institutional apostolates (the university, the high school, the downtown parish, and the retreat center at Milford). Most of the Jesuits who were retired from the university chose to move to the Faber Community. These arrangements ended the university's long standing commitment to house Jesuits employed by the university. Xavier officials then took full and complete possession of Schott Hall. (122)

In the midst of working on a three-way sustaining agreement, university trustees received an unexpected announcement from Albert Thelen, S.J., provincial of the Wisconsin province of the Society of Jesus. In early December 1989 he notified the Xavier board that DiUlio would be applying for the presidency of Marquette University. A few days later at the board meeting DiUlio acknowledged his interest in the position. After expressing disappointment over the provincial's lack of sensitivity to the needs of Xavier University, the trustees emphasized the importance for them to learn from the experience so it would not be repeated in the future. Two months later, after accepting the Marquette presidency, DiUlio submitted his resignation, effective in mid-August. During the next few weeks the board established a presidential search committee, which consisted of six trustees, three faculty members, two administrators, two students, and an alumnus. (123)

Though DiUlio's administration was shorter than expected, it nevertheless accomplished much. In addition to introducing new enrollment strategies, establishing a committee to study Xavier's core curriculum, erecting the Xavier Village complex, and laying the groundwork for the construction of a new physics building and the remodeling of Albers and Logan science buildings, DiUlio helped launch the much-needed Cornerstone Campaign. He supported and guided efforts for Xavier's Board of Trustees to acquire legal control of the properties and policies of the University. Most importantly, DiUlio's presidency helped bring much needed stabilization in the administration of the university after a period of considerable unrest during Currie's presidency.

During the initial phase of the presidential search process, the Chicago province and the Xavier University Board of Trustees approved the sustaining agreement. The university's Board of Trustees now had exclusive and explicit legal control of, and responsibility for, the properties and policies of the university. Moreover, the agreement, which included the transfer of Schott Hall to the university, defined the relationship between the Jesuit community corporation and the university and the Jesuit Chicago province. The trustees agreed to continue Xavier University "in its tradition of an institution imbued with the philosophy and educational tradition of the Society [of Jesus]." They also accepted fully "the responsibility to maintain and promote" the Jesuit character of the university. In carrying out such responsibility, they set up a permanent Jesuit Identity Committee with a two-fold charge: to maintain and promote the Jesuit traditions at Xavier and to report every three years on the status of the "Jesuitness" at the university. With its decisions to terminate President Charles Currie in 1985 and to adopt the sustaining agreement five years later, the predominantly lay board became more self-assured and clearly affirmed its identity. (124)

In keeping with the terms of the sustaining agreement, the university agreed "to employ on its faculty or in its administration members of the Society who apply to the University for such positions but with the understanding . . . that [they] . . . possess qualifications . . . consistent with the standards and policies of the University." A year earlier the trustees had approved changes in the institution's nondiscrimination policy and laws on hiring to reflect preference given to the hiring of Jesuits for faculty and administrative positions. Jesuits now served on the university faculty and administration under individual employment contracts. Their salaries, comparable to those of other employees, were paid, in total, to the Jesuit community. Though the Jesuits did not participate earlier in the university's retirement plan nor the federal social security program, the university now paid to the community an amount equivalent to such benefits for each Jesuit employed by the university. (125)

Moreover, as part of the agreement, the province promised to "retain the University as one of its ministries and [would] undertake, within the limits of its manpower resources, to make available to the University members of the Society." In addition, the provincial agreed to consult with the chair of the Board of Trustees and the president before appointing a new rector, who was an *ex officio* member of the Board of Trustees of Xavier's Jesuit community. Recalling DiUlio's premature departure, the sustaining agreement made clear that once the Xavier trustees elected a member of the Society of Jesus as president, and he had been missioned to that task by the father general in Rome, the provincial "will not request or require such person to resign as President without prior consultation with the Board of Trustees." (126)

As of May 1990, when the sustaining agreement had been fully adopted, there were no Jesuit candidates for the Xavier University presidency. According to Wild, the Chicago provincial, who attended the May meeting of the university's Board of Trustees, the lack of candidates was no reflection on Xavier. In his judgment the seven recent searches for Jesuit university presidents had "severely depleted the pool of possible presidential candidates, and rendered the remaining candidates less willing to engage in public competition." The trustees agreed to conduct a search that did not involve broad competitive scrutiny of each candidate. The provincial also offered the option of changing Xavier's charter to read "preferably Jesuit," thus opening the door to consider lay candidates. The board expressed a strong reluctance to consider the option and preferred to concentrate its efforts toward exhausting all avenues to recruit a qualified Jesuit president. The trustees adopted a new search strategy that would be slower, low key, and more sensitive to potential candidates' backgrounds and wishes. Moreover, they decided to visit candidates off campus and bring in only the final candidate for board approval and campus dialogue. (127)

Because the presidential search was delayed and a new president would not likely be on campus until the summer of 1991, the trustees saw a need for an interim president. They considered it imperative to sustain the momentum and direction of the university and assure the continued progress of such important major initiatives as the Cornerstone Campaign, the science facility construction and renovation, and the work of the University Futures Committee. The trustees selected their chair, Michael J. Conaton, to succeed DiUlio as interim president effective August 15. President and chief operating officer of the Midland Company and a 1955 graduate of Xavier with a bachelor of science degree in political science, Conaton was appointed for one year. At his first meeting with the vice presidents he cautioned "against changing decisions that have been made by DiUlio and the University Executive Committee over the past four years." As a sign of the continuing momentum, the university during his tenure secured $7.6 million in tax-exempt financing to provide for the cash flow needs for the renovation of Schott Hall for faculty offices and for use by the division for university relations and $5.2 million for the modernization of the science facilities over a five-year period. (128)

After almost 20 years of adjustments and conflict, Xavier University prepared for the challenges of the final decade of the century. The university was about to enter one of the most exciting epochs in its history.

PART IV

A NEW EPOCH FOR XAVIER UNIVERSITY 1991–PRESENT

Introduction

As Xavier University makes plans to celebrate its 175th anniversary in 2006 it holds a distinctive place in Catholic and American higher education. It is one of about 133 Jesuit institutions of higher learning in the world, 28 Jesuit colleges and universities in the United States, and approximately 1,600 independent institutions of higher learning in the country. In addition to being one of Cincinnati's oldest and most distinguished institutions, it is also the third largest private university in Ohio. Under the leadership of Jesuit presidents James E. Hoff (1991–2000) and Michael J. Graham (2001–), Xavier has evolved into an academically diverse institution, as well as a significant local and regional resource. Among the more than 900 people working at Xavier, some individuals teach and advise students and perform administrative tasks, while others cook meals, run retreats, conduct repairs, and fix leaks. Approximately 290 full-time faculty members are devoted to the university's primary mission of teaching. Their efforts in 2005 focused on over 6,600 students from 43 states and 46 countries. While offering 64 undergraduate majors, 39 undergraduate minors, 9 graduate programs, and a clinical doctoral program in psychology, the university continues to affirm through its core curriculum its central Jesuit values.

During the Hoff and Graham years, the quality of the faculty and the reputation of the university improved significantly. Faculty members were more highly qualified, dedicated, and productive. The Xavier professoriate in scholarly publication record with colleagues at comparable schools. In the 1990s alone the faculty claimed over 1,000 scholarly publications and hundreds of scholarly presentations. Ideals of academic excellence espoused in Xavier's mission statement were

— 333

clearly reflected in the recruitment and advancement of faculty members. (1)

Over the last 15 years many American colleges and universities have grown in size and popularity. Among the roughly 3,600 institutions vying for students' admission, competition for students was especially fierce among private colleges in the Midwest and Northeast. This was due largely to the declining interest in the liberal arts and regional shifts in population. Whereas in 1960 half of all students attended a liberal arts institution, forty years later only 17 percent did. From 1997 to 2002 six liberal arts schools closed.

Xavier University's student composition has changed dramatically. In the mid-1990s, for the first time in over a century, the total number of full-time students, graduates and undergraduates, surpassed the number of part-time students. The profile .of the student body also changed from a more commuter, part-time, and graduate population to a more residential, full-time undergraduate population. Xavier's academic reputation also grew during this period. Whereas in 1997 first-year applications surpassed 3,000 for the first time, eight years later they exceeded 5,400. Moreover, in response to the university's mission and the needs of adults in the metropolitan area, Xavier in 1995 launched the weekend degree program for adult and part-time students. The "adult" student, over 25 years of age, had become a major factor in enrollment growth nationally. In 1970 there were 2.4 million adult students. Thirty years later there were approximately 7 million. In addition, by 1990 enrollment at American institutions of higher learning had become predominantly female. Though opposition to complete coeducation had been strong within the Jesuit order before 1945, in 1988 nineteen of the Jesuit colleges and universities, including Xavier, enrolled more women than men. Six years later undergraduate and graduate women comprised 56.8 percent of students nationwide. At Xavier women represented 57.2 percent. (2)

Moreover, since the mid-1980s, community service and volunteerism were on the rise virtually everywhere. Consistent with its long tradition and vision, Xavier also continually renewed and expanded its service dimension. Centrally located in the city of Cincinnati within the boundaries of three demographically distinct communities—Evanston, North Avondale, and the city of Norwood—Xavier continued to figure prominently in the life of the city and drew stronger ties with its immediate neighbors and the metropolitan area. While affirming its Jesuit core values, which included the ideals of service of faith and the promotion of justice, it understood that the health and vitality of the university and the greater Cincinnati community were connected.

A significant change in American higher education during the past twenty years has also been the accessibility of information technology. The new computer-generated electronic sources of information and data retrieval made a dramatic change in the lives of students and faculty on American campuses. While more and more faculty members communicated with their students and with each other by e-mail, course syllabi and assignments were also often conveyed to students via e-mail or Web sites. In addition, many colleges and universities expanded their distance education programs and course offerings. In response to the challenges of the new information age, in 2001 Xavier University established a new division of information resources. Two years later it began implementing the SCT Banner system and the Luminis Portal that would over a three-year period significantly change the way the institution communicated electronically and conducted business. (3)

To help meet increased expenditures for faculty and staff salaries, construction, health care, and operations, colleges and universities continued to raise tuition. Private institutions had the highest increases. At private four-year colleges, tuition and fees and room and board costs increased from an average of $4,514 in 1978–1979 to $17,207 in 1995–1996 and $27,516 in 2004–2005. That same year Xavier's equivalent costs were $28,230, the sixth lowest among the 28 Jesuit colleges and universities. During the same period the national patterns of financing a college education changed. More financial aid came from loans than from grants. In 1981–1982 federal grants constituted 54.6 percent of a student's financial aid and federal loans 41.4 percent. The neediest population of students received the federal grants. By 2004 federal grants were at 38 percent and federal loans at 56 percent. Relative to the many types of institutions, namely four-year public, two-year public, and community colleges, among others—Xavier, like most private institutions, has had lower federal grant participation and higher loans for its population. In 2004–2005 federal grants at the university were at 6 percent and loans 93 percent. (4)

During the Hoff and Graham presidencies the university witnessed significant physical growth. The Xavier community notably raised its "sights" and "expectations." The campus, which had grown in spurts, chiefly in the 1920s and 1960s, acquired a new look. The 1990s and early 2000s featured widespread renovations and new buildings. In addition to the overhaul of the Kuhlman and Husman residence halls, the closing of Ledgewood Avenue, and the creation of the residential and academic malls was the restoration of Hinkle, Schmidt, and Alumni buildings, the latter renamed Edgecliff Hall in 2000, construction of the Cintas Center (2000), creation of a student recreation park (2001), the building of a new student housing complex, the commons (2001), and the construction of the Charles P. Gallagher Student Center (2002). Whereas in 1990 there were 88.93 acres, with the acquisition of new properties the university in 2006 embraced 146 acres and 65 buildings. (5)

In the sixth year of James Hoff's presidency, the university launched the Century Campaign. When completed in 2001 it had raised $125,101,900, almost quadrupling the Cornerstone Campaign that had been completed ten years earlier. In 2004 the university began the silent phase of the new campaign. Over a fourteen-year period, 1991 to 2005, the university, by rededicating itself to its Catholic and Jesuit tradition and enlisting the support of its many constituencies, increased the endowment by $76 million to $100 million, attracted a more academically talented and diverse student body and faculty, and renewed and strengthened its academic foundation. Simultaneously, the faculty grew both in numbers and quality. Midway during Hoff's tenure the faculty adopted a new constitution that established a new model of faculty governance. Throughout the next decade, especially during Graham's presidency, faculty members began exercising a greater and more meaningful role in the governance and direction of the institution. In 2002 they drafted, in collaboration with a few administrators, the Academic Vision Statement that would be a principal driving force behind the new campaign.

The university has also initiated new academic programs. It established the academic service learning semesters in Nicaragua, Nepal, Over-the-Rhine district in Cincinnati, India, and Ghana; Xavier's Center for Excellence in Education to help train inner-city school teachers in mathematics and science; a third honors program in philosophy, politics, and the public; a minor in Catholicism and culture; and, in partnership with the Archdiocese of Cincinnati Schools office, the Initiative for Catholic Schools to help train principals and elementary school teachers in mathematics and science in the local Catholic schools. In 2004 the university also launched the new provost structure. By conjoining four divisions—academic affairs, information resources, mission and ministry, and student development—the university further unified the learning environment and its mission "to educate students intellectually, morally, and spiritually . . . toward lives of solidarity, service, and success."

During this epoch Xavier experienced academic excellence, athletic distinction, and facility change unmatched in its history. A century and a half earlier the institution was on the brink of closing, had to discontinue its boarding school, and experienced what was described as the school's "darkest hour." In contrast, this latest pivotal moment, with its accomplishments, solid foundation, and potential was Xavier's brightest hour.

— 9 —

XAVIER'S NEW LEADER:
JAMES E. HOFF, S.J.,
1991–2000

During Michael Conaton's tenure as interim president of Xavier University, the Presidential Search Committee, chaired by Gerald DeBrunner, a trustee, renewed its search and changed its approach from a public to a more private process. By September 1990 it focused its interest on James E. Hoff, S.J., vice president for university relations at Creighton University. However, when members of the committee made four separate telephone calls, encouraging him to consider Xavier's presidency, each time he said "no." But in late summer, after his provincial had pointed out to him "that Xavier needed him more than Creighton did" and that there was "a greater need for a greater good," Hoff finally agreed to consider the position. Three trustees and two faculty members then met with him off campus in Chicago. He made a positive impression. Upon their return to Cincinnati, one of the trustees stressed that while Hoff was "very impressive," his candidacy was "very fragile. He loves Creighton," he said, "and would be happy to stay there. As a result, confidentiality is of the utmost concern." (1)

At the fall board meeting the trustees empowered the Executive Committee to offer the position to Hoff. He accepted the appointment and in December the Board of Trustees ratified his election. "[P]leased and honored to serve as Xavier's president," Hoff said, he then announced his plan "to fall in love with Xavier and to stay long enough to have a substantial impact." In light of Albert DiUlio's premature departure as president in 1990, he also informed the trustees that he had established an understanding with his provincial about his commitment of at least six years to Xavier and, that if future opportunities were presented to him "he will happily say no to those offers." Hoff assumed his new duties as president on March 1, 1991. Seven weeks later he was inaugurated. (2)

Hoff's list of accomplishments at Creighton University included serving for two years as interim dean of the School of Medicine, spearheading the university's successful capital campaign, and serving as vice president for university relations and president of the Creighton Foundation, a fund-raising arm of the institution. Before being ordained in 1965 he received a baccalaureate degree in biology and master's in philosophy at Spring Hill College in Alabama. He also earned a master's degree in theology at St. Louis University and a doctorate, also in theology, at the Gregorian University in Rome. (3)

Academic Programs and New Core

During the transition from the DiUlio and Conaton administrations to Hoff's presidency, the faculty and administration continued to explore ways to rejuvenate academic life on campus, as well as to strengthen and introduce new academic programs. The University Futures Committee continued to meet, and Xavier officials applied the finishing touches to the Cornerstone Campaign, which had begun in 1987. What helped bring focus to the university's direction as well as energize Xavier's community was Hoff's restatement of the institution's mission into a concise statement of vision that placed students at the center of the university's operations. Over and over again throughout his presidency he reiterated his mission statement. "My vision for Xavier is simple," Hoff said in 1991. "What I want most of all is that a Xavier education be of such quality that each and every graduate will say, 'I received an absolutely superb education at Xavier.'. . . I want every Xavier graduate to say, 'I know that I am intellectually, spiritually and morally prepared to take my place in a rapidly changing global society.'" The university's "goals," he emphasized continually, "are about our students." The president's mission statement gradually filtered down to virtually everyone on campus. (4)

Early in his term Hoff introduced and supported new initiatives, including changes in his administrative team. In 1992 he replaced Arthur Shriberg as vice president for student development and appointed Sylvia Bessegato, associate vice president for student development, as acting vice president for fifteen months. Ronald A. Slepitza, associate vice president for student services at Creighton University, became Xavier's vice president for student development in the spring of 1993. Similarly, in May of 1992 the president relieved Joan Connell of her duties as academic vice president. William Larkin, professor of mathematics and computer science, served as acting academic vice president for one year. In July 1993 James E. Bundschuh, dean of the College of Arts and Sciences at St. Louis University, became the new chief academic officer. (5)

The most significant academic accomplishment during Hoff's presidency was the university's establishment of a new core curriculum. Since Xavier's last comprehensive revision of its core of studies in 1976, college and university curricula across the country had largely become more a series of electives rather than a set of central requirements. The university's Core Curriculum Committee, which had been been formed in the spring of 1988, looked at the old core and sought, while holding dearly to the university's Jesuit educational tradition, to modernize it. Committee members also found that the 75 hours of course requirements for arts and sciences students and 63 hours for business students made it difficult for some undergraduates to complete their major requirements or to take electives. In keeping with Xavier's mission, the committee proposed to develop a core that would explore ethical and religious values more fully and provide students with a greater grounding in those values. (6)

Xavier's new undergraduate core curriculum, which took three years to develop, was adopted by the Board of Trustees in the spring of 1991 and implemented in the fall of 1992. Approved by 73 percent of the 122 voting faculty members, the new core's 64-hour requirements for all students included one hour in cultural diversity entitled "E Pluribus Unum," or "Out of Many, One," three hours in fine arts, nine hours in theology, nine hours in philosophy, six hours in mathematics, nine hours in science, six hours in history, three hours in composition or rhetoric, six hours in literature, six hours in social sciences, and six hours in a foreign language. These core requirements constituted slightly more than half the 120 hours typically needed for a student to graduate from Xavier. Rooted in the foundation of Jesuit education, the new core curriculum remained strong and, in terms of requirements, it continued to be one of the heftiest among Jesuit colleges and universities. (7)

Though the new core of studies reduced the theology and philosophy requirements by three hours each from the old core, it was steeped in ethical and religious values. It introduced a cross-disciplinary ethics, religion, and society focus or module of courses designed to prompt faculty and students to consider ethical, theological, and philosophical questions in a variety of academic contexts. It included a theology course called "Theological Foundations," a philosophy course titled "Ethics as an Introduction to Philosophy," and a third course taught by the literature departments titled "Literature and the Moral Imagination." The fourth and elective course tied in with the focus requirement. (8)

Understanding world or foreign cultures also became an important additional goal in the university's core of studies. In contrast to the old core, which had no across-the-board language requirement, (although all students in the arts and sciences and many in the social sciences were required to study a foreign language), the new core had a six-hour language requirement for all undergraduate students. In those courses students were expected to demonstrate intermediate proficiency in a second or foreign language and to study that nation's culture. Another difference between the old and new core was the history requirement. All undergraduates now had to take six hours of history, exposing them to historical methodology and the development of civilizations. Under the old structure, students majoring in any business discipline were not required to take history courses. In addition, Xavier now required its undergraduates to take nine hours in the sciences in contrast to six hours under the former core. Moreover, through "E Pluribus Unum" students and faculty members explored the complexities of cultural diversity in American society. Stanley Hedeen, professor of biology and former dean of the College of Arts and Sciences, who headed up "E Pluribus Unum," realized that a one-hour course could not adequately educate every Xavier student in cultural diversity. He looked at it as a beginning to a broader discussion. "We realize full well that what we're doing," he said, "is planting the seed and not harvesting the plant." (9)

The university's new core curriculum affirmed strongly the values and vision of St. Ignatius of Loyola, the founder of the Society of Jesus. Consistent with his vision, it encouraged and assisted students to reason critically and think creatively, to communicate accurately and effectively, to be open to all worthwhile studies and endeavors, and to pursue wisdom in confidence and freedom. In keeping with the university's Catholic and Jesuit tradition the faculty hoped that the new core would help students achieve their purposes in life, learn to discern what was truly good for themselves and society, and find God in all things. "You bump into values, ethics and religious issues no matter where you turn in this place," John LaRocca, S.J., professor of history, said. "You can't get away from them. And that's what keeps this place in the Jesuit tradition. It's not the number of courses but its concerns." The core reflected not only the mind but the heart of Jesuit education. "Xavier is a leader in maintaining a viable humanities curriculum under a lot of pressure," Paul Tipton, S.J., president of the Association of Jesuit Colleges and Universities, said. "And Xavier should be saluted for this in light of the gimmicky things that are taking place in college and university curricula these days." Indeed, the core epitomized the university's commitment to educate students "intellectually, morally, and spiritually." (10)

To help strengthen a significant piece of the new core of studies, in 1997 the university received two grants to help invigorate the ethics, religion, and society program (E/RS). A $400,000 challenge grant from the National Endowment for the Humanities assisted the university in raising an additional $1.6 million in order to establish an interdisciplinary faculty chair. Moreover, a $75,000 grant for course development from the McGregor Fund enabled Xavier to use the funds to develop three interdisciplinary, team-taught courses, and to provide professional development opportunities for E/RS faculty. By 1997 approximately 90 members of the faculty had taught courses in the program. (11)

In addition to establishing a strong core curriculum, the university enhanced its academic reputation in several ways. It revivified and introduced a number of new programs, including an undergraduate degree program in occupational therapy in 1991 in the College of Social Sciences. Moreover, that year the university introduced its Montessori program in Korea and two years later in Taiwan. Approved by Xavier's Board of Graduate Studies, which consisted of the academic deans, faculty, and students and had replaced the Graduate Council in 1991, the program became the only U.S. graduate Montessori course of study exported to the Far East. Classes of students from both Korea and Taiwan flew to Cincinnati and enrolled in the program. In the fall of 1991 the academic community also implemented a Commons Hour as a pilot project over a two-year period. Its purpose was to make it possible for faculty and others to find a common time in order to engage in intellectual discourse, to share ideas, and to discuss common interests. The idea evolved from the Futures Committee discussions and from the meetings that the deans had had with their respective department chairs. Among the 221 full-time faculty surveyed, 125 endorsed the concept. At first, the Commons Hour occurred on Wednesdays between 10:30 and 11:45 a.m. during the fall and spring semesters. Two years later, the Commons Hour, scheduled on Mondays from 1:30 to 2:45 p.m., became an annual fixture. (12)

In 1993 the university established an ad hoc Technology Task Force. Three years later it created the University Technology Committee, whose charge included broad-based planning that integrated the academic and administrative technology needs of the university and provided guidance in matters of budgeting for technology. That same year Xavier joined the consortium of libraries in OhioLINK. Using Internet access, patrons could request items available at other OhioLINK libraries. In addition, online access to research acticles grew significantly. In three years' time, 1998 to 2000, the number of Internet-based databases to journals grew from a handful to over 150 databases with over 35,000 journals accessible electronically.

In 1993 the American Academy of Collegiate Schools of Business (AACSB) granted Xavier's College of Business Administration, after ten years of preparation, a five-year accreditation. Five years later the university renamed the College of Business Administration the Williams College of Business in honor of Charles Finn Williams and William John Williams, cofounders of the Western & Southern Life Insurance Company, who had given Xavier $1 million. The company's foundation donated an additional $3 million. Through the inspired leadership of the Department of Theology, Xavier enhanced its mission by approving the establishment of the Brueggeman Center for Interreligious Dialogue. Created to bring together students and authorities from all religions, the Center for Interreligious Dialogue honored the memory of Edward Brueggeman, S.J., professor of theology, who had worked to foster greater understanding of, and respect for, all religious traditions. (13)

In the spring of 1994 the English as a Second Language program (ESL), formerly known as English Language and American Culture program and established in 1970 within the Center for Adult and Part-Time Students, offered intensive English language instruction for international students who had the goal of entering American colleges or universities and wanted to improve their English for professional purposes. Approximately 65 students from more than 30 countries participated in the program in its first year. Two years later the university established the Corporate English program to offer concentrated training in language,

American culture, and international business practices to employees of multinational corporations. To provide a full training experience, the program drew on many campus resources, including ESL and the College of Business. (14)

Consistent with its long-established tradition, the university in the 1990s continued to encourage students to experience the world outside the Xavier campus and to engage in community service. During the 1994–1995 academic year Xavier introduced the first academic service learning semester in Nicaragua. Eight students spent three months in Managua living with local poor families, doing service activities, and performing academic work. The eight students and faculty member became enmeshed in the culture and had a daily class about the culture, religion, history, and government of Nicaragua. While there the students received a semester's worth of academic credits. Their 15-hour load included three credits each of theology, political science, and community service, and six credits of language. The students returned two weeks before the end of the semester to finish reflection, theology, and political science papers and to take final exams. By the end of the decade the university also sponsored academic service learning semesters and immersion experiences in Nepal and in the Over-the-Rhine district in Cincinnati. During their three months of study and experience the students kept a journal. By combining academic study with community service, all three programs helped fulfill the university's educational mission and one of the main characteristics of Jesuit higher education underscored by Father General Peter-Hans Kolvenbach in his visit to the United States in 1989. (15)

Xavier's educational mission applied to all students—undergraduates and graduates, part-time and non-traditional students. Every student mattered. In the fall of 1995 the university established a weekend degree program aimed at the adult, part-time students in the metropolitan area. By rededicating its commitment to part-time nontraditional student populations, the university also hoped to increase overall enrollment. Consisting of five 9-week sessions each year and allowing students to complete six hours per session toward a degree, the weekend degree program provided accelerated undergraduate instruction and services. Enrollment in the first semester exceeded expectations. Though the administrators of the program had projected 60 students, 87 actually enrolled. A year later the program had 188 students. (16)

In particular, faculty mentoring of students illustrated well the centrality of students in the mission of the university. Under the leadership of Max J. Keck, professor of physics and dean of the College of Arts and Sciences, Xavier in 1995 sponsored the first annual "Celebration of Student Research" program, which encouraged faculty and students to work on common research. That experience gave students a sense of excitement and greater accomplishment beyond what they received in regular courses. In Hoff's judgment that was a "moment *par excellence* for the University." (17)

Throughout the 1990s, faculty as well as student research at the university had a higher profile, playing a larger role in the daily lives of faculty members and in their progress toward tenure and promotion in rank. Many faculty members made ongoing scholarly contributions in their field. Though research had become an increasingly important aspect of the educational environment, teaching remained the university's first priority. "There is a defining moment," Hoff said, "every time a faculty member meets a student and both teaches and cares at the same time." Faculty mentoring of students in research, especially in the sciences, testified to that. (18)

A timely recognition of the contribution of the faculty in the mentoring and education of Xavier students in the sciences was a gift in 1997 by Dr. Robert McDonald, a 1955 graduate. By creating the Joan G. McDonald Award for Outstanding Teaching in the Sciences with a gift of $333,000, he made it possible for the university and faculty to recognize teachers who influenced students in a significant way during their undergraduate study in biology, chemistry, or physics. The gift provided cash awards and faculty development funds to selected tenure track faculty and laboratory instructors. It also provided stipends for students chosen to work with faculty on summer research projects. (19)

Throughout his presidency Hoff acknowledged the essential role the faculty played in the education of Xavier students and in fulfilling the institution's mission. "[O]ur graduates strengthen their communities . . . by bringing wisdom and responsibility rooted in ethical and spiritual values to their lives and their work. Xavier's faculty [members]," Hoff said, "make this happen. They are at the heart of Xavier. They are critical to accomplishing our mission. Our faculty [is] like the single tree from which a forest grows." Realizing that no institution was any better than its people, he always insisted that the university was "really blessed with its faculty. . . . The Xavier faculty has a culture of great teaching and of caring for the individual student." (20)

During the remainder of the decade, the university continued to expand its scope of academic programs and activities. In 1997 the Ohio

Board of Regents approved Xavier's clinical doctorate in psychology program. Developed for over a decade under the tutelage of the faculty in the department of psychology and Neil Heighberger, professor of political science and dean of the College of Social Sciences, the Psy.D. program focused on care for children, the elderly, and the severely mentally handicapped. It enrolled its first students in the fall of that year. That same year the Procter & Gamble Company awarded Xavier $1.5 million to help train inner-city school teachers. The gift funded for five years the university's new urban initiative project, called X-CEED, Xavier Center for Excellence in Education. While using part of the funding for scholarships for urban teachers and students, the university also equipped a model classroom with the latest educational technology and a mathematics and science curriculum laboratory. The following year the university established a new minor in environmental studies, which integrated science, economics, theology, and practical experience. At the same time, John Grissmer, a 1955 graduate and film producer and director, made a gift of $150,000 to support the theater arts program. "I started the fund," he said, "to encourage others to see that performing arts is taken seriously at Xavier." In June 2000 the radio station WVXU, which had won international, state, and local broadcasting awards, including the prestigious George Foster Peabody Award, celebrated its thirtieth anniversary. Largely under the directorship of James King, associate professor of communication arts, the tiny operation had evolved into a 26,000-watt station, the largest privately-owned public radio station in the nation. (21)

The Century Campaign and Growth of the University

During Hoff's first year in office the university completed the Cornerstone Campaign, which had achieved its goal of preparing the institution for the next generation by providing the "new cornerstone" on which the university could build for the future. The $31.4 million raised in the campaign almost quadrupled the $8.3 million collected in the Sesquicentennial Campaign that had ended in 1982. When the Cornerstone Campaign began in 1987, Xavier's endowment was $9.7 million. Upon its completion in 1992, the endowment had increased to $27.2 million, almost triple what it had been five years earlier. The total endowment, however, was still far short of what was considered mini-mally necessary. When compared to the endowments of comparable schools nationally, Xavier's endowment consistently ranked in the bottom third. Its smallness hampered a variety of activities, from student support to faculty development. A bigger endowment would not only reduce the dependence on tuition dollars, which accounted for approximately 70 percent of Xavier's annual revenue, but "could limit the size of tuition increases," Hoff said, "and keep the University affordable." (22)

In addition to providing a boost to Xavier's endowment, the Cornerstone Campaign helped to refurbish each of the residence halls and to modernize significantly the science facilities. It helped build a totally new state-of-the-art science center, budgeted at $9.1 million, which included the renovated Albers and Logan Halls and the new Carl H. Lindner Family Physics Building. Logan Hall became operational in the fall semester of 1991 and the physics building the following spring. In order to renovate Albers, during the Christmas break that year the biology department moved to Alumni Hall, which had been vacated by physics. (23)

Indeed, the Cornerstone Campaign was Xavier's most successful fund-raising program to date. Gifts like the bequest of $6.89 million from Clara Schawe helped make it possible for Xavier to experience a new period of growth. In addition, $5.6 million raised in donations during the campaign created fifteen new endowed scholarships to help Xavier attract and retain the most academically talented students. In particular, the university awarded the Father Pedro Arrupe Scholarship, donated by Xavier's Jesuit community, to minority students with strong academic credentials. Moreover, the Beckman family members—Vincent, Paul, and Irene—jointly contributed $1 million to the campaign to establish an endowed chair, the John J. and Robert E. Beckman Chair in Theology, in honor of their brothers, both Jesuits. "Without help from our generous friends," Hoff said, "Xavier would have difficulty maintaining its reputation as a first-rate Jesuit university, one where a values-centered education is a top priority." A new vitality could "be seen on Xavier's campus," he added, "and the future looks brighter than ever before." While helping to promote a new and more positive attitude toward the university, the Cornerstone Campaign also helped keep a lid on rising tuition costs. The yield from more than $8 million in unrestricted endowment funds went directly into the operating budget, thus supplementing the operating revenue generated from tuition. (24)

Until the late 1980s all endowment income had been spent on the operating budget, thus limiting the endowment's ability to grow.

Beginning in 1990 the amount of funds provided for distribution and expenditure from the university's endowment fund each year was based on the approved spending rate multiplied by the average market value per share of the pooled investment fund for the twelve quarters prior to the beginning of each fiscal year. That year the spending rate was 5 percent. The university, through the board's Investment Advisory Committee, reinvested income earned in excess of the spending rate through the purchase of additional shares in the investment pool in accordance with the restrictions or designations of each endowment fund. Reinvesting in the endowment helped ensure its long-term growth. "In the best scenario," Hoff said, "a larger endowment would allow Xavier to pump more money into the university while simultaneously reducing the percentage of endowment funds being spent." In 1996 the trustees decreased the spending rate of the endowment fund to 4.5 percent. (25)

In light of the success of the Cornerstone Campaign, President Hoff was hopeful about Xavier's future and the inauguration of a new and more ambitious campaign for the welfare of the university. Committed to nurturing "the whole person . . . in body, mind and spirit," he planned to set in motion a comprehensive process of strategic planning linked to the next campaign. But first he hoped to change the Xavier University By-laws concerning trustee membership. Hoff thought that the setup of limited terms was inadvisable and made it extremely difficult for the president to gain continuity of support over a long period of time. To him, the advantage of continuity of leadership on the board was absolutely essential. "Once a Board member gets involved and is in a position to do more for the University," he said, "it is counterproductive for the University to retire that Board member." In May the board changed the By-laws to provide for unlimited terms. (26)

In early spring 1991 the University Futures Committee completed the first phase of its work and submitted its report, titled "Xavier University—A Proposal for the Future," to President Hoff. It identified three priorities and supporting goals to help guide the university toward the year 2000. Combining Jesuit values and Xavier's mission with a renewed conviction to serve society, the priorities stressed values-oriented education and emphasized the quality and relevance of the teaching and learning experience. The adoption of the Futures Committee document by the president and the trustees in mid-July marked the close of Phase I of the university's long-range planning process and became the foundation for Phase II planning, which consisted of developing details and cost estimates for implementation of the Futures Committee proposal. (27)

While a major focus of Hoff's presidency was to raise the sights and expectations of everyone at Xavier, one of his main goals was to secure an endowment of $100 million by the year 2000. With an operating budget of about $55 million and an endowment of under $30 million, Xavier "is too much a tuition-dependent university," he argued. "That's a concern of mine." Another reason for increasing Xavier's endowment was to enable the university to attend to the underserved in society. An important priority of Jesuit education at the university "is to keep education accessible to a broad economic spectrum of American families," Hoff said, "and that [too] is a major concern of mine." While acknowledging that Xavier had a tradition of providing high-quality education, "you don't stay the same," he said. "[Y]ou either improve or lag behind." He insisted that the university "must do more to build partnerships in Cincinnati, across the country and in the global community. Xavier is clearly an institution on the move. And it has tremendous potential for greater things." (28)

To help broaden Xavier's base of support, Hoff sought to energize alumni groups. In 1991 the university, with the board's approval, further developed alumni chapters in a number of cities, maintaining that their development was essential to building a strong Alumni Association. The president hoped to form a network of thirty alumni chapters in key communities, where they would elect officers, offer calendars of events, and develop a base of volunteers to support the university. By the winter of 1992 twenty chapters had been established. Among the programs reinvigorated by the chapters were Universal Communion Sunday, receptions following Xavier men's basketball games, get-togethers to watch national telecasts of Xavier basketball, chapter dinners, and participation in the Coordinated Alumni Recruitment Effort, the student recruitment program. (29)

As the decade progressed, the continuing growth of alumni chapters around the country enabled the university to bring its mission and vision to an ever-increasing number of Xavier graduates. In mid-October 1993 the university hosted its first National Alumni Leadership Conference. Representatives from each of the then 22 alumni chapters, with a membership of more than 37,000, helped form a National Alumni Board—the first of its kind in the history of the institution. By the mid-1990s the alumni chapters participated in blood drives, built houses, and tutored children in communities coast to coast.

In the summer of 1995 over 200 members of the Cincinnati chapter alone participated in Ignatian Service Day. While service had always played a significant role in the education of undergraduate students at Xavier, until the mid-1990s among the alumni it had never been collective, but primarily individual in focus. The idea had crystallized at the homecoming weekend in 1994, when board members of the national alumni association gathered for their second annual on-campus meeting. "If we're going to have chapters that represent Xavier," an alumnus said, "I think these chapters ought to have values that represent Xavier values. So we decided that each chapter should come up with a service project of its own." Within a year, all but one of the chapters had either completed a service project or planned to do so. In 1996, when the university now had 40 alumni chapters in the national network, the Cincinnati chapter held Ignatian Service Day, involving more than 300 people for a summer day filled with roofing, painting, and cleaning at sites throughout Cincinnati. Four years later Xavier had 45 chapters, including its first Asian chapter that consisted of 36 alumni in Korea. "Building the alumni association," a trustee observed, "has brought a tremendous amount of geographic diversity, thinking and viewpoints to the University." (30)

In addition to strengthening the university's alumni base, Hoff established in 1993 the President's Advisory Council. Meeting for the first time in February of that year, the council recognized and acknowledged those individuals who had generously supported the university and who were interested in becoming more deeply involved in its advancement. Membership included alumni, parents, friends, and representatives of corporations and foundations. Each college of the university—College of Arts and Sciences, College of Business Administration, and the College of Social Sciences—had an advisory council within the group. Council members conferred with the president, vice presidents, deans, and at times with faculty on Xavier's mission and goals. (31)

While enlarging its support base, the university also enhanced its public image. Over a two-year period, 1991 to 1993, Xavier received more media coverage than at any other time in its history. News stories about Xavier people and programs appeared on CBS *Sunday Morning* and on Monitor Radio Network as well as in *Reader's Digest, USA Today, The New York Times, The Washington Post, Glamour, U.S. News and World Report,* and the *Chicago Tribune.* Three years later, in an effort to develop even further the image and identity of Xavier to its external publics, the university upgraded the office of public relations and added a marketing emphasis. (32)

By 1993 Xavier had recorded dramatic increases in three important development categories. Since Hoff's arrival it had seen an increase of over 140 percent in multi-year pledges and commitments of over 153 percent in overall cash gifts, and 26.4 percent in annual fund support. The initiation of the President's Advisory Council, growth in the 1831 Society, a reorganized phone, mail, and student caller solicitation process, and the infusion of 1,300 new donors contributed to the success of the university's fund-raising effort. In 1994 the Xavier Annual Fund, which generated critically-needed operating revenue for the institution, posted its best totals since its founding in 1952. Total gifts for the university surpassed $6.4 million, and donations from Xavier and Edgecliff College alumni passed the $3.5 million mark for the first time. Xavier also had more donors, namely 12,074 individuals, corporations and foundations, than ever before. A year later total annual gifts amounted to $7.8 million. By the end of the decade they totaled $14.8 million. To help give the Alumni Association a voice in university policies, in 2000 the president of the National Alumni Board became an *ex officio* member of the Board of Trustees and served a term of two years. (33)

Beginning in 1993 the faculty, students, administration, and staff engaged in a university-wide strategic planning process. Draft plans were completed by June and were combined into a cohesive strategic plan that was shared with the Board of Trustees during a day-long retreat in July. After Hoff presented the positive results of the feasibility study for the capital campaign, called the Century Campaign, at the March 1994 trustees' meeting the board approved a strategic plan that was contingent upon Xavier's "ability to acquire the necessary, resources." In a news release immediately following the meeting, Michael Conaton, chair of the Board of Trustees, announced approval of the direction of Xavier's 1994–2000 strategic plan, more popularly called XU2000. A "stronger Xavier University means a stronger Cincinnati," he said. "Our pasts, presents, and futures are tied with the powerful bonds of friendship. Each needs the other for its success. For Xavier, a strong city means it is better able to recruit excellent faculty and . . . students. . . . In like manner, a strong Xavier educates prepared and skilled graduates who enhance the city's businesses and community life." (34)

XU2000 listed nine elements that were critical to achieving Xavier's mission. Using the Futures Committee document as a foundation, the university's strategic plan identified academic excellence, enrollment management, student development, Jesuit identity, mission-driven intercollegiate athletics, expanding external support and involvement, resource management, human resource management, and assessment for improvement as the major priorities. However, "[t]he top priority of the Strategic Plan," Hoff said, "is to maintain and increase academic excellence. The majority of new resources that would be required to implement this plan would be directed toward academic programs and projects. To that end the plan calls for endowed professorships, faculty development, and scholarships. That's why we need to increase Xavier's endowment to $100,000,000 by the year 2000." Over $51 million of the strategic plan were earmarked for academic excellence. Moreover, part of the goal of XU2000 was to increase the university's number of full-time undergraduate students from approximately 2,850 to 3,150. More specifically, Xavier officials planned to increase first-year students from 700 to 750, transfer students from 155 to 225, nontraditional enrollments by 15 percent, and retention rates from 87 percent to 90. (35)

In 1994, in preparation for the Century Campaign, Hoff had appointed associate professor of history, Michael J. Graham, S.J., vice president for development, and John Kucia, vice president in charge of intercollegiate athletics since 1990, administrative vice president. To help guide the campaign, James W. Frick, vice president for university relations for over thirty years at the University of Notre Dame joined Xavier as a development consultant. He served in that capacity for five years. Joseph P. Viviano, a 1959 graduate, trustee, and president and chief operating officer for the Hershey Foods Corporation, chaired the national campaign. In Viviano's judgment, the Century Campaign would enable Xavier "to take a quantum leap forward." Reflecting the sentiments of the president and his colleagues on the board, he was hopeful that the campaign, which embodied an ambitious master plan for the growth of the university's endowment, programs, and facilities would "be remembered years from now as a defining moment in the history of Xavier, a moment in which Xavier grew from great to greater." (36)

When asked early in the campaign to identify his highest priority as president of Xavier University, Hoff answered that people "know I would like to see the endowment raised to $100 million. They know I would like to see new facilities, and I do. But if we had those things and our vision and mission weren't being realized in the students, then it would all be for naught. What I want most of all for Xavier is what I've wanted most of all since I arrived here. That is to have the University's mission be realized in each student who graduates." Positive in his assessment of the university's strategic plan, Arthur J. Dewey, professor of theology and chair of Xavier's Faculty Committee, acknowledged that it was "but the beginning. We, faculty, students, and administrators must continue to work together to articulate more fully," he said, "our shared vision of what committed intellectual life means." (37)

In terms of facilities, the trustees in the 1990s focused on Xavier's residential and academic space. In the spring of 1991 the trustees had approved the renovation of Kuhlman and Husman Halls in the amount of $15 million. In addition, during the 1991–1992 academic year they also approved the construction of a fifth residence hall. The record enrollment of 2,894 undergraduate students in 1991 had necessitated plans for a new residence facility. Third in Ohio in undergraduate enrollment among independent colleges and universities, the university had experienced increasing enrollment for five consecutive years and had closed admission early for four of those years. In addition to meeting the first-year class enrollment target of 675, the university's average Standardized Achievement Test (SAT) score for the incoming class was 998, the highest ever. The SAT national average was 899. Retention of first-year students remained above 87 percent. In the spring of 1992, the trustees issued up to $23,500,000 in tax-exempt bonds for construction of the new residence hall and renovation of Kuhlman and Husman Halls. In the summer Xavier broke grounds on Ledgewood Avenue for the new residence hall, the second housing complex to be built in three years, housing 205 students. (38)

While constructing the new facility, the university attempted to establish a cul-de-sac in order to create a pedestrian mall on Ledgewood Avenue. It hoped to establish a more residential and inte- grated campus by providing safe pedestrian pathways that linked student parking lots and residence halls with the main campus and with the academic buildings on the mall. Over several months, Xavier officials conducted traffic studies, which involved the neighboring property owners, in preparation of a proposal to the city of Cincinnati to vacate a portion of Ledgewood. Upon review by the Cincinnati City Planning Commission, in the summer of 1993 the City Council narrowly approved Xavier's request by a vote of 5 to 4. Later that summer, how- ever, a group of residents in the neighboring communities of North Avondale and Evanston filed suit against the City of Cincinnati and Xavier University in protest to the closing of Ledgewood. As a consequence,

Xavier officials became convinced that the university had to "become a better neighbor." In the fall the Student Development Committee of the Board of Trustees noted that though many of Xavier's neighbors held the university in high regard scholastically, many thought it was "not an active member of the community." University officials subsequently established a task force with a focus on educating students and other university members about their role and responsibility in the surrounding communities. A few months later Xavier officials established the Community Building Institute, a partnership between the university and the United Way of Greater Cincinnati, to provide hands-on training, information, and facilitation to community-based organizations and institutions that fostered strategies for community building and neighborhood revitalization. (39)

Early in 1994 the court ruled against the residents' lawsuit, thus allowing the university to close a portion of Ledgewood Avenue. The following year the city granted a "right of entry" on Ledgewood to the university in order to complete its development up to Herald Avenue. Ultimately, the move to close a portion of Ledgewood proved to be an important step in the strategic development of the campus. It allowed Xavier "to create a special place," Hoff said, "in terms of the residential mall and better safety for the students." That same year, thanks to the generosity of Fifth Third Bank and the Mary R. and Jack J. Schiff Foundation, Xavier's newest residence hall on Ledgewood, completed in August 1993 at a cost of $6,500,000, was named the Clement and Ann Buenger Residence Hall, in honor of the Buengers, long-time friends and supporters of the university. (40)

The renovation of the residential mall, completed in December 1995, and the academic mall the following year, featured brick walkways, lush landscaping, and park-like sitting areas. With the completion of the residential mall, which connected to Ledgewood Avenue, both sides of the eastern section of campus—the residence halls and the main mall—were tied. While renovating the two malls, which significantly changed and upgraded the façade of the campus, the university, at a cost of $493,000, installed cable television and student residence hall data capabilities on campus. By 1996 all residence halls were wired, allowing students to connect to the campus network, library, and Internet. Two years later the library added 40 new computer stations, and the following year the university opened a 24-hour computer lab. Moreover, by the end of the decade the university had installed a high speed fiber optic computer network across campus. (41)

Building the Clement and Ann Buenger Residence Hall, renovating the other residence halls, closing Ledgewood Avenue and creating both a residential mall and an academic mall, and wiring all the residence hall rooms and offices for both data and cable substantially improved the environment on campus. As one trustee remarked in 1996, "[t]here's a new pride at Xavier." The new vice president for university relations, Michael Graham, S.J., whose title and added responsibilities in university relations had changed in 1996, noted that the substantial changes on campus were "along the lines described by a sacramental theology taught at Xavier in an earlier era. These are, I think," he said, "'outward signs of indwelling grace,' physical manifestations of some important changes going on within Xavier. Taken together, these changes have made Xavier an even more interesting and exciting place than it was when I arrived as a Jesuit Scholastic in 1984, for they have breathed a new vitality into the university while strengthening the fundamental character that has always made Xavier a compelling place." (42)

While planning for the renovation of the residential mall, the trustees also identified completion of the west row of buildings along the university mall, which included renovation of Hinkle Hall, Schmidt Hall, and Alumni Hall and the redesign and renovation of the campus mall as a high priority. Having seen improvements from the renovation of the Albers and Logan Halls and the addition of the Lindner Family Physics Building, Hoff was determined to complete as soon as possible the west row project, especially Hinkle Hall, where a substantial number of faculty members had their offices. The board had also begun considering in 1993 a proposal for an on-campus convocation center. Hoff formed a broad-based leadership committee to assess the feasibility of Xavier constructing a convocation center, which had been a subject of much discussion since the mid-1980s. Two board members, Robert J. Kohlhepp, who later served as chair, and Joseph L. Rippe were on the committee. At the spring 1994 board meeting, the trustees also discussed possible renovation of the University Center. (43)

As part of the strategic plan of the Century Campaign, during the 1994–1995 academic year university officials initiated a task force to study and help draw up plans for the renovation of the west row of buildings along the mall. Through ambitious renovation and with the help of a $600,000 challenge grant from the Kresge Foundation, during the second half of the decade Xavier's landmark buildings—Hinkle Hall, Schmidt Hall, and Alumni Hall—reclaimed their symbolic importance. They were renovated and updated for a cumulative cost of $7.7 million. For Hinkle Hall, which underwent a $3 million renovation, the university created a three-story atrium with skylights. Funded by Robert A. Conway, class of 1949 and a trustee, the university dedicated the atrium in memory of his father, Alfred A. Conway, a 1917 alumnus. Since the earlier renovation of Hinkle Hall for faculty use in the mid-1970s, this prominent structure on campus had received little more than basic maintenance. The Century Campaign thoroughly renovated the building to provide a more dignified and fitting home for many members of the Xavier faculty. During the 1997–1998 academic year, renovation work began on Schmidt Hall as well as on Bellarmine Chapel. The latter received a new interior with movable seating, a new color scheme, and lighting. Schmidt Hall became the new home for the offices of the president, academic vice president, vice president for financial administration, and administrative vice president. The university also transformed the former Lodge Learning Lab, previously the library on the second floor of Schmidt Hall, into the Michael J. and Margaret A. Conaton Board Room. In addition to being the meeting place for the quarterly sessions of the Board of Trustees, the new board room became a center for special events and functions on campus. A $1 million gift to the campaign by Xavier's Jesuit community helped renovate Schmidt Hall. (44)

In February 1998 the university broke ground for the proposed convocation center, called the Cintas Center, located across Ledgewood Avenue beyond Kuhlman Hall. The Cintas Center, made possible by generous gifts from Robert Kohlhepp, Jack Schiff, the Farmer and Gardner Family Funds, and James Duff, a 1962 graduate and trustee, became an on-campus multipurpose home to the men's and women's basketball and women's volleyball programs, as well as a place for members of the university community to go for major celebrations, academic convocations, basketball games, and daily dining. It also afforded opportunities for members of the greater Cincinnati community to participate in events. It raised the pride and expectations of people inside and outside of Xavier and afforded many new opportunities for more people to experience the university campus in a variety of ways. Hoff was hopeful that it would help integrate and enhance the campus and surrounding communities, as well as return commencement and alumni reunions to campus. The premium seating program, administered by John Kucia, administrative vice president, helped fund the debt service for the Cintas Center. In August 2000, two-and-a-half years later, it opened. The following month the university sponsored the Millennium Peace Celebration, the first public event for the Brueggeman Center for Interreligious Dialogue. It attracted 3,000 people to the Cintas Center. (45)

In the spring of 1999, during the construction of the Cintas Center, the university restored the statue of Our Lady, Queen of Victory and Peace, standing on the hillside between Alumni Hall and Victory Parkway. Xavier also added new brick walkways on University Drive and installed better lighting. That same year the university finished the renovation of Alumni Hall and renamed it Edgecliff Hall in honor of Edgecliff College, its graduates, and its contributions to Catholic higher education. Dedicated in April 2000, the newly-refurbished facility became the new home for the Department of Music and featured four traditional classrooms, a two-tiered classroom, music technology labs, soundproofed practice cubicles, a recital hall, and space for the office of human resources. (46)

While completing the renovation of the row of buildings on University Drive, the need for more playfield space and more parking led to the gift in February 2000 of 6.765 acres of the Badische Anilin-and Soda-Fabrik AG (BASF) chemical company, located at the corner of Dana and Montgomery Avenues and a 98-year lease and partnership with the Cincinnati Park Board that transformed 21 acres of unused parkland into playfields, varsity tennis courts, a nature trail, and a new road into campus. Xavier officials invested about $4,000,000 to develop the properties and provide additional parking. A month later the university leveled the Rainbo Building, which previously housed the physical plant offices and equipment on Herald Avenue to make way for a new apartment complex for upperclass students. Moreover, in July the university began construction of the Charles P. Gallagher Student Center, the last building project of the Century Campaign, with the demolition of the former University Center. Gallagher, a 1960 graduate and Denver business leader, had established a funding challenge, matching all donations to the center up to $7.5 million. In October Xavier purchased F&W Publications on Dana Avenue, directly across Schott Hall, for the sum of $7.6 million. The 6.2 acre business property and 150,000-square-foot building promised to provide substantial space for the division of university relations and physical plant, as well as make available additional campus parking. Over a ten-year period, 1990 to 2000, the campus had grown in size from 88.93 acres to 111.3, an increase of 22.37 acres. (47)

Jesuit Identity

Throughout much of its history, Xavier University's Catholic and Jesuit identity had largely been taken for granted. Until the last quarter of the twentieth century the university's full-time undergraduate student population had been mostly Roman Catholic. Demographics shifted, however. In addition to gradually bringing many more students, faculty, and staff from different backgrounds and faiths to the Xavier community, the number of Jesuits nationwide, as was true in other religious orders, declined. In the 1980s, Jesuits at the university, like many of their counterparts at other Jesuit institutions, entered an age of greater collaboration with their lay colleagues. "It is obvious, and has been obvious for many years," Father General Kolvenbach had said in a 1989 address in Washington, D.C., "that our educational institutions cannot survive without the presence and assistance and partnership of many dedicated lay people. We have been blessed by God with many lay people who have shared our vision and our principles, and have worked in our institutions with real dedication. As time goes on, however, we need to do more—in the selection of professors, administrative staff and members of boards, and especially in ongoing formation for both Jesuits and lay people in order to create an educational community united in mission." Building upon the success of the early Ignatian programs in the late 1980s, increasingly more Jesuits and members of the university community asked questions about the nature of Jesuit education, affirmed the need to express the values and vision of St. Ignatius of Loyola, and introduced newcomers to Xavier's tradition and mission. (48)

In light of the importance of sustaining and nurturing Xavier's Jesuit identity, in May 1992 Hoff established the Division for Religious Development and appointed Leo Klein, S.J., professor of theology and former Chicago provincial, vice president to help coordinate Catholic and other religious activities, including Ignatian programs, campus ministry, and programs in peace and justice. Ignatian programs, initiated and previously funded by Xavier's Jesuit community, were now entirely sponsored by the university. What "I'm concerned about," Hoff said, "is strengthening the Jesuit identity of the University." By adding the new division to its other administrative units, Xavier affirmed more visibly and administratively the university's commitment to its mission and ministry. Throughout the decade the board's Jesuit Identity Committee and President Hoff, echoing the sentiments of the father general, who visited the university in the spring of 1996 and reiterated his plea for greater Jesuit-lay collaboration, submitted reports and ideas underscoring the need to preserve the Jesuit character of the institution. (49)

In the late 1980s and into the 1990s, Xavier's Ignatian programs ran a series of Grailville Weekends, each a twenty-four hour, off-campus, informal grouping of faculty, administrators, and support staff who discussed with one another their lives at the university, their backgrounds, and their sense of Xavier's mission. In addition, each Xavier alumni chapter had a Spiritual Development Committee to help integrate spirituality into alumni activities. Beginning in 1995 alumni also began participating in Ignatian Service Day. Graduates from Xavier and Edgecliff College and their families volunteered at one of thirty greater Cincinnati social agencies and organizations. Moreover, to help integrate Jesuit ideals even more meaningfully in the culture of the university, Jan Jantzen, the university's first associate vice president for enrollment management, made a Grailville retreat and came up with the idea of creating service fellowships. Each year the university recruited five academically talented undergraduate students with high school records of service and, like top athletes, awarded them full-ride fellowships, which were the flagship of Xavier's scholarship program. The recipients performed at least ten hours of community service each week. (50)

Throughout its history Xavier University had attempted to nourish the spiritual growth of students, providing opportunities and activities that allowed them to "find God in all things." During Hoff's presidency the office of campus ministry sponsored many such activities, with definitive emphasis on campus-wide celebrations, worship, retreats, and outreach. During the course of a year, the university provided two student liturgies each Sunday, Masses in the residence halls each week, prayer services, and numerous prayer invocations and blessings at a variety of athletic events, dinners, meetings, and special events. There were also religious retreats for various student interest groups, including nontraditional students, African American women, and Hispanic women. The retreats afforded students opportunities for reflections on the integral parts of the Catholic and Jesuit traditions. In addition, residence hall chaplains met with approximately ten to twenty students per day, and the student development staff served as advisors to student clubs, organizations, and teams. (51)

In late August 1993 the university began sponsoring the annual Spirit Celebration Sunday on campus to celebrate the start of the academic year in unity and prayer. Faithful to the institution's identity and mission, the Mass of the Holy Spirit provided the university community a moment to address God and to ask for His guidance over the approaching year and over the directions of the university. Three years later, more than 1,200 faculty, staff, students, alumni, and friends participated in the celebration. That fall the university established the Interfaith Organization for non-Catholic students. In 1997, campus ministry created the GetAway retreat for first-year students. About 85 students attended in 1998 and 170 the following year. Also popular was the Approach retreat that encouraged students to reflect on their lives and relationships with God. (52)

Throughout the 1990s the university relied more and more on its lay community to fulfill many aspects of its Jesuit and Ignatian mission. At the time there were 24 Jesuits at Xavier. "God is making fewer Jesuits these days," Michael Graham, S.J., associate professor of history and newly-appointed vice president for development, wrote in 1994. "I can't help but wonder if God, like a wise personnel director, isn't moving the professional care of His people to the care of lay persons, whose church—as Vatican II taught us—it really is." The university's plan to maintain its Jesuit identity was simple. It chose to make its Jesuit character "not the sole responsibility of Xavier's Jesuit brothers and priests," Graham said, "but the collective responsibility of all of us who together are Xavier—faculty and students, alumni and friends, parents, staff and trustees. We will share our Jesuit tradition broadly so as to bear that tradition into the future." He further pointed out that Ignatius of Loyola was not a Jesuit, nor a priest, when he wrote the *Spiritual Exercises*. "Thus," he continued, "a layman wrote the master text that found the Jesuit enterprise. To carry that enterprise forward at Xavier is God's gift and call now to us." In addition to the growing collaborative Jesuit-lay ministry on campus, lay membership and participation on the Board of Trustees assumed a greater role. In the spring of 1994 the board increased its size to 32 and, in light of the decline of Jesuits nationally and after consulting with the provincial, changed the percentage of Jesuit members on the board from 25 to 15 percent. Four months earlier Bradley M. Schaeffer, S.J, provincial of the Chicago province, had shared his thoughts on Jesuit identity with the Jesuit Identity Committee of the Board of Trustees. While maintaining that the Jesuitness of Xavier began "with hiring people who support the mission," he urged the trustees to begin making plans for a non-Jesuit president sometime in the future. (53)

In 1997 Xavier renamed the division for religious development the division for spiritual development. Becoming more integral to Xavier's identity as a Catholic and Jesuit University, it promoted and administered a greater variety of spiritual or spiritually related activities, programs, and events. These ranged from a campus-wide Mass and picnic to groups and organizations that took students off campus to everything from retreats to soup kitchens. Though students were not required to participate in these endeavors, a large percentage of them did. In the fall of 1999 the university established AFMIX (Assuming the Future and Mission of Identity at Xavier) to provide faculty and staff with further training in the Jesuit mission. "The division [for spiritual development]," as one administrator put it, had succeeded in bringing "the best of our Jesuit tradition more to life here at Xavier." (54)

Faculty

In the early 1990s the Faculty Committee discussed concerns over the lack of faculty involvement in decision-making at the university. Because the committee "was not formally approached or embraced with respect to input or participation in short- and long-term planning processess currently taking place at the University," faculty members "get the distinct message," the chair of the Faculty Committee wrote to Hoff in January 1993, "that matters which concern us, our work, our service, our future, are being decided in a vacuum, without our genuine consultation." At the time the faculty was particularly concerned over decisions pertaining to health benefits for retirees. For several years national health care costs in general had experienced tremendous inflation. To compound the problem the federal government had continually shifted expenses previously covered within Medicare, a federal program of hospitalization and medical insurance for persons aged 65 or over, to employer-sponsored retiree health plans. In 1994 the university introduced a phase-out of its health care subsidy for future retirees. While continuing to honor its promise to those retirees who were already utilizing the benefit, the phase-out extended for future retirees over a ten-year period. At the same time Xavier authorities also studied the feasibility of increasing the university's retirement contributions for employees. The administration was hopeful that enhanced contributions would allow future retirees greater ability to cover increased costs for health insurance. (55)

While discussing Xavier's health benefits package, some faculty hoped "that a better model of faculty governance would encourage faculty members to get [more] involved" in university matters. In early 1994 the Faculty Committee began a preliminary discussion of a working paper largely developed by Arthur Dewey, chair of the Faculty Committee, entitled "Constitution of the Faculty Assembly of Xavier University." He and his colleagues proposed greater involvement by the faculty in the life of the university. "Do we want to play an active part," Dewey wrote to the faculty, "in determining the vision, mission, and responsibilities of this University?" During the next several months the faculty discussed the document. (56)

In an effort to promote greater collegiality between the faculty and administration, the following year the faculty passed Xavier's second faculty constitution in the history of the university. Of the 133 ballots counted, 123 faculty members approved the new document. This gave the faculty constitution, designed to encourage more faculty participation in the formation of academic policy, a 93 percent approval rating. It outlined the makeup and responsibilities of the Faculty Assembly, which was to meet at least once every academic semester to discuss issues significant to the development of academic policy. Consisting of full-time faculty with teaching responsibilities, academic staff, and full-time professional librarians, the assembly served as the faculty's voices. Empowered to initiate or participate "in the discussion of general academic policy," the Faculty Assembly made recommendations to the academic vice president on academic policy and life as well as monitored "the execution of academic policy." The constitution also specified the duties of the Faculty Committee. While handling the Faculty Assembly's order of business, committee members were authorized to establish the assembly's agenda, conduct assembly meetings, serve as a mediator between the assembly and other academic committees, and attend to the daily concerns of the academic community. "Faculty [members] are the memory of the university," Arthur Dewey later wrote. "By adding this much-needed element of faculty governance, the constitution will bring order to, and enhance dialogue among, faculty, administration and the various academic committees." In the spring of 1995 the faculty and administration began working on a new faculty handbook that would integrate features of the new faculty constitution as well as articulate faculty rights and responsibilities. Five years later the faculty, President Hoff and the Board of Trustees approved the university's new faculty handbook. (57)

While exploring the adoption of a new faculty constitution, Xavier in 1994 celebrated the 25th anniversary of undergraduate women on campus as well as the place of women in the life of the university. At the time, women constituted about one-third of the full-time faculty, 84 percent of the academic staff, and occupied nine chairs in twenty-five academic departments. For the first time in school history women comprised a majority of the Faculty Committee. Women's basketball, rifle, soccer, tennis, and volleyball teams, among others, had brought Xavier renewed attention and prestige. Women had also emerged as student government leaders, members of the National Jesuit Honor Society, and editors of the school newspaper. Reflecting the sentiments of virtually everyone in the university community, Hoff asserted unequivocally that over a twenty-five year period women had "made Xavier a richer [and] better place." (58)

However, there was room for improvement. Though in 1994 there were 92 women among the 233 full-time faculty members, only 4 were full professors among the 58 in the university. Moreover, the Xavier community hoped to see more women in positions of high administrative leadership. During the 1994–1995 academic year women on campus established a group called Women Offering Rights, Truth & Happiness (WORTH). This group, hoping to foster a sense of community among women, sponsored discussions about stereotypes and sexual harassment and provided services to women on and off campus. That year the university also established an ad hoc Committee on the Status of Women. In the winter of 1996 the Faculty Committee and James Bundschuh, academic vice president, reaffirmed the university's commitment to promote equality of men and women in Xavier's educational mission. Consistent with the 1995 documents of the 34th General Congregation of the Society of Jesus, the university sought to "foster an environment in which the achievement of excellence in teaching, scholarship, and service is assessed impartially and without regard to gender." (59)

Athletics

In the spring of 1991 there was much discussion in the national news about new intercollegiate athletic conferences. With the departure of Marquette and St. Louis Universities from the Midwestern Collegiate Conference (MCC), the MCC considered its future. The athletic directors discussed three possible options. The first option was the consideration of merger with some other conference. The second possibility was to maintain the conference as it presently was constituted with six teams, but to develop complementary scheduling alliances with other existing conferences to improve the MCC schedule. The third alternative was to add a few new schools. The directors agreed to proceed slowly. (60)

As Xavier considered its options, Hoff established an ad hoc committee to develop a mission statement for intercollegiate athletics at the university, to evaluate the three options in light of that mission, and to consider the effect of the university's choice on other universities. By the spring of 1993 the remaining teams in the MCC agreed to an open period of time during which they would freely continue to look at their options for future conference affiliation. Xavier quietly explored its future opportunities. In December, after a thorough evaluation of data from athletic conferences, Xavier chose to join the Atlantic 10 Conference in July 1995. The university had spent sixteen years in the MCC. It had won the last three MCC regular season championships, including a perfect 14–0 regular season in 1994–1995. The decision to move from the MCC to the Atlantic 10 Conference was a strategic decision flowing from XU2000. Joining the new conference doubtlessly helped "enhance . . . the reputation of the University," Hoff said, and broaden the exposure of the university because of the location of most of its members either in the East or Midwest. "Entering the Atlantic 10," Hoff said, "has a symbolic value, which is generated from entering a more competitive conference and from establishing higher expectations for ourselves. We're continually trying to raise expectations of who we are and of what we can accomplish. And that's not only true of basketball but it's true of everything. We are raising our sights." Moreover, the move to the Atlantic 10 enhanced the rationale and business opportunity that led to the construction of the Cintas Center. (61)

During Hoff's decade, the men's basketball team participated in the National Collegiate Athletic Association (NCAA) tournament in 1993, 1995, 1997, and 1998, reaching the second round in 1993 and 1997. It also competed in three National Invitational Tournaments (NIT) in 1994, 1999, and 2000, reaching the quarterfinals in 1994. That spring, Pete Gillen, after nine years at the helm, announced he was leaving to become the head coach at the University of Virginia. Skip Prosser, who had been Gillen's assistant coach at Xavier for several years and had taken the head coaching job at Loyola University of Maryland in 1993, accepted the Xavier position. Under Prosser's leadership the men's basketball team enjoyed one of its most successful seasons ever in 1996–1997. The Musketeers finished 23–6, won their division of the Atlantic 10 Conference as a second-year member, advanced to NCAA tournament play for the ninth time in 12 years, and completed the season ranked 13th in the Associated Press poll. A year later it again won the Atlantic 10 regular season championship as well as the tournament title. From 1990 to the end of the decade, four players were drafted in the NBA draft, including three first rounders—Tyrone Hill in 1990, Brian Grant in 1994, and James Posey in 1999—and one second rounder, Torraye Braggs in 1998. (62)

In the summer of 1998 Michael Bobinski became the university's new athletic director. He thought that upon completion of the Cintas Center there would be great opportunities for Xavier athletics, particularly basketball. "This facility will give a better opportunity to better recruit top 25 or top 50 kids throughout the country. If we're able to get just a few more of those kids, then we'll have a legitimate chance to compete for a national championship, and that's one of the reasons why I came here." (63)

In the 1990s there was also progress in other men's and in women's sports. From 1992 to 2000 the rifle team, which consisted of both men and women, competed in seven NCAA tournaments, finishing seventh or better in each appearance. In 2000 it was runner-up. That year two shooters, Jason Parker and Thrine Kane, from the team participated in the 2000 Olympics in Sydney. The men's golf team claimed four MCC championships in 1991, 1992, 1993, and 1994 and the Atlantic 10 championship in 1998. In 1992, when the university added golf to the women's entourage, its women's basketball team won the MCC regular season championship. The following year it won the MCC tournament championship and made its first appearance in the NCAA tournament. After winning a team-record 24 games and advancing to the second round of the NCAA tournament, the women's basketball team in 2000 won a school-record 26 games and the Atlantic 10 Conference tournament championship, finished 25th in the Associated Press national rankings, and earned a berth in the NCAA tournament for the second consecutive year. Having won the Atlantic 10 championships in 1998 and 2000, the women's soccer team participated in the NCAA tournaments. In addition, the volleyball team won the Atlantic 10 regular season championship in 1998. (64)

Throughout the decade the university, and in particular the Department of Athletics, took great pride in the student-athlete graduation rates. Sister Rose Ann Fleming, SND de Namur, who had been appointed the principal academic advisor for student athletes by President Charles Currie in 1985, played not only a significant role in advising student athletes but in coordinating a mission-focused relationship between academics and athletics. In a survey released by *The Chronicle of Higher Education* in 1991, Xavier posted the best statistics on student-athlete graduation rates among Division I schools in Ohio, with an overall varsity athlete graduation rate of 79 percent, 100 percent for basketball. Sister Rose Ann's success prompted basketball coach Pete Gillen that year to name her the team's Most Valuable Player. In 1998 Xavier ranked first in the nation for the graduation rates of Division I student-athletes in the NCAA Graduation Rates Report. (65)

Enrollment Growth and Campus Life

Wanting to be in the growth position in both number and quality of undergraduate students, "[e]nrollment," Hoff said in 1992, "will remain a major issue." In order to remain competitive and to shape both the quality and quantity of the undergraduate student body, the university gradually awarded more financial aid. Financial aid jumped from 16 percent of tuition revenue in 1989 to about 25 percent in 1993–1994. The increase was due to a 1989 change in the formula for calculating financial aid. Total financial aid was comprised of four parts—federal aid, state aid, endowed aid, and unfunded aid. Federal aid had peaked in the early 1980s and then began declining. Xavier, like many private colleges and universities, had to supplement aid in order to remain competitive. The university administered two forms of financial aid—need and merit. These served as enrollment management tools, with the need-based portion providing access to those who could not otherwise afford Xavier. The merit or non-need aid, which increased faster than the need-based aid in the early 1990s, allowed Xavier to shape the quality of the student body. Over a five-year period, 1989 to 1993, the increase in the number of high-ability students on merit scholarships accounted for about half of the required budget increase for aid. The grand total of financial aid for 1992–1993 was $10 million, of which only about $400,000 was funded by the endowment. (66)

That same year, Xavier alumnus and trustee, Charles Gallagher, helped fund the Pacesetters Scholarship Program in Toledo, Ohio.

Through a ten-year commitment, the program helped provide scholarships for minority students in an inner-city junior high school in Toledo to attend Gallagher's alma mater, Central Catholic High School. Each year up to ten students, who graduated from Central Catholic and qualified academically, were offered full scholarships and room and board to the university. "The Xavier community doesn't reflect the society our graduates are going out into," Gallagher said. "Xavier doesn't get a lot of top-flight inner-city kids. What I've attempted to do is to create a program that develops these children and Xavier's market for inner-city kids." Five years after the establishment of the Pacesetters Scholarship Program, the William Randolph Hearst Foundation awarded Xavier a $50,000 grant to establish an endowment to help underwrite the cost of the program. The following year the foundation increased the total size of the grant to $100,000. (67)

By the mid-1990s the university's financial aid commitment continued to increase. Its financial aid budget in 1995–1996 was $13,569,000, an increase of over $3,500,000 in three years. That proved worrisome to the Finance Committee of the Board of Trustees. In the committee's judgment there was need to develop a plan to bring it "under control." The growth of unfunded financial aid, it thought, required "continual vigilance." The following year, aid increased by 7 percent to $14,000,490, which was 26 percent of budgeted tuition revenue. By the fall of 2000 the university replaced the "percentage of tuition" formula for scholarships with specific amounts for the incoming first-year class. (68)

As financial aid increased, so did the size of the undergraduate student body. In 1994–1995, for the first time since 1919 when St. Xavier College moved to Avondale, the total number of 3,167 full-time students, graduates and undergraduates, exceeded the number of part-time students. While the first-year class totaled 761, overall full-time undergraduate enrollment increased to 2,872, the second largest in Xavier's history. Since the mid-1970s Xavier's student population had changed from a more commuter, part-time, and graduate population to a more residential, full-time undergraduate population. In the fall of 1995 there were 701 first-year students, a decline of 60 from the previous year. Varying enrollment in the first-year class year after year had been Xavier's pattern throughout much of its history. Despite the annual inconsistency, since the mid-1980s Xavier's undergraduate enrollment continued to climb over time. "While enrollment has been up and down from year to year, when you plot the trend, it's steadily upward,"

David Kalsbeek, Xavier's new associate vice president for enrollment services said in 1996. "The problem is we may not be able to sustain that trend due to our current capacities for housing, parking, classroom size, and faculty teaching loads." Consistent with the goals of the Century Campaign, the university sought to stabilize the annual first-year class at about 750 students, increase transfer students from about 100 to 150, and significantly increase the number of nontraditional students, particularly those in the newly-established weekend degree program. (69)

Tuition increases, financial aid concerns, and increased competition for a smaller pool of students had raised stakes and prompted new initiatives to increase enrollment. The admission office began targeting its direct mail efforts and began sending materials to high school sophomores and juniors, instead of waiting until the students' senior year. It also began to target market more effectively based on students' academic interests, geography, and ability. First-year applications for 1997 exceeded 3,000 for the first time ever, and exceeded the previous year's total by 30 percent. So Xavier created its first waiting list for prospective students. "The success we're seeing in admissions is a reflection of the many good things happening at Xavier," the director of admissions said. "We have a good story to tell and we're telling it in a much more compelling fashion." While undergraduate tuition increased from $9,700 in 1991 to $15,680 in 2000, the aggregate high school grade point average of enrolled first-year students jumped from 3.27 in 1996 to 3.49 in 2000 and SAT scores from 1110 to 1144 over the same period. The university, which had retained a director of freshman programs in 1990, also increased its rate of retention for first-year students to 89 percent. Moreover, the geographical diversity of the undergraduate student body had changed. In 1990, fifty-six percent of students had grown up more than 35 miles from the university. Ten years later 65 percent did. (70)

At the beginning of Hoff's tenure, 71 percent of first-year students lived on campus. Nine years later, largely due to the renovation of residence facilities and the construction of the Buenger Residence Hall, 86 percent did. Ninety percent of returning sophomores lived on campus. This was a marked change from earlier times. More undergraduates now lived on campus rather than off and participated more fully in the campus community. In 1991 there were 6,680 students enrolled in the university, 4,034 undergraduates and 2,646 graduate students. In 2000, when tuition for both graduates and undergraduates represented 74 percent of the university's total revenue, there were 6,523 students, 4,019 undergraduates and 2,504 graduate students. Though overall there was a decline of 157 students, it was mainly among part-time and graduate students. The full-time undergraduate population had grown from 2,855 to 3,351, an increase of 496 students. Among the 4,019 undergraduates in 2000, 1,905 were in the College of Arts and Sciences, 999 in the College of Social Sciences, and 865 in the Williams College of Business. (71)

As the full-time undergraduate population grew, so did students' groups. In the late 1980s and early 1990s on more and more American campuses, the gay and lesbian student populations demanded to be officially recognized as legitimate groups. In the fall of 1990 the Xavier University Board of Trustees had discussed issues related to gay rights students' groups. While some trustees suggested that the university, in keeping with the freedom of inquiry nature of a university campus, should recognize the gay rights groups, others expressed concern that the stated purposes of such organizations were contrary to the philosophy of the institution. As a consequence, the university insisted that groups of gay and lesbian students take the name "Xavier University" out of the title of their organization. By the end of the decade there were considerable discussions by members of the Faculty Committee, Faculty Assembly, Multicultural Student Concerns Committee, and the Student Government Association regarding the rights of both gay and lesbian people within the Xavier community. After consulting with the vice presidents and the Executive Committee of the Board of Trustees, President Hoff in May 2000, choosing not to amend the university's official non-discrimination policy, issued a statement of welcome on sexual orientation. "The question before all of us," Hoff said, "is how Xavier University can better fulfill its mission as an institution that is both a university and Catholic, in part, by becoming a progressively more welcoming community for all its members." (72)

Students continued to attend to social issues. The Dorothy Day House served as a meeting place for campus groups active in social concerns. Groups like Earthbread, Earthcare, Students for Life, St. Vincent de Paul Society, Pax Christi, and Amnesty International used the facility. The house had become an important center where students could plan service projects and reflect on their volunteer experiences. These programs, along with the service fellowships and the United Way and Community Chest summer student community-service internships, helped shape the ethos of the campus in the spirit of Catholic social justice tradition. During the 1992–1993 academic year the university sponsored a Minority Lecture Series to advance the educational mission of the university by creating a forum in which students and faculty could learn from and respond to the work of minority scholars in a wide range of disciplines. In the spring of 1996, William J. Clinton, president of the United States, visited the university. He met with community leaders in the Lodge Learning Lab and delivered a speech on corporate responsibility in Xavier's Schmidt Fieldhouse. The faculty assembly commended Hoff for inviting Clinton and for his public statement that the university "is dedicated to open and civil discussion of the major issues facing our nation because such academic freedom is necessary for the betterment of society." (73)

The same year that President Clinton visited the campus, Xavier's Habitat for Humanity chapter raised $50,000 to build a house in the neighboring community of Avondale. It was the first house built by a student chapter in Cincinnati. The following year more than 100 students took part in Community Action Day, a neighborhood improvement project in nearby Evanston, North Avondale, and Norwood. In 1998, for the eighth year in a row, Xavier students constructed a shantytown and held programs aimed at educating and providing opportunities for students to reflect upon the many issues involved with homelessness in the community. The construction of a second student-funded and student-built Habitat for Humanity house began in October 2000. (74)

By the end of the decade about 100 student organizations and activities existed on the Xavier campus, which was an increase of about 40 since the mid-1980s. Students could join the economics, theology, or sailing clubs, become young Democrats or Republicans, or play lacrosse, ice hockey, or take up fencing. Moreover, students continued to sponsor Club Day on the academic mall, the annual fall event that became a full-fledged carnival. Representing various student organizations, from late morning until mid-afternoon students jammed the mall with color and costumes. To facilitate students' academic programs and activities, in the spring of 1996 Xavier's Department of Safety and Security introduced an evening van shuttle service. The service offered students and staff transportation to campus parking lots and neighboring homes and apartments. The number of riders increased from 27,000 in 1996 to 50,000 in 1999. (75)

A "Phenomenal" Decade

"I have announced my plan to retire as president," sixty-eight-year-old James Hoff declared publicly in late February 2000. "In my mind, there are natural cycles in university administration consisting of long-range strategic planning followed by capital development campaigns and the implementation of strategic plans." The cycle had begun in 1992, about a year after his arrival, with the announcement of XU2000, the long-range strategic plan that helped guide Xavier throughout much of the decade. The Century Campaign, inaugurated in 1996 and scheduled to end in May 2001, helped generate the financial resources necessary to implement the academic and physical goals of the strategic plan. Hoff now thought that a new cycle of planning, development, and implementation was needed in order "to further advance Xavier as a Jesuit, Catholic university. I believe a new president should lead this new cycle. . . . Xavier will benefit greatly from a new president filled with fresh ideas and a bundle of energy." In his judgment, Michael Graham, S.J., who had served as the university's vice president for development and university relations and then became his executive assistant in June 1999, was "very talented and [had] the experience needed . . . to take on the challenge." About seven years earlier the trustees had advised the president to develop a successor. In June 1999 Gary R. Massa, vice president of marketing at Midland Company became Xavier's new vice president for university relations. (76)

Shortly after Hoff's announcement, the board's Executive Committee formed a Presidential Search Committee. Anticipating that Graham would be the "likely candidate," Michael Conaton, chair of the Board of Trustees, asked him, having been approached by two other Jesuit universities about his interest in becoming their president, to prepare a curriculum vitae to be presented to the 18-member committee, chaired by Gerald DeBrunner, who had chaired the search ten years earlier that led to Hoff's appointment. In the meantime Conaton and DeBrunner invited the provincials and rectors of the American Jesuit colleges and universities to post the Xavier vacancy on their bulletin boards. In their joint letter they advised them that there was "already a strong candidate for the presidency among the Jesuits currently at Xavier." In less than two months the committee completed its search and recommended Graham. (77)

On May 12, 2000, the Board of Trustees chose Michael Graham as the university's new president. He had become vice president for development in 1994 and had run the Century Campaign for five years while overseeing the offices of development, marketing, and public relations, and the national alumni association, and had served as Hoff's executive assistant for about a year. He was to assume the presidency in January 2001. "When I announced my retirement in March," Hoff wrote, "I had originally intended to remain in office until May 31, 2001. Because the search process for a new president was handled so expeditiously and successfully, I will retire from the presidency at the end of the calendar year. Being a lame duck president for a year is not good for Xavier University and it's not good for me either." At the beginning of the new year Hoff would become the university chancellor. His new duties included various combinations of teaching, fund-raising, consulting, and priestly ministry. (78)

In his nine-plus years at Xavier, Hoff oversaw an era of overall growth and change unmatched in the history of the university. Presiding over one of Xavier's most dynamic decades, he helped renew and strengthen the academic foundation, increase the endowment by $63.4 million to $87.4 million, triple yearly fund-raising revenue, rally greater alumni involvement, attract more and better students, and engineer a more attractive and cohesive building-and-grounds campaign. Under his leadership, planning committees boldly contemplated Xavier's future and helped renew, renovate, and reinvigorate the university. Alumni who visited the campus in the late-1990s marveled at the remarkable strides that the university had made. Hoff helped turn the univeristy into a nationally recognized center of scholastic and athletic excellence. In addition to seeing the grade point average of incoming first-year students jump from 2.9 to 3.46, by one measure Xavier in 2000 was ranked seventh among comprehensive universities in the Midwest. Five years earlier it had been ranked fourteenth.

The university's accomplishments during Hoff's presidency were nothing short of "phenomenal," said James Frick, who had served as Xavier's development consultant for five years. "Xavier has been far more successful than anyone there ever dreamed it could be." The university had always been "a diamond in the rough," as one administrator put it. "We just needed someone to polish it, and he has." In many ways Hoff "raised Xavier to a totally different level, something we never contemplated in the past," James Duff, a trustee, said. "He has raised every area of the University, and only by looking at his combined impact can you truly appreciate what he's done." Any knowledgeable insider—trustee or administrator—knew that Jim Hoff was the "conductor," Michael Conaton, chair of the Board of Trustees noted. With "the baton in his hand, . . . he has led tremendously." (79)

The decade's key accomplishments were largely made possible by the success of XU2000. Hoff had "championed the creation of the plan," Conaton said, and with the support of the faculty, administration, and trustees "he was the person in charge as it was rolled out and fulfilled." The chair of the Board of Trustees further noted that without Hoff's leadership "Xavier wouldn't be where it is today. . . . He has helped lift Xavier to heights it could only have imagined in generations past. I believe that the most important thing he did for the University was to raise its sights, to convince all of us that Xavier could be better, stronger and bolder. And he succeeded without compromising the core values of this institution." (80)

— 10 —

"A RENAISSANCE OF CULTURE AND COMMITMENT": MICHAEL J. GRAHAM, S.J., 2001–PRESENT

O n January 1, 2001, Michael J. Graham, S.J., became Xavier University's 37th president and 34th Jesuit president. The 47-year-old Cedar Rapids, Iowa, native inherited a strong university. Applications for undergraduate admission and the quality of incoming students were at all-time highs. The Century Campaign was flourishing, the Cintas Center had just opened, and a new student housing complex and the Gallagher Student Center were under construction. "It's an old cliché, but Mike Graham has big shoes to fill," Michael Conaton, chair of the Board of Trustees said. "Jim Hoff has been outstanding, but Mike Graham, in my opinion, is the one to carry us to even higher levels." Conaton and his colleagues on the board believed that Graham had the "qualities and abilities necessary" to push the school into the top tier of Catholic and Jesuit institutions. "The last decade has witnessed continuous and substantial quality improvements in virtually every facet of the University," the report of the North Central Association evaluation team that visited the university in 1999 read. "Clearly, if Xavier duplicates over the next 10 years the depth and scope of the quality of improvements that have taken place over the last 10 years, the institution will move from a prominent regional University to one with a national profile." Moreover, faculty members, who viewed the new president and tenured member of the Department of History as one of their own, also had high expectations for the university under his leadership. (1)

Graham, the oldest of seven children, graduated from Cornell College in Iowa in 1975 with degrees in philosophy and psychology. Three years later he received his master's degree in psychology and in 1983 his Ph.D. in American studies from the University of Michigan. While pursuing his studies at Michigan, Graham entered the Society of Jesus. As a Jesuit scholastic he spent a year and a half as a visiting faculty member in Xavier's Department of History in the mid-1980s before leaving to finish a master's degree in divinity. He was ordained in 1988 and a year later returned to campus as an assistant professor of history. He administered the University Scholars Program, served as chaplain and faculty moderator of the rugby club, and held ministry retreats and conducted Sunday night liturgy for students in Bellarmine Chapel. In 1994 he was tenured and promoted to the rank of associate professor. The following year the president appointed him vice president for development. (2)

Having been groomed by Hoff, President Graham looked forward to the opportunity to build upon the success of his mentor. "People asked me if I'm nervous about this," Graham said. "My answer? Sure. It's a huge responsibility. This job is much larger than me. At the same time, I believe in the grace of the office and the fact that God gives what one needs to do the job." He viewed the presidency from academic and business perspectives, but first and foremost he possessed a ministerial sense of duty. "It's the ministry that binds it together," he said. "I see what I do as a service to which God calls me." Affirming the university's rich Catholic and Jesuit tradition and echoing his predecessor's oft-repeated mission statement, he asserted that "the mission of Xavier remains today what it has ever been, . . . to form students intellectually, morally and spiritually, with rigor and compassion, toward lives of solidarity and service." (3)

On September 8, 2001, at his inauguration during Mass at St. Francis Xavier Church, Graham rededicated himself to the Catholic, Jesuit mission of the university. He delivered his inaugural speech, titled "Scholars, Saints, and Citizen-Servants", at a reception and dinner that evening at the Cintas Center. Acknowledging his predecessor's immense contributions, he emphasized that under Hoff's leadership in the 1990s the university was brought "to the place where we can dream dreams, hope hopes, see visions, anticipate mountain tops that we could not possibly have attempted or challenged ourselves to a short decade ago." As part of the inaugural events, three days later the university sponsored an academic convocation. Every year since then Xavier has set aside a day, called Academic Day, for group presentations and interaction within the university community. (4)

Academic and Strategic Planning

In his initial semester as president, Graham had meetings with a broad spectrum of university groups. The "main purpose of these listening sessions," Graham said, which he viewed as a "conversation with the University community, . . . was to afford individuals the opportunity to share [their] thoughts, perceptions and concerns in an open and uncontested atmosphere." The former vice president seized upon the sessions as a "privileged time to 'reread' the University from [his] new position." (5)

Key questions posed by Graham during the meetings were: "What would it mean for Xavier to be a 'better University'? What do we want to be? What do we want to be known for? How can we better weave the Jesuit identity into the broad culture of the University? How can we best interact with the city around us?" While addressing these questions, the participants' concerns and suggestions generally touched upon the areas of facilities, students, compensation, faculty, and staff. In terms of facilities, virtually everyone agreed that Alter Hall, McDonald Library, and the O'Connor Sports Center needed considerable attention. The student participants speculated on the most desirable size, diversity, and quality of the undergraduate student body. While some pressed for more academic selectivity of students admitted in the university, others remarked "that this goal should not overwhelm other concerns such as service [and] alignment with the University's mission." Perhaps the most commonly expressed desires were to have an undergraduate student body "of greater diversity" and for the university "not to turn away good students who would benefit greatly from a Xavier education, but who are unable to afford the cost." (6)

Faculty members expressed concerns over a variety of topics, ranging from student research and faculty development to the core curriculum and compensation. A number of them pointed out that the university could improve its infrastructure to enhance the students' education through interdisciplinary work and service learning. The faculty, staff, and administrators asserted that even though the university had made progress in technology, the "systems were often cumbersome [and] service slow in coming." They recommended that teaching and learning technology needs be addressed soon, noting that technology was "very clearly the way of the future." Lastly, in virtually every listening group the various constituencies expressed "[d]iscontent over salaries." (7)

Identifying a wide range of institutional concerns and ideas, the new president realized that the listening sessions "really began the next phase of strategic planning." In late August he shared part of his personal vision of the university's future with the ad-hoc Group of 50, which had first come together in the spring and consisted of administration, faculty, and staff from across the university. In his opening remarks Graham encouraged the university community to adopt a new approach to collaborative and mutual empowering of Xavier's academic mission. Gillian Ahlgren, associate professor of theology and chair of the Faculty Committee, praised "the passion and fire and energy that was generated in [the] Group of 50 meeting" and was pleased with the description she received of what the university "might look like in the not-so-far future." Having "great confidence" in the president's academic leadership, faculty members "feel the winds of change," she further noted, "[and] have high hopes for the future." (8)

In early fall, during the final phase of the construction of the Gallagher Student Center, Graham established the ad hoc Committee on Academic Vision "to stimulate faculty participation in a constructive vision of the academic future of Xavier University." Consisting of nine members, eight faculty, and Roger Fortin, professor of history and interim academic vice president, the committee, with Ahlgren as chair, began working on an academic vision statement that would articulate the future goals of the university. Earlier that year James Bundschuh, academic vice president, had accepted the presidency of another college and the university appointed an interim chief academic officer. Consistent with the president's expectation, the Faculty Committee was optimistic that the vision document would serve as the university's "navigational tool, . . . provide a meaningful order in the prioritization of tasks," and encourage the institution "to aspire to greater goals." During the course of the year the committee engaged faculty members in facilitated focus groups to help capture their ideas and enthusiasm and reflect on the university's aspirations as an academic community. (9)

Approved by the faculty, President Graham, and the Board of Trustees in the spring of 2002, the Academic Vision Statement imagined the university in the year 2011, 180 years after its founding.

Springing primarily from the hearts and minds of the faculty, the document envisioned Xavier being nationally recognized as the leading comprehensive university in the Midwest and the leading comprehensive Catholic, Jesuit university in the United States. Consistent with the university's mission, the faculty visualized the institution offering a richer and more "collaborative learning environment" that challenged a "diverse and capable student body intellectually, morally and spiritually." Moreover, the Academic Vision Statement envisaged a core curriculum that further "stimulated critical thinking and interdisciplinary learning" and inspired "cooperative, innovative approaches to problem solving and engagement with society." (10)

The various listening sessions that the president had undertaken in the spring of 2001 and the subsequent academic vision process generated a list of "emerging priorities" that would help form the "building blocks" of the university's next strategic plan. It was time for Xavier "to think strategically and to plan for our future," Graham had written in an open letter to the university community in the fall of 2001. "I ask all of us to reflect on . . . how do we create a learning community that is at once challenging and diverse; open and engaged; that values scholarship, service and teaching; and that sustains the ethos of care for which we have been traditionally recognized?" Like a road map, Graham was hopeful that the future strategic plan would help guide the university to a higher and more integrated level of learning on campus. (11)

In November 2001 the university launched the new Division for Information Resources with Carol Rankin, associate professor of economics and former associate vice president for academic affairs, as its first vice president. Formally linking information systems and services, instructional technology services, library services, Web development, and strategic information resources, the new division immediately moved to improve service and applications of technology for teaching and learning. In collaboration with the office of the academic vice president, the division instituted an annual Information Fluency Institute, designed to assist faculty with incorporating information fluency skills and technology into their courses. In the classroom, an increasing number of faculty employed Blackboard, a learning management system which was introduced in 2000, that allowed students to access their course syllabus and assignments, participate in online discussions, exchange information with the instructor and other students, take examinations, and see and hear video and audio clips. (12)

In late fall 2001 the new Division for Information Resources led the university in the evaluation of its administrative systems. This effort resulted in a recommendation to replace the existing systems with the SCT Banner system and the Luminis Portal, which the Board of Trustees approved in December 2002. By the following fall the university made available to students and faculty additional presentation classrooms, open instruction computer labs, interactive classrooms, and public access computers, including nearly sixty wireless hookups on campus. The MyXU portal, introduced in 2004, facilitated one-stop delivery of electronic communications across campus and offered faculty and students an alternative course management vehicle. Traditional library services were improved by the introduction of additional electronic databases, covering all academic disciplines, electronic reserves, and a series of online tutorials for building library and information competency skills. (13)

By 2005 the division, under the leadership of Mary Walker, professor of marketing and acting vice president for information resources, completed the implementation of SCT Banner, which included university relations, financial administration, human resources, student records, and financial aid. At the same time, information resources professionals continued to increase wireless connectivity on campus, which included the academic and residential malls; launched new e-mail and portal systems; introduced new Web sites for all academic areas and most allied offices; and worked in collaboration with faculty to develop and implement a language lab, expand a graduate distance learning program, and pilot an electronic portfolio program. In the fall of that year the university appointed David W. Dodd, who had twenty-five years of experience in information technology, as its new Vice President for Information Resources and Chief Information Officer.

In March 2002, Graham established the Planning Steering Committee, chaired by Ronald Slepitza, who—in addition to his regular administrative duties as vice president for student development—served as special assistant to the president for planning. Charged with the responsibility of overseeing the university's "multiple activities . . . with respect to planning," the committee involved twenty-three members of the faculty, administration, staff, and student body. Hoping that progress during the next decade would "be as propitious and transformative" as the Hoff decade had been, Graham encouraged the committee to "be realistic and yet visionary, . . . [and] combine a deep commitment to the Jesuit Catholic mission of the University along with a 'market smart' approach to sketching" Xavier's future. (14)

Guided by Xavier's mission and Academic Vision Statement, during the next year significant institutional energies were expended across the university on a wide variety of strategic planning projects. Under Slepitza's direction, a whole set of task forces, consisting of faculty, students, and administrative staff, launched out in several directions. Representing strong grassroots collaboration, the groups included the Library Planning Committee, Teaching, Learning, and Technology Committee, Career Development and Lifelong Learning Committee, Community Building Collaboration Committee, and Jesuit Identity Committee. Over time a smaller work group weaved together the various individual reports into a more coherent whole, promising to capture, better than any previous attempt, "certain important themes of Jesuit education," Graham wrote, "such as care for the person and an integrated educational experience that unites a liberal arts core to a specialized program of study particular to individual students, and then unites as well the students' in-class experience to their out-of-class experience, whether on campus through various clubs and organizations or off campus through internships, co-ops, [and] service learning." (15)

While the Planning Steering Committee conducted its work, for the first time in its history the university in October 2002 began a thorough and simultaneous study of all academic departments and programs, with special care taken to ask questions about program quality, connection to the university's Jesuit Catholic mission, enrollment, and financial health. Following a self-review by each academic department, university faculty peer and curriculum committees and the academic deans conducted their own reviews. By June 2003, all academic program evaluations were available for review electronically by the faculty. (16)

To further analyze academic needs, that summer Graham authorized the formation of the Academic Planning Task Force, which consisted of seven faculty members, the academic vice president, who served as chair, and the associate vice president for academic affairs. After a national search, in June 2002 Roger Fortin had been named academic vice president. The president charged the task force to review all academic program reviews, documents, and reports and identify those programs and activities that related strongly to the mission and academic vision, to underscore marks of academic excellence at the university, and to name those programs that probably did not relate as well to Xavier's mission and academic vision and perhaps could be scaled down or discontinued. Influenced by the Academic Vision Statement, during their deliberations the task force argued that the institution had to "make significant new investments in the academic enterprise." In the members' judgment, the university had to remain true to its Catholic and Jesuit heritage by continuing to strengthen its "undergraduate programs, especially . . . the core curriculum," and to continue to foster "critical thinking, interdisciplinary learning and effective writing." (17)

Significantly, the task force also pointed out that a number of undergraduate and graduate programs needed additional resources to achieve their full potential. "Reinvesting in our undergraduate majors, graduate and professional programs," the members said, "will strengthen our commitment to forming students intellectually, morally and spiritually, for lives of solidarity, service, and success and enrich our engagement with the various communities to which we belong." Arguing that the academic future of the university depended "on the continued development of its faculty as teachers, scholars, and learners," they urged "significant new investments in faculty development," which included a center for teaching and learning to promote innovative teaching methods and interdisciplinary teaching, and the creation of a center for civic education, literacy, and engagement. While underscoring new initiatives, the members recommended the monitoring and more extensive review, as well as the possible discontinuation of a few programs and concentrations. In November 2003 the Academic Planning Task Force submitted its report to President Graham. (18)

The Task Force Report, coupled with the Academic Vision Statement and academic program reviews, provided the university with greater clarity of vision and a sharper focus that would help define the university's strategic plan as it related to academics and help drive the next comprehensive campaign. The documents clearly recommended a blueprint for academic excellence. For Xavier to continue to grow in stature nationally, the university had to focus first on its undergraduate programs. They emphasized the importance of the core, diversity, interdisciplinary teaching and learning, better coordination and more study abroad, undergraduate student research and mentoring, faculty development, strategic hiring in understaffed areas, and innovative approaches to problem solving and engagement in society. Reflecting the sentiments of his colleagues on the task force, the academic vice president in a letter to the faculty argued that "it is at the undergraduate level that Xavier promises to make a distinctive difference. It is at the undergraduate level that Xavier can truly make its mark nationally." (19)

Xavier had also been fulfilling its mission at the graduate level. For over half a century the university's two graduate programs in business and education had served the regional community. In addition, the graduate programs in Montessori education, psychology, and health services administration, which had a national outreach as well as a local and regional one, and the programs in criminal justice, English, humanities, nursing, occupational therapy, and theology, helped Xavier carry out its mission in the community. However, in terms of size and scope the two graduate professional programs in business and education, which generated approximately four-fifths of graduate credit hours, made the greatest impact locally and regionally. On the recommendation of the Academic Planning Task Force and the Board of Graduate Studies, the university in 2004 discontinued the master's program in the humanities because of insufficient enrollment. (20)

Under President Graham's leadership the university had already begun to realize parts of its academic vision. In the first three years of his presidency, Xavier established new tenure track faculty positions and new academic programs. A leading concern that had been expressed by the faculty and administration during the listening sessions was the high rate of courses in the core curriculum taught by adjunct faculty. In June 2001 Graham enjoined the interim academic vice president and the academic deans to look into the matter and report back to him with a plan. In collaboration with David Flaspohler, professor of mathematics and newly-appointed associate academic vice president for enrollment services, they conducted an intensive study and presented their findings to the president. The data clearly showed that in order to reduce the number of adjunct faculty, meet certain academic program needs, keep the size of classes small for more personal interaction between teacher and student, and execute more strongly the mission of the university, the three colleges of the university needed 24 new tenure track faculty. After consulting with his Executive Committee, which consisted of the president and the university's vice presidents, Graham proposed that a three-year plan be developed to meet the need. (21)

In early fall the interim academic vice president and Richard Hirté, vice president for financial administration, and their respective personnel, in collaboration with the academic deans and faculty on the University Budget Committee, developed a plan by which sufficient revenue would be raised to balance the existing budget of full-time faculty, which was under-budgeted by about $400,000, as well as hire 13 of the 24 new tenure track faculty. What helped the process was Graham's directive to the Budget Committee, urging the members, as they attended to the ordinary components of the budget, to provide additional revenue "to help fund the strategic initiative" to enhance the quality of teaching, research, and service on campus. As a consequence, during the 2001–2002 year the university hired 27 faculty members, which included the 13 new tenure track faculty and 14 who filled recently vacated positions. The following year the university hired 24 additional faculty members, which included 11 new tenure track faculty. In two years' time the university had established 24 new tenure track faculty positions. (22)

In addition to increasing the size of the faculty, especially in the core areas, Xavier further improved its academic offerings. In the fall of 2002 the university received a generous gift to subsidize a program to develop and sponsor courses that would include a philanthropy component. Students in each academic course were given $4,000 to invest in the community. Over a three-year period, more than a dozen courses were offered. In the spring of 2003 the trustees approved a new interdisciplinary minor, Catholicism and culture. Under the leadership of John LaRocca, S.J., professor and chair of the Department of History, the new program examined the way Catholicism and culture influence each other. Moreover, the trustees approved the recommendation by the Board of Undergraduate Studies to change the name of Xavier's Women and Minorities' Studies minor to Gender and Diversity Studies. (23)

That same spring the university established a third honors program called "Philosophy, Politics, and the Public." Modeled after a program called "Philosophy, Politics, and Economics" at Oxford University in England, Xavier's new interdisciplinary major tapped existing strengths of the university's core curriculum. Under the directorship of Paul Colella, professor of philosophy, the program invited faculty from across the university to participate. Students in the new course of study, which included a junior year summer study abroad, examined the political, social, historical, cultural, and economic dimensions of the public. In the first two years 40 students enrolled in the new program. Along with the honors bachelor of arts and University Scholars Program, the philosophy, politics, and the public honors course of study, characterized by small classes and interdisciplinary course work, affirmed Xavier's long-established Jesuit tradition of intellectual rigor, ethics, and values. Moreover, in February 2004 the trustees approved the establishment of the master of occupational therapy program, an outgrowth from the existing bachelor program. (24)

In the summer of 2003 the university had also begun making significant investments in strengthening the Williams College of Business. In addition to hiring a new dean, Ali R. Malekzadeh, former dean and professor of strategic management at St. Cloud State University in Minnesota, and an associate dean, Raghu Tadepalli, professor and former chair of Xavier's Department of Marketing, the university added two new tenure track positions. The health and growth of the accredited Williams College of Business were not only essential to provide a stellar education for the students, but necessary to ensure a more vibrant relationship with the business community, which in turn was both a source of learning and employment for students, as well as professional and financial support for the university. (25)

Similarly, the university saw great strides made in the Department of Education. Having a long and memorable history in the community, the department continued to explore new ways of fulfilling its mission and that of the university. A generous $2,000,000 gift from the Clement and Ann Buenger Foundation of Cincinnati allowed Xavier University and the Archdiocese of Cincinnati Catholic Schools office in the fall of 2003 to launch the Initiative for Catholic Schools, a program for Catholic elementary schools in the Cincinnati area. Xavier's Department of Education and Center for Excellence in Education, in collaboration with the archdiocesan Catholic Schools office, provided faculty and material resources to enhance professional development for principals and potential administrators, as well as to increase both content knowledge and pedagogical skills for teachers of mathematics and science. To help foster more emphasis on Catholic thought and education, the grant also established the Ann Buenger Catholic Lecture Series. For her total dedication to Catholic education, in December 2004 Xavier awarded Ann Buenger the St. Francis Xavier Award, the university's highest honor. In order to sustain the Department of Education's mission in the community, the university reallocated resources as well as made additional investments in its programs. (26)

In the spring of 2005 the university further enhanced its Catholic and Jesuit identity by sponsoring a first-ever exhibition, in collaboration with Cincinnati's Jewish Foundation, on "A Blessing to One Another: Pope John Paul II and the Jewish People" at its Cohen Art Gallery. The multimedia exhibit, which opened with a gala event on May 18, documented the pope's lifelong affirming relationship with the Jewish people. Honoring the Holy See's contributions to the improvement of Catholic-Jewish relations, the exhibit, under the directorship of James

Buchanan, director of the Edward B. Brueggeman Center for Dialogue, and William Madges, professor and chair of the Department of Theology, continued at the gallery until July 15, when it moved to the Pope John Paul II Cultural Center in Washington, D.C. (27)

In June 2004 President Graham established the provost administrative structure and named Roger Fortin academic vice president and provost. The provost structure, consisting of the academic affairs, information resources, mission and ministry, and student development divisions, directly impacted the university's overall learning environment. By conjoining the four divisions, the new organization brought together faculty, librarians, instructional technology specialists, mission and ministry, and student development professionals, among others, to provide the best education possible to the students. Through the provost structure, Xavier continued to explore ways to integrate the Catholic and Jesuit character of the university in its curricula, undergraduate and graduate programs, service learning, and residence life programs and activities. It made it possible for a greater number of students, faculty, and administrative staff to collaborate and participate in activities and programs that facilitated increasing interaction across divisions and the integration of intellect, morality, and spirituality in their lives. (28)

During Graham's first five years in his presidency, the university continued to grow in stature and the faculty maintained a strong influence on the life of the university. Many faculty members had records of distinction. Internationally renowned scholar, Paul Knitter, professor of theology, had generated more than a dozen books and numerous articles. Hema Krishnan, professor and chair of the Department of Management and Entrepreneurship, had multiple publications on mergers and acquisitions in premier management journals. Ernest Fontana, professor of English, had produced over 20 articles over a fifteen-year period. John Fairfield, chair and professor of history, wrote extensively on aspects of urban history. W. Michael Nelson, professor of psychology, was widely known for his research and publications in cognitive and behavioral therapy. Frank Oppenheim, S.J., and Richard Polt, professors of philosophy, had published influential works on the philosophers Josiah Royce and Martin Heidegger respectively. This is but a glimpse of faculty scholarship, as many other professors had records of high distinction.

In addition, a growing number of faculty members in their service, as well as in their teaching and scholarship, had invigorated the mission of the university. A stellar example of faculty devotion was David Flaspohler who, until his retirement in 2005, had served the university over a period of twenty-five years in the following positions: chair of the Department of Mathematics, dean of the Graduate School, director of records, registration, and institutional research, interim director of admission, associate academic vice president for enrollment services, and director of the Xavier Center for Excellence in Education. In 2005–2006 Paul Colella, professor of philosophy and founder of the Xavier summer academic programs in Rome and London, continued to serve as first director of the philosophy, politics, and the public honors program. Edmund P. Cueva, associate professor of classics, served as director of the honors bachelor of arts program and codirector of the ethics, religion, and society program. Alexandra S. Korros, professor of history, was director of the University Scholars Program as well as chair of the Faculty Committee. All three faculty members were past recipients of the prestigious Xavier Bishop Fenwick Award for Excellence in Teaching.

By the fall of 2004 *U.S. News & World Report* had ranked Xavier number 2 among the best 142 master's-level colleges and universities in the Midwest in its annual report on "America's Best Colleges." This marked the tenth straight year that the university ranked in the report's top 10. That same fall, *Princeton Review,* based in New York City, included the university in its edition of the "The Best 357 Colleges" guide and named Xavier's MBA program in its list of "The Best 143 Business Schools." By looking at the strong entrepreneurial program and active student entrepreneurship club in the Williams College of Business, which had an exemplary student-mentoring program where virtually every student was formally connected with a local business mentor, the *Princeton Review* also ranked Xavier 11th in its inaugural list of the 25 most entrepreneurial campuses in the nation. In the spring of 2006 the *US News and World Report* Ranked the university's MBA program 24th nationally.

In september 2004 the Xavier trustees honored one of their own and extended "their warm and heartfelt thank you" to Michael J. Conaton, as he concluded 18 years as chair of the Board of Trustees. During his tenure, he had provided "an unmatched, faithful, continuity of board and executive lay leadership and mentoring to four university presidents," the trustees declared, "that even included service as interim president of Xavier." In their judgment, history "will describe the Conaton years as ones of solid, steady growth, improvement and transformation of Xavier as seen in its student body and its campus and its rising reputation and position among the top institutions of higher education." In September, Joseph A Pichler, retired chairman and chief executive officer of the Kroger Company in Cincinnati, succeeded him as chair. (29)

Collaborative and Shared Governance

During the presidencies of James Hoff and Michael Graham, the faculty, building upon the faculty constitution drafted in the mid-1990s, aspired for a larger role in the governance of the university. By a vote of 102 to 27 the faculty in the spring of 1999 had recommended more frequent meetings with the president and the Board of Trustees and "a mutual and timely accountability between administration and faculty." Based on the findings of a faculty survey conducted that year, "academic concerns" did not appear to "have high priority on the university agenda." Thus, there was "a strong desire among the faculty," the Faculty Committee observed, "for much more collaboration and consultation" with university officials. At a time when American colleges and universities dealt with multi-million-dollar budgets and the command and control styles of administration relegated the voice of the faculty and staff to an advisory role rather that of a partner in the institution's success, the faculty hoped to develop and implement a governance structure that ensured participation and collegiality in academic decision-making processes. (30)

During his first year as president, Graham endorsed the faculty's request for more interaction in the governance of the university. Embracing the concept of shared governance, the Faculty Committee, academic deans, and Roger Fortin, interim academic vice president, collaborated to regularize and institutionalize practices that helped improve faculty participation in the life of the university. As Xavier looked to fulfill its mission in new and deeper ways, it sought to become wiser and more deliberative in its operation and practices. Graham encouraged and helped establish new models for collaboration, consultation, and discussion of university matters, especially those that related directly to academic life.

In September 2001 the president, Fortin, and the Faculty Committee began communicating and collaborating more fully. In addition to meeting every two weeks with the interim academic vice president, the chair of the Faculty Committee and two faculty representatives also met with Graham and Fortin each month for breakfast. Later that fall the chair of the Faculty Committee began attending the meetings of the Academic Affairs Committee of the Board of Trustees. "This has provided," the Faculty Committee wrote in its annual report, "a valuable opportunity for dialogue, particularly with respect to the evolving academic vision of the University, the tenure and promotion process, and issues in academic governance and the academic culture more generally." That same fall the chair of the Faculty Committee also began attending the quarterly meetings of the full Board of Trustees. (31)

Recognizing the need for further study of appropriate governance models, in October five faculty members and the three academic deans attended a conference on mission and governance jointly sponsored by the American Association of University Professors and the American Conference of Academic Deans. Upon their return, the eight delegates, joined by the interim academic vice president and additional members of the Faculty Committee, met regularly to discuss areas where the governance of the university could be improved by fuller collaboration between faculty and administration. Gradually the group developed a set of general principles designed to foster a climate of mutual accountability and to enable the university to achieve its goal of greater academic excellence. Approved by the faculty on April 24, 2002, the Principles of Shared Governance document reflected the community's commitment to openness, good faith, and collaboration across the entire university. "These principles," the chair of the Faculty Committee wrote, "are a statement of governance ideals that can guide institutional practice in the future." Having received President Graham's full endorsement, in the fall the chair of the Faculty Committee and Fortin presented the Principles of Shared Governance to the Academic Affairs Committee of the Board of Trustees for discussion. Acknowledging and valuing this historic moment in Xavier's history, the committee approved the document at its December meeting. The full board then unanimously affirmed "the intent expressed in the Principles of Shared Governance." (32)

In keeping with the university's Articles of Incorporation, the principles declared "shared governance and academic freedom as essential to the health of the institution. The university administration, president, and the board recognize the primacy of the faculty in academic affairs." While acknowledging "the oversight authority of the board, the president, and university administration," the faculty and administration agreed that the faculty was in the best position to determine curricular and degree requirements, to select academic colleagues and judge their work, and to determine standards for promotion and tenure. Moreover, all parties agreed that "[c]ommunication, collaboration, and negotiations between and among the faculty, university administration, president, and Board of Trustees" were to be "carried out in good faith." (33)

The Faculty Committee took seriously faculty members' responsibilities in their enhanced role in the governance of the institution. "Establishing an effective communications infrastructure is critical in this process," the chair of the Faculty Committee had earlier stated in an address to the faculty. "We encourage you to keep yourselves informed of the governance structures currently in place throughout the University, and to walk with us as we use them, responsibly and increasingly more effectively, to promote the academic interests of the University and to support the impressive contributions of its faculty." By the fall of 2002 the chair of the Faculty Committee became a regular member of the Academic Council, a newly-constituted body consisting of members of the academic administration. During the 2003–2004 and 2004–2005 academic years trustees and members of the Faculty Committee and other faculty began the practice of meeting for lunch after one of the board's quarterly meetings. (34)

Despite the progress made in strengthening working relations between the faculty and administration much remained to be done. The adoption of the Principles of Shared Governance, frequent meetings between the president and the academic vice president and provost with members of the Faculty Committee, and fuller participation of the faculty in scores of committees was not enough to insure greater collaborative governance. Over a two-year period faculty protested, with some justification, the process used in awarding tenure to an administrator and in the cancellations of a satellite downlinked speech by Minister Louis Farrakhan, head of the Nation of Islam, and of Eve Ensler's play *The Vagina Monologues*, though the latter was reinstated a few days later. In the first instance, faculty members charged that provisions for awarding tenure in the Faculty Handbook had been violated. In terms of the two cancellations, they argued that the university, especially in regards to the play, had violated academic freedom. Though the president, academic vice president, and the Faculty Committee differed on the tenure issue, Graham assured the faculty that "notwithstanding our difference in opinion on this matter, I am fully supportive of the binding force of tenure as well as the criteria, norms, and procedures for granting it as stipulated in the Faculty Handbook." (35)

The two cancellations occurred partly because of incomplete and delayed information that the office of the president had received about the scheduled events, as well as the fact that members of the administration had not consulted fully enough. In the wake of those controversies President Graham sought to broaden participation in decision making. In the summer of 2003 he announced a change in the administrative organization of the university. He replaced the Executive Committee of the University with the President's Administrative Council. It had become clear to Graham that "significant institutional points of view" were missing from around the Executive Committee table. "To insure an interchange of important perspectives . . . from a more broadly based group of individuals," he established the new council, consisting of nineteen individuals, among whom were the president, vice presidents, a member from the Faculty Committee, and other professionals representing different sectors of the university. "This larger and more diverse group of individuals," Graham wrote, "will bring to the table both their own passion for the University as a whole and their own expertise in a particular area necessary for our continued improvement." (36)

Mainly because of *The Vagina Monologues* incident there was also considerable discussion on campus regarding university protocol for outside speakers and programs. In April 2004 the university adopted the Protocol for Campus Public Speakers and Events, affirming that the university's "multiple commitments to its mission as both a Catholic, Jesuit institution and as a university require, on the one hand, a strong commitment to teach and to respect Catholic and Jesuit traditions and, on the other, an equally strong commitment to the principles of academic freedom." The faculty and administration agreed that the potential for controversy was "never in itself an acceptable reason to deny a speaker or event." The protocol document made clear that if it were known or suspected a speaker would be controversial, the new policy now made certain that the entire campus would be made aware in order to welcome the exchange of ideas and views. Consistent with the Principles of Shared Governance, there would be ample discussion and consultation with the faculty and appropriate administrative offices. By building a system of dialogue, the steps outlined in the document intended to prevent a process where a handful of administrators on their own would determine if a speaker, event, or activity were acceptable. (37)

One of the most successful examples of collaborative governance in the early years of Graham's presidency was the development of a salary enhancement package for the faculty. Throughout the fall and early spring semesters of 2004–2005 the Faculty Compensation Committee, consisting of eight faculty members, met regularly to discuss ways of improving the salary profile of the faculty. Meeting and working with Roger Fortin and Kandi Stinson in the office of the academic vice president and provost and Richard Pulskamp, director of Institutional Research, the members reviewed faculty salary data among comparable institutions. Upon the committee's recommendation and approval by the president, the university appropriated, in addition to a 4 percent merit salary increase for all personnel, significant faculty compensation enhancement dollars for 2005–2006. This was an important first step in Xavier's effort to bring faculty salaries in line with the qualify profile of the faculty and stature of the university. (38)

Campus Life and Athletics

While teaching, scholarship, and service were the major focus of life at Xavier, students' participation in student clubs and organizations also constituted valuable learning experiences. The possibilities of meeting and working with new people, organizing programs, developing and strengthening skills, and of sharing interests with others were some of the rewards for exploring the co-curricular side of university life. Coming from 43 states and 48 countries, students became involved in more than 100 academic clubs, social and service organizations, and recreational sports. More than four-fifths of the clubs and organizations were recognized by, and responsible to, Xavier's Student Government Association (SGA) and the student development staff. Throughout Graham's presidency the SGA sought to "continuously improve . . . and develop all students . . . as responsible and involved members and leaders of society." In addition to providing a forum for civic training and student participation in university governance, as well as preserving the rights and freedoms of all students, it hosted a number of annual events, including dances, large concerts, and standup comedians. Each student organization had its own charter, elected officials, and chose a faculty, staff, or administrative advisor.

Participation in social service programs among undergraduate students during Graham's presidency continued to grow. The university had one of the most active networks of peace and justice student organizations in the country. In 2001 thirty-one Xavier graduates entered the Jesuit Volunteer Corps, one of the highest numbers among Jesuit colleges and universities. That year the university renamed the office of spiritual development, the Division for Mission and Ministry. "The change of title allows us," Leo Klein, S.J., vice president for mission and ministry said, "to clarify and re-articulate our role . . . to sponsor and support programs faithful to the educational goals of the Jesuit order." The university's focus on attending to the underserved in society, especially through the division for mission and ministry, reflected a common initiative of the nation's 28 Jesuit universities to foster Ignatian identity and service programs, empowering students to become leaders in service and to help build a more just and humane world. In addition to service clubs and organizations, a variety of academic programs such as the peace studies minor, a 15-hour interdisciplinary program focusing on peace and justice issues, and the annual academic service learning semester programs in Nicaragua, Nepal, and Over-the-Rhine in Cincinnati made it possible for students to participate in the Jesuit commitment to justice. In 2004 the university also established academic service learning semesters in India and in Ghana. (39)

The peace and justice programs at Xavier continued to educate students interested in building a more compassionate world through social action and community service. Students for Life defended the unborn, poor, handicapped, elderly, and condemned in society. Voices of Solidarity focused on peace and justice issues in Latin America. Other student activities included volunteering at a pregnancy center and lobbying against capital punishment. Earthbread continued to educate about food and farming issues and supported the debt relief effort for the world's poorest countries. St. Vincent de Paul coordinated and promoted faith-centered volunteering, which included delivering Communion to elderly nursing home patients, tutoring at elementary schools, and holding a holiday toy drive. (40)

What helped enliven the campus, increase residential occupancy, and broaden students' activities was the expansion and renovation of university facilities. In August 2001 Xavier opened The Commons, its newest residence hall. Facing the Cintas Center on the south side of Herald Avenue, the 285-bed unit, built on the former Rainbo Bakery property, helped alleviate the waiting list for campus housing. "We clearly have a demand for junior and senior housing, particularly apartment housing, so this will help us meet that demand," Ronald Slepitza, vice president for student development said. It contained two-, three- and four-bedroom units, which were furnished and cable-ready. The apartment complex increased total campus housing to nearly 1,900 beds.

The following spring the four-story Charles P. Gallagher Student Center opened. Built at a cost of $18,000,000, the 75,000-square-foot building featured a bell tower, a performing arts theater, and hosted a variety of student services, which included office and meeting space, retail services, restaurants, and pub. During the spring and summer the university cleared the space between the Gallagher Center and Husman Hall and replaced it with a campus green. As the area blended more readily with both the residential and academic malls, that part of the campus also became a more vibrant and cohesive place. (41)

As campus and students' facilities expanded, Xavier officials focused more intensely on improving the students' profile and increasing enrollment. To help stimulate the overall management of enrollment services, in the summer of 2002 the university conducted a national search and appointed James McCoy, associate vice president for enrollment management. His leadership, coupled with the experiences of the professional staff in the offices of admission and financial aid, helped recruit to mission and increase enrollment. Among the new enrollment strategies, Xavier, in the fall of 2002, began leveraging financial aid more extensively, which helped improve the profile of incoming students and appropriate the various amounts of aid needed to enroll selected students. The following spring the university launched the Parent and Alumni Recruiting Team, known as PART, to give alumni and parents the opportunity to participate in making it possible for prospective students to become better acquainted with Xavier. In the summer the university reconfigured two floors of Schott Hall into a comprehensive admission and financial aid suite that provided a very friendly and welcoming feel to prospective students and their families. (42)

In light of changes and new strategies, between 2000 and 2005 university enrollment increased from 6,523 to 6,665. In 2005 undergraduate enrollment totaled 3,879 and graduate enrollment 2,786. In the fall of 2005 the university had a record 5,482 applications for the first-year class, 2,112 more than five years earlier. Becoming a more selective institution, the undergraduate acceptance rate dropped from 87.87 percent in 2000 to 65.92 percent in 2005. The 878 first-year students in 2004 comprised the largest freshman class in over half a century, second only to the class of 900 in 1946, which consisted largely of World War II veterans. The increase of 112 students in 2004 from the previous year was not typical. The university had budgeted for a class of 800. In 2005 the first-year class totalled 771, missing the projection by 29, which was due largely to the reduction in financial aid by approximately $500,000. With an all-time-high mean grade point average of 3.60 and a mean SAT of 1184, that class was one of the most academically talented to enroll at Xavier. Eighteen percent of that class were minority students, up from 13 percent two years earlier. Eighty-eight African-American students comprised 11.4 percent of the class, an increase of 34 percent over 2003. Additionally, 21.9 percent of the first-year class was first generation college students. A significant change in the recruitment process during Graham's presidency was the number of online applications. In the fall of 2000 six percent of applications were made online. Five years later it was about 84 percent. Indications were that this trend would continue.

Athletics also energized the campus and helped increase and broaden students' activities. By 2004 the university sponsored 17 National Collegiate Athletic Association (NCAA) Division I sports, having added men's and women's track that year. Since it joined the Atlantic 10 Conference in 1995, Xavier had won by 2006 a total of 12 Athletic 10 championships. From the time of Hoff's tenure in 1991 through the first five years of Graham's presidency Xavier appeared in 32 NCAA tournaments. While excelling in athletic competitions, the university continued to rank consistently among the nation's best in the annual NCAA Graduation Rates Report. Due to continued collaborative efforts among faculty, student-athletes, and academic advisors, the university's student-athletes' graduation rate of 93 percent in 2004 was ranked second among the NCAA Division I schools. By comparison, the national average was 62 percent. (43)

Among the sports programs, the men's basketball team continued to thrive and earned increasing national recognition. Since the 1982–1983 year it had been in postseason play 19 times, including 15 NCAA tournament berths. Recording eighteen 20-win seasons from 1982 to 2005, the team averaged approximately 21 wins each season. In the spring of 2001 Thad Matta, head coach at Butler University, had become Xavier's fifteenth basketball coach. The next two years the basketball team won the Atlantic 10 regular season championships. In 2002 and 2004 it also won the Atlantic 10 tournament titles. During Graham's first five years as president it participated in the NCAA tournament four times, reaching the second round in 2002 and 2003 and the "Elite Eight" in 2004, which was a first for the men's basketball program. Over a two-year period, four players were selected in the National Basketball Association (NBA) draft, including one first rounder, David West in 2003—who was named the national player of the year by the Associated Press, *Basketball Times*, and the United States Basketball Writers Association—and three second round draftees: Lionel Chalmers, Romain Sato, and David Young in 2004. Three years after Thad Matta assumed the reigns at Xavier, he became the head coach at Ohio State University. The day after the public became aware of Matta's departure, Dawn Rogers, the newly-appointed athletic director, hired Sean Miller, Matta's associate coach for three years, as the new head coach. In early 2004 Michael Bobinski, the former athletic director, had moved to the office of development as its associate vice president, and the university appointed Rogers to succeed him. In the spring of 2006 the men's basketball team won four games in four days to win the Atlantic 10 championship. Xavier was the only school in NCAA history to win four games twice for a conference championship, having won four in four days two years earlier. The following summer Rogers became associate athletic director at Arizona State University and Bobinski returned to his former post as associate vice president and director for athletics. (44)

In addition to the success of the men's basketball program, other sports fared well. The men's golf team, coached by Doug Steiner, won the Atlantic 10 championships in 2001 and 2003 and participated in the NCAA tournaments in those two years as well as in the next three years. In the nine years in the Atlantic 10 the team had been either the champion or runner-up seven times. The university's rifle team, coached by Alan Joseph, also continued its success, participating regularly in the NCAA tournaments. It was runner-up in 2003. In 2004 Jason Parker of the class of 1996, who had won the gold medal at the World Championship in Air Rifle two years earlier, competed in the Olympics in Athens. From 1990 to 2004 seventeen Xavier shooters won a total of 51 All-America honors. Notwithstanding the success of the rifle team, upon the recommendation of the Department of Athletics in the fall of 2004 the university discontinued the program. At the time there were only 36 schools nationwide that competed in the sport. That year all divisions in the university underwent a strategic planning process and most made budget reductions to enable the university to reallocate resources to help fund new strategic planning initiatives. Moreover, in 2004 the university replaced the surface at the Xavier soccer complex on Victory Parkway with ProTurf and hired, for the first time, two full-time soccer coaches for the men's and women's teams respectively. (45)

Women's sports also continued to grow and attain national recognition. After having played at the Schmidt Fieldhouse for 29 years, in its first season in the Cintas Center the basketball team, coached by Melanie Balcomb, won both the Atlantic 10 regular season championship and the tournament in 2001 and made two NCAA tournament appearances in 2001 and 2003. In the former it reached the "Elite Eight," the first time in the history of the university. In 2001 the women's volleyball team, coached by Floyd Deaton, won the Atlantic 10 tournament championship and participated in the NCAA tournament. (46)

Moreover, during Graham's presidency the university also witnessed an increased interest in recreational sports and fitness. In 2005 Xavier's recreational sports department offered a wide variety of intramural sports, comprised of individual sports, dual sports, group sports, team sports, meets, special events, and co-intramural sports. Participation continued to remain high, with over 70 percent of the first-year class participating each year. In addition, Xavier had its share of club sports. Sharing a common interest in a particular sport activity, students came together and competed on the intercollegiate and regional level. Under the auspices of the Xavier Club Sport Council, students organized and operated the various clubs. By 2005 the university had 20 different club sports, compared to 8 fifteen years earlier, and over 400 student participants. Significantly, there was also a growing interest in self-directed sport activities. Whether the program consisted of individual goals in fitness or a specific sport like basketball, students met and engaged in various activities at the O'Connor Sports Center. In particular, there had been over a period of ten years considerable growth in female fitness through such programs as aerobics, jazzercise, water aerobics, and spinning.

The Passing of an Icon

In early spring 2004, Jim Hoff, chancellor and former president of the university, was diagnosed with cancer. He learned of his diagnosis while the Xavier men's basketball team was beginning its postseason run to the "Elite Eight" of the NCAA tournament in March. His medical condition, however, did not keep him from supporting the team and attending the first and second rounds of games in Orlando, Florida, and Atlanta, Georgia. While in Atlanta he celebrated Mass for the more than 600 Xavier supporters in the team's hotel. In April the university inducted him into its Hall of Fame. In his homily at the May baccalaureate Mass for the graduates of 2004, Hoff, his voice filled with emotion, eloquently discussed faith, hope, and Jesuit ideals. "It was as if something inside of Jim knew it would be the last pulpit he'd ever have," Graham said. He died on July 23. (47)

Five days later over 500 people attended the funeral Mass at St.Francis Xavier Church in downtown Cincinnati. Public officials, representatives from area colleges and universities, Xavier students, faculty, staff, administrators, trustees, and other friends participated in the ceremony. Throughout much of the day almost 100 people at a time had stood in line on the sidewalk in front of the church, waiting to go inside to pay their respects to the former president. Luke Byrne, S.J., chaplain for Rockhurst University in Kansas City, Missouri, delivered the eulogy. Admiring the way his long-time friend had made everyone feel important, Byrne pointed out that in Hoff's "world there were no little people. We knew it. He could communicate that with us." After the Mass the participants gathered under a large white canopy outside the church. When Ann Buenger, a friend and long-time supporter of the university, later learned that Hoff had decided when he assumed the presidency "to fall in love" with Xavier, she replied, echoing the sentiments of many, "and we fell in love with him." (48)

During the last week of July there were numerous tributes for the former president. Hoff "was much more than a successful college administrator," the editorial in the *Cincinnati Enquirer* read. "He was a leader, a teacher and a spiritual guide in the best Jesuit tradition." Everyone familiar with Xavier knew that he had "raised the bar for the entire university and got us over it," President Graham said. The university would continue to build upon Hoff's inspiring legacy. His vision would endure. Professor Arthur Dewey of the Department of Theology reflected well Hoff's living presence in the life of the university in a poem he wrote in his memory. "He leaves us well, but with work unfinished," he wrote;

> unwilling to accept the true and tried,
> he leaves us at the threshold wanting more;
> more than stone and steel or bricks and mortar,
> for Xavier is a moving vision. . . .
> He's provided for a firm foundation,
> left a launching pad for education.
> For he understood well how students thrive
> through worldwide ideals, passionate, alive. (49)

Diversity and Community Engagement

A major thematic movement during the early years of Graham's presidency was diversity. One of his first administrative actions was the establishment in April 2001 of the University Committee on the Status of Women. In 1999 the faculty, by a vote of 90 to 35, had recommended that the ad hoc Committee on the Status of Women, established in the mid-1990s, become "a permanent, standing and faculty-elected committee." Its purpose was to ensure full participation and encouragement of the contributions of women in pursuing the overall mission and goals of Xavier University, to create an environment "equally supportive of the achievements of women and men," and to "assure that equal consideration be given to women and men in all phases of the University operation." (50)

Under the new president's leadership the university also pursued plans to increase the number of minorities on campus. In the fall of 2001, when the university planned to conduct searches for about two dozen new tenure track faculty members, the administration pointed out that the university had the opportunity "to enhance diversity" among the faculty. "This historic moment," the interim academic vice president said, "challenges us to be as aggressive and imaginative as we possibly can in order to recruit more minority faculty to join us in the fall of 2002. As valuable as that goal is in itself, recent studies suggest that a more diverse faculty enriches academic life." Similarly, Dean Janice Walker of the College of Arts and Sciences argued that the "breadth of courses and research topics, the variety of perspectives in lectures and discussions, and the opportunities for personal growth experiences are significantly enhanced by diversity among faculty and students." Beyond enriching the intellectual environment of the campus community, in the judgment of many faculty members and the administration diversity better prepared students for the lives they would lead in the increasingly diverse world of the future. Among the 71 faculty hires in the years 2001 to 2004, 24 enhanced diversity. Working with the executive director for diversity development, who had joined the university in the summer of 2000, 6 of the 26 newly-created tenure track positions were opened exclusively to faculty of color. (51)

The university continued to accommodate a plurality of voices and traditions. The Academic Vision Statement and the Principles of Shared Governance document made clear that the campus was fully committed to being respectful of race and ethnicity, gender, sexual orientation, disability, age, socioeconomic class, marital status, intellectual diversity, and religious and spiritual orientation in courses and in relations with one another. While fostering critical reflection and encouraging dialogues that were mutually enriching, the university tried to avoid the intellectual imperialism of any one tradition. In an e-mail to the faculty in November 2003 the academic vice president pointed out that now and then "all of us need to be reminded that as an academic community, which thrives on the free exchange of ideas, we should respect the dignity of each individual and not tolerate any disrespect and abuse, verbally and physically." That fall the university announced the joint appointment of a faculty member with the newly-established National Underground Railroad Freedom Center in downtown Cincinnati. (52)

Consistent with the university's Catholic tradition, which asserted that all human beings were made in the image and likeness of God, and the General Congregations of the Society of Jesus, which made the promotion of faith and justice a central concern, President Graham repeatedly affirmed the importance of diversity in the life of the university. In early January 2004 the President's Administrative Council participated in a Diversity and Inclusion Strategic Planning Workshop. Upon the recommendation of the president, the trustees formed the Board Diversity Task Force, which included the chair and four other trustees. Committed to making diversity and inclusion more prominent and broadly integrated into Xavier's culture, the trustees' Diversity Task Force and the University's Diversity Advisory Committee developed during the course of the year an elaborate strategic diversity plan. Moreover, that year Xavier also conducted a search for its first vice provost for diversity. In December the university appointed Cheryl Nuñez, an experienced higher education administrator, to the post. (53)

Earlier that year the academic vice president, complying with the recommendation of the Academic Planning Task Force, had charged the Gender and Diversity Studies Committee to develop a proposal to integrate diversity more meaningfully in the core curriculum. Building upon some of the accomplishments of the pioneer E Pluribus Unum program, conceived over a decade earlier as an important first step toward the formal introduction of diversity in the curriculum, the committee worked on a proposal designed to further enrich the university's course of studies. (54)

In addition, in 2004 two faculty members, Carolyn Jenkins, associate professor of social work, and Christine Anderson, associate professor of history, working with professionals across the campus, helped draft a summary document entitled "Xavier University: Ensuring a Climate of Respect." Derived from the Judeo-Christian vision of human beings as unique creations of God, the document helped promote greater respect for diversity and for each person's humanity. It reinforced the institution's commitment to eliminating violence and harassment of any kind on campus by insuring that university policies were relevant, enforced, and integrated into daily life. "Only a campus environment of mutual respect and genuine care for all individuals," the document read, "enables [Xavier's] mission to be realized. Harassment or discrimination of any kind . . . impedes Xavier's ability to carry out the mission." Moreover, the university provided a seven-days-a-week, 24-hour phone line that connected Xavier callers to a trained advocate. (55)

While championing diversity, Graham also affirmed the ideals of service of faith and the promotion of justice in American Jesuit higher education. The Jesuit theme of justice "has found remarkably fertile soil here at Xavier," he wrote in 2004, and the "call for engagement resonates readily for many faculty and staff—and students as well." While pleased with the work of the staff associated with Xavier's programs in peace and justice, which espoused justice work, and that of campus ministry, which ran an ever-increasing number of campus retreats, reflection experiences, small prayer groups, and faith communities, "the real challenge," Graham argued, "will be finding ways of integrating both of these dimensions of justice and spirituality with one another and then integrating them in turn with the academic experience proper to a university." Xavier's experience in its academic service learning semesters in Third World settings and in Cincinnati's inner-city "should prove," he thought, "to be useful models for this process of better integrating these dimensions of student experiences as we move forward." (56)

As the head of an urban Jesuit university, Graham had come to believe that he could not only advance his own ministry, but also help the university better embody the service dimension of Jesuit higher education. The "presidencies of our colleges and universities," Graham wrote to the Chicago provincial in January 2004, "afford remarkable and perhaps unparalleled opportunities for ministry and service. . . . Certainly, my own experience has been," he argued, "that I have an ability to move in and out of all manner of terribly important conversations that are central to the shaping of the life of this community now and in the future. To be able to do so as a Jesuit priest is a great privilege for me and, I hope, a blessing as well for this community, for through these conversations I am able to bring as best I can the great treasury of our Jesuit tradition to the local civic enterprise." (57)

Very early in his presidency Graham, continuing the university's long tradition of service, had understood that the health and vitality of the institution and the community were interdependent. One evening in April 2001, in the wake of racial unrest in Cincinnati, over 250 Xavier students, faculty, staff, and administrators, including the president, packed the Conaton Board Room to speak with each other about their reactions to what went on in the community. "Their passionate testimonies, comments and questions got me to thinking," Graham said, "[w]hat might it mean for Xavier" to be a better "citizen . . . within our local community?" He became convinced that Xavier could "build upon all that we now do to better engage our students, our faculty, our community as a whole with the neighborhoods and communities of which we are an integral part." That same month the Cincinnati mayor, Charles Luken, formed Cincinnati Community Action Now (Cincinnati-CAN), a diverse and broad section of concerned community leaders, and asked Graham to co-chair the police and justice action team. Meetings took place weekly at Xavier for several months. To promote additional dialogue on racism and diversity, early in 2002 Xavier's Office of Multicultural Affairs (OMA) and the Black Student Association sponsored a three-part public series on race relations and the community. In addition, the university's women and minorities' studies committee also organized a public lecture series titled "A Usable Past: Historical Contexts for Understanding Race, Violence, and Diversity in Cincinnati." Affiliated with Xavier's Black Student Association, the Student Organization of Latinos, and the Muslim Student Association, OMA also continued to assist students of color with their academic, social, and spiritual growth. (58)

While sharing in the Jesuits' worldwide devotion to engagement with questions of peace and justice, particularly concerning the poor, community engagement became an even more integral part of the life of the university. Xavier pursued more aggressively than ever before important linkages and relationships with neighborhood and city organizations and individuals. Graham's personal commitment to the welfare of the community doubtlessly provided further impetus for discussions of the university as an engaged citizen. James Eigel, class of 1956, helped actualize the university's community engagement initiative by making a generous gift to the university. His gift provided the necessary resources to create in June 2002 the Community Building Collaborative at Xavier, whose charge was to help bring together non-profits, social service agencies, and other groups to address community needs. Through conversations with neighborhood leaders and under the leadership of Byron White, director of the Collaborative as well as the Community Building Institute, the university planned to be more integrally involved with the community and to utilize the community as a learning incubator for faculty and students in a variety of areas. Community engagement was "rooted in the very character of Xavier University," Graham had observed in 2002, "for the trajectory of Jesuit education has always been outward, toward a life that takes its meaning from engagement in the civic marketplace." Xavier's future continued to be intertwined with that of the city and the well-being of the immediate neighborhoods. Increasingly, the university, under the leadership of the president and John Kucia, administrative vice president, saw itself as a catalyst in the community, realizing that it had much to offer as well as to learn. (59)

The university had an unusual opportunity to express its neighborliness when it came to the aid of Summit Country Day, a private school about three miles east of the campus. A portion of its main building had collapsed on Sunday morning, January 18, 2004. An incredible outpouring of community support followed almost immediately, and a week later Summit administrators announced that they had accepted an invitation from Xavier to provide space for their high school students. Approximately 350 students, faculty, and staff moved to the campus at the end of the month, and during the spring semester used spaces in the Alumni Center, science labs in Lindner and Logan Halls, and classroom spaces in Cohen, Hailstones, and Alter.

The following fall the U.S. Department of Housing and Urban Development awarded a $392,754, three-year Community Outreach Partnering Center (COPC) grant to Xavier University. Better known as the Evanston-Norwood-Xavier Community Partnership, Xavier's COPC grant helped integrate the neighboring communities' expressed needs with the university's academic core competencies. In November the Cincinnati City Council approved a $2 million capital appropriation for Evanston to be applied to the work being defined jointly by Evanston and the university. (60)

During Graham's presidency, significant efforts were expended to better coordinate the various marketing strategies in such areas as academics, admissions, athletics, and public relations. By establishing the

Marketing Committee in 2001, consisting of faculty and administrators, Xavier began communicating more clearly and effectively a consistent image of the university to its various external constituencies. Under the leadership of Vice President Gary Massa and Robert Hill, Associate Vice President for Marketing and Public Relations, Xavier undertook an internal study and a series of external studies to identify the perceived image of the university and to help shape the Jesuit core messages that would be threaded through all its communication efforts. During the 2003–2004 year Xavier manifested its growing stature as a Jesuit university in the *Power of X* videos that were televised locally and nationally during the Xavier basketball games. That same year Graham replaced the Marketing Committee with the Marketing Coordinating Committee. Guided by the Academic Vision Statement and the newly-completed marketing research, the new and more broadly-based committee helped hone the university's strategic focus, sharpen the expression of its Jesuit core values, and promote in a more focused manner its identity and mission to its various publics. (61)

Planning for the Future

Following the May 2001 completion of the Century Campaign, which had raised $125,101,900, the university began making plans for the next fund drive. Having exceeded the campaign's goal by over $25,000,000 and with the foundation laid by President James Hoff firmly in place, Xavier officials were optimistic about the university's future. Beginning early in Graham's presidency, various initiatives, such as the president's listening sessions, Academic Vision Statement, and the studies and recommendations of the Planning Steering Committee and the Academic Planning Task Force provided the framework for the university's strategic plan that would steer the next campaign. The key strategy of Xavier's strategic plan was to improve its "personalized approach to learning, through enhanced collaboration among faculty and staff" toward achieving the mission of the university. The plan's four overarching themes were to recruit, retain, and help form students "intellectually, morally, and spiritually . . . toward lives of solidarity, service, and success;" foster integrated learning and academic programs of distinction; create a community engaged learning network; and develop the people of Xavier. (62)

In December 2003 President Graham asked Mary Walker, acting vice president for information resources, and Carol Rankin, associate professor of economics, to cochair a steering committee of 17 faculty members and administrators to oversee the initial planning of the major capital project that had emerged from the academic planning process. Planning teams, which included approximately 50 additional members of the university community, focused on student academic success, teaching and learning, faculty development, the library, community and business integration and collaboration, and upgrading instructional space. Building upon the significant work completed by earlier strategic planning committees, the Steering Committee envisioned an "academic quadrangle." In its May 2004 report to the president, the committee, which became known as the "Academic Quadrangle" Facilities Assessment and Recommendation Steering Committee, proposed the renovation of the McDonald Library and Alter Hall, and the construction of a "learning commons" adjacent to McDonald Library and of a building adjacent to Hailstones Hall. (63)

Faculty, administrators, and students saw the academic quadrangle proposal as the primary component of the university's campaign to create a more vibrant community of inquiry. Its conceptualization promised to embed the latest instructional technologies in academic support facilities, instructional labs, open lounges, group study areas, quiet rooms, and small alcoves. Emphasizing and enhancing Xavier's commitment to student learning and success, the "academic quad," as it came to be called, would make available for students the resources, services, and support they need to become responsible and lifelong learners. Through the resources and support offered, students would also be empowered to integrate academic, practical, and technological knowledge with questions of human values and ethical concerns. Consistent with the father general's call for Jesuit universities to "'heal the fracture of knowledge through a broad and intensive emphasis on interdisciplinary studies," faculty members would find a wide range of learning spaces and information resources to support faculty development, interdisciplinary teaching, scholarly activity, and innovative teaching methods. In keeping with Xavier's Jesuit core values, faculty members and other professionals could become more engaged in an active learning environment emphasizing critical thinking, effective communication, interdisciplinary learning, and a wide range of experiential learning opportunities that encourage engagement with civic, social, cultural, and global issues.

From 2003 to 2005, the university shared parts of the emerging strategic plan with different constituencies both on and off campus. In the process, the plan was used as a tool to determine priorities for strategic reallocation of resources. During this period Xavier also retained the consulting services of Thomas Scheye, former academic vice president and provost at Loyola College of Maryland, to help conduct the feasibility study for the next comprehensive campaign and to serve as campaign counsel. In addition, in the spring of 2004 Graham appointed Richard Hirté and Roger Fortin to cochair a Strategic Resource Reallocation Task Force. Joining them in this work were three faculty members, all of them with previous experience on the University Budget Committee. The president asked the task force as well as the vice presidents in the various divisions of the university to reallocate resources from Xavier's existing operating base to new learning initiatives that had emerged from the strategic plan. By December 2004 over $900,000 were reallocated for 2005–2006. (64)

The academic vice president and provost, after consulting with the president and the Faculty Committee, established the Academic Reorganization Committee in mid December 2004 and the Committee on Career Services in January 2005. The university charged the Academic Reorganization Committee, consisting of 14 faculty members and chaired by Jo Ann Recker, SND de Namur, professor of modern languages, to evaluate the composition of the College of Social Sciences, with particular attention to the proper designation or place of the Department of Education in the university's organizational structure. The main impetus for its formation was interest in revivifying and solidifying the role the Department of Education played in the education of students and in the life and reputation of the university itself. In addition to generating more credit hours than any other department in the university, it produced more than half of the credit hours in all the other programs in the College of Social Sciences combined.

The Committee on Career Services, which consisted of faculty and administrators from the divisions of academic affairs and student development, considered the restructuring and coordination of career services support to undergraduate students from all three colleges of the university. In addition to the two committees, several committees in the academic affairs division began conversations on how best to refine and enrich the university core curriculum. Guided by the Academic Vision Statement, the Academic Planning Task Force Report, and the mission of the university, some faculty and university officials were hopeful that diversity, interdisciplinary teaching, peace and justice issues, and the ethics, religion, and society focus in the core could be more fully integrated in the core course of studies. University officials were hopeful that the deliberation on recommendations from the above committees as well as on the core would in the long run help realize Xavier's vision and affirm its mission more strongly. (65)

In early 2005 the university also established the Network for Professional Education and Leadership (XNET). An outgrowth of the Center for Management and Professional Development, formed almost forty years earlier and later called the Xavier Consulting Group in 1999, XNET was designed to better serve internal and external constituencies. It began creating a new and expanded curriculum of non-credit professional development offerings, certificate programs, and individual enrichment programs through the collaborative efforts of a network of internal professionals and experienced practitioners drawn from across Xavier's colleges and community engagement and leadership programs. (66)

In the summer and fall of 2004 Xavier officials purchased the C. W. Zumbiel Company property consisting of 9.7 acres on Cleneay Avenue, for $8.5 million. They also acquired the Cinergy Corporation property on Dana Avenue, north of Montgomery Road, for $3.5 million. Xavier officials then swapped the Cinergy property for the Cincinnati Bell Telephone Company property on Dana Avenue near the corner of Dana and Ledgewood Avenue on the edge of campus. Xavier now owned 146 acres of property, mainly because of the effective administrative efforts of Richard Hirté and John Kucia. A number of university trustees also played key roles in the transactions. In late fall the Board of Trustees directed the administration to request proposals from architectural and engineering firms to develop a campus master plan that would include all property owned by the university, as well as property anticipated to be purchased. In January 2005 the university's Facilities Planning Committee began meeting to consider the best use of the west side of the campus, commercial redevelopment of parts of the east side, organization of the central part of the campus, neighborhood redevelopment and partnership opportunities, refinement of the proposed academic quadrangle, and prioritization of future expenditures. In February the university selected the firm of Shepley Bulfinch Richardson & Abbott of Boston, Massachusetts, and Michael Schuster Associates of Cincinnati to prepare the campus master plan. In full consultation with members of the university community, the group planned to submit its ideas to the Board of Trustees by the end of the year. (67)

The campaign preplanning that took place in the early years of Graham's tenure, including the feasibility study and hundreds of personal visits and cultivations conducted by the president and the development staff, under the leadership of Gary Massa, yielded encouraging signs. Annual Fund dollars during the first three years of the interim campaign, 2001 to 2004, increased from $4,979,470 to $5,780,113. Having recorded an unprecedented Annual Fund "Million Dollar Month" of $1,102,645 in December 2004, the university was well on its way toward another record-breaking Annual Fund year. From 2001 to 2005 the alumni participation rate increased from 21 percent to 25 percent. Moreover, after visits in December 2004 through the following January with a few potential donors during the early stages of the "quiet phase" of the new campaign, the Leadership Gifts Committee of the Board of Trustees estimated initial verbal pledges of the campaign totaling approximately $35,000,000. By February the new pledges and gifts amounted to approximately $85,000,000. These were hopeful indicators that the upcoming fund-raising drive would be successful.

The signature brick and mortar piece of the campaign was the proposed creation of the James E. Hoff, S.J., Academic Quadrangle, a fitting tribute to the university's late revered president. In addition to providing a new entryway to campus, possibly beginning at the intersection of Ledgewood and Dana Avenues and stretching from the McDonald Library to the Cintas Center, it included the construction of a teaching, learning, and research facility to centralize numerous academic resources and services and provide appropriate space for collaborative learning among the students, faculty, and other members of the community; the renovation of Alter Hall and the creation of state-of-the-art technology-equipped classrooms to improve the learning environment; and the revitalization of the McDonald Library to provide easy access to books and various forms of information as delivered in the 21st century. As a first step toward this goal, in March 2005 President Graham announced the sale of WVXU-FM to WGUC-FM in Cincinnati for $15 million. The university planned to use a major part of the proceeds to help support programs and services in the proposed Hoff Academic Quadrangle. Other anticipated capital projects were the building of a new Williams College of Business, largely made possible by a substantial gift from Stephen S. Smith, class of 1968, that would be unique in concept and invite the business community to actively engage with the students and faculty, and the construction of a new residence hall to further improve campus life and meet the growing demand for on-campus housing.

Reflecting approximately four years of study and planning, the objectives of the campaign, which would help make Xavier a more prominent national university, sought to enhance the learning environment in and out of the classroom by further improving core courses in the humanities and sciences; strengthening programs in honors, business, and the sciences; increasing use of new technologies; and providing more interdisciplinary and collaborative learning opportunities on and off campus. To further improve student life and activities the university also revitalized the O'Connor Sports Center. In March 2005 President Graham, with encouragement from the Board of Trustees, authorized its renovation, which was completed in time for the fall semester. The following spring the president established the Academic Quadrangle Steering Committee to oversee the programmatic planning for the proposed James E. Hoff Academic Quad.

Significantly, by 2011 the university also anticipates raising its national profile and increasing freshman applications by 30 percent to 7,000; growing the size of the first-year class by about 6 percent to 850 and the number of graduate, adult and part-time students by 300; increasing the amount generated through the annual fund to $10,000,000; and doubling the size of the endowment to $200,000,000. The latter goal is crucial for the university to fully realize its vision and strategic plan. More particularly, a substantially larger endowment will help provide more competitive student scholarship aid and the necessary resources to attract, retain, and develop world-class faculty. Its "growth," Graham wrote, "is the necessary safeguard that will allow Xavier to go on offering new programs, building the curriculum, and maintaining Xavier's overall excellence. Most important, it will allow us to provide an education to those who need it the most." (68)

During Graham's presidency alumni activities have grown in number and influence. In 2001 five new alumni chapters were formed bringing the total to 50. Alumni events and activities increased from 10 in 1993 to over 300 in 2004. Among the more than 67,000 alumni, over 25,000 are actively engaged in the national chapter network. Their activities range from National Xavier Nights, networking and continuing education, and community service to Xavier Communion Sunday and Atlantic 10 and NCAA basketball receptions. In the tradition of St. Ignatius of Loyola and Jesuit service, Xavier alumni, family, and friends continue to return to Xavier each year for a day of service, called the Crosstown Helpout. After gathering on campus, over 1,300 volunteers spend the day in community service at one of more than 20 sites in the metropolitan area doing work that includes cleaning, making repairs, and painting. (69)

CONCLUSION

The university has come a long way since its beginning as a small diocesan college on Sycamore Street in Cincinnati. The institution has remained true to its heritage and, like other Jesuit colleges and universities, has constantly sought to retain a universal vision, while adapting to the exigencies of American culture. Dedicated to "religion and liberal arts," as the inscription read over the door of the Athenaeum, the college in 1831 respected "the religious feelings and religious freedom of others" and made "every exertion to merit the patronage of a liberal and enlightened public." Nine years later, when the Diocese of Cincinnati turned over the Athenaeum to the Society of Jesus, St. Xavier College embodied both Catholicism and the humanist tradition. Through its *Ratio Studiorum*, the Jesuits' "Plan of Studies," the faculty placed a strong emphasis on the humanities, the arts, and the sciences. One hundred and seventy-five years after its founding, the university continues to affirm strongly its commitment to Catholic and Jesuit ideals, the endowment of Xavier's founders. Renowned for academic rigor and commitment to faith and justice, the university looks back on a proud tradition of service to its students and community and has high hopes for its future. Under President Graham's leadership, the institution has never been better positioned to reach unprecedented national academic distinction. This is Xavier University's finest hour.

EPILOGUE

Personal Reflections

In the fall of 2006 I will begin my 41st year as a member of the Xavier University community. I have seen Xavier grow in size, reputation, and influence. Not only has the face of the university changed dramatically, but so has the quality of the institution. Applications for admission continue at a volume that promises a more selective and diverse student body. The quality applicants for faculty positions are evidence of Xavier's growing reputation and attractiveness. The support and learning systems of the university—in academic affairs, in information resources, in mission and ministry, in student affairs, activities, and housing, and in administrative operations—function at an all-time high. Finances are sound, and Xavier's most ambitious comprehensive financial campaign is well on its way.

Not unlike the experience of earlier generations of alumni and friends visiting the newly-developed St. Xavier College campus in Avondale in the 1920s or encountering the campus in the wake of the construction of the 1960s, today's alumni and friends marvel at the most recent developments and the academic stature of the university. Just as earlier visionaries anticipated a "new life for old St. Xavier," this generation, as it makes plans for the proposed James E. Hoff, S.J., Academic Quadrangle and the overall redrawing of the campus's learning facilities, envisions a new life for Xavier University. Just as Elet and Albers Halls in the 1920s were markers pointing to a new Xavier, today's Cintas and Charles P. Gallagher Student Centers are windows to Xavier's future. They are wide windows, envisaging a fuller Xavier. Standing symbolically on the shoulders of those individuals who made Cintas and Gallagher Centers possible, and anticipating the support of others who will help Xavier grow during the next decade, the university is carving out a new academic landscape and a new destiny.

By continuing to educate to its mission, the university asserts that learning for learning's sake is not enough. As Xavier prepares students for specific careers, its mission affirms the belief that the most valuable and practical education is one that touches individuals directly and deeply, that helps characterize individuals at their finest as human beings. That is the essence of the university's core curriculum, Xavier's distinctive expression of its Jesuit identity. In addition to helping students expand their intellectual scope, develop useful skills, apply creative solutions to problems, understand and tolerate ambiguity, explore new ideas, acquire a more integral view of the world, and bring reason and faith into fruitful dialogue with one another, the core of studies invigorates and enriches students' pursuits of academic excellence in specific majors. From the beginning, Xavier has been fueled by these ideals. The university's core curriculum has always reflected the traditional "Jesuit education," and in keeping with the flexibility that is a trademark of that Jesuit education, each generation of faculty has enriched and adapted it to changing times.

A hallmark of Ignatian and Xavier pedagogy and spirituality is the phrase "cura personalis," "care for the person." The university fosters a climate that facilitates the development of the students' powers of intellectual, spiritual, and ethical discernment, and the connection of that discernment with action. In keeping with its Jesuit heritage, Xavier continues to provide students with an educational experience that will ultimately transform them. Today's generation of faculty, administrators, trustees, alumni, and friends rekindle the sentiments of St. Xavier College faculty in the early 1840s that the "culture of the heart and mind of youth constitutes the end of this institution." (1)

Xavier is increasingly becoming more inclusive and attentive to diversity, including race, religion, gender, ethnicity, and class. The Academic Vision Statement and various levels of planning accomplished during Graham's presidency invite the learning community not only to be more responsive to diversity issues, but to become more involved in society. Students look for more ways to connect with one another and with their communities. By continuing to integrate ethics, religion, and social values, along with peace and justice and diversity issues, in its core course of studies, the Xavier of tomorrow should continue to foster a core curriculum designed to liberate individuals, to enable them to become more self-aware, more self-governing, and more understanding of the humanity of others.

Xavier's primary navigation guide throughout its history has been the content of its mission as a Catholic and Jesuit university. Not wanting to repeat the secularizing and curricular histories of many of the great Protestant universities in the nineteenth and early twentieth centuries, Xavier rightfully remains concerned over preserving its ecclesial identity and academic purpose. Consistent with Vatican II, university members educate and prepare students for a world that is diverse in terms of culture, ethnicity, and religion. Xavier's fundamental Catholic character and identity means that religion is primary among its institutional values. Religion provides the moral foundation of our nation and our university. As Xavier expresses its Catholic identity through worship and practice, it also is open to the religious values of other traditions.

The university remains committed to developing competent, compassionate, and dedicated leaders. It provides a unique service to the Church and to society—its immediate neighbors, the metropolitan area, and the broader world—by being the best intellectual community that it can be. While exercising academic freedom to the fullest, it makes it possible for the variant lines of Catholic tradition and thought to intersect with all forms of human culture. Xavier's vision of Catholic social justice is rooted in the Scriptures and the Ignatian heritage.

Focused on its purpose and direction, Xavier continues to strengthen the connection between religious faith, core Jesuit ideals, and learning. In order to promote and safeguard its mission, the university has increasingly become a shared responsibility, cultivated and strengthened by a partnership of men and women, lay and religious. Through its mission-oriented Manresa programs, it introduces new faculty and staff to the Jesuit ethos of the institution, inviting them to continue to stretch themselves intellectually, to think and work across disciplines, and to participate more fully in the culture on campus. Along with its strong pastoral and liturgical life, Xavier supports Catholic and Jesuit scholarship by integrating religion, morality, spirituality, and ethics into the life of the institution. It keeps alive the Catholic intellectual tradition and relates Catholic social teaching to service and justice activities. There are a number of academic and divisional departments and programs in the university, such as theology, history, philosophy, english, economics, psychology, education, health services administration, nursing, campus ministry, Ignatian program, Manresa, peace and justice program, residence life, library, the Edward B. Brueggeman Center for Dialogue, the Ethics, Religion, and Society program, the Center for Business Ethics and Social Responsibility, Jesuit Fellowship Program, which fosters faculty research in the Jesuit and Catholic tradition, Gender and Diversity Studies, Catholicism and Culture minor, and the Ann Buenger Catholic Lecture Series, among others, that address Xavier's core values. No one thing affirms the university's Catholic and Jesuit identity. It is a combination of activities.

The distinctive place of the faculty in the life of the university is of primary importance. For Xavier to be true to its heritage and to fare well, it must never lose sight of what fundamentally is at its heart, namely "a community of inquiry grounded in the Catholic, Jesuit tradition dedicated to engaging and forming students intellectually, morally, and spiritually, with rigor and compassion, toward lives of solidarity, service, and success." The university's history is rich with the Jesuit ethic whereby the teacher establishes a personal relationship with students, listens to them, and draws them toward personal initiative and responsibility for learning. Consistent with the university's Academic Vision Statement and latest strategic plan, Xavier fosters a climate that welcomes interdisciplinary study and cross-divisional exploration in new areas. As the professionals in academic affairs, athletics, financial administration, information resources, mission and ministry, student development, and university relations continue to collaborate to achieve common goals, Xavier's overall learning environment is enriched.

Most importantly, through collaborative and shared governance, the faculty and administration play a central role in affirming the institution's mission and determining its well-being. What has become clearer, especially during the presidency of Michael J. Graham, S.J., is that collaborative governance is critical for the future of the university. It is essential (1) to help maintain the moral legitimacy and core values of the institution as a Catholic and Jesuit university; (2) to help sustain and nurture the university's academic culture; and (3) to promote greater effectiveness in the management of the institution. The president is the main symbol of the university, affirming through his commitment and leadership its mission and vision to the internal Xavier community and to the world at large. Guided by the exemplary role and leadership of the president, administrators work collaboratively with faculty and other professionals in advancing the goals of the institution. When governance is less shared, especially with the faculty, however, the institution becomes less academic and the moral legitimacy and core values of the institution are at risk. As the primary transmitters of the culture and ethos of the university, faculty members are often in the best position to sustain the tradition and mission of the university. They are the mainstay and catalyst of the institution. As administrators and faculty continue to work more closely, and both are afforded the opportunity to participate in the strategic planning and day-to-day operations of the university, there will be greater corporate identification with the mission of the institution.

Holding the university "in trust," the trustees continue to have a profound influence on Xavier. They hold a deep respect for its tradition and educational purpose. The laicization of the Board of Trustees in 1972 has proven invaluable in the recent developments of the university. Among the thirty-eight members on the board in 2005, eight are Jesuits. Three decades earlier the first six lay members relied on the Jesuit president and members of the religious community for guidance. Over time, as their membership and influence increased, lay trustees became more confident and assertive. The "new guardians" of Catholic and Jesuit higher education, as a contemporary has called them, proved essential participants in the continued advancement of the university to a higher level of teaching, scholarship, and service. Their phenomenal success as fund-raisers, especially since the late 1980s, made much of the progress possible. They realized that the vision of the institution could be accomplished only by more intense effort on their part, which included their own personal investment in Xavier and by encouraging others to help support the university's mission. (2)

Without the support of the trustees, alumni, and other friends of the university, Xavier would not be what it is today. The generous support of alumni and friends, so critical a century ago as St. Xavier College made plans for a new campus, is just as important today as the university seeks to fulfill its new destiny. What President Paul O'Connor observed in the late 1960s, at the end of the biggest building spurt in the history of the institution, is no less true today. "What we have today," he wrote, "is the result of sacrifice, of planning, of vision on the part of those who have gone before us. And from that we take the lesson that it is our responsibility as custodians of today to project these blessings into the future." (3)

As alumni in 1913 looked forward to the new Avondale campus, an officer of the Alumni Association expressed these sentiments: "Would it be too much to hope that in the not too distant future some Alumnus, wandering back from the East or West, . . . might take his stand upon one of the nearby hills and gaze with brightening eye and throbbing heart upon the different lecture halls and colleges that dot the spacious acres of St. Xavier University?" Similarly, over ninety years later in the midst of the development of a new campus master plan, it is not "too much to hope that in the not too distant future" alumni visiting the campus might "gaze with brightening eye and throbbing heart" at the new and more vibrant academic landscape. The university's future, one that my colleagues and I could never have imagined forty years ago, has never been more promising. (4)

NOTES

Abbreviations

AAC   Archives of the Archdiocese of Cincinnati
BT   Xavier University Board of Trustees Minutes
HC   St. Xavier College and Xavier University House Consultors Minutes
MJA   Midwest Jesuit Archives, St. Louis, Missouri
SXA   St. Xavier High School Archives
XUA   Xavier University Archives

Introduction

1. Alice Gallin, O.S,U., *Negotiating Identity: Catholic Higher Education Since 1960* (Notre Dame, Indiana, 2000), 127.
2. J. A. Appleyard, S.J., "The Secularization of the Modern American University," *Conversations* (Fall 1996), 31–33

Part I   The Formative Years of St. Xavier College, 1831–1910

Introduction

1. Roger L. Geiger, ed., *The American College in the Nineteenth Century* (Nashville, Tennessee, 2000), 2; James Findlay, "Agency, Denominations, and the Western Colleges, 1830–1860: Some Connections between Evangelicalism and American Higher Education" in Geiger, *The American College*, 115–116; Colin B. Burke, *American Collegiate Populations: A Test of the Traditional View* (New York, 1982), 15–17; Geiger, *The American College*, 132–133; David Potts, "American Colleges in the Nineteenth Century: From Localism to Denominationalism," *History of Education Quarterly 11* (1971): 363–79.
2. Colin Burke, *American Collegiate Populations*, 15–17. Geiger, *The American College*, 132–133; Findlay, "Agency, Denominations, and the Western College," 130; *Catalogue of St. Xavier College, 1890–1891*; *Catalogue of St. Xavier College, 1891–1892*.
3. Geiger, *The American College*, 138–139; See Edward J. Power, *A History of Catholic Higher Education in the United States* (Milwaukee, Wisconsin, 1958), 36–48.

4. Arthur M. Cohen, *The Shaping of American Higher Education: Emergence and Growth of the Contemporary System* (San Francisco, California, 1998), 56.
5. Gerald L. Gutek, *American Education 1945–2000: A History and Commentary* (Project Heights, Illinois, 2000), 9; Geiger, *The American College*, 128; Cohen, *Shaping of American Higher Education*, 103–105, 132.
6. *Woodstock Letters* (Woodstock, Md., 1872–1969), 18, 123.

Chapter 1 Founding of a College

1. Victor Francis O'Daniel, *The Right Rev. Edward Dominic Fenwick, O.P., Founder of the Dominicans in the United States, Pioneer Missionary in Kentucky, Apostle of Ohio, First Bishop of Cincinnati* (Washington, D.C. [1920]), 309, 315–316; Roger Fortin, *Faith and Action: A History of the Catholic Archdiocese of Cincinnati* (Columbus, Ohio, 2002), 23.
2. *U.S. Catholic Miscellany*, VII, 343; O'Daniel, *The Right Rev. Edward Dominic Fenwick,* 333; Fortin, *Faith and Action*, 15–16, 24.
3. Fortin, *Faith and Action*, 23, 30–31.
4. Quoted in Fortin, *Faith and Action*, 36.
5. Quoted in Gilbert J. Garraghan, *The Jesuits of the Middle United States* (New York, 1938), 3: 159; Fortin, *Faith and Action*, 36.
6. Quoted in Garraghan, *The Jesuits of the Middle United States*, 3: 159; Fortin, *Faith and Action*, 20.
7. Quoted in Fortin, *Faith and Action*, 43; *Xavier Athenaeum*, 5: 68–69; O'Daniel, *The Right Rev. Edward Dominic Fenwick,* New York: Frederick Puslet, 1920, p. 395; Christopher J. Lucas, *American Higher Education: A History* (New York, 1994), 126; Roger L. Geiger, ed., *The American College in the Nineteenth Century* (Nashville, Tennessee, 2000), 132; Colin B. Burke, *American Collegiate Populations: A Test of the Traditional View* (New York, 1982), 15–17; Francis Joseph Miller, "A History of the Athenaeum of Ohio, 1829–1960," (Ed.D. diss., University of Cincinnati, 1964), 58–59.
8. *Catholic Telegraph,* October 22, 1831; quoted in Garraghan, *The Jesuits of the Middle United States 3:* 160–162; Van de Velde's letter found in *Woodstock Letters (Woodstock, Md., 1872–1969), 10:* 121; *St. Xavier College, 1840–1849* folder, XUA; O'Daniel, *The Right Rev. Edward Dominic Fenwick,* 234–239, 392–393; Fortin, *Faith and Action,* 43; Geiger, *The American College,* 132.
9. *Catholic Telegraph,* October 22, 1831; quoted in Garraghan, *The Jesuits of the Middle United States 3:* 160–162; *Woodstock Letters, 10:* 121; *St. Xavier College, 1840–1849* folder, XUA; Fortin, *Faith and Action*, 43; Geiger, *The American College,* ch., p. 132.

10. Daniel Hurley, *Cincinnati, the Queen City* (Cincinnati, 1982), 57; Fortin, *Faith and Action*, 56–57.

11. *Catholic Telegraph*, October 22, 1831; April 10, 1832; John B. Foote, *The Schools of Cincinnati and Its Vicinity* (Cincinnati, 1855, reprint, 1970), 10, 122.

12. Garraghan, *The Jesuits of the Middle United States*, 3: 164–165; Foote, *The Schools of Cincinnati*, 122–123; *Catholic Almanac*, 1833, 71–73; Fortin, *Faith and Action*, 43–44; Miller, "History of the Athenaeum," 66.

13. Quoted in Fortin, *Faith and Action*, 45, 48.

14. Miller, "A History of the Athenaeum," 58–59.

15. Fortin, *Faith and Action*, 48–49, 59, 61–62; O'Daniel, *The Right Rev. Edward Dominic Fenwick*, 421; Garraghan, *The Jesuits of the Middle United States*, 3: 165.

16. Mullon to Purcell, July 28, 1833, AAC; Miller, "A History of the Athenaeum," 64.

17. Quoted in Miller, "A History of the Athenaeum," 66; Fortin, *Faith and Action*, 102; *Catholic Almanac*, 1833, pp. 72, 116.

18. Fortin, *Faith and Action*, 50; quoted in *Catholic Telegraph*, August 15, 1834; Garraghan, *The Jesuits of the Middle United States*, 3: 164.

19. Fortin, *Faith and Action*, 42, 101.

20. Fortin, *Faith and Action*, 102; see the March 13, 1835 issue of *Catholic Telegraph* for concern over potential local persecution.

21. Fortin, *Faith and Action*, 102–103, 107–108. Although nativism subsided somewhat in the late 1830s, it was revived in the 1840s. Increased Catholic immigration in the 1840s and 1850s stimulated anti-Catholic and anti-foreign sentiment.

22. Quoted in Anthony H. Deye, "Archbishop John Baptist Purcell, Pre-Civil War Years" (Ph.D. diss., University of Notre Dame, 1959), 140.

23. Quoted in Miller, "A History of the Athenaeum," 73, 75, 76–79; *Catholic Directory*, 1838.

24. Fortin, *Faith and Action*, 52–53, 60; *Catholic Telegraph*, May 16, October 31, 1840.

25. Reuben Gold Thwaites, ed., *The Jesuit Relations and Allied Documents*, 69 (New York, 1959), 183; *The Jesuit Bulletin*, February 1935, MJA; quoted in Garraghan, *The Jesuits of the Middle United States*, 3: 161–162; Fortin, *Faith and Action*, 30–31. The earliest recorded visit and effort by a Jesuit in the Cincinnati area occurred in 1749. In August of that year Joseph Pierre de Bonnecamps, professor of hydrography at the College of Quebec, joined an expedition down the Ohio River. At the time the French tried to reassert their claim to the Ohio valley. The group spent four days —August 28 to August 31—near the mouth of the Little Miami River. Though the effort was unsuccessful, Bonnecamps provided the first survey and drew up the first map of the area that was to become Cincinnati.

26. Garraghan, *The Jesuits of the Middle United States*, 3: 162.
27. *Woodstock Letters, 10:* 121–124.
28. Fortin, *Faith and Action*, 59, 61–62; Garraghan, *The Jesuits of the Middle United States*, 3: 165.
29. Quoted in Garraghan, *The Jesuits of the Middle United States*, 1: 55–78, 314–315, 489–490; 3: 165–166.
30. Quoted in Garraghan, *The Jesuits of the Middle United States*, 1: 489–490; 3: 166.
31. Verhaegen to Purcell, August 10, 1840, XUA.
32. Purcell to Verhaegen, August 17, 1840, XUA.
33. Purcell to Verhaegen, August 17, 1840, XUA; Deye, "Archbishop John Baptist Purcell," 222–223; *Catholic Telegraph*, June 12, 1890; Garraghan, *The Jesuits of the Middle United States*, 3: 167.
34. Purcell to Verhaegen, August 17, 1840, XUA; Garraghan, *The Jesuits of the Middle United States*, 3: 167–168.
35. Quoted in Garraghan, *The Jesuits of the Middle United States*, 3: 169.
36. Purcell to Verhaegen, August 17, 1840, XUA; Deye, "Archbishop John Baptist Purcell," 222–223; *Catholic Telegraph*, June 12, 1890; George E. Ganss, S.J., *The Jesuit Educational Tradition and Saint Louis University* (Institute of Jesuit Sources, 1969), 31–32.
37. Fortin, *Faith and Action*, 134; quoted in Garraghan, *The Jesuits of the Middle United States*, 3: 172; St. Xavier College deed in XUA.
38. Fortin, *Faith and Action*, 62–63; *Catholic Telegraph*, September 12, 1840.
39. Quoted in Garraghan, *The Jesuits of the Middle United States*, 3: 173; St. Xavier College, 1840–1849 folder, XUA. Jesuits in Kentucky opened the St. Ignatius Literary Institution in September 1842.
40. Quoted in Garraghan, *The Jesuits of the Middle United States*, 3: 166.
41. Garraghan, *The Jesuits of the Middle United States*, 3: 170–171. A scholastic was a Jesuit, not ordained, who was assigned to teach for a period of time after completing required courses in philosophy.
42. Quoted in Deye, "Archbishop John Baptist Purcell," 224–225; *Catholic Telegraph*, November 28, 1834.

Chapter 2   Jesuits Take Charge, 1840–1865

1. *Catholic Telegraph*, March 25, May 27, June 24, 1847; *U.S. Department of Interior, Report on the Social Statistics of Cities*, Part II, The Southern and Western States (Washington, 1887), 358; quoted in Roger Fortin, *Faith and Action: A History of the Catholic Archdiocese of Cincinnati, 1821–1996* (Columbus, Ohio, 2002), 65–66.
2. Fortin, *Faith and Action*, 66.
3. Patrick W. Carey, *The Roman Catholics* (Westport, Connecticut, 1993), 31, 35; Jay P. Dolan, *The American Catholic Experience: A History from*

Colonial Times to the Present (New York, 1985), 127, 161; *Catholic Telegraph*, June 1, 22, August 10, 24, 31, September 7, 1848; Fortin, *Faith and Action*, 56, 77.

4. Quoted in Gilbert J. Garraghan, *The Jesuits of the Middle United States* (New York, 1938), 1: 513.

5. St. Xavier College 1840 Ledger Book, XUA; the first prospectus was subsequently printed in the first college catalogue, *Calendar of St. Xavier College, 1841–1842*; Vincent T. O'Keefe, S.J., "Who Owns Jesuit Colleges and Universities," *Conversations* (February 1992), 15–17.

6. George E. Ganss, S.J., *St. Ignatius' Idea of a Jesuit University* (Milwaukee, 1956), 25–29; George E. Ganss, S.J., *The Jesuit Educational Tradition and Saint Louis University* (Institute of Jesuit Sources, 1969), 3, 7–8.

7. Ganss, *Jesuit Educational Tradition*, 3–5, 23.

8. J. A. Burns, C.S.C., *A History of Catholic Education in the United States* (New York, 1937), 237; *Calendar of St. Xavier College, 1841–1842*; *Calendar of St. Xavier College, 1842–1843*; Anthony J. Kuzniewski, S.J., *Thy Honored Name: A History of The College of the Holy Cross, 1843–1994* (Washington, D.C., 1999), 38–39; Frederick Rudolph, *The American College and University: A History* (New York, 1962), 25–26; Arthur M. Cohen, *The Shaping of American Higher Education: Emergence and Growth of the Contemporary System* (San Francisco, 1998), 75; Roger L. Geiger, ed., *The American College in the Nineteenth Century* (Nashville, Tenn., 2000), 139. St. Xavier College, like most colleges in antebellum America, was not large enough to offer specialized academic departments exclusively. Chemistry, mathematics, and natural philosophy were taught in most of the institutions, but anyone skilled in any branch of science usually would also teach the other branches.

9. *Catholic Telegraph*, July 7, 1855; *Catalogue of St. Xavier College, 1854–55, 1855–56*; Garraghan, *The Jesuits of the Middle United States*, 3: 120; Robert F. Harvanek, S.J., "Jesuit Education and Its Contemporary Focus," *Loyola University Phoenix* (November 10, 1978), 7–8; Christopher J. Lucas, *American Higher Education: A History* (New York, 1994), 132; Rudolph, *The American College and University*, 134; Cohen, *Shaping of American Higher Education*, 76–77, 81.

10. *Catholic Telegraph*, January 9, 1841; the advertisement was dated December 26, 1840.

11. *Catalogue of St. Xavier College, 1869–1870*; Geiger, *The American College*, 141; Rudolph, *The American College and University*, 113–114.

12. *Woodstock Letters* (Woodstock, Md., 1872–1969), 5: 117–118; Garraghan, *The Jesuits of the Middle United States*, 3: 174; *Catholic Telegraph*, December 12, 1840; *The Calendar of the St. Xavier College, 1841–1842*, XUA.

13. *Catholic Telegraph*, September 26, 1840; *Calendar of St. Xavier College, 1841–1842*, XUA; James Findlay, "Agency, Denominations, and the Western Colleges, 1830–1860: Some Connections between Evangelicalism and American Higher Education" in Geiger, *The American College*, 117.

14. *Calendar of the St. Xavier College, 1841–1842*; *Catalogue of St. Xavier College, 1849–1850*, XUA; *Woodstock Letters*, 5: 117.

15. *Calendar of St. Xavier College, 1841–42*; *Catalogue of St. Xavier College, 1845–1846*; *Catalogue of St. Xavier College, 1849–1850*, XUA; *Woodstock Letters*, 5: 117.

16. Garraghan, *The Jesuits of the Middle United States*, 3: 174; *Catholic Telegraph*, December 12, 1840; February 27, 1841?.

17. Minutes of Philopedian Society, January 19, 1941, XUA; *Calendar of St. Xavier College, 1842–1843*, XUA. Other charter members of the Philopedian Society were William Armstrong, Samuel Black, Thomas Burts, Edward Conway, Andrew Francisco, John Goodin, George Guilford, William Hart, and Timothy O'Connor; Sheldon Rothblatt; *The Modern University and Its Discontents: The Fate of Newman's Legacies in Britain and America* (Cambridge, Mass., 1997), 160; Rudolph, *The American College and University*, 137.

18. Minutes of Philopedian Society, January 19, 1841, XUA; *Calendar of St. Xavier College, 1842–43*, XUA; *Catholic Telegraph*, May 6, 1847; Lucas, *American Higher Education*, 130.

19. *Catholic Telegraph*, February 27, 1841.

20. Quoted in Garraghan, *The Jesuits of the Middle United States*, 3: 113–114.

21. Quoted in Garraghan, *The Jesuits of the Middle United States*, 3: 170–172; St. Xavier College deed in XUA.

22. BT, March 5, May 9, 1842, XUA; *Catalogue of St. Xavier College, 1898–1899*, XUA; Cohen, *Shaping of American Higher Education*, 84.

23. The trustees first met to organize the board on May 9, 1842; BT, May 9, 16, June 1, 1842, XUA. The Jesuits Louis M. Pin and J. Y. Gleizal and the bishop's brother, Edward Purcell, served as trustees. *Calendar of St. Xavier College, 1841–1842, 1843–184*, XUA. By 1880 there were still seven members.

24. *Calendar of St. Xavier College, 1841–42*; *Catalogue of St. Xavier College, 1864–1865*, XUA; Garraghan, *The Jesuits of the Middle United States*, 3: 175; *The Collegian*, April 1887, XUA.

25. *Calendar of St. Xavier College, 1841–1842*; *Catalogue of St. Xavier College, 1845–1846*, XUA; Julie Ann Bubolz, "College As It Was in the Mid–Nineteenth Century" in Geiger, *The American College*, 83.

26. Garraghan, *The Jesuits of the Middle United States*, 3: 120, 175; *Catholic Telegraph*, February 27, 1841; *Calendar of St. Xavier College,*

1841–1842, 1842–43; Catalogue of St. Xavier College, 1867–1868, XUA; Cohen, *Shaping of American Higher Education*, 68.

27. James J. O'Meara's Diary, 1865, XUA.

28. *Calendar of St. Xavier College, 1841–1842; Calendar of St. Xavier College, 1842–1843*, XUA.

29. *Calendar of St. Xavier College, 1843–44; Catalogue of St. Xavier College, 1849–1850*, XUA; *Xavier University News*, November 1, 1922, XUA.

30. A Sketch of Xavier University, Ms, SXA; Garraghan, *The Jesuits of the Middle United States*, 3: 176, cites *Catholic Telegraph*, May 6, 1847.

31. BT, June 12, 1842, XUA; *Calendar of St. Xavier College, 1842–1843; Catalogue of St. Xavier College, 1849–50; Catalogue of St. Xavier College, 1848–1849*, XUA; also formed in 1847 was the Cosmopeon Society, which consisted of students who belonged to the lower-junior classes and looked to the "qualifying of its members for entering the higher Societies."

32. Charles Cist, *Cincinnati in 1841*(Cincinnati, 1841), 118; *Calendar of St. Xavier College, 1843–1844; Catalogue of St. Xavier College, 1858–1859*, XUA; in 1845–1846, it is referred to as catalogue; *Xavier University News*, December 22, 1922, XUA; *Catholic Telegraph*, February 3, 1844; *Cincinnati Gazette*, February 1, 1844; Colin B. Burke, *American Collegiate Populations: A Test of the Traditional View* (New York, 1982), 47–48; The first mention of a librarian appeared in the *St. Xavier College Catalogue, 1894–1895*, XUA; Cohen, *Shaping of American Higher Education*, 91; HC, November 4, 1897, XUA. The museum specimens in the first 25 years were largely collected by the Jesuit scholastic, John Baptist Duerinck. In 1897 St. Xavier College made "the students' library a 'Free Library.'"

33. *The Catholic Calendar and Laity's Directory, 1841*; Lloyd D. Easton, *Hegel's First American Followers: The Ohio Hegelians* (Athens; Ohio, 1966), 44; John Bernhard Stallo, *The Concepts and Theories of Modern Physics*, ed. Percy W. Bridgman (Cambridge, Mass.,1960), viii; Garraghan, *The Jesuits of the Middle United States*, 3: 184.

34. *Catholic Telegraph*, September 2, 1847; *Catalogue of St. Xavier College, 1846–1847*, XUA; Garraghan, *The Jesuits of the Middle United States*, 3: 195.

35. BT, July 6, 1846; July 20, 1847, XUA; Garraghan, *The Jesuits of the Middle United States*, 3: 179; St. Xavier College, 1840–1849 folder, XUA.

36. *Woodstock Letters*, 5: 121–123; *The Collegian*, April 1887, XUA; St. Xavier College, 1840–1849 folder, XUA; *Catholic Telegraph*, September 2, 1847; August 31, 1848; February 3, 1849; *Calendar of St. Xavier College, 1843–44; Catalogue of St. Xavier College, 1846–1847*, XUA;

Catholic Almanac, 1849; Garraghan, *The Jesuits of the Middle United States*, 3: 195.

37. Garraghan, *The Jesuits of the Middle United States*, 3: 180, 193; *Catholic Telegraph*, August 31, 1848; *Catalogue of St. Xavier College, 1847–48*; *Catalogue of St. Xavier College, 1848–1849*, XUA.

38. Diary of Julius Johnston, S.J., 1850–1851, XUA; the College sold the mansion property on April 30, 1873, for $89,229.03, nearly thirteen thousand dollars an acre. Garraghan, *The Jesuits of the Middle United States*, 3: 180, 195; St. Xavier College, 1840–1849 folder, XUA; O'Meara's Diary, 1865, XUA; *Catalogue of St. Xavier College, 1849–1850*; *Catalogue of St. Xavier College, 1898–1899*; *Xavier University News*, May 25, 1956, XUA. Julius Johnston's personal diary began on October 1, 1850, and continued to June 8, 1851.

39. *Catholic Telegraph*, June 14, 28, July 5, 12, 1849; "Holy Mary" Students' Vow, June 27, 1849, XUA; *Catalogue of St. Xavier College, 1848–1849*, XUA; O'Leary alludes to Robert E. Manning, S.J., "Vignettes of Xavier," *Xavier University News*, April 12, 1940.

40. *Catalogue of St. Xavier College, 1849–50*; *Catalogue of St. Xavier College, 1850–51*; *Xavier University News*, May 25, 1956, XUA; Diary of Julius Johnston, 1850–1851, XUA; *Woodstock Letters*, 5: 121–123; *The Collegian*, April 1887, XUA. In the summer of 1852 Brother William Hayes was also a victim. Garraghan, *The Jesuits of the Middle United States*, 3: 188–189, 192.

41. *Calendar of St. Xavier College, 1841–1842*; *Catalogue of St. Xavier College, 1861–1862*, XUA; Fortin, *Faith and Action*, 77–80, 86–91; Garraghan, *The Jesuits of the Middle United States*, 3: 176–177.

42. Mrs. William J. Cummins, "Genealogy Department," *Cincinnati Historical Society Bulletin*, 24, 4 (October 1966): 343–344; *Catalogue of St. Xavier College, 1847–1848*; *Catalogue of St. Xavier College, 1848–1849*; *Catalogue of St. Xavier College, 1850–1851*; *Catalogue of St. Xavier College, 1898–1899*, XUA.

43. *Catalogue of St. Xavier College, 1848–1849*; *Catalogue of St. Xavier College, 1850–1851*; *Catalogue of St. Xavier College, 1851–1852*, XUA; 1850 Census, *Cincinnati Historical Society Bulletin*, 24, 4 (October 1966).

44. *Catalogue of St. Xavier College, 1841–1842; 1848–1849; 1849–1850*, XUA; Garraghan, *The Jesuits of the Middle United States*, 3: 176–177; *Woodstock Letters*, 5: 118.

45. Garraghan, *The Jesuits of the Middle United States*, 3: 506; Cummins, "Geneaology Department," 342–344.

46. "Biblical" Letter of Augustine L. Helm, "Alumni Notes," *The Xavier Athenaeum 4*, 2 (February 1916): 88, XUA; *Memorials of [Provincial] Visitations*, XJA, March 11, 1845; March 7, 1850; June 22, 1851; Fortin, *Faith and Action*, 96.

47. Quoted in Garraghan, *The Jesuits of the Middle United States*, 3: 177. According to Garraghan, in 1856 the hundred or so day students registered were all, with a single exception, Catholic..

48. Garraghan, *The Jesuits of the Middle United States*, 3: 121, cites Jesuit leadership's wish for only one boarding school in the province; Fortin, *Faith and Action*, 108–110.

49. John Quincy Adams, "An Oration Delivered Before the Cincinnati Astronomical Society, on the occasion of laying the cornerstone of an astronomical observatory, on the 10th of November, 1843," (Cincinnati, 1843), 54–56; *Catholic Telegraph*, November 17, 1843.

50. Fortin, *Faith and Action*, 107–110; "Popery in the United States," *Christian Observer*, September 1847.

51. Fortin, *Faith and Action*, 114–116; "Years of Struggle," *The Xavier Athenaeum 4*, 3 (April 1916), p. 116; *Historia Domus* (House History, St. Xavier College), 1854.

52. Quoted in *Catholic Telegraph*, September 23, 1854; Fortin, *Faith and Action*, 110.

53. Fortin, *Faith and Action*, 154–155; *Catholic Almanac*, 1843, 1844, 1845; Donald Middendorf, "Xavier Celebrates 106th Anniversary," *Xavier University News*, October 21, 1937, XUA; Father Nota also appears for the first time in a St. Xavier College Catalogue in 1845–1846; Garraghan, *The Jesuits of the Middle United States*, 1, 504; 3: 178.

54. Fortin, *Faith and Action*, 154–155; Edmund M. Hussey, *A History of the Seminaries of the Archdiocese of Cincinnati 1829–1979* (Norwood, Ohio, 1979), 11–13; Garraghan, *The Jesuits of the Middle United States*, 3: 178–179.

55. Garraghan, *The Jesuits of the Middle United States*, 3: 172, 178–179; Elet to Purcell, [n.d.] 1847, AAC.

56. Garraghan, *The Jesuits of the Middle United States*, 3: 185–186 cites *Catholic Telegraph* (c. 1846)

57. Quoted in Garraghan, *The Jesuits of the Middle United States*, 3: 186.

58. Garraghan, *The Jesuits of the Middle United States*, 3: 187–188; *Catholic Almanac*, 1848; *Catholic Telegraph*, February 1841; June 26, 1845; April 21, 1869; *Litterae Annuae*, 1842–1849, XUA; *Clerus Cincinnatensis: A Directory of Clergy and Parishes of the Archdiocese of Cincinnati, 1821 to 1996* (Cincinnati, 1996), 52.

59. Fortin, *Faith and Action*, 73; BT, September 1849, XUA; quoted in Garraghan, *The Jesuits of the Middle United States*, 3: 201.

60. Fortin, *Faith and Action*, 135–136.

61. Garraghan, *The Jesuits of the Middle United States*, 3: 198; Fortin, *Faith and Action*, 91; *The Daily Times*, March 1, 1860; *Catholic Telegraph*, April 13, 1862.

62. Quoted in Garraghan, *The Jesuits of the Middle United States*, 3: 184, cites in footnote 47; Elet to Purcell, c. 1845, Archives of Mt. Joseph-on-the-Ohio.

63. Anthony H. Deye, "Archbishop John Baptist Purcell, Pre-Civil War Years" (Ph.D. diss., University of Notre Dame, 1959), 330; Fortin, *Faith and Action*, 150; Garraghan, *The Jesuits of the Middle United States*, 3: 185; Van de Velde to Purcell, June 2, 1848, AAC; Mary Agnes McCann, "Archbishop Purcell and the Archdiocese of Cincinnati" (Ph.D. diss., Catholic University of America, 1918), 53.

64. Fortin, *Faith and Action*, 113, 115; Garraghan, *The Jesuits of the Middle United States*, 3: 181; *Catholic Telegraph*, July 29, 1849; *Catholic Almanac*, 1849, 153.

65. Garraghan, *The Jesuits of the Middle United States*, 3: 183; BT, July 13, 1848, XUA; Elet to Purcell, June 26, 1848, AAC. DeBlieck later served as president of St. Joseph's College in Bardstown and St. Ignatius College in Chicago.

66. Garraghan, *The Jesuits of the Middle United States*, 3: 192–193; Henry F. Brownson, *Orestes A. Brownson's Latter Life: From 1856 to 1876* (Detroit, 1900), 139.

67. Garraghan, *The Jesuits of the Middle United States*, 3: 193, 255; *The Collegian*, April 1887, XUA; HC, May 12, 1885, XUA.

68. Quoted in Garraghan, *The Jesuits of the Middle United States*, 1, 138; 3: 193–195.

69. Garraghan, *The Jesuits of the Middle United States*, 3: Garraghan, 196; Holy Cross, pp. 37–38; Bledstein, *Culture of Professionalism*, 242; Lucas, *American Higher Education*, 128.

70. Garraghan, *The Jesuits of the Middle United States*, 3: 196; Kuzniewski, *Holy Cross*, 37–38; Burton J. Bledstein, *The Culture of Professionalism: The Middle Class and the Development of Higher Education in America* (New York, 1978), 242; Lucas, 128.

71. Quoted in Garraghan, *The Jesuits of the Middle United States*, 3: 196–197; *Catholic Telegraph*, September 9, 1854; St. Xavier College, 1850–1859 folder, XUA; *Woodstock Letters*, 5: 189; *Catalogue of St. Xavier College, 1853–1854*, XUA; BT, March 5, May 9, 1842, XUA.

72. *Catholic Telegraph*, July 7, 1855; June 5, 1856.

73. William S. Murphy to _____, March 17, 1855, Midwest Jesuit Archives; Garraghan, *The Jesuits of the Middle United States*, 3: 197–198.

74. Quoted in Garraghan, *The Jesuits of the Middle United States*, 3: 197–198, cites DeSmet to Duerinck, October 1855.

75. St. Xavier College, 1840–1849 folder; September 12, 1856–July 16, 1861 folder, XUA; Garraghan, *The Jesuits of the Middle United States*, 3: 198; *Woodstock Letters*, 16: 316.

76. Garraghan, *The Jesuits of the Middle United States*, 3: 198–199, cites De Smet to Oakley, January 14, 1857; De Smet to Beckx, June 1, 1858;

Rudolph, *American College and University*, 219; *Catalogue of St. Xavier College, 1898–1899*, XUA.

77. Garraghan, *The Jesuits of the Middle United States*, 3: 200, cites Keller to Beckx, January 19, 1854; quoted in *Catholic Telegraph*, July 7, 1860.

78. Quoted in Garraghan, *The Jesuits of the Middle United States*, 3: 120, 124; *Catalogue of St. Xavier College, 1869–1870*, XUA.

79. Garraghan, *The Jesuits of the Middle United States*, 3: 197; Hussey, *Seminaries*, 19; Fortin, *Faith and Action*, 147; Geiger, *The American College*, 145, 152; Rudolph, *American College and University*, 219; Raymond Walters, *A Historical Sketch of the University of Cincinnati* (Cincinnati, 1940), 16.

80. *Catalogue of St. Xavier College, 1860–1861*; *Catalogue of St. Xavier College, 1861–1862*, XUA. The four lay faculty members were H. Brusselbach, H. Gerold, A. Picket, and D. Donovan.

81. BT, July 15, 1861, XUA; Garraghan, *The Jesuits of the Middle United States*, 3: 200, cites Schultz to Beckx, c. 1861 (AA); Ferdinand Coosemans, first provincial of Missouri, pointed out to the general that Schultz had made a great personal sacrifice in accepting the presidency at St. Xavier College. His passion was in his missionary work with the Native Americans.

82. Quoted in Garraghan, *The Jesuits of the Middle United States*, 2: 156–157.

83. *St. Xavier College Catalogue, 1861–1862*, XUA.

84. M. P. Dowling S.J., "The Jesuits in Cincinnati," *Woodstock Letters*, 5: 195; Garraghan, *The Jesuits of the Middle United States*, III, 200–201; Diary of the Prefect of Studies, SXA; G. Wallace Chessman, *Ohio Colleges and the Civil War* (Columbus, Ohio, 1963), 13; *Catalogue of St. Xavier College, 1864–1865*, XUA.

85. Rocky, J. L., et. al., *History of Clermont County, Ohio, 1795–1880* (Philadelphia, 1880), 238; *Catholic Telegraph*, September10, 13, 1862; Diary of the Prefect of Studies, September 2, October 6, 1862, SXA.

86. *Catalogue of St. Xavier College, 1863–1864*, XUA; *Woodstock Letters*, 5: 119–120; *Historia Domus*, 1863–1864, XUA; Eugene C. Murdock, "The Bounty System in Cincinnati," *Bulletin of the Cincinnati Historical Society*, 24, 4 (October 1966): 279–301; The Jesuits drafted were John DeBlieck, John Kuhlman, and James Halpin.

87. *Historia Domus*, 1862–1863, XUA; Fortin, *Faith and Action*, 144–145.

88. *Catalogue of St. Xavier College, 1858–1859*, XUA; O'Meara's Diary, 1865, XUA.

Chapter 3   A More Secure St. Xavier College, 1865–1911

1. *Catalogue of St. Xavier College, 1865–1866*, XUA; Gilbert J. Garraghan, *The Jesuits of the Middle United States* (New York, 1938), 3: 202.

2. *Woodstock Letters* (Woodstock, Md., 1872–1969), 5: 116–177; James J. O'Meara's Diary, 1865, XUA; *Catalogue of St. Xavier College, 1867–1868*, XUA; F. Moeller, S.J., "Xavier University History and Remembrances," (unpublished ms. [n.d.], XUA; *Catholic Telegraph*, Centenary Edition, 1931.

3. O'Meara's Diary, 1870, XUA; Garraghan, *The Jesuits of the Middle United States*, 3, 201–202.

4. *Catalogue of St. Xavier College, 1867–1868*; *Catalogue of St. Xavier College, 1898–1899*, XUA.

5. *Catholic Telegraph*, May, 1867; O'Meara's Diary, 1867, XUA; *Catalogue of St. Xavier College, 1867–1868*, XUA; *Catholic Telegraph*, Centenary Edition, 1931.

6. *Catalogue of St. Xavier College, 1867–1868*; *Catalogue of St. Xavier College, 1920–21*, XUA; quoted in O'Meara Diary, 1870, XUA.

7. F. Moeller, "History and Remembrances," XUA; *Xavier University News*, October 21, 1937, XUA.

8. BT, May 20, 31, 1869; August 20, 1877, XUA; *Catalogue of St. Xavier College, 1868–1869*, XUA. On June 4th a copy of a resolution entitled 'an Act to Provide for the incorporation of St. Xavier College' was sent by Hill and J. A. M. Fastre, S.J., secretary of St. Xavier College (both acting for the Board of Trustees) to the Secretary of State of Ohio, who accepted the resolution on June 5. Letters of Incorporation of St. Xavier College, XUA; Act of the Legislature of the State of Ohio, "To Provide for the Incorporation of St. Xavier College," May 5, 1869, XUA; Vincent T. O'Keefe, S.J., Who Owns Jesuit Colleges and Universities? (*Conversations*, February 1992), 15–17; Donald P. Gavin, *John Carroll University: A Century of Service* (Kent, Ohio, 1985), 40.

9. Roger Fortin, *Faith and Action: A History of the Catholic Archdiocese of Cincinnati, 1821–1996* (Columbus, Ohio, 2002), 150; *Catalogue of St. Xavier College, 1898–1899*, XUA; Raymond Walters, *Historical Sketch of the University of Cincinnati* (Cincinnati, 1940), 15–21.

10. BT, April 10, 19, 1872; February 26, 1873, XUA; *Woodstock Letters*, 3: 76; *Catalogue of St. Xavier College, 1873–1874*; *Catalogue of St. Xavier College, 1898–1899*, XUA.

11. BT, September 19, 1876, XUA; *Catalogue of St. Xavier College, 1876–1877*, XUA; HC, February 23, 1888; August 31, 1949, XUA, The first recorded minutes of the House Consultation are dated September 16, 1881. The consultors were the Jesuits Tracy, Driscoll, DeBlieck, and Bosche. Bosche was secretary. House Consultation minutes were written from September 16, 1881, to August 31, 1949, at which time the minutes read: "At this point it is the wish of Fr. Rector (James F. Maguire) to discontinue writing reports of consultors. They will be *typed* and saved."

12. Minister's Diary, June 22, 1876, XUA; *Woodstock Letters*, 5: 120; O'Meara's Diary, 1876–1879, MJA.

13. *Historia Domus*, May 21, 1898; April 12, 1901, XUA; Minister's Diary, June 22, 1876, XUA; *Woodstock Letters*, 5: 120; O'Meara's Diary, 1876–1879, MJA; *The Collegian*, April 1887, XUA; HC, February 10, 1897, XUA.

14. Minister's Diary, November 7, 1885, XUA; BT, January 28, February 20, 1884; April 14, May 15, July 2, 1885, XUA; *Catalogue of St. Xavier College, 1898–1899*, XUA. Patrick Poland donated $1000 "towards the completion of the new classroom building." *Catalogue of St. Xavier College, 1898–1899*, XUA; HC, January 28, February 20, 1884; March 5, May 12, 30, 1885, XUA; *Xavier University News*, October 21, 1937, XUA. The Moeller Building extended seventy-six feet westward along Seventh Street and was forty feet wide,

15. *Catalogue of St. Xavier College, 1867–1868*, XUA; BT, September 16, 1869, XUA.

16. *Catalogue of St. Xavier College, 1865–1866*; *Catalogue of St. Xavier College, 1869–1870*; *Catalogue of St. Xavier College, 1871–1872*; *Catalogue of St. Xavier College, 1874–1875*; *Catalogue of St. Xavier College, 1888–1889*, XUA; Diary of the Prefect of Studies, October 19, 1869, SXA; O'Meara's Diary, 1870, XUA.

17. O'Meara's Diary, 1870, XUA; Diary of the Prefect of Studies, October 19, 1869, SXA.

18. *Calendar of St. Xavier College, 1841–1842*; *Catalogue of St. Xavier College, 1867–1868*; *Catalogue of St. Xavier College, 1868–1869*; *Catalogue of St. Xavier College, 1879–1880*, XUA; Minister's Diary, October 6, 1871, XUA.

19. Minister's Diary, November 25, 26, 28, 1870, XUA; O'Meara's Diary, 1871, XUA.

20. *Catalogue of St. Xavier College, 1868–1869*, XUA; Sadlier's *Catholic Almanac*, 1878, XUA; HC, August 1, 1882, March 29, August 6, 1883, XUA; BT, September 1, 1894, XUA; Minister's Diary, December 6, 23, 1871, XUA; O'Meara's Diary, 1870, XUA; *The Official Catholic Directory*, 1911; Memorial Visitation, March 14, 1890, MJA.

21. Minister's Diary, December 6, 23, 1871, XUA; O'Meara's Diary, 1870, XUA; Garraghan, *The Jesuits of the Middle United States*, 3, 426; Frederick Rudolph, *The American College and University* (New York, 1962), 288.

22. BT, October 12, 1874, January 3, 1879, August 14, 1879, XUA; Manning Folder, XUA; Minister's Diary, January 1, 11, August 13, 1879, XUA. During Meyer's term, there were new programs, such as the special evening lectures for alumni. He also got the roof repaired on the Athenaeum building. Meyer went to St. Louis University in the summer

of 1881. He would later serve as president of Marquette University, provincial of the Missouri province, and assistant to the general of the Society of Jesus in Rome for English-speaking provinces.

23. BT, August 20, 1881, August 25, 1884, January 27, 1886, XUA; HC, January 27, 1886, XUA; O'Meara's Diary, 1881, XUA; Garraghan, *The Jesuits of the Middle United States*, 3, 432. Shortly after President Coghlan took office he ordered a set of bells for the church tower, which were installed during Holy Week in preparation for Easter Sunday.

24. BT, May 12, 13, 1870, XUA; Minister's Diary, May 20, 1870; November 11, 1872, XUA; O'Meara's Diary, 1867, 1871, XUA.

25. O'Meara's Diary, 1884, XUA; *Woodstock Letters*, 7: 48–52; *Catalogue of St. Xavier College, 1876–1877*; *Catalogue of St. Xavier College, 1877–1878*, XUA; HC, June 21, 1886, XUA; Thomas F. Maher, "The Reveries of an Alumnus," *The St. Xavier Fair News*, January 5, 1895, XUA; Roger L. Geiger, ed, *The American College in the Nineteenth Century* (Nashville, Tenn., 2000), 146, 148.

26. Henry A. and Kate B. Ford, *History of Cincinnati, Ohio* (Cleveland, 1881), 532.

27. O'Meara's Diary, 1870, XUA; *Catalogue of St. Xavier College, 1886–1887*, XUA; HC, September 29, 1903, XUA.

28. *Catholic Telegraph*, January 7, 1886; May 19, 1887; *Woodstock Letters*, 16: 209–210; Garraghan, *The Jesuits of the Middle United States*, 3, 425.

29. *The Collegian*, April 1887, XUA.

30. *The Collegian*, April, May, June, July, August, September, 1887, XUA; HC, January 9, 1885, XUA.

31. *Catholic Telegraph*, July 5, 1887.

32. O'Meara Diary, 1911, XUA; Garraghan, *The Jesuits of the Middle United States*, 3, 447; HC, June 2, 1912, XUA; *Catalogue of St. Xavier College, 1876–1877*; *St. Xavier College Catalogue, 1883–1884; Catalogue of St. Xavier College, 1897–98*; *Catalogue of St. Xavier College, 1920–21*, XUA; Arthur M. Cohen, *The Shaping of American Higher Education: Emergence and Growth of the Contemporary System* (San Francisco, 1998), 109.

33. Geiger, *The American College*, 146, 148, 267–268; *Catalogue of St. Xavier College, 1890–1891*; *Catalogue of St. Xavier College, 1891–1892*; *Catalogue of St. Xavier College, 1904–1905*; *Catalogue of St. Xavier College, 1908–1909*, XUA.

34. Students in the Colleges of the Missouri Province, October 1, 1903, XUA.

35. *Catalogue of St. Xavier College, 1906–1907*, XUA; Provincial to Grimmelsman, July 25, 1910, XUA; HC, December 29, 1911; April 17, 1913, XUA; Frederick Rudolph, *The American College and University: A History* (New York, 1962), 294; *Xavier Alumnus*, January 1969, XUA.

36. Peter Dobkin Hall, "Noah Porter Writ Large?: Reflections on the Modernization of American Higher Education" in Geiger, *The American College*, 264; Rudolph, *American College and University*, 244, 277; Christopher J. Lucas, *American Higher Education: A History* (New York, 1994), 153.

37. Quoted in Charles F. Donovan, S.J., David R. Dunigan, S.J., Paul A. Fitzgerald, S.J., *History of Boston College: From the Beginnings to 1990* (Chestnut Hills, Massachusetts, 1990), 108–109; Rudolph, *American College and University*, 255, 290; Lucas, *American Higher Education*, 165–167, 210. The main spokesman in post-Civil War America for the traditional curriculum was Noah Porter, president of Yale University. He doubtlessly affirmed the thinking of the Jesuits at St. Xavier College when he wrote in 1878 in his classic, *The American Colleges and the American Public*, that the college course was "preeminently designed to give power to acquire and to think, rather than to impart special knowledge."

38. O'Meara's Diary, 1882, XUA; Fortin, *Faith and Action*, 91–92; HC, April 17, 1882, February 1, 1883, XUA; *Catholic Telegraph*, July 12, 1883.

39. O'Meara's Diary, 1865, XUA; *Clerus Cincinnatensis: A Directory of the Clergy and Parishes of the Archdiocese of Cincinnati, 1821 to 1996* (Cincinnati, 1996), 76; Fortin, *Faith and Action*, 145–146. *The Collegian*, April 1887, XUA.

40. O'Meara's Diary, 1865, XUA; *Clerus Cincinnatensis*, 76; Fortin, *Faith and Action*, 145–146. On December 20, 1868, property was acquired on the east side of Sycamore Street between Fifth and Sixth Streets for the St. Xavier Parish school.

41. BT, January 7, 1873, XUA; O'Meara's Diary, 1865, XUA; HC, March 5, 1885; November 10, 1887, XUA; *Litterae Annuae*, June 1909, XUA; In 1938 St. Ann Parish was united with St. Edward's Parish on Clark Street. It closed in 1965. *Clerus Cincinnatensis*, 76; Fortin, *Faith and Action*, 145–146.

42. *Catholic Telegraph*, July 9, 1931 for general information; Garraghan, *The Jesuits of the Middle United States*, 1, 577–579; BT, February 26, 1873, XUA.

43. Fortin, *Faith and Action*, 152.

44. Fortin, *Faith and Action*, 152.

45. M. Edmund Hussey, "The 1878 Financial Failure of Archbishop Purcell," *The Cincinnati Historical Society Bulletin* 36 (Spring 1978): 16; *Catholic Telegraph*, December 26, 1878; Fortin, *Faith and Action*, 152–153; Minister's Diary, December 18, 1878; January 1, 1879, XUA.

46. Fortin, *Faith and Action*, 154; BT, February 14, 1881, XUA.

47. Quoted in Hussey, "The 1878 Financial Failure of Archbishop Purcell," 21, 27; HC, January 14, 1889, XUA; Fortin, *Faith and Action*, 167, 170. Upon appeal the Ohio Court, though upholding the judgment of the

lower court decision that Purcell had held the church property in trust, decreed that the cathedral was liable for $114,182.92; the cathedral school for $15,442.48; Mt. St. Mary's of the West Seminary for $8,635.18; and St. Joseph cemetery and other assets collected from the Purcell estates, the amount awarded to the creditors was $409,384.61.

48. *Catalogue of St. Xavier College, 1868,1869*; *Catalogue of St. Xavier College, 1907–1908*, XUA; Minister's Diary, March 8, 1878, XUA; *The Collegian*, April 1887, XUA.

49. *St. Xavier College Catalogue, 1883–1884*; *St. Xavier College Catalogue, 1885–1886*, XUA; *Xaverian News*, February 1, 1922, XUA; *The Collegian*, April, 1887, XUA; HC, January 14, 1889, February 15, 1893, XUA; *Woodstock Letters*, 20: 146.

50. HC, December 19, 1887, September 25, 1891, December 4, 1901, June 8, August 24, 1906, XUA.

51. HC, May 18, 1889, XUA; *Catalogue of St. Xavier College, 1899–1900*, XUA; *Litterae Annuae*, October 17, 1901, XUA; *Woodstock Letters*, 36: 177–178.

52. *Catalogue of St. Xavier College, 1898–99*; *Catalogue of St. Xavier College, 1901–1902*, XUA; Diary of the Prefect of Studies, September 20, 1865, XUA; *Xavier Magazine*, Fall 1998, XUA; O'Meara's Diary, 1865, XUA; *Historia Domus*, July 31, 1899, XUA. Rudolph, *American College and University*, 373–374.

53. W. C. Wolking, class of 1883, was the first secretary and H. M. Calmer, S.J., the first moderator of the Alumni Association. *Catalogue of St. Xavier College, 1872–1873*, XUA; Xavier *Alumnus*, January 1969, XUA; *Alumni Association Minutes*, December 12, 1888, XUA; *Athenaeum*, 5: 143–144, XUA; *Cincinnati Commercial Gazette*, May 2, 1889; Manning folder, XUA; HC, August 28, 1887, XUA; BT, October 6, 1887, XUA. Francis Cloud was president of the Alumni Association for two years, 1889 and 1890.

54. *Woodstock Letters*, 18: 123; quoted in *Cincinnati Commercial Gazette*, May 2, 1889; *Xavier University News*, September 25, 1940, XUA; *The Collegian*, April 1887, XUA.

55. William Bocklage, ed., "Seven Decades of Service: A Brief History of the Xavier University Alumni Association," *Xavier University Newsletter*, March 1958, XUA; HC, November 4, 1888, XUA; *Woodstock Letters*, 19: 425–426.

56. BT, May 27, 1890, XUA; HC, November 4, 1888, XUA; *Athenaeum*, Christmas 1918 issue, XUA; *Cincinnati Commercial Gazette*, June 17, 1890; *Xavier University News*, September 25, 1940, XUA.

57. HC, December 1, 1889, March 12, April 14, 29, June 22, 1890, XUA; BT, May 27, August 19, 1890, June 5, 1891, XUA; *Historia Domus*, 1890–91, XUA; *Woodstock Letters*, 19: 424–426; Bocklage, "Seven Decades of

Service . . . of the . . . Alumni Association," *Xavier University Newsletter*, March 1958, XUA.

58. *Historia Domus*, 1890–91, XUA; Bocklage, "Seven Decades of Service . . . of the . . . Alumni Association," *Xavier University Newsletter*, March 1958, XUA; *Woodstock Letters*, 19: 425–426; 20: 300; 21: 142–144.

59. *Historia Domus*, December 29, 1891, XUA; *Woodstock Letters*, 21: 142–144, 280; HC, October 25, 1899, XUA; *The College Mirror* (n.d.), XUA. The gymnasium contained two ladders, a bridge and upright ladder, a climbing pole and a climbing rope, two punch bags, parallel and portable horizontal bars, swinging and travelling rings, a vaulting horse, four pulley machines, a pulley machine with rowing attachment, numerous dumbbells, among other equipment.

60. Memorial Visitation, January 15, 1892, MJA; *Historia Domus*, December 24, 1898, XUA; HC, August 24, 1906, XUA.

61. *Litt Ann*, December 1893, XUA; Bocklage, "Seven Decades of Service . . . of the . . . Alumni Association," *Xavier University Newsletter*, March 1958, XUA; BT, December 26, 1893, XUA; Garraghan, *The Jesuits of the Middle United States*, 3, 433. The Alumni Association held the annual dinner series for fifty years to 1952.

62. BT, June 7, 1897, XUA; *Historia Domus*, November 10, 1896, XUA; HC, March 24, 1896, February 10, 1897, XUA; see *Catalogue of St. Xavier College, 1896–97* for O'Connor's status; *Woodstock Letters*, 26: 195; *St. Xavier College Bulletin*, May 1930, XUA.

63. Consultors' Meeting, May 25, 1897, XUA; "Scheme for the Endowing of the Class of Philosophy," [n.d.] 1897, Midwest Jesuit Archives; HC, May 25, 1897, XUA; Geiger, *The American College*, 150; Fortin, *Faith and Action*, 212. In 1885 John Poland, S.J., began a home for working boys on East Fifth Street in Cincinnati.

64. HC, May 25, 1897, XUA; "Scheme for the Endowing of the Class of Philosophy," [n.d.] 1897, MJA.

65. *The Collegian*, April 1887, XUA; O'Meara's Diary, 1870, XUA.

66. Poland to Grimmelsman, August 25, 1904, MJA; HC, March 3, 12, April 2, 1905, XUA; *Historia Domus*, March 3, 15, 1905, XUA; Fortin, *Faith and Action*, 177.

67. HC, February 15, 1901, March 3, 12, April 2, 1905, XUA; *Historia Domus*, February 2, 1901; March 3, 15, 1905, XUA; BT, February 15, 1901, XUA; Fortin, *Faith and Action*, 177.

68. Fortin, *Faith and Action*, 188–193.

69. HC, February 18, March 2, 15, 1906, XUA; Dutton to Dierckes, May 8, 1906, MJA; *Historia Domus*, May 8, 1906, XUA.

70. BT, August 24, 1906, XUA; HC, May 28, July 11, August 24, September 29, October 1, 1906, XUA; *Woodstock Letters*, 35: 303–304; Garraghan, *The Jesuits of the Middle United States*, 3, 447–448.

71. *Woodstock Letters*, 35: 303–304; *Historia Domus*, January 23, 1907, XUA; HC, January 8, 25, March 3, April 23, 1907, XUA.
72. HC, March 3, April 23, May 6, June 11, November 5, December 23, 1907; February 4, March 24, May 13, 1908, XUA.
73. *Historia Domus*, March 3, 1908, XUA; BT, March 19, 1908, XUA; Garraghan, *The Jesuits of the Middle United States*, 3, 431.
74. *Historia Domus*, March 3, 1908, XUA; BT, March 19, 1908, XUA; Provincial to Archbishop Moeller, April 23, 1909, XUA; Garraghan, *The Jesuits of the Middle United States*, 3, 431.
75. Grimmelsman to Meyer, March 8, 1909, MJA; *Memorial of Provincial Visitations*, February 26, 1911, XUA.

PART II   "A New Life for Old St. Xavier": A University is Born, 1911–1945

Introduction

1. Christopher J. Lucas, *American Higher Education: A History* (New York, 1994), 227; David O. Levine, *The American College and the Culture of Aspiration, 1915–1940* (Ithaca, N.Y., 1986), 14; Arthur M. Cohen, *The Shaping of American Higher Education: Emergence and Growth of the Contemporary System* (San Francisco, 1998), 110.
2. *Diamond Jubilee Bulletin*, January 20, 1915, MJA.
3. Lucas, *American Higher Education*, 201–203.

Chapter 4   A New Campus, 1911–1931

1. Meyer to Grimmelsman, March 2, 1911, MJA; *Athenaeum*, May 16, 1919, XUA.
2. Meyer to Grimmelsman, March 2, 1911, MJA.
3. Quoted in Heiermann to Meyer, July 21, 1911, MJA; *Historia Domus*, September 19, 1911, XUA; *Athenaeum*, 1: 43–45; 182–184; *Diamond Jubilee Bulletin*, January 20, 1915, MJA; *Catalogue of St. Xavier College, 1911–1912*, XUA; *Woodstock Letters* (Woodstock, Md., 1872–1969), 41: 125; HC, July 11, 1911, January 30, March 24,1912, XUA; BT, July 20, 1911, XUA.
4. HC, March 13, July 11, 20, 1911, XUA; BT, July 20, 1911, XUA; Heiermann to Meyer, July 21, 1911; Thomas M. Smith, S.J., to Meyer, July 24, 1911, MJA.
5. Heiermann to Meyer, July 21, 1911, MJA; *Historia Domus*, September 19, 1911, XUA; HC, March 10, 1913, XUA; BT, March 17, 1913, XUA.
6. William J. Harrington, S.J., to Meyer, July 24, 1911; Foley to Meyer, July 22, 1911; George A. McGovern, S.J., to Meyer, July 22, 1911; Finn to Meyer, July 29, 1911, MJA.

7. HC, July 28, September 11, 1911, XUA.
8. BT, September 18, 1911, XUA; *Historia Domus*, September 19, 1911, XUA; Archbishop Henry Moeller to Rev. Francis Heiermann, S.J., February 26, 1912, XUA; *Athenaeum*, I, March 1912, XUA.
9. In accordance with the advice of real estate agents the college gave the city a quit claim deed, not a warranty deed. HC, December 3, 1911, March 13, 1912, January 5, March 10, 1913, XUA.
10. In January 1912 Mrs. Poland donated $1,000 to the Avondale school. Upon her death two months later college officials, faculty, and students attended the service. On Wednesday, January 24th, the Jesuits celebrated Mass for the first time at the Avondale campus. O'Meara's Diary, 1911, XUA; Xavier Diary, December 28, 1911, XUA; *Athenaeum*, I, 43–45; 182–184; *Diamond Jubilee Bulletin*, January 20, 1915, MJA; *Catalogue of St. Xavier College, 1911–1912*; *Catalogue of St. Xavier College, 1915–1926*, XUA; *Woodstock Letters*, 41: 125; HC, January 30, March 24,1912, XUA; Minister's Diary, January 24, 1912, XUA.
11. James J. O'Meara's Diary, 1911, XUA; William Bocklage, ed., "Seven Decades of Service: A Brief History of the Xavier University Alumni Association," *Xavier University Newsletter*, March 1958, XUA.
12. *Woodstock Letters*, 18: 263; William T. Burns, "Twenty-five Years: A Retrospect," *Athenaeum*, I (April 1913), XUA; *Catalogue of St. Xavier College, 1913–1914*, XUA; *The Xaverian*, 1924, XUA. The four alumni were William A. Byrne, Thomas P. Hart, Richard Ryan, and William C. Wolking.
13. *Memorial of Provincial Visitations*, December 19, 1913, XJA; Xavier Diary, May 12, 1914, XUA; HC, February 6, 20, March 8, 12, April 13, May 11, 1914, XUA; *Xavier University News*, September 25, 1940, XUA.
14. St. Xavier Diamond Jubilee Fund Committee, January 25, 1915, MJA; *Athenaeum*, III, 67; IV, Intro. (1915–1916); Xavier Diary, August 25, 30, 1915; October 4, 1915; May 8, 1916, XUA; Heiermann to Alumni, October 25, 1915, MJA; *Diamond Jubilee Bulletin*, January 20, 1915, XUA, Midwest Jesuit Archives; *Catalogue of St. Xavier College, 1913–1914; 1914–15; 1915–16*, XUA. In the fall of 1915 the architectural firm submitted a supplemental set of plans, which included a chapel, a research laboratory for the graduate department, an arboretum, and an open-air theater.These plans were never implemented.
15. St. Xavier Diamond Jubilee Fund Committee, January 25, 1915; *Diamond Jubilee Bulletin*, January 20, 1915, MJA.
16. HC, May 15, 1914, XUA; BT, April 3, May 20, 1914, XUA; HC, December 21, 1915, January 3, 1916, January 17, 1923, XUA; *Diamond Jubilee Bulletin*, January 20, 1915, MJA.
17. *Diamond Jubilee Bulletin*, January 20, 1915, MJA.

18. O'Meara Diary, 1911, XUA; Gilbert J. Garraghan, *The Jesuits of the Middle United States* (New York, 1938): 3, 447; HC, June 2, 1912, XUA; Arthur M. Cohen, *The Shaping of American Higher Education: Emergence and Growth of the Contemporary System* (San Francisco, 1998), 109; David O. Levine, *The American College and the Culture of Aspiration, 1915–1940* (Ithaca, N.Y., 1986), 15, 58.

19. O'Meara Diary, 1911, XUA; Garraghan, *The Jesuits of the Middle United States*, 3, 447; St. Xavier College of Commerce, Accounts, and Finance, Announcements for 1912–1913, p. 3, XUA; HC, June 2, 1912, XUA; Teacher to Heiermann, May 8, 1913, XUA; *Catalogue of St. Xavier College, 1914–15*; *Catalogue of St. Xavier College, 1915–16*, XUA; *The Official Catholic Directory*, 1911.

20. *Catalogue of St. Xavier College, 1915–1916*, XUA; *Catholic Telegraph*, Centenary Edition, 1931; *The Musketeer Yearbook, 1925–26*, XUA

21. *Woodstock Letters*, 48: 278.

22. HC, June 2, 1912; May 15, June 26, 1914; August 20, 1915, XUA; Xavier Diary, January 1, 1917, XUA; BT, January 7, 1917, XUA.

23. BT, January 5, 1919, XUA; *Catalogue of St. Xavier College, 1920–21*, XUA; *Woodstock Letters*, 48: 278; McCabe to Burrowes, January 7, 1919, Midwest Jesuit Archives. The board approved the proposal for a law school. Two women, Anne M. Overman and Mary L. Prout, were members of the first class.

24. The woman student was Miss Anne Overman. *Xaverian News*, October 1, 1922, XUA; *Catalogue of St. Xavier College, 1920–21*, XUA.

25. *St. Xavier Catalogue, 1912–1913*; *Catalogue of St. Xavier College, 1920–21*, XUA; *Xaverian News*, December 15, 1919; May 27, 1925, XUA.

26. *Diamond Jubilee Bulletin*, January 20, 1915, Midwest Jesuit Archives; Heiermann to Parents, March 15, 1913, XUA.

27. *Regulations and Practical Suggestions for the Students of St. Xavier College*, April 1916, XUA; HC, March 21, 1916, XUA. As makeup examinations imposed an additional burden on the faculty, they had to be taken on the day appointed; if not, the college charged a fee of $1.00 for each examination.

28. *Athenaeum*, I, 166–168, XUA; Moeller to Heiermann, February 1912, XUA; *Catholic Telegraph*, Centenary Edition, 1931.

29. HC, May 15, 1917, XUA; Xavier Diary, June 17, 1917, XUA.

30. Xavier Diary, January 16, 29, April 25, 1917, XUA; *Athenaeum*, V, 219; VI, 117, XUA; HC, April 16, 1917, XUA.

31. *Athenaeum*, I, March 1912, 58, 70–75; Gilligan was present when football was discontinued in 1973; VI, 38–40, XUA; Xavier Diary, September 9, 1920; Frederick Rudolph, *The American College and University: A History* (New York, 1962), 384–385. The five alumni who headed the

St. Xavier College Athletic Association were Eugene O'Shaughnessy, Harry Rieckelman, Clifford Carberry, William Leaver, and Harry Gilligan.

32. HC, November 30, 1914, XUA; *Catalogue of St. Xavier College, 1914–15*, XUA; *The Xavier Athenaeum*, IV, 94, XUA; *Xavier Alumnus*, February 1970, XUA.

33. HC, June 2, 1912; April 17, 1913; April 16, June 10, 1917, XUA; *Catalogue of St. Xavier College, 1925–1926*, XUA; McCabe to Burrowes, July 13, 1917, Midwest Jesuit Archives; Garraghan, *The Jesuits of the Middle United States*, 3, 447. Patrick Poland, a Cincinnati businessman, bequeathed a generous portion of his estate to his sons, John A. and William F. Poland, both of them Jesuit priests of the Missouri province. The novitiate at Florissant became the beneficiary of John's share while William's was conveyed to his alma mater, St. Xavier College.

34. *The Xavier Athenaeum*, November 1, December 13, 1918, XUA; Levine, *The American College and ... Culture of Aspiration*, 27–28.

35. In 1927 the college dedicated the fountain on the first floor of Alumni Science Building, now Edgecliff Hall to his honor. *The Xavier Athenaeum*, January 24, 1919, XUA.

36. HC, February 4, April 16–19, November 17, 1916, XUA.

37. McCabe to Burrowes, January 17, 1919, MJA.

38. McCabe to Burrowes, January 17, 1919, MJA; Cohen, *Shaping of American Higher Education*, 164; Christopher J. Lucas, *American Higher Education: A History* (New York, 1994), 189.

39. BT, January 5, June 11, 1919, XUA; *Historia Domus* II, June 24, April, July 7, 1919, XUA.

40. Xavier Diary, August 28, 1919, XUA.

41. In October 1921 the board secured from the Western and Southern Life Insurance Company a loan of $125,000 at 6 1/2 percent interest, payable in ten years. BT, September 12, 1920; May 25, July 22, 1920; November 7, 1921, XUA.

42. Dormitory Circular, 1924, XUA; Brockman to Robert L. Kelly, March 7, 1929, XUA; Diary of St. Xavier College, September 14, November 14, 1920, XUA; HC, August 9, 1920; November 9, December 4, 1921, XUA; Georg Schurhammer, S.J., "Francis Xavier: His Life, His Times," I, Europe 1506–1541, translated by M. Joseph Costelloe, S.J., 1973, *The Jesuit Historical Institute* (Rome, 1973).

43. St. Ignatius College in Cleveland disputed the claim that St. Xavier was the largest Catholic college in Ohio; *Xaverian News*, November 1, 1920; May 1, June 1921, XUA; *Woodstock Letters*, 51: 84; President Paul L. O'Connor's Comments, Cleveland Chapter, Alumni Association, February 8, 1969, XUA.

44. Proposed Dormitory Circular, 1924, XUA; Brockman to Donnelly, February 25, 1924, XUA; HC, January 23, 1924, XUA; *Woodstock*

Letters, 51: 84; *Xaverian News*, November 1, 1920; May 1, June 1921, XUA; *Xavier Alumnus*, October 1970, XUA; Rudolph, *American College and University*, 384, 388; Cohen, *Shaping of American Higher Education*, 122. The college named Corcoran Field in honor of John and E. B. Corcoran, major contributors to the stadium fund.

45. BT, April 1, 1923, XUA; Brockman to Noonan, April 28, 1923, XUA; *Woodstock Letters*, 51: 84.

46. HC, October 18, November 22, 1922, XUA; *Xaverian News*, April 15, May 1, 1921, XUA.

47. HC, October 18, November 22, 1922; January 17, 1923, XUA; BT, May 29, 1923, XUA; To Whom It May Concern, President, St. Xavier College, October 10, 1923, XUA; Bocklage, "Seven Decades of Service," *Xavier University Newsletter*, March 1958; *Xaverian News*, April 15, May 1, 1921, XUA; Geiger, *The American College*, 150–151.

48. Proposed Dormitory Circular, 1924, XUA.

49. BT, May 29, 1923, XUA; *Catalogue of St. Xavier College, 1924–25*, XUA; *Woodstock Letters*, 52: 144; HC, May 21, 1924, XUA; Proposed Dormitory Circular, 1924, XUA; Brockman to Robert L. Kelly, March 7, 1929, XUA. Initially a few trustees had thought the dormitory should have been named after an individual who donated $100,000. When rebuilding the automobile drive behind the clubhouse, the driveway had been completely destroyed by a landslide that occurred when excavating for the athletic field in the rear of the clubhouse.

50. *Woodstock Letters*, 53, 1924; 54, 1925.

51. *Xaverian News*, September 21, 1927; September 24, 1930; October 27, 1932; September 20, 1934, XUA.

52. Proposed Dormitory Circular, 1924, XUA; *The Xaverian*, 1924, XUA; *Catalogue of St. Xavier College, 1923–24*, XUA. From the 1920s through the mid-1950s the terms College of Liberal Arts, College of Arts and Sciences, College of Arts, and College of Liberal Arts and Sciences were used interchangeably.

53. Proposed Dormitory Circular, 1924, XUA; Brockman to Donnelly, February 25, 1924, XUA; *The Xavier Newsletter*, June 1953, XUA.

54. Proposed Dormitory Circular, 1924, XUA; Brockman to Donnelly, February 25, 1924, XUA; Schmidt to Brockman, April 25, 1924, XUA; HC, January 23, 1924; February 2, 1925, XUA; *St. College Xaverian*, 1924, XUA.

55. Xavier Diary, II, May 27, 1925, XUA; *Woodstock Letters*, 54: 133–134; *Cincinnati Enquirer*, June 9, 1927; *The Musketeer*, 1926, 50, XUA.

56. Xavier Diary, II, January 28, Mary 27, 1925, XUA; *Woodstock Letters*, 54: 133; BT, March 31, 1926, XUA; HC, May 9, 1928; March 20, 1929, XUA; Brockman to Robert L. Kelly, March 7, 1929, XUA; *Xaverian News*, December 22, 1922, XUA. In 1926 the Board of Trustees authorized

President Brockman to borrow approximately $75,000 to complete payments on the library building, which had a frontage of more than 90 feet and a depth of 125 feet or more.

57. Xavier Diary, II, August 20, 1925, XUA.

58. *Woodstock Letters*, 54: 133; *Xaverian News*, October 10, 17, 1928, XUA; *Catholic Telegraph*, Centenary Edition, 1931.

59. Brockman to McCabe, February 21, August 16, September 17, 1926, XUA; *Woodstock Letters*, 56: 369; BT, March 22, September 30, November 22, 1922; December 10, 1926; March 8, 12, 1927, XUA; HC, January 17, 1923; March 25, 1927, XUA; *Cincinnati Enquirer*, June 9, 1927. On December 10, 1927, the Frederick A. Schmidt Co., which was a trustee of an irregular tract of land fronting 580 feet on the west line of Woodburn Avenue (now Ledgewood Avenue) 75 feet north of Herald Avenue, and of another tract fronting 745.20 feet on the east line of Herald Avenue, leased the two tracts to the college with the privilege of purchase. On the same day the company transferred the property by deed to the Title Guarantee and Trust Company. On September 9, 1940, Xavier University acquired the warranty deed to the two tracts for $128,750.

60. *Xavier Alumnus*, April 1966, XUA. In 1973 the Alumnae Association and the Alumni Association became a single organization.

61. BT, March 11, 1927, XUA; HC, January 13, 1926; March 12, November 8, December 5, 1927, XUA; Provincial to Brockman, August 7, 1926, XUA. In the winter of 1927 Walter Schmidt added $25,000 to his security note.

62. Brockman to Robert L. Kelly, March 7, 1929, XUA; Xavier Diary, II, March 7, 1928, XUA; *Woodstock Letters*, 57: 548–549; *Cincinnati Enquirer*, June 9, 1927; HC, January 10, April 3, 1928, XUA; *Xavier Alumnus*, February, October 1970, XUA; *St. Xavier College Bulletin*, May 1930, XUA. A registered architect, Coach Joe Meyer assisted in the design of the Xavier fieldhouse.

63. *Cincinnati Enquirer*, June 9, 1927; Brockman to Cooper, June 12, 1929, XUA. The newly-elected governor of Ohio, Myers Y. Cooper, delivered the main address at the 1919 commencement.

64. HC, January 9, 25, 1927, XUA; McCabe to Brockman, January 29, March 25, 1927, XUA.

65. Xavier Diary, April 14, 24, May 7, 1927; *Woodstock Letters*, 54: 132.

66. Brockman to Othmar Knapke, C.PP.S, October 26, 1928; Brockman to B. J. Cottingham, October 23, 1928; Brockman to Cooper, August 30, 1929; Brockman to Robert L. Kelly, March 7, 1929, XUA; Diary of St. Xavier College, II, September 19, October 2, 1927; November 23, 1929, XUA; *Xaverian News*, January 4, 1928, XUA. William Arbigast was the auditor.

67. Xavier Diary, II, November 23, 1929, XUA; Brockman to Cooper, August 30, 1929; Brockman to Robert L. Kelly, March 7, 1929, XUA; *Woodstock Letters*, 58: 246; Sloctemyer to White, October 26, September 22, 1931, XUA; *Xavier Alumnus*, October 1970, XUA. The expanded football stadium rose up to a height of 425 feet above the field level.

68. *Catalogue of St. Xavier College, 1928–29*, XUA; Brockman to C.G. L. Yearick, October 6, 1928, XUA.

69. HC, February 2, 1917; February 2, September 15, October 23, 1928, XUA; Brockman to Robert L. Kelly, March 7, 1929, XUA.

70. The actual cost of the building was $150,000 plus $32,000 for laboratory equipment and various furnishings. *Woodstock Letters*, 58: 706–707; HC, April 17, September 23, 1929, XUA; Garraghan, *The Jesuits of the Middle United States*, 3, 448; Xavier Diary, II, June 9, 1948, XUA.

71. *Woodstock Letters*, 58: 706–707; HC, April 17, September 23, 1929, XUA; Garraghan, *The Jesuits of the Middle United States*, 3, 448; Xavier Diary, II, June 9, 1948, XUA. Ohio Senator Robert O'Brien was also a personal friend of Francis J. Finn, S.J., the famed author of twenty-one books.

72. *Woodstock Letters*, 58: 706–707; *Catholic Telegraph*, Centenary Edition, 1931; Brockman to Richard A. O'Brien, S.J., April 15, 1930, XUA; Brockman to Edward J. Whalen, S.J., March 31, 1930; Brockman to Robert Keel, S.J., Tokyo, Japan, February 22, 1930, XUA.

73. Brockman to O'Brien, September 23, 24, 1929, XUA. *Xaverian News*, September 18, 1929; March 19, 1930, XUA.

74. *Xaverian News*, September 24, 1930; October 27, 1932; September 20, 1934, XUA.

75. Brockman to Kroger, January 31, 1930, XUA; HC, September 23, 1929; September 22, 1930, XUA.

76. *Xaverian News*, December 1920, XUA.

77. *Xaverian News*, December 21, 1921; January 15, 1922, XUA; *Catholic Telegraph*, Centenary Edition, 1931; description of CSMC in Fortin, *Faith and Action*, 229; *The Xaverian*, 1924, XUA; *The Musketeer*, 1926, 171, XUA; *Catalogue of St. Xavier College, 1923–24*, XUA.

78. *Xaverian News*, May 1, 1923; May 27, 1925; September 30, 1937, XUA; *Xavier University News*, September 30, 1937, XUA; *Catholic Telegraph*, Centenary Edition, 1931; Fortin, *Faith and Action*, 234.

79. *Xaverian News*, December 21, 1921; January 15, 1922, XUA; *Catholic Telegraph*, Centenary Edition, 1931; Fortin, *Faith and Action*, 229.

80. *Catholic Telegraph*, Centenary Edition, 1931; *Xaverian News*, February 8, 1923; February 4, 11, 1931, XUA. The Clef Club was sometimes known as the Father Finn Clef Club.

81. Burrowes to Heiermann, October 30, 1913; Thill to Burns, January 22, 1937, XUA; *Xaverian News*, January 15, 1923; October 21, 1925;

February 12, 1930; April 15, 1931; March 3, 1932, XUA; *The Xaverian*, 1924, XUA; *Xavier Magazine*, Fall 1999. In 1925 the college officials approved an informal Christmas dance. Moreover, during this period and into the 1930s Archbishop McNicholas of Cincinnati forbade students of Xavier University to send an invitation to the students of Our Lady of Cincinnati and Mount Saint Joseph Colleges requesting participation in the junior prom and in the selection of a young woman as "Prom Queen." The archbishop thought that "this servile imitation of the world in its beauty bathing contests and carnival activities [was] at all worthy of the idealism that should be evident in everything pertaining to Christian education."

82. *Xaverian News*, December 1, 1921; Annual Pictorial Edition, 1922; October 15, 1923; April 8, 1925; April 4, 1935, XUA; Rudolph, *The American College and University*, 369; Cohen, *Shaping of American Higher Education*, 247–248. Until 1935 attendance at Student Council meetings was limited to the student representatives. That year meetings were also opened to students.

83. *Xaverian News*, October 15, 1922; April 1, 1923; November 3, 1926; May 16, 1928; September 24, October 8, 1930, XUA; *Catalogue of St. Xavier College, 1927–1928*, XUA.

84. *Woodstock Letters*, 56: 370; *Cincinnati Enquirer*, June 9, 1927; Proposed Dormitory Circular, 1924, XUA.

85. *Woodstock Letters*, 56: 370; *Cincinnati Enquirer*, June 9, 1927; Proposed Dormitory Circular, 1924, XUA; Sloctemyer's Presidential Report, 1932, XUA.

86. *Woodstock Letters*, 56: 370; Proposed Dormitory Circular, 1924, XUA; Sloctemyer's Presidential Report, 1932, XUA.

87. BT, December 26, 1924, XUA; Xavier Diary, March 22, 1925, XUA; Provincial to McCabe, April 11, 1917, XUA; Cohen, *Shaping of American Higher Education*, 151; William P. Leahy, S.J., *Adapting to America: Catholics, Jesuits, and Higher Education in the Twentieth Century* (Washington, D.C., 1991), 38–39.

88. *Cincinnati Enquirer*, June 9, 1927; Sloctemyer's 1931 Commencement Address, XUA; *Xavier Alumnus*, February 1963, XUA. The university continued to use the seismographs in the basement of the Schmidt Library Building. In 1962 it installed a new seismological observatory on the Jesuit farm near Milford, Ohio. The sensitivity of new seismometers, acquired through an air force grant, made it necessary to locate them away from busy traffic on Victory Parkway and Dana Avenue.

89. *Xaverian News*, October 27, November 15, December 1, 1922, XUA; *Xavier University News*, September 25, 1940, XUA; Levine, *The American College and . . . Culture of Aspiration*, 19.

90. *Xaverian News*, October 1, 1922; February 8, 1923; February 4, 11, 1931, XUA.

91. Schmidt to Brockman, June 29, 1923, XUA.

92. *Xavier Alumnus*, April 1965; August 1969, XUA; Xavier Diary, November 7, 1925, XUA; *Xaverian News*, October 7, 1925, XUA. In 1925 Finn was honored for his twenty-five years of service in Cincinnati. The mayor of Cincinnati and a committee of prominent public men gave their congratulations in person and provided him with a purse of more than $5,000 on the occasion of his silver jubilee.

93. Brockman to Ankenbauer, December 9, 1925, XUA.

94. Brockman to McNichols, January 23, 1926; Brockman to provincial, August 6, 1926, XUA.

95. Brockman to Cloud, February 5, 1926; Cloud to Brockman, January 29, 1926; Grace to Brockman, February 2, 1926; Agnew to Brockman, February 9, 1926; McNichols to Brockman, February 17, 1926, XUA.

96. Brockman to provincial, August 6, 1926; Brockman to Cloud, May 15, August 5, 12, 1926; Brockman to Agnew, May 24, August 2, 12, 1926; Cloud to Brockman, August 14, 1926; Mathews to Brockman, August 12, 1926; Sullivan to Brockman, August 20, 1926; Chairman to [Friends], April 15, 1930; Brockman to Sullivan, August 30, December 29, 1926; Brockman to DuBois, May 5, 1930, XUA.

97. Frank Gauche, President, St. Xavier Alumni Association, to alumni, May 9, 1927, XUA.

98. Leahy, *Adapting to America*, 73–74; Heiermann to provincial, May 27, 1915; Sister Monica to _____, April 17, 1915; Mother Mary Florence to Heiermann, October 4, 1916; Brockman to McNicholas, September 1926, XUA; *Catalogue of St. Xavier College, 1916–17*; *Catalogue of St. Xavier College, 1919–20*; Ursuline College at New Rochelle, New York, did not require a year's residence for the women religious enrolled in the school.

99. Heiermann to provincial, May 27, 1915; Mother Mary Florence to Heiermann, October 4, 1916; Brockman to McNicholas, September 1926, XUA; *Catalogue of St. Xavier College, 1916–17*; Rudolph, *The American College and University*, 339; Cohen, *Shaping of American Higher Education*, 168.

100. *Athenaeum*, 6: 70, XUA; Garraghan, *The Jesuits of the Middle United States*, 3, 447; BT, March 22, 1922; June 17, 1918, XUA; *Catalogue of St. Xavier College, 1917–18*; *Catalogue of St. Xavier College, 1919–20*, XUA.

101. *Woodstock Letters*, 47, 1918; 48, 1919; *Catalogue of St. Xavier College, 1919–20*, XUA; *Xavierian News*, August 1918, XUA.

102. President to Moeller, June 17, 1920, XUA.

103. Schmidt to Moeller, September 10, 1920; Schmidt to Moeller, [n.d.], 1920, XUA.

104. Schmidt to Moeller, [n.d.], 1920; Schmidt to Moeller, September 10, 1920, XUA; *St. Xavier College Catalogue, 1920–21*, XUA.
105. Moeller to McCabe, October 23, 1920, XUA.
106. Schmidt to McCabe, October 30, 1920, XUA.
107. McCabe to Moeller, November 5, 1920, XUA; BT, September 12, October 26, 1920, XUA.
108. BT, March 22, 1922, XUA; Fortin, *Faith and Action*, 330.
109. An Address to His Grace the Archbishop of Cincinnati, presented by the Alumni Association of St. Xavier College, February 12, 1924, XUA; Brockman to Donnelly, February 25, 1924, XUA.
110. Brockman to Ulery, January 4, 1926; Brockman to McCabe, February 21, 1926; Brockman to McNicholas, September 1926, XUA.
111. McCabe to Brockman, January 29, 1927, XUA.
112. Brockman to Schmidt, April 5, 1927; Ulery to McNicholas, April 19, 1927; McCabe to Brockman, May 12, 1927, XUA; *Cincinnati Enquirer*, June 9, 1927.
113. McNicholas to Brockman, July 9, 1927; Brockman to Mother Superior, July 12, 1927; Brockman to Ulery, July 16, 1927, XUA.
114. *Catholic Telegraph*, August 2, 1928; Brockman to Blakely, March 2, 1932, XUA; Sister Mary Callista Flanagan, O.S.B., *Jesuit Education in the Archdiocese of Cincinnati in the Past One Hundred Years* (unpublished master of arts thesis, University of Notre Dame, 1940), 43; Fortin, *Faith and Action*, 330–331.
115. Brockman to Mother Mary Bernardine, S.M., January 11, 1928, XUA; *The Official Catholic Directory*, 1922 through 1940; Sloctemyer's Presidential Report, 1932, XUA; *Woodstock Letters*, 56: 370.
116. Father F. X. McMenamy to Father James McCabe, August 9, 1919, XUA.
117. L. N. Steltenpohl, secretary of St. Xavier Alumni Association to Rev. James McCabe, January 13, 1922; Brockman to Wolking, February 29, 1924, XUA; *Xaverian News*, February 21, 1924, XUA.
118. BT, December 26, 1924; HC, January 13, February 24, April 21, 1926, XUA; *Xaverian News*, February 21, 1924, XUA; Brockman to McNichols, January 23, 1926; St. Xavier Foundation Resolutions, December 13, 1927, XUA.
119. Louthian to Brockman, January 11, 1927, XUA.
120. Certificate of Amendment to Articles of St. Xavier College, July 31, 1930, XUA; BT, July 31, 1930, XUA; HC, April 27, 1931, XUA; Brockman to McCabe, January 6, 1928, XUA. The left half of the shield on the seal had stripes of silver and blue from the coat of arms of the home of Xavier. The upper quarter of the right side displayed the arm of St. Francis Xavier, holding the crucifix. The lower quarter contained three sea shells, indicating that Xavier "is an apostle transmarinus" ["coming from beyond the sea"].

Chapter 5   Depression and War, 1931–1945

1. *Cincinnati Enquirer*, February 13, 1931; *The Xavier Newsletter*, June 1953, XUA.
2. Xavier Diary, II, April 23, 1931; *Xavier University Catalogue, 1930–1931*, XUA.
3. *Cincinnati Enquirer*, April 23, 1931; *Xaverian News*, April 29, 1931, XUA.
4. Sloctemyer's 1931 Commencement Address, XUA.
5. Sloctemyer's 1931 Commencement Address, XUA.
6. Bunker to Sloctemyer, September 29, 1931; J. A. Smith to Sloctemyer, September [n. d.], 1931, XUA.
7. The following universities and colleges participated in the competitions: St. Louis, Loyola, Saint Mary's, Kansas; Creighton, University of Detroit, Marquette, John Carroll, St. John's University, Toledo, Rockhurst, Regis. Sloctemyer's Presidential Reports, 1931, 1932, 1933, XUA; *Xavier University Catalogue, 1929–1930*; *Xavier University Catalogue, 1930–1931*, XUA; *Catholic Telegraph* Centenary Edition, 1931.
8. Sloctemyer's 1931 Commencement Address, XUA.
9. Sloctemyer's 1931 Commencement Address, XUA.
10. Earl Winter, director of publicitity at the University, to Brockman, July 18, 1930; Brockman to Haburton, August 19, September 24, October 7, 1930; Haburton to Brockman, November 7, 1930; January 14, 1931; Sloctemyer's 1931 Commencement Address, XUA.
11. Sloctemyer's 1931 Commencement Address, XUA.
12. Sloctemyer's 1931 Commencement Address, XUA.
13. Louthian to Bredestege, November 14, 1931, XUA.
14. Sloctemyer to Louthian, December 11, 1931; Louthian to Sloctemeyer, December 14, 1931, XUA.
15. Sloctemyer to Blakely, March 2, 1932, XUA.
16. Sloctemyer to Dr. Hugh Graham, John Carroll University, September 21, 1934; Sloctemyer to Hugh Graham, September 26, 1934, XUA.
17. Mother M. Lucy to Sloctemyer, May 2, 1934; Sister Maximma, Provincial House, Sisters of Notre Dame, Covington, to Sloctemyer, May 2, 1934; Mother Lisba, Villa Madonna Academy, to Sloctemyer, May 3, 1934, XUA.
18. Sloctemyer to Rev. Mother Mary Lucy, St. Anne Convent, May 7, 1934, XUA.
19. Christopher J. Lucas, *American Higher Education: A History* (New York, 1994), 176–177.
20. Sloctemyer's President Report, 1932, XUA; *Xaverian News*, November 16, 1933, XUA; Sloctemyer's 1931 Commencement Address, XUA; *Xavier Alumnus*, February 1970, XUA. The talented Xavier University basketball hall of famers John Tracy, John "Socko" Wiethe, Kenny

Jordan, Hal Pennington, and Leo Sack also helped generated interest in the program.

21. Sloctemyer's 1931 Commencement Address, XUA.
22. Walter Schmidt to Sloctemyer, February 16, 1933; Sloctemyer folder, [n.d.], XUA.
23. Sloctemyer to Bunker, July 10, 1933, XUA.
24. Sloctemyer's Presidential Report, 1932; Dean to Brockman, October 9, 1929, XUA.
25. Sloctemyer to Bunker, July 10, 1933, XUA.
26. Sloctemyer to Bunker, July 10, 1933; Art Leibold to Sloctemyer, July 14, 1933, XUA.
27. The two examiners were Dr. Homer P. Rainey, president of Bucknell University, and Dr. Raymond A. Kent, president of the University of Louisville. Report of the Board of Review on Higher Education of the North Central Association of Secondary Schools and Colleges, March 21, 1934; William P. Leahy, S.J., *Adapting to America: Catholics, Jesuits, and Higher Education in the Twentieth Century* (Washington, D.C., 1991), 44–45; Philip Gleason, *Contending with Modernity: Catholic Higher Education in the Twentieth Century* (New York, 1995), 186.
28. Report of the Board of Review on Higher Education of the North Central Association of Secondary Schools and Colleges, March 21, 1934, XUA; Faculty Meeting, November 2, 1934; October 20, 1939, XUA.
29. Report of the Board of Review on Higher Education of the North Central Association of Secondary Schools and Colleges, March 21, 1934, XUA; Faculty Meeting, November 2, 1934; October 20, 1939; Report of the Supplementary Inspection of Xavier University, Cincinnati, Ohio, April 18, 1934, XUA; Burns to Alumni, August 21, 1935, XUA.
30. *Catholic Telegraph*, May 1, 1934, XUA.
31. Dr. Raymond Walters to Father Hugo F. Sloctemyer, May 7, 1934, XUA; Xavier University release, [n.d.], 1934, XUA.
32. Sloctemyer to Stephens L. Blakely, Blakely & Murphy, Covington, May 19, 1934; Sloctemyer to John C. Thompson, May 19, 1934, XUA.
33. HC, December 18, 1934; January 2, 1935, XUA; Father Charles Cloud, S.J., to Father Hugo Sloctemyer, S.J., December 22, 1934, XUA. In 1930 the father general had urged Jesuit schools to comply with standards for accreditation.
34. Sloctemyer's text on Board of Athletic Control, 1934–35, [n.d.]; Sloctemyer folder, [n.d.], XUA; Faculty meeting, February 1, 1935, XUA. The four Jesuits on the Board of Athletic Control were Terence Kane, Aloysius A. Breen, John I. Grace, and Frederick Miller. The layman was William E. Chancellor.
35. *Xaverian News*, March 10, 1935, XUA; BT, March 25, 1935, XUA. The second NCA team consisted of John Dale Russell of the University of

Chicago and Father Alphonse Schwitalla, dean of the Medical School of St. Louis University. Report to the Committee on Review of the Commission on Institutions of Higher Education, North Central Association of Secondary Schools and Colleges, March 1935. After a rest period, Sloctemyer was eventually stationed at the Novitiate of the Sacred Heart at Milford. He became regent of the Loyola University School of Law in Chicago and professor of jurisprudence on the Loyola faculty.

36. Bunker to Burns, April 16, 1935; Cloud to Burns, October 14, 1935, XUA; HC, April 16, 1935, XUA; Gleason, *Contending with Modernity*, 187.

37. Burns to Provincial, May 14, 1935; Schmidt to Burns, July 24, 1935, XUA;

38. Burns to Provincial, May 14, 1935; Schmidt to Burns, July 24, 1935, XUA; HC, May 15, 1935, XUA.

39. Burns to Provincial, May 14, 1935; Schmidt to Burns, July 24, 1935, XUA.

40. Schmidt to Burns, July 24, 1935, XUA; HC, July 22, September 7, 1935, XUA.

41. *Cincinnati Times-Star*, August 20, 1935. The various committees of the Athletic Advisory Council consisted of the Finance, Publicity, Ways and Means, Budget, Promotion and Pass, Schedule, Seating, Grounds, Ushers, and Scoreboard Committees

42. Burns to Alumni, August 21, 1935; Cloud to Burns, October 14, 1935; Stephens L. Blakely and James R. McGarry to Burns, October 9, 1935; Meyer to Burns, October 8, 1935; Burns to Provincial, October 16, 1935, XUA.

43. Burns to Provincial, October 16, 1935; Cloud to Burns, August 18, 1936, XUA; HC, November 19, 1935; February 20, October 7, 1936, XUA.

44. Resolution, Council of City of Cincinnati, December 15, 1937, XUA; Raymond Walters to Gilligan, December 7, 1937, XUA; *Xavier University 2003–04 Media Guide* (2003), 158–159, XUA..

45. HC, February 9, 16, October 26, 1938; January 11, June 5, 1939; September 6, 1940; January 5, 1941, XUA.

46. HC, January 4, 1940, XUA; *Cincinnati Enquirer*, August 22, 1949; Xavier Diary, II, May 18, June 19, 1939, XUA; Roger Fortin, *Faith and Action: A History of the Catholic Archdiocese of Cincinnati, 1821–1996* (Columbus, Ohio, 2002), 202–203.

47. Bracken to Steiner, February 5, 1941, XUA; *Xavier University 2003–04 Media Guide*, (2003), 159; Faculty Meeting, February 14, 1941, XUA.

48. Policy of Intercollegiate Athletics, [1943], XUA.

49. Arthur M. Cohen, *The Shaping of American Higher Education: Emergence and Growth of the Contemporary System* (San Francisco,

1998), 164–165; David O. Levine, *The American College and the Culture of Aspiration, 1915–1940* (Ithaca, N.Y., 1986), 185–186.

50. HC, November 16, 1931; January 5, 1932, XUA; Provincial to Sloctemyer, May 9, 1931, XUA.

51. Memorandum, probably dated January 17, 1931, XUA; HC, November 16, 1931; January 5, 1932; September 1, 1941, XUA; Lay Professors, XU, Avondale, December 11, 1931, XUA; *Xaverian News*, October 1, 1931, XUA; Xavier Diary, II, February 24, March 17, 1933, XUA; *Xavier University Catalogue, 1931–1932*; *Xavier University Catalogue, 1932–1933*, XUA.

52. HC, April 27, May, [n.d.], November 16, 1931; March 28, 1932, XUA; *Xavier University Catalogue, 1931–1932*; *Xavier University Catalogue, 1932–1933*; *Xavier University Catalogue, 1933–1934*, XUA; Sloctemyer's Presidential Report, 1932, XUA. In June 1932 Sloctemyer noted that the "student body has not decreased."

53. HC, October 2, 1928; September 7, 1931, XUA; Fortin, *Faith and Action*, 305–310.

54. HC, February, n.d., 1932, March 28, 1932; June 4, July 22, 1933; October, [n.d.], 1933; November 26, 1934; November 16, 1936; February 9, 16, 1938; February 6, 1939; September 6, 1940; September 1, 1941, XUA; Sloctemyer's Presidential Report, 1933, XUA; *Catalogue of Xavier University, 1933–1934; Catalogue of Xavier University, 1938–39*, XUA; Cloud to Sloctemyer, July 1, November 25, 1933, XUA.

55. HC, February, [n.d.], 1932, March 28, 1932; June 4, July 22, 1933; October, [n.d.], 1933; November 26, 1934; November 16, 1936; February 9, 16, 1938; February 6, 1939; September 6, 1940; September 1, 1941, XUA; Sloctemyer's Presidential Report, 1933, XUA; *Catalogue of Xavier University, 1933–1934; Catalogue of Xavier University, 1938–39*, XUA; Cloud to Sloctemyer, July 1, November 25, 1933, XUA; Levine, *The American College and . . . Culture of Aspiration*, 185–186, 203.

56. HC, February, [n.d.], 1932, March 28, 1932; June 4, July 22, 1933; October, [n.d.], 1933; November 16, 1936; February 6, 1939; September 6, 1940, XUA; Sloctemyer's Presidential Report, 1932; Sloctemyer's Presidential Report, 1933, XUA; *Catalogue of Xavier University, 1938–39*, XUA; *The Jesuit Bulletin*, February 1935, Midwest Jesuit Archives; Sloctemyer to Albers, September 5, 1934, XUA; *Xavier University News*, May 25, 1956, XUA; *Xavier Alumnus*, August 1969, XUA.

57. HC, February 9, 1938; September 1, 1941, XUA; Cloud to Burns, August 17, 1936; Fitzgibbons to Burns, September 30, 1936, XUA.

58. HC, January 11, June 5, 1939, XUA; *Xavier University Catalogue, 1936–1937*; *Xavier University Catalogue, 1938–1939*; *Xavier University Catalogue, 1939–1940*, XUA.

59. *Xaverian News*, October 26, 1934; March 5, 1936, XUA; *Xavier University News*, April 5, 1940, XUA.

60. *Xaverian News*, May 14, October 1, 1936, XUA; *Xavier University News*, September 23, 1937, XUA; Fortin, *Faith and Action*, 263; Gleason, *Contending with Modernity*, 154–156. The last issue of *Xaverian News* was published on May 20, 1937.

61. *Xaverian News*, October 1, 15, November 5, 1936, XUA; *Xavier University News*, February 19, May 7, 1941, XUA; Fortin, *Faith and Action*, 299–300.

62. Xavier Diary, II, January 24, 1937, XUA; HC, February 9, 1938; June 5, 1939, XUA; BT, October 9, 1939, XUA; *Xavier University News*, October 6, 1939; December 12, 1941, XUA. The first contingent of ROTC officials arrived on campus on September 16, 1936.

63. Xavier Diary, II, January 24, 1937, XUA; *Xaverian News*, April 2, October 1, 1936, XUA; *Xavier University News*, October 6, 1939; December 2, 1941, XUA; HC, June 5, 1939, XUA; BT, October 9, 1939, XUA.

64. Xavier Diary, II, April 30, 1939; April 10, September 29, November 24, 1940, XUA; Meeting of the Faculty of Liberal Arts and Sciences, April 21, October 20, 1939; January 18, 1940; February 14, 1941, XUA.

65. BT, August 26, 1940, XUA; HC, September 6, 1940, XUA; Diary of St. Xavier College, II, August 26, 1940, XUA. After leaving Xavier Burns taught at John Carroll University, the University of Detroit, before joining the Loyola faculty in 1956.

66. HC, September 1, 1941, XUA; Benson to Steiner, February 9, 1941, XUA.

67. HC, September 1, 1941, XUA; BT, August 26, 1940, XUA.

68. Faculty Meeting, February 14, 1941, XUA.

69. *Xavier University News*, November 3, 1939; February 19, 26, 1942, XUA.

70. Xavier Diary, II, May 29, 1942, XUA; *Xavier University Catalogue, 1980–1982*, XUA; *Xavier University News*, February 19, 29, 1942, XUA.

71. Xavier Diary, II, December 17, 1942; January 30, 1943, XUA; *Xavier University News*, October 8, 1942, XUA.

72. Xavier Diary, II, February 1, 3, 4, 10, 1943, XUA; HC, February 9, 1938; January 7, [1943], XUA.

73. Xavier Diary, II, January 30, February 1, 3, 4, 10, 1943, XUA; *Xavier Magazine*, Winter 1996.

74. Steiner to Sullivan, February 13, 1943; Steiner to Parents, March 10, 1943, XUA; Xavier Diary, II, February 1, 3, 4, 10, 1943, XUA.

75. Steiner to Parents, March 10, 1943; Steiner to Fathers Breen and Englum, March, 1943, XUA; Xavier Diary, II, February 1, 3, 4, 10, 1943, XUA; *Xavier Magazine*, Winter 1996, XUA.

76. Xavier Diary, II, February 1, 3, 4, 10; March 20, 1943, XUA; *Xavier Magazine*, Winter 1996; Professor William Marcaccio to Rev. Paul L.

O'Connor, S.J., April 3, 1969; Cincinnati City Manager C. O. Sherill to Fr. Steiner, S.J., November 29, 1943, XUA; *The Xavier Newsletter*, September 10, 1943; June 16, 1944, XUA.

77. *The Xavier Newsletter*, September 10, October 29, 1943, XUA.
78. Raymond J. Fellinger, Registrar, to Steiner, March 3, 1943, XUA; *The Xavier Newsletter*, September 10, October 9, 1943; January 5, 1945, XUA; *Xavier University News*, March 1, 1946, XUA. *Xavier University News* was suspended after the January 28, 1943, issue. It resumed on March 1, 1946.
79. "DAILY ORDER AND RULES," Dana Hall, February 5, 1944, XUA.
80. *The Xavier Newsletter*, October 29, 1943, XUA; *Xavier University News*, March 19, October 22, 29, December 17, 1942; January 28, 1943, XUA.
81. *Cincinnati Post*, July 16, 1943; *The Xavier Newsletter*, September 10, 1943; June 16, August 25, 1944, XUA; Mimeo XU News, August 19, 1943, XUA.
82. *The Xavier Newsletter*, September 10, 1943; June 16, August 25, 1944, XUA; Mimeo XU News, August 19, 1943, XUA. Clem Crowe, a University of Notre Dame alumnus, became the head basketball coach and assistant football coach at his alma mater.
83. HC, April 3, 1944, XUA; *The Xavier Newsletter*, June 16, 1944, XUA; Xavier University Faculty, 1943–1944, XUA.
84. *The Xavier Newsletter*, August 25, 1944, XUA.
85. Xavier Diary, II, February 1, 3, 4, 10, 1943, XUA; Steiner to Sullivan, February 13, 1943, XUA; *Xavier Magazine*, Winter 1996.
86. *The Xavier Newsletter*, June 16, 1944; January 5, 1945, XUA.
87. *The Xavier Newsletter*, August 25, 1944; January 5, 1945; *Woodstock Letters* (Woodstock, Md., 1872–1969), 74, 1945.
88. Robert W. Horton, United States Maritime Commission, to Rev. Celestin J. Steiner, President, January 29, 1945; Lieutenant Daniel H. Heekin, March 7, 1945, XUA. The *S.S. Xavier Victory*, 455 feet in length, was longer than one-and-a-half football fields.

PART III   A Modern University, 1945–1990

Introduction

1. Arthur M. Cohen, *The Shaping of American Higher Education: Emergence and Growth of the Contemporary System* (San Francisco, 1998), 175
2. Cohen, *Shaping of American Higher Education*, 239–240.
3. Christopher J. Lucas, *American Higher Education: A History* (New York, 1994), 228; David O. Levine, *The American College and the Culture of Aspiration, 1915–1940* (Ithaca, N.Y., 1986), 13, 22.

4. Levine, *The American College and . . . Culture of Aspiration,* 13; Gerald L. Gutek, *American Education 1945–2000: A History and Commentary* (Project Heights, Illinois, 2000), 222; Lucas, *American Higher Education,* 227–228; Alice Gallin, O.S.U., *Negotiating Identity: Catholic Higher Education Since 1960* (Notre Dame, Indiana, 2000), 47.
5. Cohen, *Shaping of American Higher Education,* 187, 191–193.
6. Gallin, *Negotiating Identity,* 111–113, 128.
7. Gallin, *Negotiating Identity,* 1–3, 125.
8. Cohen, *Shaping of American Higher Education,* 398.

Chapter 6   The University's Postwar Challenges, 1945–1955

1. Xavier's Case Before the Community and the Nation, October 1945, XUA.
2. HC, n.d.[likely late fall, 1944], XUA.
3. Xavier's Case Before the Community and the Nation, October 1945, XUA; *Cincinnati Post,* May 17, 1945; *Cincinnati Times-Star,* May 17, 1945.
4. HC, March 28, 1945, XUA; Letter of Archbishop John T. McNicholas to Pastors of Archdiocese, April 16, 1945, XUA; *Cincinnati Post,* May 17, 1945; *Cincinnati Times-Star,* May 17, 1945; *Cincinnati Enquirer,* May 12, 1946. St. Xavier High School alone made a contribution of $10,000 to the drive.
5. Steiner, Xavier University and Cincinnatians, [1946], XUA; Alice Gallin, O.S.U., *Negotiating Identity: Catholic Higher Education Since 1960* (Notre Dame, Indiana, 2000), 73–74.
6. *Xavier Must Be Ready When They Come Back,* [1945], XUA.
7. *Xaverian News,* November 12, 1930, XUA; HC, September 12, 1945; February 1, March 12, 1946, XUA; *The Xavier Newsletter,* April 1952, XUA. According to the provisions of the Logan will, part of the money would be used for a science building and part for endowment.
8. Albers to Charles F. Williams, April 6, 1946, XUA; HC, March 12, 1946; Xavier Diary, II, April 26, 1946, XUA; Resolution, Council of the Cincinnati of Cincinnati, April 10, 1946, XUA.
9. Steiner to Zema, July 30, 1946; Steiner to Mrs. Hinkle, February 27, 1951, XUA; Presidential Report, Commencement, June 1951, XUA; *The Xavier Newsletter,* February 1955, XUA.
10. Steiner to Zema, July 30, 1946, XUA; HC, January 29, 1948, XUA; *Cincinnati Enquirer,* August 22, 1949; *The Xavier Newsletter,* October 1953, XUA.
11. Arthur M. Cohen, *The Shaping of American Higher Education: Emergence and Growth of the Contemporary System* (San Francisco, 1998), 182; *Xavier Magazine,* Winter 1996; Minutes of Faculty Meeting, August 16, 1946, XUA.

12. "Know These Facts?" issued by the Citizens' Committee of the Xavier University Fund and Goodwill Campaign, [1946?], XUA; Xavier Diary, II, March 8, 1946, XUA; *The Xavier Newsletter*, January 5, 1945, XUA.

13. Steiner to Miller, November 25, 1946; Wheeler to Steiner, January 27, 1947; Steiner to Miss Marianne Miller, February 25, 1947; Steiner to Miss Florence M. Hornback, May 5, 1947; Steiner to Mary E. Dixon, April 26, 1948, XUA; HC, September 12, October 13, 1945; March 6, November 3, 1947, XUA; *Xavier University Catalogue, 1945–1946*, XUA.

14. William P. Leahy, S.J., *Adapting to America: Catholics, Jesuits, and Higher Education in the Twentieth Century* (Washington, D.C., 1991), 129; *Xavier Communique*, December 1975, XUA; Xavier Diary, II, April 12, 1946, XUA.

15. *Xavier University News*, October 1, 1946, XUA; HC, May 6, 1946, XUA; Steiner's "Xavier University and Cincinnatians" [1946], XUA; *Xavier University Catalogue, 1944–1945*, XUA; Gerald L. Gutek, *American Education 1945–2000: A History and Commentary* (Project Heights, Illinois, 2000), 9–14; Cohen, *Shaping of American Higher Education*, 182–183; Minutes of Faculty Meeting, November 21, 1946, XUA.

16. Rev. J. Peter Buschmann, S.J., "Students Bunked in Fieldhouse," *Xavier Communique*, October 29, 1971, XUA; *Xavier Magazine*, Winter 1996.

17. Presidential Report, Commencement, June 1949, XUA; Xavier Diary, II, September 12, October 14, 1946, XUA; General Information on Temporary Housing, [n.d., probably 1951 or 1952], XUA. The barracks were located on the later site of Alter Hall, the McDonald Library, and Schott Hall.

18. Steiner to Appleby, October 4, 1946, XUA; quoted in *Xavier Magazine*, Winter 1996.

19. HC, February 1, 2, March 12, June 18, 1946, XUA.

20. *Xavier University News*, October 1, 1946, XUA; HC, May 6, 1946, XUA; Steiner's "Xavier University and Cincinnatians" [1946], XUA; Gutek, *American Education*, 11.

21. *Xavier University News*, December 13, 1946; May 21, 1954; October 18, 1957; February 27, 1959, XUA.

22. *Xavier University News*, February 8, 1951; March 21, 1952; March 20, 1959, XUA.

23. *Xavier University News*, February 14, May 2, 9, 1947; April 28, 1949; November 11, 1951; March 20, May 8, 1953; February 24, 1956; May 2, 1958, XUA.

24. *Xavier University News*, October 14, 1948, XUA.

25. *Xavier University News*, March 1946; November 19, 1951, XUA.

26. *The Xavier Newsletter*, April 1956, XUA; Gallin, *Negotiating Identity*, 5–7.

27. Quotes Minutes of Faculty Meeting, November 7, 1946, XUA; Steiner to Lausche, March 1, 1946, XUA.

28. Steiner to Lausche, March 1, 1946, XUA; Quotes Minutes of Faculty Meeting, November 7, 1946, XUA.

29. Quotes Faculty Meeting, November 7, 1946, XUA; *Xavier University Catalogue, 1945–1946*, XUA.

30. Faculty Meeting, November 7, 1946, XUA.

31. Faculty Meeting, November 7, 1946; November 12, 1947, XUA.

32. HC, March 6, 1947, XUA; *The Xavier Newsletter*, April 1953, XUA.

33. *Xavier University News*, October 10 to December 12, 1947, XUA; HC, February 14, 1948, XUA; *The Xavier Newsletter*, June 1952, XUA; Press Release on Maguire, 1955, XUA; *Xavier Alumnus*, April 1964, XUA. Dr. Albert Anderson, professor of education, succeeded Moser as director of Operation Youth in 1963. Professor William Smith from the Department of Accounting had the longest term, serving as director from 1973 to 2001.

34. HC, August 24, November 26, 1946, XUA; *Xavier University News*, January 17, 1947, XUA; *Cincinnati Enquirer*, August 25, 1949. Rev. Fr. Rector went to Chicago and obtain Fr. Provincial's approval.

35. *Xavier University News*, January 17, 1947, XUA; Faculty meeting, January 13, 1947, XUA; *Cincinnati Enquirer*, August 22, 1946; HC, December 7, 1946; April 3, June 27, 1947, XUA. Members of the Lay Advisory Board were William H. Albers, Richard LeBlond, Joel L. Bowlby, Roger Ferger, Eugene A. O'Shaughnessy, Bolton Armstrong, Charles Williams, Walter Verkamp, D. J. O'Conor.

36. Steiner to Carl W. Rich, July 31, 1947, XUA; *Woodstock Letters* (Woodstock, Md., 1872–1969), 79: 338–339.

37. Steiner to Carl W. Rich, July 31, 1947, XUA; *Woodstock Letters*, 79: 338–339.

38. Presidential Report, Commencement, June 1949, XUA; HC, February 14, 1948, XUA; Xavier Diary, June 9, 1948, XUA; Steiner to Whom it may Concern, May 18, 1948, XUA. On March 1, 1949, the university published a report of gifts received during the past three years. As of December 1, 1948, $100,000 was used for emergency purposes; $122,672 reserved for endowment; and $245,344.19 designated as building fund. Of the latter amount $173,000 was applied to the new armory. Upon completion, the armory had 3,102 square feet of floor area, containing classrooms, drill hall, garage, storage space, and firing range.

39. *Xavier University News*, September 20, 26, 1947; October 7, 1948; February 24, 1949; September 14, 1950; Presidential Report, Commencement, June 1949; Steiner to Hinkle, January 25, 1951, XUA. In addition to 25 states being represented, there were in 1947 undergraduate students from China, Austria, Hawaii, Puerto Rico, British Honduras, and the British West Indies.

40. *Xavier Alumnus*, June–July 1963, XUA; *Honors Course Bulletin*, January 1949, Midwest Jesuit Archives; Xavier Diary, II, January 25, 1949,

XUA; Presidential Report, Commencement, June 1949, June 1950, June 1955, XUA.

41. *Xavier Alumnus,* June–July 1963, XUA; *Honors Course Bulletin,* January 1949, Midwest Jesuit Archives; Philip Gleason, *Contending with Modernity: Catholic Higher Education in the Twentieth Century* (New York, 1995), 250–252.

42. *The Xavier Newsletter,* June 1952, XUA; Press Release on Maguire, 1955, XUA; Presidential Address, Commencement, 1950, XUA; *Xavier Alumnus,* July 1960; April 1964; Presidential Report, Commencement, June 1951, XUA. In 1980 the university transferred the cash balance in the Chaswill Foundation Student Loan Fund to its Emergency Student Loan Fund.

43. *Xavier Alumnus,* October, 1962, XUA; *The Xavier Newsletter,* October 1952; April 1953, XUA; Presidential Report, Commencement, May 1953, XUA.

44. Presidential Report, Commencement, June 1955, XUA; *The Xavier Newsletter,* September 1954, XUA.

45. *The Xavier Alumni Newsletter,* May 1958, XUA; *Xavier Alumnus,* February 1970, XUA; *Xavier University Basketball 2003–04 Media Guide,* (2003), 159.

46. *Cincinnati Times-Star,* December 5, 1946; *Cincinnati Post,* December 6, 1946; HC, July 11, 1947, XUA; *Xavier Magazine,* Fall 1998. The best football season thereafter came in 1965 when it went 8-2.

47. Eligibility Rules Governing Participation in Collegiate Athletics, October 20, 1947, XUA.

48. Steiner to Gordon Nead, January 16, 1948, XUA.

49. HC, November 10, 1948; Xavier Diary, II, September 6, 1949, XUA.

50. *Cincinnati Enquirer,* August 22, 25, 1949, XUA; *Xavier Communique,* October 29, 1971, XUA.

51. *Cincinnati Enquirer,* August 22, 25, 1949; *Xavier Communique,* October 29, 1971, XUA.

52. *Cincinnati Enquirer,* August 22, 25, 1949. During his years at Xavier, President Steiner served as a member of the Board of Directors of the Community Chest, member of the Board of Directors of the Cincinnati and Hamilton County Chapter of the American Red Cross, vice president and member of Cincinnati's Board of Directors of the Better Housing League, vice president and member of the Board of Directors of the Mayor's Friendly Relations Committee, and vice president and member of the Board of Directors of the city's Adult Education Council. Beginning in 1947 he also served as pastor of Bellarmine Chapel at the university, though more in an overseeing capacity.

53. Xavier Diary, II, August 21, 1949, XUA; *Cincinnati Enquirer,* August 22, 1949; *Xavier Alumnus,* December 1960. On December 4, 1960, Xavier University awarded him the St. Francis Xavier medal.

54. Minutes of Faculty Meeting, December 11, 1949, XUA.
55. Steiner to Mrs. Hinkle, February 27, 1951, XUA; Presidential Report, Commencement, June 1951, XUA.
56. Alumni Directors Meeting, Chicago Province, May 17, 1947, XUA; HC, October 13, 1948, XUA; Xavier Diary, November 20, 1948, XUA; *The Xavier Newsletter*, February, April 1952; April 1953, XUA. By this time *The Xavier Newsletter* was published six times a year. The goal of the second phase of the campaign was $50,000. In addition to an alumni chapter in Indianapolis, the six alumni chapters in Ohio were in Cincinnati, Columbus, Portsmouth, Dayton, Hamilton, and Cleveland.
57. *Xaverian News*, November 12, 1930, XUA; *The Xavier Newsletter*, April 1952; April, June, September, 1953; November 1954, XUA; Presidential Report, May 1953, XUA. The Logan century depository contained a number of objects of special scientific interest, ranging from science textbooks and samples of chemistry elements discovered by mid-century to student research papers and faculty publications.
58. *The Xavier Newsletter*, April, September 1953; June 1955, XUA; Presidential Report, May 1953, XUA.
59. Presidential Report, Commencement, May 1953, XUA; *The Xavier Newsletter*, December 1952; October 1953; December 1954, XUA.
60. *The Xavier Newsletter*, February, April, November 1954, XUA; Presidential Report, Commencement, May 1953, XUA; Businessmen Mobilized for Xavier University, [n.d.], XUA; Milestones, News from The Century Campaign of Xavier University, Fall 2000, XUA; O'Connor's LEF Talk, March 10, 1967, XUA. According to Milestones, Fall 2000, BMX "is short for business mobilized for Xavier." It started in 1953.
61. *The Xavier Newsletter*, February 1954, September 1954; April, September 1955, XUA; Presidential Report, Commencement, June 1955, XUA.
62. Presidential Address, Commencement, 1950, XUA.
63. Minutes of Faculty Meeting, October 20, 1948; Minutes of Organizational Meeting of Faculty Organization, March 9, 1952, XUA; O'Connor to Maguire, September 25, 1953, XUA.
64. O'Connor to Maguire, September 25, 1953; O'Connor to Father Lemmer, September 20, 1953, XUA; Faculty Committee Minutes, April 2, 1954, XUA.
65. Faculty Committee Minutes, November 20, 1953; April 2, May 21, 1954, XUA; *The Xavier Newsletter*, April 1956, XUA; *Xavier University Faculty Handbook*, 1956, XUA.
66. *The Xavier Newsletter*, September 1955 XUA. President Maguire had been a member of the Advisory Committee of the Community Chest,

Mayor's Friendly Relations Committee, and Cincinnati's Better Housing League.

67. *The Xavier Newsletter*, September 1954, XUA. John Carroll University and University of Detroit were members of the Chicago province from 1928 to 1955, at which time they joined the newly-established Detroit province in 1955.

Chapter 7 Xavier University Transformed: The Presidency of Paul L. O'Connor, S.J., 1955–1972

1. *The Xavier Newsletter*, September 1955, XUA; *Xavier Communique*, November 25, 1974, XUA.

2. *Xavier University News*, September 30, 1955, XUA; *The Xavier Newsletter*, September, December 1955, XUA; Memorial Resolution to O'Connor by the Commercial Club, November 1974, XUA.

3. *The Xavier Newsletter*, September, October, December 1955, XUA.

4. *The Xavier Newsletter*, September 1956; X. . . as I see it, Fall 1957, XUA.

5. O'Connor's Address, Queen City Association, December 3, 1959, XUA.

6. "X. . . as I see it," Fall 1957; New Release, June 1957, XUA; *The Xavier Newsletter*, October 1957, XUA; *Xavier University Catalogue*, 1957–1958.

7. *The Xavier Newsletter*, June, September, 1957, XUA. Schmidt, former president of the Xavier Alumni Association, died on July 16, 1957.

8. *The Xavier Newsletter*, March 1958, XUA; Alice Gallin, O.S.U., *Negotiating Identity: Catholic Higher Education Since 1960* (Notre Dame, Indiana, 2000), 28–29.

9. *The Xavier Newsletter*, December 1955, XUA; Remarks of the Very Reverend Paul L. O'Connor, S.J., May 1, 1958, XUA; *The Xavier Alumni Newsletter*, May, 1958, XUA; *Xavier Alumnus*, May 1959, XUA.

10. Remarks of the Very Reverend Paul L. O'Connor, S.J., May 1, 1958, XUA; *The Xavier Alumni Newsletter*, May, 1958, XUA; Operation Party Line, LEF Talk, March 30, 1967, XUA.

11. O'Connor's Address, Queen City Association, December 3, 1959, XUA; *Xavier Alumnus*, July 1960, XUA; E. M. Orlemann, Secretary, City Planning and Boundaries Committee, to Mr. Edward P. Vonderhaar, July 2, 1958, XUA; BT, April 12, 17, 1966, XUA; Faculty Committee Minutes, December 10, 1957, XUA. The land developed east of Herald Avenue would eventually become designated as the University Mall.

12. *Xavier Alumnus*, May 1959; October, December 1960; October 1961, XUA. When construction of the new classroom building began in early summer 1959 the university had more than $600,000 in its annual fund earmarked for it.

13. O'Connor's address Queen City Association, December 3, 1959; O'Connor BMX Talk, 1964, XUA; VonderHaar to O'Connor, [n.d., March 1960], XUA; *Xavier Alumnus*, May 1959; October, December 1960; March, October 1961, XUA.

14. President Report, Commencement, June 1960, XUA; *Xavier Alumnus*, July 1960; October 1961, XUA; *Xavier News*, January 8, 1965, XUA.

15. Presidential Report, Commencement, June 1960, XUA; BT, January 6, 1972, XUA; Helmes to Mulligan, August 24, 1971; O'Connor to William H. Zimmer, April 13, 1964, XUA; *Xavier Alumnus*, July 1960; October 1961, XUA; *Cincinnati Post & Times-Star*, April 6, 1964.

16. *Xavier Alumnus*, October, 1961, XUA.

17. *Xavier Newsletter*, June 1960, XUA; *Xavier Alumnus*, July, 1960; December 1962, XUA; Rev. Paul L. O'Connor, S.J., Chapel Dedication, December 16, 1962, XUA. At the Bellarmine Chapel dedication ceremonies O'Connor pointed out that it "embodies, in a sense, the challenge to our times. That is to take the marvelous advances in scientific accomplishment and to dedicate them to larger purposes."

18. O'Connor's Address, Queen City Association, December 3, 1959, XUA; *Xavier Alumnus*, July, 1960, XUA; BT, September 18, December 31, 1963, XUA; *Xavier Alumnus*, February 1963, XUA.

19. O'Connor's Address, Queen City Association, December 3, 1959; O'Connor's LEF Talk, 1964; O'Connor's BMX Talk, November 4, 1965, XUA; *Xavier Alumnus*, July, 1960; February 1963, XUA; BT, September 18, December 31, 1963, XUA; Gallin, *Negotiating Identity*, 36.

20. O'Connor's BMX Talk, 1964; O'Connor's LEF Talk, 1964; O'Connor's Comments, Louisville, Alumni Association, April 14, 1967, XUA; BT, April 10, 1963; September 3, 1964; January 22, 1965, XUA; *Xavier Alumnus*, November, 1959, XUA.

21. BT, January 22, 1965; January 6, 1966, XUA; *Xavier Alumnus*, January, October 1965, XUA; O'Connor's BMX Talk, November 4, 1965, XUA.

22. Certificate of Amendment to Articles of Xavier University, February 5, 1966, XUA; Roger Fortin, *Faith and Action: A History of the Catholic Archdiocese of Cincinnati, 1821–1996* (Columbus, Ohio, 2002), 310–311. On September 12, 1945, President Steiner asked the treasurer "to obtain legal advice on the limitation in our original charter for the educating of 'White youth'." According to the House minutes, "[a]fterwards Fr. Breen found that such a change in the charter had already been made." HC, September 12, 1945.

23. BT, March 10, 25, 1965, XUA.

24. Malone to O'Connor, November 8, 1965; O'Callaghan to O'Connor, November 11, 1965; O'Callaghan to Dr. Don Cosgrove, October 12, 1973, XUA; BT, November 19, 1965, XUA; Faculty Committee Minutes, November 5, 1965, XUA

25. *Xavier Alumnus*, April 1966, XUA. When Clement Barnhorn, the sculptor, died in 1935, he willed his entire group of original plaster models to the university. The Alumni Association mounted selected pieces in the Mary G. Lodge Reading Room in the Schmidt Building. Other artists in the university's collection consisted of Henry Farny, John Rettig, Martin Rettig, Matt Daly, Martin Dumler, Elizabeth Nourse, Louis Vogt and others. Later acquisitions included paintings by Thomas Lindsay, John Sharp, John Weis, E. T. Hurley, and Herman Wessel among others.
26. BT, November 6, 1964, XUA; *Xavier Alumnus*, January 1965, XUA.
27. O'Connor's Indianapolis Alumni Association Talk, April 12, 1967, XUA; *Xavier Alumnus*, May 1967, XUA. The Mary Lodge Learning Laboratory eventually occupied the second floor of the Schmidt Building.
28. BT, November 19, 1965; January 6, May 17, June 15, August 18, December 8, 1966, XUA; *Xavier Alumnus*, April 1968, XUA. Total enrollment in the 1967–1968 school year was 2,341 in the undergraduate day programs, 968 in the Evening College, and 2,653 in the Graduate School.
29. O'Connor's BMX Talk, November 4, 1965; O'Connor's LEF Talk, March 30, 1967; O'Connor's Remarks at the Dedication of the Musketeer Plaza, November 2, 1968, XUA; *Xavier Alumnus*, September 1966, XUA.
30. O'Connor's LEF Talk, April 14, 1966; March 30, 1967, XUA; BT, June 15, 1966; May 4, 1967, XUA; *Xavier Alumnus*, September 1966; January 1969, XUA. Hilda Rothschild in the Department of Education was instrumental in establishing Xavier University's Montessori program. In 1966 seven women earned the distinction of being the first students in the country to receive master of education degrees in Montessori.
31. BT, September 18, 1963; September 13, 1965, XUA; HC, September 18, 1965, XUA; O'Connor's LEF Talk, 1966, XUA; *Xavier Alumnus*, April 1970, XUA.
32. O'Connor's LEF Talk, 1966, XUA.
33. BT, February 12, 1965; March 18, September 29, 1966, XUA; *Xavier Alumnus*, September 1966, XUA.
34. BT, December 8, 1966, XUA.
35. BT, January 5, 24, March 7, April 27, 1967, XUA; O'Connor to Board of Trustees, May 1, 1967; Connery to O'Connor, April 22, 1967, XUA.
36. BT, March 7, April 27, 1967, XUA; O'Connor to Board of Trustees, May 1, 1967; Connery to O'Connor, April 22, 1967, XUA; *Xavier Alumnus*, April 1970, XUA.
37. O'Connor to Paul C. Beckman, March 9, 1970, XUA.
38. *Xavier Alumnus*, April 1965, XUA. By 1965 sixty-two persons had been named to the Musketeer Legion of Honor.

39. *Xavier Alumnus*, April 1965; September 1966; April 1968, XUA. The mural, made possible by the class of 1966 remembrance fund, was drawn by the Cincinnati artist, William H. O'Neill.

40. *Xavier Alumnus*, April 1968, XUA; O'Connor Remarks at the Dedication of the Musketeer Plaza, November 2, 1968, XUA.

41. O'Connor's Notice to Jesuit Community, April 28, 1966; O'Connor to Board of Trustees, April 12, 17, 1966, XUA; *Xavier Alumnus*, September 1966, XUA; *Xavier Newsletter*, September 1954, XUA; *Xavier Magazine*, Winter 1996.

42. Arthur M. Cohen, *The Shaping of American Higher Education: Emergence and Growth of the Contemporary System* (San Francisco, 1998), 245–246; *Xavier Alumnus*, October 1961, XUA.

43. O'Connor, BMX Talk, 1964; O'Connor Comments, Cleveland Chapter, Alumni Association, February 8, 1969; O'Connor's Comments, Louisville Chapter, Alumni Association, April 14, 1967, XUA; *Xavier Alumnus*, April 1968; January, June, October 1969; April, June, December 1970, XUA.

44. *Xavier Alumnus*, June, October 1969, XUA.

45. Faculty Committee Minutes, October 7, 1963; April 10, September 30, 1964; May 20, 26, 1966, XUA; O'Connor to Chair of Faculty Committee, June 13, 1966, XUA; *Xavier University Faculty Handbook*, 1956, XUA; Gallin, *Negotiating Identity*, 60, 121; Lawrence Andrew Dorr, "Academic Deans in Jesuit Higher Education: A Comparative Study of Deans, Jesuit and Lay," (Ph.D. diss., University of Michigan, 1966), 19–21.

46. Faculty Committee Minutes, October 7, 1963; April 10, September 30, 1964; May 20, 26, 1966, XUA; O'Connor BMX Talk, 1964; O'Connor's LEF Talk, 1964; O'Connor's Comments, Louisville, Alumni Association, April 14, 1967, XUA; O'Connor to Chair of Faculty Committee, June 13, 1966, XUA; Gallin, *Negotiating Identity*, 60, 121.

47. O'Connor to Trustees, June 16, 1970, XUA; BT, June 15, 1966; August 6, 1970, XUA; Faculty Committee Minutes, May 6, 1969, XUA; A Report to the University Board of Trustees on the University Senate, March 1974; Fortin's Report on the History of the University Senate, December 1973, XUA; Gallin, *Negotiating Identity*, 123.

48. *The Xavier Newsletter*, May 1957, XUA; Presidential Report, Commencement, June 1960, XUA; *Xavier Alumnus*, November 1959; October 1964; June 1970, XUA.

49. "X. . . as I see it," Summer 1957; *The Xavier Newsletter*, May, June 1958; X Newsletter, June 1958, XUA; O'Connor BMX talk, 1964, XUA; Presidential Report, Commencement, June 1959; June 1960, XUA; O'Connor to W. Homer Turner, April 15, 1958; *Xavier Alumnus*, November 1959; May 1961; October 1964; April 1965; April, September

1966; June 1970, XUA. In June 1960 Xavier awarded its first master's degrees in hospital administration.

50. *Xavier Alumnus*, May, October 1961, XUA.

51. *Xavier Alumnus*, December 1962, XUA. The scientists from the Israel Institute of Technology, Princeton, Harvard, and Yeshiva Universities were Nathan Rosen, Eugene P. Wigner, Wendell H. Furry, and Yakir Aharanov respectively.

52. BT, September 18, 1963, XUA; O'Connor's LEF Talk, 1964, XUA.

53. BT, December 28, 1964, XUA; *Xavier Alumnus*, October 1965, XUA; O'Connor's Indianapolis Alumni Association Talk, April 12, 1967, XUA. The computer center included a 1620 IBM computer and served the university in three primary areas—research, education, and administration.

54. *Xavier Alumnus*, January 1970, XUA.

55. Presidential Address, Commencement, June 1967, XUA; *Xavier University Catalogue, 1965–1966*, XUA.

56. FAX, October 11, 1967, XUA; BT, May 16, 1968; January 23, April 15, September 11, 1971, XUA; *Xavier University Catalogue, 1969–1970*, XUA; Academic Council, Minutes, May 14, 1971, XUA. The graduate counterpart to the Academic Council was the Board of Graduate Studies.

57. Gallin, *Negotiating Identity*, 57–58, 196.

58. Quoted in Gallin, *Negotiating Identity*, 56.

59. O'Connor to Board of Trustees, January 27, 1966; Nieporte to Mr. H. J. Siebenthaler, October 19, 1970, XUA; BT, February 14, 1968; December 16, 1970, XUA.

60. *The Xavier Newsletter*, September 1956; "X . . . as I see it," Summer, 1957, XUA; BT, March 10, May 25, 1962; February 2, 1963, XUA; Rank and Tenure Committee Minutes, February 11, 1957, XUA; *Xavier Alumnus*, October 1964, XUA; Gallin, *Negotiating Identity*, 41.

61. *The Xavier Newsletter*, September 1956; "X . . . as I see it," Summer, 1957, XUA; BT, March 10, 1962; February 2, 1963; March 20, 1964; February 12, 1965; December 8, January 6, 1966; February 14, 1968; February 24, 1971; February 12, 1972, XUA; FAX, October 11, 1967, XUA; Faculty Committee Minutes, May 7, 14, November 2, 1965, XUA; Chair of Faculty Committee to O'Callaghan, October 22, 1965; O'Callaghan to Chair of Faculty Committee, October 26, 1965; Hailstones to Chair of Faculty Committee, October 20, 1965; Minutes of the Committee on Rank and Tenure, February 6, 1969; O'Callaghan to O'Connor, February 18, 1969, XUA; AAUP Report for 1969–1970, March 11, 1970, XUA.

62. BT, December 8, January 6, 1966; February 14, 1968; February 24, 1971; February 12, 1972, XUA; FAX, October 11, 1967, XUA; O'Callaghan

to O'Connor, February 18, 1969; Chair of Faculty Committee to O'Callaghan, October 22, 1965; O'Callaghan to Chair of Faculty Committee, October 26, 1965; Hailstones to Chair of Faculty Committee, October 20, 1965, XUA; Faculty Committee Minutes, November 2, 1965; Minutes of the Committee on Rank and Tenure, February 6, 1969; AAUP Report for 1969–1970, March 11, 1970, XUA.

63. O'Connor's Tuition Statement, February 11, 1963, XUA; O'Connor to Parents, October 28, 1964, XUA; *Xavier Alumnus*, January 1965, XUA.

64. *Xavier Alumnus*, May, 1961, XUA; Buschmann, "Xavier Faces The Admissions Crisis," XUA; BT, March 17, 1962, XUA.

65. *The Xavier Newsletter*, May 1957, XUA; Presidential Report, Commencement, June 1959; June 1960, XUA; *Xavier Alumnus*, May 1961; June 1970, XUA; O'Connor's BMX Talk, November 4, 1965, XUA. The topic of the Intercollegiate Essay Contest in 1969 was "Literature and the Search for God Today," with papers submitted by students from nine Jesuit universities and colleges.

66. *Xavier University News*, January 16, November 11, 1952; January 22, 1954; October 26, 1956; January 13, 1958; February 26, 1959, XUA. Harry Gold graduated with honors in June 1940. The lowest grade he received at the university was ironically in a course entitled "Principles of Ethics." On December 9, 1950, he received a 30-year prison sentence. He was released on parole in 1965,

67. *Xavier University News*, October 21, 1960, XUA; *Xavier News*, September 25, 1964, XUA; BT, April 17, 1966, XUA; Presidential Address, Commencement, June 1967, XUA; Members of the class of 1967 had much to do with the establishment of Faculty and Students Talk and Faculty and Dorm Students in Conference.

68. *Xavier Alumnus*, May 1962; April–May 1963; February 1970, XUA; *The Xavier Alumni Newsletter*, May, 1958, XUA; Faculty Committee Minutes, November 6, 1958, XUA. McCafferty's record [91-71] was the second best in Xavier history behind Clem Crowe's 97-78. During his last year he had been combination coach and athletic director.

69. *Xavier University News*, October 5, 12, 19, 1962, XUA.

70. *Xavier University News*, October 19, 1962, XUA; *Xavier Alumnus*, May 1962; April–May 1963; February 1970, XUA. A university committee made the selection of the 54 all-time greats that constituted all five all-decade teams.

71. *Xavier Alumnus*, June–July, 1963; October 1964, XUA; *Xavier University News*, May 18, 1956, XUA; *Xavier News*, March 20, 1964; April 9, 1965, XUA.

72. *Xavier Alumnus*, November 1959; December 1960; December 1963, XUA.

73. *Xavier Alumnus*, October 1963, XUA; Faculty Committee Minutes, January 17, 1964, XUA.
74. O'Connor to Edward Brueggeman, Chair of the Faculty Committee, February 5, 1964, XUA; *The Communique*, February 5, 1964, XUA; BT, April 17, 1966, XUA.
75. *Xavier University Magazine*, Fall 1998. Tim Wooner confessed to the prank at his 40th class reunion in 1998.
76. *Xavier Alumnus*, November, 1959, XUA; Presidential Report, Commencement, June 1960, XUA; William J. Larkin, Chairman, Faculty Committee, to P. H. Ratterman, S.J., March 4, 1964, XUA.
77. *Xavier Alumnus*, March 1972, XUA.
78. FAX, October 11, 1967, XUA; Gallin, *Negotiating Identity*, 54.
79. *Xavier Alumnus*, January 1969, XUA; Gallin, *Negotiating Identity*, 23, 57.
80. Minutes of Meeting, Religious Development Committee, February 17, 1969, XUA; BT, February 25, 1969; August 4, 1970, XUA; Gallin, *Negotiating Identity*, 24-25.
81. *Xavier News*, March 22, September 27, October 4, 1968, XUA.
82. *Xavier News*, October 22, 1965; February 4, 25, October 28, 1966; February 10, April 14, May 19, 1967, XUA.
83. *Xavier Magazine*, Fall 1999; Editorial, "Awareness at Xavier University," *Cincinnati Enquirer*, October 22, 1969; *Xavier Alumnus*, August, October 1969, XUA; *Xavier News*, October 1, 22, 1969; October 28, 1970, XUA; Cohen, *Negotiating Identity*, 247–248.
84. Academic Council Minutes, February 12, 1969, XUA; *Xavier Alumhus*, March 1969, XUA; BT, March 10, 1965; February 25, 1969, XUA; *Xavier News*, October 28, November 11, 18, December 2, 1966; March 8, 22, April 5, May 3, 10, 1968, XUA; Report by ROTC Investigation Committee, [n.d.], 1968, XUA.
85. *Xavier Alumnus*, February 1970, XUA; BT, September 25, October 2, 9, 1964; October 14, 1966; November 10, 1967; November 27, 1969, XUA; O'Connor to Faculty on Racial and Justice Committee, November 17, 1965, XUA; General Faculty Meeting, October 20, 1965, XUA.
86. *Xavier Alumnus*, February, April 1970, XUA; BT, November 27, 1969, XUA; *Xavier News*, March 7, 1969; January 12, 1972, XUA; Gerald L. Gutek, *American Education 1945–2000: A History and Commentary* (Project Heights, Illinois, 2000), 228. In the spring of 1969 students had organized the first Black Culture Program. Statistics about the racial composition of the university's student body are virtually nonexistent before the late 1960s. The first full-time non-tenure track black faculty member was Mark Cummings in the Department of Mathematics in 1962. Five years later the university hired William Edward Gordon as associate professor of economics and finance, becoming the first full-time tenure track African American faculty member at Xavier

University. A year later a second tenure-track black faculty member was hired in the Department of Mathematics. In the fall of 1970 Napoleon Bryant joined the Department of Education.

87. O'Connor Comments, Indianapolis Chapter, Alumni Association, April 12, 1967, XUA; BT, March 25, June 28, 1965, XUA; Humbert, S.J. to O'Callaghan, S.J., May 25, 1965, XUA.

88. O'Connor's Address, Queen City Association, December 3, 1959; O'Connor's Notice to Jesuit Community, September 29, 1969; O'Connor BMX talk, 1964; O'Connor's LEF Talk, 1964, XUA.

89. *The Xavier Alumni Newsletter*, September 1958, XUA; *Xavier Alumnus*, March 1960; October 1961; March, October, 1961; March 1962; April–May 1963, XUA.

90. O'Connor's LEF Talk, 1964, XUA; *Xavier Alumnus*, April 1966, XUA.

91. BT, June 14, 1967, XUA; *Xavier Alumnus*, September 1967, XUA; O'Connor's Statement on Tuition, February 12, 1969, XUA.

92. O'Connor to W. Homer Turner, April 15, 1958, XUA; O'Connor's LEF Talk, 1964; BMX Talk, 1964; O'Connor Comments, Louisville Chapter, Alumni Association, April 14, 1967, XUA; *Xavier Alumnus*, April 1968; March, October 1969; April 1972, XUA.

93. John A. Moser to O'Connor, October 18, 1967, XUA; FAX, October 11, 1967, XUA.

94. George A. Brakeley to O'Connor, April 22, 1969, XUA; O'Connor Comments, Cleveland Chapter, Alumni Association, February 8, 1969, XUA; BT, April 15, 1969; April 29, 1970; June 14, 1971; June 14, July 18, 1972, XUA; Faculty Committee Minutes, December 1, 1969, XUA.

95. *Xavier Alumnus*, March 1969; June 1970, XUA; Paul L. Burkhart to O'Connor, August 21, 1969; O'Connor to Board of Trustees, August 2, 1965; January 7, August 25, 1969; Beumer to Board of Trustees, February 17, 1970, XUA; BT, September 23, 1961; July 27, 1962; April 4, 1963; June 14, 1972, XUA; FAX, October 11, 1967, XUA; O'Connor's LEF Talk, 1964, XUA.

96. William P. Leahy, S.J., *Adapting to America: Catholics, Jesuits, and Higher Education in the Twentieth Century* (Washington, D.C., 1991), 85; *Xavier University News*, December 12, 1947; July 23, 1956, XUA.

97. BT, September 23, 1961; June 20, October 11, 1963: March 7, 1967, XUA; O'Connor Speech, Indianapolis, [n.d., 1967], XUA; Gallin, *Negotiating Identity*, 80–81. Edgecliff College went coed in 1970; the College of Mt. St. Joseph in 1986.

98. O'Connor Speech, Indianapolis, [n.d., 1967], XUA; *Xavier Alumnus*, January 1969, XUA; *Xavier News*, April 28, 1967, XUA.

99. Student Council Poll Results, [n.d.,] , XUA.

100. BT, December 14, 1968, XUA; *Cincinnati Enquirer*, February 3, 1969.

101. O'Connor to Board of Trustees, January 17, 1969, XUA; *Cincinnati Enquirer*, February 3, 1969; September 1, 1970; Gallin, *Negotiating Identity*, 80–81.

102. O'Connor to Board of Trustees, January 17, 1969, XUA.

103. O'Connor to Board of Trustees, January 17, 1969, XUA; *Xavier Alumnus*, March 1969, XUA; Gallin, *Negotiating Identity*, 72.

104. O'Connor to Board of Trustees, January 17, 1969, XUA; *Xavier Alumnus*, March 1969, XUA.

105. Arrupe to Harvanek, February 11, 1969; Harvanek to O'Connor, February 21, 1969, XUA; BT, January 17, 1969, XUA.

106. *Xavier Alumnus*, August 1969, XUA; Frederick Rudolph, *The American College and University: A History* (Athens, Ga., 1990), 323; Gallin, *Negotiating Identity*, 79.

107. *Xavier Alumnus*, April 1970, XUA; *Xavier University Magazine*, Winter 1995.

108. *Xavier Alumnus*, February 1970, XUA.

109. *Xavier Alumnus*, September 1972, XUA; *Xavier University Magazine*, Winter 1995; *Xavier University News*, October 14, 1960, XUA. The first woman faculty member in the undergraduate day division was Gertrude Lum in the Department of Biology. However, the first full-time tenure track woman faculty member was Marjorie Dew, who was hired in 1965 as assistant professor of English.

110. Cohen, *Shaping of American Higher Education*, 151.

111. Quoted in Gallin, *Negotiating Identity*, 116.

112. Quoted in Gallin, *Negotiating Identity*, 43–44; Charles Ford and Edgar Roy, *The Renewal of Catholic Higher Education* (Washington, D.C., 1968); Vincent T. O'Keefe, S.J., Who Owns Jesuit Colleges and Universities?, *Conversations* (February 1992), 15–17. See Paul A. FitsGerald, S.J., *The Governance of Jesuit Colleges in the United States, 1920–1970* (Notre Dame, Indiana, 1984).

113. BT, March 18, April 17, 1966, June 29–30, 1966; January 24, 1967; October 4, 1968, XUA; Gallin, *Negotiating Identity*, 43.

114. O'Connor Comments, Indianapolis Chapter, Alumni Association, April 12, 1967, XUA.

115. O'Connor to Board of Trustees, October 3, 1968, XUA; Gallin, *Negotiating Identity*, 43–45.

116. O'Connor to Board of Trustees, October 3, 1968, XUA; Gallin, *Negotiating Identity*, 43–45; 46–47; *Catholic Institutions: Canonical and Civil Law Status* (Washington, D.C., 1968).

117. O'Connor to Board of Trustees, October 3, 1968, XUA.

118. O'Connor to Board of Trustees, October 3, 1968, XUA; BT, October 4, 1968, XUA.

119. BT, October 4, 1968; January 17, 1969, XUA; Deters to O'Connor, March 20, 1970, XUA.
120. BT, September 6, 1969, XUA; Survey of Current Jesuit College and University Governing Structures, 1970, XUA; Gallin, *Negotiating Identity*, 44. Among the 66 Catholic institutions who were members of the Middle States Association of North Central, 32 percent of the boards of trustees had a majority of lay people.
121. BT, September 6, October 8, 1969; August 24, December 8, 1970; January 23, 27, 1971, XUA; *Xavier Alumnus*, April–May, 1963; October 1970, XUA; O'Connor's Notice to Jesuit Community, January 28, 1970; O'Connor to Board of Trustees, September 3, 1969; January 21, 1971, XUA. In the fall of 1969 the trustees granted President O'Connor a leave of absence in order to undergo a thorough medical checkup. For a few months Victor Nieporte, S.J., executive vice president, served as acting president.
122. *Xavier Communique*, January 8 1971, XUA; O'Connor to Fr. Richard E. Twohy, S.J., President, Gonzaga University, September 22, 1970, XUA; BT, January 11, 1971, XUA. The new Jesuit board members were Reverend A. William Crandall, S.J., president of the Association of Jesuit Colleges and Universities; Richard E. Twohy, president of Gonzaga University, in Spokane, Washington, and Lawrence V. Britt, dean, College of Arts and Sciences at John Carroll University in Cleveland.
123. BT, April 15, September 11, 1971; July 18, 1972, XUA; Gallin, *Negotiating Identity*, 111, 119.
124. BT, April 6, 1972, XUA; Vince Beckman to O'Connor, May 26, 1972, XUA.
125. Board of Trustees Committees, 1976–1977, XUA.
126. BT, September 23, October 14, November 11, 1961, XUA.
127. BT, December 26, 1970, XUA.
128. Committee on Rank and Tenure, February 16, 1971, XUA; Mulligan to O'Connor, February 18, 1971; O'Connor to Trustees, February 23, 1971; David Tom to Roderick Shearer, November 8, 1971, XUA; BT, January 4, 1971, XUA.
129. BT, December 26, 1970, XUA; Student Survey on Xavier University Football, October 16–17, 1971, XUA; Michael Conaton to Shearer, [n.d.], XUA; Committee on Rank and Tenure, February 16, 1971, XUA.
130. Mulligan to O'Connor, October 26, 1971, XUA; Committee on Rank and Tenure, February 16, 1971, XUA.
131. VonderHaar to Mulligan, November 17, 1971, XUA.
132. BT, December 12, 1971, XUA; Report of the Football Subcommittee, [n.d.], received December 1, 1971, XUA; Report on the Progress of the Three-Year-Cost-Reduction Plan for Football, December 21, 1972, XUA.

133. XU On-Campus Press Release, August 30, 1972, XUA; BT, June 14, September 29, 1972, XUA; O'Connor to William J. Keating, November 8, 1972, XUA; *Cincinnati Post*, September 11, 1974. Xavier University had had a position of chancellor in its administration from 1922 to 1962.

Chapter 8   Adjustments and Conflict: A Mature University in Transition, 1972–1990

1. *Xavier News*, September 27, 1972, XUA; *Xavier Alumnus*, November 1972, XUA; *Xavier Communique*, December 8, 1972, XUA; BT, September 25, 1974, XUA.
2. *Xavier Communique*, December 8, 1972, XUA.
3. Report of the President, 1972–1973, XUA; BT, September 26, 1973, XUA.
4. Report of the President, 1972–1973, XUA.
5. Report of the President, 1972–1973, XUA; BT, September 25, 1974, XUA.
6. BT, September 26, 1973; December 17, 1975, XUA; *Xavier News*, December 6, 1972; May 16, 1973, XUA.
7. *Xavier Alumnus*, November 1972, XUA; Executive Committee Meeting, December 20, 1972, XUA; BT, January 5, June 1, 1973; September 26, 1973, XUA; Report of the ad hoc Committee on Athletics to the University Senate, April 1973, XUA.
8. BT, December 19, 1973, XUA.
9. BT, December 19, 1973, XUA; *Xavier Magazine*, Fall 1999. The lay faculty member who voted to retain football was Michael J. Conaton of the class of 1955.
10. BT, December 19, 1974; December 15, 1976, XUA. The surplus in June 1976 was $29,619.
11. Mulligan to Board of Trustees, May 24, 1977, XUA; BT, December 14, 1977; Student Affairs Report, December 5, 1984, Board of Trustees, XUA.
12. BT, May 24, 1978, March 14, 1979, XUA; *Musketeer Sports News*, February 3, 1979, XUA.
13. BT, March 14, May 9, September 12, 1979; May 7, 1980, XUA; *Xavier News*, October 29, 1980, XUA. Upon the hiring of Bob Staak, Jim McCafferty, the former athletic director, became director of the newly-built O'Connor Sports Center.
14. BT, December 16, 1981, XUA.
15. Mulligan to Administrative Offices and Faculty, September 18, 1973; O'Callaghan to Dr. Don Cosgrove, October 12, 1973, XUA; Faculty Committee Minutes, November 2, 16, December 7, 1973, XUA; BT, September 26, 1973, XUA.

16. BT, September 25, 1974, XUA; University Planning Committee Report, May 1, 1985, XUA; Faculty Committee Minutes, November 12, 1960; April 20, 1961, XUA. In 1960 Xavier faculty led by W. Henry Kenney, S.J., professor of philosophy, had proposed the establishment of "an Honors Program other than the H.A.B. program," with special two-hour interdisciplinary seminars in English, history, and theology and basic courses in political science and economics on "Man and Society" in the first two years. It never materialized.

17. Mulligan to Administrative Offices and Faculty, September 18, 1973, XUA; BT, September 26, 1973; September 25, 1974; September 27, 1978; September 12, 1979, XUA; Academic Vice President's Report to the Trustees, September 21, 1977, XUA; University Planning Committee Report, May 1, 1985, XUA; *Xavier Alumnus*, June 1970, XUA.

18. BT, September 25, December 19, 1974, XUA; Academic Vice President's Report to the Trustees, September 21, 1977, XUA; Brennan to Joseph Angilella, August 20, 1976, XUA.

19. BT, March 23, 1977, XUA; Mulligan to Trustees, May 24, 1977; December 13, 1978, XUA.

20. BT, December 17, 1975, XUA; Report of the North Central Association of Colleges and Secondary Schools Visit, March 13–15, 1978, XUA; *Xavier University Catalogue, 1976; Xavier University Catalogue, 1978–1980*, XUA

21. Report of the North Central Association of Colleges and Secondary Schools Visit, March 13–15, 1978, XUA; BT, March 27, 1974, XUA.

22. Report of the North Central Association of Colleges and Secondary Schools Visit, March 13–15, 1978, XUA; BT, March 21, September 27, 1978, XUA; University Planning Committee Report, May 1, 1985, XUA; FAX, October 11, 1967, XUA.

23. BT, September 27, 1978; May 9, September 12, 1979; September 4, 1980, XUA.

24. BT, May 5, 1982, XUA; Academic Vice President's Report, May 5, 1982, XUA; University Planning Committee Report, May 1, 1985, XUA; Arthur M. Cohen, *The Shaping of American Higher Education: Emergence and Growth of the Contemporary System* (San Francisco, 1998), 126.

25. Mulligan to Fletcher E. Nyce, February 24, 1975, XUA; Academic Vice President's Report to the Trustees, May 25, September 21, 1977; Mulligan to Board of Trustees, May 24, 1977, XUA; BT, March 19, May 28, October 1, 1975; September 27, 1978; May 9, 1979, XUA. The Office of Admission and Recruitment was placed under the jurisdiction of the academic vice president in 1975.

26. Report of the President, 1972–1973, XUA; BT, May 6, 1981; May 4, 1983, XUA; Academic Vice President's Report, May 5, 1982, XUA; University Planning Committee Report, May 1, 1985, XUA.

27. Report of the President, 1972–1973, XUA; Enrollment Statistics, April 1973, XUA; BT, June 1, 1973; March 27, September 25, December 19, 1974, XUA; "Freshman Inquiry and Applicant Information, 1961 to Present"; "Xavier University Fall Enrollment Trends;" Enrollment Statistics, April 1973, XUA; Mulligan to Board of Trustees, May 24, 1977, XUA; Alice Gallin, O.S.U., *Negotiating Identity: Catholic Higher Education Since 1960* (Notre Dame, Indiana, 2000), 81. According to the Board of Trustees minutes of December 13, 1978, the number of freshmen increased from 389 in 1974 to 574 in 1978;

28. BT, September 29, December 15, 1976; March 23, May 25, 1977, XUA. Xavier retained the consulting services of the Northlich Stolley Company.

29. Report of the North Central Association of Colleges and Secondary Schools Visit, March 13–15, 1978, XUA; BT, May 25, 1977; September 16, 1981, XUA; "Summary Data Freshman Class, 1977 to Present," XUA.

30. BT, March 23, 1977; September 12, 1979, XUA; Report of the North Central Association of Colleges and Secondary Schools Visit, March 13–15, 1978, XUA.

31. BT, March 23, 1977; September 12, 1979; September 4, 1980; September 16, 1981; September 15, December 15, 1982, XUA; Report of the North Central Association of Colleges and Secondary Schools Visit, March 13–15, 1978, XUA; Report of the Academic Vice President to the Board of Trustees, May 9, 1979, XUA; "Freshman Inquiry and Applicant Information, 1961 to Present"; "Xavier University Fall Enrollment Trends," XUA; Gallin, *Negotiating Identity*, 49. In 1982 Xavier University's first online registration had a successful debut.

32. BT, September 15, 1972; September 26, June 1, 1973; December 19, 1974; December 8, 1989, XUA; Shearer to Trustees, May 29, 1973, XUA. To help promote financial giving on a higher plain the university designated the $500–$999 level as the Elet Society.

33. Corbett to Mulligan, September 16, 1974; Mulligan to William Whittaker, June 4, 1974, XUA.

34. Mulligan to Trustees, November 16, 1974; Mulligan to William Whittaker, June 4, 1974, XUA.

35. BT, September 15, 1972; September 26, 1973; December 19, 1974; March 19, 1975; March 24, 1976, XUA; Mulligan to Trustees, November 16, 1974; Mulligan to Executive Committee of the Board of Trustees, May 16, 1974, XUA; *Xaverian News*, May 16, 1928, XUA. A gift from the Harpenau-Elsaesser families helped pay for the construction of four new tennis courts.

36. BT, October 1, 1975; September 29, 1976, XUA; Report on Capital Fundraising at Xavier, Board of Trustees, December 3, 1986, XUA.

37. BT, September 29, 1976; September 21, December 14, 1977; September 12, 1979; September 15, 1982, XUA; Report on Capital Fund-raising at

Xavier, Board of Trustees, December 3, 1986, XUA. The Sesquicentennial Campaign received its largest gift from an alumnus in the amount of $605,000. Moreover, a National Endowment for the Humanities Challenge Grant of $500,000, awarded in 1977 and designed to provide improvement in such areas as the library holdings and renovations of humanities facilities, helped stimulate the campaign. In addition to the fund-raising success of the Sesquicentennial Campaign, the total cost per dollar raised was 18.2 cents compared to 21.5 cents per dollar from 1970 to 1976 during the Advancement Fund Campaign. Moreover, in 1979 the university's total indebtedness was slightly more than $3,000,000, $2,750,000 in long-term mortgages and $270,000 in debt service.

38. BT, March 21, May 9, September 27, 1978, XUA; *Xavier University Magazine*, Winter 1992.
39. U.S. Shoe News Release, November 13, 1978, XUA; BT, December 13, 1978; September 12, 1979; March 11, May 6, December 16, 1981; May 5, September 15, 1982, XUA. U.S. Shoe donated land worth over $2,165,000 that became the site of Xavier's A.B. Cohen Center.
40. BT, June 1, 1973; December 15, 1976; September 12, December 12, 1979, XUA.
41. Report of the President, September 16, 1981; December 5, 1984, Board of Trustees, XUA.
42. O'Connor to Trustees, September 3, 1969, XUA; BT, September 6, 1969, XUA.
43. BT, December 12, 1979, XUA; Faculty Committee Minutes, January 21, 1980, XUA.
44. BT, March 12, 1980, XUA; Gallin, *Negotiating Identity*, 79.
45. BT, March 12, 1980, XUA. Many spouses of Edgecliff Alumnae were Xavier alumni.
46. Brennan to Xavier Faculty, March 12, April 29, 1980, XUA.
47. BT, May 7, 1980, XUA; regarding effective date of option: BT, March 11, 1981; September 15, 1982, XUA.
48. Rev. Francis C. Brennan, S.J., April 29, 1980, XUA.
49. Academic Vice President's Report, September 4, 1980, XUA; BT, September 4, December 17, 1980; March 11, September 16, 1981, XUA.
50. BT, May 6, September 16, 1981, XUA; "Freshman Inquiry and Applicant Information, 1961 to Present"; "Xavier University Fall Enrollment Trends," XUA.
51. BT, September 16, 1981, XUA.
52. BT, September 27, 1978; September 12, 1979; September 4, December 17, 1980; September 16, 1981, XUA; Daniel W. Geeding, Chairman, Faculty Committee, to Robert Mulligan, November 16, 1981, XUA. The university had only one remedial course in mathematics and none in English.

53. BT, March 10, May 5, 1982, XUA.
54. BT, May 5, 1982, XUA; Academic Vice President's Report, May 5, 1982, XUA.
55. BT, December 15, 1982, XUA; *Xavier News*, October 10, 1974; March 6, 1975, XUA; *Xavier Newswire*, September 7, 1988, XUA.
56. Mulligan to Members of the Executive Committee, August 8, 1978, XUA; BT, September 27, 1978; September 4, December 17, 1980, XUA.
57. BT, May 6, 1981; September 15, 1982, XUA.
58. BT, May 6, 1981; September 15, 1982, XUA.
59. BT, May 6, 1981; May 5, September 15, 1982, XUA.
60. BT, September 15, December 15, 1982; October 5, December 14, 1983, XUA.
61. Report of the Academic Organization Task Force, January 18, 1984, XUA; BT, October 9, 1985; October 8, November 19, 1986, XUA.
62. BT, May 25, 1977, XUA; University Planning Committee Report, May 1, 1985; Executive Committee, Board of Trustees, April 29, 1987, XUA. In 1987 the University hired an Affirmative Action Officer.
63. Currie to The University Community on Strategic Planning Process, September 3, 1984, XUA; Academic Affairs Committee Report, December 5, 1984, Board of Trustees, XUA.
64. University Planning Committee Report, May 1, 1985, XUA; *Xavier University Catalog, 1986–1988*, XUA.
65. University Planning Committee Report, May 1, 1985, XUA; "Xavier University Fall Enrollment Trends," XUA.
66. University Planning Committee Report, May 1, 1985, XUA; "Xavier University Fall Enrollment Trends," XUA.
67. BT, December 14, 1977, XUA; University Planning Committee Report, May 1, 1985, XUA.
68. University Planning Committee Report, April 19, May 1, 1985, XUA; BT, May 5, 1982, XUA.
69. BT, September 15, 1982; March 16, 1983, XUA.
70. BT, September 15, 1982; March 16, May 4, 1983, XUA.
71. Report of the President, December 5, 1984; October 15, 1985, Board of Trustees, XUA; BT, October 10, 1984; March 12, December 4, 1985; Faculty Committee Minutes, May 6, 1983, XUA. The deficit in 1984–1985 was $432,000.
72. Chair, Faculty Committee, to John Minahan, January 23, 1984; President Currie's Memo, January 24, 1984; Faculty Committee Minutes, February 2, 1984, XUA.
73. Charles L. Currie to Faculty Committee, February 2, 1984; Ann Beiersdorfer, R.S.M., to Charles L. Currie, February 2, 1984, XUA.
74. Report of the President, December 5, 1984; October 15, 1985, Board of Trustees, XUA; BT, October 10, 1984; March 12, December 4, 1985,

XUA; Faculty Committee Minutes, February 2, 1984, XUA; "Xavier University Fall Enrollment Trends," XUA.

75. Faculty Committee Minutes, May 3, 1984, XUA.

76. Minutes of the Finance Committee of the Board of Trustees, October 10, 1984; March 11, 1985, XUA *Xavier Magazine*, Spring 2000; BT, October 10, 1984; May 15, December 4, 1985; December 3, 1986; April 29, May 13, September 30, 1987, XUA; University Planning Committee Report, May 1, 1985, XUA. In terms of tuition and fees Xavier University ranked 22nd out of 28 Jesuit colleges and universities. While a board member warned of tuition increases that could price Xavier out of the market, another warned of "selling the product too cheaply."

77. *Xavier Magazine*, Spring 2000; BT, May 15, December 4, 1985; December 3, 1986; April 29, May 13, September 30, 1987, XUA. Ewing Industries, developer, purchased the Edgecliff property.

78. *Xavier University 1989–90 Fact Book*, XUA.

79. *Xavier Magazine*, Spring 2000. By the year 2000 Edgecliff alumni funded over $50,000 in grants.

80. BT, October 10, 1984, XUA; Report of the President, December 5, 1984, Board of Trustees, 1985; Currie to Board of Trustees, May 8, 1984, XUA.

81. AAUP packet, 1985, XUA; BT, March 11, 1985, XUA.

82. BT, Report of the Chair, March 11, July 30, 1985, XUA. Currie abstained from voting on March 11, 1985.

83. BT, March 12, 1985, XUA.

84. BT, March 12, 1985, XUA.

85. Currie to Board of Trustees, May 8, 1985, XUA; BT, May 15, 1985, XUA.

86. BT, July 30, 1985, XUA; Faculty Committee Minutes, March 28, 1985, XUA. Francis "Frank" V. Mastrianna, dean of the College of Business Administration, was scheduled to be named provost.

87. BT, July 30, October 9, December 4, 1985, XUA. Members of the board: Kluener, Fr. Beckman, Mr. Beckman, Fr. Biondi, Fr. Blumeyer, Fr. Bradley, Mr. Buenger, Fr. Carter, Fr. Cavanaugh, Fr. Currie, Geier, Hoenemeyer, Juilfs, Mrs. Lanier, Lawrence, Fr. O'Halloran, Fr. O'Malley, Pepper, Fr. Toland; excused Mr. Dugan.

88. Currie to Minahan, August 12, 1986; Faculty Committee to Currie, August 16, 1985, XUA; *Cincinnati Enquirer*, August 15, 1985; BT, October 9, 1985, XUA. Before being asked for his resignation, on several occasions the chief academic officer had announced his intention to leave Xavier University by the end of the 1985–1986 academic year.

89. BT, December 4, 1985; "Father Currie's Closing Remarks to the Board of Trustees, December 4, 1985, XUA; interview with Professor David Flaspohler, March 13, 2001.

90. "Father Currie's Closing Remarks to the Board of Trustees, December 4, 1985, XUA.

91. BT, December 4, 1985; May 14, 1986, XUA.

92. BT, December 4, 1985; May 14, 1986; March 4, 1987, XUA; Development Committee Report to Board of Trustees, October 8, 1986; Academic Affairs Committee Report, May 11, 1990, XUA; University Planning Committee Report, May 1, 1985. In 1990 salaries for Xavier professors were at the 48.5 percentile of IIA schools, associate professors at the 48.2 percentile, and assistant professors at the 51 percentile.

93. Xavier University Fall Enrollment Trends, 1974 to 2000, XUA. From 1982 to 1985 the number of undergraduate students decreased from 3,985 to 3,615 and graduates from 2,965 to 2,622.

94. BT, December 4, 1985; May 14, 1986, XUA. Melissa Lanier, a trustee, chaired the Presidential Search Committee.

95. Minutes of the Academic Affairs Committee, Board of Trustees, March 5, May 14, 1986, XUA; Mean Grade Point Average Comparison Study, 1986, prepared by Director of Minoity Affairs, Debora Jones, BT, December 3, 1986; March 4, 1987; Report, Office of the Academic Vice President, September 24, 1986; December 9, 1987; Minutes of the Executive Committee of the Board of Trustees, September 17, 1986; April 29, November 18, 1987, XUA. In the spring of 1986 seven faculty opted to participate in Xavier's Early Retirement Opportunities Program. The university realized long-term savings of approximately $700,000 from the success of the early retirement program.

96. Gallin, *Negotiating Identity*, 162–163; "Xavier University Fall Enrollment Trends, XUA.

97. Development Committee Report, Board of Trustees, May 14, October 8, 1986; March 4, 1987; Executive Committee, April 29, November 18, 1987; Report of the President, October 8, 1986, XUA. The trustees discontinued the theatre arts major in the spring of 1987.

98. Report of the President, October 8, 1986; Finance Committee Report, Board of Trustees, September 30, 1987, XUA.

99. Report on Capital Fundraising at Xavier, Board of Trustees, December 3, 1986; Executive Committee Minutes, November 14, 1986; February 12, 1987; Academic Affairs Committee, February 18, 1987, XUA.

100. Minutes of the Executive Committee of the Board of Trustees, September 17, 1986; Academic Affairs Committee Report, November 19, 1986; April 29, 1987, XUA; BT, September 30, 1987, XUA; Academic Deans to Faculty, March 22, 1999, XUA. The Board of Trustees approved the new mission in September 1987.

101. Development Committee Meeting, Board of Trustees, March 4, 1987, XUA; Buenger to DiUlio, July 13, 1987, XUA.

102. Executive Committee Minutes, Board of Trustees, April 29, September 8, 1987; September 12, 1989, XUA; BT, March 2, 1988, XUA. Retained the services of the firm of Hogan, Nolan, and Stites.
103. BT, December 9, 1987; March 2, May 11, 1988; September 28, 1990, XUA. Dr. Neil Heighberger, professor of political science, became dean of the College of Social Sciences. At the time Dr. Daniel Geeding, professor of marketing, was dean of the College of Business Administration and Dr. Stanley Hedeen, professor of biology, dean of the College of Arts and Sciences.
104. *Xavier University Magazine*, Fall 1993.
105. BT, September 28, November 15, 1988; March 8, September 12, 29, December 8, 1989; February 27, March 9, May 11, 1990, XUA; Executive Committee Minutes, Board of Trustees, November 15, 1988; November 13, 1989, XUA. At the Executive Committee of the Board of Trustees in the summer of 1988 Richard Hirte submitted a tax exempt financing proposal to restructure university short-term debt that would lessen impact on operating dollars and free up capital for other uses. Through the Ohio Higher Education Facility Commission the board approved the Buenger $14,265,000 Higher Education Facilities Bond Issue, which sold very quickly. The trustees also obtained additional tax-exempt financing of approximately $6 million for the acquisition of a campus telephone system, parking expansion and demolition of the old football stadium, and reimbursement for university expenses incurred in the renovation of the A. B. Cohen Center and Elet Hall, which became by the summer of 1990 the new home for the Departments of Education, Psychology, and Social Work.
106. Finance Committee, Board of Trustees, December 7, 1990; BT, Academic Affairs Committee Report, May 11, 1990, XUA; BT, March 4, 1987; May 11, 1988; December 8, 1989; March 9, 1990, XUA.
107. Shriberg to Board of Trustees, November 18, 1988, Athletic Five Year Plan, December 7, 1988, XUA. The university's new athletic director was Jeff Fogelson. Before moving to the Cincinnati Gardens for the 1983–1984 season the men's basketball team since after World War II had won 326 games and lost 129 in the Schmidt Fieldhouse.
108. Shriberg to Board of Trustees, November 18, 1988, December 7, 1988; President's Report, October 15, 1985, XUA. Though the department of athletics's five-year plan discussed the possible reinstitution of football, it recommended "that a Football program not be started during the next five years." It urged the university "to remain sensitive to annual changes that could impact on any future programs."
109. BT, September 25, 1974, XUA; *Xavier News*, October 23, 30, 1975; August 25, 1983, XUA; *Xavier Magazine*, Spring 1998. In 1977 Ben Urmston, S.J., began a radio program in response to the Jesuit order's renewed commitment to integrating faith and justice.

110. *Xavier News*, February 21, 28, March 7, 21, May 16, October 24, 1973, XUA.

111. BT, December 19, 1974, XUA.

112. BT, Protest Statement, December 19, 1974; March 19, 1975, XUA; Minutes of the Budget Review Committee, October 23, 1980, XUA. In 1981 there three undergraduate students and one graduate student on the University Budget Committee.

113. *Xavier News*, January 31, February 7, March 5, September 10, October 22, 29, November 5, 1980; February 11, 1981, XUA.

114. *Xavier News*, April 19, 26, 1979; January 31, February 7, 1980, XUA.

115. *Xavier News*, October 5, 1978; March 18, November 18, 1981; October 14, 28, 1982; September 27, 1984; January 24, XUA; *Xavier Newswire*, October 16, 23, 1985; April 29, November 11, 1987; March 9, 1990, XUA.

116. BT, September 27, 1978; March 12, May 7, 1980, XUA.

117. *Xavier University News*, March 13, 1975, XUA; *Xavier Newswire*, February 19, 26, March 5, 1986, XUA; Student Affairs Report, Board of Trustees, March 4, 1987; December 8, 1989; September 28, 1990, XUA.

118. Executive Committee Minutes, Board of Trustees, September 18, 1987, XUA; BT, May 13, September 30, 1987, XUA.

119. Mulligan to Board of Trustees, May 24, 1977, XUA; BT, October 8, 1986; September 29, 1989; September 28, December 7, 1990, XUA. Student Life Committee Report, Board of Trustees, September 28, 1990, XUA; Xavier University Factbook, 1989–1990, XUA. Ratterman Hall provided housing for ten women. The Xavier Village was built on the Peggy Becker Jackson 5.6 acres of property purchased in 1988.

120. BT, December 9, 1987; May 11, 1988, XUA.

121. BT, May 14, 1986; May 17, 1989, XUA; *Xavier University Magazine*, Summer 1993.

122. Finance Committee of Board of Trustees, December 8, 1989, XUA; BT, September 25, 1974; May 17, December 8, 1989; March 9, 1990, XUA.

123. Xavier University Factbook, 1989–1990, XUA; BT, December 8, 1989; May 7, 1993, XUA. At the December 1989 board meeting the trustees also revised the University Statutes, stipulating that the board would consist of not less than 15 nor more than 35 trustees. If the total number of trustees were a number evenly divided by four, the number of Jesuits would not be less than one-fourth of the total number of trustees plus one. If the total number of trustees were a number not evenly divisible by four, the number of Jesuits would not be less than that number that was the next highest whole number above the fractional number obtained when the total number of trustees was divided by four.

124. Obligations of the Jesuit Community, February 5, 1990, XUA; BT, December 8, 1989; March 9, 1990; May 7, 1993, XUA.

125. BT, September 29, 1989, XUA; Financial Report, May 31, 1993; Vincent T. O'Keefe, S.J., "Who Owns Jesuit Colleges and Universities," *Conversations* (February 1992), 16.
126. Obligations of the Jesuit Community, February 5, 1990, XUA; BT, March 9, 1990, XUA.
127. BT, May 11, 1990, XUA.
128. Board of Trustees to Members of the University Community, May 11, 1990; BT, May 11, September 28, 1990, XUA; Executive Committee Minutes, Board of Trustees, September 10, 1990; February 26, 1991, XUA. When fully renovated by the end of 1991 the Schott project had cost approximately $2.270 million. BT, September 28, December 7, 1990. To reflect more accurately the university's financial operating cycle, the board at its December 1990 meeting approved the recommendation of the administration to change the fiscal year to one beginning on June 1 and ending May 31. Previously it had begun July 1 and ended June 30.

Part IV A New Epoch for Xavier University, 1991–Present

Introduction

1. Scholarly Presentations, 1992–1996, Xavier University; Scholarly Presentations, 1996–2000, Xavier University, XUA.
2. Alice Gallin, O.S.U., *Negotiating Identity: Catholic Higher Education Since 1960* (Notre Dame, Indiana, 2000), 47; William P. Leahy, S.J., *Adapting to America: Catholics, Jesuits, and Higher Education in the Twentieth Century* (Washington, D.C., 1991), 85; *Xavier Magazine*, Summer 2001; *Digest of Education Statistics*, 2005.
3. Gerald L. Gutek, *American Education 1945–2000: A History and Commentary* (Project Heights, Illinois, 2000), 320–322.
4. Gutek, *American Education*, 319; The College Board: *Trends in Student Aid – 2004*. In 2005–2006 tuition and fees and room and board costs at Xavier University were $30,490.
5. *Xavier Magazine*, Fall 1999; President's Report, 2000, XUA.

Chapter 9   Xavier's New Leader: James E. Hoff, S.J., 1991–2000

1. BT, September 28, 1990, XUA; Fortin's interview with Chancellor James Hoff, S.J. June 9, 2004.
2. BT, September 28, December 7, 1990, XUA.
3. *Xavier Magazine*, Winter 1991; A Message from the Chairman of the Board, President's Report, 1991, XUA.
4. A Message from the President, President's Report, 1991, XUA; *Xavier Magazine*, Fall 1996.

5. BT, March 5, 1993, XUA.
6. *Xavier Magazine*, Fall 1993.
7. Core Curriculum Committee to Faculty, March 22, 1991, XUA.
8. BT, May 10, 1991, XUA; Core Curriculum Committee to Faculty, March 22, 1991, XUA; *Xavier Magazine*, Fall 1993.
9. *Xavier Magazine*, Fall 1993.
10. BT, May 10, 1991, XUA; Core Curriculum Committee to Faculty, March 22, 1991, XUA; *Xavier Magazine*, Summer, Fall 1993; President's Report, 1996, XUA.
11. *Xavier Magazine*, Fall 1997; Spring 1998; President's Report, 1998; 2000, XUA.
12. Academic Affairs Committee, Board of Trustees, December 7, 1990, XUA; Board of Undergraduate Studies Minutes, April 5, 1991, XUA; BT, December 3, 1993, XUA; Bill Larkin to Faculty, August 24, 1992; Hoff to Faculty, April 27, 1998, XUA; Faculty Committee Minutes, September 9, 1996, XUA; President's Report, 1998, XUA; *Xavier Magazine*, Fall 1993; Summer 1998. Charles F. and William J. Williams led Western Southern from its founding in 1888 to 1952. Regarding the Commons Hour the initial proposal recommended seven roundtables, one cultural event, four college or department meetings, and two division meetings per year.
13. President's Report, 1996, XUA; *Xavier Magazine*, Summer, Fall 1993; Spring 1994; Summer 2000.
14. President's Report, 1996, XUA; *Xavier Magazine*, Summer, Fall 1993; Spring 1994; Summer 2000. Employees of Procter & Gamble and Itochu Corporation, headquartered in the United States and Japan respectively, enrolled in the the corporate ESL program.
15. Jesuit Identity Committee Report, Board of Trustees, May 4, 1994, XUA; *Xavier Magazine*, Spring, Winter 1996; President's Report, 1995, 2000, XUA.
16. BT, December 2, 1994; September 22, 1995, XUA; Faculty Committee Minutes, September 9, 1996, XUA; President's Report, 1996, XUA; Weekend Degree Program Self Study, 2001–2002, XUA.
17. President's Report, 1996, XUA; *Xavier Magazine*, Winter 1997.
18. President's Report, 1996, XUA; *Xavier Magazine*, Winter 1997.
19. *Xavier Magazine*, Winter 1997.
20. President's Report, 1993, XUA; *Xavier Magazine*, Fall 1996.
21. *Xavier Magazine*, Winter 1997; Winter 1998; Spring 1999; Spring 2000; President's Report, 1997, XUA.
22. *Xavier Magazine*, Winter 1992; President's Report, 1993, 2000, XUA.
23. President's Report, 2000, XUA; Executive Committee, Board of Trustees, February 26, 1991, XUA.
24. *Xavier Magazine*, Winter 1992; President's Report, 1993, XUA.

25. BT, September 28, December 7, 1990; December 3, 1993; December 2, 1994, XUA; *Xavier Magazine*, Spring 1996.

26. *Xavier Magazine*, Winter 1992; Jesuit Identity Committee Report, Board of Trustees, May 4, 1994; Nominating Committee Meeting, Board of Trustees, March 8, 1991, XUA.

27. Executive Committee, Board of Trustees, February 26, 1991, XUA; Xavier University Strategic Planning Process, [n.d.], XUA

28. BT, December 6, 1991, XUA; *Xavier Magazine*, Winter 1991; Fall 1996; A Message from the President, President's Report, 1991, XUA; Xavier University Presidential Vision Statement, 1994, XUA.

29. BT, May 10, 1991, XUA; *Xavier Magazine*, Winter 1992.

30. *Xavier Magazine*, Summer 1993; Spring, Fall 1996; Spring 1999; Winter 2000; President's Report, 2000, XUA.

31. *Xavier Magazine*, Spring 1993. Council members also served as potential candidates for future positions on the University's Board of Trustees.

32. From the Chairman of the Board, President's Report, 1993; President's Report, 1996, XUA.

33. BT, September 24, 1993; March 4, 1994, XUA; President's Report, 1994, XUA; *Xavier Magazine*, Summer, Fall 1996; Milestones, News from The Century Campaign of Xavier University, Fall 2000, XUA.

34. BT, March 5, 1993; March 4, 1994, XUA; Xavier University News Release, March 4, 1994, XUA; "Our Partnership," Michael J. Conaton, Chairman of the Board, President's Report, 1994, XUA.

35. BT, March 6, 1992; March 5, 1993; March 4, 1994, XUA; Xavier University News Release, March 4, 1994, XUA; *Xavier Magazine*, Spring 1994; President's Report, 1994, XUA.

36. BT, May 10, 1991; March 6, 1992; May 4, September 23, December 2, 1994, XUA; *Xavier Magazine*, Winter 1997. In 1991 James Frick had visited the university and appraised its development operations.

37. Xavier University News Release, March 4, 1994, XUA; *Xavier Magazine*, Fall 1996.

38. President's Report, 1991, XUA; *Xavier Magazine*, Winter 1992; Winter, 1993; BT, March 6, September 25, December 4, 1992, XUA. The bonds were issued through the Ohio Higher Educational Facilities Commission for the specific purpose of refunding 1989 series debt.

39. BT, September 3, 24, 1993, XUA.

40. BT, September 25, 1992; March 5, May 7, December 3, 1993; March 4, 1994; December 1, 1995, XUA; President's Report, 1996, 2000, XUA; *Xavier Magazine*, Winter 1996. Clement Buenger graduated in 1953. He and his wife, Ann, also created a $1 million charitable remainder trust to fund scholarships for Xavier students.

41. BT, September 23, 1994; March 3, September 22, 1995, XUA; *Xavier Magazine*, Winter 1999; Financial Report, Board of Trustees, May 31,

1993; President's Report, 1994, 1996, XUA. In 1993 the university installed a computer software system designed to support financial accounting and budget control, human resources, alumni and development, and student information. Savings from the university's medical plan in the amount of $450,000 and $300,000 from the annual Repair and Renovation Fund provided the funds for the Campus Mall project. To pay for the installation of cable installation and data capabilities in the residence halls, the university took $100,000 from the Annual Equipment Fund and borrowed $395,000 from the endowment, amortizing it over six years at 6 percent and paid the loan back by establishing a new $100 student residence technology fee. Moreover, at the end of the 1994–1995 fiscal year the university transferred approximately $1.2 million from its operating budget to the Plant Fund, part of which was used to help fund the residential mall project.

42. President's Report, 1996, XUA; *Xavier Magazine*, Winter 1999.
43. BT, May 7, 1993; March 4, December 2, 1994, XUA; President's Report, 1996, XUA. Richard Hirté and John Kucia also served on the committee to draw up plans for the convocation center.
44. *Xavier Magazine*, Winter 1997; Fall 1998; Spring 1999; President's Report, 1997, 1998, XUA. The gift by the Jesuit community also helped renovate the residential and academic malls.
45. *Xavier Magazine*, Fall 1999; President's Report, 2000, XUA.
46. President's Report, 2000, XUA; *Xavier Magazine*, Spring, Fall 1999; Summer 2000.
47. Milestones, News from The Century Campaign of Xavier University, Fall 2000, XUA.
48. Address of Peter-Hans Kolvenbach, superior general of the Society of Jesus, June 7, 1989, Washington, D.C.
49. BT, March 6, 1992; May 4, 1994, XUA; *Xavier Magazine*, Fall 1996; President's Report, 1996, XUA.
50. Jesuit Identity Committee Report, Board of Trustees, May 4, 1994, XUA; *Xavier Magazine*, Summer 1993; Winter 1996; Summer 1997; President's Report, 1997; 2000, XUA. The Service Fellowship program was featured on the national news program, CBS *Sunday Morning*.
51. Student Life Committee Report, Board of Trustees, September 28, 1990, XUA; North Central Association of Colleges and Universities Report, April 19–21, 1999, XUA.
52. *Xavier Magazine*, Spring, 1996, Winter 1996; Winter 1999.
53. "Our Jesuit Character," by Michael Graham, S.J., Vice President for Development, President's Report, 1994; *Xavier Magazine*, Winter 1997; BT, December 3, 1993; May 4, 1994, XUA. In 1997 there were 3,934 Jesuits in the United States and approximately 24,000 worldwide. As of 2004 the trustees have kept intact the requirement that the president of Xavier University must be a member of the Society of Jesus.

54. *Xavier Magazine*, Spring 1996; President's Report, 2000, XUA. In 1998 Richard W. Bollman, S.J., succeeded Joseph Bracken, S.J., as rector of the Xavier Jesuit Community.

55. Riga to the University Community, January 20, April 19, 1993, Board of Trustees, December 4, 1992; also alluded to in Board of Trustees, March 5, May 7, 1993; March 4, 1994; Chair of Faculty Committee to Hoff, January 15, 1993. Beginning in the fall semester of 1993 the university discontinued the 100 percent tuition remission for spouses and dependents of faculty and staff, reducing it to 90 percent. However, the recipients were no longer charged the 10 percent dependency user fee. In terms of Xavier's retirement plan, from 1994 to 2002 the university increased its contributions to its employees' plan by 3 to 3.5 percent.

56. Faculty Committee Minutes, November 6, 1992; March 1, 1993; January 14, February 4, 1994, XUA; Chair of Faculty Committee to Hoff, January 15, 1993; Chair of Faculty Committee to Faculty, January 21, 1994, XUA.

57. *Xavier Magazine*, Winter 1995; Faculty Committee Minutes, September 27, 1995, XUA.

58. *Xavier Magazine*, Winter 1995.

59. *Xavier Magazine*, Winter 1995; Statement on Academic Climate, February 27, 1996, XUA; Ernest Fontana and Robert Rethy to Faculty, April 26, 1999, XUA.

60. BT, March 8, 1991, XUA.

61. BT, March 8, 1991; December 3, May 7, 1993; May 4, 1994 XUA; *Xavier Magazine*, Fall 1996.

62. BT, May 4, 1994, XUA; President's Report, 1997, XUA.

63. *Xavier Magazine*, Fall 1998.

64. President's Report, 1999, 2000, XUA.

65. President's Report, 1991; 1999, XUA; BT, September 23, 1994, XUA.

66. BT, September 28, December 7, 1990; March 8, May 10, 1991, XUA; Academic Affairs Committee Minutes, Board of Trustees, December 4, 1992; March 5, September 24, December 3, 1993, XUA.

67. President's Report, 1993, XUA; *Xavier Magazine*, Summer 1996; Fall 1997; Fall 1998; Milestones, News from The Century Campaign of Xavier University, Fall 2000, XUA.

68. BT, September 23, December 2, 1994; December 1, 1995, XUA.

69. BT, September 23, 1994, XUA; President's Report, 1995, XUA; *Xavier Magazine*, Fall 1996.

70. President's Report, 1997; 2000, XUA; *Xavier Magazine*, Winter 1996; Summer 1997; Fall 2000. Graduate tuition in the 1990s increased generally from $270 per credit hour to $420. In 1990 the university hired Adrian Schiess as director of freshman programs. His office proved instrumental for the university's successful first-year retention rate.

71. Fall Enrollment Trends, 2004, XUA; *Xavier Magazine*, Fall, Winter 2000.
72. Student Life Committee Report, Board of Trustees, May 11, December 7, 1990, XUA; BT, September 28, 1990, XUA; Message from the President, May 5, 2000, XUA.
73. President's Report, 1993, 1996, XUA; *Xavier University Magazine*, Summer 1996; Faculty Committee Minutes, April 1, 1996, XUA; Student Life Committee Report, Board of Trustees, September 28, 1990, XUA.
74. President's Report, 1997; 1998; 1999, XUA; *Xavier Magazine*, Spring, Winter, 1996; Fall 1998; Spring 2000.
75. BT, December 1, 1995, XUA; President's Report, 1996; 2000, XUA; *Xavier Magazine*, Spring 2000.
76. *Xavier Magazine*, Spring 2000; interview with Gerald DeBrunner, a trustee, January 4, 2005.
77. Conaton and DeBrunner to Provincials, February 21, 2000; Conaton and DeBrunner to Rectors, February 21, 2000, XUA.
78. *Xavier Magazine*, Summer 2000.
79. *Xavier Magazine*, Spring 1999; Fall 2000.
80. "A Message from the Chairman of the Board," Michael J. Conaton, President's Report, 2000, XUA.

Chapter 10   "A Renaissance of Culture and Commitment": Michael J. Graham, S.J., 2001 – Present

1. *Xavier Magazine*, Fall 1999.
2. *Xavier Magazine*, Winter 2001. President Graham received his master's degree in divinity at The Weston School of Theology in 1988.
3. *Xavier Magazine*, Summer 2000; Winter 2001.
4. Inaugural Talk, Michael J. Graham, "Scholars, Saints and Citizen-Servants," September 8, 2001, XUA. The presentations were on "Engaging Our World of Complexity," "Dialogue on Black/White Community Building," and "Globalization: Ethics, Economics and Culture in an Age of Globalization." The academic convocation on September 11, 2001, consisted of three interdisciplinary presentations, involving faculty and administration, followed by closing remarks by the president.
5. Graham to University Community, November 1, 2001, XUA.
6. Graham to University Community, November 1, 2001, XUA.
7. Graham to University Community, November 1, 2001, XUA.
8. Ahlgren to Graham, email, August 26, 2001, XUA.
9. Ahlgren to Graham, August 27, 2001; Faculty Committee Annual Report, 2001–2002, XUA.

10. Academic Vision Statement, 2002, XUA.
11. Graham to University Community, November 1, 2001, XUA.
12. Graham to University Community, November 1, 2001, XUA; *Xavier Magazine*, Spring, Winter 2001; BT, Information Resources Committee, February 21, 2003, XUA. In January 2001 Xavier signed a five-year comprehensive service relationship with Cincinnati Bell and its parent company, Broadwing Communications, to have the company be the school's exclusive provider of on-campus communications. Including the telephone systems upgrade, the university that year spent more than $5 million on technology, which was an in increase of a little more than $1 million in 2000 and $870,000 the previous year. Xavier used money from a capital equipment fund to lease personal computers, which were on a four-year replacement plan. Regarding the division for information resources, in 2004 Web development became known as Web resources and services.
13. In 2003 Carol Rankin had opted to return to the faculty. Her successor remained in office for only a few months. By the fall of 2003 the university introduced forty-four presentation classrooms, six open instruction computer labs, and five interactive classrooms, over 400 public access computers, including nearly sixty wireless hookups in the library and Gallagher Student Center. Moreover, there were over 200 electronic databases installed in the library. In the spring of 2005 the university moved the all day, seven days a week computer lab to a more prominent place in the Gallagher Student Center.
14. Graham to Members of the Planning Steering Committee, March 13, 2002, XUA.
15. Graham to Provincial, January 30, 2004, XUA.
16. Academic Affairs Committee, Board of Trustees, September 27, December 6, 2002, XUA; Mary Walker to Faculty, June 20, 2003, XUA. As the associate vice president for academic affairs Mary Walker oversaw the academic program reviews in 2002–2003. The programs' responses to the deans' reports were also available electronically to the faculty.
17. Academic Affairs Committee, Board of Trustees, September 26, 2003, XUA; Academic Planning Task Force Report, November 24, 2003, XUA. Among the seven faculty members on the Academic Planning Task Force, three were from the College of Arts and Sciences, two from the College of Social Sciences, and two from the Williams College of Business. The two administrators served as *ex officio* non-voting members. Besides reviewing the reports of the various academic departments and committees, pertinent financial data, and other sources of information, in the fall of 2003 the task force met with the three academic deans and Richard Pulskamp, director for institutional research. The

Academic Planning Task Force further recommended that Xavier continue to "encourage and support the faculty effort to understand more fully the logic of the core and the connections among its various parts" as well as "communicate the logic and the intellectual richness of the core curriculum earlier and more completely" to the first-year class.

18. Academic Planning Task Force Report, November 24, 2003, XUA. In 2004 the university discontinued the master's degree program in the humanities and the pre-mortuary science program in the Department of Chemistry.

19. Fortin to Faculty, October 22, 2003, XUA.

20. Fortin to Faculty, October 22, 2003, XUA. In 2004 the university also discontinued the pre-mortuary science program in the Department of Chemistry.

21. Quality Improvement Initiative to Faculty, November 9, 2001, XUA. In some departments, such as modern languages and theology, adjunct faculty taught over 50 percent of core courses.

22. Quality Improvement Initiative to Faculty, November 9, 2001, XUA; Academic Affairs Committee, Board of Trustees, September 27, 2002; September 26, 2003, XUA.

23. Fortin to Faculty, September 27, 2002, XUA; Faculty Assembly Minutes, March 14, 2003, XUA; Academic Affairs Committee, Board of Trustees, February 21, 2003, XUA.

24. Academic Affairs Committee, Board of Trustees, February 21, 2003; February 20, 2004, XUA.

25. Fortin to Faculty, October 22, 2003, XUA.

26. For Ann Buenger's total dedication to Catholic education, in December 2004 Xavier awarded her the St. Francis Xavier Award, the university's highest honor.

27. The exhibit was expected to tour Jewish and Catholic universities throughout the United States and Europe before becoming a permanent display in Israel. In 2002 the university changed the name of the Brueggeman Center for Interreligious Dialogue to the Edward B. Brueggeman Center for Dialogue.

28. Roger A. Fortin, "The Provost Model: What it Means for Xavier," Provost Workshop, June 7–8, 2004, XUA.

29. BT, September 24, December 3, 2004.

30. Ernest Fontana and Robert Rethy to Faculty, April 26, 1999, XUA; A Report from the Faculty Committee, 1999, XUA.

31. Faculty Committee Annual Report, 2001–2002; 2002–2003, XUA.

32. Academic Affairs Committee, Board of Trustees, May 17, September 27, 2002, XUA.

33. Principles of Shared Governance at Xavier University, April 24, 2002, XUA.

34. Ahlgren's talk, September 17, 2001, at the Academic Affairs Assembly, XUA.

35. Faculty Committee Minutes, April 9, 2003, XUA; Graham to Dennis Long, Chair of the Faculty Committee, May 5, 2003, XUA; *Xavier Newswire*, March 12, 19, 2003, XUA; Faculty Committee Annual Report, 2002–2003, XUA; Faculty Assembly to Graham, Fortin, and Michael Conaton, March 14, 2003, XUA. In the judgment of the Faculty Committee the cancellation in March 2003 of *The Vagina Monologues*, which prompted an emergency meeting of the Faculty Assembly, "constituted a threat and challenge to academic freedom at Xavier University." Over a three-day period the president, academic vice president, and vice president for student development met with students, faculty, and various constituencies to discuss principles underlying academic freedom. On March 14, four days after the initial cancellation, student actors, joined by fellow students, held a rally titled "Our Lips are Sealed: Students Against Xavier Censorship." While on a business trip to Florida, Graham commented on the rally. "I heard the disappointment and frustration of our students when I met with them earlier this week," he said. "I commend them for coming together . . . to passionately express their opinions and concerns. Like other members of the academic community, I am fully supportive of the principles of academic freedom." Over the weekend the Xavier Players, a student group that produced main stage productions as well as directed workshops, put on the play in the Gallagher Student Center as part of a faculty member's class that dealt with gender issues. Though pleased with the eventual showing of the play, faculty members found its presentation in the context of a class as "an inadequate response." They saw the production as "a student initiative that exemplified student concerns about women's issues" and should have been approved at the outset.

36. BT, February 21, 2003, XUA; Graham to Members of the University Community, August 21, 2003; Graham to Trustees, April 23, 2003, XUA.

37. University Protocol for Campus Public Speakers and Events, April 1, 2004, XUA; Academic Affairs Committee, Board of Trustees, February 20, May 7, 2004, XUA.

38. The Faculty Committee met regularly with the academic vice president and provost and often consulted with Richard Pulskamp, professor of mathematics and director of institutional research, and Kandi Stinson, professor of sociology and interim associate vice president for academic affairs. The university appropriated over $273,000 for faculty compensation enhancement.

39. *Xavier Magazine*, Spring 2001.

40. *Xavier Magazine*, Spring 2001.

41. *Xavier Magazine*, Summer 2000; Milestones, News from The Century Campaign of Xavier University, Fall 2000, XUA. Xavier decorated the second floor of the Gallagher Center with photographs taken from around the world by William J. Rielly, a 1939 graduate. Rielly, who donated $300,000 to the construction of the Gallagher Student Center, gave to the university 57 photographs, 20 of which were to be used at any given time for teaching and for expanding the students' imagination. The Commons was built at a cost of $13,955,000.

42. Academic Affairs Committee, Board of Trustees, September 27, 2002, XUA.

43. *Cincinnati Enquirer*, November 1, 2004; David Hellkamp to Faculty, August 20, 2003, XUA. In the fall of 2004 Xavier University Division I sports consisted of men's and women's basketball, men's and women's golf, rifle, volleyball, men's and women's soccer, men's and women's tennis, baseball, men's and women's cross country, men's and women's track, and men's and women's swimming.

44. From 1990 to 2004 Xavier had nine players drafted in the first or second round of the NBA draft. In 2004–2005, during Sean Miller's first year as head coach, the team, in a rebuilding year, won 17 games and lost 12.

45. In the history of the university the rifle program produced two Olympians, Jason Parker and Thrine Kane, class of 2003. In 2005 Xavier officials planned to commemorate the success and many proud accomplishments of the rifle program, its athletes, and coach with a significant presence in an Athletic Hall of Fame display being planned for installation in the Cintas Center.

46. *Xavier Magazine*, Summer 2001.

47. *Cincinnati Enquirer*, July 29, 2004.

48. *Cincinnati Enquirer*, July 29, 2004; Fortin's conversation with Ann Buenger and others, January 13, 2005.

49. *Cincinnati Enquirer*, July 26, 2004; Arthur Dewey, Reflections by Xavier faculty and staff, July 27, 2004.

50. Ernest Fontana and Robert Rethy to Faculty, April 26, 1999, XUA; Graham to Xavier University Community, April 10, 2001, XUA.

51. Fortin to Faculty, November 12, 2001, XUA. The new faculty hired in the collective diversity pool joined the Departments of Communication Arts, History, Philosophy, Psychology, and two in Theology respectively.

52. E-mail, Fortin to Faculty, November 24, 2003. While teaching in the department of psychology the joint appointment consisted of duties at the Freedom Center that helped implement its mission to move people higher in the achievement of freedom through history.

53. Cheryl Nuñez assumed the new duties on May 2, 2005; Academic Affairs Committee, Board of Trustees, February 20, 2004, XUA. The Diversity and Inclusion Strategic Planning Workshop was run by Global Lead

Consulting, a Cincinnati firm. In addition to the trustees, the academic vice president and provost and Dean Janice Walker, who was chair of the university's Diversity Advisory Committee, served as *ex officio* members.

54. Academic Affairs Committee, Board of Trustees, September 26, December 5, 2003; February 20, 2004, XUA; Fortin to Gender and Diversity Studies Committee, February 18, 2004, XUA.

55. Xavier University: Ensuring a Climate of Respect, October 11, 2004, XUA. The 24-hour phone line that connected callers to a trained advocate was a joint project with Cincinnati's Rape Crisis & Abuse Center and the Young Women's Christian Association (YWCA) Battered Women's Shelter.

56. Graham's homily, November 5, 2000, XUA; Graham to Provincial, January 30, 2004, XUA.

57. Graham to Provincial, January 30, 2004, XUA.

58. *Xavier Magazine*, Summer 2001. The signing of the landmark Collaborative Agreement between the Cincinnati Black United Front, the American Civil Liberties Union of Ohio, the City of Cincinnati, and the Fraternal Order of Police took place at Xavier. Moreover, working with colleagues in the division of student development, the Office of Multicultural Affairs also sponsored diversity workshops and cultural programs to raise cultural, racial, and ethnic awareness and understanding among students.

59. President's Report, 2002, XUA; Graham to Provincial, January 30, 2004, XUA. In collaboration with the United Way of Greater Cincinnati, the university also expanded significantly the Community Building Institute by bringing in two individuals—one funded by Xavier, one funded by the United Way—who helped to network the university better beyond itself and by helping internal university constituencies come to know better the remarkable resources available to them in the surrounding communities.

60. Xavier's COPC grant focused on four goals: creating a partnership school between the Xavier education department and Hoffman Elementary School in Evanston; establishing a more desirable and marketable residential community in Evanston; developing the Montgomery Road business corridor from Dana and Montgomery south to the Interstate 71 interchange; and promoting leadership development in Evanston and Norwood.

61. Graham to Provincial, January 30, 2004, XUA. In 2002 and 2003 Thomas Hayes, professor of marketing at Xavier, helped develop and implement internal and external marketing studies. Moreover, Cincinnati's Procter & Gamble Company assisted the university in conducting the studies. Both sets of studies clearly affirmed the Jesuit core values of demonstrating care

through personal attention; ensuring broad, challenging academic experiences; fostering faith, values, morals, and spiritual growth; embracing diversity of people and perspectives; engaging the city of Cincinnati and its business, culture, and communities; and preparing students for successful lives and careers. In 2004 Robert Hill's title changed to associate vice president for marketing and printing services.

62. Roger Fortin, "The Provost Model: What it Means for Xavier," Provost Workshop, June 7–8, 2004, XUA. The university's various strategic and planning sessions underscored five main imperatives: renewed commitment to intellectual excellence and academic rigor in a number of programs, ranging from pre-med and honors to business and education; more interdisciplinary study and attention to the university core; a more vibrant center for learning, engagement, and reflection; greater diversity and engagement in society; and rekindling of Xavier's Catholic and Jesuit identity.

63. Message from the President, December 22, 2003, XUA; Graham to Trustees, January 26, July 13, 2004; Academic Affairs Committee, Board of Trustees, May 7, 2004, XUA. The idea for the academic quadrangle stemmed from a collaborative effort from the Academic Vision Statement, the Academic Planning Task Force Report, and subcommittees of the University Planning Steering Committee. Carol Rankin was the first vice president for information resources.

64. Graham to Trustees, January 26, 2004, XUA.

65. *Xavier Magazine*, Winter 2001; Fortin to Faculty, October 22, 2003, XUA. The Academic Reorganization Committee and the Career Services Committee submitted their reports in mid-April 2005.

66. While serving internal and external constituencies, XCEL sought to grow student enrollment, enhance revenue generation, and expand external engagement.

67. Graham to Trustees, January 18, 2005, XUA. The Zumbiel Company planned to continue its operation at the Cleneay location until 2007, thus providing time for the university and the city of Norwood to plan the redevelopment of the property. Upon the acquisition of the Cinergy property in November 2004 for a price of $3.5 million, it exchanged it for the Cincinnati Bell property, valued at $1.75 million, while the university retained 55 percent ownership in the Cinergy property.

68. *Xavier Magazine*, Winter 1995.

69. During 2004–2005 Alumni Relations staff also helped coordinate several alumni and admission receptions and began to become more integrated with development activities by participating in peer screening for the campaign, promoting the Annual Fund, implementing a financial assistance program for students, and directing development efforts with potential parents of Xavier students.

Epilogue   Personal Reflections

1. *Catalogue of St. Xavier College, 1845–1846.*
2. Alice Gallin, O.S.U., *Negotiating Identity: Catholic Higher Education Since 1960* (Notre Dame, Indiana, 2000), 119; cites Martin Stamm, "The New Guardians of American Catholic Higher Education: An Examination of Lay Participation" (Ph.D. diss., University of Pennsylvania, 1979).
3. O'Connor Comments, Cleveland Chapter, Alumni Association, February 8, 1969, XUA.
4. William T. Burns, "Twenty-Five Years: A Retrospect," *The Xavier Athenaeum*, I, (April 1913), 164, XUA.

Index

489